In their own words

Liam Swords

In their own words
The Famine in North Connacht
1845-49

the columba press

First published in 1999 by

the columba press

55A Spruce Avenue, Stillorgan Industrial Park, Blackrock, Co Dublin

Designed by Bill Bolger
Origination by The Columba Press
Printed in Ireland by Colour Books Ltd, Dublin

ISBN 1856072479

Acknowledgements
Quotations from Fr Bernard McGauran are taken from *Eyewitness Grosse Isle, 1847,* by Marianna O'Gallagher and Rose Masson Dompierre, published by Carraig Books, Sainte-Foy, Quebec. The Sligo shipping lists are taken from *Famine Immigrants,* edited by Ira A. Glazier and published by The Genealogical Publishing Co Inc., Baltimore, MD.

CONTENTS

List of Illustrations

List of Abbreviations

Correspondence	*Correspondence relating to the measures adopted for the relief of distress in Ireland*
CSORP	Chief Secretary's Office Registered Papers
DDA	Dublin Diocesan Archives
DP	Distress Papers
Grosse Isle	*Eyewitness Grosse Isle 1847*
JP	Justice of the Peace
OP	Outrage Papers
OPW	Office of Public Works
PLG	Poor Law Guardians
RLFC	Relief Commission Papers
RM	Resident Magistrate
SC Irlanda	Scritture riferite nei Congressi, Irlanda
SFFP	Society of Friends' Famine Papers
Transactions	*Transactions of the Central Relief Committee of the Society of Friends during the Famine in Ireland in 1846 and 1847*

Preface

I was struck by a remark made to me by Mrs Nash O'Conor Don some years ago to the effect that her family was fortunate in that every hundred years or so it produced a historian. What was true of the O'Conor Don family was probably equally true of Achonry diocese. Just then Liam Swords had arrived back from Paris where he had published a number of books on the history of the Irish in France. I suggested to him that he should write a history of the diocese. The result was *A Hidden Church*, describing the history of the diocese in the eighteenth century. It is a splendid volume which more than amply rewarded my confidence in him.

Now, scarcely eighteen months later, he has produced a second large volume on the Famine from 1845 to 1849. *In Their Own Words* graphically recounts the experiences of those who lived and often died during the unparalleled horrors of those terrible years. The parishes of the diocese were then divided between six Poor Law Unions, Sligo, Boyle, Castlerea, Swinford, Castlebar and Ballina. Only the Swinford Union was situated within the diocese itself. Two neighbouring Unions, Westport and Ballinrobe, were added and thus North Connacht became the scope of the book.

The Famine had enormous consequences, not least upon the diocese of Achonry. Its pre-Famine population was estimated in the region of 150,000 which has since eroded to some 32,000, largely the result of the Famine and its long legacy of emigration. *In Their Own Words* will not only be of great interest to the general public but should prove a great boon to the numerous local hostory societies all over North Connacht.

✠ *Thomas Flynn*
Bishop of Achonry
3 March 1999

Introduction

This is not a book *about* the Famine; it is a book *of* the Famine. *In Their Own Words,* as the title implies, recounts the experiences, words and reflections of eye-witnesses of the events described. Some are the words of the victims themselves; many others come from pleading letters written by priests and ministers, resolutions of Boards of Guardians or reports of local constabulary or Poor Law inspectors. Numerous petitions were sent to the government by individuals imploring help for themselves and their starving families. All are named, whether it be victims as in the case of inquests or evictions, or signatories, often running to several hundreds, of a single petition. The Appendices alone contain over fifty pages of names of inhabitants of towns, villages and parishes.

It follows a diary or journal form, with an entry for almost every day, and several for some days, of the four years while the Famine lasted. Sometimes, incidents, though separated in time, are linked together, to facilitate the reader. Each entry describes a happening in some town, village or parish throughout the region. The names of these places are highlighted in the wide margins and a list of those marginalia is provided in the preliminaries. Thus a reader whose primary interest is in his own town or parish can pick his way selectively through these to follow the sequence of events in his own neighbourhood.

My thanks are due to Bishop Flynn who has encouraged and generously supported this venture as part of the on-going history of the diocese of Achonry; the Director and staff of the National Archives, Dublin, who are always helpful and courteous; Valerie Ingram, Librarian, Office of Public Works; David Sheehy, Dublin Diocesan Archive; Bill Bolger, designer, Mary Ann Bolger, and Seán O Boyle of The Columba Press.

Dramatis Personae 1845-49

Prime ministers: Sir Robert Peel (1841-46), Lord John Russell (1846-52)

Permanent secretary to the Treasury: Charles Trevelyan

Lord Lieutenants: Baron Heytesbury (– July 1846), John George Brabazon Ponsonby, Earl of Bessborough (1846-7), George William Frederick Villiers, Earl of Clarendon (1847-52)

Chief Secretaries: Sir Thomas Freemantle (1845), Earl of Lincoln, Henry Labouchere MP (1846), Sir William Somerville (1847-49)

Under Secretaries: Richard Pennefather (1846), Thomas N. Redington (1847)

Relief Commission: 20 November 1845, Edward Lucas, chairman, Sir James Dombrain, Colonel Harry Jones, Sir Randolph, Edward Twistleton, John Pitt Kennedy and Sir Robert Kane. In January 1846 Sir Randolph Routh became chairman and Colonel Harry Jones was removed.

Secretary: William Stanley

Commissariat Department, Dublin Castle: Commissary General: Sir Randolph Routh,

Assistant Commissary General, Sligo: Charles G. Adams,

District Assistant Poor Law Commissioner: Caesar George Otway,

Temporary Poor Law Inspectors, March 1847: Richard Bourke, Lt William Hamilton (Ballina), Richard Hamilton (Belmullet), Capt A. E. Burmester, (Boyle), Capt. R. P. Farren (Castlebar), James Auchmuty (Castlerea), Capt Geo. G. Wellesley, Capt. W. E. D. Broughton, Capt. Hanley (Swinford), Capt. J. Gilbert (Sligo)

Board of Works: Colonel Harry Jones, chairman, Henry R. Paine, secretary

County Surveyers: Henry Brett (Mayo), N. R. St Leger (Sligo)

Inspector General: Colonel Duncan McGregor

County Inspectors: (Mayo) James F. O'Connor, (Sligo) Samuel H. Lawson

Sub-Inspectors: Mayo: John S. Kelly (Ballaghaderreen), William Caldwell (Ballina), J. S. Bindon (Ballinrobe), H. B. Blake (Belmullet), Benjamin Jackson (Castlebar), Richard Singleton (Claremorris), Edward Hunt (Swinford), Denis Walshe (Westport). *Sligo:* E. S. Corry (Ballymote), John Grant (Riverstown), J. S. Stewart (Tubbercurry)

Coast Guard Inspector General: Sir James Dombrain.

Inspecting Commanders: Mayo: Lt William Dawson (Belmullet), Lt A. Henri

(Killala), Frederick Carey (Drumkeehan), Capt. Edward Holland (Ballycastle)

County Officials of Mayo and Sligo:

Lieutenants: Earl of Lucan, Castlebar (Mayo). Colonel Arthur Francis Knox Gore, Belleek House, Ballina (Sligo).

Magistrates of Mayo and Sligo: Alexander Perceval, Templehouse, John Armstrong, Chaffpool, Ballymote, Daniel Jones, Banada Abbey, Charles King O'Hara, Annaghmore, Edward Howley, Belleek Castle, Ballina, George Vaughan Jackson, Carramore, Ballina, Bernard Owen Cogan, Collooney, Charles Joseph MacDermot, Coolavin, Joseph A. Holmes, Clogher, Ballaghadereen, Richard Gethen, Earlsfield, Ballymote, Alexander Crichton, Ballymote, Edmond Taaffe, Swinford, Edward Deane, Carrogowan, Ballavary, George Rutledge, Brabazon Park, Swinford, Charles Strickland, Loughglynn.

Chairmen of Boards of Guardians: Ballina, Edward Howley; Boyle, Oliver D. J. Grace; Castlebar (paid vice-Guardians), William R. Leckey, A. Thomas, Capt. W. Carey; Castlerea, Thomas George Wills; Sligo, C. K. O'Hara; Swinford, George Vaughan Jackson.

Winter 1845-46

The Blight

A disease which attacked the potato crop was first reported in Ireland early in September 1845 but it was not observed in the west of the country until towards the end of October. By the late summer and early autumn it had spread throughout the greater part of central and northern Europe. One source of the disease was thought to have been South America, particularly Peru, but it was more likely to have originated in the eastern United States where it largely destroyed the potato crops of 1843 and 1844. Vessels from New York and Philadelphia could easily have brought diseased potatoes to European ports. The blight first attacked the leaves of the stalks and then spread to the potatoes. It was described as having the appearance of soot. The plant decomposed rapidly, turning black and rotting, producing a putrid smell. In Ireland the failure of the potato crop in 1845 was only partial, as the early crop escaped entirely but the unusually wet weather in the later season contributed to the rapid spread of the disease.

RLFC 2/Z.13210

Constabulary Reports:

Tubbercurry

Saturday 20 September 1845. J. S. Stewart, sub-inspector, to Capt Lawson, County Inspector, Sligo

'There has been a small failure in a few instances but it is of a very trifling nature. The general opinion in the country is that there has not been so good a crop of potatoes for some years.'

Ballymote

Monday 22 September. Sub-inspector to Col Duncan McGregor, Inspector General

'No complaints of failure of the potato crop have reached me from any quarter of this district but that on the contrary it presents every appearance of a most abundant return in this part of the country. In fact, more so than has been observed for some years past.'

Ballinrobe

Tuesday 23 September. J. S. Bindon, sub-inspector to the Inspector General

'The potato crop … is both ample and good and it was a matter of congratulation at the Ballinrobe Agricultural Meeting last night, the principal speaker having pronounced the crop bountiful and healthy.'

Ballina

Wednesday 24 September. William Caldwell, sub-inspector to the Inspector General

'No desease nor failure whatever complained of in this district. The crop is a most abundant one and considered beyond an average one of former years. The markets are well supplied … and the current prices are from 2d. to 2½d. per stone for the best description, viz. peelers.'

Swinford

Friday 26 September. Edward Hunt, sub-inspector, to James T. O'Connor, County Inspector, Castlebar

'Up to this period there is not any complaint of any failure in the potato crop, nor any rise taken place in the sale of potatoes.'

Ballaghaderreen

Saturday 27 September. John S. O'Kelly, sub-inspector to James T. O'Connor, County-Inspector

'After the minutist inquiry, I find that the potato crop in this district is free from disease and promises to be an average one.'

O'Connor reported to Dublin:

'From what I have seen and heard, having visited a large portion of the county lately … there never was to all appearances a finer crop of potatoes in this county … The general crop will not be dug until November but no failure has appeared in the early crop.'

Ballaghaderreen

RLFC 2/Z.14282

Monday 20 October 1845. John S. Kelly, sub-inspector to the Inspector General

'Incipient disease of the potato crop has shown itself in a partial way in this district within the last few days … I cannot ascertain what particular denomination of potato is most infected and in what peculiar soil the disease is most prevalent. In some instances it has appeared in boggy tillage and in other places, in what is in this vicinity called spudaur? or tag lands. General digging begins in the beginning of November.'

21 October. Sub-inspector's report to the Inspector General   *Ballina*
'For the first time yesterday this subject has been the matter of anything like serious consideration and this from the fact of an example of diseased potato was exhibited in the board room of the Poor Law Guardians by Mr G. V. Jackson of Carramore who said that he unexpectedly discovered this failure in one of his best fields only the day prior, and which to all external appearances was a most healthy crop.'

Wednesday 22 October. Edward Hunt, sub-inspector, to the Inspector General   *Swinford*
'The potatoes in this district are universally afflicted with the rot, in conse-   RLFC 2/ Z.14344
quence of which a general panic has arisen in all classes, both of farmer and householders. At yesterday's market potatoes which I purchased on the 14th for 1s. 6d. per cwt, I had to pay 2s. 10d. yesterday. Oats at 16s. for 24 stone brought £1 5s. to £1 7s. yesterday, and oatmeal in like proportion.'

Thursday 23 October. Pilsworth Whelan RM to Richard Pennefather   *Co Sligo*
'Ten days back the tops rapidly faded and dried, particularly on high ground   RLFC 2/ Z.14316
and soon after small patches of brown colour appeared on the potatoes ... These progressively spread on the outsides of the potato, the part affected became tainted and rotten as the disease advanced and if in this state the crop was put into a pit, both good and bad became alike rotten. The farmers put the diseased potatoes aside and only pitted the sound ones. The potato disease is universal throughout this district (all Co Sligo and the part of Mayo adjoining Ballaghaderreen) ... The alarm amongst all classes is considerable and at the requisition of Mr Cooper of Markrea Castle, a meeting of the principal gentry of the county took place today at the Meldan Hotel in the town of Sligo ... It was admitted by all that the disease was universal. It was suggested to apply to the government requesting a stop to the distillation of corn and that there be a subscription for buying oatmeal to store and sell in the country. Nothing final was agreed on ... The oat crop is average but the wheat is deficient in quality. The market price of potatoes rose considerably for the last two markets but this day fell again, finding that the price in the English markets did not warrant those in Sligo ... The actual loss in the potato crop is not yet material.'

Saturday 25 October. John Coghlan CC to Sligo Champion   *Gurteen*
'It is utterly impossible to convey to you a true picture of the alarming state of dispondency into which the people of this parish have been thrown by the extensive rot in the potato crop. There are eleven hundred families in it and

there is scarcely one that has not suffered, many have all their potatoes totally lost … It is quite common that a potato field tried today may be good and sound and in three days after in a state of melancholy putrefaction … My heart bleeds to contemplate the dark future that appears before the suffering people. They have neither oats, nor money, nor potatoes, nor the hope of relief from a kind and indulgent landlord.'

Tubbercurry
RLFC 2/Z.14920

Friday 31 October. John Connor, head constable, to the Inspector General
'The disease in the potato crop has become general in this district. In the parish of Kilmactigue more than one half has failed and in a few instances almost the entire. Several persons who, when pitting their potatoes, considered them safe, after examining them in a few days found them greatly injured … In the remaining parishes of this district the injury is not considerable and the disease is not supposed to be making much progress and from the abundance of the crop, it is believed that if not more than one fourth be damaged, there would still be a sufficiency.'

Ballina
RLFC 2/Z.15250

Tuesday 4 November 1845. Sub-inspector to the Inspector General
'I do not believe that 5% or one twentieth of the potato crop is yet destroyed. The markets hold steady. Yesterday in this town there was rather a fall in prices, 15d. to 22d. per cwt (a fall of 2d.), with a good supply and in only a few odd cases a taint appeared. The weather has been charming without a drop of rain for the last seven days or since 29 October. The corn crop is safe in the haggard and it now appears so abundant. A fall has also occurred in the oat market, from 21s. & 22s. to 18. 6d. to 20s. for a sack of 24 stone. People heed the instructions to store the potatoes dry but turning them into flour or starch, they regard with contempt.'

Foxford
RLFC 2/Z.15348

Saturday 8 November. George Vaughan Jackson JP to the Chief Secretary
'On our way to Foxford Petty Sessions we observed a vast deal of destruction done by floods caused by a fall of rain within the last four days that in severity is almost unprecedented. In the estate of Lord Limerick at a place called Coolcronane the poor people met us on the road and showed us acres of potatoes that were entirely covered with water and ruined. We also saw poor creatures up to nearly their knees digging potatoes to save them. In some districts the population were obliged to leave their houses … All along the banks of the river Moy the injury done the potato crop is quite deplorable. The bridge of Ballylahan we hear is torn down …'

Ballaghaderreen
RLFC 2/Z.15500

8 November. John S. Kelly, sub-inspector, to the Inspector General
'Since my report of 26 October, the rot has become general, there being no instance in which the crop has wholly escaped the infection … The rich uplands, where the potato grows to a large size, have suffered most. The peo-

ple are actively employed in separating the diseased from the sound and cutting off the part affected. The general opinion, particularly since the wet weather has set in, is that at least one half of the whole crop will be destroyed before the first of next month.'

11 November. Sub-inspector to Inspector General

'Scarcely any which is altogether free from this distemper ... Individuals have, no doubt, in many cases been altogether deprived of their crop by this disease but others again (and these latter are the nine-tenths) have been only partially visited ... The supply of potatoes is equal or more ample than that of last year ... One-third of last year's crop was used for feeding pigs for the market ... The new potato crop was early in July this year ... The present crop would have more than seven months consumption ... The disease has not affected the market prices, 1½d. to 2d. per stone. Heavy rain last Wednesday and Thursday has affected the digging out and storing of the potatoes.'

15 November. Same to same

'A great quantity of potatoes have been dug since my last report and almost in every instance more or less diseased. Quite sound potatoes pitted a fortnight ago and one-third at least was found diseased. The crop from boggy lands is sound as yet ... If one-third of the crop can be saved, it will come up to what is called 'a bad year'. There is still in this district a great part of the crop in the ground.'

Monday 17 November. James Henry PP to Sligo Champion

'We regret we must confirm the rumour of a very general failure of the potato crop in this county. It is impossible to say precisely what amount of injury has been done, but we fear we are not over the mark, when we surmise that one third of the crop is entirely lost ... If the failure were local, confined to one particular district, the contributions of benevolent individuals might save the peasantry from starvation, but it is, alas, universal. From all quarters the accounts are most disheartening, and yet the grain is leaving the country as fast as it can be exported, in order to enable the tenants to meet the demands of the landlords. All this is very distressing, but we must only hope that Providence will not desert the people in their extremity.'

Sunday 23 November. Henry Brett, county surveyor, Castlebar, to Henry R. Paine, Secretary, Board of Works

'The prevalent disease has committed great ravages in most parts of this county, and it appears to be daily getting worse ... The potatoes in pits are in most cases worse and it is generally believed better to leave them undug ... The disease is most capricious, attacking in some places one kind of potato,

Ballina
RLFC 2/Z.15796

Castlebar
RLFC 2/Z.16036

Bunninadden

Co Mayo
RLFC 3/1/101

in others nearly all kinds. 'Cups' seem to be the least affected. It is gratifying to find that the districts which suffered most in former years of famine, are at present comparatively free from the disease, namely, Erris, Achill, the sea coasts and mountain districts. God grant they may continue so ... There is almost a total cessation of the sale of grain, the markets continue at moderate rates and from the great abundance of the potato crop, the present loss (which cannot be less than one-third or one-fourth) can be afforded.'

Ballymote
RLFC 2/Z.16462

Monday 24 November. Rev J. Garrett, Vicar of Emlefad, to the Lord Lieutenant
'Of the potatoes that are partially diseased, the sound parts are used for pigs, poultry and grating into starch. The general opinion is that the farmers have an abundance of provisions, that the prices of young cattle, pork and butter are better than they have been for many years, that the grain crop was abundant and, bearing the price it does, a very small portion of it will suffice to meet the usual demands and consequently the rents may be paid in almost every instance without endangering a scarcity. But there is a labouring class who depend entirely on conacre potatoes as a support and who pay the rent of their cabins and conacre by what they have earned in England in the harvest or perhaps in their own locality. These poor beings can't obtain any employment at this season They have already few sound potatoes and will probably be destitute before the first of March ... I propose that a depot of rice and oatmeal be provided in each union and employment given to these people, such as making crossroads, levelling old ditches and making new ones, under the superintendance of local engineers. On Saturday night wages of 10d. per day should be paid, partly in food at the rate of 10s. per cwt. for oatmeal. The government may in this way put to silence all the discontent and clamour, which the dissaffected have raised and may avert much misery and remedy the national calamity, which has fallen most severely on the poor working classes. It is clear to every thinking man that opening the ports or prohibiting the export of farm produce would be the ruin of Ireland ... Our only resource is agriculture. We have no manufactuory and consequently we must have a universal bankruptcy if our grain, beef, pork and butter are not exported. In such a season, I feel that every individual is called upon to sustain the government in an endeavour to avert the evils that attend upon the scarcity of food, and it would be a blessing to Ireland if the base agitators who pretend to be patriots were driven from the surface of society and not permitted ... to goad the unhappy peasantry into rebellion and the now unhappily too prevalent system of assassination of the resident gentry.'

Sligo
RLFC 2/Z.16838

Thursday 27 November. Francis Knox Gore to Sir Thomas Freemantle
'I attended the meeting of the Poor Law Guardians of the Sligo Union. They

are of the opinion that the central part of the county will not have a suffi-cient supply of potatoes for the winter and spring. The meeting was adjourned for a fortnight when the necessity of organising committees in particular districts will be discussed but to take this step till absolutely nec-essary would be ... to unsettle the minds of the people and distract their attention from endeavouring to save what remains of their potato crop. The county gentlemen recommend the Lord-Lieutenant to establish simple but principal mills in the districts where the crop is most injured, to convert the bad potatoes into Farina, making the mills also depots for the Farina (dry or wet) manufactured by the peasantry ... It is too much to expect private indi-viduals to undertake this when others besides their tenants might benefit ... Unless this is done much of the diseased potatoes will be lost ... It would stimulate the people to make the Farina themselves, to keep food in the country which would be lost or given to cattle ... People will receive a fair price for bad potatoes or Farina.'

Friday 28 November. Edward Hunt, sub-inspector, to the Inspector General
'Since my report of 29 October, the disease is not progressing and panic among the people has greatly subsided and the price of potatoes has fallen.'

Swinford
RLFC 2/ Z.16886

Saturday 29 November. Henry Brett, Castlebar, to Henry R. Paine, Board of Works
'It would appear that the disease is not making the rapid advances heretofore observed, but it nevertheless still continues to make inroads on those in pits as well as on those undug.'

Co Mayo
RLFC 3/ 1/112

Wednesday 10 December. Resolution of Sligo Board of Guardians
'That the potato disease has prevailed and continues to progress in the four inland baronies of this county to an alarming extent and that a considerable portion of the crop has perished. That numbers of the poorest classes, totally dependant on their conacre potato crops which have particularly suffered, must be driven to the markets for food which it will be impossible for them to purchase unless afforded early, special and continued employment ... That depots or stores of provisions should be established to supply food on rea-sonable terms ... That we apprehend the worst results unless prompt and adequate measures be adopted.'

Sligo
RLFC 2/ Z.17842

Monday 19 January 1846. Petition of James Henry PP to the Lord Lieutenant on behalf of 1,100 families
'That there is no part of this county, perhaps of the entire kingdom, where the potato disease prevails and with more violence, than in this parish. That

Bunninadden
RLFC 2/ Z.1218

it is now beyond all doubt that the potato food will be exhausted before two or three months. That one half, if not more, of the people here depend exclusively for their subsistance on potato food. That 400 families of this parish have no means at all of support but conacre potatoes. That almost the entire of the above class have not at this moment a potato fit for human use.

I pray therefore on their part that your Excellency will institute some public employments in this neighbourhood to enable the poor people to earn something to preserve themselves from starvation. This can be readily done as there are many localities entirely shut out from the public roads for the want of anything in the shape of a public pass to their villages, and the people are at present obliged to carry the produce of their own land on their backs to the high road.'

Gurteen
RLFC 2/Z.1220

Monday 19 January. Memorial of the inhabitants of the parish of Kilfree, signed by Peter Brennan PP, chairman and Thomas R. MacDermot, secretary, to the Lord-Lieutenant

'That in this parish the destruction of the potato crop has been great and universal; that two-thirds of the entire have been totally destroyed or rendered unfit for use; that famine with all its accompanying horrors is rapidly approaching a peaceful district remarkable for the industry and quiet demeanour of its inhabitants; that under present alarming circumstances they confidently appeal to the wisdom and humanity of your Excellency to shield them from the impending danger by ordering some works useful to the community at large and affording salutary employment to the poor ... In the peculiar danger which now threatens to overwhelm them, memorialists venture to address your Excellency earnestly imploring that such works may be ordered speedily in this district before famine and disease shall have visited it.'

Loughglynn
RLFC 3/1/404

Friday 23 January. Charles Strickland to J. P. Kennedy, Dublin Castle

'Up to so late a time as the end of December, the loss of the potato crop, tho' severe in some places, did not much alarm me. Much use was made of the diseased potatoes in feeding cattle and pigs and in many cases for human food by cutting off the affected parts...Within the last fortnight and even the last few days the potatoes in pits are nearly all diseased or quite rotten ... When sowing time comes it may be difficult to find a sufficient quantity of sound seed for the next year's crop ... During the last fortnight we have had very unusually fine weather and warmer than any weather since the crop was dug and the disease seems to be much increased by it.'

Kilmactigue
RLFC 3/1/393

Friday 23 January. Jemmet Duke to J. P. Kennedy

'The district from Banada to Aclare and Belclare has suffered extremely from the disease and, as is generally the case, the good clay ground is the worst, the moory lands not so badly affected. I do not however think that district in a much worse condition than the circumjacent country and the centre of the county … The extract from the report of Rev Daniel Mullarkey went too far as he said that all would be lost in December. I do not think any are yet entirely exhausted. Public works are required in this district where there is a dense population without any means of procuring wages for their labours … The disease is progressing more latterly than it had been for some time previous, with the exception of its first appearance.'

Tuesday 27 January. Resolutions of the Swinford Board of Guardians (See Appendix 1M)

Swinford
RLFC 3/1/484

'That the gloomy and alarming prospects of a scarcity of provisions occasioned by an extensive failure of the potato crop throughout the whole of this extensive and thickly populated Union are such as to call for the most prompt measures to avert the famine with which the poor, over whose interests we preside, are threatened. That the disease has progressed to an alarming extent since our last report to the Poor Law Commissioners. We then were in hopes that the potatoes which were apparently safe, and which had been stored in a safe state, and depended on for a future supply of food and seed, would continue so, but unfortunately (as we find that in pits opened within the last few days in most cases at least two-thirds were useless), our hopes are frustrated, and we much fear a great scarcity and consequently dread a famine unless the government shall afford prompt and efficacious assistance. That we therefore trust your Excellency may be graciously pleased to take this memorial into your immediate consideration and by your rendering pecuniary aid to the poor of this Union in the shape of public works and prevent a people, as remarkable for their orderly and peaceable conduct as for their industrious habits, from enduring excessive privations, if not perishing from want, as the crops of many families are already exhausted.'

To His Excellency The Lord Lieutenant of Ireland

We the Guardians of the Poor of the Poor Law Union of Swinford in the Counties of Mayo and Sligo, beg to present to your Excellency the following Resolutions agreed to, at a Special Meeting of our Board held this day by requisition, owing to the urgency of the occasion—

That the glaring and alarming prospects of a scarcity of provisions occasioned by an extensive failure in the Potatoe Crops throughout the whole of this extensive and thickly populated Union, are such as to call for the most prompt measures to avert the famine with which the poor, we whose interests we preside, are threatened,

That we regret being obliged to state, that the disease has progressed to an alarming extent since our last report to the Poor Law Commissioners, we then were in hopes, that the Potatoes which were apparently safe, and which had been stored in a safe state, and depended on for a future supply for food and seed, would continue so: but unfortunately (as we find that in fits spend within the last few days, in most cases at least two-thirds, were useless) our hopes are frustrated, and we much fear a great scarcity, and consequently dread a famine unless the Government shall afford prompt and effective assistance—

That we therefore trust, Your Excellency may be graciously pleased, to take this our Memorial into your immediate consideration, and by your rendering aid to the poor of this Union, on the shape of Public Works and prevent a people as remarkable for their orderly and peaceable conduct as for their industrious habits from incurring excessive privations, if not perishing from want, as the crops of many families are already exhausted.—

That the foregoing Resolutions be transmitted to His Excellency, by our Chairman—

Board Room
January 27th 1846.

Signed on behalf of the Board of Guardians

Spring 1846

Relief Measures

A Poor Law had been introduced to Ireland in July 1838. To enable the implementation of this act, the country was divided into into 130 new administrative units known as 'unions'. The unions in north Connacht were Sligo, Boyle, Castlerea, Swinford, Ballina, Castlebar, Westport and Ballinrobe. Each union consisted of a group of electoral divisions made up of a number of townlands. Swinford Union comprised 12 electoral divisions, Sligo 23, Boyle 16, Ballina 17, Castlebar 10, and Castlerea 18. A workhouse was established in the principal market town of each union. This was administered by a Board of Guardians who were a mixture of elected and ex officio local men, usually chosen from the wealthy and propertied classes. Swinford had 21 elected Guardians, Sligo 39, Ballina 33, Castlebar 21 and Castlerea 27. The workhouses were financed locally by the poor rates on the principle that 'property should pay for poverty' and to force landlords take a greater interest in the management of their estates an act was passed making landlords liable to pay poor rates on land valued at under £4 per annum.

Individuals could not enter the workhouse, but paupers had to enter as whole family units. Once inside, families and sexes were to be strictly segregated. Nobody was to be idle in the workhouse, as the name suggests. Breaking stones in the workhouse yard for gravelling roads or other such work was mandatory for men and women and used as a deterrent to any pauper remaining too long. Food was inferior and monotonous. Destitution was the only criterion for admission to the workhouse.

To offset the impending distress due to the failure of the potato crop, the British prime minister, Sir Robert Peel, in November 1845 secretly arranged for the purchase and importation into Ireland of £100,000 worth of Indian meal (maize) from America. He also established on 20 November the temporary Relief Commission. In January 1846 Randolph Routh was appointed chairman. Their duties were to advise the government and supervise and co-ordinate the local relief committees. These were comprised of local notables, including landlords, clergymen, magistrates and large farmers. The local committees were to purchase and re-sell the Indian corn which was stored in government depots at ports such as Sligo and Westport. They were financed by raising local subscriptions which were matched by a government grant of

Memorial of the Swinford Board of Guardians to the Lord Lieutenant, 27 January 1846

up to 100%. Originally these local committees were based on the barony as a unit such as those for the combined baronies of Costello-Gallen in Mayo or Corran or Leyny in Sligo but as the crisis deepened they became centred on smaller units like parishes.

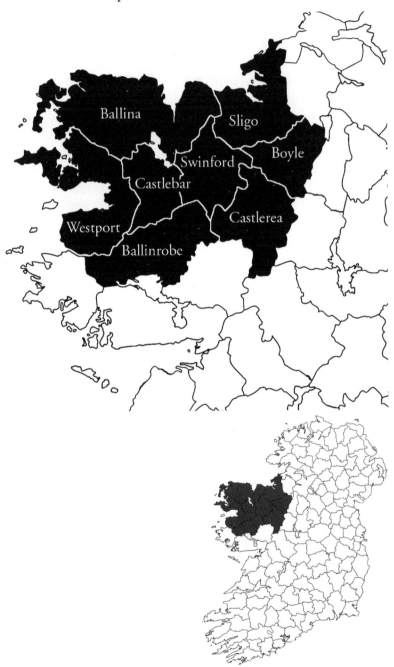

Map of the eight Unions of North Connacht

Friday 6 February 1846. J. A. Holmes, Hanover Square, London, to J. P. Kennedy   *Ballaghaderreen*
'Up to a month ago when I had to leave home on business, I had been   RLFC 3/1/494
unwearied in inspecting the state of the crop of upwards of 500 families who
are under my charge. I do not know of one whose crop was totally destroyed
and from the information which I have received since, am I aware of any of
these families having been obliged to resort to the market ... I have been in
constant communication with the different landlords ... who are anxious to
do anything in their power to assist their tenantry and I purpose to return to
my residence at the end of this month to remain permanently and give any
assistance in my power to relieve anyone who may require it.'

Monday 9 February. Rev J. Garrett to T. N. Redington   *Keash*
'I do not know how far our store of food may be safe and the mob kept off   OP 26/80
during the distribution of cooked supplies. One station in part of the country under the mountain of Keash, where several outbreaks have been committed and where some police have been till lately stationed, should have the
police restored.'

Thursday 12 February. G. V. Jackson to the Poor Law Commission   *Ballina*
'Messrs Gallagher of Ballina are particular friends of mine. They have exten-   RLFC 3/1/537
sive mills for storing and grinding Indian corn. They are known on the Corn
Exchange of London and Liverpool as of the highest character. I will be
obliged if you can get them the grinding of any corn that may be consigned
to this port.'
Draft reply, 14 February: 'The storing will be at Sligo and if they find it worth
their while, they will have an opportunity of competing.'

Monday 16 February. Rev M. Tyndale, Rector of Kilmactigue to the Chief Secretary   *Kilmactigue*
'Unless some measures be immediately taken for the relief of the people, the   RLFC 2/Z.3098
consequences must be dreadful to contemplate ... There is not a single land-
proprietor within a circuit of ten miles of this place, nor a magistrate, whose
influence might be beneficially exerted in this or any other emergency ...
There is an immense population of able-bodied men most anxious for
employment, several thousand acres of undrained bog and a great want of
public roads.'

Tuesday 17 February. G. V. Jackson to the Lord Lieutenant   *Swinford*
'The circumstances of this Union are very peculiar and call for more atten-   RLFC 2/Z.3910
tion than that of most other Unions in Ireland, there being few if any resident proprietors, there being many properties under the courts, others
belonging to lunatics and minors on which little employment if any has been

or can be given. Others also being vested in trustees whose only object, having but a passing and temporary interest, is likely to be the repayment of monies advanced by them. A further particularity is that there are many remote localities thickly peopled, far away from high roads and public communications and almost beyond the reach of any assistance the Guardians can afford. I request that you will have a supply of Indian corn and maize stored in this poorhouse.'

Extract from Guardians' minutes:

'That having conferred with each other as to the state of the potato disease in the various parts of the Union since our last meeting of the Board, we regret to find that all the evidence agrees as to the case being alarming and imminent in some electoral divisions of the Union, and that in consequence we made arrangements to open this house and prepare for the approaching difficulty with the least possible delay. The master of the poorhouse has thrown out as useless four barrels of potatoes out of thirteen grown on the ground attached to the house.'

Dublin

DP 73

Saturday 28 February. Instructions to committees of relief districts

'That Lieutenants of counties be requested to form committees ... to be comprised of, Lieutenant or deputy-Lieutenant of the county, magistrates of Petty Sessions, officer of the Board of Works, clergymen of all persuasions, chairman of the Poor Law Union, Poor Law Guardians and resident magistrate. That they will promote by every means in their power the most profitable and most natural resources of employment in their district, by stimulating private enterprise ... That landholders and other rate-payers are the parties both legally and morally answerable for affording relief to the destitute poor ... That the measures to be adopted by the officer of the government are to be considered merely as auxiliary ... That the local committee should solicit subscriptions ... a list of the sums subscribed, together with a list of the landlords who do not subscribe should be brought under the notice of the Lord-Lieutenant who will determine on the sum to be contributed from the funds at his disposal in aid of the local subcription ... That the government will be prepared to supply to the local committee, at a moderate price such reasonable quantity of Indian meal and oatmeal ... for distribution to destitute persons employed by them or for sale at or under first cost, with a view of enabling the poorer classes obtain a sufficiency of food, with the wages ordinarily earned ... A task of work shall be required from every person capable of giving it, who applies for relief. The payments for the work performed shall be made in food ... as will be sufficient to support the workman and the helpless persons of his family ... Gratuitous relief shall be afforded only to those persons who are entirely incapable of giving a day's work and their reception in the workhouse, from want of room, is impracticable … Tickets should be given to such only as are without means of providing food for their families.'

Friday 13 March 1846. Extract from engineer's report
'The progress of decay increases. In the month of February a greater quantity of potatoes rotted than in the previous two months. Letting the potatoes remain undug in the ground was the best way of preserving them. This method was adopted extensively in Co Sligo. The small farmers (those who pay £4 to £20 annual rent) expect their supply of potatoes will be exhausted by the middle of May … The supply of cottier tenants or labourers is now nearly consumed. The impoverished condition and squalid misery of this class of the people of the county, has not yet arrived at any extraordinary degree of distress but there is an apprehension of famine that in itself is frightening … Between 16 March and 20 May the farmers will afford to the labourers full employment in tilling the ground … From 20 May to 10 September public works will be the best means of preventing famine.
The poorer the ground the sounder were the potatoes. In the mountainous districts where the potatoes were planted in a peat soil, disease made less progress than in the more cultivated parts of the country.'

Corran, Leyny & Coolavin
RLFC 3/1/724

Wednesday 18 March. Rev J. Garrett to Dean of Ferns
'Magistrates and cess payers should appoint overseers to select the labouring classes in the public works and not confine the operations to contractors who will only give employment to a few of their own servants and dependants.'

Ballymote
RLFC 3/1/1190

Wednesday 18 March. John Coghlan PP to Bernard Owen Cogan JP, Collooney
'Weeks have passed since the magistrates and cess-payers of this unfortunate half barony specified the public works to give employment to the starving population of this district … When are we to expect relief? We are daily surrounded by the hunger-stricken poor seeking food or the means to procure it. Typhus is now ravaging this district. In the name of our common humanity, I call upon you, Sir, who well knows this barony and its destitution, to lay before his Excellency the heartrending situation of this district. You are aware how peaceable and quiet they have been at all times. I fear that as hunger breaks their will, so will their quiet peaceable habits be very shortly turned to procure the means of subsistence in violation of order and the laws that hitherto regulated their conduct … I have the greatest fear for the safety of the people and the stability of the peace and order which always characterised this barony. We have adopted everything contained in the act of parliament for our guidance. Was it to mock our distress that nothing has been done?'

Kilmovee
RLFC 2/Z.5748

Gurteen
RLFC 2/Z.5748

Thursday 19 March. Peter Brennan PP to Bernard O. Cogan JP, Collooney
'O Sir, had you witnessed the scenes at which I must be hourly present and had you heard the melancholy reports which are every succeeding moment carried to me by many of my parishioners, you would censure me most severely for having deferred so long to press this matter on your attention. Many of my people, having for many weeks continued to subsist on deseased potatoes, have not now even that description of food on which to subsist. Fever is very prevalent in the villages throughout my parish caused by the use of unwholesome fruit ... Unless the people get employment, the result will, I dread, be most melancholy ... The people are willing to labour at any employment to which they may be sent.'

Tubbercurry
RLFC 3/1/863

Thursday 19 March. John Meekings MD to the Poor Law Commission, suggesting the building of a fever hospital for the 'approach of fever which is now generally believed will rage as an epidemic this summer. Such would be built for £200 to £250. I think that the government could give a grant of £110 and £50 could be raised by subscription. As it would be a public work, half the cost would thus be raised.'

RLFC 3/1/1616

17 April. Same to J. P. Kennedy, seeking a grant of £100 to build a fever hospital, having already £100.
'The period of its requirement may not be far distant ... We are the centre of a large and populous district, more than 20 miles from any hospital, having three towns, of which Tubbercurry contains 1,000 inhabitants. By commencing the work at once, labour and mechanics could be now easily procured which as the season advances ... could not be had without exorbitant rates of wages. Many of the landlords are absentees, in fact nearly all, and therefore we are obliged to seek assistance from the government which a more favoured neighbourhood might not require ... Fever may break out suddenly and it will be a heart-harrowing circumstance to find that no means have been adopted to meet this exigency or to isolate the disease.'

Swinford
RLFC 3/1/1181

Tuesday 31 March. Extract from the Guardians' minutes
'Having conferred with each other as to the state and progress of the potato disease since our last meeting, we regret to be obliged to arrive at the conclusion that the disease prevails universally and rapidly increases in every part of the Union.'

Coolavin
DP. 140 & 162

Tuesday 31 March. Michael Gethen JP, Theo. Sherlock, Martin Callaghan and James Powell, cesspayers, to the Lord-Lieutenant
'The great number of roads, bridges, pipes and gullets in the half barony are under contract and there is no obligation imposed on the contractors to

Straide, Wednesday 25 March. Michael Davitt was born, the second child of Martin Davitt and his wife Catherine

employ destitute persons able and willing to work … Townlands are shut up and have no access to high roads for horses and cars.' They recommend that overseers be appointed and that the labourers be certified as in want by the resident magistrate, Poor Law Guardian or Protestant or Catholic clergyman.

Thursday 2 April 1846. John Armstrong JP to Richard Pennefather, enclosing a memorial from the magistrates and cesspayers at a Special Sessions in Coolaney, 1 April

Coolaney
DP 169

'We are prohibited from passing any new roads or works … Those we are authorised to pass must be given to contractors … They are no relief to the labouring poor as contractors will employ their own horses and carts and those who are either their under-tenants or those who may be indebted to them.'

Wednesday 22 April. Resolutions of a public meeting

Sligo
DP 686

'That from want of employment, consequent on so many being discharged from the merchants' provision yards, corn stores etc, as well as from the high price of food, that the labouring classes in Sligo town are in a sad state of want and destitution. That an application be made without delay to the Commissioners to put the Indian meal now warehoused here on the market at a moderate rate which will have the effect of lowering the price of potatoes, oatmeal and other food. That a public meeting be called by the Mayor, of aldermen, magistrates of the Petty Sessions, chairman of the Board of Guardians, Poor Law Guardians, clergymen and such other intelligent gentlemen and merchants as he may approve of, for the purpose of relieving the existing distress in this town and neighbourhood.'

Kilfree, Co Sligo
DP 775

Tuesday 28 April. Bernard Whelan RM to the Chief Secretary
'At the Petty Sessions of Mullaghroe held on 28 April 1846 in the county of Sligo, upwards of two-hundred of the peasantry assembled. The Revd Messrs Brennan and Coghlan addressed the magistrates, stating that the people were in want of food, that they thought employment would be given them and that they could not control the people longer and that Roscommon peasantry intended to cross into Sligo to swear the people there not to work under the wages given in Roscommon, and that they would not starve whilst provisions were to be found.'

RLFC 3/1/5084

Wednesday 29 April. J. A. Holmes JP to the Lord-Lieutenant
'I explained to them the great anxiety of the government to cooperate in giving employment, and considered it adviseable to take the declaration of many that they are at present out of provisions. I examined each person most minutely and permitted no person whatever to sign the declaration who was not actually at the time in a state of destitution and I beg leave to remark that most of these persons are cottier tenants merely holding a cabin and small garden.' *(See Appendix 11)*

Holmes also enclosed a memorial signed by Peter Brennan PP, Myles MacDermot, Thomas MacDermot, Andrew Baker, John Coghlan CC, Thomas Costello, Terence Finn & Michael Finn:
'That we were in daily expectation that works would have been commenced, in order to give employment to the distressed poor who were able and willing to work. That we now find that there appears no immediate prospect of giving employment without the slow formality of a new meeting ... That your Excellency will direct that some of the works will be immediately commenced as the people are starving ... the road leading to Carroontemple churchyard, commencing at Monasteredan, and also the road leading to the churchyard of Templeronane commencing at Mahanagh, and also the levelling of hills on the main road from Boyle to Ballina, commencing at Mountirwin and ending at Cloonloo, the mearing of the county. That those three works, of such great public utility, are situate in those districts where famine is most rife ... That we implore your Excellency in the name of suffering humanity and for the preservation of the peace of this hitherto peaceable district ... that those works will be at once commenced. 750 human beings are without any description of food or means of procuring it. That the call for labour is now nearly at an end as the oats will be planted in a day or two ... That several other families have not more provisions than will suffice for a week and several others have not more than will suffice for a fortnight.'

Summer 1846

Public Works

Legislation had been introduced in March paving the way for the establishment of public works to provide relief. Most of these works consisted in the repair and construction of roads. The money was provided by a Treasury grant, half of which was to be repaid by the locality, the other half being a free grant. The distressed area had to send a memorial to the Lord Lieutenant requesting assistance. This was forwarded in turn to the Relief Commissioners and the Board of Works for their comments. It was then sent to the local surveyor for his inspection. When the Board of Works received his report they made their decision and if they accepted it they made a recommendation to the Lord Lieutenant, who then asked for the sanction of the Treasury. Only after this cumbersome procedure could the works commence.

The local relief committees were responsible for selecting the labourers among the destitute to whom they issued work tickets. There was much criticism of some committees and of some individual members in their choice of labourers who often were not only not destitute but were expressly chosen to enable them to pay the arrears of rent due to their landlord. The labourers were paid a daily rate of 9d or 10d. Five-sixths of all those employed were concentrated in only seven counties, including Galway, Mayo and Roscommon. In June the number of people employed daily was approximately 21,000. In July it increased to 71,000 daily and it peaked in the second week of August at almost 98,000. On 21 July 1846 the Treasury announced that all the public measures introduced to meet the emergency were to be brought to a close as soon as possible in the expectation that the potato harvest would render them unnecessary.

Kilcolman
RLFC 3/1/3169

Monday 11 May 1846. Memorial of poor and distressed individuals to Board of Works

'The poor and very distressed individuals of the parish of Kilcolman ... most humbly implore, beg and beseech your Honours will be good enough to favour them with some relief to support nature, as their very distressed state may be better conceived than described, and we unanimously and most humbly presume informing your Honours that it had been agreed on that a line of road was necessary to pass from Redhill through Fawleens to Monasteredan, which was approved by one of her Majesty's engineers ... Your complained *(sic)* will learn each and every of the said distressed individuals to pray to Almighty God to relieve and shelter your souls in Heavenly bliss.' *(Reply to be directed to Mr Burns, Ballaghaderreen for Patt Gallagher, Fawleens.)*

Swinford
RLFC 3/1/2467

Tuesday 19 May. Extract from the Guardians' minutes

'We consider a relief committee ... necessary for this district, and we request Mr Vaughan Jackson will convene the persons appointed to constitute that committee, to a meeting to be held at the boardroom, Swinford, 26th of this month.'

RLFC 3/1/2678

26 May. Resolutions of Gallen & Costello Relief Committee.

'That two sub-committees be formed for Costello barony and two for Gallen barony. That all persons possessing property or deriving an income from these two baronies be asked to subscribe to relieve the distress of the population and that an account be opened in the Provincial Bank, Ballina. That Mr Strickland be appointed chairman of the sub-committee for Ballaghaderreen, Francis R. O'Grady for Aghamore and Mr Deane for Gallen. That each member of the committee attend a meeting this day fortnight with information on the state of destitution in his district.'

G. V. Jackson recommended Daniel Keane of Kilduff as pay clerk of Gallen barony, who had applied for the post and was willing to deposit £200 to £300 as security. 4 June 1846, Board of Works rejected the recommendation as 'extremely unadviseable as officers appointed by them should be free agents'.

Gallen
RLFC 3/1/2510

Saturday 23 May. Extract from Capt Peebles' report

'Generally speaking, the labourers have a sufficient supply of potatoes to last them for a month to come ... At the same time I should mention that the potato disease continues, and if it assumes a more aggravated form, the stock will probably not last so long ... From the barony a very considerable number of labourers go usually at this season of the year (or a little later) to England in search of employment ... It might be adviseable not to undertake the whole of the works I have recommended ... although I think it probable that being now in expectation of work in their own country, they may be induced to remain on the spot.'

Thursday 28 May. James Henry PP to the Lord Lieutenant   *Cloonoghill*
'In Cloonoghill there are 700 families without food or the means to procure   DP 1593
it. Many of these poor people subsisted for the last few weeks by borrowing
a little meal from those whose stock was not then exhausted. I had influence
over the poor up to this time to prevent an outbreak, by holding out encouragement that the works would soon be commenced. Memorials were procured many weeks ago but nothing has been done. If some immediate step is
not taken by the government to relieve these suffering people, the peace of
the country as well as the lives of the people are at stake.'

Monday 1 June 1846. Walter James Bourke to the Lord Lieutenant   *Killala*
'This day I have been waited on by a large number of the labouring classes   DP 1838
of this town for the purpose of stating that they were unable to procure a sufficient supply of potatoes on the market on Saturday last, in consequence of
the number of vessels along the coast shipping them for other ports. They
wished to know from me how they were to act. I promised I would at once
write for your Lordship's directions. This has for the present satisfied them.
There is in this country plenty of provisions I hope for a long time but if
allowed to be taken out of it, there will be none left. Should this not be
immediately prevented, the people would be driven to acts of violence.'

Friday 5 June. G. V. Jackson to the Relief Commission   *Foxford*
'Some men asked me for work or food as they were starving in the town of   RLFC 3/1/2916
Foxford yesterday evening, as I was returning from Swinford Special Sessions.
I made as much enquiry as the lateness of the hour and the circumstances
would admit into the accuracy of what they said … I was assured by persons
that what these poor men stated … was perfectly true. A channel of employment should be opened at once. It is reported that the recent hot weather has
so injured all the potatoes that remain as to make them unhealthy as food.'
Draft reply:
'No application has been made for public works in the district. Local relief
committees should raise subscriptions … and the government will be prepared to add a donation immediately.'

Tuesday 9 June. Resolutions of the meeting of the Gallen & Costello Relief   *Swinford*
Committee   RLFC 3/1/3088 & 3181
'That the government be urgently called upon to have the public works com-
menced to give employment to the able bodied and the destitute poor … We

have reason to apprehend from the threatening attitude which some persons are assuming in some localities caused by extreme destitution and we fear the results may be very serious. That a depot is necessary for Indian meal and maize at Foxford, Swinford, Ballaghaderreen, Ballina and Ballyhaunis. That we feel a pride and pleasure in recording that even under the pressure of distress, the exemplary character of the population of these baronies remains unchanged.'
Wednesday 10 June. G. V. Jackson to William Stanley
'Distress is general and in some places extensive. Public safety imperatively requires that employment be given at once. It has been stated from more place than one, that the people declare "whilst sheep and cattle are to be found, they will not perish from hunger". The district is peculiarly circumstanced, there being no resident gentry to assist or give employment, many localities being remote and thickly peopled … I cannot too forceably urge the absolute necessity of this representation being at once attended to.'

Bunninadden
RLFC 3/1/3271

Sunday 14 June. Memorial of James Henry PP, John Finn CC and 29 parishioners of the parishes of Cloonoghill, Kilturra and Kilshalvey to the Relief Commission (See Appendix 1F)
'We … beg most respectfully to inform you of the state of extreme destitution of many of the poorer classes in these districts in which there is no resident landed proprietor and consequently but little employment can be obtained by the able bodied labourer, nor has any public work been as yet undertaken altho' applied for long since and no relief committee has been formed that we are aware of for the barony of Corran in which these parishes are situated and from our want of means we fear that any subscriptions we may be able to collect will appear so trifling in your eyes as scarcely to justify our demand of relief, which we are however most urgently compelled to make. In default of a baronial committee we have formed a parochial one and shall proceed to make application to our non-resident landlords for subscriptions and in the meantime implore some immediate relief from the funds in your hands or a supply of Indian meal from the depot at Sligo.
Draft reply: 'Forward list of subscriptions however small … and a grant in aid will be recommended. Indian meal can be purchased at Sligo depot by any duly constituted relief committee.'

RLFC 3/1/3634

26 June. John Armstrong JP to the Relief Commission

Memorial of the inhabitants of Cloonoghill, Kilturra and Kilshalvey, 16 June 1846

'There is no relief committee for the parishes of Cloonoghill and Kilturra in Corran barony. A parochial one was set up but not sanctioned by the Relief Commission. Considerable distress exists, there are no resident landlords or householders of sufficient means to employ the poor able to work.'
Armstrong asks that a grant be made towards the relief of the destitute.

RLFC3/1/3271

JU 16 1846

Gentlemen

We the undersigned Inhabitants of the Parishes of Clooneghell, Killerra and Kilshalvy in the County of Sligo beg most respectfully to Inform you of the State of extreme destitution of many of the poorer classes in these districts in which there are no resident landed proprietors and Consequently but little employment can be obtained by the able bodied labourer, nor has any Public work been as yet undertaken altho' applied for long Since and no Relief Committee has been formed that we are aware of for the Barony of Corran in which these Parishes are Situated and from our want of Means we fear that any Subscriptions we may be able to Collect will appear So trifling in your eyes as Scarcely to Justify our demand of Relief which we are however most urgently Compelled to make — In default of a Baronial Committee we have formed a Parochial one and Shall Proceed to make application to our non resident Landlords for Subscription and in the mean time implore Some immediate Relief from the funds in your hands or a Supply of Indian Meal from the Depot at Sligo —

Please to Communicate your Reply to the Revd Mr Henry P. P. Bunnenadden, Ballymote or to John Armstrong Esq Chappool Ballymote the nearest Resident Magis=trate to whom we refer you for the accuracy of our Statement.

Draft reply:
'There are vacancies in Boyle workhouse and also in Sligo workhouse. There is a constabulary depot in Ballymote already.'

Kilmactigue
RLFC 3/1/3288

Monday 15 June. Extract of Major Whittingham's report
'It appears indeed that the loss of potatoes (by the figured map supplied to me) in the electoral division of Kilmactigue has been less there than in all the other divisions except Achonry. In Coolaney for instance, the loss appears by that map to have been twice as great as in Kilmactigue, and whether the map is correct or not, it is most assuredly an imperfect index of the real state of the barony at present.'

Ballinrobe
RLFC 3/1/3602

Saturday 20 June. J. S. Bindon Corbet to the Inspector General
'Between 8 and 9 o clock this morning a number of distressed people attempted to force themselves on the public works, repairing the streets of Ballinrobe. They said "if they could not get work, they would break into houses for provisions".'

Balla
RLFC 3/1/3586

Tuesday 23 June. Paul McGreal PP to the Relief Commission, complaining that the Catholic curates are excluded from the relief committee. 'The district has 2,000 families, 1,900 of whom are Catholics.'
Draft reply, 26 June. 'Curates should be at once admitted.'

Gallen & Costello
DP 2661

Wednesday 25 June. G. V. Jackson to the Under-Secretary
'The district contains 19 parishes with scarcely a resident magistrate ... All their recommendations having been disregarded, the committee are induced to adjourn *sine die* and inform the people accordingly and let events take their course. Every safeguard of the committee has been rejected, public works, depots etc and their deliberation absurd and cruel (especially compared with wealthy districts where employment is found and depots given) ... Are the poor of the district to starve? The formation of depots, however small, would remove apprehension. The works under the Extraordinary Petty Sessions don't cost the government a farthing. The population of the parishes of Toomore and Knock must perish (from the evidence given at their meeting on Tuesday), if employment be longer delayed. All the other parishes are approaching the same state ... I am in the painful position of having parties coming day after day long distances and finding no result.'

	Gallen		
Parishes	no. of families	amount granted	no. of men employed per day for 60 days
Attymass & Kilgarvan	750	£563 1s. 4d.	200
Killasser	750	£133 6s. 6d.	40
Kilconduff & Meelick	1600	£510 13s.	150
Kildacomogue & Straide	1100	£340	110
Bohola	800	£114	25
Toomore	900	£100	35
Costello			
Kilbeagh	1800	£653	200
Kilcolman & Castlemore	1600	£445	150
Kilmovee	1100	£480	160
Total		*£2061*	*664*
Aghamore	1500	£300	100
Annagh	1000	£378 8s. 4d.	120
Bekan	800	£675 13s. 4d.	225
Knock	800	£33 6s. 8d.	10
Total		*£2965 8s. 4d.*	*985*

Gallen

Thursday 25 June. John Armstrong to the Relief Commission
'From the report of the Roman Catholic clergyman extreme distress prevails in the upper half barony of Leyny, containing a population of 7,500. The funds are only £190 and no public works have commenced. The committee fears that the extreme destitution will compel them to dole out a considerable portion of our small means without being able to exact work in return.'
Draft reply, 27 June:
'Under no circumstances can gratuitous relief be sanctioned except for the infirm poor and then only in the event of there not being any vacancies in the workhouse. Employment must be provided and the commissioners cannot conceive that any part of the country is in such a state as not to present a variety of small public works of utility, suitable both for males and females.'

*Coolaney,
Cloonacool,
Tubbercurry*
RLFC 3/1/3585

Saturday 27 June. James McHugh PP Cloonacool, James Gallagher PP Achonry, Daniel Mullarkey PP Kilmactigue, & John Flynn PP Curry, to the Under-Secretary
'Very great distress exists in these parishes from the total failure of the potato crop of last year and the inability of the inhabitants to purchase other provisions from want of money. It appears from the returns which have been made

Tubbercurry
DP 2807

Tubbercurry

to the relief committee of the district that upwards of 7,500 persons are in actual distress at this moment and that to relieve all those persons only two small works have been ordered to be carried on, altho' several others were approved of at the Extraordinary Sessions, which if carried on would greatly relieve those who have no means to purchase and who are willing to labour if they could find employment ... Unless something is done immediately to relieve the distressed, we are quite certain it will be no easy matter to restrain those who are at present suffering from hunger.'

DP 2878

1 July. James McHugh PP to the Relief Commission

'Week after week passed in vain expectation of getting some employment by which they could support their starving families that were deprived of that means by that awful visitation, the potato rot. Now after their patience being worn out, expecting relief every other week, they got quite exasperated on hearing that Mr Ormsby Gore got public work for his tenantry in the next parish, Kilmactigue, and not contributing one pound more towards the funds for public works, than their landlord, Thomas Meredith Esq. whose letter for £100 was laid before the magistrates on the day of the Sessions. Major O'Hara also got public works to give employment to his tenantry, the people best accommodated with roads in the entire county of Sligo. But the misfortune of Mr Meredith's tenants is that he is absent from this country, an officer in one of her Majesty's regiments. The distress of the generality of the people is such not from any scarcity of meal but for want of means to purchase it. I dread in spite of all I can do to keep it down, they will break out and take the stock off the fields to stay their hunger. As the addage has it, "Hunger would make a hole through a stone wall." I assert without fear of contradiction, that there is not a more useful line of road in Co Sligo than the line from Tubbercurry to Sessua Common. The people living along that line, though paying very heavy county cess, must carry their grain etc on their backs more than a mile to the nearest road to them, and some of them a mile and a half and must wade their way through rivulets, hedges and ditches, a distance of three miles coming to church or chapel on Sunday and to markets and fairs to this town. For want of any other guardian to represent their galling distress, they are every other day running to me crying for redress and it not in my power to relieve them. Now with due submission I beg leave to lay their appalling condition before their natural guardians.'

The Claddagh,
Galway
DP 3018

Wednesday 1 July 1846. Petition of the Claddagh fishermen to the Lord Lieutenant

'That amounting to 4,000 souls, they are sufferers in common with the poor of the district, both by the failure of the potato crop and there being no demand for sea-weed during the last two months, upon which they support their families at this season of the year ... That for the last three weeks they have been engaged in fishing and that after three weeks toil at sea, each man's earnings have not amounted to more than the miserable sum of 5d for the entire week, and that many of us would have died from want had we not been relieved by a portion of the Calcutta Relief Fund, distributed among our families by the clergymen of the West Chapel ... That no fishery exists at present ... until the harvest herring fishery may set in about the latter end of August or the beginning of September. That they request the erection of a pier to give employment at this season of want ... when they are compelled to pawn their clothes and fishing tackle to purchase provisions.'

Wednesday 1 July. Richard Kyle to G. V. Jackson   *Swinford*
'Market prices yesterday in Swinford: oatmeal 16s. per cwt (an increase of 2s. 6d. on last market), potatoes from 3s. 8d. to 4s. per cwt (an increase of 1s. 9d.). Consequently, men are anxious to obtain work on the line from Swinford to Ballyvary.'

7 July. Resolutions of Gallen & Costello Relief Committee:
'The delay in the works is a cause of extreme anxiety ... A proper staff of over-seers and assistants should be supplied ... Contractors who are declining to fulfil their obligations will be prosecuted ... 80 tickets to be given to William McHugh PP for his parish ... 8s. a week to be paid to all stewards ... The county surveyor is to furnish a schedule of all the public works in each parish and to provide a set of rules for stewards, gangmen and labourers.'

8 July. Capt Gordon to Board of Works   RLFC 3/1/4165
'The Swinford Committee earnestly request that a depot of Indian meal be established at Swinford, as there is none nearer than Ballina.'

Monday 6 July. Edward Cooper, Markrea Castle, re 'threatening letter' he   *Collooney*
received from the Relief Committee of the upper half barony of Leyny who intend   RLFC 3/1/4061
to return the names of landlords who do not subscribe
'In April I directed my agent to employ three or four trustworthy men to report on the prospects of the poor before the harvest on my estates who have a right to be relieved from starvation by me ... On 16 May I received a letter from the chairman requesting my subscription as a landlord in the district. On 18 May I replied that persons having claims for relief from me should not seek aid from any board and that I would not provide for the poor on other men's estates ... I received another letter from Mr Brett with a list of town-lands on my estates with 242 persons in need of relief ... I sent this to my agent requiring the names of the heads of families in want. Of 19 in the town-land of Rathscanlan, eight are selling meal and otherwise comfortable and of the seven from Ogham, one is selling meal and three of them have cows.'

Partry
DP 3525

2am Tuesday 7 July. Peter F. Conway CC to the Lord Lieutenant
'I am just arrived in my room, being called during the night to administer the last rites of our holy religion to a poor man whose soul is perhaps before his Creator whilst I write these few lines. The name of the unfortunate man is Patt Lydon of Toureen in this parish. Should he die, I have no doubt his death was caused for the want of food or from the effects of very bad food. He has eight in family. I would not acknowledge this awful fact to have occurred in the parish where I preside, but that this poor man received from me during the summer nearly £2. From what I can learn, I believe a poor woman, a native of the mountain district of this parish, died of starvation a few weeks since … Unless the people are employed … before many weeks we will have many more victims in this parish … I have used every influence with the people to keep them quiet for the last two months. I have exhorted them daily to bear patiently for a while their distress and I promised them frequently from my altar that they would get the means of support. Now as they see no sign of relief, they are I find becoming discontented and I fear something will occur to disturb the peace of the country unless the people are employed.'

Foxford
RLFC 3/1/4143

Wednesday 8 July. G. V. Jackson to Relief Commission
'This day at Foxford I met Capt Gordon and H. Brett, county surveyor and asked them to visit the village of Shanwaer, the property of W. Cuffe in the parish of Toomore, represented with many others to me as being in the worst state of distress. For the people of 15 dwellings, Brett laid out a small work to the extent of 4 cwt of meal to meet the urgency … £21 17s. 6d. was collected in the town of Foxford with which Indian meal will be purchased tomorrow.'

Ballina
RLFC 3/1/3929

Thursday 9 July. G. V. Jackson to William Stanley
'I regret the smallness of the subscriptions for Mayo as compared with Clare. Many posponed payment, not knowing how subscriptions are to be applied etc.'
Draft reply: 'The proper mode of expending the funds is to purchase Indian meal or oatmeal or other food which may be either sold at a moderate price to distressed inhabitants or granted to able-bodied persons in return for work. Under no circumstances is it to be distributed gratuitously. The Commission regards such a practice as demoralising. With regard to impotent persons and others unable to work, relief should be afforded to them in the workhouse of the Union to which they belong.'

Sunday 12 July. John F. Meekings MD & treasurer of the Relief Committee of *Tubbercurry*
upper Leyny, to the Relief Commission RLFC 3/1/4223
'Destitution and starvation are now increasing so rapidly in this district that I consider it the duty of everyone, even in the individual capacity, to urge upon the Relief Commissioners the necessity for extraordinary exertions to ward off a calamity so awful and truly heart-rending to those obliged to witness it. As physician of the dispensary of this locality, independently of being one of the Relief Committee, I have opportunities of correctly ascertaining the wants of the poor and I know instances in which whole families have been a day without food, ashamed to beg, yet suffering serious privation. Many of this class are daily surrounding my door craving for work and most willing to obtain even a slender support for their families. They are fully impressed with the idea that we have been armed with powers to employ all that present themselves. I therefore earnestly appeal on behalf of suffering humanity that some of the public works approved of would be commenced without delay and such particularly, to enumerate two which are in localities where distress exists in an aggravated form ... a new road round the hill of Mucketta and one from the town of Bellaghy to Cully. Both are lines of great utility and would satisfy the hopes of many suffering poor. As far as our moderate funds permit, we as a committee have studied small works thro' the district but they can only act as a drop of oil upon the expansive ocean of misery around ... I feel I would be culpable if I failed to lay before the Commission this statement and to earnestly entreat their immediate attention to it.
P.S. Gratuitous relief in a limited and well-guarded form would be required, since infirm persons are around us, having children to support and if they are sent to the workhouse they must of course leave their cabins and small holdings to the mercy of their neighbours.'
Draft reply, 17 July:
'The true cause of not having works in progress is to be found in the absence of the requisite local exertions for providing the means of relief in due time.'
25 July. John Meekings MD to the Relief Commission, re the new road to avoid RLFC 3/1/4737
Mucketta hill
'The poor immediately around this are in very great distress ... Thirty men are only employed while hundreds are applying for help. In the parish of Kilmactigue, where much destitution exists, the Committee placed about 600 men for a new line of road now in progress between Aclare and the mearing of Co Sligo. The county surveyor, on visiting it, has reduced the number to 200, by which 400 were at once thrown out of employment at a time when the worst trying and pinching period of the year has come. Something should be devised to continue the people in the work. I do not think the Committee should be confined in regard to the numbers they employ.'

Swinford
RLFC 3/1/4520

Tuesday 14 July. Resolutions of the meeting of the Gallen & Costello Relief Committee

That the sale of meal by the Foxford sub-committee be authorised. That Daniel Keane be appointed to pay the Extraordinary Sessions monies in Gallen, on his getting £400 security and similarly Pat Dogherty in Costello. That the Board of Works be requested again to approve the new road from Kiltimagh between the mill at Cloonfallagh and the main road at Cahir, as the inhabitants are in the greatest state of want. That £20 be assigned to Foxford for employment in the parish of Toomore. That Pat Laven be requested to proceed at once with his contract from Kiltimagh to Bohola. That Capt Gordon be requested to make arrangements for children to break stones by the box and to have the boys and girls that have worked up to this day paid for their labour. That gratitude be expressed for the meal depots at Swinford and Ballaghaderreen and that one be requested for Ballyhaunis. That Mr Brett be requested to enquire about Austin Battle, a contractor who urged the men in Kilgarvan to hold out for a shilling a day. That Anthony Durkan, overseer in Kilgarvan, be dismissed for rating the wages contrary to the order of the Committee. That proper pay sheets be provided for all parishes. That the county surveyor be requested to have all the works put into operation at once.

RLFC 3/1/4329

15 July. G. V. Jackson to the Relief Commission

'Mr Stevens attended the meeting yesterday in Swinford and his arrangements gave the Committee sincere pleasure … These depots are producing the most important results. The Indian meal is of the best quality and greatly liked by the population; mixed with oatmeal it is largely used and is such a blessing to large families where cheapness is of such consequence.'

17 July. Minute of the Gallen & Costello Relief Committee

'Meal was given to the wives and children of fathers in England … It is absolutely necessary to have work provided in the parishes of Attymass, Kilgarvan, Killasser and Toomore. They request the Inspector General of police to arrange for the deposit and sale of small quantities of meal to the distressed poor in the police stations in the baronies of Gallen & Costello.'

Upper Leyny
RLFC 3/1/4319

Thursday 15 July. Dean Edward N. Hoare to the Relief Commission, enclosing a subscription list for the upper half barony of Leyny, amounting to £237 as well as the names of the non-subscribing land proprietors. A grant of £67 is recommended. (See Appendix 3E)

'No public works have been undertaken in the half barony with the exception of those at Kilmactigue and a small work near Tubbercurry. The Committee have several useful works approved by the county surveyor and upon these employ so many persons that they expend 4 to 6 tons of Indian meal each week.'

Saturday 18 July. Charles Strickland, chairman, Ballaghaderreen Relief Committee, to the Relief Commission

'£54 was collected and I have sent for 3 tons of Indian meal … The town of Ballaghaderreen alone has a population of nearly 1,500, many of whom are unable to work and are completely destitute … No credit being now given in the country as was heretofore the custom, those poor persons who depended on it in other years and have no means of obtaining provisions, are in a deplorable state and require immediate relief.'

Ballaghaderreen
RLFC 3/1/4398

Saturday 18 July. G. V. Jackson to the Relief Commission, enclosing the Foxford subscription list, amounting to £21 17s. 6d. and signed memorial. A grant of £15 was recommended by the Relief Commission. (See Appendix 31)
Memorial to the Swinford Relief Committee

'We the undersigned residents in the town of Foxford beg the favour of your allocating from the funds at your disposal a sum for each of the following works in which all the inhabitants of the town and its vicinity are interested and we further freely undertake the superintendance of the men employed in these works free of any charge or personal benefit.

Foxford
RLFC 3/1/4484

1. opening the brook leading through the town plots of Foxford to the river to prevent the plots being injured as they now are in rainy weather or by floods. 2. repairing the road to Collingmorra, where a man lost his life in April 1846, and on whom an inquest was held, owing to the badness of the road. 3. making a foot passage over the ford at the yellow river at Moorbrook, to enable the parishioners to come to divine service or to the market. A man was drowned here. 4. repairing the passage through the fair green of Foxford to Shragarra. 5. repairing a part of the road from Foxford to Aclare at Muckro.

These works would cost comparatively small sums and would be of great public benefit … We felt compelled to distribute Indian meal in cases of utter destitution and illness … *(See Appendix 1G)*
Resolution of the Swinford Relief Committee

'We find on investigation that the meal given away was chiefly to the wives and children of persons who had gone to England and who are not admissible to the poorhouse without the father being admitted with them.'
Jackson writes:

On 16 July I accompanied Capt Peebles, the reporting officer of the Board of Works, thro' north of the barony of Gallen … The potatoes are all gone and the population are subsisting on oatmeal procured by the sale of cattle or other property or by money obtained from usurers at from 20% to 50% p.a. or on securities, IOUs, at £1 or 25s. per cwt. This system must lead to the bankruptcy of the tenantry and as a consequence to that of the landlords. No works are undertaken in the north of the barony of Gallen, consisting of the parishes of Toomore, Attymass, Kilgarvan and Killasser and the employment provided by the Extraordinary Sessions is nearly run out. The population of these parishes are in a deplorable state of destitution and absolutely need employment ... The new potato crop is everywhere attacked by the disease of last year or one like it. The exertions of the Committee to relieve the existing misery of the population are largely embarrassed, in consequence of old professional beggars having gone about thro' the villages, reporting that the inmates of the poorhouse are half-starved on one meal a day, confined in dark cells and can never get out again if once admitted. Unluckily, some old persons have recently died in the Swinford poorhouse. This has spread alarm and created a feeling among a mass of destitute wretches that it is better for them to die of hunger out of the house than to have torture added to hunger before death in the house ... There is an impression generally prevailing among the population that their condition is being consulted for, and they therefore bear privation with patience.'

24 July. Board of Works to the Under-Secretary, approving the works, reported by Capt Peebles, to the amount of £2,150.

'The distress is very great in the barony and the necessity for employment is most urgent.' *(See Appendix 4D)*

Corran
RLFC 3/1/4677

Thursday 23 July. Rev J. Garrett to the Relief Commission enclosing subscribtion list, amounting to £244, of the Corran Relief Committee (See Appendix 3C)

'The early potato crop is already so far destroyed that the poor, who usually subsisted in August and September on the produce of their early potato gardens, will be thrown into abject destitution.'

RLFC 3/1/4707

25 July. Report of Capt Gordon

'I visited the barony to ascertain if destitution exists there and I am happy to state that I did not find distress to any extent anywhere except Bunninadden and the hill at Knockdinogue? ... all the labourers that were able having gone to England. On the Curlew mountains there are some cases requiring assistance by means of public works. The new potatoes ... which a few days ago looked so well, have failed completely, all the stubbles being withered and the young potatoes quite rotten. I observed this in the town of Ballymote itself.'

Swinford

Tuesday 28 July. Resolutions of the Gallen & Costello Relief Committee (See Appendix 2E)

Satisfaction expressed at the establishment of a government depot for meal, as a result of which the price of meal fell from £1 to 13s. 6d. Requests 5 tons of meal to be provided from Ballina to Foxford. Want of tools prevents the men being employed. Re the prevalence of distress in the parishes of Attymass, Kilgarvan, Toomore and part of Killasser and other parts of the barony where no works are provided and where there are no resident proprietors, request Bernard Durcan PP, Bernard Egan PP with the Rev Mr Tighe or Mr Coghlan from Costello, to go to Dublin to describe to the Relief Commission the condition of the population in their localities. The prospect of the present potato crop presents features that are truly alarming and as the premature digging of the new crop begins, the consequences must be disastrous. No payment to be made to Thomas Geraghty, contractor, till it is ascertained by Mr Deane whether he has employed persons not requiring relief.

Wednesday 29 July. Rev J. Garrett to the Relief Commission
'Lord Lorton lodged his £150 to be expended in this barony on the road from Boyle to Ballymote. Colonel Perceval and Mr Phibbs are ready to do the same if the road from Templehouse to Oldrock is approved by the Board. These sums are at the disposal of the Committee on condition that they are applied only to these roads. Subcriptions paid to Richard Gethen amount to £64. Sir Robert Gore Booth, Sir Alexander Crichton, Lord Palmerston, and Thomas Jones, landed proprietors to a considerable extent in the barony, with many others of minor estate, have not replied. We adjourned our meeting to Friday next to the no small mortification of many poor labourers expecting sustenance and employment.' *The Relief Commission recommended a grant of £45.*

30 July. Rev J. Garrett to the Relief Commission
'Sir Robert Gore Booth has generously taken into his own hands the employment and support of the population on his own estate, the rental of which is £2,000 a year, and thus greatly lightened the labours of our committee.' *(See Appendix 3C)*

Ballymote
RLFC 3/1/4890

Autumn 1846

Total Failure

Blight once more attacked the potato crop in 1846 but this time much earlier and caused much more destruction than in the previous season. 'Both early and late crops are a total failure,' Sub-Inspector Edward Hunt reported from Swinford on 25 August. Similar reports came from all over the west. The great famine had begun.

In June the Whigs under Lord John Russell took over from the Tories. By August, when the total potato failure became almost certain, food supplies in the government depots were critically low. The new government made some small purchases of Indian corn and other foods, some of which they sent directly to the ports of Westport, Ballina and Sligo. The largest issues of food were made from the depot in Sligo, which served the north-west, where acute distress became evident as early as mid-August. Over 650 tons of Indian meal and oatmeal were distributed from here between 10 August and 19 September.

To add to the distress, food prices rose dramatically during the autumn. This was partly due to farmers hoarding their grain and merchants making exorbitant profits. Bernard Durcan, parish priest of Swinford, reported to the Lord Lieutenant on 13 September that Indian meal 'before last week was at 10s per cwt. Last week it was raised to 11s and this week it is further raised to 12s.' During the same period oatmeal went from 14s. a cwt to 18s. 6d. By 1 October it was £1 2s. a cwt. At a meeting of the Gallen and Costello Relief Committee on 13 September, Fr Coghlan and Fr Muldowney proposed a resolution condemning the 'speculation of heartless selfish merchants' who had 'raised food even beyond famine prices.' 'They have and are exacting the pound of flesh,' they declared.

Saturday 1 August 1846. Memorial signed by James O'Hara PP and 173 inhabitants of the parish of Drumrat and Kilshalvey, to the Lord Lieutenant (See Appendix 1H)

'That your memorialists have come up cheerfully and peaceably under the great loss of their former crop of potatoes, and subsisted during this hard summer without as yet any government work or food. And now your memorialists are totally run out of the old provision or money to buy it, and have nothing to feed themselves or their families, as they have lost their early potatoes by the rot, and the stalks of the late crop being blighted. Your memorialists are in destitution and despair and most humbly beg for work.'

Rev J. Garrett, who forwarded it to the Lord-Lieutenant, wrote:

'I do believe every word in this memorial verified as it is by the signature of Priest O'Hara, a most respectable man.'

*Keash &
Bunninadden*
DP 4207

Tuesday 4 August. Resolutions of the Gallen & Costello Relief Committee

'That Rev Mr Brennan will transmit to Capt Gordon at once the names of the parties who he supposes to have suffered unjustly from stewards. 200 men to be employed on the road from Attymass to Rooskey, 200 on the road from Kilgarvan to Bonniconlon, 200 in Toomore, 100 breaking stones from Bohola to Ballylahan, 40 at Grallagh, 100 cutting hills at Straide. The state of the potato crop is very alarming, more particularly within the last few days when the influence of lightening etc appear to have had a destructive effect upon it. That the closing of government stores on 15 August will produce extreme misery. The price of meal rose today to 17s. per cwt. That Board of Works start eight works on roads in Costello and two in Gallen.' *(See Appendix 4C&D)*

Swinford
RLFC 3/1/5091

6 August. Relief Commission to T. N. Redington, informing him that they have received a subscription list amounting to £33 from the Swinford Relief Committee and recommending three tons of meal for the Committee.

DP 4050

Wednesday 5 August. Petition of 61 inhabitants of the islands of Inniskea to the Lord Lieutenant

'That their potato crop up to 12 July showed a most delightful appearance of a productive and abundant crop to reward their toils but from that period the disease attacked this crop, first by a foeted burning fog, by sultry nocturnal breezes and noxious dews, with some trifling rain, all of which, in short, every change from heaven, has proved a pestilence to this vegetable, so that now no symptom or vestige remains thereof but the part laid down for an early crop which had some strength when attacked and the growth of the vegetable then is now its only produce, of which one out of twelve is scarcely edible and even the pick, the fowls and swine refuse to eat, though used by

Erris Head
DP 4650

Memorial of the
clergy and inhabi-
tants of the parish
of Toomour to the
Lords Justices

your memorialists, striving to live by even those, but these are now gone and
with them our chief support, we dread, forever. As for corn, it grows not on
the gritty soil of these islands and our barley crop has been destroyed and
over much blighted by black smut. And even this poor crop the landlord
claims for the rent as the only merchantable commodity in memorialists' possession, so that immediate starvation will be their doom, unless speedily
relieved by some public works (until) God shall please to relieve or release
them and their crops from this pestilence ... That those islands on the main
are the mariner's only home in his distress, when it fails him to make the har-
bours of Blacksod or Broadhaven, which is often the case. Yet those islands
have been so far neglected that there is not even a symptom of even a common or regular landing place on either island, nor a pier to shelter a fishing
boat, nor a perch of a common passage or road to carry a load or lumber by,
or direct a passenger by night or day ... That the description of these islands
can be given by every mariner passing round Erris Head, or this kingdom, as
they cannot be passed unnoticed. They ask for the construction of 640 perches
of road and the erection of a pier as a shelter from the storm to the sea-tossed
mariner in his distress.'

*Saturday 8 August. Rev J. Garrett to the Under-Secretary, enclosing a memorial
signed by James O'Hara PP and over 380 inhabitants of Keash (See Appendix 1H)*
'All their potatoes are destroyed, and the late crop, as well as the early gardens
quite useless ... An engineer officer may be sent, if their distress be still
doubted ... That the public works ... be forthwith commenced to prevent
actual starvation.'
Garrett writes:
'It is quite melancholy and alarming to see the grief and sorrow of the inhabitants of this district who have not their accustomed food for their families
and have not the means of purchasing flour or oatmeal to sustain them. 173
of these people signed the memorial which I put before you last week and no
reply, to which you did me the favour to say that it was referred to the Board
of Works. This reply has sadly aggravated the sufferings of the expectant population as they have experienced before from the Board many disappoint-
ments ... The present condition of a great many of them is most lamentable.'

*Saturday 8 August. Relief Commission to T. N. Redington, informing him that
they have recieved from the Swinford Relief Committee an additional subscription list amounting to £16 and recommending £12 grant.
G. V. Jackson to Relief Commission, enclosing the name of Col Kirkwood who
subscribed £10 and the Relief Commission recommended £10 grant.*

To the Right Honorable: the Lords Justices
of Ireland.

The Memorial of the undersigned Clergy:
and inhabitants of the Parish's of Tumour, and Barony
of Corran, most humbly sheweth.

That Memorialists have lately before forw^d
a Memorial thro the under Secretary for Ireland, to the Gov-
-ernment; and Stated, that, their early Potatoes were partially,
Tainted. And that they wanted food, and employment; how
Much worse than, when the Engineer officer, Made his Report,
Memorialists have, now again; with grief, and sorrow, to leave
their sufferings before Government, and to State, that now all their
Potatoes are destroyed, and the late crop, as well as the early Garden,
quite useless. Memorialists beg, that an Engineer officer, May be
sent, if their distress be still doubled; and that the Public works
solicited for the Barony of Corran, by the Cess payers, and
Magistrates, and approved by the Engineer officer, and County
Surveyor, be forthwith Commenced, to prevent actual starvation
in the Parish of Tumour, And Memorialists in duty bound,
will ever pray. Dated 8th of August 1846.

James O'Hara P. P. Tumour
Francis Soden   Thomas x Mulvanny   Mich^l Grey
And^w Nealon   John Wenery   Patt x Higgins
Hugh Mannon   Luke M^c x Gowan   Thomas Higgins
Patrick Cryan   Mich^l M^c x Gowan   Patt Wenery
John x Cryan   Math^w x Cryan   James x Cryan
Walter Wenery   Mich^l Maddin   John x Forry
Patt x Lyden   James x Cryan   Peter x Higgins
James M^c x Gowan   Dennis x Cryan   John Forry
John Wenery   Edward Wynne   Darby x Brehony
Patt Cryan   Patt x Kilmartin   Patt Candon
John x Mulvanny   Roger x Cryan   Daniel x Brehony

'Great alarm prevails everywhere here as to the potato crop. The early gardens seem to have failed all round and the markets threaten to rise rapidly. The peasantry seem anxious to get to America or any colony to avoid the difficulty that seems approaching. Meal has increased from 13s. 6d. to 17s. 6d. a cwt at Swinford within a few days.'

RLFC 3/1/5272   *9 August. Richard Kyle to Relief Commission, enclosing an additional subscription list amounting to £33 and G. V. Jackson sent a further two subscriptions (See Appendix 3F)*

Ballymote   *Monday 10 August. Rev J. Garrett to the Under-Secretary*
DP 4207   'You will think me troublesome and intrusive. It has for years been my desire to destroy all religious differences and to earn as far as I humbly could the confidence of my parishioners of every religious persuasion. We now most providentially are free from agitators and demagogues and the people flock in numbers to me to plead for them. I was comparatively silent till the distress became urgent. I beg, Sir, that you will follow up your benevolent instructions and those of the present government, by ordering the Board of Works to send an engineer forthwith and begin to employ and sustain the poor people. You must now perceive that it becomes necessary to continue the erection of relief committees and to extend the supply of food up to the end of September to catch the new oats. The new potatoes are all gone.'

Upper Leyny   *Monday 10 August. J. Armstrong to William Stanley*
RLFC 3/1/5228   'I received your circular regarding the cessation of the Relief Commission of Ireland on 15 August and that 10 August was the last day for issuing grants. Our funds will be exhausted by next week's distribution and the situation of the country will be very deplorable indeed. Our early crop of potatoes has so generally failed that little relief can be afforded by it and our prospects as to the coming year worse than ever remembered in this country. It would be a great object to continue relief for another fortnight. I must implore on behalf of the destitute portion of our population some further donation from your board.'
Draft reply: 'Relief Commission is unable to recommend a donation. The committee should refer their application for relief to the Board of Works.'

DP 4273   *10 August. J. Armstrong to T. N. Redington*
'Our committee after this week cannot render any further assistance, our funds being completely exhausted. Heretofore, we have been able to expend £60 weekly on Indian corn, for which we have given much employment in small public works. If we could carry on these works one week longer, employment would be afforded by harvest labour.' *He asks for another grant*

of £60. 'We despair of procuring any further subscriptions from private individuals and cannot describe the misery that daily presents itself to those residing in this country. The committee has already spent £400 …'

Thursday 13 August. Board of Works to T. N. Redington   *Dublin*
'The Treasury has authorised the Board of Works to instruct engineers and   DP 4310
inspecting officers to close the works from time to time as the harvest works
in the different localities commence … Where labourers are living on their
own crop of potatoes, the numbers employed on the public works should be
reduced.'

Thursday 13 August. Resolution of the Corran Relief Committee (See Appendix 2C)   *Ballymote*
'That the state of the potato crop, which this committee declare to be totally
lost, render it absolutely necessary that a respectful application be made to
government requesting and urgently pressing that the Board of Works shall
forthwith be directed to grant the public works set forth … and that the old
provision being exhausted, the poor will be in actual destitution immediately
if not employed forthwith.'

Rev J. Garrett to Relief Commission, enclosing additional subscriptions amount-   RLFC 3/1/5396
ing to £32 (See Appendix 3C)
17 August. Same to the Relief Commission
'The potato crop being quite useless it is now more than ever imperative
upon the government and all the communities to extend their exertions and
by no means to think of ceasing as was first the intention.'

18 August. Same to the Under-Secretary   DP 4389
'Daily applications are made by numbers in a state of starvation and we don't
know why we are left in the background while the barony of Coolavin is in
full work … The case is most urgent and we beg an immediate reply to
endeavour to peacify the wretched people.'

Thursday 14 August. G. V. Jackson to Relief Commission, asking to have the three   *Swinford*
tons of Indian meal donated to the Swinford Relief Committee, to be delivered to   RLFC 3/1/5389
Ballina to save the carriage costs
'The store in Foxford is run out and market prices have risen excessively. In
fact the position of this country is most alarming in every view. I fear the supply of grain available for food will not enable the population to carry on till
the harvest is in. More meal is wanted at the government store in Ballina as
the supply is run out.'

18 August. Resolution of Swinford Relief Committee, passing a motion of thanks   RLFC 3/1/5502
to the Relief Commissioners
'Under the blessing of Divine Providence, the means provided by them have
saved society from convulsion and ruin.'

Ballina
RLFC 3/1/5426

Friday 15 August. Report of Frederick Cary, coast guard
'The people are without food, money or employment, are endeavouring to sell their cattle at half their value to sustain their families, and have at present to travel 30 and 50 miles on foot for two or three stones of meal. All of them are living on one bad meal *per diem* and the people are in very great alarm and will, I fear, proceed to help themselves if not employed and relieved promptly.'

Drumcliffe
DP 4357

Monday 17 August. Thomas Hamilton, coast guard, to Sir James Dombrain
'The potato crop … from Sligo to Donegal is at present almost a total failure. The fields without exception are as black as they usually were in November from the natural ripeness of the potato crop. It requires much labour to dig and select a sufficiency of the unripe bulb for the use of a family … Large numbers of the population, labourers, tradesmen and farmers are indulging the most serious apprehensions and are beginning to give expression to sentiments at once discreditable and dangerous, such as, "We want while others have", "Hunger will break thro' stone walls".'

Ballymote
DP 4407

Friday 21 August. Resolution of the Corran Relief Committee (See Appendix 2C)
'Multitudes are in utter destitution … Actual starvation will visit and lay waste many of the most populous villages of this district and members of this committee are witnesses of the deplorable state of very many creatures already without food … that an officer be sent to view the state of things … that destitution will force them to break into houses where they may expect food and kill the cattle of their neighbours to allay the cravings of hunger.'

DP 4492

22 August. Rev J. Garrett to the Chief Secretary
'It is absolutely necessary to order us immediate employment to avert scenes of horror, bloodshed and plunder. The slowness of the proceedings under our pressure of destitution aggravates the great sufferings of the people of this barony, usually most peaceable, and they have special ground of complaint against the Board of Works who continue deaf to almost all applications from this barony.
P.S. The oat crop here is late. None will be available for a month and the potatoes are all lost.'

RLFC 5/26/2

23 August. Edward S. Corry, sub-inspector to the Inspector General
'For the last three weeks the people have been using the early crop of potatoes but have great difficulty in procuring a sufficient quantity. Some in the vicinity of the town have given up digging for potatos and are supporting themselves with meal.'

Friday 21 August. C. K. O'Hara to the Relief Commission   *Lower Leyny*
'The recent general calamity of potato rot or blight has deprived a large por-   RLFC 3/1/5492
tion of the population of their only means of subsistence … The corn will
not be ripe for three weeks … Having few substantial farmers little employment will be afforded and until then food must be provided for numbers
who have not a sound potato at this moment. The district comprises the
parishes of Killoran, Kilvarnet and Ballisodare, including the villages of
Ballisodare and Coolaney, containing about 10,500 inhabitants, 1,600 of
whom are agricultural labourers, partly partial or occasional labourers with
small holdings and partly actual labourers, holding only a cabin and conacre.
Of these I have during the year employed on my own works 350 daily and
supplied them with £500 worth of meal. 200 are employed on small works
granted by the Board of Works, amounting to about £422 … (I lodged £45
for a new road to Court Abbey burying ground.) About 150 men have been
occasionally employed on county works, making in all 700. Of the 900
remaining, at least 400 require immediate relief till corn cutting starts. £400
to £500 will be required for Indian meal earned in small local works … As
the principal proprietor, I have spent £1,200 extra on employment and food
for my own poor. My funds are now exhausted and I cannot support the poor
of other districts. The floods of the last three days have greatly increased the
distress and destroyed a quantity of meaow, flax and corn.'
*O'Hara enclosed a subscription list for lower Leyny Relief Committee amounting
to £159 (See Appendix 3D)*

Monday 24 August. Memorial of parish priest and inhabitants of the parish of   *Erris*
Kilmore Erris to the Lord Lieutenant   DP 4467
'Our poor, deprived of the potato, their almost only food, have congregated
in crowds in the town of Belmullet demanding something wherewith to support themselves and their starving families. Their number was great and their
demeanour peaceable, but how long a peasantry goaded by hunger may continue peaceable, no one can calculate. Our potatos, diminutive in size, are
totally unfit for use. Our part of the country … is productive of little or no
corn. How are we to live? … Think not, my Lord, that we demand idle
bread. Give us but work and we shall earn our bread by the sweat of our
brow, but give it speedily, my Lord, and drive not a starving peasantry to the
public violation of existing law. A peasantry, more willing to labour and more
obedient to the law of the land, never existed, but who can stand the cravings of an empty stomach or die content while his neighbour's cattle walk the
fields?'

Ballaghaderreen
DP 4465

Monday, 24 August. Memorial of the Ballaghaderreen Relief Committee to the Lord-Lieutenant (See Appendix 2A)
'The poor in this district are in a deplorable state from the loss of their potato crop, so much so that there is reason to fear that some will actually die of starvation if not very speedily relieved either by a gratuitous distribution of provisions or by giving immediate and extensive employment. The works at present in progress are totally insufficient. Two cases have been this day brought before the committee, of two persons who are now confined to their beds and not expected to recover entirely from want of food, and many others have been mentioned of the poor unable to work any longer.'

DP 4446

25 August. R. M. Whelan RM to T. N. Redington
'Yesterday upon arriving here for Petty Sessions, I found assembled at the courthouse several hundreds of the peasantry, nearly one hundred of whom carried spades and shovels. They were exceedingly excited and, appealing to me, complained that the workmen employed on the public roads had not been paid their wages for nearly three weeks and many of them were in a state of starvation. That on a road near the town at a place called Drumacoo?, where 75 had been employed at 10d. per day, their wages had been reduced to 8d. per day, while at the same time, upon a line of half a mile of road, the number of overseers had been increased at a rate of much higher wages. The crowd also clamoured on account of their wages having been kept back from them on the previous time of payment until half past eight at night, and then given to them when whiskey was selling, in order that they should give drink to the stewards under whom they had been employed. I have therefore felt it my duty to call your attention to these circumstances, as from the very extreme distress which prevails, it is probable that violence will be resorted to against the persons or properties of individuals in a district remote from military or police protection.'

RLFC 2/Z.14378

28 August. Charles Strickland to T. N. Redington, requesting 600 parchment tickets for the labourers to be employed on the public works in the barony of Costello
'Words cannot describe the distress of the poor who are waiting with the utmost anxiety to get work on these lines. The lists are prepared but there are no tickets to be had in Swinford.'

DP 5134

1 September 1846. Board of Works to T. N. Redington
'In reference to the memorial of the Ballaghaderreen Relief Committee that the poor in their district are in a deplorable state of destitution and that the works at present granted and in progress are few and insufficient. Another work has been ordered on 29 August for £100.'

Tuesday 25 August. John Stewart, sub-inspector, to the Inspector General   *Tubbercurry*
RLFC 5/26/7
'Both the early and late crops of potatoes have been injured to an alarming
extent. Of the early crop but a small portion of it remains, as it early became
available for food, and with every prospect of being a fair average crop, but
in one week the disease set in with a virulence that soon destroyed all hope.
To procure sufficient food to support his family, a man would have to dig,
not for half an hour as in former years, but for nearly the whole day, so that
at this moment there is as much potato ground dug up as there used to be in
the middle of October, so that of the early crop a very small portion only now
remains, not more than a quarter. Of the late crop, it is very difficult to speak
with any certainty. It may be a gracious Providence will show that man's
extremity is God's opportunity, but at this moment the general opinion is
that the late crop is totally lost, for if the healthiest stalks be dug up, the produce is a few hardly formed tubers, in which the disease is perfectly visible.
For the last three weeks the young potatoes have not increased in size and if
this continues there will not be a potato in the barony of Leyny on 1
December … The use of diseased potatoes by those who have nothing else to
live on must be injurious to their health. In fact the smell of the potatoes generally after being boiled is so bad as to prove they are not fit food for any creature.'

Tuesday 25 August. Edward Hunt, Sub-Inspector, to Inspector General   *Swinford*
RLFC 5/21/19
'Both early and late crops are a total failure. A stone of potatoes is not to be
had. Such as are not rotten, are not larger than marbles and only fit for fowl.
Absolute starvation compels the people to eat rotten potatoes. I don't think
this district could produce for any sum one barrel of potatoes. I have stood
by and seen from one to ten perches of potato ground dug for potatoes for
dinner for a family consisting of eight persons and the produce did not
exceed 7 lbs and those of so bad a quality and small as to render them next
to useless for any purpose. The greatest consternation prevails among all
classes from their dread of famine. The peasantry state firmly but peaceably
that they will not give their oats to be sold for landlords' rents, that they will
not starve, and all the conacre tenants whose entire support was their potato
crop, declare that if not fed by the government, they will take food, either
cattle or corn, from those who have it. I myself have not had a potato for use
in my house for the last six weeks and am substituting vegetables and meal
for potatoes.'

Wednesday 26 August. Board of Works to T. N. Redington recommending work   *Tirerrill*
to the extent of £100   DP 4712
'A considerable number of labourers have gone to England in search of work
but many remain from the want of means to defray their expenses and are in

a state of great distress, caused by the absence of employment and the total failure of the potato crop.'

Swinford
DP 4561

Wednesday 26 August. Memorial of the Gallen & Costello Relief Committee to Lord John Russell (See Appendix 2E)
'While we cannot but feel grateful to her Majesty's government for the sympathy expressed for the sufferings of our starving population and the measures contemplated for their relief, we at the same time cannot find words to express the utter state of destitution in which they are now placed and the urgent want and the urgent necessity there exists for giving them the most prompt and immediate assistance. The potato crop has totally and irretrievably been lost and, from the lateness of the harvest in this part of Ireland, the oat crop will not be available for a month or six weeks. With the utmost alarm the consequences that will inevitably result should not instant employment be given to carry the people over this most trying period. An inquest has been already held in a neighbouring parish, in which the verdict returned has been 'death caused by stavation', and clergymen members of this committee have stated at this meeting that during the past week they have been called on to attend persons in a dying state, reduced to it solely by the want of food.'

Kilmactigue
DP 5311

Friday 28 August. Henry McCarrick, Aclare, to T. N. Redington.
'Almost the entire potato crop is rotten. The safe potatoes are few indeed, for a family of five or six persons cannot obtain so much free from the disease in two or three cwt of them as they would consume at one meal. It is reported that in the mountainous and poorer districts, the people are actually getting weak from hunger, having no food but diseased potatoes and that they are not able to dig sufficient ground, from which they would obtain so much of these as would do to satisfy their wretched families at one time. A woman has just related to me the horrifying statement of the people's wretchedness, that where she lives she particularly noticed a child, who six weeks ago was a fat and plump child as she ever beheld, but that on yesterday it was reduced to a skeleton from the unwholesome food which it received and that she observed it fall beneath the pigs, who if they wished could devour it, and that in general all the poor people are getting weak and have a sickly appearance. Really, it is awful to contemplate the dreadful prospect that awaits the unfortunate inhabitants of this parish, unless the government gives them employment immediately. The people await with patience the commencement of public works etc. in this backward and neglected neighbourhod. Five or six weeks hence, have been commenced here about a mile and a half of public roads which is now almost completed. 150 men obtained employment on

this road at the rate of 9d. per day and notwithstanding this low wage, the scenes of discontent and jealousy, which daily occurred, showed plainly how miserable and impoverished the wretched people are and how willing to work for a trifle. There are in this parish at least 2,000 unemployed men who at present have scarcely the means of subsistance. Such shocking reports, as are hourly circulating of the destitution, wretchedness and privations of the unfortunate peasantry, are enough to appal the heart of the stoutest man. Some ruffians and evil-minded persons there are who say that "so long as cows, sheep, meal etc remain in the country, they cannot and shall not starve", but there are a hundred for one who are determined to wait patiently the employment which they daily expect from the government.'

Friday 28 August. Sworn statement of Andrew Baker, Redhill, Mullaghroe, before M. Crofton JP, Boyle

Coolavin
DP 4557

'I am a large landholder, holding about 500 acres in the barony of Coolavin under stock. I have built an excellent house within the last two years, laying out about £1,000 upon it. Last year there was a considerable loss of the potato crop in my neighbourhood and that numbers in consequence were supported by the many Dublin works undertaken in the barony of Coolavin up to last Tuesday week when about 800 persons were dismissed. The failure of the potato crop has been so complete this season that the population around me is already in a state of starvation. On Tuesday last, 25th instant, about 500 persons came to my house and declared that they were starving and that unless they were supplied with work, they must have recourse to killing cattle and seizing whatever they could get, rather than perish, but that would be their last resort. Since last Tuesday parties of twenty and thirty have been continuously coming, expressing the same sentiments, whom I know to be without any means of support. In the neighbourhood of Mullaghroe alone I have about 70 head of cattle and 250 sheep, besides stock elsewhere, and I and my family have been filled with dread apprehension this last week that we shall be ruined by the destruction of our property, if the most speedy and prompt measures are not taken to relieve the starving population. Already I have lost about £600 this year from the people not being able to pay their conacre rents and tho' the persons that assembled stated that I would be one of the last (on account of my usefulness in assisting them) that they would injure, yet I have the deepest apprehensions on account of their distress.'

Friday 28 August. Rev J. Garrett to William Stanley, enclosing a further subscription list amounting to £50 (see Appendix 3C)

Ballymote
RLFC 3/1/5553

'If you don't extend your bounty to us, we must stop our poor labourers on Tuesday or at furthest Wednesday, and I know not what they will do.'

Leyny

DP 4714

Saturday 29 August. Capt R. P. Farren to Board of Works

'I visited yesterday the central part of the barony, having previously passed over its north-eastern and southern extremities ... The following is the result of an examination I made a few days since in a field one acre in extent, situated in the north-western part of the barony ... In a line dug across 30 ridges there were but 51 sound potatoes and these were of a small size, in many cases not larger than a marble ... The crop is worthless and will not pay the expense of digging ... The condition of the labourer, the cottier with his few perches, those dependent on the conacre system for food, is therefore most lamentable and the small holders of from two, three to four and eight acres, which are the most numerous portion of the community, are scarcely less distressed. The failure in the last potato crop pressed heavily on all. Many during the summer season obtained meal on time and loans of money ... The difficulties of the present season have rendered the majority unable to repay these advances. The oat crop which is a good one, will afford the cottier class (the small-holders) the means of support, but the custom is usually to leave that part of the farm produce for the rent. The former class (the labourer) (those excepted who, having left the country in search of employment during the English harvest, are fortunate enough to return with their earnings) have neither means of support or wherewith to pay their rent ... With respect to the barony, there are however particular districts somewhat more distressed than others. The southern and western part of the parish of Kilmactigue is one of these. Also the district at the foot of the chain of mountains running parallel with the road from Coolaney to Ballina, the town of Tubbercurry and the southern portion of the parish of Achonry. A great portion of the last mentioned parish, the western and south-western part, is a wild mountain district with a dense pauper population clustered in villages having no means of support. The next locality alluded to, parallel to the Ballina and Coolaney road, is also a poor district, and the portion of the parish of Achonry described, is thickly peopled. In the first and last mentioned districts some relief is afforded by means of public works. The rest and indeed the whole and central portion of the barony, being considerably more than one half its whole extent, is without assistance in this respect.

In conclusion, it would appear that the field or late potato crop, upon which the great bulk of the people depend for existence, having totally failed, the early potato gardens being nearly exhausted, the employment to be looked for from agricultural transactions being temporary and insufficient to meet the wants of the distressed, and that given by resident gentlemen (there are but three or four in the whole district, an area of 121,625 acres) being comparatively of trifling amount, the state of destitution amongst the labouring classes in the barony, will in a short period be extreme and, as the people already talk openly of taking the cattle from the fields, it is apprehended that crime will follow.'

Sunday 30 August. Rev J. Garrett to the Under-Secretary   *Ballymote*
'This district has been thrown into great consternation by the very unex-   DP 4545
pected intelligence that the County Surveyor has orders to stop all the works,
so long expected here, and only commenced in the last three days! The cup
has just been held to the lip of the most patient peasantry of Ireland and is
dashed suddenly from their grasp without slaking their hunger or thirst. I beg
and implore that you will consider this matter and not force these poor
beings to use violence which it may be very difficult to avoid. Our crops are
generally late and won't be fit for reaping for ten days more. Of course the
new oats can't be ready to make meal for a month and the people have no
money to buy Indian meal. If his Excellency could only view the haggard
countenances of the half starved wretches, one thousand of whom must,
under this order, stand idle in this one barony, where relief in public works
has only been three days extended to them in the recent grants, and would
direct that for ten days more the county surveyor should have permission to
continue the works ... Where it is possible to employ greater numbers, it
would be a great mercy to the peasantry and remove the great discontent
experienced under the present system.'

Monday 31 August. E. J. Mulloy to Capt C. E. P. Gordon   *Partry*
'All order and regularity appear to be thrown overboard, the goverment rules   DP 4715
violated and not merely by the uncivilised peasantry but by men of education. Also the good intentions of the government abused and the money
granted for the misery of the country people, placed by priest and landlord
in the reach of wealthy landholders, while the miserable homeless wretches
group about in every place I turn and tell me that men who could live at
home are employed on the works while they cannot procure half the necessaries of life ... The deluded people are led to believe their condition will be
bettered by quitting their work and assembling in large numbers to show
themselves and their strength to the landlords ... for the purpose of making
the government believe that more distress exists than really does and besides
to deter the landlords from asking for their rent. I am of the opinion that if
half the people who were at work in my district would be properly chosen
and got fair wages, allowing two or three from distressed houses, there would
be very little distress to be found after ... I learned from the Rev Mr Conway
CC that on Saturday the 23rd, while at prayers, he observed strangers in his
chapel, who came there for the purpose of swearing the people of this locality not to work for low wages or pay rent. He, Mr Conway, horse-whipped

them out of his chapel and admonished the people not to be led astray by any unlawful behaviour and to pay their rents if they were able.'

Sligo
DP 4679

Tuesday 1 September. Memorial of builders, masons, carpenters, etc. to the Lord Lieutenant

'They are suffering severely from the want of employment which is chiefly occasioned by the visitation of providence in the failure of the potato crop. That the incapacity of the tenantry to pay their rents in a great measure deprives the landlords of the means of giving that employment which under ordinary circumstances they were in the habit of giving ... That the mercantile and commercial classes of this town have felt the shock as well as the landlords ... That they derived a great deal of their employment from these classes, whose wonted energies seem paralysed by the above-mentioned visitation ... Hence they have no hope for their usual employment ... They request the government to provide money to build a military barracks, police barracks, proper custom house, dock for repairing ships, extension to the county infirmary, and town hall ... That there are 700 persons in Sligo whose support depends on labour in the building line.'

Swinford
RLFC 3/2/21/42

Wednesday 2 September. Bernard Durcan PP to George Vaughan Jackson

'We all regretted much the cause of your absence and sincerely hope to hear soon of your being recovered from the effects of the accident you met with ... There came a supply of meal to the depot here last week, seven tons of Indian meal and three of oaten. There has been a very great demand for it. I have been at the store a while ago and found that the oaten meal was disposed of except about a half a ton which was not likely to stand till 12 o clock today. There was about three tons of the Indian meal and there has been a ton of it ordered to Kiltimagh today. It is very necessary to keep a good supply for the next fortnight or three weeks and it would be therefore well to order more for Swinford without delay. The works have been stopped since Saturday with no reason given. Much hardship is still felt from the non-payment of the labourers.'

DP 4680

2 September. Memorial of the inhabitants of Kilconduff and Meelick (Swinford), signed by Bernard Durcan PP, James Devine CC, P. Spelman CC, and B. W. Eames, vicar and about ninety inhabitants to the Lord Lieutenant (See Appendix 1M)

'That the suspension of the public works ... has reduced the great mass of the inhabitants of these parishes, consisting of a population of 9,000 souls, to a state of the most utter destitution, nothing short of absolute starvation. That the depot for the sale of oat and Indian meal in Swinford ... cannot be continued as they have no means of purchasing them ... Therefore most humbly but most urgently implore your Excellency to have some instant steps taken to give some relief to the poor or the consequences will before a week be such as your Excellency will deplore and every man possessed of a human heart lament.'

3 September. Richard Kyle, secretary, Costello and Gallen Relief Committee, to George Vaughan Jackson, enclosing a bank bill for £22 from the Lords Justices and the reply of Lord John Russell to the memorial of the committee.   RLFC 3/2/21/42

'On 38 August 1846 three tons of Indian meal arrived in the depot but is now all disposed of … Thousands came long distances for meal and were obliged to return without it, declaring they had not a morsel to eat, nor their family … The market price of meal is 18s. a cwt.'

Draft reply to above, 7 September, Sir Randolph Routh to George Vaughan Jackson: 'The urgency of distress requiring further supplies of food will receive prompt attention from Commissary-General Stevens. Allowance must be made for difficulties arising from the sudden increase of demand … produced by an exigency that could not have been anticipated.'

Wednesday 2 September. Treasury Chambers to T. N. Redington informing him that the Lord Lieutenant had authorised the immediate execution of certain works in counties Mayo, Sligo and Cork to the amount of £1,100, 'but these are the last that will be authorised.'   *Dublin*
DP 4720

Thursday 3 September. Police constable to George Vaughan Jackson, stating that he 'has had no meal for the last eight days excepts five cwt of Indian meal sent with your own horse and cart on Friday evening last, one bag of which was sold on Saturday. When the people found I had meal on Monday morning, there were great numbers at an early hour who came a long distance. The other bag did not last a half an hour. I told the people I expected three tons that you ordered. Many have come every day since in expectation of getting meal and some returned in tears.'   *Foxford*
RLFC 3/2/21/40

He regrets Jackson's recent accident and hopes for a speedy recovery 'in common with the people in general, who feel a loss in your absence.'

Thursday 3 September. Thomas D. Tolan to T. N. Redington regarding the Claddagh fishermen   *The Claddagh, Galway*
DP 4613

'Their present condition is most deplorable. Many of them to my knowledge have every particle of furniture, that would be taken as a pledge, in the pawn office. Over 500 feather beds have been pawned in order to fit themselves out for the herring fishery which I am sorry to say is not as productive as it was this time twelve months. Out of all the boats which were fishing last night, only twenty or twenty-five were successful. The remainder had not as much as would support themselves and their families for one day. Is it not a hard case to hear a poor man declare that he went out to fish on yesterday evening fasting and that he returned this morning without the means of purchasing a meal for himself and his family? The £100 we received from the trustees of the Calcutta Fund is exhausted and unless some relief is afforded to this numerous colony, the result will be dreadful.'

Ballina
DP 4649

Saturday 5 September. George Vaughan Jackson to T. N. Redington
'The new crop of grain is excellent in quantity and quality, but not yet fit for use and the mills cannot grind enough for food … The supplies sent to Swinford and Ballina are inadequate … I tried at Westport for two tons of Indian meal from a merchant for the people of Foxford. He could not give it, the demand was too great … An ample supply at Ballina would feed all the adjacent points … Great privation is felt by the poor between the exhaustion of one supply and the arrival of another at the government stores … No merchant has contemplated the introduction of Indian meal at Ballina or Killala … Intense suffering is entailed on the labourers and their families, not being regularly and promptly paid their wages.'
Draft reply to above from T. N. Redington to George Vaughan Jackson:
'The gentlemen of Ballina and its neighbourhood should enter some arrangement for their support and not at this early period rest exclusively on the assistance of the government without any effort of their own.'

Boyle
DP 4642

Saturday 5 September. M. Crofton JP to the Under-Secretary, enclosing a ballad
'which was taken from a ballad singer this morning in the market … There are no doubt persons anxious to excite and aggravate the feelings of the famishing part of the population by the circulation of such papers … A considerable number of persons presented a petition to the Board of Guardians stating that they were starving and asking for employment before they were driven to the adoption of unlawful means. The Board of Guardians gave them the option of entering the workhouse which they declined, not wishing to abandon their houses in expectation of shortly getting work … Should employment be withheld beyond a few days, anarchy may be the result.'

Ballinrobe
OP 21/23951

Sunday 6 September. Extract of a letter from the High-Sheriff of Mayo
'The people are assembling in thousands. Tomorrow the peasantry of this and the adjoining districts are to march into Ballinrobe. No one knows the authority under which they are required to assemble; but a notice was posted on the chapel to that effect. These multitudes have assembled elsewhere. They appear peaceable and seem to be acting under the orders of leaders. I fear this is only the beginning of evil. The Roman Catholic clergy take no part in these proceedings but do not sanction (condemn) them. If the people

A New Song called

The

ADVICE.

Air—'Granuaile.

Ye landlords of Erin I would have ye beware
And of your poor tenants in time to take care
For the rot of potatoes has made them this year
From the crutch to the cradle to tremble with fear

Ye see that starvation would meet us in the face
Only for relief coming from some foreign place
So sell your cattle and dont keep a tail
Before ye do part with corn or meal

Number of acres you will find in one field
To see the potatoes rotten it would make your
      heart bleed
You petitioned your Queen and yours prayers did
      prevail
For she opened the ports both for corn and meal

But now try our landlords and see what they will do
They know how the rot is in the country althrough
Tell them for the rent you will give them good bail
And not make you sell off our corn or meal

If with your request they will not comply
Tell them on the spot that ye would sooner die
That your families are starving ye never will fail
But fight till ye die both for corn and meal

Balladsheet seized at
the market in Boyle,
5 September 1846

find no benefit from these day-meetings, they will assuredly have recourse to others of a more dangerous character by night.'

Ballymote
DP 4622

Sunday 6 September. Rev J. Garrett, to T. N. Redington.
'Numbers daily apply in a starving state for work who cannot be admitted in the local works now in progress and these will all close for want of funds in the next week. An engineer should be sent down to co-operate with the relief committee so that works might be forthwith commenced. Delay will frustrate our combined efforts to avert anarchy and violence among the starving population.'

Dublin
DP 4718

Sunday 6 September. Board of Works to Henry Labouchere
'Lists of persons who are to be employed to be prepared by the Board's engineer to prevent the jobbing and irregularities which were committed last season in the issue of tickets, a safeguard that gross injustice and partiality are not practised in the selection. Who are to be considered – the labouring poor. The government's aim is two-fold – to afford the distressed a subsistance and to preserve the peace of the country. Some guard must be taken to prevent every man in the country who wishes for employment being forced upon the works, which was attempted in many districts last summer.'

Gurteen, Co Sligo
DP 4768

Tuesday 8 September. Peter Brennan PP to the Lord Lieutenant
'My Lord, many hundreds are completely destitute of food for their famishing children. They are thrown on the world, sad victims of hunger and despair. It is on behalf of such I venture to solicit your Excellency's mercy … In the discharge of my ministerial duties, I am, my Lord, in the way of encountering much misery and you will, I hope, make allowance for the feelings of a pastor who sees starvation and death impending over his people.'

Foxford
DP 4997

Wednesday 9 September. Rev Geoff Mostyn, Protestant curate, to T. N. Redington
'In Toomore there is not a single resident landlord or in the town of Foxford one merchant or trader to employ constantly the poor creatures that are anxious for work. The population is immense for miles around and from the scantiness of land are compelled to give any money demanded for it. More than one half of the people have got no oats and have lost all their potatoes. No road under the Board of Works has been begun this year tho' long expected … The poor are quiet and wonderfully patient and will remain so if employed … The poor tradesmen are in a wretched way, no potatoes, no oats or money to buy the yellow meal … A small sum should be placed at my disposal or that of a committeee for very urgent want, lest any might perish thro' need of timely aid.'

Thursday 10 September. Rev B. W. Eames, Vicar of Kilconduff, to the Relief Commission, stating that the supply of Indian meal for the Swinford depot is quite inadequate and begs them 'to take pity on the miserable population here and order a larger quantity for this district which may avert all the horrors and consequences of starvation.'

Swinford
RLFC 3/2/21/42

Draft reply to above, 11 September: 'As much as is possible is being done, considering the sudden nature of the exigency which has arisen. The want of local exertion for promoting importations of food is much to be lamented but it is still to be hoped that the arrangements for the government sales, which are to be auxiliary only to trade supplies, will encourage the traders in Ballina and other towns to make the importations.'

Friday 11 September. Capt Burmester to the Poor Law Commission
'I find already in many localities people are suffering very severely and I recommend that no time be lost in getting supplies of provisions into the country. With the exception of Lords Mount Sanford and Lorton, I do not hear of any exertions being made by the gentry on this point and I do not think from what I have seen that persons engaged in trade are of a class to depend on from want of capital and enterprise.'

Co Roscommon
DP 4885

Saturday 12 September. George Vaughan Jackson to the Lord Lieutenant
'Every post brings me letters upon letters from all parts of North Mayo, stating that the population are starving, that disease is now appearing owing to the use of diseased potatoes, that if food be not imported largely and rapidly, the population cannot but perish of hunger … Many persons, whose minds are intent on doing all they can to assist in meeting this terrible calamity, get discouraged and speak of leaving their homes to avoid witnessing horrors they cannot alleviate … Had we at Ballina an ample supply of cheap food … we should feel encouraged to persevere and to do all in our power to assist the efforts of the government to the utmost to meet the difficulty we are placed in.'

Ballina
DP 5454

Saturday 12 September. E. A. Lucas, secretary, Tirerrill Relief Committee, to T. N. Redington, asking 'to procure the services of the police in selling Indian meal, stores of which have been opened for the convenience of the people in several villages in the barony convenient to the barracks.'

Collooney
DP 4865

Saturday 12 September. Ulic Burke, physician, Swinford, to H. Labouchere
'As medical officer of the dispensary for the barony of Gallen, I have the most intimate acquaintance with the condition of the poor. No official report, no public memorials, no even private accounts can convey or give an adequate

Swinford
RLFC 3/2/21/42

idea of the misery our people are still patiently enduring. I am here at the centre of a union containing 74,000 souls. There is not a single resident landlord who could give constant employment to five persons and no such person as a merchant among us nor a mill that would be capable of grinding a ton of corn in the day ... The supply to Swinford depot is totally unequal to the wants of the people, some of whom have to come a distance of more than 10 miles for a miserable half stone of meal and have sometimes to wait an entire day before they obtain it.'

DP 4797   *13 September. Bernard Durcan PP to the Lord Lieutenant, enclosing a memorial signed by him and his curates, Patrick Spelman and James Devine, as well as the vicar, B. W. Eames and 51 inhabitants of Swinford. (See Appendix 1M)*

'The unexampled distress accompanied with actual famine which at present affects this district, and which, unless timely relief is afforded, will inevitably lead to the most deplorable consequences ... There is an absolute necessity of keeping the depot at Swinford constantly supplied and establishing other depots in the district ... Evil consequences of varying the price at which the meal is sold. The week before last it was at 10s. per cwt. Last week it was raised to 11s., and this week it is further raised to 12s. ... Nothing is so calculated to alarm the minds of the people and drive them to desperation as this weekly rise ... during the cessation of the works which gave them employment and means to procure their miserable pittance. No people in the world could be more patient under their unparalleled suffering than the people in this part of the country, but really their endurance cannot go much further.'

Belmullet   *Monday 13 September. George Crumpton? JP to the Lord Lieutenant*
DP 5044   'The only means of sustenance to be had for money in Belmullet is flour at 2s.6d. per stone and the people in the country are trying to exist by grinding their oats and barley in querns (their being no mills in the country) and some of them on shell fish ... In a large village in this neighbourhood their are two or three of these querns kept at work day and night. They are worked by hand and the villagers have to wait their turn before (after several hours paid labours) they have the means of providing a meal for themselves and family ... A large body of them to meet tomorrow ... and threats are held out that they will do mischief to stores and to a vessel lying at the pier to carry away corn from one of the merchants here ... Have a supply of meal sent in here. There is no dependance to be placed on the exertions of the merchants here.'

Ballymote   *Monday 13 September. Rev J. Garrett to Sir Randolph Routh*
RLFC 3/2/26/18   'There is no meal in the Ballymote depot for the last four days and the poor people have been left at the mercy of hucksters, who charge enormous profit. This is deplorable as the labourers employed in the public works, whose

wages reduced to 8d. a day was small enough without the additional misery of a simultaneous rise in the price of provisions, by reason of there being no meal in the store.'
Draft reply to above, 14 September 1846:
'It is adviseable that the possessors of properties in the distressed districts should co-operate for the purpose of encouraging traders to make importations of food by ordering supplies through them for their tenantry and dependants.'

Wednesday 15 September. James Conry to T. N. Redington   *Castlebar*
'Undue and exorbitant prices have been demanded and paid in the provision   DP 4899
markets of this town and in the other markets of this county. Oatmeal which had up to a very late period been selling here at 14s. per cwt (112lbs), has within the last two weekly markets here risen to the exorbitant price of 18s.6d. per cwt, placing it almost beyond the reach of the great bulk of the population … Flour and meal of every other description have risen proportionately in price and this too at a time when all employment, either upon public works or from farming operations, has ceased. The people have therefore of necessity been compelled in increased numbers to resort to the government depot here for Indian meal to support existence. Up to yesterday this meal was supplied (in quantities not exceeding 7lbs for each applicant) at the rate of 10s. per cwt or 1s.3d. per stone, but strange to say, as if to countenance and sustain instead of checking the exorbitant prices demanded by the provision merchants, the parties in charge of the depot advanced the price of Indian meal yesterday to 12s. per cwt or 1s.6d. per stone, an advance in one day of 20% … Indian meal is issued here through a small window about two feet square, attended by only one person and the consequence is that many of the unfortunate parents of young and weak families are kept waiting amongst a crowd outside this window, consisting of hundreds of persons, for one, two or three hours before they can obtain a miserable pittance of meal to keep alive their wretched offspring and, as if to aggravate the evil, this store is not opened until the hour of ten o clock in the morning and it is closed for the day at the hour of five in the afternoon.'

Wednesday 15 September. Joseph Kilgarrif, teacher of Balla National School, to   *Balla*
the Lord Lieutenant   DP 5166
'Meal of every description has risen within the last week to an enormous price by a few heartless forestallers who scruple not in exacting from the wretched human beings, three prices for what provisions they are capable of purchasing.'

Ballyhaunis

RLFC 3/2/21/24

Wednesday 16 September. Charles Strickland to Mr Stevens, Sligo

'I am much surprised by your letter of yesterday's date that you can give me only five tons of Indian meal for the Ballyhaunis Relief Committee. Finding the supply of meal in the barony of Costello so much less than was absolutely required, we formed a relief committee at Ballyhaunis and entered into subscriptions to the amount of about £100 for the purchase of Indian meal for that very distressed locality from 10 to 25 Irish miles from any depot. It gives us now the greatest possible alarm to find that we have taken this onus upon ourselves and with our money ready to pay, we cannot be supplied with the food in sufficient quantity to keep the poor alive. The heart-rending accounts I have heard, and what I have myself frequently seen, show beyond all question of doubt that if this supply cannot be fully kept up the poor will starve, with money in their hands to pay for provisions. You can well see the state of public opinion as to the want of provisions for this locality when private subscriptions of from £20 to £3 and even 10s. each has been given to bring in meal for sale only, and this supply, what we long but uselessly sought, from the government. The markets have not been supplied with the usual quantity of meal. Persons with capital are afraid to buy for fear of its being taken from them at the outbreak which they consider inevitable, and those who have any store are afraid to own it for the same reason. I have been so pressed on one or two occasions to buy meal from one or two persons who were found out to have a few cwts of meal for their own use that I have bought under the market price for the purpose of selling again in small quantities to the poor at cost price. Many would rather sell it at any price than keep even a small quantity in their houses when they were known to have it.

The supply must really be kept up for at least two months until the poor small landholders can get their corn ground. This country is entirely in the hands of small occupiers without any potatoes and with from a half to three or four acres of oats. The population of the barony is ... above 66,000 souls ... and with but one depot at one end of it. Mills are but very few, not above ten in the barony, and but half of those worth speaking of, and you may calculate how long it must then take before any general relief can be felt from these mills when every small landholder gets his own small quantity ground. It cannot be sooner than six or eight weeks and in the mean time Indian meal is the sole support of fully one-third and I might say half the population.

I entreat of you to let me know when I can send the carts and for what quantity. From 10 to 12 tons a week is as little as we could do with to give the necessary relief. The old stores are run out and the new not come in and cannot come in for some weeks.'

DP 5179

17 September. Eugene Coyne PP to the Lord Lieutenant

'If the government were to witness the scenes of misery and wretchedness that I daily meet with, they would not be so dilatory in sending substantial relief ... The murmuring of these hungry, half-naked persons, after having pawned their clothes to purchase a stone of meal and could not get it, should soften the hardest heart to compassion.'

Thursday 17 September. Rev J. Garrett to William Stanley   *Ballymote*
'The poor are badly harrassed at the Ballymote depot as there is only one   RLFC 3/2/26/18
man weighing the meal and many, after standing the whole day, faint with
hunger, return that evening without the expected food to their families ...
He cannot supply the multitude that crowd about his office for food. It
would require two men more ... More than a hundred poor are at the
moment waiting ...'
18 September. List of subscriptions, amounting to £146, paid to Richard Gethen,
treasurer of the Corran Relief Committee (See Appendix 3C)

Thursday 17 September. Resolution of a meeting of magistrates and associated cess-   *Swinford*
payers under the chairmanship of George Vaughan Jackson (See Appendix 1M)   DP 5222
'That the provisions of the Poor Employment Act are altogether unequal to
meet the calamity that now presses on us ... National works are indispensable for the safety of the country in its present melancholy position. That in
the ten parishes of Gallen there are no merchants thro' whom it can be
expected a supply of food be provided for the people ... that if Commissariat
stores of food are not established at Swinford, Kiltimagh, and Foxford the
population must inevitably starve.'

Friday 18 September. P. C. Lynch, High Sherrif of Mayo to T. N. Redington,   *Mayo*
enclosing a resolution of a meeting held yesterday   DP 5164
'That the destitute situation of the tradesmen and mechanics of Mayo is by
the failure of the potato crop of the present season greatly aggravated ...
Those very circumstances have had the effect of putting a stop to almost all
employment. That the mechanics, artificers and tradespeople of this county
... are entitled to the same consideration ... as the claims of the labouring
population.'

7080

Lurgan Lodge, Colloony, County Sligo.

September 17, 1846.

Sir,

Not having been favoured with a reply to the Circular which I had some time since the honor of sending ; soliciting a subscription from you, as one of the Landed Proprietors of the Barony of Tyrerill, in this County, towards the Funds of the Relief Committee ; I have been directed to write to you again on the subject.

In doing so permit me further to say that whatever doubt might have then *existed*, has since given place to certainty. There is *not* this year as last, a partial failure, but the entire destruction of the Potatoe crop. *Millions* have lost their twelve months' supply of Food ! ! *Thousands* and tens of thousands even now are almost starving ! ! !

Surely then the christian duty, " to deal thy bread to the hungry," was never more imperative on those who are blessed with the means than at the *present moment*. The relief which the committee hope to be able to afford—by the subscriptions which may be collected—will be impartially extended over the whole Barony ; so that your Tenantry will equally participate in the benefits of it ; and hoping for an immediate and favourable reply.

I remain Sir, with much respect;

Your faithful humble Servant,

E. A. LUCAS.

SUBSCRIPTIONS ALREADY RECEIVED :—

12 = 12 = 0

	£	s.	d.			£	s.	d.
E. J. Cooper, Esq.,	50	0	0	Rev. E. A. Lucas,	....	2	0	0
Mrs. O'Gore,	10	0	0	Rev. D. Durcan,	....	2	0	0
Wm. Weir, Esq.,	10	0	0	John Gethin, Esq.,	....	5	0	0
C. W. Cooper, Esq.,	10	0	0	Rev. L. Cullenan,	....	2	0	0
Rev. W. French, Esq.,	5	0	0	John Duke, Esq.,	....	2	0	0
W. Phibbs, Esq.,	5	0	0	B. O. Cogan, Esq.,	....	5	0	0
K. D. Loyd, Esq.,	1	0	0	John Wynne, Esq.,	....	5	0	0
John Ormsby, Esq.,	10	0	0	Michael Kough Esq.,	....	10	0	0
John Ffolliott, Esq.	5	0	0	Rev. Barry Phibbs,	——	5	0	0
E. Frazer, Esq.,	2	0	0	Rev. E. Feeny,	....	2	0	0
N. O. Fury, Esq.,	2	0	0	Thomas Phibbs Esq.	....	1	0	0
Sir G. King,	10	0	0	Rev. E. Elwood,	....	1	0	0
Rev. R. Cage,	2	0	0	Roger Duke, Esq.,	——	5	0	0
John Grant, Esq.,	2	12	0	Charles Langley, Esq.,	——	10	0	0
				Earl of Zetland,	——	30	0	0

3 = 0 = 0

127 = 12 = 0

214 = 12 = 0

Thacker, Printer, Sligo

Friday 18 September. Memorial of the inhabitants of Tubbercurry, Carrentubber, Ballyara, Tullacusheen, Clooneen, Sessua Common, Tullavella, Frenchford, Mullaun, Cloonacool, Sessua Garry, Sessua Kilroy in the parish of Achonry to the Lord Lieutenant

Tubbercurry
DP 5301

'At an extraordinary presentment sessions held at Tubbercurry on the 16th inst. … an application was made for making 1,219 perches of a new road was approved of by the presiding magistrates & cesspayers. The above named townlands contain a population of 4,200 who are destitute of food owing to the total failure of the potato crop and must inevitably perish from hunger unless they get employment on the above named work whereby they may purchase provisions. In addition to giving employment, the road in question is one of very great utility to the public at large and particularly so to the persons living along the line, all of whom were heretofore obliged to carry their corn and any other commodity, which they had to dispose of, on their backs to market. There is not any other public work in the neighbourhood on which they may get employment.' *(See Appendix 1N)*

Monday 21 September. James McHugh PP to the Lord Lieutenant, enclosing a memorial signed by the inhabitants of Tubbercurry and other townlands:

'As there is not a single landlord or magistrate in this very populous parish of Cloonacool, including a population of 1,000 families, to represent the pressing distress of the people, and as I am placed over them by God as their spiritual guardian for want of better, I must now come forward on their behalf to do the best I can to represent their galling destitution as temporal guardian. Therefore, with due submission I beg leave to call your Excellency's attention to the accompanying memorial, requesting you will be graciously pleased to order the new line of road between this town and Sessua Common to be opened forthwith … as being a very useful and necessary line, and capable of giving employment to a 1,000 starving people. I assert without fear of contradiction that one-third of the population in the district are without a four-footed beast or a grain of corn in the world, as they depended chiefly on daily labour and conacre potatoes, which are all lost by this awful visitation of Providence. The rich and poor are included in this dire calamity. There is not a potato in the country. The people are now idle, as the harvest is cut down and in the haggard and, if they are allowed now without employment to brood and ponder over their miseries and awful destitution, God only knows what may be the result. I shudder at the idea! Though otherwise as moral, as peaceable and amenable to the law of God and man as any other in the kingdom, and for a corroboration of this assertion, I beg leave to refer your Excellency to one of your own officers, the sub-inspector of the district, a gentleman that is entitled to the greatest praise and merit for his tenderness and humanity towards the distressed poor of this locality. As the Lord God

Circular letter soliciting subscriptions for the Tircrrill Relief Committee

has been pleased to call on you to rule the destinies of this country, as the first Irish nobleman for more than half a century, which we all hail with delight, I trust you will look with a benevolent eye on this portion of Her Majesty's subjects, situated in this locality, and not allow them to perish for want of employment. With all possible submission, I beg leave to make two remarks to your Excellency. The first, that you will order public prayers to be offered in every church and chapel in the kingdom, on some convenient Sunday, to avert the anger of the Almighty, which we have deserved by our manifold crimes; and secondly, that you will order a depot of government provisions to be kept at every police barracks in this district to convenience the working classes, and to be sold to them on moderate terms; and you may rely on it that this step will be more conducive to the peace and tranquility of the country than if you scattered all the Queen's troops among them. Food on reasonable terms, and employment to earn the price of same, will supply the place of the troops that are talked of being sent into the country. Oh! May the God of wisdom, that has laid the burden of ruling his subjects in this country on your shoulders, guide and direct you in the prudent discharge of that onerous duty, and give you life and health to see your native land restored to peace and plenty.'

Swinford
DP 5325

Saturday 19 September. Bernard Durcan PP to T. N. Redington
'I deeply regret to be obliged to say that our apprehensions ... have been already in a great measure realised. The store of meal in the sub depot of Swinford, having been exhausted since the 15th and there being no fresh supply received since or intimation of any being exported, the natural consequences have been that the private vendors have raised the price of meal beyond the reach of the poor, whom hunger and despair stare in the face. In the famine that exists, private credit, which even the poorest enjoyed to some extent heretofore, is totally stopped so that thousands are destitute of any better food than a scanty meal of the half-rotten miserable root, which they have in lieu of the potato. To procure a sufficiency of even this wretched substitute for wholesome food, occupies a great part of the family the greater part of the day and when collected together, cannot be used except in a sort of compound. I need not say how prejudicial to health this species of diet must be and it is alreay producing its natural results, viz. fever, cholera, morbus, dysentery, etc. which are becoming very prevalent in this locality. I deemed it my duty to lay this plain statement of facts before you in the full confidence that you will see that such prompt and efficacious measures be adopted as will meet the urgency of the case. It is essential that not only the depot at Swinford be abundantly and constantly supplied but also that other depots be established in the neighbouring towns and that a moderate and invariable price be adhered to.'

22 September. Memorial of the clergy and inhabitants of Swinford asking to increase the supplies of meal to the depot there and the formation of depots throughout the county
Reply to above:
To meet the exigency which has so suddenly arisen, there are not foreign supplies of corn as yet in the ports and cannot be expected to arrive before the end of October or during November. Gentlemen of local influence should therefore unite their exertions to have the produce of the home harvest brought largely into the markets for the subsistence of the population.

Swinford
RLFC 3/1/5863

Sunday 20 September. Lieutenant Dawson, coast guard, to Sir James Dombrain
'A great number of country people came into my yard this day complaining heavily of their starving state and praying that I would use any means in my power to obtain food for them and that the whole country would be in to me on Thursday. I requested that no such demonstration should be made, that I would write this evening and that if anything could be done, I was sure no time would be lost, that arrangements were being made for a large supply of meal for sale. The want here seems to be increasing every day.'

Belmullet
DP 5687

Monday 21 September. Sub-Inspector Denis Walsh to Pierce G. Barron RM, Westport
'Mr Graham, a merchant of this town, had five carts employed in conveying oats to the quay to be shipped this morning. Between 600 and 700 persons made the carmen return to the store with it, stating at the same time that they would not allow one grain of corn to leave the country as they were starving. They did not offer the slightest violence.'

Westport
OP 21/26029

Monday 21 September. Memorial signed by John Brennan CC, James Jordan, secretary, and Brownslow Lynch, Protestant minister, to the Lord Lieutenant
'There are no resident landlords nor any relief whatever from them. There are one or two instances of death caused by starvation and unless immediate relief be given many will meet with premature graves. There are many instances of families living during the last ten days on turnips and cabbages and fever and other diseases are rife in the parish and a meal depot should be permanently established in Kiltimagh.'

Kiltimagh

Tuesday 22 September. John Corley PP to the Lord Lieutenant
'Yesterday there was not a stone of meal in this town and many persons who came to buy were fainting in the streets. Unless your Excellency will order a regular supply for this locality, the people will die of want, for those towns where large supplies are to be had are too inconvenient to them, who cannot

Foxford
DP 5360

Foxford   purchase more than a stone or half stone at a time. I hope your Excellency will pay immediate attention to this communication as the crisis does not admit of delay.'

RLFC 3/1/5863   *22 September. Relief Commission Office to Rev Geoff H. Mostyn, Foxford*
'At present, gentlemen of influence should unite in exertions to have supplies of home produce augmented in the markets, as the importations will not arrive in sufficient quantity before the end of October or during November. It is not proposed to place money at the disposal of individuals; but relief committees collecting local subscriptions will obtain grants in aid of them.'

DP 5523   *23 September. Rev Geoff H. Mostyn, to T. N. Redington*
'Many must perish from hunger, specially some of those who were employed as stone breakers on a projected road near this village. I have seen the poor things come in day after day, week after week, for their few shillings hard-earned indeed and they were told by the paymaster that they could get no money as the pay sheets were not forwarded to him. There is gross negligence somewhere. Such cruelty to those starving creatures! Their tears of complaint are truly heart-rending and in my opinion many of them will perish.'

DP 6384   *9 October. Board of Works to T. N. Redington concerning Rev Geoff Mostyn's complaint about the delay in paying the wages of labourers and enclosing the report of the Board's officer:*
'I lost no time in sending to the paymaster urging the immediate discharge of the monies due to the labourers in the district of Foxford for stone breaking and have this day 1st inst. ascertained that he has been paying the parties referred to and I hope no further ground for complaint will be found to exist.'

DP 5473   *23 September. George Vaughan Jackson to the Chief Secretary*
'At Foxford I found the supply of the store quite exhausted and great demand for food and no supplies in the hands of private parties. The same state of things existed in Swinford. The weather prevents any of the mills working ... The position at the moment is most critical ... The population will break loose if this state of things continues much longer ... No supplies can be obtained at Ballina, Westport or Sligo. There is great discontent at the works not being recommenced and at the labourers in some places not being paid altho' wages are a long time due.'

DP 6386   *16 October. Board of Works to T. N. Redington re G. V. Jackson's letter, 23 September.*
''Tis true there were and may be still, claims from persons thrust on the works by the committees without tickets and without any regard to the limit necessarily prescribed for each work. In numerous instances the committees totally disregarded the arrangements of the officers of the Board and the natural result was confusion, waste of funds, the non-execution of the works and all kinds of irregularities.'

Thursday 24 September. John Corley PP to George Vaughan Jackson
'In haste I beg to state that the people are preparing to come into or rather
to march on this town. There is no time to spare. Take some steps to prevent
it or deter them from it.'

Jackson sent above to the Chief Secretary, commenting:
'Foxford (Toomore) is a parish with 900 families and no food and no
employment of any kind, their being no resident proprietor, nor any merchant or other person to employ the population. I have taken all the steps I
could take under the emergency. I waited on Mr Waters. He proceeded at 8
am to Sligo to wait on Commissary Dobree. We called on the officer commanding the *Warrior,* a government steamer, in the port at Ballina. He sails
at 7 am tomorrow, weather permitting, for Sligo to be at the disposal of the
government officers there. There are but fifteen tons of oaten meal in Ballina,
none at Killala, nor at Crossmolina, Foxford, Swinford, etc. There is no other
kind of food available for the population. The mills in the country are all at
a stand for want of water. The position of affairs is most perilous. From my
knowledge of the poor here I am persuaded that nothing but the last extremity would make them violate the law but everywhere I go the cry of the
unhappy people assails me, "We are starving". With great difficulty I
obtained two tons of meal for Foxford which will not answer the demand for
two hours. Mr Corley renders me the best service in exhorting the poor to
patience and observance of the law and greatly relieves the distress by acts of
charity … If large supplies of food are not thrown into Ballina and if employment on the works … is not resumed … it is impossible to calculate on what
the consequences may be. If meetings of the population in masses once begin
it will extend without limit. Were orders for the resumption of work arrived,
it would give confidence and allay the alarm that at present is intense.'

Wednesday 23 September. Corran Relief Committee to Sir Randolph Routh
'The present wages of 8d per day are quite insufficient to sustain the labourers and their families. We request that, the harvest being completed, wages
will be raised.'

Thursday 24 September. J. G. Wills JP to T. N. Redington
'We have a large suburb belonging to Mr Lloyd of Rockville which numbers
more poor and utterly destitute people than the whole of the two large estates
belonging to Lord Sandford and my father. This gentleman has neglected to
assist in the support of his own poor or even to answer our application as a
relief committee. He has not given one farthing to the relief fund … The
multitudes of hungry people pressing into the town are likely to attack private property in the madness of their hunger.'

Foxford
DP 5484

Ballymote
RLFC 3/2/26/18

Castlerea
DP 5485

Castlerea
DP 5574

26 September. H. B. Wray RM to T. N. Redington

'The melancholy fact, under existing circumstances, that our food market is rising and that we are at this moment without a pound of meal or biscuit in the government sub depot here, for use of the hundreds of poor labourers who are (in consequence of the neglect of their landlords) entirely dependant on food from that store. And added to this deplorable condition, no public works of any kind are yet in progress in my district to enable the people (ready and willing to work) to procure food at the present high market prices … The consequences to private property may be fearful. The disappointment of the many wretched beings who came to the store this day, at finding there was no issue of meal or biscuit, caused such apprehension that I felt it my duty to hold the troops and police in readiness to protect private property should any attempt at violence be made upon it. Happily none occurred.'

Collooney
DP 5515

Thursday 24 September. E. A. Lucas to Henry Labouchere, enclosing a resolution passed this day by the Tirerrill Relief Committee

'That the hardships and privations which numbers in this barony are unfortunately at present undergoing are so great that they can be no longer endured and that this committee would be insensible to all the better feelings of human nature if they were allowed to pass without respectfully calling on the government to commence without delay some of the numerous public works in each district approved of at the Special Sessions at Collooney, Monday 14 September and to give additional assistance to Capt Gilbert to report thereon to the county surveyor for laying out and carrying on the same.'

Tubbercurry
DP 5888

Friday 25 September. Memorial of Martin Scanlon, John Brennan and Edmund Durkan, near Tubbercurry, to the Lord Lieutenant

'That they are highly distressed for the want of an accommodating road from the backward and retired situation of their place of residence to the mean *(sic)* road, being a space of one mile and three-quarters, of which the Grand Jury of County Sligo granted a presentment for repairing about three-quarters of a mile, but being neglected ever since, which so discommodes them as to be under the necessity of carrying their oats and other burdens on peoples' backs, notwithstanding paying taxes and all other legal impositions … All the relief they got from the government's bounty was a ton of meal and work for a few pounds a day. The relief committee excludes them from participation in this as their landlord, James Knox of Rappa Castle, did not contribute but £5.'

Coolavin
DP 6576

Friday 25 September. J. A. Holmes JP, Clogher, Ballaghaderreen, to T. N. Redington, requesting that the commissariat depot be continued in Coolavin

'There is neither market nor village in the barony … If it is closed grievous results may follow as I don't know one trader in the barony who either has the capital or means to import one week's provisions for that portion of the inhabitants who must be purchasers.'

He encloses a resolution of magistrates and cess-payers on 23 September asking for a grant towards building a bridge across the ford of Clooncunny at Lough Gara:
'That considering the very great and general distress now prevalent ... without giving any obstruction to merchants in the free importation of corn to this country or to the equitable traffic of the same in our markets, measures will be speedily adopted by the government to prevent the alarming and exorbitant rise in the price of the poor man's food, as otherwise the present rate of wages must prove wholly inadequate to the purposes of substantial relief.'

Friday 25 September. Memorial of four parish priests, four curates and two Augustinians of Ballyhaunis and its vicinity, to the Lord Lieutenant, requesting a food depot in Ballyhaunis
'We now most respectfully in the name of our starving parishioners beg to impress upon your Excellency the necessity of immediate attention to the prayer of the memorial or else the consequences are likely to be dreadful.'

Saturday 26 September. Joseph McTucker PP to Henry Labouchere
'It was with the utmost consternation I heard this morning that the poor people who went to work on the public works were to get but 8d. per day. I, as one of those best acquainted with the circumstances of the poor in this locality, have been most particular in selecting the greatest objects for employment, and owing to the vast numbers that were seeking it, I was obliged to deny employment to any save one member in each family. Looking to the present price of Indian meal, which is the cheapest kind of food he could provide, how could a poor man obtain sufficient food for his family with the small sum of 4s. per week? It cannot be that the government will allow such a lingering process of starvation to be introduced. The poor people have privations enough to endure, being compelled to labour or rather expend their physical exertions, when they cannot have even a sufficiency of food. I earnestly entreat of you to give directions that for this week they may get 10d. per day, the sum allowed two months since.'

Sunday 27 September. Rev J. Garrett to Sir Randolph Routh
'There is no meal in Ballymote since Friday morning and multitudes have gone away in sad disappointment. Richard Gethen, treasurer, had three tons of Indian meal to pay workmen on Sir Robert North's estate, which he sold out on Friday and yesterday to the most destitute. This is the most critical moment.'

Coolavin

Ballyhaunis
DP 5631

Boyle
DP 5552

Ballymote
RLFC 3/2/26/18

1 October. Same to Sir Randolph Routh
'Corran Relief fund is exhausted ... It would now particularly be a charity to fund us half to buy the provisions from our farmers and retail them at a reduced price.'

Belmullet
DP 5688

Tuesday 29 September. Lieutenant William Dawson, coast-guard, to the Inspector-General, enclosing an application signed by fifty-eight tradesmen of the town, including three tailors, one clothier, ten shoemakers, two victuallers, five masons, two nailors, one carrier, two hatters, one baillif, three dealers, two teachers, three carpenters, four smiths and one sawyer
'That he will procure them a supply of Indian meal from whatever quarter he thinks proper, for which they are willing to pay a fair price and thereby save themselves and their families from utter famine.'
Dawson wrote:
'I know them to be suffering greatly from the scarcity of provisions. There is not any oatmeal to be had in the town for the last week and the few potatoes that are brought to the market are not sufficient to supply the wants of one-tenth of the townspeople. The little flour that is sold is 2s.10½d to 3s. a stone. Numbers of the country people are continually thronging in here and meeting me on the roads, to know if I can give them any hope of speedy supplies of provisions and work, for there are many of them almost starving, since the sudden stoppage of the sale of meal.'

Ballisodare
DP 5735

Wednesday 30 September. Memorial of fifty-two labourers living in the town or immediate neighbourhood, to the Lord Lieutenant (See Appendix 1C)
'They are at present in a state bordering on destitution for want of employment ... They therefore most humbly suggest that an old road leading from the bridge of Ballisodare to Ardcotton, a distance of about two miles, and meeting the public road between Collooney and Coolaney, if opened would be of incalculable advantage to those generally passing that way, together with affording employment to memorialists ... having no funds at their disposal to enable them to procure for their desolate families even a scanty supply of the common necessaries of life, whom with few exceptions depending on day labour for the support of their families.

Swinford
DP 5916

Thursday 1 October 1846. Bernard Durcan PP to Henry Labouchere, informing him of '... the melancholy and alarming state of destitution and misery to which the people in this part of the country are reduced ... Swinford is the centre of an extensive and densely populated district as poor as any in Ireland. There is not a single resident landlord in the barony (Gallen), of which it is the chief town, who can give the least relief, or agent who takes any interest in procuring it. There was a depot established in it for the sale of Indian corn and oatmeal in small quantities, from which, whilst the supply was kept up, much advantage was derived, as the people had the opportunity of getting even the smallest quantity at a moderate price and the markets were kept down. But alas! they have been deprived of even this advantage. There has been no meal in the depot for the last ten days nor are there any hopes held out of its being continued at all. The consequence is that oatmeal which, while the depot was in operation, sold for 16s. or 17s. a cwt., has risen in the local markets to £1 2s. I am told that the reason for giving up the depot is that the people are supposed to have the oat crop now available. It is true the greater part of the holders of land have; but then there are thousands of poor families who have no land or who, having a small portion of boggy land, have no oats and these, having no employment for the last six months and no earthly means of procuring any food, are suffering all the miseries of famine and disease. Even those who have oats cannot convert it to use for want of a sufficiency of mills to grind it. There is no appearance of the works, which were presented at the Extraordinary Sessions, being commenced. From all these causes, the peoples' minds are alarmed beyond calculation. The calamity has been so great that nothing but giving employment on the most extensive scale, and keeping an abundant supply of provisions in the country, could prevent unusual famine and all its accompanying horrors. Sanguine hopes were hitherto entertained that the government were resolved to adopt the necessary measures to prevent so dreadful a state of things. These hopes were founded partly, on the character of the several members composing the present government, and partly on the promises made by them, but alas these hopes seem now to be dissipated and a universal gloom is coming over the minds of the people which, in all probability will end in violence and plunder and universal confusion.'

Thursday 1 October. E. Howley JP, chairman of the Ballina Poor Law Guardians, to Henry Labouchere   Ballina
DP 5826
'On Tuesday last, while a number of magistrates here assembled for the election of an officer ... a large crowd of wretched-looking persons came in as a body to the doors of the house and sent up the accompanying document to the board room:

"Mr Chairman and Gentlemen,
... We beg leave to submit to your notice that there is a certain individual in this town shipping oats at the present time, when the poor of Ballina are starving for want of food, and no employment to be had. Gentlemen, we ask you is it lawful to let the grain out of the country, when such a state of things is allowable, and if so, you and every one of ye, may look to the consequences."

After reading it, and consulting with my brother magistrates for a few min-

utes, I proceeded to address a few words to them on the illegality of attempting to prevent the exportation of grain and the bad consequences which were
likely to result from such an imprudent course; at the same time, holding out
to them the strongest assurance of the immediate increase of the public works
and the introduction of a large quantity of Indian meal to Ballina. Indeed,
before I left the board room, we entered into a large subscription to purchase
at once a cargo of Indian corn and to have it ground here, and sold by us at
first cost to the poor. This had the effect of inducing them to disperse quietly,
assuring me they would strictly follow my advice and not attempt to trans-
gress the law. Meal and every description of food is very scarce and dear here
and the people without employment ...'
*Howley strongly recommended the immediate resumption of public works to
enable the numerous starving poor to get employment for six months to come.*

Lower Leyny
RLFC 3/2/26/25

Thursday 1 October. C. K. O'Hara to William Stanley
'The subscriptions placed at the disposal of the Lower Leyny Relief
Committee are at present applied to providing supplies of Indian meal and
other foods for sale weekly at Coolaney, in the smallest quantities at cost
price, on an average of from three to five tons weekly.'

DP 5956

*3 October. Commissariat Relief Office to T. N. Redington informing him that
they had received a subscription list from the barony of Lower Leyny amounting
to £189 and recommend a grant of £90. (See Appendix 3D)*

Gallen
DP 5871

*Saturday 3 October. Board of Works to T. N. Redington recommending £12,538
18s. 4d. for 63 specified and costed public works in the barony of Gallen. (See
Appendix 4D)*

Corran
DP 6137

*Saturday 3 October. Treasury Chambers to T. N. Redington informing him that
Board of Works have been directed to proceed with works in the barony of Corran
to the amount of £5,117 10s. (See Appendix 4B)*

DP 5957

*5 October. Commissariat Relief Commission to T. N. Redington informing him
that they have received subscription lists amounting to £63 from the Corran Relief
Committee and recommending a grant of £30. (See Appendix 3C)*

Ballyhaunis
RLFC 3/2/21/24

Saturday 3 October. Eugene Coyne PP to Sir Randolph Routh
'This inland country is in an awful state of destitution and many of them
would be now rotting in their graves only for the sum of £130 contributed by
the shopkeepers, a few of the gentry, and the clergy, who gave from £1 to £5
to purchase Indian meal for those who could buy it and by that means keep
down the markets which are getting up to famine prices. We are now in a bad
way and unless the government come to our assistance with meal and money,

the people will die in hundreds. I now call on you, Sir, in the name of heaven, before there are any more lives lost, to send us funds to relieve the destitute poor.'

Tuesday 6 October. John Corley PP to the Lord Lieutenant
'The scanty payment? given did not, nor does not, reach a third of those who would require it, even of those on the verge of starvation. Such as are employed are fast sinking under the weight of labour, owing to their having no nourishment. When they first commenced, persons gave them some meal on credit, until they would receive their pay, but when that was delayed, as it has been for the last fortnight, they would get no credit and were obliged to live on cabbage, without any other species of diet. It would, I think, be more merciful to treat them as did Bonaparte his wounded soldiers, than thus leave them a prey to famine and victims to all those diseases and afflictions which accompany it. I hope, my Lord, you will attend to this appeal and see justice done to the most indigent and wretched people on earth.'

Foxford
DP 7874

Tuesday 6 October. Richard Gethen, chairman, and Rev J. Garrett, secretary of the Corran Relief Committee, to Henry Labouchere
'In consequence of the limited extent of employment, many of the destitute have four miles to go to work and thus the roads granted become most indiscriminately crowded, while many wretches who are excluded are nearly driven to madness by their hopeless condition, witnessing that some of their neighbours, in their own condition as to destitution, are employed.'

Ballymote
DP 6221

Tuesday 6 October. John Armstrong, Chaffpool, Ballymote, chairman of the Upper Leyny Relief Committee, to Sir Randolph Routh, asking him for a depot to be set up in Tubbercurry 'for that district where nothing can equal the misery of the poor people but their patience. There are very few resident gentlemen and a population of about 30,000 souls with very little public works. The price meal has arrived at will preclude the purchase of sufficient food for the labourer and his family.' *If the depot is not granted Armstrong asks for 20 tons of Indian meal weekly.*

Tubbercurry
RLFC 3/2/26/26

Wednesday 7 October. Memorial of the Costello Relief Committee to the Lord Lieutenant, signed by J. A. Holmes JP, J. Seymour JP, Vicar of Castlemore, Denis Tighe PP, Ballaghaderreen, Charles Strickland, JP, chairman, Thomas Philips JP, Cloonmore House, John Coghlan PP, Kilmovee & William McHugh PP.
'Words cannot describe the famishing state of the people ... The works selected for immediate employment are quite inadequate to meet the immediate distress. Employment of 1,000 men in a barony with a population of 50,000 is

Ballaghaderreen
DP 6179

a mere nothing ... The peace of the country is endangered. The patience of the people is now exhausted as they see no prospects of the works commencing. God only knows where it will end if the seriously threatened outbreak should once commence.'

DP 6189

7 October. Board of Works to T. N. Redington recommending £21,899 for specified and costed public works in the barony of Costello (See Appendix 4C)

Upper Leyny
DP 6105

Wednesday 7 October. Board of Works to T. N. Redington, recommending £6,126 5s. for three public works (See Appendix 4E)

Corran
DP 6191

Thursday 8 October. Board of Works to T. N. Redington, recommending £798 to make a new road, 633 perches long, leading from the road from Ballymote to Tubbercurry at Woodhill to Ballinaleck

Ballina
DP 6387

Sunday 11 October. George Vaughan to Henry Labouchere recommending works in which women and children could be employed, such as fencing with rough walls made of stones collected from fields, and removing whins, brushwood, rocks and other obstructions to the cultivation of farms

Kiltimagh
DP 7055

Sunday 11 October. Memorial signed by inhabitants of the parish of Killedan (Kiltimagh) to the Lord Lieutenant (See Appendix 1J)

'The parish of Killedan contains about 1,200 families, 500 of whom are in possession of no land and were obliged consequently to live upon conacre potatoes, by the total failure of which crop, these 500 families are quite destitute of any means of support. There are also 400 families among us who have no cattle of any description, nor on average one stack of oats. The diseased potato, while it was capable of being procured, afforded a miserable subsistence to the most distressed and, alas! from the baneful effects of such food, pestilence to a frightful extent is spreading among us. The number of persons daily snatched away, both by the pestilence and by the effects of hunger, is rapidly increasing.

While labouring under these unparalleled sufferings, we have violated no law, we were guilty of no crime. The most wretched of us, being now driven to desperation by the effects of hunger and disease, are beginning to disregard the admonition of the most peaceable. Hundreds, able and anxious to labour for their subsistence, are at this moment about to become the victims of hunger. Placed in this sad and miserable condition, we most earnestly implore your Excellency, both with a view of preserving the public peace and also the lives of her Majesty's most dutiful subjects, to take into your immediate consideration these ungarnished and unexaggerated statements of facts, which are alas too true and which we are prepared, if necessary, to verify by affidavits.'

Tuesday 13 October. Eugene Coyne PP to Sir Randolph Routh requesting a depot in Ballyhaunis   *Ballyhaunis*
'Meal is now beyond famine prices, which would not be the case if the memorials and letters of the resident clergy were attended to. I now call on you, in the name of heaven, to look to this inland country or the consequences are likely to be fatal to life and prosperity.'

Tuesday 13 October. G. M. Trevelyan, Treasury, to T. N. Redington informing him that he has directed Board of Works to proceed with works in the barony of Leyny to the extent of £6,126 5s. (See Appendix 4E)   *Leyny*

Tuesday 13 October. Resolution of Swinford Board of Guardians   *Swinford*
'That the chairman, G. V. Jackson, will represent to the Lord Lieutenant the   DP 6733
utter impossibility of our carrying on the relief of the destitute through the Poor Law, owing to the unlooked for and unprecedent calamity in which we are plunged, unless a loan is made to meet the intense urgency of the present moment, to be paid by the rate at a future period.'
Observations of Mr Otway, assistant commissioner, on above:
'It is almost impossible to get any rate in … to get anyone to pay 1s. of any rent or tax … It is difficult to take coercive measures against a whole district … There is extreme poverty, which not only forces the destitute to seek admission into the workhouse, but also deprives the rate payers of the means of paying the rate, at the time it is most required.'
13 October. Resolutions of the Gallen & Costello Relief Committee (See Appendix 2E)   DP 6581
Resolution, proposed by Edward P. McDonnell and seconded by Revd John Coghlan PP:
'That the deaths of masses by starvation and that convulsion that will shake society to its centre, must take place at once if public work on the largest scale is not provided for the population.'
Resolution, proposed by Revd Bernard Egan and seconded by Richard O'Grady:
'That from the masses that apply for employment who are absolutely starving, we feel our further meetings will only tend to increase the dangers of our unfortunate position, by exciting delusive hopes and exasperating feelings already stimulated by hunger, if government do not at once give employment on the most extensive scale.'
Resolution, proposed by Revd Mr Coghlan PP, and seconded by Revd Mr Muldowney:
'That we call upon the government to establish provision depots in every parish of the baronies of Gallen and Costello as we have no confidence in the merchants of the country (with the exception of the Westport merchants) as the others have taken advantage of the poverty of the people and have raised

food even beyond famine prices. They have and are exacting the pound of flesh. We therefore solicit the interference of the government, to prevent the people from starvation, to which they are reduced by being left to the speculation of heartless selfish merchants.'

Resolution, proposed by Edward P. McDonnell and seconded by Revd Mr Coghlan PP:

'That this being our last meeting, before we separate we deem it due to Charles Strickland Esq., agent to Lord Viscount Dillon, to hear our unqualified testimony, not alone to his indefatigable zeal and his valuable assistance in carrying into effect the objects of this committee, but for his very great and laudable exertions in being the means of procuring a large quantity of the provision for the poor in this, the barony of Costello, and thereby enabling many poor and destitute families to prolong for a short time a wretched and miserable existence.'

Resolution, proposed by Revd Mr Coghlan PP and seconded by Edward P. McDonnell:

'That ... we, the representatives of Costello, cannot permit this dissolution to take place, without expressing our unbounded gratitude and kindest acknowledgements to our chairman, G. V. Jackson Esq., whose zealous discharge of his arduous duties we admire and appreciate. The urbanity of his gentlemanly demeanour commands our lasting gratitude.'

Ballymote
DP 6668

Wednesday 14 October. Richard Gethen, chairman, and Rev J. Garrett, secretary, to T. N. Redington

'The Relief Committee of Corran has laboured to revise and correct the labour lists with a view to select the really destitute and exclude such as can support themselves and their families by their own means, and finding it difficult, if not impossible, to obtain accurate information ... that the Lord Lieutenant order the constabulary to make out a correct inventory of the substance and extent of the holdings of the population, from whence the deserving objects for relief may be selected.'

15 October. Rev J. Garrett to Sir Randolph Routh

'The work of Corran Relief Committee has become very onerous and requires the services of a competent person to keep the accounts, to register the labourers employed, and to keep all official documents and correct books, where the more destitute are chosen to the exclusion of those who are richer.'

Costello &
Corran
DP 6699

Thursday 15 October. G. M. Trevelyan, Treasury, to T. N. Redington, informing him that he has directed Board of Works to proceed with the works in the barony of Costello, to the extent of £21,899 and in the barony of Corran to the extent of £798 (See Appendix 4B&C)

Friday 16 October. Denis Tighe PP to the Lord Lieutenant   *Ballaghaderreen*
RLFC 3/2/21/23
'The Ballaghaderreen Relief Committee has raised over £100 and seeks a government grant ... Fever is becoming very prevalent and a few have already
fallen victims to hunger. Even this day I met two men unable to walk from
hunger ... The public works are not yet commenced. We are all in the greatest fears of an outbreak against property. I fear life itself will not be secure if
the people are not immediately relieved. Most of my parishioners are now living on one meal in the day.'

Friday 16 October. Memorial of the Relief Committee to the Lord-Lieuntenant   *Upper Leyny*
(See Appendix 21)   DP 6989
'It is a very remote and poor district with a population of 37,000 ... The sum
of £3,397 was allocated for public works (£2,729 was allocated to Lower
Leyny with a population of 9,913) ... They feel they have every reason to
complain ... The officer of the Board of Works should be ordered to select
out of the list forwarded, some others of the most useful lines of roads or
other works to give employment to our miserably distressed population,
many of whom are literally starving.'

Friday 16 October. John Coghlan PP to the Lord Lieutenant   *Kilmovee*
DP 662
'I was prevented by the want of a road conveyance from accompanying Mr
Strickland on a deputation to wait on your Excellency and request your most
humane and timely interference to rescue my poor people from the horrors
of starvation. They are literally starving before my eyes. There is not a single
labourer out of a population of 5,844 human souls at this moment in employment and only a promise of 280 men. What are they to do? Must they perish after being promised relief from the late act? A month has now elapsed.
There is no employment. They have borne all patiently, not even an act of
petit larceny, except two sheep which were stolen, has occurred. I beg, I
entreat your Excellency will order that at least 1,500 men be employed on
Monday next. If not, they perish. May God in his mercy relieve them.'

19 October. John Coghlan PP to Sir Randolph Routh   RLFC 3/2/21/27
'Indian meal much required for the starving multitudes, by which we are surrounded. A depot in this place is quite indispensable.'

21 October. Francis R. O'Grady, chairman, Kilkelly Relief Committee, William   RLFC 3/2/21/25
McHugh PP, John Coghlan PP Kilmovee, Richard Prendergast PP Aghamore, to
Sir Randolph Routh, asking for depots in Ballyhaunis and Kilkelly 'because of
the high price of meal at the market and thus we will be able to keep the
already starving poor from outrage.'

Draft reply, 21 October:
'It is not at present practicable to increase the number of depots or supply all

those already established ... Where depots shall be established, it is not intended to sell the food at first cost, but at such prices as will enable traders, selling at the same rates, to realise their profits.'

Ballymote
DP 7686

Monday 19 October. Richard Gethen & Rev J. Garrett, Corran Relief Committee, to T. N. Redington
'That in the task work at breaking stones, it may hereafter be competent for the overseers to permit feeble boys or women, who can scarcely earn anything in this description of labour, to avail themselves of the assistance of a child or brother to assist in breaking the stones, to enable them to receive the labours of both, when the stones are measured, to sustain the wretched families. We are aware that in some cases a poor boy cannot earn more than 6d. a week at breaking stones and the utmost would be 2s. a week for a woman to earn.'
Reply, 3 November. Board of Works to T. N. Redington:
'The Board's proper officer reported that it would completely destroy the system of task work, or even any regularity of conducting the employment of the poor, if the plan proposed by Mr Gethen was accepted.'

RLFC 3/2/26/18

23 October. Rev J. Garrett to William Stanley
'It is truly painful to have to report the death of an able-bodied labourer, whose wages of 8D. a day had been unpaid for ten days. He and his family were forced to subsist on cabbage for the last four days, and being at work in a drain in this inclement weather, he was siezed with Irish cholera and lost his life, leaving a desolate widow and six children. It is truly lamentable to think that, the price of provision being 2s. 8d. per stone for oatmeal and 2s. 3d. for Indian meal, the unfortunate men are unable to sustain themselves and their families on 8d. a day, and tho' willing to try task works, it has not been offered to them in a tangible shape, the overseers not understanding how to agree for tasks and at what price ... Deaths will daily increase from starvation unless the wages are increased.'
Garrett encloses a subscription list of the subscriptions of Corran Relief Committee for the month ending today, totalling £31 2s. Commissariat Relief Office recommended a grant of £15 (See Appendix 3C)

Leyny
DP 6895

Wednesday 21 October. Board of Works to T. N. Redington recommending works to the extent of £1,271 (See Appendix 4E)

Gallen &
Costello
DP 7075

Wednesday 21 October. Board of Works to T. N. Redington re the meeting of the Gallen & Costello Relief Committee in Swinford, 13 October, with reference to the immediate employment of the poor
'The county surveyor has been instructed already to commence works in Gallen to the extent of £12,538 18s. 4d. and in Costello to the extent of £21,899.' *(See Appendices C&D)*

Wednesday 28 October. Roger Palmer JP to the Lord Lieutenant, enclosing a notice posted on the courthouse door

'We do hereby give notice to all the boys in the parish of Kilbride, Lackan, Doonfeeny and the mountains, to attend at Ballycastle on Friday, 29 Oct. 1846, to hold on it a vestry? of our own on the gentlemen of the country. Any man who stops at home, he will be sawed and quartered. It is their due to support us. If they don't do it, we will have it out of their houses and gardens by night or by day. We are not liable to starve and they having our earning and our forefathers' earning. If they do not relieve us immediately, we will take it ourselves. Any man who is found out to take down this notice, he may as well have his coffin made. But any man that fails and stops at home, he may be making his own coffin.'

Friday 30 October. Rev J. Garrett to Henry Labouchere

'I have strongly represented a fortnight since the sad destitution of the inhabitants of Lackagh, Doorley, Mocknegroagh? and Drumfin, who live out of reach of any public works ... Capt Gilbert witnessed the distress of this district and suggested a memorial to the Board ... and tho' road no. 5 on the list of the county surveyor was duly passed and approved by him, and would afford relief to the suffering families consisting of 600 souls, we have failed to obtain an answer from the Board of Works.'

Saturday 31 October. Extract from the Guardians' minutes Resolution proposed by A. Crean Lynch and seconded by Dr Dillon

'That we find the collection of the outstanding rate wholly impracticable, that we are without any contractors and that £1,000 is due to former contractors, as well as the salaries of our officers. That but for the kind aid of the Earl of Lucan for the last four weeks, our inmates would have starved. That we therefore feel ourselves reduced to the painful necessity of refusing further admissions, until the government makes an advance.'

Observations of C. G. Otway on above:

'A letter should be sent to the Board of Guardians pointing out the illegality and the cruelty of the Board of Guardians refusing admissions, at a time when relief is most required. If the Guardians persist in refusing to admit the poor and strike a new rate, the Poor Law Commission should dissolve them.'

Winter 1846-47

Deaths from Starvation

Prices continued to spiral and the supply of food became increasingly scarce. The first reports of deaths from starvation were recorded. Fr O'Flynn, PP of Attymass, reported on 19 November to George Vaughan Jackson that four persons had so died in his parish recently. The workhouses became overcrowded and large numbers of applicants were refused admission. The Swinford Board of Guardians recorded on 10 November: 'There are upwards of 100 persons in the workhouse over the number the house is calculated to contain and the Board of Guardians decline to admit any more altho' there were 200 persons at the door seeking relief.' Even those lucky enough to gain admission were also in danger of starving. Whatever rates were collected were quite inadequate to meet the expenditure. Those who had contracted to provide food for the inmates refused to do so on credit. Only the generosity of the chairman, G. V. Jackson, and one or two other members, who funded the workhouse out of their own pockets for a few weeks, prevented its closure and the expulsion of the inmates. Bad weather added considerably to the sufferings of the people. Winter came early. There was heavy snow in November and again early in December.

A new system of public works was devised in August but did not come into operation until the end of October. By Christmas there was a total of 18,321 persons employed on the roads in Co Mayo and 10,720 in Co Sligo. A month later it had risen to 36,931 in Co Mayo and 14,035 in Co Sligo. The new system was to be funded totally from local taxation and carried out exclusively by the Board of Works with little or no input from local committees. Labourers were to be paid not by the day but on the basis of task work. As they became progressively more debilitated from lack of nourishment, there earnings consequently fell to little more than starvation wages, while food prices continued to rise. As the measurement of task work was time-consuming, there were sometimes considerable delays in the payment of wages.

Sunday 1 November 1846. Francis Knox Gore, Belleek Manor, to Sir Randolph Routh, urging the necessity of keeping up supplies of meal in the depots of Sligo and Ballina, the latter supplying a great part of Sligo

Ballina
RLFC 3/2/26/2

'I am strongly urging the farmers to bring in their oatmeal to market and have succeeded to a certain extent. I hope to get over the difficulties till supplies from America will reduce prices to moderation.'

Draft reply to above, 1 December:

'The government depots are only intended as auxiliaries, not as the chief source of maintenance for the population.'

Monday 2 November. Bernard Durcan PP, chairman, and Ulic Burke MD, secretary of the Swinford Relief Committee, to the Commissary General

Swinford
RLFC 3/2/21/42

'The Swinford Relief Committee was established to purchase meal and issue it in small quantities and at first cost to the suffering poor. We enclose a list of subscriptions raised from persons who are not by any means affluent but who have the absolute necessity of making some exertions to assist the poor by keeping down if possible the markets in which provisions now rate with famine prices, oaten meal selling at 24s. a cwt by retail. There is not a single resident landlord who could afford to assist us. We request the highest possible donation.' *(See Appendix 3K)*

3 November. Relief Committee of the Swinford district, comprising the parishes of Kilconduff, Meelick, Killedan and Bohola, signed by Edward Deane, to the Lord Lieutenant

RLFC 3/2/21/39

'They have done all in their power to alleviate the present calamity and if evil consequences to the peace of the country ensue, the blame should be attributed to the proper quarters. They think it is as unnecessary as it has been hitherto useless, to say one word as to the heartrending scenes of appalling distress, misery and famine by which they are surrounded. The parishes contain a rural population of 21,968 individuals. It is an underestimate to say that one in four require relief by way of labour. This would give 5,424 individuals the means to provide for the wants of the rest. Two months ago the Extraordinary Sessions voted large sums for many works approved by the Board of Works. There were only 1,000 persons employed within the last three or four days. There exists in some quarter or other a want of inclination or competence to give the people work … Unless immediate steps are taken to give the people employment, the committee feel they should no longer hold out delusive hopes to a suffering and too patient people, but they will resign an invidious, onerous and thankless office, the duties of which, by the unwillingness of others, they are prevented from discharging, either with satisfaction to themselves or advantage to the poor.'

Swinford
RLFC 3/2/21/42

6 November. Ulic Burke MD to the Commissary General requesting the use of part of the constabulary barracks, that has been used before by the commissariat as a depot, for the purposes of storing and disposing whatever meal their funds will enable them to purchase
Draft reply to above, 13 November:
'Request cannot be acceded to as the barracks does not belong to the commissariat. Suggests that the committee find people willing to store and sell the meal at prices to be fixed, sufficient to repay first cost with all charges, including a commission of £5 per cwt. In this way the relief fund vested in food would be kept undiminished and constantly providing supplies.'

Foxford
DP 7954

Friday 6 November. G. V. Jackson to the Lord Lieutenant
'The reports made to me, as chairman of the Foxford Relief Committee, of the sufferings entailed on the poor labourers, by not being regularly and promptly paid their wages, are dreadful.'
27 November, Board of Works to T. N. Redington re above:
'The Board of Works officer reported that the pay-clerk of Gallen had to make payments in two different baronies, which rendered delay in some cases unavoidable. Now there are two pay-clerks in Gallen alone.'

Collooney
DP 226

Sunday 8 November. E. A. Lucas to Henry Labouchere, enclosing a resolution of Tirerrill Relief Committee
'That there are some well authenticated cases of persons having perished from hunger … that fever, disease and destitution prevail to the most fearful extent … That the Board of Works be directed at once to commence all works approved without a moment's delay … That the poorhouses are closed and not a single person has been employed for the last three weeks.'

Swinford
CSORP O.718

Tuesday 10 November. Extract from Guardians' minutes
'Met today after adjourning yesterday. There are upwards of 100 persons in the workhouse over the number the house is calculated to contain and the Board of Guardians decline to admit any more altho' there were 200 persons at the door seeking relief. Unless a loan is given by the government to meet the intense urgency, we will be reluctantly obliged to close the workhouse.'
Observations of C. G. Otway on above, 18 November:
'I urged the Board of Guardians on Tuesday to hasten the rate collection and that the money coming in of the present rate will support the full number in the workhouse for two or three months.'

RLFC 3/2/21/42
Bernard Durcan PP and Ulic Burke MD to the Commissary General, enclosing a list of additional subscriptions, amounting to £15 and a grant of £7 10s. was recommended (See Appendix 3K)

12 November. Memorial of the parishes of Meelick, Kilconduff, Killedan and Bohola, to the Lord Lieutenant, signed by Edward Deane, chairman, Edward Hunt, sub-inspector, Bernard Durcan PP Kilconduff & Meelick, Thomas McNicholas PP Bohola, Daniel Mullarkey PP Killedan, and B. W. Eames, Vicar of Kilconduff

Swinford
DP 8220

'That the works sanctioned by the Board of Works were even then quite insufficient to afford relief. That distress is since fearfully increased and continues to increase more and more every day in consequence of the exorbitantly high prices of provisions ... That many of the works ... must be soon completed. That the Lord Lieutenant should call another Extraordinary Sessions of the barony as soon as possible to provide employment.'

Reply to above, 27 November: Board's officer reported that 'if the lists were duly scrutinised and none but the persons really in distress put in, I have no doubt that the numbers already stated would be sufficient for the present.'

Thursday 12 November. Memorial signed by 13 inhabitants of the parish of Bohola to the Lord Lieutenant (See Appendix 1D)

Bohola
DP 7949

'That this parish with a population of 4,800 is suffering under the awful calamity with which it has pleased Divine Providence to visit this affliction. That more than three-quarters of this number are in a state of the most frightful destitution, endeavouring to prolong a miserable existence, more like the beasts of the fields than human beings, while their astonishing patience under such unparalleled misery, deserves the highest praise and the warmest sympathy. That employment is provided for only 230 persons or not more than one for every sixteen persons requiring it.'

Reply to above, 26 November:

'Board's officer reported that employment is provided for 480 individuals, which appears very close to a proper proportion ... The population appears to be better off than in other districts of the barony ... If there should still appear to be destitute persons unemployed, they will increase the numbers on the works in operation.'

Tuesday 17 November. Memorial of William Kellaghan to the War Office

Ballyhaunis
CSORP M.548

'That he is a pensioner from the 36th Regiment of Foot ... has ten in his family, six boys and four girls, all to be supported on 11d. a day and four of them able to work with himself, but neither landlords, agents, priests or friars will give or allow petitioner or his children in any works or employment whatever. That they are not admitted into the workhouse and no outdoor relief will be given to them. It would be an act of charity to grant petitioner and his family a passage to upper Canada.'

War Office to the Lord Lieutenant re above, 6 January 1847, suggesting that the

Lord Lieutenant should give orders to the relief committees that pensioners should be received on the public works, if they are really in a state of destitution.

Swinford
CSORP O.20934

Thursday 19 November. G. Vaughan Jackson, chairman, Swinford Board of Guardians, to the Lord Lieutenant
'The unlooked for calamity by which the country is oppressed, renders it imposssible for the Board to continue relief unless assisted by a loan. The Revd Mr O'Flynn, Catholic clergyman of Attymass parish, reports to me, as the chairman of the Relief Committee for that district, that four persons have died in the parish recently, from the effects of destitution.'
Jackson encloses a resolution of the Swinford Board of Guardians:
'That as this workhouse is now almost full, we request our chairman to represent to the Lord Lieutenant the utter impossibility of our carrying on the relief of the destitute thro' the Poor Law, owing to the unlooked for and unprecedent calamity in which we are plunged, unless a loan is made to meet the intense urgency of the present moment, to be repaid by the rate at a future period.'

CSORP O.21482

21 November. Richard Kyle, clerk of the Swinford Union, to G. V. Jackson.

State of the workhouse:
Remaining on the previous Saturday: 705
Admitted during the week: 52
Total: 757
Discharged during the week: 117
Died: 4
Remaining: 636
Of these, 207 in the workhouse were unclad.

'The expenses for provisions, fuel, etc. exceeds £60 a week. Ready money only will be accepted. We are unable to obtain contractors or credit. Were it not that you kindly gave £50 last week to buy supplies, and that Daniel Keane before that cashed cheques for £120 for the same purpose, it would have been impossible to support the house during the last three weeks. The amount in the treasurer's hands this day is £16 4s. 4d., and a cheque given on last meeting day for £25 to puchase meal remains unpaid for want of funds … I fear that unless we again trespass on your kindness, or that the Poor Rate collectors (to whom I have written) bring in on Tuesday as much as they possibly could collect, there will be no alternative but to discharge the paupers on Tuesday.'
25 November. Poor Law Commission to T. N. Redington stating that 'they entertain some serious doubts whether the Swinford Board of Guardians will be able to continue the relief of the destitute poor in the workhouse.'

Saturday 28 November. Leyny Relief Committee to the Lord Lieutenant, signed by Dean Edward Hoare, vice-chairman, and John Hamilton, clerk

Tubbercurry
DP 9291

'Extraordinary Presentment Sessions have become necessary because the hills of Innavolty? and Achonry, in part cut down and not finished for want of funds, are now impassable. Work on the road from Curry to Swinford has stopped a few days ago for the same reason. Many of the works will be completed in a week or ten days and great numbers will be thrown out of employment. Some labour of a reproductive character should be instituted hereafter … and thus task work in a tangible shape be offered to the destitute.'

Edward Hoare to Sir Randolph Routh, enclosing a resolution passed today at a meeting of the Upper Leyny Relief Committee

RLFC 3/2/26/26

'That the chairman urge upon Sir Randolph Routh the necessity of storing Indian meal in Tubbercurry, in case communication between this district and Sligo be interrupted by snow during the winter.'

'A heavy fall of snow last night and this day shows up the danger of leaving a large district like this dependant to a great extent for the supply of provisions on mills and stores at a distance of twelve or fifteen miles. Is a reserve depot to be opened only in case of necessity?'

Draft reply to above, 2 December:

'Relief Committees should enlarge subscriptions and donations to keep up supplies sufficient for a period when road travel is impeded by snow, but does not recommend that the government should do so.'

Saturday 28 November. Board of Works to T. N. Redington re complaints about the restriction of work in the barony of Costello

Costello
CSORP W.3840

'Up to 12 November, 4,000 labour tickets have been issued. In the absence of Lieutenant Cox, who has charge of the district, we cannot say how many were issued after that date. The total number of names, furnished by the relief committees to the present time, exceeds 6,000. The committees are too numerous to allow the inspecting officer to attend their meetings. Regarding employment of two or more members of a family, it would be impracticable with the present staff of engineers and assistants.'

Monday 30 November. Memorial of Gallen Relief Committee to the Lord Lieutenant, signed by Edward Deane, chairman, B. W. Eames, vicar, Bernard Durcan PP, Daniel Mullarkey PP Killedan, Thomas McNicholas PP Bohola, Edward Hunt, sub-inspector

Gallen
DP 8869

'That in the four parishes of Bohola, Kilconduff, Meelick and Killedan, with a population of 21,698, who are with scarcely one exception, in the utmost possible state of destitution. That the sums voted at the last Extraordinary Sessions early in November are not adequate to give employment to one-third of those requiring relief. These works will only continue until the second week of January ... The poor deserve the highest praise for the unexampled patience with which they have borne and are enduring sufferings almost without parallel in the history of Ireland.'

Lower Leyny
DP 9122

Thursday 3 December. C. K. O'Hara, chairman of the Lower Leyny Relief Committee, to T. N. Redington, with the full agreement of Alexander Perceval
'That Upper Leyny, comprising the parishes of Achonry and Kilmactigue, and Lower Leyny, comprising the parishes of Killoran, Kilvarnet and Ballisodare, be constituted separate districts and that Extraordinary Presentment Sessions be called for Upper Leyny alone. This county has yesterday suffered a great and irreparable loss in the death of Mr Armstrong of Chaffpool, chairman of the Upper Leyny Relief Committee and a resident magistrate. He died of typhus fever, caused by his indefatigable exertions as a magistrate and chairman of the relief committee.'

Swinford
CSORP O.21936

Thursday 3 December. Poor Law Commission to T. N. Redington re rates
'The entire arrears amount to £1,800, of which £1,450 are arrears of the last rate, which was made in May 1846, the remainder being the arrears of a rate made in December 1843. The Commission has written to Assistant Commissioner Otway to report on the class of rate payer in arrears.'

CSORP O.22340

Otway's report, 5 December:
'Some few extensive landowners as immediate lessors, and large and respectable occupiers, have paid or will pay their rates at once, but the great mass of the ratepayers are delaying to pay their rate on the ground of inability. It is difficult to obtain rates from two classes. Occupiers of small holdings, valued over £4 and under £8 or £10, are wholly unable to pay, owing to the failure of the potatoes and having to purchase food at high prices and every day they will become less and less able to pay. The other class are immediate lessors of small and embarrassed properties, of whom there is a larger number in this Union than in any other Union. The occupiers rated at and over £10, from the high price of corn and all the other produce of their farms, and the immediate lessors of the large estates, are able to pay the rates. Sufficient rates to support the workhouse with a full complement of inmates ... could be collected from this class of ratepayer.'

Riverstown,
Co Sligo
RLFC 3/2/26/29

Friday 4 December. Sub-Inspector John Grant to the Inspector General, enclosing the verdict of the inquest on the afternoon of 3 December at Glan, Ballinakill parish, on the body of Bryan Waters, about 56 years old
'That the deceased Bryan Waters came to his death by the absolute want of food to support life.'

12 December. E. A. Lucas, Collooney, re above: RLFC 3/2/26/42
'Waters did not belong to that district, but was returning from Arrigna, Co Roscommon, and was taken ill and died on the way. It does not appear that he sought employment in the place in which he would have been entitled to it.'

Saturday 5 December. James Hughes PP to Henry Labouchere   *Claremorris*
'The relief committee here consists of Maurice Hewson, chairman, John   CSORP W.22012
Gray, secretary, Richard Singleton, sub-inspector and myself. The three first gentlemen know little of the poor of the parish and have little communication with them. Making up the lists of the suffering poor to be sent to the public works devolves on me principally – my curates are excluded from the committee. There are 450 families, the great bulk of whom are starving. I made up a list of 185 heads of families to receive tickets for work a fortnight ago. It was sent to Capt Farren but there was no reply. When the chairman sends a list he gets work tickets, but the connection of my name with any application is fatal. In one work with eleven gangs of ten men ... some of these from extreme hunger are not now able to crawl to work. Some gangs working with all their might, receive only 3d. per day and that withheld more than three weeks. They are obliged to get meal at usurer's prices. The present employment is only a slow but sure system of starvation for innumerable families.'

Wednesday 9 December. Rev Francis Kinkaid, secretary of Ballina Relief Committee,   *Ballina*
to the Lord Lieutenant   DP 9482
'The workhouse contains more than 1,200. Besides those provided with work, 1,700 widows, orphans and infirm poor, remain wholly destitute and for them alone are the committee anxious to provide a scanty existence of one meal a day gratuitously.'
10 December. Andrew Fraser, head constable, to the Inspector General   CSORP Z.326
'The importation of food since 1 Oct. 1846 is small and as follows: American & British flour, 171½ tons, Indian meal, 59 tons, barley, 108 tons, oats, 51 tons, oatmeal, 49½ tons, wheat, 30 tons, rye, 2 tons, rice 1½ tons.'

Wednesday 9 December. G. V. Jackson to the Poor Law Commission   *Swinford*
'The Board of Guardians sat until 5 pm yesterday. The number of applicants   CSORP O.22994
exceeded 200, of which 113 were admitted, bringing the total in the workhouse to 798. Such was the awful state of the applicants that the Board could not reject them. The sums collected weekly are quite insufficient to meet the weekly expenditure. The Board of Guardians will be prevented from relieving the fearful destitution now pressing upon them unless funds be provided.'
£600 of the 2nd Rate, 19 May 1846, at 10d in the £1, were collected by the collec-

tors, Dillon Cassidy, Michael Tully, D. Mullarkey, M. Durkan, J. Steevens, J. Dogherty, J. Sheridan

Ballaghaderreen
CSORP z.326

Thursday 10 December. J. S. Kelly, sub-inspector, to the Inspector General
'The markets are kept down by the purchase of supplies at Sligo week after week by Mr Strickland.'

DP 9513

11 December. Ballaghaderreen Relief Committee to the Lord Lieutenant, signed by J. A. Holmes, Charles Strickland, chairman, Thomas Philips, Denis Tighe PP Ballaghaderreen, James Henry PP Kilturra, and D. O'Kane PP Carracastle
'The distress is increasing to an alarming extent, so much so that several cases of deaths have occurred and there are not sufficient works granted to employ the numbers requiring relief.'

DP 9701

12 December. Denis Tighe PP to the Lord Lieutenant
'The poor of this parish are in the most awful state of destitution and, if not immediately relieved, many of them will die of hunger. The public works at present in operation are totally inadequate to give them anything like a support. Scarcely one-fifth of them are employed ... The poor are dying of hunger in my parish, and if they are not immediately relieved, 'tis hard to say what the consequences may be.'

Ballymote
CSORP z.326

Friday 11 December. Edward J. Corry, sub-inspector, to the Inspector General
'At Ballymote meal is sold at cost price which is procured by R. Gethen, local magistrate, and at Clogher a store has been opened by Joseph A. Holmes, where meal is sold at cost price. The consumption there is one ton per day.'

Collooney
DP 9528

Friday 11 December. E. A. Lucas to T. N. Redington, enclosing a resolution of the Tirerrill Relief Committee
'That as the money granted for public works has now been expended, leaving the roads in a very unfinished and inconvenient state, they request the Lord Lieutenant to fix the earliest possible date for holding Special Sessions, for finishing those roads and giving employment.'

Sligo
CSORP z.326

Saturday 12 December. J. N. T. Enfin, sub-inspector, to the Inspector General
'There has been, and is, almost daily arrivals of Indian corn, flour, buck wheat, barley, peas etc, which at present is more than equal to the demand.'

Swinford
CSORP z.326

Saturday 12 December. Edward Hunt, sub-inspector, to the Inspector General
'A private relief committee here has imported about six tons of Indian meal, which is sold at a reduced price. The markets are rising considerably, both for oats and meal.'

Saturday 12 December. John Gray, chairman, and Rev John Hamilton, secretary of the Upper Leyny Relief Committee, to the Lord Lieutenant

Tubbercurry
CSORP W.22796

'There has been a total suspension of the public works because of the inclemency of the weather. Thousands of human beings, thrown out of employment and exposed to inevitable starvation and certain death, presents a spectacle so appalling that we can find no language adequate to describe our feelings on the subject. We urge the Lord Lieutenant to secure to the labourers the continuance of their pay as heretofore when employed. We call to the Lord Lieutenant's attention the crying injustice under which the labourers are employed on the public works in this district by the non-payment of their wages for several weeks. On the Aclare to Drumartin road, the men have not been paid since 18 Nov. and on all the other roads since 25 Nov.'

Sunday 13 December. Sworn statement of Anthony Walsh at the inquest on Pat Loftus from Knockfall, near Straide

Straide
OP 21/35577

'On Friday night last deceased was carried into my house in a very weak state by Patt Newcomb and Patt Reilly, my neighbours. Deceased was a stranger. I asked him his name. Deceased weakly articulated that his name was Patt Loftus from Knockfall (near Straide). I then got some warm milk for deceased and when in the act of giving him some, he grasped at the porringer? as if pinched with hunger. He was not able to take much of the milk. I then gave him some gruel and a bit of bread. I have no doubt that deceased was in a starving state. Deceased died that night about 12 o clock. He had no property, only one halfpenny, and a pair of spectacles and was miserably clad.'

Monday 14 December. C. G. Otway to the Poor Law Commission

Castlebar
CSORP O.718

'The minutes of the Board of Guardians of 28 Nov. & 5 Dec. show that the Board of Guardians refused to admit the destitute poor to the workhouse. I attended their meeting on 21 Nov. and used every exertion in my power to get the Board of Guardians to admit the destitute poor into the workhouse and although the state of destitution in the town and Union is extreme and although cases of the most urgent distress besought admission, I was unable to succeed. I stated the claims and rights of the starving poor to food and shelter in the almost empty workhouse, a house with accommodation for 600 with only 135 in it ... I had hoped that the force of public opinion, if not the increasing inroads of famine, would have led the Board of Guardians at a subsequent meeting to admit the poor and I implored the Board of Guardians to reconsider the subject ... The refusal of the Board of Guardians at such a time to admit more poor into the workhouse was a cruel neglect of their highest duties. The Board should be dissolved if they do not admit the poor.'

Swinford
CSORP O.22994

Monday 14 December. G. V. Jackson to the Chief Secretary

'The heavy fall of snow and my reposing about 18 mile from the poorhouse, will prevent my attending the Board meeting tomorrow. At the last meeting 98 paupers were admitted over the number intended for the house, owing to the dreadful extent of destitution that prevails in the Union. On 11 December the master of the workhouse reported that he had no milk or funds to buy any. Ten days ago I sent three tons of Indian meal on my own security. I cannot individually further assist the Board in funding the food of the paupers, as I have not received anything like the amount of rent hitherto paid at this period, nor any prospect of ever receiving it … I see no prospect open in this matter other than that the paupers must perish in the house from starvation or be turned out to perish abroad.'

CSORP O.718

15 December. Extract from the Guardians' minutes

'Altho' there are 720 paupers in the workhouse, from the misery and destitution of the applicants before us this day, we cannot possibly eject them in this inclement season of the year altho' funds are totally embarrased.'

Observation of Mr Otway on above:

'I cannot advocate the government granting a loan … Surely a much greater portion of the rate could be collected.'

Upper Leyny
RLFC 3/2/26/26

Tuesday 15 December. Dean Hoare to Sir Randolph Routh, informing him that he is now chairman of the Upper Leyny Relief Committee, following the death of John Armstrong and enclosing an additional subscription list amounting to £60. The Relief Committee recommended a grant of £60 (See Appendix 3E)

'At my own glebe house I have established a depot at my own cost. I payed 4d. per cwt for carriage, being 10 miles from the mills. The same sum is allowed for loss in weighing and for the payment of the woman who weighs it out. I sell it for 1d. per stone above the price I pay to the mills. I sell about two tons a week, whereby the poor are saved going four or five miles to a market town and obtain the meal at a less price than it is sold for at the hucksters … I occasionally give a free ticket to a poor person to be paid for by myself and which ticket is returned to me as cash by the person employed to sell the meal, who accounts with me every second day … I am altogether unassisted in this undertaking and desirous to extend the plan to other parts of the district.'

Draft reply, 19 December:

'While the workhouse is full, free tickets for food may be given to the actually infirm poor who are destitute. In all other cases food should be sold at a price sufficient to repay first cost with all other charges including £5 for storing and selling.'

Wednesday 16 December. Henry Brett, county surveyor, to T. N. Redington
'Farm operations are everywhere totally neglected. There is nothing done or doing to provide for the future crop … Unless some measures are taken to have this attended to, the consequences will be fearful.'

Castlebar
DP 9919

Saturday 19 December. Relief Committee of Upper Leyny to the Lord Lieutenant
'The present system of road making for the employment of the poor will prove ruinous to the country … withdrawing both the small farmers and the labourers from agricultural employment … the fields lying waste and over-run with weeds, all husbandry suspended and scarcely any preparations mak-ing for the necessities of the ensuing years … The labourers should be sup-plied with tickets from the lists prepared by the relief committees and be placed under the direction of the occupying tenants … The numbers of labourers supplied thus to the farmer shall be apportioned according to the rates of each farm … Work would be more generally spread over the coun-try and brought nearer to the poor … While the proprietors and occupying tenants will have to bear the burden, they should also reap the benefit.'

Upper Leyny
DP 10114

Sunday 19 December. Report of the medical officer of the workhouse
'The defect in diet, in warmth, as well as in the other arrangements of this house at present, are calculated to be not only detrimental to the health but, if continued, destructive to the lives of the inmates. The week now ending was I believe the severest from snow, rain and cold we had this season, and during this trying week, the destitute inmates of this workhouse were with-out fuel, there being scarcely as much turf as would prepare their food … They got their breakfast, such as it was, at or about 2 o clock, and their din-ner, such as it was, at or about 5 pm daily. From 5 pm to 2 pm the following day, being 21 out of the 24 hours, they are left in their large, damp and com-fortless rooms, without fuel, without food and without suitable clothing, weak from hunger, trembling from cold and sick from both … If the present mode of treating these wretched human beings be not speedily altered, dis-ease to a frightful extent will be engendered … and may end in some weekly returns of fearful mortality.'

Castlebar
CSORP 0.719

Tuesday 21 December. John S. Stewart, sub-inspector, to the Inspector General,
replying to the query: 'has any considerable importation of food taken place to meet the wants of the district?'
'A few truggers bring up principally to Tubbercurry about 4 tons of Indian or other meal and the late John Armstrong and Dean Hoare had private depots for the sale of meal, about 2 tons per week each. Last Monday oats sold at about 36s. per sack of 25 stone. There were only 30 or 40 sacks for sale instead

Tubbercurry
CSORP Z.326

of the normal 200 or 300 sacks. Farmers will not part with their oats on any terms, nor make any exertion for the ensuing crop. There is a notion among them that the government will be obliged to cultivate and seed their ground for them.'

Balla
CSORP W.23596

Tuesday 21 December. Sir Robert Lynch Blesse, chairman of the Balla Relief Committee, to Henry Labouchere
'Owing to the want of proper tools in the making of roads, the labourers are not earning sufficient to support one person, much less a family, in some instances only 2d. a day. There was an inquest today on James Byrne of Brieze who died on 18 December. He had been employed on the relief works between Balla and Brieze. The verdict was that he died of starvation ... His wages were not paid regularly ... A smith living near the town of Balla has been owed money by the engineer since last August.'

CSORP W.586

9 January 1847. Henry Brett, county surveyor, to Board of Works re above:
'The reason why people were earning bad wages was chiefy owing to their total unwillingness to do any work whatever. They were under the impression, and I have no doubt it was instilled into their minds, that they should get work whether they wrought or not.'

Sligo
CSORP O.342

Thursday 23 December. Resolutions of a meeting of landed proprietors and cess-payers in Sligo
'We fully agree with the exemption of any proprietor, consenting to take the proportion of the sum assessed on his electoral division to be applied in reproductive labour, from further taxation. Taxation for the relief of the poor should be so arranged as not to throw too heavy a burden on proprietors of lands adjoining over-peopled districts ... We urge the expediency of affording facilities for emigration to those who wish to leave the country ... There should be increased facilities for owners of estates encumbered with debt, of selling portions of their properties with little legal expense. A general meeting should be held in Dublin and Colonel Knox Gore, Sir Robert Gore Booth, John Wynne, E. J. Cooper and Charles O'Hara were deputed to attend.'

Swinford
DP 10160

Thursday 23 December. Swinford Relief Committee to Henry Labouchere (See Appendix 2H)
'The relief committee comprises the parishes of Kilconduff, Killedan, Bohola and Meelick, with a population of 22,948, 31,846 families, 3,402 rated under £6 (1841 census). There are 2,020 employed. Not one in ten are employed and the remuneration can scarcely afford sufficient food for even that one. The numbers now requiring relief are more than double what it was three months ago ... The sums granted by the Extraordinary Sessions are very

nearly exhausted and the works must soon stop … There is neither a resident landlord, farmer, merchant or factory of any description in the district … These plain facts are stated without exaggeration, in terms as cold as if we had not hearts to feel the misery around us.'

Friday 24 December. Lord Sligo to the Lord Lieutenant
'The merchants in Westport inform me that they have now on the water supplies of food to the amount of £100,000 but that unless some further protection be afforded them, they must direct the ships to discharge elsewhere … The merchants are most anxious that cavalry should be sent there … The people, if not prevented by the certainty of failure, will attack the food stores, confining their combination to the supplies alone, the entire supply or nearly so of the county of Mayo. The effect of a want of protection preventing their risking their entire wealth in the trade would be too frightful to contemplate.'

Westport
OP 21/37185

Saturday 25 December. The O'Conor Don to T. N. Redington
'The two clergymen of this parish and some hundred men are here complaining of the mode of payment. The men were offered 1s. 6d. a day and are paid 3d. a day, working in bogs up to the calves of their legs in water. Payments are mostly made one batch by the day … Some of the men are in tears. Their children are starving.'
Report of Capt Burmester, inspecting officer, 29 December re above:
'The men have nothing to complain of. If they were to cease to be dishonest and give a fair day's work for a fair day's wages, they would find that they could support themselves and their families. By their indolence, they baffle the calculations of the engineer and defraud the public, and on any attempt being made to induce them to exertion, they assemble in bodies to annoy and endeavour to intimidate their superiors.'

Castlerea
CSORP W.23668

Saturday 26 December. Report of the workhouse medical officer
'19 December, the sick in the hospital got no food from 5 pm the previous day to 7 pm this evening. 23 December, no. 367, Anthony Leonard, aged 31 years, who had paralyses affections for 10 years, and got diarrhoea on 15 November but was cured, died from exhaustion. 26 December; no. 769, James Lyons, aged 72 years, died of diarrhoea and infirmity.'

Castlebar
CSORP 0.719

Saturday 26 December. Dean Hoare to William Stanley
'It would be better to allow a certain rate of allowance per ton for storing and selling meal as I cannot see any good reason why the person storing and selling should be remunerated in proportion to the price, instead of according to the quantity of provisions sold.'

Upper Leyny
RLFC 3/2/26/26

Swinford
RLFC 3/2/21/42

Saturday 26 December. Bernard Durcan PP and Ulic Burke MD to the Commissary General, enclosing an additional list of subscriptions, amounting to £17 and a grant of £17 was recommended (See Appendix 3K)

'If the state of any district would justify you in deviating from the usual amount given in aid, ... the destitute state of the people here would be more than ample justification.'

Achonry
SFFP 2/505/5

Monday 28 December. Joseph Bewley and Jonathan Pim, Society of Friends, to Dean Hoare remitting £20 (See Appendix 6A)

Kilmactigue
SFFP 2/505/5

Monday 28 December. Bewley and Pim to Rev Tyndale, rector, remitting £20 (See Appendix 6Q)

Claremorris
CSORP W.23992

Wednesday 30 December. James Hughes PP to Henry Labouchere

'The people in this parish and surrounding districts are starving in multitudes. Already nine have died of starvation and ten times nine are ready to follow them, whose constitutions are irreparably destroyed by hunger. These deaths I pronounce so many murders. I must attribute them to the officials of the government ... Six weeks after the Sessions approved public works, they were only partially commenced. The government officials did not use the ordinary means in their power to save the lives of the people. On 17 December the officials declared that the poor starving people would spend a merry Christmas, that their wages due for more than eight days and sometimes for a fortnight, would be paid and all these promises have been violated. Not one man up to yesterday had been put on the public works for the last six weeks. Lists of the starving poor (more than 300) have been sent to the government official in Castlebar more than nine days ago and up to yesterday not one of these poor people has been put to work. The pay clerks are walking about the streets of this town with the public money in their pockets, not being able to pay these wages to the poor, not having been given the pay sheets. The local engineer leaves his district on Saturday and does not return until Tuesday night, with the tickets or lists in his possession ... The Board of Works always backs their own officers. At the market today, oats was 14s. 7d. a cwt and meal, £1 7s. a cwt.'

The Claddagh, Galway
CSORP Z.121

Wednesday 30 December. Memorial of four priests of the Claddagh parish to the Lord Lieutenant

'The attempt now making to relieve them by employing them on public works is productive of wasteful expenditure of public money, tends to demoralise them and increases the distress of the poor generally by reducing the supply of fish ... There would be a great gain in employing these poor men in fishing. They would be well content to go to fish for a subsistence and thus help the public whilst they serve themselves … They are so reduced to want as to be unable to furnish themselves with provisions to go to sea or to redeem out of pawn offices their fishing tackle. The Lord Lieutenant should distinguish between distressed fishermen and the distressed labouring poor and provide some means by loan or grant to afford relief to fishermen through the medium of employment at sea as for the labouring poor on land.'

Thursday 31 December. Rev J. Garrett to Henry Labouchere, re suspension of the works for a week in the hard weather. 'The Board should be ordered to pay for 180 stone of meal by which these creatures were kept alive at that crisis.'

Ballymote
DP 16

Saturday 2 January 1847. Report of the workhouse medical officer
'27, 28, 29, 30 & 31 December 1846, the sick in hospital did not get the diet prescribed for them. 1 January 1847, the sick got no food until after 1 pm and the sick as well as the other inmates of the workhouse got one meal, and on this day, 2 January, they have got no food up to 12 o clock.'

Castlebar

7 January. Poor Law Commission to the clerk of the Castlebar Union re the medical officer's report
'At a trying period, Castlebar Board of Guardians have abandoned their post and neglected their duty and it is to the Commissioners a subject of concern and indignation to know that in the midst of a public calamity the Guardians have not only shut the door of their workhouse against the starving poor, but have likewise omitted to take proper.steps to provide effectually for the food, fuel and clothing of the comparatively few individuals who are already inmates of that establishment. The Poor Law Commissioners call on the Board of Guardians duly to discharge their duty and in the event of continued default, they will dissolve the Board of Guardians.'

CSORP 0.718

8 January. Richard Gibbons PP to T. N. Redington
'It is unhappily too well known by the reports of the local journals transcribed into the Dublin newspapers that the house is closed against the admission of paupers during the present trying visitation on the poor … I am a frequent visitor of the workhouse, often inspecting each class of the inmates, and I am pained to have to state that almost every individual of the 100 or more, is showing striking signs of haggard and famished looks … Indian meal is supplied very irregularly, often not sent to the house until an advanced hour of the day … and never in a large or satisfactory supply. Fuel, turf is most irregularly supplied, on many days not at all … Breakfast is deferred to 1 pm or 2 pm. On Wednesday 1 January, the paupers had only one diet and that at a late hour. The master states that he is obliged to per-

CSORP 0.362

mit the paupers to confine to their beds ... the children pining away by
hunger and cold ... Coffins are with difficulty procured for those that die ...
Those able to creep out prefer ... to dying from cold and hunger inside.'

CSORP O.719   *9 January. Report of the workhouse medical officer*
'4 January, the sick in hospital and the other inmates have not got breakfast
up to 3.30 pm. 5, 6, 7, 8, 9 January, the sick did not get the bread prescribed
for them.'

Swinford   *Saturday 2 January. Extract from Guardians' minutes*
CSORP O.718   'Striking a new rate, with so much of the former rates uncollected, would be
an act of injustice and oppression towards these rate-payers who have freely
paid the rates hitherto. Some of the Guardians, whose means admitted of it,
have assisted to relieve the difficulty of the Union, but this class of assistance
can no longer be considered available as a large majority of proprietors in the
Union are non-resident and financial pressure on all classes of society, caused
by the calamity of famine, is intense. If money is not advanced by the state
no means can prevent the inmates of this house (this day 664) from perishing by starvation. To prevent the death of the inmates from starvation until
this day week, the chairman, vice-chairman and deputy vice-chairman are
requested to provide the necessary supplies on their own security. The supply
of food, of all kinds inclusive, in this district is wholly insufficient for the
wants of the population and the enormous price of food and the fluctuating
of prices are destructive to the means of all classes who make a livelihood by
industrial resources.'
Observations of C. G. Otway on the above:
'I believe a large portion of the uncollected rate is collectable. I will attend at
Swinford on Tuesday and confer with the Board of Guardians and advise
what is best to be done.'

CSORP O.342   *5 January. Richard Kyle, clerk of the Swinford Union, to the Poor Law Commission*
'Fearful distress and starvation at present existing in all parts of the Union.
The enormous prices of all kinds of provisions and the want of sufficient
employment have driven a vast number of the population to seek relief in the
workhouse. At this moment there are upwards of 150 persons outside the
door seeking admission but who could not be admitted, there being upwards
of 700 in the the house and the supplies being obtained on this day on the
personal security of the Board, who have paid £1 6s. per cwt for oatmeal,
being the market price this day. Unless the government give a loan, relief in
this workhouse cannot be continued much longer.'

CSORP O.176   *6 January. G. V. Jackson to the Chief Secretary*
'The price of food begins to cause great alarm, as well as its scarcity. One
Guardian stated yesterday that in Costello barony oatmeal was sold at 4s. a

stone, and passing through Foxford I was informed that Indian meal was sold at 2s. 8d. a stone.'

Monday 4 January. Extract from Guardians' minutes
'From the bankrupt state of the Union (contractors are owed £2,000), further accommodation is impossible and unless government funds are given we must immediately close the workhouse … The dearness of food would consume all the means of persons hitherto independant.'
Observations of C. G. Otway on above:
'A Union comprising so rich a portion of Co Mayo, of so large an extent and of so great annual value, should be able to support the workhouse … The rich barony of Tyrawley, with so many resident gentry as any barony in Ireland, ought and is able to support its workhouse and its indoor poor. I will attend the Board of Guardians next Monday and do all I can to get the rate collected.'

Ballina
CSORP O.718

Thursday 7 January. Edward Hunt, sub-inspector, to the Inspector General
'I was this day engaged with Capt Stirling (inspecting officer of the Board of Works for the barony of Gallen), arranging some misunderstanding amongst the persons employed on one of the public works from Culmore to Cloonfinish at which road 100 persons are employed, but the number of starving half-clad people who entreated that they also might get employment, exceeded 80 men. My own personal knowledge of the starving mass of the people in the district, you would be horrified could you only see the multitude of starving men, women and children, who daily and hourly swarm the town, soliciting with prayers and tears one meal of food. What I would beg to impress truly and without the slightest exaggeration on your mind is that money is almost useless. There is not a sufficiency of food, even of the coarsest quality to support animal life in my district for one month. I most respectfully entreat that you will use your high influence from your public position to have food sent immediately to the very peaceable, orderly people of this district, who though famishing from want of food, up to this period have observed the rights of property with the strictest honesty and forbearance. I attended the meeting of the Poor Law Guardians of Swinford Union yesterday and regret to inform you that, but for the humane conduct of the chairman, deputy chairman and vice-chairman, in undertaking out of their own private finances to supply the paupers, 715, with food, there was not one single pound of oatmeal to feed them for the current week. The markets have gone beyond the reach of people who were once comfortable. The supply is getting shorter daily and if the oats (their sole support) now in this district were converted into meal, one month would consume the entire. No prepa-

Swinford
DP 414

Swinford

ration is made or making for the ensuing spring. The people appear to be paralysed from starvation. They tell me they must use their little seed for food, and when that is used they say "they must lie down and die". They have no internal resources, no manufactories, no mills, no resident landlords to look to, to provide them with seed. I again most respectfully beg your earnest and humane consideration of the true and unbiassed statement I make on behalf of the famishing people of this district. The market prices of yesterday were a follows: Potatoes, none; oats, 24 stone, £2 6s. 8d.; oatmeal per cwt, £1 11s. 3d.; rice, none; turnips per ton, £1 8s.; milk (very scarce) per quart, 4½d.

CSORP O.345

8 January. Richard Kyle to G. V. Jackson

'I have sent this morning three carmen and a police escort for meal to Foxford. After the meeting on Tuesday there was not 1lb of meal in the house until a shopkeeper in the town named Fleming, kindly advanced his money to pay for 6 cwt of meal and this morning we were again obliged to call upon him to pay for 5 cwt more, which I returned to him today … Contractors have declined to supply the house in future. Milk and turf being supplied by at least 80 persons, who dispose of these necessaries to purchase meal for themselves, several of whom have solemnly declared that they had no means to procure a morsel for their families, until paid for what they had delivered to the workhouse. The baker has also refused to give bread in future. It is lamentable to see the groups of poor with which the house is beset since Tuesday, crying and bawling, craving admittance. The enormous price and demand for meal since the last market in this town has driven thousands into actual madness. Droves of beggars are to be met in every quarter, pining from cold and starvation. Altho' the time is short until the next meeting of the Board, I fear the establishment will be knocked up before then as the two tons of meal which you kindly gave is of no consequence without the other necessaries.'

Kyle enclosed a memorandum showing the sums due for the supplies of the last two weeks:

> Balance of money due to D. Keane, advanced to buy meal, £8
> Milk for one week to 2 Jan. due to 74 poor persons, £18 14s. 5d.
> Turf purchased in ass-loads, due to at least 50 persons, £4 16s. 2d.
> Milk for 2nd week to 9 Jan. due to 82 persons, £19 15s.
> Baker to Sat. 2 Jan (having declined to accept cheques there being £68 odd due to him, and ordered by the Board to be paid weekly in future) £17 8s.
> Total £68 13s. 7d.

CSORP Z.370

8 January. Capt J. Stirling to Colonel Jones

'Destitution is greater than can well be described even at present, but what will it be in the course of two or three months, no one can foretell. The price of food is enormous and even were the markets down to the usual rate, unless an abundant supply of foreign provisions shortly comes into the country, the consequences must be most disastrous. Next year will be much worse than this ... There is nothing like a sufficiency of grain to crop the lands, not taking into consideration the numbers of acres formerly planted with potatoes, as well as the fact that whatever quantity of land may be needed, owing to the want of manure, no great return can be expected. Altogether it is a very disheartening state of affairs. At least it strikes me as such, being a stranger to the scenes I witness and the backward state of cultivation. I was present yesterday at the meeting of the Guardians for the Swinford Poor Law Union, and positively had not Mr Jackson and two other gentlemen come forward and entered into personal security for the payment of provisions for one week, 650 paupers must have been turned out of the poorhouse and taken to begging, by which they could, as things are at present, get nothing and could only add to the claimants for relief works which are already over burdened. My life is a constant roving from morning until night. My house is beset with men, women and children, all crying together, saying I can save them by giving them an order to work. They have an idea that my power is unlimited and that I can authorise the expenditure of any sum of money.'

9 January. G. V. Jackson to the Chief Secretary   CSORP O.345
'Not having received half my ordinary payments of rent, I am personally unable to render any assistance to the Union, that at any other period would have been a grateful office to me.'

12 January. Poor Law Commission to T. N. Redington   CSORP O.1607
'The Lord Lieutenant will be prepared to direct Sir Randolph Routh to place at the Commissioners' disposal such sums of money requisite for the maintenance of the Glenties, Swinford and Tralee Unions and wishes to obtain security from the Boards of Guardians for repayment of such advances.'

Sunday 9 January. Dean Hoare to Deputy Commissary General Dobree, enclosing a subscription list mounting to £35 and hoping for a grant similar to the subscriptions collected (See Appendix 3B)   *Upper Leyny* RLFC 3/2/26/26
'I am planning to set up seven soup kitchens in localities far removed from each other but near to individual members of the committee who will oversee them ...'

Saturday 9 January. John Mulligan to the Lord Lieutenant   *Swinford* OP 21/48
'Last Wednesday I sent to Mr Gallagher's mills in Ballina, £132 payment for 120 cwt of meal. He promised to send an escort with the meal on this day from Ballina to Foxford and the Swinford police to meet it there. He said he sent them a requisition to do so by post. We applied to the officer and he refused two or three men, having no magistrate residing nearer than four

miles to this town, which is very inconvenient to the police. Our nine carriers were certain the Ballina escort would not disappoint them when starting at a quarter to ten this morning with the meal from Ballina. When the escort refused, the carriers had not proceeded more than a mile when they were attacked on the mailcoach road by men, women and children and beaten and cut with knives etc. One of our horses was struck with a knife in the face and knocked down. One of the carts was broken, the sacks cut with knives and the carriers faced with knives. Sacks of meal were carried off, 3 cwt off one cart and 2 cwt off another ... The mailcoach passing brought intelligence to Ballina. When the police and officers arrived in cars, the thieves had escaped to their houses, principally the inhabitants of a village a mile from Ballina ... We shall bring no more provisions, or any friends of ours, to this town while the country people are allowed to commit such outrages and highway robberies, by the negligence of the police authorities.'

Blacksod Bay
OP 21/53

Tuesday 12 January. Statement of the captain of Clyde of Glasgow
'About 3 o'clock yesterday afternoon, while lying at anchor in Elly harbour, I was boarded by about 100 countrymen determined to plunder the cargo, which consisted of flour and barley of about 100 tons. On their coming on board they said they had come to take away the cargo and that hunger and starvation had driven them to it, but that they did not in any other way intend to meddle with the vessel or any of the crew ... I perceived a boat belonging to H.M. Steam Vessel, *Rhadamanthus,* with two officers and boat's crew and on my waving to them, they immediately came to my assistance. The officer gave the word to fire ... The mob began to jump into their boats as fast as possible ... There were at the time about 500 men, women and children waiting on the beach to assist in discharging the boats on their landing.'

Ballina
CSORP 0.718

Thursday 14 January. C. G. Otway to Poor Law Commission
'I will attend the meeting of the Board of Guardians next Monday ... There is a want of workhouse accommodation in this large Union, the largest in Ireland ... The workhouse should be considerably enlarged or a workhouse built in another part of the Union ... An adequate and separate fever hospital should be attached to all workhouses.'

Kilmactigue
DP 577

Thursday 14 January. Patrick Stenson to T. N. Redington enclosing a resolution of a meeting of gentry
'That a depot for the sale of meal be established in Aclare for the purpose of reducing the price of provisions to a more moderate standard.'
Stenson writes:
'Extreme wretchedness of this unhappy district ... numberless deaths from

starvation are daily occurrring … By what giant strides famine is desolating the land.'

Thursday 14 January. Report of C. G. Otway to Poor Law Commission   *Swinford*
'There are 719 inmates in the workhouse on the week ending 9 January and   CSORP O.718
the doors of the house were thronged on the evening of Tuesday 5 January by
applicants for admission who, for want of accommodation, could not be
admitted, although known to be in an actual state of starvation. The credit
of this establishment has failed and the supplies of the house for the previous
three or four weeks had to be obtained through the generosity of the chairman, G. V. Jackson and some of the members of the Board of Guardians …
The current expenditure is £70 a week. Of the last rate (May 1846), £742 has
been collected and £1,172 uncollected. It will be extremely difficult, if not
impossible, to induce the Board of Guardians to strike a new rate under the
peculiar circumstances of the country, and the amount of rate that must necessarily remain uncollected from the distressed state of many of the rate-payers and if this is not done, the inmates must starve in the workhouse or, being
turned out, starve outside … There is not an adequate supply of clothing and
bedding, especially bedding, in the workhouse … The contractor is so poor
and, not being able to get cash for Guardians' cheques, he has been unable
to supply the orders in sufficient time and quantities. It would take £100 or
£160 for a full supply of clothing and bedding.' *(See Appendix 5)*

Friday 15 January. Denis Tighe PP to the Lord Lieutenant   *Ballaghaderreen*
'There are over 2,000 persons in my parish, able-bodied and not yet   DP 639
employed. The hand of death is rapidly doing its work of destruction among
them. My home is filled every hour of the day with walking skeletons who
must necessarily sink into their graves, if not relieved within a few days. Five
persons have died from want within the last three days. The people are getting outrageous. I fear I will have no control over them. I have promised
them since the Sessions at Ballyhaunis on 26 December, that they would get
work. They and I are beginning to despair. The life of my parishioners are in
your Excellency's hands.'

Friday 15 January. Bernard Durcan PP to the Lord Lieutenant   *Swinford*
'The people are starving, my Lord. Deaths from starvation are much more   DP 660
numerous than can be imagined even from the number recorded by the coroner's inquests … Much, if not all of the blame, it appears to me, lies at the
door of the Board of Works … At the end of November there was a total
insufficiency of works then in progress … Magistrates and cess-payers assembled on 11 December and passed works to the amount of £1,700 which was

Swinford deemed very moderate, as it only sufficed to give employment at very moderate wages to one out of every five for two months … Up to the present, sanction for these works has not been received from the Board … The people are daily and hourly crowding this little town and besetting my door, imploring work and nothing can equal their despair when I am obliged to tell them that it is not in my power to give them any. The intensity of the distress is fearfully increased by the enormously high prices of provisions in our markets, oaten meal selling at £1 7s. a cwt … If works are not commenced forthwith, numbers must inevitably starve and their deaths will be caused by not getting that employment which the magistrates and cess-payers deemed necessary and agreed to provide.'

13 February, Board of Works to T. N. Redington re above:
'We have already given as much employment in this district as the works presented will admit of … A new Sessions has been proclaimed on 13 February.'

Erris *Friday 15 January. G. V. Jackson to Society of Friends*
SFFP 2/507/3 'A dreadful instance of misery has come before me this day. I held an enquiry into the death of Michael Crowe found dead. His widow, aged 20, is in rags and I think dying from the effects of suffering and misery. I never saw a more painful picture of human suffering than this unhappy woman presents. If any clothes remain on hands, some flannel dress, stockings and a blanket would be a mercy to this sufferer. The Guardians here ordered a weekly allowance of money but I think she is dying of consumption and she is unwilling to enter the infirmary as she says she wants air.'

Castlebar *Saturday 16 January. Report of the workhouse medical officer*
CSORP O.719 'Useless to continue to prescribe bread. 10 January, the sick with diarrhoea, for whom rice and milk have been prescribed have got neither up to 2 pm. 12 January, 12.30pm, the inmates have not got breakfast. 15 January, the inmates got one meal at 5 pm, being without food for the previous 24 hours. 12 January, Celia Barrett, an idiot, helpless and disabled from infancy, died of diarrhoea. 15 January, no. 480, Ulick Staunton, aged 72, died of diarrhoea. 16 January, diarrhoea and dysentery prevalent, 12 cases and 2 deaths. All are suffering from the intense coldness of the house from want of fuel and food.'

16 January. Extract from Guardians' meeting
Resolution proposed by Dr Ronayne and seconded by Edward Deane:
'That we view with deep concern the state of the few inmates of the Castlebar workhouse, amounting to 112, who must have been discharged or permitted to starve but for the charitable exertions of the Earl of Lucan. That from the general destitution prevailing … the collection of the Poor Rate is impossible, a vast number of rate-payers being now reduced to pauperism and the

non-payment of rents rendering others unequal to such an impost ... A sum was raised in this town and neighbourhood to open a soup kitchen where 1,200 to 1,500 receive soup daily.'

17 January. C. G. Otway to Poor Law Commission   CSORP O.905
'I arrived in Castlebar on 15 January ... The statements of Mr Gibbons are true (8 Jan). Since 21 November the paupers were left without any breakfast on three days, 1, 2, & 15 January (the master had no fuel to cook it). The agent of Lord Lucan supplied meal but not bread since 26 December and only now and then turf. The master had only one-third of the turf required and left the paupers in bed for want of heat. The coffin contractor would not supply coffins as he was not paid. Lord Lucan, Sir J. O'Malley, Lord Kilmaine and Mr Kearney, vice-chairman of the Board of Guardians, and many other persons of rank and property have not paid the rates rated on them ... A workhouse closed at such a time in a wretched town and county, where some of the people have died of starvation and where two-thirds of the rates are due by lessors of the largest property of the Union, while the few inmates (123) are left in the state described by the medical officer.'

Saturday 16 January. Poor Law Commission to the clerk of the Union   *Ballina*
'The Guardians must continue relief during the severe distress which is well   CSORP O.718
known to exist in the Ballina Union. The duty of providing for the paupers at present in the workhouse is one of the most sacred obligations upon all those who are possessed of any property in the Union.'

Saturday 16 January. G. V. Jackson to the Under-Secretary   *Swinford*
'My own decided conviction that the magnitude of the calamity the country   CSORP O.862
suffers under, the peculiar position of the Swinford Union and the entire absence in that Union of agencies of relief that abound elsewhere, will render it quite beyond any powers the Board of Guardians posssesses, unaided by a loan on the security of the rates, to meet the difficulties the Union is placed in. The mass of applicants alone for admission to the house ... would render new agencies of relief, never contemplated by the law at present, indispensible for the safety of the lives of the population. Unless the present system of collecting the Poor Rate be changed and an efficient organ for that branch of the system be established, the striking of any number of new rates would now and will at any future time, in my opinion, be nugatory.'

Monday 18 January. John Atkinson, Coroner, Co Mayo to Lord Lieutenant,   *Ballina*
enclosing a list of 34 people who died and upon whom he held inquests where the   DP 938
verdict of death by starvation were returned between 11 December 1846 and 17
January 1847.

Ballina
CSORP O.718

Ballina, Monday 18 January. C. G. Otway to Poor Law Commission
'(Many) had left the country. One townland near Killala has only 3 occupiers left out of 26; in another, one left out of 10 and in another, only 3 out of 17. The migration from this part of the country is almost incredible. There are 1,060 inmates in the workhouse today; expenditure, £110 a week. The average weekly collection of rates for the last six weeks was £85. The meal and bread merchants, when food is so scarce and valuable, are not willing to be out of their money for even a short time, when they can so easily get ready money for their goods. This day the chairman had to advance £100 out of his own pocket for the current week. About £2,100 is due to contractors. I will urge the Guardians at the meeting next Monday to strike a new rate of nearly £8,000 to provide expenses for the next 8 months. A rate of 1s. 6d. in the £1 would net £7,300.'

Ballaghaderreen
DP 581

Tuesday 19 January. Denis Tighe PP to the Lord Lieutenant
'The awful scenes I have this day to communicate are heartrending. Two persons have died today from starvation. One of them, Mark McCaen, declared a few hours before his death, that he had not eaten a full meal for twelve days previously. I had over 200 persons at my house today crying out for work or food. Their patience is great considering their wants … If they are not relieved within a few days … they cannot hold out much longer. Their appearance is frightful. We have only two principal lines where the people are employed and one-quarter of those who want work are not on them. If the Board of Works delay much longer … we will have to record in dozens the deaths of the people.'

Carracastle
DP 580

Wednesday 20 January. Denis O'Kane PP to the Lord Lieutenant
'I am beseiged by applicants for relief … and am moved by the many heartrending scenes I witness in visiting the sick and indigent in this locality … Nothing less than the dire necessity of these creatures to whose calls I must attend, would make me ask your Excellency for funds … I hope the entreaties of the poor, whose cries are now ringing in my ears, will meet with favour. Public employment is doled out with a sparing and niggardly hand, wages are miserable, prices of provisions are rising … sickness is increasing, deaths are multiplying …'

Swinford
CSORP O.806

Wednesday 20 January. G. V. Jackson to the Under-Secretary
'The Board of Guardians has struck a new rate and taken every means to collect the rate now unpaid. I had however to undertake to find food for the inmates of the house for 15 days and I have transmitted a supply for that period from Ballina, there not being enough in Swinford. I cannot under any cirum-

stances continue to do this, the non-receipt of rent forbids it. The people in this Union (Ballina) and in the Swinford Union are dying of starvation. The relief works are run out, the drainages not ready to be commenced, food at a famine price, the people cannot but perish. Were a weekly sum given from the funds of any of the relief associations for a soup kitchen at Foxford, Swinford and other parishes around here, I would endeavour to have them established at once and in this way save some lives.'

Thursday 21 January. J. A. Homes JP and Charles Joseph MacDermot JP to the Lord Lieutenant, asking him to appoint a Board of Health in Coolavin.   *Coolavin*
CSORP H.782
Proposed members: Joseph A. Holmes JP, Charles J. MacDermot JP, Harwood O'Farrel MD, Peter Brennan PP, C. Cosgrave PP, Rev E. Powell, Rector of Kilfree, Edward Costello PLG, James Powwell PLG, Andrew Baker, Theo Sherlock, Dominick Corr JP, Thomas MacDermot, Charles Costello
'Fever and dysentery are raging to a frightful extent in the district. There is neither a dispensary or apothecary resident ... The fever hospital in Boyle is not yet open and if it was, it would not contain one-tenth of the fever patients of the Union. These two diseases are carrying off our population in great numbers.'

Thursday 21 January. G. H. Moore to the Lord Lieutenant   *Ballyglass?*
DP 965
'Able-bodied men can no longer obtain two quarts of meal for a day's work, which has to be divided amongst six individuals ... We have sent from this house several times to Westport within the last fortnight without being able to procure meal. The merchants in this county ... are apprehensive that the enormous profits they have been making will soon be interfered with ... There is a necessity of having provisions in government depots, sold to the people at a reasonable price ... If not done, serious and alarming outbreaks are likely to take place. A meeting which will be attended by enormous crowds of people has been convened for Monday next.'

Friday 22 January. Bernard Durcan PP and Ulic Burke MD to the Commissary General, enclosing a subscription list amounting to £75 and a grant of £100 was recommended (See Appendix 3K)   *Swinford*
RLFC 3/2/21/42
'The horrid scenes we are every day compelled to witness, no language can describe ... The stock of provisions in the country is wholly exhausted, nor can we with our utmost efforts, at any of the seaports, at the highest prices, obtain enough to supply our little store. Oatmeal is £26 and Indian meal £21 per ton.' *They request to be supplied from the government depot.*
'Thus we can depend on supplies and our carmen not having to wait three or four days and then bringing not half the quantity we expect ... The

Assistant Commissary General visited our store on Tuesday and in no part of the country has he met with more distress or a place with fewer resources … Our poorhouse is now overcrowded with more than 150 above the number it was intended to accommodate.'

Castlebar
CSORP O.987

Friday 22 January. Report of the workhouse medical officer
'17, 18, 19, 20, 21, & 22 January, the sick in hospital did not get the bread prescribed for them. 21 January, no. 412, Michael Regan, aged 50 years, died of diarrhoea.'

23 January. P. Ronayne MD to the acting chairman of the Board of Guardians
'Dysentery is on the increase … 10 cases were admitted this week … It is necessary to change the present diet by substituting bread for stirabout for at least one meal daily. The sick have not got the rice prescribed for them from 5 pm Thursday to 10 pm Saturday, thus leaving those wretched creatures about 41 hours to struggle against disease, unaided by such nutriment as is deemed essential to and prescribed for their recovery.'

23 January. C. G. Otway to Poor Law Commission
'I was unable to induce the Board of Guardians to strike a rate. The master of the workhouse stated that after 2 pm he was without meal or fuel and that a pauper had died and was upwards of two days unburied because there was no coffin. Mr Ormsby, Lord Lucan's agent, promised him meal and turf but no other necessaries. The clerk, the master and the medical officer subscribed for a coffin for the dead man.

Otway urges strongly that the Board of Guardians be dissolved:
'It is necessary to take steps to provided for the adequate support of the paupers in the workhouse. If this is not done the unfortunate creatures now in the workhouse must actually starve in it.'

CSORP O.1231

29 January. Poor Law Commission to I. O'Malley, clerk of the Castlebar Union, informing him that the Board of Guardians has been dissolved
'On 23 January, at a period when the severest distress was known to exist in the Castlebar Union, the Guardians maintained in the workhouse only 106 inmates, although it was built to accommodate 600, and did not adequately provide for the relief even of the few destitute individuals admitted. A new Board is to be elected and if they fail, paid Guardians will be appointed.'

29 January. Poor Law Commission to Stephen Bourke, master of the workhouse, authorising him 'to purchase during the next week the necessary food, clothing, bedding, fuel and other necessaries for the workhouse inmates and will guarantee tradesmen the payment of bills. Whatever food the medical officer deems necessary for the health of the inmates should be supplied to them.'

Saturday 23 January. Memorial of the inhabitants of Foxford to the Lord Lieutenant (See Appendix 1G)

Foxford
OP 21/94

'We have no depot for purchasing food except in Ballina, 10 miles distant … Within the last few days property conveying to us and our neighbourhood has been taken from the carriers in open day. Public works have ceased in many places near us which has thrown a starving population on its own resources … More frequent attempts at robbery may and will take place. We have a barracks capable of containing 100 men fit and ready for their reception, now occupied by five of the constabulary who are insufficient to attend the escorts of provisions coming from Ballina here day after day, and who are obliged to protect the public carriers to Swinford, a distance of 8 miles. We implore your Excellency to order the military here for the purpose of protecting our persons and properties.

P.S. While this memorial was in preparation, the property of Widow Fox and Mr Patrick Davis, provision dealers, comprising flour, meal etc., had been plundered between Ballina and here.'

Saturday 23 January. W. H. Cox, inspecting officer, to J. C. Walker

Belmullet
OP 21/80

'A small schooner bound for Limerick, which came into Blacksod Bay near Belmullet, was boarded by a large number of men in boats. The crew made no resistance and the cargo, consisting of flour amounting to the value of about £1,000 or between 50 and 60 tons, was carried off on 17 January. Information was brought into Belmullet by the pilot who contrived to escape. A small party of soldiers, police and coastguards went down and succeeded in capturing 12 persons in boats with flour on board … An armed vessel is required for Blacksod or Broadhaven Bays … None of the prisoners who were taken were engaged on the public works.'

Monday 25 January. N. R. St Leger, county engineer, to Archdeacon Verschoyle, chairman of the Leyny Relief Committee, Coolaney

Lower Leyny
DP 4192

'My assistant, Mr Brennan, reports to me that very great destitution exists in the lower half of the barony of Leyny and, as many of the works there must be suspended for want of funds, you should apply to the Lord Lieutenant for another Extraordinary presentment Sessions.'

Tuesday 26 January. Constabulary report

Swinford
OP 21/81

'A depot has been formed at Ballina for the supply of Ballina, Swinford, Foxford, Crossmolina and Ballaghaderreen and relief committees can obtain there any meal which their funds will purchase … Foxford District Relief Fund has not yet been formed. No subscriptions have yet been received from Ballaghaderreen but a fund has been collected and food provided. Assistant

C. G. Adams has been instructed to proceed to these districts and report on the actual state and wants of each. The Ballina workhouse contained 1,151 persons and Swinford workhouse 722 inmates on the last return.'

29 January. Report of Charles G. Adams, Assistant Commissary General, to Sir Randolph Routh

'I found on my arrival in this town on the 19th intant ... that the day had been appointed for a special meeting of the Poor Law Guardians to consider the insolvent and very critical situation of that asylum. There were in it upwards of 700 paupers, for whose support on that day there were only 11 stone of meal, and it was stated to be hopeless to expect to obtain credit to procure any further supply or to provide fuel etc for its maintenance any longer ... The Guardians generally entertained strong objections to strike a new rate ... The measure was, however, carried reluctantly after a lengthy discussion, and thus the serious apprehension entertained of the great additional destitution, which must have prevailed, and the dreadful consequences which might have followed, if the paupers had been turned out on the town and neighbourhood, were much allayed. Credit for food was obtained and a further number of paupers admittted ... I found meal, obtained from Sligo out of the funds of the relief committee, was selling at 2s. 9d. per stone, and that about two and a half tons remained in hand, besides a balance in money: on market day meal was not sold. Dr Burke, who had undertaken to superintend the relief thus afforded, exhibited to me his accounts and managements which appeared to be satisfactory. I urged upon those influential gentlemen with whom I conversed on the subject, the urgent necessity of circulating a local subscription list but they all considered it would be next to useless. Some of the non-residents who had been applied to ... would or could not contribute, urging their pecuniary difficulties and embarassments in consequence of the non-payment of their rents, and others had not even replied to the pressing applications made to them. I returned here today ... Indian meal was selling by the committee, of which there were about 26 cwt in store, at 2s. 6d. per stone; the market price of oatmeal yesterday was 3s. 6½d. The balance on hand was £84 0s. 7d. (exclusive of £100 expected from the Relief Office) with which it was intended to send to the depot at Ballina for 4 tons of meal. I did not fail strongly to recommend the establishment of a soup kitchen, but at present it is generally considered expedient to economise the funds in their present employment.

Foxford: I yesterday accompanied G. V. Jackson to this neighbourhood, and ... we found the locality to be in an extreme state of destitution. The land is generally very sterile and it appears to be surprising how many of the poor creatures could ever have raised a sufficiency of food for their support. Nothing but the potato could have afforded it. We visited several cabins, some in the village of upper Shanwaer, and the inmates presented objects of the most appalling misery. Steps will be immediately taken by Mr Jackson, by circular letter to solicit local subscriptions but in the meantime I respectfully but earnestly recommend that a donation may be immediately placed at the disposal of the relief committee in Foxford of which that gentleman is chairman, and I feel satisfied that every precaution will be taken to economise its distribution in relief in this locality; and that as soon as it can be effected a soup kitchen will be established. I beg to submit that the commissariat office in Ballina may be permitted to sell to each of the committees in Foxford and Swinford to the extent of 4 tons of Indian corn or meal per week.'

Wednesday 27 January. Rev J. Garrett to the Under-Secretary *Ballymote*
CSORP W.1354
'A useless and unnecessary road, no. 11 on the schedule, is about to be commenced in opposition to the gentry and to the great injury of my glebe. I hope the government will stop this wanton waste of public money … Engineer Fitzgerald stated to Mr St Leger that the number of destitute in Corran was 18,000. At last census the population of the barony, men, women and children, was 18,489. The letter was concocted to follow up his application for the obnoxious and useless road, no. 11. We have nearly 4,000 at work. If the roads commenced are proceeded with we shall be able to keep the destitute employed until reproductive work begins. There have been many admitted on the roads, smuggled on the lists by some of the priests in proportion to the liberality with which they paid their Christmas dues, and our committee are working hard to take them off the lists and force them to thresh corn and live on it and to employ the destitute only.'

29 January. Same to Sir Randolph Routh, enclosing a subscription list amounting to £72, since 26 October 1846, to the Corran Relief Committee. A grant of £120 was recommended (See Appendix 3C) RLFC 3/2/26/18
'We want to establish soup kitchens in our barony and liberal funds are indispensable to save the lives of many starving creatures.'

31 January. Same to T. N. Redington DP 1055
'Sessions should be called without delay for finishing the roads, now in a deplorable state and quite impassable … Destitution abounds in the locality … If any delay is made, we shall have multiplied deaths. Food is daily becoming dearer and private benevolence is now become so much checked by the impossibility of collecting rents, that we cannot hope to stem the tide of starvation.'

Thursday 28 January. Memorial of the magistrates and householders to the Lord Lieutenant *Sligo*
CSORP H.913
'A meeting was held between the above and the medical practitioners at the

courthouse on 1 January. Fever and other contagious diseases, which have appeared to an alarming extent amongst the poor inhabitants of the town and county … We request the Lord Lieutenant to appoint a Board of Health. The county fever hospital is unable to meet the demands.'

Ballintubber
CSORP Z.1205

Friday 29 January. Memorial of the parishioners of Kilgifin, Co Roscommon, to the Lord Lieutenant
'Since the 7th century of the world, a greater calamity had not befallen the land of the brave … The parish is deprived of the benefit of public works for want of forward gentlemen, which parish is situated in a mountainy remote place … the greater portion of the inhabitants are fled to England and absconded …'

Foxford
DP 1176

Saturday 30 January. G. V. Jackson, chairman of Foxford Relief Committee, to the Lord Lieutenant
'Since our last weekly meeting, four inquests have been held and verdicts of death from starvation returned in each case … No resident proprietors, nor merchants, nor others of the independant classes, to assist the poor; the rocky and mountainous character of the country in most places, forbids employment as to reproductive work … the soil is poor, the quantity of produce small, the quality is bad. The population is dense … This day we arrive with pain and alarm at a conviction that in the parishes of Toomore, Attymass, Kilgarvan and Killasser there are about 3,000 families who are in danger of perishing from starvation … if other agencies are not suddenly brought to their relief. In many parts the supply of food is already gone, the relief works are run out and we can see no prospect before the unhappy people but death by masses … The poorhouses at Ballina and Swinford are both full to overflowing and numbers in each case are refused admission for want of room. Surrounded by a fearful array of human suffering and wretchedness, we feel our position to be one of no ordinary responsibility.'

Swinford
DP 1102

Saturday 30 January. Bernard Durcan PP to the Lord Lieutenant
'A number of 310 persons in this parish in a state of utter destitution and kept a whole week out of employment through the culpable neglect of the district engineer. I reported the case on Wednesday last to Mr Brett, county engineer, but there has been no redress yet. It is monstrous that after so many delays from other causes, so many should be, tho' in a state of extreme destitution, deprived of relief through the misconduct of a paid officer.'
Report of Mr Brett re above, 20 February:
'All the persons referred to in the letter of Mr Durcan have been at work upwards of a fortnight. The assistant engineer could not do more than he was doing to set all in operation.'

31 January. Memorial of Swinford Relief Committee to the Lord Lieutenant (See Appendix 1M)

DP 1177

'The sums granted by the Extraordinary Sessions are not at all adequate to meet the hourly increasing demands for relief. The works will be very shortly left incomplete for want of funds and … the men will be thrown out of work and thus a fearful increase will be made to those who are now depending on a casual and every day more and more precarious charity. It is absolutely necessary that a Presentment Sessions for this barony be held at the earliest possible moment.'

Saturday 30 January. Cardinal Franzoni to Archbishop Murray, Dublin, enclosing bills for £730 sterling, offerings of the clery and citizens of Rome for the relief of famine sufferers

Rome
DDA MURRAY PAPERS

'The Pope is sending £1,000 of his personal money and the Propaganda Cardinals, £500. The Archbishop will know how best to divide this among the four Metropolitans, giving most where there is the greatest need and seeing that the suffragan bishops in districts badly affected receive a just allocation.'

Spring 1847

Quakers and Soup Kitchens

In November 1846 the Society of Friends (Quakers) met in Dublin and set up the Central Relief Committee of the Society of Friends. Joseph Bewley and Jonathan Pim were appointed joint secretaries. At the same time the Society of Friends in England decided to raise funds for famine relief in Ireland. The Dublin Committee published an address, copies of which were sent to England and even more importantly to America, particularly to the Quakers in Philadelphia. Funds began to pour in first from the Quakers in Ireland itself, then from those in England and later from the Friends in America. By December they began their relief operations, especially in the most distressed unions of the west of Ireland. On 28 December Dean Hoare of Achonry and Rev Tyndale of Kilmactigue each received a donation of £20 to help in establishing soup kitchens to feed the starving. For the next two years they continued to make grants of money, boilers, food and clothes to numerous parishes for distribution amongst the most needy. In 1847 the Quakers provided approximately £200,000 for the relief of distress which was spent almost exclusively in the west of Ireland. While they were strictly non-sectarian, making their grants to ministers and priests, Protestant and Catholics, they showed a certain preference for Protestant ministers, for practical reasons only. Joseph Bewley stated to a parliamentary committee that ministers made better agents as they usually had the help of wives and daughters, while priests were already over-stretched ministering to the dying.

At the beginning of February the government passed the Soup Kitchen Act providing direct relief in the form of cooked food or soup through the establishment of soup kitchens. The public works continued to expand. Early in February the total number employed on the roads in Co Mayo was 39,366 and a little over a month later it had risen to 49,425. Thereafter it began gradually to taper off. Deaths from fever and dysentery continued to rise during the spring. Ballina workhouse recorded 87 deaths for the week ending 3 April and during the same week Castlerea had 256 inmates suffering from fever. The workhouses continued to suffer from an acute shortage of funds until the government finally agreed in late February to grant a weekly loan to cover current expenses.

There was a sharp rise in emigration among that class who could still muster the passage money. On 25 March Pius IX issued an encyclical letter requesting three days of public prayers in Catholic churches worldwide when alms should be collected for the relief of the starving in Ireland.

Prospects for the 1847 harvest were bleak. On 30 March it was reported from Ballina that 'people say that they are not able to till the land because of bodily weakness and they have neither seed nor money.' The same was true of all the north-west.

Ballina
CSORP O.8579

Monday 1 February 1847. Extract from Guardians' minutes. J. J. Joygner, manager of the Provincial Bank, to Edward Howley, chairman of the Board of Guardians, re £600 loan
'The only way in which an advance to that extent would be granted, would be on the personal security of the members of the Board of Guardians. *Resolved:* That £26, the whole amount of funds in the treasurer's hands, be used to support 1,200 paupers in the workhouse and that the chairman be asked to make up the balance. Otherwise we will be obliged to close the workhouse this day.'
1 February. T. N. Redington to Edward Howley, Belleek Castle
'The circumstances of the Union urgently require that a new rate should be struck to meet the daily increasing demand upon the funds … On the security of such rates, an advance may be made by the treasurer.'

Costello barony
SFFP 2/506/19

Monday 1 February, Charles Strickland to Society of Friends (See Appendix 6)
'I should like to put up two or three soup shops as soon as possible. We have practically ascertained the quantities of several articles to make a really good and nourishing soup and have got in a store of articles ready to carry us for a little time in anticipation of your kind and generous assistance … Distress is much increasing and not a moment's delay must unnecessarily take place further upon our parts.'
Draft note: 'Grant 1 ton of rice for immediate distribution. C. Strickland proposes to have boilers ferried by canal to Longford, 1 of 130 gallons, 1 of 100 gallons and 1 of 70 gallons.'

Ballaghaderreen
DP 1178

Monday 1 February. Ballaghaderreen Relief Committee
'Unanimously resolved to call on the government to have Sessions called at Ballaghaderreen, to finish the footpaths in Ballaghaderreen, £300, the roads from Hawkesford to Doocastle, £700, from Baroe to Shragh, £300, from Cross to Float, £200, from Ballaghaderreen to Carracastle, £560, from John Moran's house to the mailcoach road at Doogerry, £100, and from Cloonmene to Cross, £200.'

Coolavin
SFFP 2/505/5

Tuesday 2 February. J. Bewley and J. Pim to J. A. Holmes (See Appendix 6M)
'The Committee will grant £20 in aid of the soup shop … recommending very prompt measures towards establishing it, as it appears from the statement that disease and death are woefully prevalent in the district. This grant will be payable as soon as the establishment is in an efficient state and likely to be so mainteined … We would suggest thy purchasing a ton of rice at Sligo to be paid by this Committee and have it distributed if possible daily in a cooked state amongst the most destitute and especially those afflected with sickness.'

Tuesday 2 February. Extract of letter of Wm. J. Spenell?   *Belmullet*
'The sufferings of the people here for want of food are frightful. It is difficult   DP 1306
to pass through the streets, so many surround you, and it is truly heartrending to see the wretched state which many, very many are reduced to, and to
hear their cries is trying to the sternest heart.'

Tuesday 2 February. Luke Dolan, blacksmith, Doon East, to the Lord Lieutenant   *Coolavin*
'Last November I made and delivered 6 dozen stone hammers to Pat   CSORP W.I447
Meehan, steward on the new line of road at Clonsellagh, for which I never
since received a penny and I am on the verge of being thrown on the world's
wide waste, endeavouring to support a long family, destitute and helpless …
The species of tradesmen in this country are so immediately pressed by
poverty, owing to the manner of their being paid for their annual labour, by
getting 8 stone of potatoes from every family in their district once a year.'
Board of Works to T. N. Redington re above, 2 March:
'Dolan has been paid since.'

Tuesday 2 February. Dominick Noone CC to T. N. Redington   *Cliffony*
'Did you hear the screams, the execrations, the lamentations of the people at   CSORP W.II40
this announcement *(to stop a line of road in progress),* could you even in imag-
ination reach a conception of the peoples' feelings, you would press on the
Board of Works not to follow up their instructions. The people have become
desperate and we succeeded for this day in suppressing riots and calming
their tempers in some measure. So for mercy's sake and for suffering humanity, lay our case before the Lord Lieutenant and the Board of Works. As the
people have sworn fearlessly in our hearing that they would no longer suffer
hunger but would take all the property that they would meet … You will
have wholesale plunder and insubordination and a violation of all laws will
be the melancholy consequence … Clerical influence will no longer prevail.'

Wednesday 3 February. Rev Wm. Tyndale to Society of Friends re £20 grant (See   *Kilmactigue*
Appendix 6Q)   SFFP 2/506/19
'I purchased and erected a boiler containing upwards of 60 gallons at a cost
of £8 5s. We give out soup four times in the week to 98 of the most destitute
families gratuitously. We endeavoured to make sale of a portion to some persons in employment at a penny a quart but could only procure 2s. since the
commencement…There are to my certain knowledge many poor families
entirely subsisting on this supply of soup etc, some with the addition of
watercresses. We are also obliged to give oatmeal, rice and barley, together
with medicine, to many who are labouring under different diseases and yet,
I lament to say, deaths from these diseases are of almost daily occurence.'

Emigration
Transactions p. 255

Wednesday 3 February. Jonathan Pim to Jacob Harvey
'Emigration this year will certainly be enormous. Inclement as is this season, they are going already. A ship left Sligo just before Christmas and instead of the sorrow usual on leaving their native country, there was nothing but joy at their escape, as from a doomed land. The country in many places is becoming depopulated. The people are deserting their families, crowding into towns and cities; spreading themselves over our eastern counties, where destitution is less because the people have been accustomed to rely on wages for their support; and when they can beg their passage, crossing over to England and Scotland.'

Swinford
CSORP W.2132

Thursday 4 February. B. W. Eames, Vicar of Kilconduff, to Henry Labouchere
'There is a great grievance the poor people here labour under since Capt Stirling, the late inspecting officer, was replaced … When a person working on the roads was unable from sickness (which I lament to say is increasing to an alarming extent) to attend, he is prevented by the overseers to send any of his family in his place, although on his wages depend the sole support of his family.'
Board of Works to T. N. Redington re above, 17 March:
'In the event of the relief committee's deeming it adviseable to recommend the substitution of any individual from sickness or other causes, an authority is sent to the overseer by the inspecting officer to that effect.'

Ballina
CSORP O.8579

Thursday 4 February. A. McMunn, clerk of the Union, to C. G. Otway
'Our chairman is keeping the paupers in the workhouse supported at his own expense, in money advanced from his own reources at about £120 a week, unassisted by the treasurer or a single Guardian, and altho' he is determined to make every sacrifice rather than allow our poor to be turned out and left to die, still it is quite impossible for the private resources of any one private indiviual to support 1,240 or 1,300 weekly in our house.'
6 February. C. G. Otway to Poor Law Commission
'I fear the worst consequences if some means are not at once adopted to get the treasurer to make an advance to the Union. The chairman has latterly been providing funds out of his own pocket to support the workhouse but this cannot last long.'

Collooney
CSORP Z.1278

Thursday 4 February. Resolutions of the Tirerrill Relief Committee
'That the numerous deaths which are occurring every day from starvation in this barony, when importunate people are unable to procure coffins, the immediate attention of the government be called to this subject and the Lord Lieutenant be requested to provide a fund for this purpose and prevent the

spread of pestilence, which otherwise inevitably will take place, as bodies have been a week in some cases unburied.

That in consequence of the several deaths that are daily occurring in this barony, an enormous expense will be incurred. The committee requests the government to direct the coroners not to hold inquests, in cases where there can be no question as to the cause of death, if the expense is to be defrayed by the county, as the cess-payers are already overburdened by taxation.

That the committee write to Sir Randolph Routh, requesting 10 boilers of 180 gallons each for 10 locations including Collooney.'

Draft reply, 6 February: 'His Excellency has no funds to provide coffins.'

Thursday 4 February. Denis Tighe PP to William Stanley, requesting 2 boilers of the largest size, as the population of the parish is 12,000.

4 February. J. Bewley and J. Pim to Denis Tighe PP

'We are in receipt of thy favor of the 2nd inst. and on a careful examination being made we do not find that any application from thee was received. We have made a grant to Charles Strickland of Loughglynn for general relief measures in this district to whom we accordingly beg leave to recommend thee.'

Ballaghaderreen
RLFC 3/2/21/23
SFFP 2/505/5

Thursday 4 February. Rev J. Garrett to William Stanley

'I intend to establish 5 soup kitchens in the barony of Corran ... I have procured 1 boiler from the Irish Association of 100 gallons and I need 4 more of 60 gallons each. The population comprises 18,489 souls and we calculate that we will need to feed at least 4,000 gratuitously ... Many wretched creatures are unable to work, tho' included in our labour lists ... It is a most enormous labour and difficulty to put off the rich, whom some of the priests smuggled into our committee. It would be highly desirable if some mode could be devised of procuring an accurate inventory of the substance of the farming population thro' the constabulary or some disinterested agency, for if not, it will be quite impossible to prevent the most profligate waste of food, by these men returning their rich parishioners and the fund will be speedily exhausted.'

Ballymote
RLFC 3/2/26/18

Thursday 4 February. Memorial of Martin Connor, Baronagh, Blacksod Bay, to the Lord Lieutenant

'On Sunday, 17 January last, the schooner, *Glasgow of Domfrieze* with Captain Ekins, bound from Glasgow to Limerick, laden with wheat and flour, put in and anchored in Elly Bay, Blacksod ... in consequence of a head wind which blew rather fresh. At 3 o'clock, he as pilot went on board the schooner, which required shifting to safer anchorage, and being some short time on board, the coastguard galley, having David and Owen Lloyd Jr (boys) therein, came also on board. When he was about half an hour on board, he saw several boats

Belmullet
OP 21/149

manned pulling from the shore towards the *Glasgow*, the crew of four of which came on board and immediately proceeded to break the hatches and bid him to join and assist them. He replied that, though he was in as great want of provisions as they were, he would not. Some of those depredators then said that he ought to be lashed to the mast, others that he ought to be quartered, upon hearing which, at the hazard of his life, he leaped from on board into the galley and was brought by the boys, who also quit the vessel at the same time. On coming ashore the report was spread that he was for giving information to the proper authorities at Belmullet. The road and direct way to which town was set with watches to obstruct him therefrom, but he went byeways, running a distance of upwards of six Irish miles on foot and gave his information to Lieutenant Dawson at Belmullet, who promptly sent some of the coastguards, police and a party of the 49th Regiment, to succour and save the schooner and cargo from being plundered, with whom he proceeded back to the schooner and remained all that night on board and piloted said schooner and all that remained of her cargo (something more than three-quarters thereof) safe to the pier of Belmullet … Thirteen of these predators, apprehended on board, have been committed for trial to Castlebar gaol. That he is envied and has been repeatedly threatened for giving such information and is in dread of his life from his neighbours … He humbly hopes and prays that your Excellency will deign to take the service so rendered into your humane consideration and order him such reward as the nature of such a case merits.'

Castlebar
CSORP O.1696

Thursday 4 February. Stephen Bourke, master of the workhouse, to Poor Law Commission
'I have scarcely as much provision as will answer until Saturday morning. There are contractors for soap, candles, meat, milk, sugar, barley, rice, wine, pepper and mustard for the hospital but no contractors for straw, meal and bread. The present ready money prices and quantity required per week is as follows: 6 cwt of oatmeal at £1 7s. per cwt, £8 2s.: 180 lbs of bread at 2¾d per lb, £2 1s. 3d: turf at 5s. per horse load, £2 18s. 4d. The Earl of Lucan pays for those foods and fuel he sends here. There is no scarcity of money at all … but of food … Regarding the admission of paupers, the medical officer thinks that those with fever and dysentery, now so prevalent, should not be admitted, as it would be cruel to bring disease among the inmates seeking refuge from hunger.'
5 February. Poor Law Commission to Sir Randolph Routh, requesting him to send £20 to Stephen Bourke, master of the workhouse.

Foxford
OP 21/143

Friday 5 February. Rev Geoff Mostyn to T. N. Redington
'I only heard this day that a memorial was forwarded to the Lord Lieutenant

praying that troops would be sent to the village of Foxford. I have not seen the memorial, its getting up being a hole and corner affair and, as far as I can learn, passed upon the interested views of two individuals. I refer you to the police authorities, who will inform you no outrage is committed or outbreak dreaded in this immediate locality. A few of the constabulary are wanted as an escort for the bread stuffs etc.' *See 23 January.*

Saturday 6 February. Resolutions of the Board of Health   *Sligo*
'That the Charter House be rented from John Wynne at £10 a month. That Drs Homan and Knott of the Fever Hospital extend their care to above at an equal salary to what they already receive and that Dr McMunn be appointed apothecary at £35 p.a. That John Morris be appointed steward at £20, with a porter, head nurse and six nurses, kitchen maid and laundress. That advertisements be placed in the Sligo papers for beds, bed-ticks, bolsters, calico shirts, blankets, rugs, night chairs, pans, chamber pots, straw, oatmeal, tea, sugar, sweet milk, beef, bread, buttermilk, soap, candles and coal.'

Saturday 6 February. J. J. Joygner, manager, Provincial Bank, Ballina, to   *Swinford*
Swinford Board of Guardians
'Favoured with your letter of the 5th instant, asking the probable amount of loan the London directors would be likely to sanction on the rates … They have declined advancing on them and if no other security of a business like character be offered, it is useless to repeat any application.'

Sunday night 7 February. G. V. Jackson to the Lord Lieutenant   CSORP O.1411
'The master and the clerk of Swinford poorhouse report by this night's post that the paupers in the house, 668 in number, are in bed for want of fuel and that there is not a shilling's worth of food in the house for their support tomorrow. 56 were admitted last week, making it 733 or 33 more than the house was intended to contain. I sent at once to Swinford £20, (confided to me by a friend to relieve the poor), to meet this instant pressure … We individually can go no further than we have already gone in personally assisting the Union. No combination of local efforts can contend with this fearful visitation and if a foreign agency does not come to our assistance, be it governmental or the offspring of public benevolence, the poor of this house must perish of starvation. Nothing can save them. I assume no language of complaint. It is my own conviction that the government in each department has done and is doing all that any government can do to mitigate the horrors of the calamity we suffer under; but my own experience satisfies me that it is beyond the reach of human means to meet.'

7 February. Resolutions of Swinford Board of Guardians   CSORP O.1908
'That the thanks of the Board of Guardians and the Union at large, is due to

our chairman, George V. Jackson for sending £20 to the clerk to enable him to purchase food for the paupers, who would be without food this day had he not sent the above sum and having on other occasions procured meal for the house.

That we cannot too strongly impress upon the government the necessity of affording us immediate assistance in the way of a loan to relieve the awful destitution prevailing in this Union and save the lives of 690 paupers in the house. That owing to the charitable feelings of our chairman, on whose responsibility the establishment has been supported during the last month, we were enabled to afford shelter and relief to our starving fellow creatures and keep the house open ... We consented to strike a new rate amount of £2,373 in the hope that government would give us a loan on the security of this rate. That unless the government send us immediate assistance, it is impossible for us to act as Guardians of the poor, being this day without funds to provide food or fuel for the inmates and have no other alternative left, except being compelled again to apply to our chairman to send us what quantity of meal is being required until our next meeting. We put the fearful state of things before the government and the Poor Law Commission, to which we implore their earnest and immediate attention.'

Ballymote
DP 1249

Sunday 7 February. Rev J. Garrett to T. N. Redington, requesting that
'the Lord Lieutenant will call a Special Sessions to finish works already begun. Two hills, Ballybrennan and Camross?, are left from want of funds in a most dangerous state ... 180 men employed on them have been a whole week idle ... Several other roads, on which the funds are exhausted, which will throw the body of men employed on them into utter destitution.'

RLFC 3/2/26/18

Same to Sir Randolph Routh:
'Sir Robert Gore Booth has given £100 and hopes to be granted an equal sum and send for 4 boilers to Sligo ... The hucksters are extorting lately and the poor are suffering the most awful destitution with astonishing patience ... Deaths multiply weekly.'
Draft reply: £100 donation was recommended.

Ballaghaderreen
SFFP 2/506/19

Monday 8 February. Denis Tighe PP to Society of Friends
'The population of this parish over which I preside is 12,000 souls, the most of whom are in extreme want, several hundreds of them are entire days without tasting food, and many, very many obliged to give up the public works from hunger. Fever and dysentery are spreading to an alarming extent and "deaths from starvation" is the awful news that reaches me from every quarter. I am indeed in a most wretched state, witnessing their misery, listening to their cries and seeing them falling on the road from hunger and declaring

in the presence of God that death would be a relief to them ... I have written to the Society of Friends in Liverpool, Birkenhead and Leeds and to you and have not received a single shilling ... I will appeal to them again ... and to all the other relief committees of the Society of Friends in England whose address I can make out. I will thus discharge my duty to God and my fellow creatures and then when I see them fall around me as I do every day, my conscience will acquit me of blame.'

Monday 8 February. Relief Committee of Cloonoghill, Kilturra and Kilshalvey to the Lord Lieutenant, requesting him to order an Extraordinary Presentments Sessions for the barony of Corran (See Appendix 2B)   *Bunninadden*
DP 1435

'400 of the most destitute now employed on the public works in those parishes will in three or four days be thrown out of employment, funds being exhausted.'

Monday 8 February. Resolutions of the Board of Guardians, proposed by G. V. Jackson and seconded by John Perkins   *Ballina*
CSORP O.3475 & O.8579

'That a rate of £12,000 be struck to support the expenses of the Union for 12 months and that the chairman be requested to wait on the Lord Lieutenant and urge on him the absolute necessity of an immediate loan to keep the house open. That the rate should be apportioned according to the number of paupers sent in from the different electoral divisions.
Ballina, 4s., Backs, 3s., Attymass, 3s., Kilgarvan, 1s. 8d., Dromore West, 1s. 3d., Easky, 1s. 8d., Kilglass, 1s. 8d., Castleconnor, 1s. 6d., Ballysokeary, 4s., Killala, 2s., Lackan, 3s. 4d., Ballycastle, 1s. 8d., Kilfian, 3s., Crossmolina, 2s. 6d., Belmullet, 1s. 3d., Binghamstown, 1s. 3d.
Upwards of 140 persons who are almost starved appeared. We could not put them on the books, the workhouse being full. That our chairman be again requested to advance another £100 to support the paupers in the house, which we should have long since turned out, only for his kind and humane assistance heretofore ...'

Monday 8 February. Memorial of Kilkelly Relief Committee to the Commissary general (See Appendix 2G)   *Kilkelly*
RLFC 3/2/21/27

'The population of the Kilkelly Relief district contains at least 18,500 human beings ... fully 18,000 of them are in the deepest distress and destitution ... Every day several are dying of starvation ... We have no provisions in the mountainous district ... Hundreds must perish of malnutrition unless a depot for the sale of meal be established in Kilkelly ... No food can be provided for the people nearer than Sligo or Ballina, a distance of nearly 30 miles. We therefore in the name and on behalf of a famishing population call upon you, Sir, to relieve our deplorable famished stricken condition by establishing at once a depot for the sale of meal in Kilkelly.'

Kilmactigue
SFFP 2/505/5

Monday 8 February. Bewley and Pim to Rev William Tyndale (See Appendix 6Q)
'We beg leave to acquaint thee that the Committee has granted £20 in aid to relief measures in operation in thy district. Permit us to suggest whether thy distribution of cooked rice would not be useful especially to those suffering from sickness. Rice might probably be purchased on reasonable terms at Sligo. We beg leave to enclose a letter of credit for £20.'

Coolavin
SFFP 2/505/5

Monday 8 February. Bewley and Pim to J. A. Holmes
'We are directed by the Committee to express their approval of the suggestion of purchasing the rice in Liverpool provided that in the meantime the poor people are not permitted to suffer.'

Kilmactigue
CSORP Z.1711

Tuesday 9 February. John S. Stewart, sub-inspector, Tubbercurry, to the Inspector General
'On yesterday I attended an inquest at Annagh, parish of Kilmactigue, held on the body of Nancy Kelly, a beggar woman, who died in her brother's house on Sunday morning, the 7th instant, of absolute want of any food. The verdict of the jury was 'death of starvation'. I trust I am not going out of my province in making the following statement. I found the body lying in Patrick Kelly's, her brother's house, on a wisp of straw laid over a few boards and a creel. The brother himself was sitting without a coat nursing a child, which was quite evident was rapidly hastening to the grave, as the doctor said from want of food and he has three other children, from eight to three years old, mere skeletons, hunger painted on their shrunken cheeks, the mother being gone to work on the Banada and Cully public works in order that she might earn something for her famishing children and there was nothing in the miserable cabin but some old bed clothes, a box and two plates.
It was proved in evidence that this wretched man, hearing that his sister was unable to go about begging as usual, and that the storm had rendered her little hut totally uninhabitable, had borrowed an ass and brought her a distance of nearly two miles to his own place and gave her a division of his own miserable supply of food. This amounted to one pound of meal and one quart of sowens? during a period of six days, and death mercifully closed her eyes and put an end to her sufferings. After the inquest, Meredith Thompson Esq. of Knockadoo, was requested to allow something to provide a coffin and to interr her body. He said he would give it out of his own pocket; he did not think he had the powers as the act gave him no power to provide coffins for anybody on which an inquest was held, but for the bodies of strangers. I

Inscription on a headstone in Ballyara Cemetery

The 'Pride of Ballyara'
tread softly o'er the spot,
his blood can give nobility;
a noble steed was he
His sire was blood
and blood his dam
and all his pedigree.

This slab is in memory of a famous thoroughbred
that netted a fortune for the Mullarkey family.
In 'black '47' – the famine years –
Dr J P Mullarkey purchased two cargo of oat meal
and two cargo of potatoes and carted them to
Drumartin, Aclare, Tubbercurry as a gift.
We shall ne'er see his like again.
Photo: Fr Paddy Kilcoyne

urged him that this woman was nearly two miles from where she had usually resided, and that it was self-evident her brother could not provide a coffin, if it was only to cost sixpence, on which he kindly gave 7s. 6d. to provide a coffin and to get her interred, saying at the same time, he was nearly confident he would not be allowed one farthing of it.

I beg to remark that if the coroner has no power under the new act to provide coffins for the utterly destitute on whom inquests may be held, that they will have to buried without them, as in this poor locality the only persons who can be supposed able to contribute to the purchase of them, are the few members of the relief committee, and it is a regular tax on us everyday of meetings, making up subscriptions among ourselves to bury the destitute. Perhaps if the coroner be bound by the new acts to provide coffins only for strangers, some temporary remedy during this period of distress and destitution would be ordered by the government, if you thought it right to bring the circumstance under the notice of the proper authorities.'

Ballisodare
SFFP 2/505/5

Tuesday 9 February. Bewley and Pim to Patrick McTucker, secretary relief com-
mittee (See Appendix 6E)
'We beg leave to acquaint thee that the Committee are willing to aid in establishing a soup shop and to inquire whether an order on Ballina for a boiler
would be desirable as we have a few at our disposal there and if so what size
can thy committee undertake to keep fully at work.'

Ballinacarrow
SFFP 2/505/5

Tuesday 9 February. Bewley and Pim to Rev Henry Perceval (See Appendix 6D)
'We beg leave to acquaint thee that the Committee will grant £20 as a donation to the soup shop fund to encourage an extension of its operations,
payable as soon as it is in an efficient state and distributing 100 gallons or
upwards daily or three or four days in the week. We would strongly recommend the distribution of cooked rice.'

Sligo
CSORP H.1677

Wednesday 10 February. Minutes of Board of Health
'As many bodies of paupers be for a considerable time unburied for want of
coffins, thro' the different parts of the town and vicinity, coffins shall be supplied at the expense of the Board.'

Report: (See Appendix 5)	
cases of fever in the fever hospital:	41
cases of fever in the workhouse:	164
cases of dysentery in workhouse:	168
non-contagious diseases:	204
Total:	536
Deaths from fever in the workhouse:	6
Deaths from dysentery:	12
Total:	18

Castlebar
CSORP O.1880

Thursday 11 February. C. G. Otway to Poor Law Commission
'I considered and I consider a cruel dereliction of duty by the Castlebar
Board of Guardians, at a most trying time, the unpardonable neglect of the
few inmates that were allowed to remain in the workhouse ... I repeatedly
and anxiously remonstrated, not only with the Board of Guardians as a body,
but by every influence and entreaty that I could use with individual members
of the Board, I endeavoured to bring the Guardians to a sense of their duty
and prevent the lamentable and cruel course that has been pursued ... The
Earl of Lucan was the chief person who opposed me.'
Poor Law Commission to Sir George Grey, Home Office, London, 16 February:
'The Earl of Lucan is legally bound to pay the whole of the amount for which
he stands rated. The Commissioners express the high sense they entertain of
the energy and fearlessness of Mr Otway actuated solely ... by a desire that,

for the future, relief should be duly administered to the destitute poor in the Castlebar Union.'

Thursday 11 February. Dean Hoare to William Stanley
'I have seen the beneficial results of acting in accordance with the regulations of the Commissary General. I have sold at the house of a servant on my land, meal to the amount of £200 (besides rice, cheese and other provisions); and this has not cost me a shilling (except the inconvenience of keeping a float of about £30). By adding £1 per ton to the price paid at the mills (at a distance of 10 miles), I have covered all my expenses and provided a poor carman (with a family of 12), and for the person who weighs and sells the meal (with a family of 8), to the amount of £4 each, within 10 weeks. The advantage to the neighbourhood has been very great. For a mile in every direction around me, the private dealers sell at a reasonable profit. If I had sold at a loss (supposing I could have afforded it), I should have stopped the private dealers, and thereby limited the supply in the country; and if I had not sold at all, prices would have been higher in the neighbourhood, as they are in other parts of the district.'

Upper Leyny
RLFC 3/2/26/26

Friday 12 February. Bewley and Pim to Archdeacon Joseph Verschoyle (See Appendix 6L)
'The Committee directs us to acquaint thee that they will grant £30 ... towards the establishment and maintenance of a soup shop on a scale somewhat commensurate with the wants of the district ... Have the goodness to inform us what thou considers the exigency such as to require aid towards the immediate distribution of food pending measures for establishing a soup shop.'

Coolaney
SFFP 2/505/5

Friday 12 February. Resolution of Boyle Relief Committee, Viscount Lorton in the chair
'That the melancholy and alarming state of the destitute at the present moment in consequence of a great fall of snow, and the Board of Works being only authorised to pay 4d. a day until they could resume their work, and the workhouse is now full and every channel through which relief be afforded is overstocked, we urge the government to authorise the payment of full wages (8d. a day) during the continuance of the snow. In order to preserve the lives of the labourers, we authorise the engineer, Henry Buck, to pay full wages.'

Boyle
CSORP W.1705

Saturday 13 February. J. A. Holmes to Society of Friends (See Appendix 6M)
'My thanks for the donation of clothing ... Our soup kitchen is now in full operation and of the greatest use. The ton of rice granted by your Committee is being daily distributed ... Never did a donation come in such good time

Coolavin
SFFP 2/506/19

and never was greater benefit derived by poor people than from this grant. I only wish any member of the Society of Friends Committee could witness the daily distribution of it and the eagerness and thankfulness with which it is received.'

Ballaghaderreen
SFFP 2/506/19

Sunday 14 February. Denis Tighe PP to Laurence Gurney, Society of Friends, London
'On an average 20 deaths from starvation have occurred every week since 1 January and that number is frightfully increased the week just ended on account of the heavy fall of snow. On yesterday two beggars died immediately near my house as they were crawling to it to get relief. That unfortunate class is completely gone. They are found in every direction lying on the roads either dead or breathing their last...We have no claim but that of charity. In the name of the God of charity I ask your aid to feed the hungry.'

Ballymote
SFFP 2/506/19

Monday 15 February. Rev J. Garrett to Society of Friends
'By the sad procrastination of the government officials and Board of Works, we are now surrounded by 640 labourers thrown out of employment on the public works and starving with their families. It is most lamentable to witness their sad condition, food at a famine price and no money to buy it. We have been forced to give some gratuitous food to one hundred this day to rescue them from the jaws of death, but our store won't last a week and deaths will multiply.'

Carracastle
SFFP 2/505/5

Monday 15 February. Bewley and Pim to D. O'Kane PP
'The Committee ... directs us to express their regret to notice the want of that organisation in thy impoverished district, which appears to be essential for the proper carrying out of relief measures. The Committee would willingly grant some assistance if such organisation be effected.'
22 February. Same to same
'The Committee has directed us to acquaint thee that they have entered into arrangements with Charles Strickland of Loughglynn, who has undertaken with their assistance to set forward relief measures for the barony of Costello generally and we accordingly beg leave to refer thee to him.'

Ballaghaderreen
RLFC 3/2/21/23

Monday 15 February. Charles Strickland to Poor Law Commission, enclosing a subscription list amounting to £165 for the Ballaghaderreen Relief Committee (See Appendix 3G)
'If a grant of boilers could be made to us, they would be of infinite service in providing a cheap, warm and nutritious food, as well in the town of Ballaghaderreen as in the country districts.'

Tuesday 16 February. Edward Howley, Belleek Castle, to Edward Twistleton   *Ballina*
'A very heavy fall of snow prevented me travelling. Unless a loan is granted   CSORP O.3475
we must close Ballina workhouse and turn out the paupers as we have neither funds nor credit … I am advancing from my private resources £105 a
week and altho' I am determined to expend the last farthing I have, sooner
than let the poor people starve, I cannot much longer hold out to support
1,235 paupers now in the house. We would have as many more if we had
acommodation and funds. We owe contractors £3,000 and they are naturally
most clamourous in their demands. For charity's sake, do all you can for us.
£12,000 rate was struck last Monday … cannot be collected sooner than next
October as property here is in a most embarrassed state.'

Tuesday 16 February. Dean Hoare to Society of Friends (See Appendix 6A)   *Upper Leyny*
'We gratefully acknowledge two contributions of £20 each from your benev-   SFFP 2/506/19
olent Committee…We are now expending £23 weekly in support of 9 soup
kitchens and we are also expending £52 10s. per week in free distribution of
meal. Our funds will not enable us to carry on this relief … beyond the 6th of
next month and as that time draws nigh, I feel anxious to obtain further aid.'

Tuesday 16 February. Bewley and Pim to Ulic Burke MD. (See Appendix 6V)   *Swinford*
'The Committee grants £30 as a donation to the soup fund and they express   SFFP 2/505/5
a hope that it will be established on a scale somewhat commensurate with the
wants of the district. We beg leave to submit to the committee of which thou
are secretary, whether some prompt relief measures ought not to be adopted
and we would suggest that immediate arrangements be made for distributing
rice in a cooked state amongst the most destitute of the poor, especially those
afflicted or threatened with dysentery.'

Wednesday 17 February. Lord Lieutenant to Sir Randolph Routh, authorising   *Workhouses*
him to place at their disposal such sums as may be requisite for the following   CSORP O.1667
workhouses: Swinford, Castlebar, Ballina, Tralee, Glenties, Carrick on Shannon,
Cavan, Dunmanway and Bantry.
Wednesday 17 February. Poor Law Commission to T. N. Redington, requesting   *Castlebar*
£20 for the maintenance of Castlebar workhouse during the past week.   CSORP O.1696
Swinford, Saturday 20 February. Poor Law Commission to T. N. Redington,   CSORP O.1810
requesting £60 for the maintenance of the Swinford workhouse for the ensuing week.
Tuesday 23 February. Poor Law Commission to T. N. Redington informing him   *Ballina*
that £100 is requisite for the maintenance of the Ballina workhouse for the ensu-   CSORP O.1923
ing week.

Ballymote
SFFP 2/506/19

Wednesday 17 February. Society of Friends' query form completed and signed by Richard Gethen, chairman, Rev J. Garrett, secretary, Rev James Flemimg, Presbyterian minister and Bernard O'Kane PP
'We daily expect two boilers. We mean to have five soup kitchens. We shall be doomed to see thousands die of starvation if we don't receive liberal subscriptions from the humane and charitable. Unhappily a vessel laden with provision for our chief landed proprietor, Sir Robert Gore Booth, has been lost and that fatality greatly aggravates our present grievous destitution. Those that die now are in many cases carried out at night and buried without coffins. Funerals even when coffins are obtained seldom appear attended by any number and deaths have become so common that the natural feelings appear to be quite blurted among the population. Beggars at length are driven from door to door without alms, quite a new feature in the Irish peasant's character. Even the gentry are forced to deny what formerly they freely gave.'

Swinford
RLFC 3/2/21/42

Friday 19 February. Ulic Burke MD to the Commissary General
'We have appropriated £175 to establish a soup kitchen as soon as we receive the necessary boilers … The assistance already received has saved hundreds from a premature and dreadful death. We cannot help expressing our fearful conviction that no human efforts can save thousands from perishing.' *(See Appendix 3K)*

Foxford
CSORP Z.1901

Friday 19 February. Resolution of Foxford Relief Committee (See Appendix 2F)
'They view with great alarm the effect in this district of the operation of Sir G. Grey's letter to the Lord Lieutenant … The non-residence of proprietors, the number of properties in trust, under the courts, under decrees of the courts for sale, cases where there are no representatives of the proprietors present, will interpose insurmountable obstacles in this district to the general employment by the proprietors as a general rule … The amount of money parliament is ready to advance for the relief of the present visitation, if applied in one way, will hasten the overthrow and downfall of the country, while if applied in another way, will tend to its restoration, solvency and general improvement. Cultivation of the soil and carrying out great drainages are the best means to follow … Were a sufficient supply of seed provided, the population, exclusive of any parties employed by the Board of Works, especially females who are accustomed to work, would suffice to cultivate the land.'

Upper Leyny
RLFC 3/2/26/26

Saturday 20 February. Dean Hoare to William Stanley, enclosing a new subscription list amounting to £109, since 4 February (See Appendix 3E)
'The district comprises 97,000 acres and contains 30,000 inhabitants, of

whom two-thirds are in a state of destitution. We have 9 soup kitchens in operation and the cost of these, added to free tickets for meal to the infirm destitute, is £50 weekly. With a smaller expenditure we could not effect anything. Even this is insufficient for the necessities of so large and so poor a district. There is not a single landed proprietor or agent, or resident magistrate residing in the district ... all devolves on the resident clergy. We have on two several occasions, addressed a circular to all the landed proprietors, in number 38, and the valuation of their estates, £24,000 per annum. The result has been subscriptions to the moment, since last August, of £128. Of this sum, £20 (in addition to £30 last summer), was received from our late chairman, and £50 now reported from his widow for a soup kitchen on her property, while £10 (in addition to £20 last summer) from a gentleman whose property in the half barony does not amount to £50 p.a. Thus, from 36 landed proprietors, possessing estates to the value of £22,000 p.a., we have received only £68, nor do I see any hope of obtaining more.

The state of the district is fearful and I am apprehensive of being compelled to discontinue out-door relief, by which the lives of thousands have been saved, unless we receive a large grant in aid from the government. We have now only £5, in addition to £50 from Mrs Armstrong appropriated to a particular locality. We are to receive £100 from the General Relief Association in Dublin next week, but with this sum we cannot carry on our present relief beyond 6 March.

I write in haste, in the midst of interruptions, attending to the calls of a starving multitude by whom my house is continually surrounded.'

Saturday 20 February. Rev J. Garrett to Sir Randolph Routh, enclosing a list of subscriptions for Corran amounting to £80 and a grant of £30 was recommended (See Appendix 3C)   *Ballymote*
RLFC 3/2/26/18

'The boilers have not yet arrived ... 6 tons of oatmeal were given in gratuitous relief to starving poor famiies to save their lives.'

Saturday 20 February. Bewley and Pim to J. A. Holmes (See Appendix 6M)   *Coolavin*
SFFP 2/505/5

'We are directed to transmit thee £20 in fulfilment of grant and to express satisfaction at being informed of the efficiency of the soup establishment and confidence in all due exertions for its future maintenance.'

Monday 22 February. Lord Lieutenant to the Board of Works   *Foxford*
CSORP W.1874

'The Earl of Lucan informed me that the Foxford Relief Committee have placed on the public works' lists, 49 persons having upwards of 200 cows, 50 horses and asses, several sheep and a quantity of oats.'

Ballaghaderreen
SFFP 2/506/19

Monday 22 February. Denis Tighe PP to Society of Friends
'I had a letter this morning ... from that benevolent and truly charitable man, Laurence Gurney, London enclosing a draft for £10, his own personal subscription. He recommended me to write again to you. At his kind suggestion I do and respectfully request a share in your charities to feed the hungry who are dying around me in every direction.'

Achonry
SFFP 2/505/2

Monday 22 February. Bewley and Pim to Dean Hoare (See Appendix 6A)
'The Committee ... direct us to transmit to thee £20 as their third donation and we beg leave to express a hope that the times may not be far distant when more effectual means may be found of supporting extensive relief operations as the funds of a private relief association would hardly supply so long a demand from all the distressed districts.'

Costello barony
SFFP 2/505/5

Monday 22 February. William Todhunter, Society of Friends, to Charles Strickland
'The ton of rice was forwarded to thee on the 16th inst. by canal boat to Longford. The boiler we had not yet been able to set off.'

Ballina
SFFP 2/505/5

Wednesday 24 February. Bewley and Pim to Oliver C. Jackson JP
'The Committee directs us to acquaint thee that they expect to land in Ballina supplies of provisions now on the way from Liverpool in a steamer lent by the government for this service and will cheerfully appropriate a share for thy district, but some organization appears wanting, and we submit for thy consideration whether a committee of respectable inhabitants ought not to be formed and local subscriptions raised before obtaining assistance elsewhere.'

Straide
CSORP Z.2219

Wednesday 24 February. Memorial of housekeepers and widows to the Lord Lieutenant
'The regret on our hearts at present for not being able to afford sending our children to the Straide National School, is incomparably grievous and that in consequence of the scarcity of provision and having no means for their support or to pay the teacher for his attentive instruction. We ... implore your Excellency will not see the school closed for want of attendance and also that you will send some relief to be given weekly to the following persons who do deplore the idea of not having the youth educated.' *(See Appendix 1L)*

Ballymote
SFFP 2/505/5

Thursday 25 February. Bewley and Pim to Richard Gethen (See Appendix 6F)
'The Comittee are in receipt of thy letter on behalf of the Ballymote relief committee in reply to which we are directed to transmit thee £20 as a second donation to the district relief fund.'

Thursday 25 February. Archbishop MacHale to Archbishop Murray, Dublin, thanking him for £240 of the Roman money for distribution among the poor of Connacht through the bishops of that province.

Tuam
DDA MURRAY PAPERS

Friday 26 February. Jonathan Pim to Joseph C. Harvey, Sligo (See Appendix 6K)
'The application of Collooney respecting rice was not fully considered. How is the rice to be forwarded to Collooney? It would be well to make enquiry in Sligo as to the price of rice there. See the quality and let us know and we can make arrangements for having it delivered as you may wish.'

Collooney
SFFP 2/505/5

Friday 26 February. Bewley and Pim to John Coghlan PP. (See Appendix 6R)
'The Committee directed us to acquaint thee that they have made grants to Charles Strickland of Loughglynn to aid him in establishing soup shops in the barony of Costello and conclude that thy parish will have a share of it. They will nevertheless as a means of present relief have forwarded to the relief committee on behalf of which this application is made a half ton of rice if arrangements can be made for distributing it in a prepared or cooked state daily or three or four times in the week amongst the most destitute of the poor, especially those afflicted or threatened with dysentery.'
1 March. John Coghlan PP to Bewley and Pim (See Appendix 6R)
'I am honoured with your kind favor promising half a ton of rice provided I get it distributed in a prepared state to those numerous people affected in my unfortunate parish ... Ballina or Sligo would be the most convenient sea port to this mountainous district.'

Kilmovee
SFFP 2/505/5

SFFP 2/506/19

Saturday 27 February. Jonathan Pim to Joseph C. Harvey, P.O. Tubbercurry re Denis Tighe PP
'The writer of the enclosed (Denis Tighe PP) has been unremitting in begging from all quarters. He got £10 from Samuel Gurney. We wrote on the 4th in reply to his applications that we considered the district as included in that for which we made a grant of £100 to Charles Strickland. Please inquire about him as to respectability etc and the district. Is there any one else attending to it or is it under Strickland's care?'
27 February. W. Todhunter to J. C. Harvey
'I send you sundry letters received from Denis Tighe PP of Ballaghaderreen ... I fear from the – conduct of Tighe that he is not exactly the proper sort of person to entrust with funds to distribute assistance to the destitute ... We should take care not to allow parties to bully us out of money by much talking when it is really wrong to trust them and we must equally guard against a sanguine man as if he was too desirous of handling the money. Please return the four letters of Tighe's ... as soon as you are leaving Ballaghaderreen.'

Ballaghaderreen
SFFP 2/505/2

SFFP 2/505/5

4 March. Bewley and Pim to Denis Tighe PP
'A deputation from this Committee being in thy neighbourhood, their report was only received this morning. Although the Committee have already made arrangements with Charles Strickland ... for relief measures in the barony of Costello by establishing soup shops, for which they have provided boilers and £100 in money, which is perhaps a full proportion of their funds for one district, yet in consideration of the great destitution prevailing in this neighbourhood, they have resolved to place at thy disposal one ton of rice value £25.' *(See Appendix 6C)*

Ballina & Swinford
CSORP O.2295

Saturday 27 February. Poor Law Commission to T. N. Redington, enclosing bills from contractors who have supplied clothing for the inmates of Ballina and Swinford Unions. Ballina, £47 0s. 3d., Swinford, £84 7s. 6d., and requested another £100, in addition to the £100 already granted for Ballina workhouse for the ensuing week.

Ballina
CSORP Z.3356

Sunday 28 February. Robert Atkenson to T. N. Redington
'I have 120 acres within one and a half miles of Ballina ... It was set to small tenants but they have all fled and left the country, taking the rent due with them, which has deprived me of the means of farming it. I want to know if grants are available to improve my property and to give employment to the poor.'

Sligo
CSORP H.2235

Sunday 28 February. Report of Dr W. Colles
'There are few good streets but many horrid lanes with rows of most miserable cabins on each side. The lanes are very dirty, no attention being paid to the cleansing of them. The cabins also are small, dirty and wretched. The great scarcity of provisions and want of fuel has induced many to dispose of every article of furniture so that they have only the bare walls and a heap of bad straw and not more than one or two sods of turf constituting a fire.
The appearance of the people is most wretched. There are to be seen an immense number of squalid, thin, worn-out figures, half clad and many hardly able to walk. The children also, worn down almost to skeletons, look like withered old persons.
The failure of the potato crop drove a great number of poor from the country. These crowded the town, seeking food and employment. This want of provisions and the bad quality and scanty supply gave rise to a dysentery which appeared about September ... It has always a tendency to end in chronic diarrhoea, which is most obstinate and will wear out the patient from one to three months. The dysentery is contagious especially in the cabins where the morbid evacuations are allowed to remain and profound cleanli-

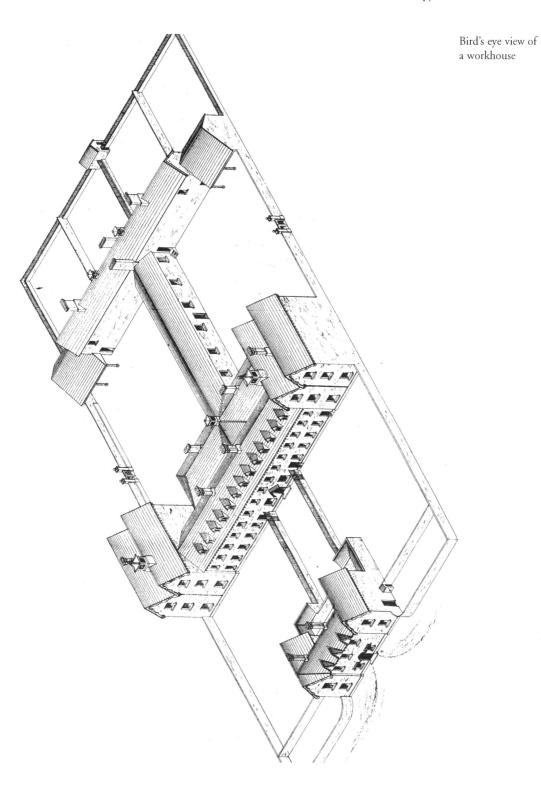

ness not attended to ... It cannot be cured without proper nourishment as medicine cannot supply the place of food ...

I next inspected the workhouse ... At each side of the boardroom are two large cesspools or reservoirs ... 2 feet large and 12 deep ... I have been told the affluence can be smelt a hundred yards off ... There are also two other similar cesspools at each side of the infirmary and one large one at the rear. All these are within the enclosure walls which must confine the unwholesome affluence from them. Behind the main building is the laundry with a small enclosed yard and a cesspool in the centre ...

Dormitories: The beds were placed on the floor (two and three often in each), thus preventing the free circulation of air round them. There were no close stools, the patients were obliged to pass their evacuations into a bucket which often remained all night in the room. There are no lights allowed and no fireplace to warm their drinks or assist ventilation, so that it was not to be wondered if the patients, especially the children, preferred passing their evacuations under them. The garrets, under the slates exposed to extremes of heat and cold, were low. In one ward of 24 beds there were 57 patients ... I cannot conclude this report without bearing testimony to the great anxiety shown by all persons whom I met to share in trouble or expense to relieve their suffering countrymen.'

CSORP H.2241

2 March. Travelling expenses of Dr Colles:
'I left Dublin on Sunday 21 February for Sligo and returned on Friday evening, 26 February, being employed five days and one night, besides one day making up the report. My travelling expenses owing to the hospitality of the Sligo gentry scarcely exceeded £5.'

Ballaghaderreen
CSORP W.3606

Monday 1 March. James Conlon, potter and tile maker, Crennane, to the Lord Lieutenant
'I took a holding of ground from Charles Strickland, made a boundary fence and drained it and possessed it for two and a half years and paid two years' rent ... 14 September 1846, Mr Strickland sent the bailiff who seized the effects, served notice for me to quit on 1 May 1847 and stripped my workshop of shelves and racks and left me unable to earn 6d. a day at my trade ... I went to Mr Strickland and asked him to put my son on the public works and myself as steward but he refused in order that I and my family might starve and perish. My son has read arithmetic, algebra, Euclid and mensuration.'

Carbury
Correspondence p. 181

Tuesday 2 March. Capt O'Brien to Col Jones
'Having proceeded to Sligo ... I became aware that great destitution existed ... especially in the barony of Carbury. I therefore acceded to the desire of

Sir Robert Gore Booth, that I should personally satisfy myself by inspection of the exact state of affairs there. The first place I visited was a wretched hamlet of three cottages containing three families, numbering in all 32 persons, belonging to three brothers, the whole having lived on 12 acres of land ... Last year they thought themselves so well off, they refused to take £60 to give up the lease and depart. Now they are starving. One of the brothers and three others of the families had died during the previous week. The widow was lying on the ground in fever, and unable to move. The children were bloated in their faces and bodies, their limbs were withered to bones and sinews, with rags on them which scarcely preserved decency, and assuredly afforded no protection from the weather. They had been found that day, gnawing the flesh from the bones of a pig which had died in an out-house ... On 27 February, Sir Robert Booth took me to a place called the "Sands" on the north shore of Sligo Bay ... contains 60 huts ... with a population of five to each hut ... With Sir R. Booth, I went into five of these huts. In the first, into which I crawled with difficulty, lay a coffin holding the owner's wife, who had died three days before, of want. The owner stood near the door, having come from the public works (where he had been earning 8d. per day) to see to burying his wife, and he told us he was about to depart "to dig a hole to put her in, and try to get a couple of men from the works to help him carry her there". A skeleton of a living child was in a cradle, in a corner near the fire. A woman, a neighbour, was sitting by it and rocking the cradle, and said it would be dead before morning, and added (truly!) "It would be better if we were all dead". The child's cradle and a broken table, comprised the entire furniture.

The door of the second hut we came to, was shut. We called and knocked. A voice answered from within. The door gradually opened, and out of this hole, appeared the head of a man ... His face and lips were colourless. His entire clothing consisted of a dirty coarse shirt, in shreds. When he saw us, he called out "Send for the priest to me; I will be gone before morning; I am dying of the starvation." ... Sir Robert Gore Booth asked him if he had any one to send to the meal depot, which was two miles distant. He called a little girl from the hut, but when Sir Robert was giving her directions where to obtain a half a stone of meal, the man cried out, "Can you give any bread, I will be dead before the meal comes, give me bread now; there is a shop not a mile off; give me a bit of bread now." I doubt that he is now alive.

From the door of the third hut, which we stopped at, came a tall strongly made man, followed by a woman with a child in her arms, and two little girls. The child in arms was evidently dying. I asked the man had he been at work. He showed me his feet, and asked how any man could work with feet in that state; they were so swelled the skin appeared ready to burst ... he could not have moved a step on the hard road. He had within the previous week buried his mother and his sister.

Into the fourth hut we came to, we crawled backwards on our hands and knees. On a bedstead with a little straw over it lay a man covered only by an old quilt; his face was so swollen his eyes were scarcely to be perceived; his feet and ankles also much swelled; his knees and thighs, which he showed, wasted to the bone ... His wife was cowering over an iron pot, suspended above a turf fire, with a young child in her arms. Three other children were sitting about, and a young man was preparing a fishing line ... The mother held up the infant, bared its body, and discovered to us its little bones almost starting through the skin ... The young man said he was going out to fish in the morning, as he hoped to do more in that way, to "stop the starvation", than he could by earning 8d. a day on the public works. I asked what was in the iron pot; the woman answered that it was barley she had begged in the morning. She stirred up the liquor with a ladle; we could see no barley, save a grain or two; the liquor was not more nourishing than so much hot water. The fifth hut was on the verge of the sands ... There was evidence that things here had been better at no very distant period; the dresser, and a few odds and ends of crockery, were clean ... The family were eight in number ... The mother was lying on the ground huddled near the fire, attenuated and moaning. Two lads of the ages of 16 and 18 in a bed, where they had been for two days, not able to go to the public works, upon which they had been previously earning 6d. each; and they presented in their thin limbs, swelled and yellow faces, and sunken eyes, the unquestionable effects of famine. The only healthy person of the family was a daughter, probably 22 years old. She told us she had been on the public works earning 6d. a day; but as that was nothing among so many, she thought it better to stay at home and mind the sick in the house ...

Sir Robert Booth's estate is large, and the supplies he has procured would keep those of his own well enough, were he not pressed also to feed his neighbours' tenants. At his own place, Lissadell, he has established two soup boilers ... He gives gratuitously 280 gallons of this soup per day, every day including Sundays. He sells, six days in the week, 150 loaves per day ... and 30 tons of Indian corn per week ...

In the baronies I have alluded to, the people are dying from starvation by dozens daily ... Many cannot crawl to the public works, much less do anything when there ... In the neighbourhood of the poorhouse they come to die in order that they may receive a decent burial. Typhus fever and dysentery have added to their horrors ... There were in the Sligo poorhouse on 24 February, 208 cases of fever and 145 of dysentery. The master of the poorhouse and his four sons, the matron and her daughter, the schoolmaster and his assistant were among them; eleven had died the previous night; the matron is since dead.'

Wednesday 3 March. William Bennett's account of his journey in Ireland
'We left Dublin on the 12th by day coach for Boyle ... From Boyle we took a car across the county to Ballina. The shores of Lough Gara are wild and dreary and the whole district increasingly so on approaching the small town of Tubbercurry. Here we first encountered the public works so-called ... It was melancholy in the extreme to see the women and girls labouring in mixed gangs on the public roads. They were employed not only in digging with the spade and with the pick, but also in carrying loads of earth and turf on their backs and wheeling barrows like men and breaking stones, while the poor neglected children were crouched in groups, about the bits of lighted turf in the various sheltered corners along the line.'

Tubbercurry
Transactions p. 161

Wednesday 3 March. Memorial of the Swinford Relief Committee to the Lord Lieutenant (See Appendix 3K)
'This district has been hitherto most unfairly dealt with and deprived of its due proportion of the relief given to the country generally. Altho' there is not one district where destitution prevailed to a greater extent and consequently where employment was more required, yet up to the present moment, instead of one in five, the number allowed by the Board of Works, not more than one in six or one in seven of the destitute have procured employment. At the last Extraordinary Sessions for this barony held on the 17th ult. large sums, sufficient to allow of the required extended employment, were grant-ed; and resolutions were adopted, that in consequence of the hourly increase to the numbers of the destitute and in consequence of the enormous rise in the price of provisions, it was absolutely indispensible to give, in future, employment to one in four of the population. Nevertheless, instead of this extended employment being given, which had been hitherto afforded, it has been restricted. Some of the works, for the completion of which sums had been granted at these Sessions, have been altogether suspended. The most frivolous and vexatious delays and impediments are thrown in the way of the relief committee by the officers of the Board of Works: for instance when heads of families, named in the lists, are prevented from illness from attend-ing to the role, no other member of the same family will be permitted to take their place, without a transfer of names and a reference to the inspecting offi-cer in Castlebar, which frequently caused a fortnight's delay. From all these causes the most intense suffering has been produced and very many deaths have occurred which might have been avoided and prevented, if the measures provided for relief were made available.'

Swinford
DP 4276

Report of H. Brett, county surveyor, 24 March, re above:
'I have just completed arrangements with the inspecting officer of this district (Capt Wellesley) for the immediate resumption of all the works suspended in the locality ... with reference to an extension of employment I cannot recommend any such step to be taken, when the new meaures of relief are likely to be soon in operation.'

RLFC 3/2/21/42   *4 March. Bernard Durcan PP and Ulic Burke MD to the Commissary General*
'The totally exhausted state of the resources of this most densely populated and most distressed district, and the entire absence of every proprietor who could afford us the slightest possible local assistance ... We request £180 for the soup kitchen on which the lives of thousands will have to depend ... and boilers to be sent with all possible dispatch.'

Kiltimagh   *Thursday 4 March. Letter to the editor of the Mayo Telegraph signed 'a Kiltimagh man'*
'In the village of Treenagleragh ... all the oats belonging to three of the most destitute in the parish have been seized and canted by his lordship's (Lord Lucan) driver and subsequently ejectment decrees have been obtained against them at the last Ballina sessions ... They petitioned him personally to leave them their small quantity of oats, their only means of subsistence, and that they would cheerfully give up their holdings ... It was by his lordship's special directions the notices to quit were served on those parties ... The persons thus treated are Anthony Durcan, John Kelly and Widow Kilgallin. Again, what think you of the time that had been fixed for exacting the last November rent? During the late frost, deep snow and storm!
There is one circumstance that should not be overlooked. A poor man named Pat Jennings, whose abject poverty and almost roofless cabin are beyond description, is confined to his bed of death from the brutal treatment he received from the iron-hearted driver of his lordship, when seizing for the November rent about one-half hundred of meal and about the same quantity of oats, the only property he possessed in the world and which of course had been as dear to him as life, and in his struggle to save the above little property from the grasp of this driver, he was knocked down and left almost dead by this worthy official with the butt-end of an old rusty bayonet that is almost worn out in the service.
In this parish on another property quite contiguous are to be found the traces of sorrow and affliction, accompanied by the widows' cries and orphans' tears, and poor labourers with long families are to be seen actually obliged to work at 6d. per day, without support, 5d. of which they must pay for one quart of meal ... Such as endeavour to make up the rents are treated with barbarian cruelty by a certain excoriating agent not living many miles from

Castlebar, whose serpentine temper is proverbial. But in justice I must acknowledge there are some landlords whose sympathy for the starving poor cannot be exceeded.'

Friday 5 March. Memorial of Relief Committee to the Lord Lieutenant (See Appendix 2G)

Kilkelly
DP 4225

'The holdings of the tenantry in the district varies from 2 to 5 acres. The number of householders is about 3,696. At least one sixth of the entire population are cottier tenants without any land, whose only support was derived from conacre potatoes and casual day's labour in spring and harvest. Unless the entire cottier tenants are left on the public works and a proportionate number of those having lands, they must perish by thousands. The time they will take to make their tillage will be about a fortnight or three weeks ... This poor mountainous district, comprising the parishes of Kilmovee, Kilbeagh West and Aghamore, is different from other counties where holdings are large. Unless the people are supplied with seed, they will be utterly unable to till their lands ... The entire people are most anxious and willing to make a larger tillage than ever, if they had the means.'

Friday 5 March. Captain O'Brien to Mr Walker, re Jobbing on Public Works article in Morning Chronicle, 24 February, 1847

Sligo
Correspondence
pp. 184-6

'It is quite true that among them (pay-clerks) are to be found the sons of a clergyman, of a magistrate, and possibly of a grand juror; but it must be remembered that a heavy pecuniary is attached to the situation of pay-clerk, and in every case two securities are required, each in the sum of £400 ... They must also have a knowledge of accounts. Hence a certain extent of education is necessary ... Whereas their toil is considerable while their wages is comparatively small ... For this toil the pay is £2 per week ... The sons of a clergyman are the two Mr Yeates ... Mr Whelan is the son of a stipendary magistrate ... Mr Neynoe is the second son of Mr Neynoe of Castle Neynoe, who I believe has been on the grand jury of Sligo ... Among the remainder are gentlemen who hold and cultivate land and there are two officers of the militia ... The appended list of pay-clerks shows the districts to which they belong, the dates of their appointments and the times when they commence and finish their weekly payments.

Coolavin, William A. Sherlock, 19 December, 1846, commences his payments on Monday ... finishes on Thursday. On Saturday goes to Sligo, 22 miles, for cash.

James Elwood, 15 December, 1846, commences his payments on Monday ... finishes on Thursday.

Corran, Richard Fleming, 28 November, 1846, commences his payments on

Thursday ... finishes on Tuesday.

Abraham Motherwell, 26 August 1846, commences his payments on Friday, finishes ... on Tuesday.

Thomas McDermott, 15 January 1847, for two weeks commenced payments on Saturday, having balances on hand, and terminated on Thursday.

Leyny, L, Pilsworth Whelan, 17 December 1846, commences his payments on Monday ... finishes on Thursday.

Leyny U, Martin Cochran, 23 December 1846.

Charles O'Connor, 17 November 1846.

Ballina
SFFP 2/506/19

Monday 8 March. Hugh Conway ADM to Wm Todhunter, Society of Friends

'Three days previous to the receipt of your very kind and consoling letter of the 20th ult. I was taken very ill of a severe cold or influenza brought on by over exertion and mental anxiety ... This is the second attack which I had since your visit to Ballina. I took to bed with but little hopes or even a desire of recovery. My slight hopes of recovering were principally influenced by a foreboding that I was called to follow my most worthy and esteemed colleague, (Rev) Mr Kinkaid, who shortly before died of a fever, and whose death considerably increased my difficulties. While I welcomed death as a happy release from the difficulties before me, but your very consoling letter considerably altered those feelings and made me desire to see your benevolent exertions give comfort in their affliction to my most miserable people. The condition of our people in town and also of those in the country has been every day getting worse since you have been amongst us. Sickness, added to their other miseries, has rendered their condition no longer tolerable and is now hastening them in scores to the grave. The number of deaths in this parish for the last 6 weeks is about 22 per day. It is true that starvation did not strike the deathblow in all those cases but in all of them it was the principal agent and brought dysentery, fever or some other of the multiplicity of sicknesses, with which the people are afflicted, to its aid only to strike the death blow. It may be a matter of surprise with many why misery should be accumulating in spite of all exertions to allay it. The cause is the people are not supplied with food nor with means to purchase it. They have sold every article of dress, furniture and every other earthly source of comfort which they might possess to get food, and now the want of all of them combined with the sicknesses that have been generally influenced by their miseries, will desolate the country if not speedily and plentifully supplied. Hitherto the people in the country had some little grain crop and while that lasted they never refused assistance to those in distress. This was a constant relief to the misery of the town. But now the grain has disappeared, I may say, entirely from the country, the cows, the sheep, the horses and asses are

rapidly disappearing with it, and everything seems now thrown into the cru-
cible to be melted into food. The poor of the town thus left to the abundance
of their own misery, the streets and thoroughfares of the town are not now so
crowded with beggars as at the time you were here. Yet you meet with a sufficient number of them to mark the progress of misery. But enter the camp
of misery, enter their wretched dwellings and there you find them stretched
in sickness and in want, unable to move. Agricultural pursuits are now lost
sight of and employment on the public works is looked to as the only means
of relief. Those public works as managed here, instead of being a relief, have
been in very many cases a most potent engine of death owing to the competition for employment and to the limited extent to which employment had
been given. Only one person in a family, no matter how numerous, could be
employed. His wages seldom exceeded 3s. 6d. in the week and when the
worth of it in provisions, now so very dear, was divided among 7 or 8, often
10 in family for a week, the share of the earner was very little. Yet he strug-
gled a while at the work until labour and weakness overpowered him and
sunk him to the grave. Thus are affected very many of the deaths that are
dayly occurring. You may easily infer how much the want of clothes and of
every other earthly comfort may contribute to the work of death. But as facts
speak more forcibly than words I will mention what I one day witnessed in
a part of this town, and from it you may infer the misery of the entire.
Mr Crosfield of Liverpool sent 10 bags of rice for the relief of the poor of
Ballina and by an order of Mr Forster it was placed at the disposal of the Rev
Messrs Kinkaid, Armstrong and myself. Mr Armstrong and I divided the rice
into two parts, and also divided the town, leaving one half to be attended by
each in order to facilitate the distribution and to prevent imposition. As so
small a quantity would give but little relief amid so much destitution, we
intended to give it only to those who were sick in dysentery, and for the purpose of ascertaining who were sick I commenced to make a visit of enquiry.
In the first street that I visited, called Bohernasop, and which consists of
about 147 houses and contains double that number of families, there were
only 34 houses in which I did not find from one to five persons sick, all of
them of dysentery. Among the sick I found 47 families consisting of 183 individuals, and of those there were only 18 persons able to leave their houses to
seek relief for the rest. The amount of comfort and furniture which they
seemed to possess was as follows: five wooden boxes, which in better days
answered for a keeping place for clothes, but in one of them I found on that
day a dead child put there to screen it from the view of its dying mother,
about twenty small iron pots some of them broken, 13 bed rugs and occasionally some small articles of delph such as a cup, a broken plate or mug to
drink water out of. Generally speaking each family had a tin can to convey

soup from the soup kitchen. There they lay, each family grouped together on a little dirty straw on the earthen floors of their cabins, without bed or bed clothes, without fire or food or anything to sustain life.The filth and wretchedness, which the peculiar nature of their sickness added to their misery, rendered their condition indescribably wretched. Suffice it to say that I, though now familiar with poverty and misery in its most appalling features, cannot forget the scenes which I witnessed on that day. I made this visit during the fall of snow that was about three weeks ago, and when I still think of the snow falling though the broken roofs and smoke holes or the pale and withered countenances of those poor victims of misery and sickness, I cannot but extol the provision that had saved many of them from death. It took me three days to complete my visit and from beginning to end it was mostly a repetition of the same scenes. Such is the condition of our people here at present and from appearances I omen still worse for the future.

The landlords have flattered their tenants in the early part of the year to sell their grain to pay a half year's rent, promising to forgive the other half on condition of such payment being made. But no sooner has the half year's rent been paid, processes were served for all outstanding arrears. The tenants, in order to escape the execution of the decrees obtained against them are flying from the country. Such of them as can are going to America, and such as cannot are going to England or flocking into this town. Thus notwithstanding the great drain on our people by death, yet the population in town is rapidly on the increase. The lands by those means are left untilled, for the landlords are unwilling to purchase seed and the tenants who remained on the lands are unable to procure it and in this position of affairs there is no preparation making, nor disposition shewn by either party to cultivate the land. What then is to become of the country next year? Add to this fever of a most malignant character is now beginning to shew itself here. 73 cases of fever have taken place in the Ballina workhouse within the last 8 days. Therefore when some of those strangers now flocking to the town, and on whom those long resident in the town look with a jealous eye as intruders on the charity intended for their own relief, when, I say, those strangers take their disease, and, as it is to be feared, die of it, their neighbours both from a fear of the disease and a want of sympathy for them, will not go near them, until they become decomposed, and generate a plague which might soon depopulate the country. Those considerations caused me to make a resolution for the formation of a board of health, but those possessing influence and character in the place are taken up with their thoughts about their present difficulties, that they have lost all sight of the future, and have contented themselves with merely adopting the resolution. Such are the prospects before us.

Dear Sir, you have been kind enough to ask my opinion about the clothing of the poor as one of the most important branches of your extensive relief. I think nothing can be more desirable at present as the government have made some provision for the feeding of the poor. The description of clothes most required are warm and strong trousers and loose jackets for the men, petticoats and wrappers for the women, and shoes especially for the old men, for many of them have died with swollen legs and inflated countenances from the cold caught from want of shoes. The fact is, all ages among the poorer classes now require clothes, for the miserable rags that they have on them are now rapidly melting away under the influence of wear and tear and age and weather, for they serve them as bed clothes by night and dress by day. But of all descriptions of clothes there is none more required than bed clothes. If a strong description of ticking to keep warm, strong sheeting, a blanket and rug could be had for those who are now obliged to sleep in their rags on the floor on some dirty straw, it would contribute exceedingly to their comfort, and by contributing to the cleanliness of their persons would prevent the otherwise rapid spread of disease.'

Monday 8 March. Bewley and Pim to Rev E. A. Lucas (See Appendix 6K)
'The Committee has directed us to transmit thee £20 as a donation to the fund for the establishment and maintenance of a soup shop and we would recommend an application to the government for further assistance.'

Collooney
SFFP 2/505/5

Monday 8 March. Bewley and Pim to Henry Joseph McCarrick (See Appendix 6B)
'The Committee has directed us to transmit thee £10 to enable thee to purchase half a ton of Indian meal to be distributed in small portions from time to time amongst the most destitute of the poor.'

Aclare
SFFP 2/505/5

Tuesday 9 March. List of inspecting officers nominated by the Relief Commissioners, including Capt W. E. D. Broughton, Richard Bourke, Lieut William Hamilton, James Auchmuty, Capt R. P. Farren, Capt A. E. Burmester, Capt J. Gilbert

Dublin
CSORP Z.3551

Wednesday 10 March. Dean Hoare to William Stanley, enclosing a new list of subscriptions since 20 February, amounting to £109, for which a grant of £109 was recommended (See Appendix 3E)
'Certain portions of the contributions included on this list being appropriated by the desire of the donors to particular localities, the general fund of the committee is nearly exhausted. The district contains a population of about 27,000 inhabitants of whom about 20,000 are in a state of destitution. There are 9 soup kitchens in operation and if funds allow we hope to set up 3 more.'

Upper Leyny
RLFC 3/2/26/26

Boyle
SFFP 2/506/19

Wednesday 10 March. Emily Irwin to Society of Friends
'There is nothing else to be found in Boyle in any considerable quantity but oatmeal or Indian meal, which the poor find does not agree with them. It comes in casks and is not freshly ground, but the rice they begin to appreciate and like very much … I fear the same would discourage ourselves in endeavouring to assist them did we not know that He, who has in righteous judgement sent this calamity, can in mercy cause it to work for His own glory and the salvation of souls. Many now send their children to our school and would gladly have the gospel preached, who before could not be persuaded to do so.'

Charlestown
SFFP 2/506/34

Thursday 11 March. Michael Muldowney CC to Miss Anne Forster, Ladies Society, London
'The destitution in the parish of Kilbeagh of which, owing to the serious indisposition of the parish priest, I am administrator, is so great and universal that unless such charitable society as yours come to their immediate relief my poor starving population amounting to 4,580 human beings must perish of inanition. Fever and dysentery are committing frightful ravages amongst them. Each day the deaths average from two to three.'

Templehouse
SFFP 2/506/19

Thursday 11 March. Rev Henry Perceval to Society of Friends
'The boiler of the soup kitchen at Templehouse … contained about a hogshead and a half. This is filled three times a week and given gratuitously to the poorest people of the neighbourhood. In addition to the 7lbs of food given away each week at Templehouse, we have lately commenced giving a dinner of cooked rice every day to all the children at our male and female schools which amount to upwards of 100 and this number is likely to increase considerably.'

RLFC 3/2/26/27

12 March. Colonel Perceval to Sir Randolph Routh, enclosing a subscription list, amounting to £235 7s. from the Templehouse Relief Committee (See Appendix 3L)
'Exclusive of the purposes to which this money is applied, Col. Perceval has been for months supplying upwards of 45 families with soup in considerable quantities three times a week. He has also kept a depot here and in a second locality six miles off, since the close of the last session of parliament, where all kinds of bread stuffs have been supplied at wholesale prices, independant of other means of relief.'

Swinford
DP 4878

Friday 12 March. Bernard Durcan PP to T. N. Redington
'… melancholy and deplorable state to which the people in this district are reduced in consequence of the sudden and unexpected suspension of the works. No less than nine of them have been suspended in the parishes of

Kilconduff and Meelick. The local engineer informs me that several others
are to be suspended in a few days. Thus 860 persons, representing nearly as
many families, almost all of whom depended wholly on their wages for subsistence, are thrown out of employment at once, without any previous provision being made for their relief otherwise. For all those works large additional sums were granted at the last Extraordinary Sessions held in Swinford
on 17 February. The people are allowed to starve because the legal means provided for their relief will not be applied by those whose duty it is to apply
them. If after the new measure comes into operation the labourers were to be
withdrawn gradually as recommended in the Treasury Minute, it would be
fair enough, but hitherto no arrangements have been made to put that measure into operation and the people are turned off en masse to perish of
hunger. Yes, the people are perishing and unless prompt steps be taken to
remedy this evil and the works be forthwith resumed, thousands must
inevitably die of want and a heavy responsibility will rest on those who could
and ought to avert that calamity.'

Sunday 14 March. Rev J. Garrett to Sir Randolph Routh
'The boilers have not arrived except one from the Irish Association ... The
intention is to boil every day 80 pounds of beef at 4d. a pound, 3 stone of
oatmeal at 3. 6d. per cwt and 2 stone of wheat? meal at 2s.'

Ballymote
RLFC 3/2/26/18

Monday 15 March. John Coghlan PP to the Lord Lieutenant
'On this day orders were sent by the assistant engineer of this district to the
men to sit idle and starve as a necessary consequence. In the west end of my
ill-fated parish, Kilmovee, 523 individuals living solely by the wages which
they earned on the public works. In the name of the living God, I entreat
your Excellency to direct their officer to allow the above number resume their
works or substitute for the men their wives and children. If not, they of
necessity perish. It would be a blessing to suspend the works, provided the
people were allowed subsistence while cultivating their little holdings ... The
holdings of my unfortunate poor famine-stricken parishioners vary from 2 to
5 acres. Of course their small farms do not require that time to cultivate,
which other larger farm districts stand in need of ... From my intimate
knowledge of their dire destitution even while working, unless your
Excellency will order at once the resumption of the several works ... the
entire of that great number will be found among the dead before many days.
They are perfectly destitute, without money or value or food or seed of any
kind, unless that, I think, one-tenth of them may have snatched from famine
a few stones of seed oats. I earnestly implore your Excellency, in the name of
the Great Giver of goodness, to direct that either wages or food be provided

Kilmovee
DP 4912

for them while preparing their little holdings. Their landlords have done nothing for them, nor is there any appearance of their assisting them with either food or spring seeds. Their only recourse is to fly to me for succour. My only hope of relieving them is an appeal to your Excellency's humane benevolent interposition.'

Tubbercurry
CSORP Z.3819

Monday 15 March. Dean Hoare to William Stanley
'The Upper Leyny Relief Committee has been dispensing soup since the first week of January and I have no doubt many lives have been saved by this means. We are anxious for the new relief measures to come into operation, as we find it impossible to raise funds to meet the demand for relief. We have no boilers and are in great need of them. It is better to commence with as large pots as we could procure, without waiting, like another committee of which I am a member, have done to this day, while the poor are perishing of famine.'

15 March. Upper Leyny Relief Committee to the Lord Lieutenant (See Appendix 21)
'We pledge ourselves to exert all our influence with the peasantry, to urge them to use every exertion, by cultivation and sowing of the land, to secure the country, with the blessing of providence, against a recurrence of famine in the ensuing year ... We find a disposition on the part of the tenants to sow their land if they had the seed required for that purpose and in all cases where the landlord has provided seed for their poorer tenants, to be paid for at next harvest, the people are busily employed cultivating the land and sowing the seed ... With some exceptions, landlords are not supplying seed, including those possessing the largest estates. Neither have they contributed to the funds of this committee, which are expended in saving from starvation the poor on the estates of non-subscribing landlords.'

Ballinrobe
CSORP O.3895

Wednesday 17 March. Rev James Anderson, vicar, to the Under-Secretary
'The master and clerk of the workhouse lie dead. The lives of the doctor and matron are in the balance. For God's sake, dispatch from Dublin proper persons to take charge, by tomorrow's night mail. Things are in an awful state and we are all overwhelmed. For myself, I am quite prostrated as to strength.'
Thursday, 18 March, same to same:
'The doctor of the workhouse died. There are upwards of 700 inmates, all more or less ill with dysentery, themselves under no control and 5 cwt of meal in the house. For God's sake, send proper persons to take charge, medical men etc, and give us means for the support of the house.'

Coolaney
OP 26/117

Thursday 18 March. G. Knox RM to the Under-Secretary
'The Coolaney Relief Committee have got threatening letters (signed Molly

Maguire), ordering them to turn certain persons off the public works and place on them a great number from each family ... We have 5,000 men and plenty of ball and powder ... Coolaney Relief Committee treated the matter with great contempt.'

Thursday 18 March. Bernard Durcan PP to T. N. Redington   *Swinford*
'If the works ... are not resumed and the people employed until the new   DP 4963
measures come into operation, it is my firm conviction that a vast portion of
the people must inevitably perish, who would otherwise be saved. I cannot
understand why the general rule should not be observed in this district.
There is an order for reducing the men on the work generally 20%. But here
they are all turned off en masse ... More are to be stopped immediately.
About 1,100 men are already turned off in the two parishes (Kilconduff and
Meelick). A great number are idle a whole month. The country is in a dreadful state in consequence. It has prevented numbers from tilling their holdings, having been obliged to consume the seed they had reserved for that purpose, in consequence of being deprived of every other source of sustainment.'

18 March. William Forster, Society of Friends, to Bewley and Pim   SFFP 2/506/19
'I wish to submit to your prompt attention the case of the very destitute population of the towns of Swinford and Foxford ... that a supply of meal, rice
and biscuit be sent to both places. I should be inclined to deal liberally, perhaps as much so as in any other grant ... I should think you could not do
better than communicate with Dr Burke, Swinford and – Mostyn, curate at
Foxford. I made a grant of a ton of meal at Swinford to meet the heavy pressure of their present exigency, which in consequence of the many persons
thrown out of work, by the suspension of certain lines of roads, was at that
time very great. It is more than probable that by this time that supply is nearly
if not entirely consumed and tho' it is possible their soup kitchen may be in
operation, it will be far from affording adequate relief.'

Bewley and Pim to Ulic Burke MD and Rev G. H. Mostyn re above, 20 March   SFFP 2/505/5
(See Appendices 6N&V)
'We now enclose the accompanying order upon our friends, Hugh Gallagher
and Co, merchants, Ballina for the following provisions viz. 10 barrels of
Indian meal, 10 bags of peas, and half a ton of biscuit, value £46' (for
Swinford and similarly for Foxford).

G. H. Mostyn to Bewley and Pim. 24 March: SFFP 2/506/34
'Your kind order reached me on 21st and yesterday I got from Gallagher's of
Ballina 10 barrels of Indian meal, 10 bags of peas and half a ton of biscuit.
Our committee met this day and adopted rules for its distribution. Each
member has his district to be visited tomorrow. The aged and infirm get help
three days a week gratis ... Anyone able to gather limestones should do so.

When burned into lime their houses should be well whitewashed, plastered and floored with mortar. Can you give me any aid in money towards making the houses of the poor clean and comfortable as this prevents the spread of disease?'

Coolavin
SFFP 2/506/19

Thursday 18 March. J. A. Holmes to Society of Friends (See Appendix 6M)
'I purchased in Liverpool one ton of rice to be distributed in a cooked state … The amount is now due and I would feel exceedingly grateful by a remittance for the amount … I have already reported to the Committee the great benefit the poor people have received from this donation. Dysentery is still making awful havoc among them … The stinted allowance of food … is now thinning the population in this district and deaths are daily increasing.'

SFFP 2/505/6

25 March. Bewley and Pim to J. A. Holmes:
'We are directed to transmit thee £28 19s. 9d. to pay for the rice and £10 for the relief of the exigencies of the present time … We hope that the gentry of the neighbourhood will come foward liberally to assist the poor who may be discharged from the public works and who consequently may suffer great distress … We authorise the purcase of another ton of rice at Liverpool or Sligo.'

RLFC 3/2/26/15

19 March. J. A. Holmes to William Stanley
'We need two soup boilers, each holding 150 gallons. There are two already in operation, supplied by private individuals but they are far too small for the demand.'

DP 8104

20 March. Commissariat Relief Office to T. N. Redington, informing him that a subscription list for £137 0s. 6d. was received from Coolavin and recommending a grant of £137 (See Appendix 3B)

Tubbercurry
RLFC 3/2/26/26

Saturday 20 March. Dean Hoare to Sir Randolph Routh, enclosing a resolution of Upper Leyny Relief Committee
'The funds at the disposal of this committee (inclusive of grants expected from the government and promised subscriptions) do not exceed £40, in addition to provisions to the value of £100, granted by the British Relief Association … We solicit extraordinary aid to enable us to continue the measures of relief which we have been carrying on for the last three months, until the new relief measures shall have come into operation … as our funds are so much reduced … that we have not means to carry on those measures of relief for more than a fortnight hence, viz. to 3 April.'
Hoare writes:
'The circumstances of this case are very pressing, inasmuch as the district … is, at the same time, the most extensive and poorest and the most neglected by proprietors, of any in this county. There is no resident proprietor and only one landlord has any representative residing in the district – a family doing

much good in the neighbourhood. The proprietors of upwards of one half of the district have refused to contribute towards the relief of the existing distress ... Our expenditure since Christmas, when out-door relief was first allowed, has been £640. The district ... contains upwards of 28,000 inhabitants, of whom at least two-thirds are in a state of destitution. For the supporting of 9 soup kitchens a weekly sum of £30 is required ... We feel apprehensive that the new relief measures will not come into operation for 3 or 4 weeks; and in the meanwhile, not only are 20% to be struck off the public works, but the assistant engineer has this day received an order from the county surveyor to suspend all the works, upon which the money sanctioned has been expended; and the results will be ... that nearly 4,000 (out of 5,000) labourers will be thrown out of employment next week. It is fearful to think of the destitution which these measures will cause and what maybe the consequences ... I trust that you will recommend to the Lord Lieutenant that a grant be made not only £47 in aid of the list enclosed, but also a grant of £210 in consideration of the grants received from Relief Associations.' *(See Appendix 3E)*

Tuesday 23 March. Thomas Mulcheen, Redford, to Lord Lieutenant
'I have 7 in family, 5 of them females, the eldest 19 and the youngest 8, without one pound of food or a four-footed beast, with one and a half acres of bog and moury land. In the past I maintained my family by the benefit of a public school. Now my school is diminished. My priest, E. Coyne PP Annagh, sent for two tickets for my family but by fraud of the local clerks or mischance, we got none ... Lord Lieutenant should order Mr Bell, public works' officer in Ballyhaunis, to examine my case.'

Ballyhaunis
CSORP Z.4104

Tuesday 23 March. N. J. Browne, Bakens, to T. N. Redington
'It was reported maliciously through the parish that it is due to me writing to the government that people have been struck off the roads and armed gangs have been going about, swearing the people not to vote for me as Poor Law Guardian, as I opposed Mr Bourke, the other candidate on the relief committee, to get the government to raise the wages to 2s. a day ... I never attended a relief committee ... I have no tenants, I graze my land with 100 to 150 black cattle, and the same number of sheep. I also hold a grass farm in the parish from Sir Roger Palmer. On Sunday night two of my bullocks were killed, the flesh carried off and the skins left. The government should make the parish or townlands liable for these thefts. I give more employment than all the parish put together and pay my men in cash every week ... The labour bill is frequently above £5 a week. I have no conacres, receive no duty work or presents ... I have no tenants to persecute or eject.'

Castlebar
CSORP W.4408

Boyle
MACDERMOT PAPERS,
COOLAVIN

Wednesday 24 March. Julia MacDermot to her brother Edward MD, Bath, Somerset

'Revd Mr Tucker called here for the purpose of telling Mamma that his brother, Doctor Tucker of Castlerea, intends very shortly to leave for America: he has not as yet told any person except his brother of his determination. Revd Mr T. wishes you should at once be made aware of the vacancy, and also of the yearly income Doctor Tucker had that you might judge for yourself whether you would come in his place before another takes possession. For the workhouse he has £80 yearly. His salary was doubled lately as there are at present in the house twelve hundred, all or nearly all, in fever etc. For the Loughglynn dispensary he has £70 ...

Poor Toby Peyton died of fever, he has left thirteen children. The MacDermot Roe is dead, he is much regretted, he also died of fever ... Mr Robertson of the Abbey is dead. Mrs Irwin of Rushfield ditto and of fever. There is not a day in which we do not hear of the departure of some one whose face at least we knew. If you look at a newspaper you will see the state of poor dear Ireland. The poor are dying in hundreds. The Protestants are fasting today and praying that the famine may in the mercy of the Almighty be averted. For the same purpose we had public prayers on three days last week. I would like to know what they think of fasting. The last they had was at the time of the cholera. One good has been derived from the famine which is most remarkable in this Orange town, the Catholics and Protestants are so united.

Harry Jordan of Roslevin Castle is dead. My obituary of eminent persons recently deceased is coming to a close. I have only to mention Miss Cranston, sister of the attorney, Mrs O'Malley of Newcastle, Co Mayo, and dear little Vicky, the favourite of poor Uncle Hugh. Aunt Jane was in a great grief at her death. Unless I wished to give a very short letter I could not avoid the list of the dead as there is nothing of a gay nature spoken of. Not one here married since the potatoes failed except Mr Conmee of Kingsland ...

I can only hear the ticking of the clock and the music of my pen as Mamma is asleep. The house is very quiet and John being away adds to the stillness ... He is secretary to the relief committee and is indeed kept very busy. The ladies of Boyle and the neighbourhood have formed a society for clothing the poor and giving employment (to poor women and girls) I am a member of the committee. Mrs Lefroy, daughter of Lord Lorton is our chairwoman.'

Rome

Thursday 25 March. Pius IX issued an encyclical Praedecessores Nostros to Patriarch, Primates, Archbishops and Bishops of the whole Catholic world in favour of the famine victims of Ireland. He asked them to appoint three days of public prayer and to exhort their people to give alms for the relief of the Irish people.

Friday 26 March. 11 stone masons to Lord Lieutenant   *Newport*
CSORP Z.4201
'We are reduced to the lowest ebb of poverty in consequence of the wages of
this county being so low and provision rating so high and no employment
worth notice to be had, which leaves ourselves and our families in the grasp
of death.' *They ask the Lord Lieutenant for help* 'by imigrating us and our families to British America, where we will work for the government, until our
passage money was paid back … One month hence, unless saved by divine
Providence, will leave us in our graves.'

Friday 26 March. Rev George Griffiths to Society of Friends   *Ardcarne,*
Boyle
SFFP 2/506/19
'A day or two ago I was asked to turn into a house "to see a sight" and it was
a sad one. Extended on the floor lay the dead body of a man, naked, almost
a skeleton. His legs had recent sores where they had burst owing to dropsy.
Huddled up in the corner of the cabin lay two boys, 18 and 20 years of age.
One of them is since dead … Has it been observed in other places that far
more men die now than women?'

Saturday 27 March.   *Blacksod Bay*
OP 21/226
'The sloop *Ann Cook* was plundered this morning by several boats, of about
12 tons of meal in Blacksod Bay.'

Tuesday 30 March. Denis Tighe PP to Lord Lieutenant   *Ballaghaderreen*
DP 5304
'The most rude and ill-judged dismissals off the public works has been carried into effect in this parish by order of the government official. I wrote to
him to allow our relief committee to make the selection. He has taken no
notice of my letter but proceeded to strike off with blind and cruel indifference the names just as it pleased him. The consequences are that the very
poorest are now left to starve and die. Already the wretches are suffering all
the agonies of hunger. They have no lands to crop. They have no wages to
get. They will most certainly die or be driven to acts of desperation, if they
are not immediately returned. Oh! 'tis a cruel thing to strike off at once 860
poor starving fellow creatures and to sign one morning their dimissal, I may
say, their death warrants. I implore your Exellency's clemency in their favour.
We are in this barony an exception to the world for poverty and misery. In
the name of God, who will judge our acts and reward the charitable, extend
your clemency to those starving creatures and allow them to live. There is not
a moment to be lost. We have funds enough in the public grants for roads to
keep them alive and in the name of heaven allow us not to starve.'
15 April. Same to Lord Lieutenant: RLFC 3/2/21/23
'I received your reply to my letter of 30 March, complaining that Capt
Primrose had struck off labourers … I again distinctly state that this com-

mittee was not consulted and that some of the poor struck off are suffering dreadfully. I will give you a few examples: John Cunif, Ballaghaderreen, John Duffy, do, Billy Cunif, do. I could add many others who have no land, or the least means to get relief, who were included in this sweeping cutting off of the poor.'

Ballina
CSORP Z.4727

Tuesday 30 March. William Caldwell, sub-inspector, to the Inspector General
'I made a special tour of inspection through the entire district during the past week ... There is almost a perfect absence of any preparation for sowing or spring tillage. Not one fiftieth of the county is either ploughed or dug. There is no apparent inclination of the peasantry to commence the usual spring work. It is melancholy to see the vast superficies of fine potato soil lying neglected and without a grain of barley or oats even likely to be sown. The only exceptions are the country gentlemen and a few of the more rich and independant farmers ... but for the future wants of the community there is comparatively nothing. People say that they are not able to till the land because of bodily weakness and they have neither seed nor money. The population is thinning fast either thro' emigration or death. Funerals are ten-fold the usual ratio ... Crowds of the middle order of farmers, such as can command from £20 to £30, are daily deserting their farms and quitting with their families for America. Among the class under this amount, they are necessarily fixtures and a general paralysis prevails and a total absence of anxiety or energy as to the future and they are only scantily existing upon the wage obtained from the public works. Regarding the still higher orders, despondency in many cases exists ... and difficulties and embarassments anticipated at no very distant prospection ... The present prospects are very gloomy and unless within the ensuing month of April, exertions of a very extraordinary active nature be then made to remedy the existing state of neglect, and to crop the land in some shape, nothing but the most dreadful foreboding can present itself to any reflecting mind, as to the lamentable result hereafter and the appalling deficiency of home-raised corn or food for the ensuing season.'

Ballavary
CSORP Z.4727

Tuesday 30 March. Michael Coggers, Anthony Cannon, John Coggers, John Lavan and Pat Mulderrig to Lord-Lieutenant, complaining that they were not paid 8d. a day for the use of their asses on the line of road from Springhill to Balla in the barony of Gallen.
C. Kavanagh, assistant engineer, Swinford to Capt Fitzmaurice, superintendant in charge, re above, 21 April:
'I distinctly told the labourers that the price allowed was for cutting and removing the earth and that I would pay neither horse, ass or mule. In allotting the set of tasks, the price was set from 8d. per cubic yard to 5d., the difference of 3d. for moving the earth.'

Thursday 1 April 1847. Patrick Fenerty to Lord Lieutenant   *Crossmolina*
'I am a very poor man, with a wife and three helpless children, a linen weaver   CSORP Z.4460
by trade. I have no employment whatsoever and in a state of poverty, seeing
my wife and three children starving and cannot relieve them. I beg your
Excellency to grant me and my family a passage to any part of the Kanadies,
you thinks proper.'

Thursday 1 April. Denis Tighe PP to Sir Randolph Routh   *Ballaghaderreen*
'The people are in the greatest want … There are three dead this morning in
this town from starvation and their friends are not able to buy a coffin or
shroud to have them interred. There were 860 persons dismissed from the
public works a few days ago, which has frightfully increased the sufferings of
the poor … Many of them will die if they are left many days without relief
… For God's sake hasten to relieve us.'
*15 April. Same to same, stating that he had not yet received the government dona-
tion*
'The people are suffering dreadfully. All my funds are exhausted … I beg of
you to send me at your earliest possible convenience what we are entitled to.'

Saturday 3 April. Rev W. Tyndale to Society of Friends   *Kilmactigue*
'The dismissal of the poor who have been labouring on the roads to the   SFFP 2/506/19
amount of 2,000 has caused the greatest consternation and alarm amongst
them … I understand that they will all be dismissed next week … Our new
relief committee is only just organised but has not yet commenced operations. After receiving your last grant of 8 February we commenced to fill our
boiler with soup and rice porridge alternately and we have now on our list
124 who are almost all the heads of families … Fever is, I thank the Lord, on
the decline amongst us but dysentery still prevails and in this case rice is certainly the best and safest food.'
7 April. Bewley and Pim to Rev W. Tyndale   SFFP 2/505/6
'We are directed to transmit herewith an order in thy favour for one ton of
rice to be distributed in a cooked state or in small quantities to distressed
families that thou art aware know how to cook it properly.' *(See Appendix 6)*

Saturday 3 April. Rev G. H. Mostyn to Society of Friends (See Appendix 6N)   *Foxford*
'Your grant of 10 barrels of meal, 10 bags of peas and half a ton of biscuit has   SFFP 2/506/19
been a most timely relief to the poor of this place … Numbers of starving
creatures bless the Friends for their kindness. 160 families each day receive
their portion … The Friends may deem it necessary to give a fresh grant. If
such be the case I would have nothing to do with it unless I had the entire
control. Where there is a numerous committee, one man pulls this way and
another that.'

SFFP 2/505/6

Reply to above, 14 April:
'We are directed by the Committee to transmit herewith an order in thy favor on H. Gallagher and Co, Ballina for 10 barrels of Indian meal and half a ton of biscuit. Please inform us whether the local committee have a soup boiler and if not, how the peas last sent were made use of ... Canst thou distribute rice in a cooked state ... If so we would make thee a grant.'

Collooney
DP 3429

Monday 5 April. P. Durcan PP to T. N. Redington, requesting that his senior curate, Dominick O'Connor, be appointed a member of Coolaney Relief District, as Durcan is a member of the relief districts of Ballisodare and Collooney and utterly impossible for him to attend the Coolaney Committee.

Belmullet
CSORP Z.4946

Monday 5 April. 9 persons to Lord Lieutenant
'Because of the wretched state of misery that we are in since the destruction began to prevail on our crops, we have no means left whatsoever. These people, who were appointed for the purpose of giving relief to the poor, are not giving them any but letting them in a starving condition, feeding their own friends and servants with the relief money, and the clothes also that was sent to them, they distribute to their own servants and the poor get very little ... They are dying as numerous as bees on a harvest day, burying them in their own clothes, without a coffin or any other thing requisite for them to defray their funeral charges. They will be from seven to eight deep and without being interred and some of the poor creatures taken upon a man's back to the burying place and putting them down there ... The relief men are getting from a quart to two quarts for 8 in family of Indian meal gruel and a small quantity of rice, poor men working from six in the morning to six at night, at 6d. a day ... Indian meal is at 2s. 6d. a stone and rice 3s. 6d. a stone. To make a long story short ... we could not describe the poverty and desolation and famine that we are in now and in the remotest part of Ireland, having no person ... to arrange or state our distress to foreign places or to get some relief for us. There are but 4 boilers in the half barony of Erris. Let us know what we ought to do about our land. The landlords are wanting to get our poor holdings. We don't know how to act, whether we will give possession or not.'

Aclare
SFFP 2/506/19

Wednesday 7 April. Henry Joseph McCarrick to Society of Friends (See Appendix 6B)
'I have distributed provisions for the handsome sum of £10 which you were pleased to send me ... To the poorest (and indeed alas! they are all wretchedly poor), I have given from a half to one stone of Indian meal on two days a week. To others whom I did not consider in a dying state I have given from a quarter to half a stone. To people who were ill of dysentery, fever etc I have given some small quantities of rice which I have purchased for a few pounds

sterling sent to me by a few charitable individuals. But now all being almost distributed ... I know not really what the starving creatures of this town and district will do ... Your indeed truly charitable and humane brethern beyond the Atlantic have probably responded to the call of their perishing brothers in this now alas desolate isle. I hope that you will be graciously pleased to send but a few pounds ... Eternal gratitude, as well as eternal happiness to yourselves as well as your noble brethern in the far West.'

Reply to above, 10 April: SFFP 2/505/6
'We are directed by the Committee to enquire whether thou couldest distribute rice in a cooked state and whether thou canst purchase rice in Sligo at or under £23 per ton, the price here being £21 for rice of good quality. If so, a ton may be purchased.'

Henry Joseph McCarrick to Society of Friends, 15 April. enclosing a bill for £23   SFFP 2/506/19
5s. for one ton of rice purchased from Dominick Henry, merchant, Sligo
'I have no boiler established. The way I distributed the meal was from a quarter to three-quarters of a stone to a family on separate days of the week. The rice can be distributed in the same way. The inhabitants of this town and district have a pretty good knowledge of cooking. To the poor and ignorant portion I can give all the instructon in my power ... Never, never indeed did the poor wretched inhabitants require something to put a stop to dysentery so much so as on the present occasion, when hundreds are weekly carried by it to their final resting place.'

Reply to above, 21 April, enclosing a letter of credit for £23 5s.:   SFFP 2/505/6
'It was not our intention that thou shouldest have purchased any unless to distribute in a cooked state. However, we hope thou will be careful of it, only giving it in cases where thou art satisfied the parties know how to cook it. We beg leave to transmit herewith an order in thy favor on the government depot in Sligo for half a ton of Indian meal ... We are quite aware of the poverty of this district.'

Friday 9 April. Dean Hoare to Society of Friends (See Appendix 6A)   *Achonry*
'There are two soup kitchens in my parish ... one in an outhouse on my own   SFFP 2/506/19
premises; the other at the village of Tubbercurrry, under the active superintendance of my curate, Rev John Hamilton ... From these we distribute about 120 gallons daily ... The relief committee have expended upwards of £1,000 in gratuitous relief since last December ... but having no money we cannot continue the soup kitchens. I shall be very grateful to your Committee for a grant to carry on the two soup kitchens a little longer ... I dispense some cooked rice daily at my own house.'

Reply, 14 April: SFFP 2/505/6
'We are directed by the Committee to transmit herewith an order in thy favor

on J. O'Connor, Sligo for four tons of rice, one for each of the soup kitchens mentioned by thee.'

Ballymote
SFFP 2/506/19

Friday 9 April, Rev J. Garrett to Society of Friends (See Appendix 6F)
'I have attended upon the distribution of soup and bread to the relief in the last week in this parish of 360 families, averaging 6 in every house and my family have given out needlework and knitting to a large body of young women put off the public works ... Our funds are now exhausted. If you will now help us we shall have 9 additional soup kitchens and bakeries in operation in a week and without funds we cannot save the lives of the unemployed and starving people.'

SFFP 2/505/6

Reply to above, 19 April:
'We are directed by the Committee to transmit herewith an order in thy favour on John O'Connor of Sligo for half a ton of rice and 6 barrels of Indian meal to enable thee to continue and extend the distribution of soup.'

Claremorris
CSORP W.4878

Saturday 10 April. Michael O'Conner, Crimline, to Lord Lieutenant
'I have seven in my family, all females, and am without land, means or support ... in a deplorable state of famine ... Nothing in the world to subsist on but a cold hut ... and got no tickets for the public works this year, although this poor wretched creature applied to the clergy, engineers and committees.'

Ballina
CSORP Z.4977

Monday 12 April. Finance Committee to Chief Secretary
'It is impossible for the constabulary to render us all the assistance in escorting food, protecting store etc ... As the revenue police have at present but little to do as regards illicit distillation, we consider they could be made available.'

Liverpool
CSORP Z.5037

Monday 12 April. Whitehall to T. N. Redington
'We have received urgent representations from the parochial authorities of Liverpool, of the alarming spread of fever in that town, owing to the continued influx of large numbers of Irish paupers; and that it is stated that several have recently arrived at Liverpool from Ireland with the typhus fever upon them.'

20 April. City of Dublin Steam Packet Company to T. N. Redington
'It would seem to be attended with great difficulty, if not wholly impracticable, to ascertain who may or may not be infected with any particular disease, when the number of passengers of the lower order now proceeding to Liverpool from this port, ranges from 600 to 1,000 daily, few of whom come near the vessel until a short time of her sailing.'

Tuesday 13 April. Lord Lieutenant to Poor Law Commission   *Ballina*
'Lord Lieutenant is against advancing £140 to Ballina Union ... Since the for-   CSORP O.4864
mer advance the Guardians have incurred a further £350 liability and only £5
and £17 10s. rates were collected in the previous two weeks ... The maintenance of the workhouse is being thrown on the government by the Guardians
... It would be dangerous if this procedure was generally adopted. The Lord
Lieutenant does not doubt that this and many other Unions will be unable,
through want of sufficient funds, to maintain the existing number of inmates
in the workhouse.'

Tuesday 13 April. Extract from Guardians' minutes   *Swinford*
'Altho' there have been 63 deaths in the poorhouse within the last three weeks   CSORP O.5019
... matters are getting better. Fever is not increasing, which we attribute to the
precautions taken by the medical officer and the constant attention paid to the
sick, as well as a sufficient number of nurses having been provided by the
Board, altho' we regret that we are unable to have the necessary improvements
in ventilation carried out, from the terror of disease that prevails, which prevents the clerk getting a mason or carpenter at any price to enter the house.'

14 April. Poor Law Commission to T. N. Redington, concerning charges of cruelty   CSORP O.4959
towards the inmates of Swinford workhouse, by the master, Mr O'Grady
'It is reported that O'Grady died from fever caught in the discharge of his
duties. The Poor Law Commission will forward the charges to assistant commissioner and the Board of Guardians.'

20 April. Extract from the Guardians' minutes   CSORP O.5298
'In reference to a complaint against the late master of the workhouse for cruelty etc, we feel it due to his memory to put on record our conviction that
the charges against him are both false and libelous, and we also consider the
charges against the matron and porter of the house as false and unworthy of
notice, but we shall make inquiry into the circumstances of the case, when
the subsidence of fever and disease in the house admits of our doing so ...
That the balance of salary, £10 due to the late lamented master, as he lost his
life in the service of the house and as his wife is but slowly recovering from
the disease to which he fell victim, and as his family are left in great distress,
we hope the Poor Law Commission will kindly allow this sum to be paid out
of the monies they kindly lend ... and that they will allow payment to be
made for white-washing the house and other small matters, recommended by
the medical officer, in consequence of the disease in the house ... and that
the nurses' weekly wages be similarly paid ...
Only £5 rates were collected during the preceding week. A special meeting
was called for 27 April to take measures to expedite the collection and the
solicitor has been called to report on his proceedings.'

CSORP O.5580

26 April. Poor Law Commission to T. N. Redington, enclosing the resolutions of Swinford Board of Guardians, 20 April 1847, and recommending that the Board be allowed to pay £10 owed to the family of the late master and the weekly wages of the nurses out of the £60 weekly remitted.

Ballina

CSORP O.9759

Wednesday 14 April. Poor Law Commission to T. N. Redington
'The report of 7 April showed that the number of inmates was 929, of which upwards of 500 were in fever and dysentery. The Poor Law Commission sent three experienced nurses from Dublin and advanced £140. We heard today from the master of the workhouse to remit a further amount for immediate supplies.'

CSORP O.5102

16 April. William Somerville, Whitehall, to T. N. Redington
'I laid before Sir George Grey your letter concerning Ballina Union ... It cannot be permitted that the wretched inmates of these workhouses should be turned loose upon the world for the want of funds to support them.'

CSORP O.5121

17 April. Report of Mr Otway, assistant commissioner, stating that the following are required: 100 men's shirts and material for 100 more, i.e. 300 yards of strong shirting linen, 100 women's shifts and material for 100 more, i.e. 300 yards of strong calico, 60 towels, 50 pairs of blankets, 75 pairs of sheets, 70 rugs, 70 bedticks and 70 bolsters. Poor Law Commission has sent several articles of bedding and towels, received from the Ordinance department and recommends that Guardians be authorised to buy shirts and shifts from local contractors.

CSORP O.5208

19 April. Poor Law Commission to clerk of the Union
'All the Guardians must sign a resolution that they will pay all the sums advanced and the commission wishes to get an account of how the money is spent, the cost of the maintenance of the workhouse for the period between the advances, and the amount of rate collected for each period.'
21 April. Poor Law Commission to T. N. Redington
'Ballina Board of Guardians will not be able to support the workhouse without a further sum of £140 for the week beginning 24 April.'

CSORP O.5657

Whitehall, 21 April:
'Sir George Grey entirely approves, under the circumstances stated, of £140 being advanced to Ballina Guardians.'

Ballaghaderreen

SFFP 2/505/6

Wednesday 14 April. Bewley and Pim to Denis Tighe PP (See Appendix 6C)
'We are directed by the Committee to transmit herewith an order for one ton of rice to be distributed in a cooked state...We will also deliver a boiler of 100 gallons to any carrier producing at this office an order signed by thee.'

Friday 16 April. Statement of the mate of the schooner Mavis of Dumfries (76 tons)
'We sailed on 11 April from Greenock for Galway with 62 tons of wheat, 11 tons of coal and 25 tons of pig iron. On 14 April at noon, then off the Black Rocks (Achill Head), two rowboats with 14 men pulled alongside … The men got on board, seized the helm and brought the ship up in the wind, when 8 more boats came alongside, and finding the vessel was laden with wheat, they broke open the hatches with axes of their own and filled the sacks which they had in their boats, about 30 in number, as well as the sacks which were on board the schooner. They then filled their boats in bulk and pulled away in the direction of the Black Rocks. The boats' crew did not offer any personal violence but merely said that they wanted the wheat to eat.'

Achill
OP 21/240

Saturday 17 April. Lieut. A. R. Dunlop, H. M. steam vessel Acheran, to Rear-Admiral Sir Hugh Pigot
'On Thursday, 15 April, three vessels were being plundered outside those islands (Iniskea) during the calm that then prevailed. Lieut Wylde reported that he had secured three men in the overt act of carrying away meal from one of the plundering boats, and also two sacks of the meal, one having the government mark on it, and that he left four more sacks on the beach, for want of means of transport. There were about 200 people assembled on the beach, cutting the bags open and carrying away as much as they could; having secured his prisoners, he caused them to march to Barracktown, a distance of two and a half miles, and there confined them in a hut with a sentry over them, but the people assembled in the front and rear of the hut during the night and while the sentry was endeavouring to keep them off the door, they unroofed the back of the house and assisted the prisoners to escape. Lieut Wylde however ascertained the prisoners' names and residences … and the police are now in search of them.'

Blacksod Bay
OP 21/242

Saturday 17 April. Chief-Secretary to Lieut Peterson, emigration agent, concerning the class of vessels advertised to sail with emigrants from that port, amongst others, the Albron and Josephine, the latter of which is reported not to be sea-worthy.

Galway
CSORP Z.5066

Saturday 17 April. John Finn, John Gallagher and Thomas McCormack to Lord Lieutenant. Finn has 7 in family on two and a half acres, Gallagher 8 in family on four acres, and McCormack 10 in family on four acres, 'all without means of support but daily labour. In January they sent a memorial to the Lord Lieutenant that the Cloontearn line might not be deviated from its original destination, so as to destroy their small holdings, but it was, as a continuation of the Drumlusnagh line with which it had no natural connexion, which

Kilfree
CSORP W.5131

was sanctioned by the parish priest, as they were poor and unable to contribute largely towards his collections. They were dismissed from the public
works, leaving their famishing families a prey to the terrors of famine and
destitution ... Their cabbage and potato gardens are uprooted by this line,
leaving them no prospects for the ensuing year. They beg the Lord
Lieutenant to order them employment, to avert the destruction that seems
impending over their forlorn families.
P.S. Michael Finn, the overseer of the Drumlusnagh line, has 60 acres and
keeps men belonging to the Board of Works employed on his own farm and
when they refused, they were immediately discarded.'

Ballymote   *Sunday 18 April. Rev J. Garrett to Sir Randolph Routh*
'Treasurer has not yet got the money. If the £25 is not remitted, you should
have told us before we had gone into debt laying in provisions ... We must
stop of course our relief to the destitute daily given in cooked rations to 506
individuals.'

Boyle   *Sunday 18 April. Julia MacDermot to her brother Edward MD, Bath, Somerset.*
MACDERMOT PAPERS,   'I send you one of our circulars. Pray do what you can for us, and if you have
COOLAVIN   no hope of success, send it back to me. The printing of them comes a little
higher than we can afford. We are therefore very saving of them. Mrs
O'Farrell wrote to the Queen of the French. She has, I am told, got an answer
and 300 francs.'

CSORP O.5303   *20 April. C. G. Otway to Poor Law Commission*
'I had a meeting yesterday with Lord Lorton, Capt Duckworth and Mr
Hackett, Guardians of Boyle Union ... I recommend to the commissioners
to quarantee the payment of interest on £2,000 for a limited period to meet
the present wants ... I also recommend an advance of £80 to meet current
expenses and support of the inmates for next week ... A large amount of the
rates are uncollectable from the total want of present or probable future
means on the part of a considerable number of rate-payers.'

Drogheda   *Wednesday 21 April. Mayor of Drogheda to T. N. Redington.*
CSORP H.5373   'The immense influx of paupers from the West is increasing to an alarming
extent, a visitation which has been fearfully pressing on us during the year.'

Foxford   *Wednesday 21 April. Bewley and Pim to Rev G. H. Mostyn (See Appendix 6N)*
SFFP 2/505/6   'We are directed by the Committee to transmit herewith an order in thy favor
on H. Gallagher of Ballina for 10 barrels of Indian meal to be distributed in
small portions from time to time amongst the most destitute of the poor.'

25 April. Rev G. H. Mostyn to Bewley and Pim.   sffp 2/506/36
'Your letter of the 21st has reached me with an order for one ton of rice and 10 barrels of meal … But for your Society hundreds in this district would most assuredly have died within the last month … A grant of 50 articles of clothing sent from your office per the Longford boat never has come to hand as yet.'

Wednesday 21 April. Bewley and Pim to Capt G. G. Wellesley, inspecting officer   *Swinford*
'We feel the difficulty of the present state of transition from one mode of   sffp 2/505/6
relief to another and are desirous of giving such assistance as the means placed at our disposal may enable us. We are fully aware of the distress which prevails in the Unon of Swinford … If thou would kindly recommend judicious and trustworthy agents, we should be glad to afford some assistance.'
Same to same, 23 April:
'We would be much obliged by any information thou will kindly afford us, respecting the best means of assisting a locality, which we know to be much distressed and to which we have hitherto given very little assistance for want of suitable agents.'
Reply of Capt Wellesley, 27 April: sffp 2/506/19
'I know not where, except in one or two electoral divisions, to turn to find a person in whom I could place confidence. We are in a most wretched state. I am endeavouring by aid of a grant from the British Association to put the committees to work … To enable me to assist them I would ask your assistance. This is certainly a Union of paupers, for there are very few who will not require gratuitous relief. There is little difference in the condition of all parts of it that I should find it difficult to state which is the most destitute. All grants sent to me I apply to all parts of the Union as near as possible to the proportion of the population … It would do much good if it were possible to give a little rice in addition to those suffering from dysentery.'

Wednesday 21 April. Board of Health, Dublin to T. N. Redington   *Castlerea*
'We have received a letter from the vice-chairman of the Board of Guardians   csorp H.5238
of Castlerea, stating that the medical officer is in fever and that the only other medical practitioner there had already resigned from the workhouse and was leaving for America and that the master of the workhouse was ill and that a medical practitioner be sent down from Dublin. The Board is sending Dr Custes by the next mail and he will be paid one guinea a day and travelling expenses.'

Thursday 22 April. Bewley and Pim to Margaret Furey, Ardnisbrack (See   *Collooney*
Appendix 6K)   sffp 2/505/6
'The Committee directs us to inquire whether thou hast any expectation of

being able to sell in the neighbourhood the flannel or drugget which thou mayest get manufactured or be good enough to say how it is expected it can be sold or disposed of.'

Broadhaven
OP 21/270

Friday 23 April. Report of Capt Thomas of the cutter Jane & Agnes of Belfast
'The cutter was bound from Belfast to Limerick with 664 bags of meal. When becalmed on 23 April off Erris Head, Broadhaven, he was boarded by three boats, being those used on the coast called carracks *(sic)* and made of canvass, containg 10 to 12 men; the first boat carried off 9 sacks of meal, the second, 10 and the third, 5, making in all 24 sacks. They at first took possession of the helm, threatening to run the vessel on shore and take the lives of the crew, if they resisted.'

Blacksod Bay
OP 21/293

23 April:
'The *George Lord* of London, between Achill Head and Dervillan Island, was boarded by several boats full of country people, who broke open the hatches, threatened, if any resistence was made by the crew, they would be thrown overboard. They plundered the cargo, consisting of barley, meal, rice and biscuit, which they carried away.'

Ballina
SFFP 2/505/6

Friday 23 April. Bewley and Pim to G. V. Jackson
'The Committee are in receipt of thy letter and beg to say if any means of relief are being carried on under thine own superintendance they shall be glad to assist thee pending the necessary arrangements for bringing the new act into force.'

Coolaney
SFFP 2/505/6

Friday 23 April. Bewley and Pim to Archdeacon Verschoyle
'The Committee beg leave to inform thee that their funds have been contributed by persons of all persuasions with injunctions in very many cases to distribute them without reference to sect or party. The Committee cannot make a grant to a school which is evidently sectarian but having full confidence in thee shall be quite ready to make another grant for general distribution when the present is expended.'

SFFP 2/506/19

Reply to above, 29 April:
'Returns his most sincere thanks to the Society of Friends for their most kind offer of further assistance and begs to solicit a further supply which is at present most urgently required in consequence of the cessation of the public works ... He also requests to know whether any further grant may be distributed by himself ... in consequence of the words "having full confidence in thee" being used in their much esteemed letter.'

Monday 26 April. Bewley and Pim to Patrick Groarke CC (See Appendix 6P)   *Kilkelly*
'The Committee directs us to transmit herewith an order in thy favor on the   SFFP 2/505/6
government stores in Ballina for 8 sacks of Indian meal ... The Committee
are desirous to know whether there is any boiler in thy district and whether
thou couldest distribute cooked rice or if the people know how to dress it
themselves.'
Reply to above, 23 May:
'I received your letter of the 13th inst. stating that you would make me a
grant of rice ... I am sure that nothing could benefit the poor sick of this district more. The better way would be to send it in a raw state ... The people
by little instructions could be shewn to cook it themselves. Allow me,
Gentlemen, to give you the sincere thanks of the many that your grant of 8
sacks of Indian meal made to me relieved. I will in a few days return you a
list of the many poor starving people relieved therewith.'

Wednesday 28 April. Society of Friends clothing query completed and signed by   *Coolaney*
Kate P. Thompson (See Appendix 6L)   SFFP 2/506/36
'About 700 in need of clothes ... calico, flannel, in short what will create
cleanliness and warmth for men and women ... Every possibility to have
them made locally. It will give employment to our women and help to place
them again within doors.'
30 April. Mrs Verschoyle to Society of Friends.   SFFP 2/506/19
'She begs leave to address the Society of Friends, having been recommended
by Capt. Gilbert to lay before them for consideration the destitution of most
of the female children of the peasantry in her neighbourhood from the scarcity
of food and their parents' want of means to purchase it. She hopes to be
favoured with a grant from your most benevolent Society, which may enable
her in some degree to alleviate their distress by a prudent and limited distribution.'

Summer 1847

Emigration and Piracy

In the middle of May the first shipload of emigrants from Ireland arrived at Grosse Ile in the St Laurence River about thirty miles downstream from the city of Quebec. Despite its name, it was a tiny island about a mile and a half long and a half mile wide, which was used every year from mid-May to mid-November as a quarantine station. On 24 May the *Jessie* arrived from Sligo with 243 immigrants. No less than 11 ships arrived from there in June, four of them on the same day, 10 June. In all 27 ships arrived that year from Sligo and a further five from Killala with a total of 6,962 passengers. 523 died on the voyage and of these 139 were lost at sea following the shipwreck of the *Carricks* from Sligo off Cape Rozier on 19 May. There were only forty-eight survivors. The death rate on most of the ships during the voyage ranged from four to ten but the *Larch,* which arrived from Sligo on 20 August, lost 110 at sea and a further 86 in quarantine. With 440 on board it had the largest passenger list of the Sligo ships and its high mortality may have resulted from overcrowding. Most of the ships contained from 127 to 303 passengers. There were 337 deaths of passengers from the Sligo and Killala ships while in quarantine in Grosse Ile. These deaths normally ranged from one to ten per shipload, although the *Wolfeville,* which arrived from Sligo on 10 June, had forty-eight deaths, having already lost thirty-seven at sea. The last ship to arrive at Grosse Ile before the end of the navigational season was the *Richard Watson* from Sligo on 8 November with 170 on board.

The first priest to be sent there to minister to the dying was the Ballisodare-born Bernard McGauran, who had been ordained the previous year for the diocese of Quebec. His letters to the Archbishop of Quebec give a harrowing account of the sufferings and deaths of many of the Irish immigrants. McGauran was among the first priests to be struck down by typhus. Once recovered, he returned again and again to minister in Grosse Ile and he was the last priest there at the end of 1847.

A total of 11,200 emigrated from Sligo in 1847. Of these the great majority went to Canada, with just over 1,000 going to the U.S.A. A little over 3,000 emigrated in 1848 , with 746 going to the U.S.A. In 1849 there were almost 4,000 emigrants, of which 1,665 went to the U.S.A.

The number of persons receiving gratuitous soup rations peaked at over two and a half million in July. There were wide regional diversities with the highest proportion of the population depending on them in the west. Over 94% of the population in the Ballinrobe Union were receiving rations, over 85% in the Westport Union, 84% in Swinford, over 78% in Ballina and almost 76% in Castlebar union. The Poor Law Amendment Act in June introduced the 'Gregory' or Quarter Acre Clause, which stated that any occupier of more than a quarter of an acre of land could not be deemed destitute and was not eligible to receive relief paid for by the poor rates. It was proposed by Sir William Gregory who later became the husband of Lady Gregory of Abbey Theatre fame. While the act itself authorised for the first time 'outdoor' relief, the Gregory Clause was a draconian measure that condemned countless occupiers of small patches to starvation. Henceforth, any person who occupied more than a quarter of an acre who applied for a place in the workhouse or for food for his family had to give up his patch of land or face starvation.

During the winter and spring many of the poor had to pawn all their possessions, including their clothes to provide food for themselves and their families. They were now virtually reduced to nakedness. The Quakers set up a sub-committee to oversee the distribution of clothes and a query form seeking information on the quantity and kind of clothes most needed was widely circulated in the west of Ireland. Local ladies' societies were established and they undertook to have garments made locally from the bales of cloth provided by the Quakers. Thus not only were the poor clothed but employment was provided for poor local tailors and shoemakers who were themselves facing starvation.

Some of the destitute resorted to desperate measures to feed themselves and their families. Fishermen living on the Atlantic seaboard carried out daring acts of piracy on the high seas. Putting to sea in their curraghs they raided and robbed ships carrying meal from America and elsewhere. The first such incident took place in Blacksod Bay at the end of March when 12 tons of meal was carried off. More acts of piracy were carried out in April. The government increased the number of coastguard stations and provided extra steamers to patrol the north-Mayo coast.

Following the papal encyclical, money began to pour in to Propaganda in Rome, particularly from Italian and Swiss dioceses, for the relief of the destitute Irish. Other dioceses worldwide sent their contributions directly to the Archbishop of Dublin. The Roman money was distributed among the western bishops in July. The bishops of Achonry, Killala and Elphin received £50 each. By the end of that month the province of Tuam had received £750 for distribution among the most needy.

Cong
CSORP Z.5670

Saturday 1 May 1847. Edward Waldron PP to Lord Lieutenant
'There is no police station or resident proprietor in the parish and if the distribution of breadstuffs is attempted here, it would be attended with the loss of food and perhaps of lives. You know it is not an easy duty to control a starving people ... 150 of the poor of these parishes (Kilmolane and Ballycolla) died of sickness and starvation these three months past. I fear many more will soon be on the same list.'

CSORP I.6336

Friday 21 May.
'The Cong Relief Committee resolved that from the threatened food riots, manifestations of which have already taken place by marching into Cong with a flag, demanding food or work, and threats having been made to attack the commissariat stores here, our chairman be requested to communicate with Mr Redington and request that Capt Bindon, constabulary, be directed to reside at Cong and reinforce by even a few men the station at Cong.'

Castlebar
CSORP O.5636

Saturday 1 May. C. G. Otway to Poor Law Commission
'The Guardians of Castlebar Union are not able to enter contracts for milk, coal, soap and candles as they have no money. The medical officer has not been able to obtain milk, whey and flummery ... No parties are willing to give the Board of Guardians credit ... A weekly advance of £20 should be sent as a loan ... The high constable of Carra was appointed as Poor Rate collector.'

Newport
CSORP H.5973

Monday 3 May. Report of Dr Daly
'Not one-third of the population can survive this year. Hospital relief is no use: what is required is one large provision establishment or convalescent depot, for if dismissed from the fever hospital apparently well, they must inevitably relapse and die for want of restorative nutriment.'

Ballymote
OP 26/153

Tuesday 4 May. Sworn statement of Patt Finan, Branchfield
'On Wednesday or Thursday, 21 or 22 April, late in the evening, James and Michael Maginness of Branchfield called and asked me to go with them to make out some sheep ... I said I was too weak from hunger. They replied, "It was little matter to be hungry when I would not provide." They persuaded me. They were about three or four hours on the mountains and caught six sheep, which they drove into a channel, tied in couples four of them, and killed the remaining two. On the following day, James Maginess brought me one of the sheep and two days later brought me a head, shoulders and four feet of another sheep.'

Tuesday 4 May. J. A. Holmes to Society of Friends

'The invoice is for 2 tons of rice, having purchased and distributed the second out of my own limited resources and I shall feel very much obliged if the Committee will order me payment for the one ton. The demands on us for food are daily increasing and it is quite impossible we can meet them. 146 families are daily supplied with good soup and 4lbs of cooked rice each, the latter being provided by your Committee. Our supply will only last a few days … Your Committee has been so generous to us that I do not wish to trespass too much on their funds … I am quite certain if in your power to give us further assistance … you will take into consideration the wild and poor district in which I live and the absence of any resident proprietor but myself to look after these wretched people.'

Coolavin
SFFP 2/506/19

Wednesday 5 May. J. G. Wills, vice chairman, to T. N. Redington, requesting a loan of £2,000 to clear liabilities

'The members of the Board paid the treasurer £225 to support the workhouse for a week and three days, i.e. to 15 May … If the loan is not advanced, the only alternative is to close the house and turn out a mass of infection on a community already too much oppressed by sickness … If the loan is not given, we must hand over the house to a set of paid Guardians, washing our hands of the whole matter.'

Castlerea
CSORP O.5792

Wednesday 5 May. Joseph Duggan, clerk of the Union, to Poor Law Commission, enclosing two resolutions of the Board of Guardians

'The Board of Guardians wishes to erect board sheds in the male and female yards, for the immediate accommodation of the numerous paupers requiring admission. The Board requests a loan of £1,000 to prevent the necessity of turning out the paupers and requests the chairman, Lord Lorton, to make the application.'

Boyle
CSORP O.567

Thursday 6 May. Denis Tighe PP to Society of Friends (See Appendix 6C)

'I continue to give out in a cooked state the rice you were pleased to send me for the poor. It has already saved the lives of hundreds … We have only one boiler of 180 gallons. It was prepared in the morning and again at night. A second boiler is much wanted. 286 families or 1,430 persons relieved by one bag of rice and 5 stones of oaten meal (3 April).'

8 May. Same to same

'The people are generally so poor that I am not aware of any of them to have bought clothing during the Spring. We have great reason to be truly grateful to your benevolent Society. At the time the last ton of rice reached us we had not a single ounce of food to give them but as the bulk of the people are

Ballaghaderreen
SFFP 2/506/19

starving everything we get for them in the way of charity disappears in a few days … The poorhouse in Castlerea is about to be closed for the want of funds. Fever and dysentery are increasing and the cry of the poor to get food was not so great this year as during the week just ended. This was occasioned by all the public works being suspended. A good many have died from want in the last 10 days.'

Draft reply, 12 May:

'Send order on Sligo for 10 sacks of Indian meal and 10 sacks of barley meal. We hope the boilers are kept at work.'

Ballina
CSORP O.6088

Tuesday 11 May. Extract from letter of E. Howley, chairman

'The master cannot get one farthing's worth of provision without ready money and the paupers would have starved on yesterday, had I not gone security to one of the merchants for meal and bread, the price to be paid on tomorrow. Deaths and disease are increasing considerably and we had more than 80 admissions last week.'

Kilcolman
(Ballaghaderreen)
SFFP 2/506/19

Tuesday 11 May. J. A. Holmes to Bewley and Pim (See Appendix 6C)

'I beg leave to solicit a grant from you for the poor of the parish of Kilcolman. I live immediately on the borders of it and am a member of its relief committee. There is no resident proprietor living in it. They are in a most wretched state … I don't feel myself at liberty to give them any of your last grant. Indeed if I did it would not last 6 days … If the Committee entrust me with a grant for these wretched people, it shall be as their other grants are, distributed by a member of my own family … Never did the Committee send a donation to a people more in want of it.'

SFFP 2/506/20

Same to same, 16 June re above:

'I enclose an account of the distribution of a ton of Indian meal … to the poor of the parish of Kilcolman. I now beg leave to solicit another grant to this district … Fever is very prevalent, in many cases entire families being ill of it. It is for these unfortunate objects I now claim the bounty of the Society.'

Draft reply, 21 June:

'Send order on Sligo for a ton of Indian meal and 5 bags of biscuit.'

Belmullet
OP 21/190

Wednesday 12 May.

'The *Defiance of Cardigan* (master, Thomas Davies) on a voyage from Belfast to Galway, was boarded and plundered by upwards of 150 persons off the coast of Belmullet. 34 plunderers were taken prisoner. The coastguard at Ballyglass put to sea and captured 10 curraghs, loaded with Indian meal and manned by 34 men.'

Saturday 29 May. 34 prisoners to Lord Lieutenant
'We were all then and there put in the Bridewell of Belmullet, where we have been detained untried ever since (18 days this day), in a narrow dungeon of only four narrow cells, without fire, candle, bed or a seat to sit on but the cold flags, while our long families have been in a state of starvation at home, and eight of our families died of starvation since they have been so confined, some of them leaving their destitute forlorn orphans to seek relief where they may, or die of starvation.'

Wednesday 12 May. G. V. Jackson to Society of Friends
'Thanks for the 8 sacks of Indian meal and 20 bags of biscuit ... I saw Capt. Wellesley yesterday, government inspector of the Swinford Union, as well as Rev J. Corley, RC clergyman, Foxford ... I propose to give the remainder to 30 or 40 families thro' Rev Mr Mostyn, Rev J. Corley and Mr John Fitzgerald of Foxford.'

Foxford
SFFP 2/507/3

Friday 14 May. G. Knox RM to Dublin Castle
'It would be adviseable to have the stations of Tubbercurry, Cloonacool and Chaffpool strengthed by a few additional police to each. The people appear discontent at the stoppage of the public works and have in two instances sent threatening letters to the relief committees. Should there be any attack on any of the provision stores, the force would be quite inefficient. There are only six policemen at Tubbercurry.'

Tubbercurry
OP 26/162

Friday 14 May. Rev J. Garrett to T. N. Redington, transmitting a petition presented this day by 477 able-bodied men,
'who peaceably assembled at the Committee room of the Toomour electoral division and begged us to forward it to the government or the Board of Works. I strongly advise that this fine body of men be forthwith employed and not permitted to brood over their privations in idleness and plot some outrages to satisfy the craving of their appetites. A pound of Indian meal is quite insufficient for such a man as any of these for twenty-four hours and it would be an economy to employ them.'
Petition of 477 men over 17 and under 50 to Toomour Relief Committee (See Appendix 1H)
'Petitioners are in a most deplorable state at present owing to the great distress existing ... beseech the gentlemen of the committee will take their distress into their charitable consideration by granting them present employment on the Knockoconnor line of road, to prevent actual starvation in the electoral division of Toomour and petitioners and families will ever pray as in duty bound.'

Keash
DP 5821

Sunday 16 May. P. J. O'Connor CC to Society of Friends re an order on Westport which was recalled (See Appendix 6G)

'The Almighty alone knows how many many lives may be lost thro' the disappointment. Dysentery rages to such an alarming extent and prepared rice is considered to be one of its best cures and consequently the recalling of the order has deprived many a poor creature who could not afford one farthing towards purchasing it … I still hope you will still manage so as to enable me have an order … In your communication to me of the 15th ultimo you have intimated that your Committee has considered it unnecessary to have sent any relief in meal in consequence of rations of meal being distributed in the parishes … Pray allow me state for your information and to have such an impression removed from your benevolent and charitable hearts, that the distributions doled to the poor are both inadequate and unsatisfactory and I am certain you will agree with me when I state the facts. First, the system adopted in Templemore (Straide) and Ballavary is that meal is distributed only once in the fortnight and on that day only one pound allowed each adult and half a pound to those under 16 years, This proportioned to time allows 1 ounce per day to each individual and a quarter ounce for these under age and is that sustenance as sufficient to prevent starvation? I am certain, respected Sirs, your humane feelings will suggest the answer that it is not and the consequence of this inhuman and injust treatment is that each day we have to add to the gloomy catalogue of deaths from starvation. This very day I have to record the death of a man named Patrick Mulderrig of Grallagh who was found dead in his cabin and it cannot be ascertained when he died or how long he remained unheeded and unheard of but the fact of the greater part of the human visage viz. his nose, eyes and mouth and also his fingers and toes been eaten of by rats, tells he must have remained there unheeded for a considerable time and also in the townland of Lacull, I can prove to satisfaction were it it investigated that 39 human beings have perished in a few months of the direct want and actual starvation. Volumes could not contain all the painful examples I could instance and every day scenes, the most horrifying are occurring, scenes so gloomy and shocking to the feelings of humanity that my heart yearns and my tongue falters at the recital of them. Consequently, I once more importune you in the name of charity to have reissued me whatever pittance your charitable feelings will suggest. I can challenge Ireland this day for misery and real want and I am certain the greatest object, my poor flocks, are in such destitution and do on that account expect an immediate answer and relief for them.'

Draft reply, 31 May:

'Send an order on the government depot, Westport, for half a ton of meal and 5 cwt of rice to be distributed in small portions in a cooked state amongst the most necessitous of those who are not provided for under the government relief measures.'

Tuesday 18 May. Joseph Brown, Ashbrook, Ballavary, on behalf of the inhabitants of the parishes of Straide and Kildacomogue, to Lord Lieutenant   *Straide &*
'The poor of these parishes are in a most distressed state, dying of hunger and   *Ballavary*
burring *(sic)* without coffins. There are instances of being one week dead   DP 5852
without a human person to visit them until their eyes and many portions of
their bodies have been eaten by rats. The donations given by the Ballavary
Committee is so very small. Only three and a half pounds of Indian male
(sic) for seven in a family, from Friday until Tuesday following, making it five
days for some to live on that small portion.'

Tuesday 18 May. Patrick Manning, constabulary pensioner, to Lord Lieutenant   *Foxford*
'I am a pensioner at 8d a day or £12 3s. 4d. per annum. In consequence of the   CSORP I.6226
extreme destitution unhappily prevailing throughout the country, I am
unable to support myself and my family of four. I wish to emigrate to the
Canadas but my means are so limited that I am unable to do so without assistance. I humbly solicit your Excellency to direct our passage to be paid under
the following terms, namely, to deduct a year's pension from me commencing on 1 July next in lieu of same, myself supplying my family with sea store
… Once in Canada I could very well do without my pension for a year, as I
have several friends there in good circumstances, who, together with my own
industry and that of my family, would be sufficient for our support.'

Wednesday 19 May. Poor Law Commission to T. N. Redington   *Ballina*
'On 7 April we received a letter from E. Howley requesting additional paid   CSORP 0.6258
nursetenders. There were 800 in the workhouse with fever and dysentery and
nurses were required as they could not be found in the country. On 9 April
experienced and competent nurses were despatched to Ballina, their expenses to and from Ballina and one guinea a week to be paid. Since then the number of sick was reduced from 800 to 300 and only eight fever cases. One of
the nurses has caught the fever and there is little hope of her recovery. Their
salaries have not been paid and the Poor Law Commission request that, as in
the case of the Swinford Union, the salaries of the nurses will be paid from
the sums advanced to meet the current expenses of the workhouse.' *See
Appendix 5A.*

Wednesday 19 May. Samuel Bourus to Wm Todhunter, Society of Friends   *Belmullet*
'I am no London banker but a poor country shopkeeper … My conscience   SFFP 2/506/20
tells me I have done my duty and I leave the event to Him who knows the

secrets of hearts … Whilst writing the above, I was called out to see a woman with three very young children, who fell from exhaustion in my yard; she is now in my kitchen in a dying state. I must put down a large pot to boil peas in every day for the poor who flock here for assistance, my boiler which contains only 60 gallons being quite too small … The last supply given by your benevolent Committee will very soon be exhausted and then unless another be granted, all must starve. They are sinking daily and becoming weaker and weaker … But for the supplies granted by the Society of Friends, hundreds, now dragging out a weary existence, would months ago have died a lingering death.'

Kilmactigue
SFFP 2/506/36

Wednesday 19 May. Society of Friends clothes query form completed and signed by Mrs Jones, Banada Abbey (See Appendix 6Q)
'The whole of the working portion of the peasantry are reduced to all but nakedness. Men are obliged to work in this harsh weather without their coats that their wives who are on the public works may wear them. There is one instance of this in our own employment. His name is John Lendsdy? I just heard it by chance.
Kind of clothes: Frieze for the old men, barrogan and corduroy for young men and boys and drugget and calico or stuffs for the women and little girls.
Nothing short of starvation would induce the peasantry of this neighbourhood to sell or pawn their clothes. Many consider it a disgrace to do so. However, within the last winter many have done so in every family. One woman pawned her shawl to give bread to her family.'

Boyle

Friday 21 May. E. and R. Irwin to Society of Friends, enclosing a list of 159 families to whom they have distributed relief, with comments on each.
'Those marked S have one or more children receiving scriptural instruction and fed once every day. There are 152 children in the school, all fed daily and on the last day of the week we have for some time past given to one child out of each family (84) a quarter stone of meal for the sabbath day … This we were led to do finding many were fasting that day and missed the boiler which we do not use on that day … The biscuits were of great benefit. We gave them chiefly to the labourers who came at dinner time to the boiler, many having no other dinner, that one quart of soup which was often divided with his son.'

Dromahair
CSORP W.6581

Sunday 23 May. H. Allnut to Board of Works
'Today a priest, Thomas McKeon, publicly threatened or denounced me in his chapel and incited his people against me, saying that I had been transported and recommending the next time I visited work no. 19, to strip me

and duck me and that when my shirt was off they would see the marks of the Cat etc. The people were informed that I could give them employment if I pleased and that I have unlimited means at my disposal … There are great abuses. Persons were being paid that had not attended the works for two or three months, and two or three of the one family were employed. Some poor creatures had not one (of their family) on the works … I placed a Catholic and honest man as overseer, who brought to light numerous tricks … I have no doubt the priest could stir the people up to acts of violence.'

Monday 24 May. Fr Bernard McGauran to Archbishop of Quebec
'We have at present thirty-two of these vessels which are like floating hospitals, where death makes the most frightful inroads, and the sick are crowded in among the more healthy, with the result that all are victims to this terrible sickness … There are usually four or five hundred on board. Today I spent five hours in the hold of one of these where I administered the sacraments to a hundred people, while my very welcome colleague was on board another…While we are on the ships, there are people dying in the hospital without the sacraments. I have not taken off my surplice today: we meet people everywhere in need of the sacraments; they are dying on the rocks, and on the beach where they have been cast by the sailors who simply could not carry them to the hospitals. We buried twenty-eight yesterday, twenty-eight today, and now (two hours past midnight), there are thirty dead whom we will bury tomorrow. I have not gone to bed for five nights. The spectacle, My Lord, is heart-rending. Once these halpless people are struck down by this strange malady, they lose all mental and physical powers and die in the most acute agony! We hardly give anyone Holy Communion because we do not have the time…I am not at all afraid of the fever, I have never felt happier than in my actual state. The Master Whom I serve holds me in His all powerful hand. Night and day we are in the midst of the sick where there are many sudden deaths. We can hardly stop to take a rest, but someone comes in haste to summon us. There are already a great number of orphans, whom I recommend to your Grace … My Lord, it is impossible that two priests will do, my legs are beginning to bother me, because I am always on my feet.'

Grosse Ile, Canada
Grosse Isle pp. 50-51

Fr Bernard McGauran. Born in Ballisodare, Co Sligo, on 14 August 1821, son of George McGauran, merchant, and Brigid Colleary. Came to Quebec as a young man, where he studied for the priesthood and was ordained on 23 April 1846. He was among the first priests posted to Grosse Ile in 1846. His first tour of duty lasted a month. He was struck down by typhus but returned several times and was the last priest still there in the autumn of 1847.

Ballymote
SFFP 2/506/20

Monday 24 May. Rev J. Garrett to Society of Friends (See Appendix 6F)
'I have held over your kind grant for barley meal and Indian meal in the hope that rice might be procured instead of the barley meal … I have been enabled thro' your kindness to deliver out rice and Indian meal porridge with the happiest results among the poor afflicted with bowel complaints, dropsy and dysentery and if I had hopes that your late order would be given in rice it would be a great relief. Pray inform me if this is probable.'
Draft reply, 31 May: 'Send an order on the government depot, Sligo, for ½ ton of rice.'

Doocastle,
Bunninadden
SFFP 2/506/23

Monday 24 May. Joseph MacDonnell to Society of Friends (See Appendix 6I)
'Fever and dysentery prevail to an awful extent and many who have escaped those dreadful diseases are almost as great sufferers from want of the common necessaries of life … There is no fever hospital at Gurteen, 7 miles from this, three doctors having died successively of fever and no medical man as yet could be found to undertake this perilous duty. I know not what would become of the population here only for the indefatigable exertions of that truly amiable and charitable man, the Revd James Henry PP of Bunninadden. Several applications are daily made to me for green crop seeds … I will take upon myself the superintending of the cultivation of green crop seeds, should the Committee give the seeds.'
Draft reply, 26 May: 'Order on Sligo ¼ ton of Indian meal and ¼ ton of rye.'

Knockcrohery
CSORP Z.6371

Monday 24 May. John Brehony, pensioner of 27th Infantry Regt, to Lord Lieutenant
'I applied to the local relief committee for help but was refused … I am in deep distress, bordering on starvation. I humbly suggest that this is too bad to suffer a man, who fought and bled on the well-contested battlefield of Badajos, where he lost an arm, to perish of hunger, and that within a furlong of where he drew his first breath.'

Ballina

Wednesday 26 May. Palmer Kirkwood, rate collector, Killala to Poor Law Commission
'£85 rates still due … I had 450 civil bills served at the last Ballina Quarter Sessions. In 60 or 70 cases the parties left the country before the Sessions; 85 were entered for trial, half of those fled the country, several others were destitute paupers; I only obtained 12 decrees and recovered the rates from five. The other seven fled the country, one died and one became insolvent.'
John Irwin, rate collector, Greyfort, Ballina, to Poor Law Commission
'I had £20 in decrees against persons, some of whom have left the country, others … their property taken from them. Also a great number of persons

have absconded the country, leaving no property behind them and no person to pay the rate … In this district of Ballina … poverty extends to such a pitch that it is almost impossible to describe.'
Robert McAndrew, rate collector, Ballina, to Poor Law Commission
'£140 arrears due by persons from whom there were no means of procuring payment. Included in the arrears, £20 due by Capt Atkinson, who is non-resident and £12 due by Lord Clanmorris, non-resident and now dead and was tenant for life. £30 due by James Anderson, who is never to be seen, pays no person and who has no chattell property available. The remainder is due by paupers or persons who have emigrated or died.'

Friday 28 May. Report of Capt Lawson
'The case against Abraham? Martin for illegally fishing for and killing salmon in April … was brought before the Petty Sessions court of Sligo yesterday, but the witness, Terence Rogers, did not appear, although he had been apprized … and yesterday morning I myself warned him to attend. The charge of course, in the absence of the only witness, fell to the ground.'

Sligo
CSORP 1.6649

Sunday 30 May. Bernard McGauran to Archbishop of Quebec
'The *Saint George* has just moored beside the ship where I have been hearing confessions for the last four hours … I have gotten over my fatigue, not that I have been resting. But being used to it now, I do not feel as tired as I did in the beginning. I assure you, my Lord, that I have never felt so much consolation in my entire life, the blessings bestowed on us by the sick and the dying soften our hardships … mortality increases on board the ships, we have buried almost fifty today taken from these vessels. But I still hope that matters will gradually improve.'

Grosse Ile
Grosse Isle p. 59

Sunday 30 May. Cardinal Chanelli to Cardinal Fransoni
'I undertook to publish a notice (of the encyclical) by ordering that in the cathedral churches of Corneto and Montefialcone, as well as in all the collegial and parochial churches of the diocese, a solemn triduum be held, and by communicating to all those who wished to obtain the indulgence granted by the Holy Father, I ordered equally that in the said two cathedrals, suitable sermons be preached to move the souls of the faithful in favour of the poor Irish and I deputed in all parts, subjects, both ecclesiastical and lay, who besides making a collection in the churches during the triduum, would gather alms in their respective countries. The sum collected came to 159 *scudi* and 56 *baj.*'

Corneto,
Italy
SC IRLANDA
vol 29, f.988rv

Ballaghaderreen   *Sunday 30 May. Labourers and tenants to Lord Lieutenant (See Appendix 1B)*
DP 5925   'There are over 14,000 able-bodied men in the district … Altho' being deprived of the means of sustaining nature, we forbear to commit a breach of the law. The public works have been suspended and a temporary relief committed to peculent and fraudulent rulers, who are not content by seeing thousands of their fellowmen consigned to an unhallowed grave. We would most respectfully and earnestly solicit your commissioners, ere it was too late, to look with mercy on Her Majesty's loyal subjects of this district, by forthwith commanding the resuming of the public works.'

Coolaney   *Monday 31 May. Kate P. Thompson to British Ladies Clothing Association*
SFFP 2/506/36   'Having passed the winter on the public works men and women are reduced to a most pitiful state of nudity; mens' coats worn over a tattered petticoat on our women and the men somewhat indecent in their torn garments. My sick list is overburdened in a population of 1,100 who daily attend the soup kitchen. I have 400 on the sick roll, not one of them could provide one meal for themselves and are wholly dependant on the 1 lb of meal porridge they get at the soup kitchen which is not sufficient to sustain a man's strength. It is fearful to see men willing to work made a public beggar of.'
12 June, British Ladies Clothing Association completed and signed by Kate P. Thompson:
'1,200 are more like spectres in rags than human beings … We have a ladies association … manufacturing flannel, drugget and linen, besides making clothes for sale and knitting stockings … Our people are willing and anxious to be employed. There is hardly a house where there is not one or two with fever and dysentery, to whom we bring nourishing food and medicine … We have in our depository a supply of clothes for sale suitable for distribution.
Previous grants: £10 from Mrs Fowler, Tottenham and £10 from the Belfast Ladies Association.
Ladies Committee: Miss Gray, Miss McDermot, Mrs Thompson, Mrs O'Connor.

Ballina   *Monday 31 May. Resolution of Ballina Relief Committee*
'That a Board of Health be formed with the following members, William Atkinson, Edward Howley, Rev Hugh Conway, Rev Mr Lees, Rev Pat McHeal, Thomas Jones and William Whittaker … Capt Cox, inspecting officer of the Union, brought an order from the central Board of Health, calling upon them either to erect or rent a house as a hospital for fever patients from the electoral divisions of Ballina, Ardnaree and Backs.'

Grosse Ile   *Thursday 3 June. Fr Taschereau to Archbishop of Quebec*
Grosse Isle pp. 84-5   'It is a very painful thing to say and even more difficult to believe, but it is,

in my opinion, the expression of the truth, spoken by a captain whom I met today: "It would be better just to send a battery of artillery from Quebec, to sink these ships to the bottom rather than let all these poor people die in such an agonising manner: if things don't change, they will all die …" How can we wish them health when all breathe the foul air of the between decks, walk on flooring covered with muck; consider the unwholesome food and dirty water that they take for their meals! Most of them have for a bed the boards or a few filthy wisps of straw that do more harm than good: still, how many more after a month and a half of the crossing, are wearing the same clothes and the same shoes that they had when they came on board ship, and which they have not taken off day or night? I have seen people whose feet were so stuck to their socks that I could not anoint them! … I have already begged Mr McGauran to get some rest since our arrival; but he was satisfied simply with returning sooner to his house and getting to bed a little earlier than before. Yesterday, he complained of great weakness and this morning of a painful headache. After breakfast I almost commanded him, I don't know from what authority, to rest. Since he felt better he went aboard a few ships and came back towards one o'clock this afternoon with a severe fever.'

Sunday 6 June. Bishop of Castrimarius to Cardinal Ortinio, remitting 150 Neapolitan ducats, collected for the poor Irish.

Lucerne, 6 June. Apostolic Nuncio to Cardinal Franzoni, remitting the sum of 5,758. 65 French francs, collected in the diocese of Fribourg for the poor Irish 'The country is naturally poor and this year has suffered much from a scarcity of provisions. Besides, some radical cantons have forbidden the Bishop of Basle to publish the encyclical. Nevertheless, I am confident I will be able soon to send your Eminence another such sum.'

10 June. Same to same, remitting 7,630 French francs collected in the canton of Lucerne for the poor Irish 'and which exceeded my expectations. Of this sum, 1,000 francs were given by the Cistercian monastery of St Urban. In this year of scarcity and at a time in which all the Catholic cantons and especially Lucerne, are threatened by an armed invasion …'

11 June. Same to same, remitting a further sum of 3,672 frs and 60 centimes, to complete the collection from Fribourg diocese.

Sunday 6 June. Michael Groarke to Lord Lieutenant
'I contracted to make some drains on the sides of the road from Ballyhaunis to Sligo … Henry Brett, county surveyor, certified the payment of same at a special Sessions for the barony of Costello, 19 May to the amount of £10 but I cannot get the money until the next assizes … I and my family are in a state

Castrimarius, Italy
SC IRLANDA
vol 29, f.990rv &
f.166rv

ibid, ff.172rv

ibid, ff.174r

Ballyhaunis
CSORP W.6892

of starvation and implore the Lord Lieutenant to order payment and save me and my family from famine and death which will surely follow.'

Belmullet
CSORP Z.8922

Monday 7 June. Report of Henry B. Blake, sub-inspector
'On the evening of the 3rd inst. the *Wellington* of Belfast, bound for Westport, was passing the islands of Inniskea ... About ten miles off at sea, she was boarded by several curraghs, manned by country people, who plundered her of about forty tons of Indian meal and corn ... Up to the present date the plunderers are unknown ... The *Wellington* was on her passage from Virginia to Westport, with Indian meal for Martin Thompson, merchant, Westport.'

Sligo
CSORP Z.7139

Saturday 12 June. Petition of Denis Monaghan, Cloonagh, Killadoon, a prisoner in Sligo gaol, on a charge of having in his possession some beef which was supposed to be part of a bullock, stolen from John Gethen, Kingsboro, Sligo, to Lord Lieutenant
'Petitioner was committed to Sligo gaol on 26 March 1847 and was brought to the last Quarter Sessions in Ballymote to stand trial ... and still remains in custody, having applied to the Clerk of Peace for Sligo at Ballymote to be discharged ... What agrivates (sic) your poor petitioner's case is the circumstance of his having a wife and large helpless family solely dependant on your petitioner for support, and now left in a most destitute condition ... He humbly throws himself on your Excellency's clemency and mercy ... to order his release and restore him to his poor family, from which he is unjustly separated ... Under the circumstances of these fearful times of famine and disease, God only knows the consequences of what may befall his poor destitute wife and children, already a long burden on a heavy taxed and unfortunate country.'

Kilcolman
(Ballaghadereen)
SFFP 2/506/36

Sunday 13 June. Society of Friends clothing query completed and signed by Arabella Macdermot, Coolavin House (See Appendix 6C)
'*Number needing clothes:* about 200 mostly females.
What kind?: Flannels, calicos and check with corduroy.
Can they be made locally? It is much wanted to encourage female industry.
Are there any local manufactures? Knitting and spinning with a little sewing.
Can you get corduroys and moleskins made into jackets and trousers or frieze made into coats? We can. Our tailors are all idle.'
Draft note: 1 piece flannel, 1 piece calico, 1 blue print, 1 corduroy, 1 B. worsted, 1 B. cotton.

SFFP 2/506/20

13 June. Frances Kelly, Ladies Committee to Society of Friends
'A number of females have been employed by Rev Mr Tighe in making up

the material granted for clothing by your Society. These are now exhausted and there have been many applications to us for knitting which the committee was obliged to refuse from want of funds to provide the necessary materials … The boiler of the relief committe being out of order, it would be more convenient to our committee to distribute the rice uncooked … We shall willingly undertake to superintend its distribution at the dispensary according to the recommendation of the medical attendant … The public works are all stopped, the unfortunate poor worn out from poverty and disease and multitudes perishing from fever and dysentery or, if escaped from death from these diseases, certain to perish from want of better nourishment than that scantily doled out by the relief committee. The best proof of the wretchedness of this town is that a pawnbroker's shop not more than a few months established contains £700 worth of property, principally bedding and wearing apparel sacrificed to ward off the approach of hunger by tradesmen always remarkable for sobriety and who have hitherto been able to support their families in decent independance.'
Draft reply, 21 June: 'Order in Sligo half a ton of rice and 5 bags of biscuit … It would be much preferable to distribute the rice cooked.'

Tuesday 14 June. Rev B. W. Eames to Society of Friends (See Appendix 6V)   *Swinford*
'I should feel much obliged if you would let me have some rice for the poor   SFFP 2/506/20
of my parish suffering from dysentery. Your charitable Society will be glad to
hear that the condition of the poor is much improved since the government
relief has come into operation.'
Draft reply, 21 June: 'Order at Ballina half a ton of rice, half a ton of Indian meal and 5 bags of biscuit. This grant … is intended for the sick and for children and any destitute who from whatever cause may not be receiving rations under the Act … When this grant is expended … we shall be willing to make a further grant.'

Wednesday 16 June. Elizabeth Holmes to J. Bewley (See Appendix 6M)   *Coolavin*
'I am induced in my brother's absence for a short time to again throw our-   SFFP 2/506/20
selves on their kindness for a further supply of rice … A further one, if received, would be given altogether to children, of whom (since the closing of our soup kitchen on the last day of last month) 150 have been receiving each day one cooked meal … The quantity at present cooked is 4 stone per day and this if continued for some time longer would greatly ameliorate the condition of many families.'
Draft reply, 16 June: 'Order on Sligo for 1 ton of rice.

Castlebar
CSORP O.7844

Thursday 17 June. Poor Law Commission to clerk of Castlebar Union
'Amongst the most considerable (rate) defaulters are the Earl of Lucan, Sir R. Palmer, Sir Samuel O'Malley, Col McAlpine, Lord Kenmare, Wm Kearney, John Cheevers, Michael Rowland, James Hardiman, John H. Payton and John Bodkin … three of whom, viz. Lucan, McAlpine and Kearney, are members of the Board of Guardians … Since their re-election in March, they have taken no effectual steps to recover the rates due from the parties named. They can be recovered by action or suit in the superior courts.'

Ballymote
OP 26/198

Thursday 17 June. G. Knox RM to Under-Secretary, enclosing a notice sent by John Patterson, head constable, which he found posted up on the chapel wall and the market cross at the fair day in Ballymote on 14 June:
'This is to give notice to the labouring class of the barony of Corran to assemble on Wednesday next in Ballymote in quest of labour or support. It is better for the country gentlemen and farmers to co-operate with us than to see the result of this distressed class. Will commence at 9 o'clock in the forenoon.'

Ballaghaderreen
SFFP 2/506/20

Friday 18 June. Charles Strickland to Society of Friends (See Appendix 6C)
'It is the wish of your Committee to relieve as far as possible that class of persons who are not upon the relief lists but yet whose means are insufficient to afford them sufficient support without their disposing of everything in the way of stock which they may be possessed now, to their utter ruin hereafter. I request your kind assistance towards the relief of that class in the electoral districts of Loughglynn, Ballaghaderreen and Castlemore, in each of which I am chairman. The last fortnight's estimates for Ballaghaderreen and Castlemore were £591 but in all three divisions a very considerable number of persons now possessing some means are left off.'
Draft reply, 23 June: 'Send order on Castlerea for 3 tons of Indian meal and half a ton of wheaten meal. Oatmeal and wheaten meal mixed makes good bread.'

Ballaghaderreen
DP 7142

Friday 18 June. James Doyle to Lord Lieutenant
'He is a poor tradesman having five in family and no mains *(sic)* of support but in a state of starvation … got no relief, either work or meal, for his little weak family the whole year notwithstanding the many hundreds of pounds and tons of relief meal sent to the destitute of Ballaghaderreen and its vicinity but the poor did not get it. It was and is given in plenty to favourite persons under the superintendance of the committee, Charles Strickland and Joseph Holmes, who have given the management of the relief meal to a man, Edmund Duffy, a national schoolmaster and he can give or keep. He has a salary of £10 per year for attending the school but since the commencement of the relief meal being given, there is no attendance given

by him to that school. He is treble paid by the meal. A relief of clothing has been sent to the destitute in care of Revd Denis Tighe PP Ballaghaderreen, which by his influence to the friends of both Higgins and wife they get the greater and the best of the clothes, while poor destitute widows, orphans and other poor are left weak and starving. Also a great quantity of meal has been sent to the Revd Gentleman for the destitute that has been dealt with in like manner, people in good opulence getting it in plenty and those who are getting relief meal has also got their share of said meal and on the 17th inst. his reverence got *(illegible)* of dividing a few tons of meal and left hundreds of poor creatures starving of both town and country lying on the streets.

Also the money given by the charitable Quakers for the relief of the poor tradesmen of the town has been given to favourite persons, by giving under colour of charity, a few lbs of yellow meal to tenants and country people. But of all the relief that has been sent, he is denied of except one stone of meal which was given him by the request of Doctor Dillon who, seeing the little weak children in want, he got one stone of meal for him. This is the truth. He humbly implores your Excellency's fraternal protection of both himself and weak family by ordering immediate relief to support nature and not allow both him and family to perish. He refers the truth of the memorial to the books where the names of those getting relief are inrold *(sic)*. In fact the relief sent to the poor is squandered and taken away by persons in trust and out of every pound sent for their relief they get 5 oz.'

20 June. Michael Towey and James Kelly, Taunamucklagh, to Lord Lieutenant   DP 7204
'We never got one ounce of relief this year and … are in an awful state, having fourteen in family and no means of support … We do not know the reason why we would not get relief and hundreds of more wealthy in the neighbourhood getting relief. We would sooner die than commit any crime to shame and convict us to be prisoners … There is a report that the government is sending relief to the gentlemen and the clergy in this part of the country for distribution among the tenantry … If your Excellency was informed of the manner the tenantry and the poor are treated, your Excellency would be surprised, as all the relief is converted by the interest and affection of the committees and gentlemen to well-wishers of their own and the poor in an awful state of starvation and trampled on …'

Friday 18 June. Resolutions of the Board of Guardians   *Boyle*
'That the supply for last week was ordered by Mr Flavett, otherwise the pau-   CSORP O.7371
pers would have been without a morsel to eat and that the Commissioners be requested to forward the sum applied for on this day week and £100 for the ensuing week.

That Andrew Baker and James Fleming be approved as securities for Thomas

McDonagh, rate collector for Toomour electoral division and Martin Callaghan of Mullaghmore and Terence Finn for the electoral divisions of Kilfree and Coolavin with Andrew Baker and Pat McDonagh as their securities.'

Turlough
CSORP Z.7367

Saturday 19 June. Sworn statement of Charles Lestor, sent by Rev W. C. Townsend, chairman of Turlough Relief Committee, to Lord Lieutenant
'I was put in charge of the meal store in Turlough and given the key with instructions not to give it out without orders from Wm Malley, acting treasurer. On 19 June Edward O'Malley CC and M. O'Donnell CC came to the meal store and asked for the key to get a quantity of Indian meal. I refused. Thereupon Rev Edward O'Malley and Rev Michael O'Donnell endeavoured to break open the door and called for a crowbar or spade, and having failed to break the door, O'Donnell broke a window with a stick and afterwards, assisted by Rev Edward O'Malley, effected an entrance and took four carts of Indian meal, containing about 12 cwts each … In consequence of the crowd of people then present, amounting to upwards of one hundred, I was unable to resist such forcible entry.'

CSORP Z.8091

15 July. Magistrate's report:
'The case regarding the incident of 19 June came before the bench at Castlebar Petty Sessions this day. The magistrates present were Kearney, Dillon, Ormsby and above. Edward O'Malley CC was unable to attend owing to illness. Two witnesses were examined, Lester and the treasurer of Turlough Relief Committee. Lester appeared not to be anxious to press the charge and we could not elicit anything from him. The treasurer stated that the accused took the meal as members of the committee and also took the book with the names of those to receive rations and ticked off the names of those to whom they gave meal and they returned the book the next day and a small quantity of meal. The magistrates ruled that the store had been broken open and the meal taken but without felonious intent. The case was dismissed but they expressed their opinions that the conduct of the Reverend Gentlemen was most reprehensible.'

Keash
SFFP 2/506/20

Saturday 19 June. Abby Fleming to Bewley and Pim (See Appendix 60)
'My grateful thanks to your benevolent Society for the grant of 4 sacks of Indian meal made in May last … It has enabled me to alleviate in some degree the sufferings of 63 destitute families whose number amounted to 370. I distributed it three times a week … from 2 to 4lbs at a time, according to the number each had in family. Fever and dysentery prevails to an alarming extent in this locality … Up to the present period several poor creatures have not yet got relief at the government stores.'
Draft reply, 23 June: 'Send an order on Sligo for ½ ton of Indian meal and ¼ ton of rice.'

Tuesday 22 June. Edward Howley, Belleek Castle, to Poor Law Commission *Ballina*
CSORP O.7498
& O.7495
'We are in a most deplorable state for want of funds to purchase the necessaries for the inmates of the workhouse, having only received £100 for three weeks' maintenance. On yesterday we had not a morsel of bread for the children and the sick … and how we are to keep the house open and the inmates alive, I really do not know. We owe about £6,000 to our contractors, who are hourly importuning us for payment … I hope to have collected a large portion of the rates from the principal landed proprietors, altho' they are very much opposed to its payment. In the meantime, for pity's sake, come to the rescue of our poor workhouse inmates by an immediate and liberal advance of money for the provisions we have been getting for the last three weeks back … Fever is again very much on the increase and if, through want of funds, the unfortunate patients should want nourishment etc, I apprehend the most fatal consequences to all the inmates of the house.'

Wednesday 23 June. Petition of David Tarpey, Cahir, to Lord Lieutenant *Aghamore*
DP 7243
'Petitioner is a man that has five in family and spent all the means he had in the whole world to keep himself and his family from starving. Since November last the committee chairman of the said parish did not allow your petitioner one pound of the outdoor relief or one penny to earn on the public works … He begs and implores your Excellency will order or send your petitioner some relief to keep him and his family from starving.'

Thursday 24 June. Report on fisheries *Westport*
CSORP O.8472
'37 hookers, rigged with one mast and three sails and badly fitted, and 480 boats registered, with 2,171 fishermen. Fish include herring, haddock, ling, turbot, cod, sole, plaice, mackerel, pollock, whiting, bream, gurnet, raye, skate, congor eels, crabs, lobsters and oysters in abundance. The markets are Westport, Newport and supplied by cadgers to Castlebar. None are packed or cured for export and there are no stores or curing stations. A superior construction of boats is suggested.'
'There are 146 serviceable boats with 2,507 men and 35 boys. Fish include *Ballycastle* herring, cod, ling, turbot, sole, fluke, mackerel, lobster, bream, gurnet, pollock and salmon. The markets are Ballina, Killala, and Crossmolina. Owing to the famine the fishermen are too poor to keep their boats and tackle in order. Boat ports with good piers should be built.'
'There are 104 yawls and curraghs. There are immense quantities of fish on *Drumkeehan?* the banks, as fine as any in the world, but few are taken. In the market in Belmullet there are no fish or very few to what there used to be. The fishery

has gone to ruin since the last awful calamity has fallen on the country. The people have been unable to fish as they were wont to do in consequence of their want of food … Their boats and curraghs need to be repaired. They need to be supplied with fishing gear and fed for a season and in fact clothed also, more than the means of prosecuting the fishery here. I have no hesitation in saying that the whole population are in a state of utter prostration in mind and body, without money or means of any kind.'

Durlairgh? 'There are 595 boats with 2,653 men. Fish include, cod, ling, haddock, bream, glasson, halibut, turbot, salmon, herring and oysters. The markets are Belmullet, Crossmolina and Ballina. Larger hookers are required as the fish are more abundant at a considerable distance from the shore.'

Donegal to Ballina 'There are 500 square-sterned boats and yawls, averaging about two tons and pulling four oars, with 2,883 and 84 boys. Fish include, herring, mackerel, sprat, haddock, cod, ling, glasson, hake, sole, turbot, plaice, horse mackerel and many others. There is no established market. Carriers come to the fishing station to buy and supply the interior and neighbouring towns. There is no curing or packing. Suggested improvements include a curing station, bounties and better boats.'

Pullendira, Co Sligo 'There are 117 boats and 720 men. Fish include, salmon, sole, plaice, cod, glasson, herring, turbot and lobster. The markets are Ballina, Easky and Sligo.'

Ballina CSORP O.7498 *Friday 25 June. Poor Law Commission to T. N. Redington, requesting a further £100 for Ballina workhouse*
'Since 22 May the Poor Law Commission paid £5 14s. 6d due to a nurse who died of fever and £5 10s. to another nurse who caught the fever but recovered sufficiently to enable her return to Dublin.'

Tubbercurry DP 7213 *Tuesday 29 June. Anonymous letter to Lord Lieutenant*
'I beg your Lordship will order Capt Gilbert of Sligo and Capt Wellesely of Swinford to look after the quality of the meal, the committees of this locality are getting for the poor. It is of the very worst description, by means of influential persons having friends selling such in Sligo. They are getting it through them. The meal is near rotten.'

DP 7152 *Dean Hoare to Capt Gilbert re above:* 'On one occasion I heard complaints about the meal … Our treasurer, Mr Brett, purchased 10 tons at Sligo from a friend of his, Dr Conlon, at 10s. less per ton than he paid at Mr Culbertson's mills at Ballisodare. Of this meal I heard some complaints. On another occasion, Brett purchased 12 tons from a friend and relation of his in Sligo, Mr Dan Henry … Brett is a most upright man.'

Tuesday 29 June. Extract from Guardians' minutes
'No money lodged by the collectors since the last meeting, the collectors
attending the Ballina Sessions, recovering arrears due by some immediate
lessors, on whom civil bills were served by the Board's solicitor.
Resolved: that our solicitor be directed to take the most summary proceedings
against Charles Forde, late collector, and his securities for his gross neglect in
not having paid the rate collected by him.'

Swinford
CSORP O.7758

Tuesday 29 June. J. A. Holmes to Bewley and Pim (See Appendix 6M)
'I have distributed the 2 tons of Indian meal and 1 ton of barley meal granted
me by the Society of Friends on the 7th and 15th of last month. There are a
few stones yet in hand. The distress still continues very much among a class
of farmers whose holdings are valued too high to get relief from the relief
committees and who in consequence are great sufferers … Disease is very
prevalent, particularly fever, and these people require great care, their confinement precluding them from carrying anything to support them … I trust
the Society will grant me another supply for the district of Coolavin.'
Draft reply, 5 July: 'Order on Sligo half a ton of wheaten meal, 1 ton of rice
and 5 bags of biscuit to be distributed to the destitute who are not entitled to
receive relief under the Act.'

Coolavin
SFFP 2/506/20

Wednesday 30 June. Memorial of John Judge to Lord Lieutenant
'Memorialist was check clerk under the Board of Works from 2 December
1846 to 12 January 1847, on a new line of road from Swinford to
Ballaghaderreen. He never received payment despite repeated applications to
the assistant engineer, Mr Halpen, and government inspector, Capt Lyndy …
He humbly implores that your Excellency will display the same spirit of justice as practised by your noble predecessors … His wages were 15s. a week …
His situation at present is extremely precarious, his pecuniary resources are
entirely exhausted, the awful condition of the times press heavily upon him.
In the name of charity, justice and benevolence and with a suppliant air,
memorialist begs your Excellency will have his money paid him, which on
affidavit he can prove to be due.'

Ballyhaunis
CSORP W.7580

Wednesday 30 June. Mark H. Devlin, medical officer, to Edward Howley
'I have just been at the workhouse where I found the inmates in a sad state
from want of food. I was unable to order anything for the sick, except what
could be supplied from the surgery. There has been no bread in the house for
the last twenty-four hours. Neither has there been wine, porter or meat. The
convalescents from fever and dysentery are dying from want of nourishment.
The healthy portion of the house are becoming faint from hunger; and fever

Ballina
CSORP O.7706

is spreading rapidly among them. It is hopeless to think that the healthy can escape disease, or that the lives of the unfortunate sick poor can be preserved, if such a state of things … continues.'

1 July. Edward Howley to Poor Law Commission
'We are in a very bad way in the workhouse for want of provisions, as the £100 sent weekly, if even sent regularly, is totally inadequate to purchase a supply … The poor people are dying rapidly and even those just recovering from fever are actually carried away for want of nourishment. Fever is very much on the increase again and if things are allowed to go many days longer as they are, I shudder to contemplate the fearful consequences. I got on yesterday a small supply of bread from the baker and one ton of meal from Mr Callaghan on my own account, but this is now nearly consumed and what we are to do for the remainder of the week, I really do not know, as the £100 expected today is long since due and must be at once paid away … *Howley implores the Poor Law Commission* 'to come at once to the assistance of the poor famishing inmates of the workhouse.'

CSORP O.7814   *5 July. Report of Mark H. Devlin, medical superintendent*
'The inmates have suffered very much, particularly during the past week, from insufficiency of food … On one occasion there was no bread in the house for twenty-four hours and frequently neither wine, porter or meat are at all procurable … The recovery of the convalescents is considerably retarded from want of sufficient nourishment and some lives are lost from the same cause. Fever has latterly increased … The fever sheds are almost completed. At least 50 bedsteads should be immediately ordered. The patients should be removed to the sheds as soon as possible.'

Belmullet
CSORP S.7602

Wednesday 30 June. William Mague, Ballina, to T. N. Redington, advising that the Quarter Sessions should not be held in Belmullet on 6 July, because of the prevalence of fever there. He encloses a statement signed by Peter Shiels, W. O'Donel, Walter Bourke, Edward Bolingbroke, Thomas MacAndrew, Robert Paget, Charles B. Jordan, Ignatius Kelly, Myles Jordan and Robert Mostyn, that 'it would entail the most destructive consequences and that they decline to attend.' *Also enclosed a statement of Thomas Fergus, process-server, residing in the town of Belmullet, who* 'verily believes it would be dangerous to the safety of the court to congregate there from the prevalence of fever of the most frightful and virulent description, which afflicts more than half the population of Erris and more particularly the town of Belmullet … There are vast numbers at present lying with fever … There are several cases of fever in Belmullet Bridewell … At least every second house in the town of Belmullet has either inmates lying in typhus fever or recovering from same or has had numbers swept away by this disease … Many of the persons who shall attend at the Sessions must, from the miserable condition of the remaining peasantry and the prevalence of fever and dysentery, become victims of these distempers.'

Thursday 1 July. Poor Law Commission to clerk of Castlebar Union   *Castlebar*
'One of the (rate) defaulters is the chairman of the Union, the Earl of Lucan.   CSORP O.7844
Others of them are either members of the Board of Guardians or gentlemen
of rank and consideration in the Union … It is most unfortunate that claims
were not conclusively pressed against members of their own body at a time
of universal and severe distress. During the five years that the Union was in
operation, the greatest number of inmates in the workhouse was 202 and at
the present time of famine and disease is 405. Seven inquests found the persons died of starvation in a period of six months.' *The Poor Law Commission
calls for the dissolution of the Board of Guardians to be replaced by paid
Guardians. E. T. B. Twistleton signed and sealed the act of dissolution of the
Castlebar Board of Guardians.*

Friday 2 July. Charles Strickland to Society of Friends   *Ballaghaderreen*
'A good portion of the population are left off the relief lists and many of these   SFFP 2/506/20
persons require some aid to prevent them becoming paupers … Very much
good might be done by relieving that class who are not now in that state of
destitution to enable them get the present relief.'
4 July. Same to same
'I have been obliged to buy many tons of meal at my own risk … in anticipation of government funds. However, all is now going on well, I believe. A
good deal of this confusion was owing to the violence of the people, chiefly
of those in better circumstances, who threatened the committee on one or
two occasions, if they would not put all on indiscriminately for relief.'
Draft reply, 8 July:
'Send C. Strickland an order on Castlerea for half a ton of barley meal and
half a ton of wheaten meal.'

Saturday 3 July. Memorial of Thomas Williams, captain, George Cann and John   *Broadhaven*
Browne, first and second mates of Richard Watson to Lord Lieutenant   OP 26/242
'The *Richard Watson* on voyage from New York to Sligo, with a cargo of
Indian meal, while becalmed off Broadhaven on the night of 3 July, was surrounded by upwards of 30 boats carrying more than 150 men. The three
aforementioned cut the ropes which attached the boats to their vessel, drove
off the pirates and took seven of them prisoner and carried them to Sligo.'
*They ask the Lord Lieutenant for compensation, as they were detained by the trial
and lost earnings on other vessels.*

Sligo

Sunday 4 July. Sister Mary Francis de la Salle, Convent of Mercy, to Cardinal Franzoni, thanking him for the donation of £20 for the relief of poor children and others in this afflicted district.

Elphin & Killala
SC IRLANDA
vol 29, ff.184rv 187r

Monday 5 July. Bishop George Browne, Elphin, to Cardinal Franzoni, acknowledging the receipt on 5 June of £100 sterling (£50 for the poor of Elphin and £50 for Bishop Thomas Feeney of Killala).

Broadhaven
OP 26/242

Monday 5 July. Statement of John Doyle, master of the smack Emily Maria
'The smack *Emily Maria* of Dublin from Sligo bound to Westport laden with Indian corn, was openly attacked at sea by six curraghs consisting of 17 men, east-south-east of Broadhaven. I and my crew kept them off and did not let them board us, but in my effort to protect our lives and property, two of my men were severely wounded by a number of stones they hove on board of us, some of them 2 and 3lbs weight.'

Swinford
SFFP 2/506/20

Monday 5 July. Ulic Burke to Society of Friends (See Appendix 6V)
'The number of applications that are to be considered, the necessary forms that are to be complied with and the many unfortunate delays that frequently occur, may and indeed must prevent relief being given as promptly as is to be desired … Unfortunately fever like famine will not wait until they are complied with … I can however, only endeavour to discharge my duty to the best of my power and wait with patience until I am enabled to do so more efficiently … The crops have a most healthy and luxuriant appearance and present every prospect of an early harvest.'
Draft reply, 9 July: 'Send £5 more … We should be glad to place some rice and biscuit in the hands of any trustworthy person you might recommend who would undertake to distribute it to the sick.'

Coolavin
CSORP H.7954

Tuesday 6 July. Board of Health, Coolavin, to T. N. Redington, requesting a grant of £102 0s. 4d., signed by J. A. Holmes, chairman, Constantine Cosgrave PP, Edward Costello, Peter Foreman, secretary, and James Bourke?
'The population in the 1841 census was 10,206. The principal landlords are Lords Lorton, De Freyne, and Palmerston, and Mr O'Farrel Cadet. The resident magistrates are the Prince of Coolavin and J. A. Holmes. The gentry are Capt Sherlock of Mt Irwin, Edward Costello of Kilfree and Andrew Baker of Redhill. At present there is no description of employment since the public works were suspended and the small farmers have no need of labour.'

Shrule
SC IRLANDA
Vol 29

Wednesday 7 July. Michael Phew PP to Alexander Barnabo, Propaganda, Rome, acknowledging receipt of letter and bank bill payable to Rev Dr Cullen, to the amount of £20 for relieving the poor of his parish.

'The poverty and destitution here is great in the extreme. There are great numbers of them dying for want of food. There is fever and other sicknesses, the usual accompaniments of destitution, very general amongst them. There are many of the deceased buried without any coffin but a little straw tied about them. The people very generally look pale and emaciated because they have not half enough to eat. They are, notwithstanding, very religious and patient in their suffering. I hope you will be pleased to represent their wants and privations to those in Rome who are charitable, in the hope that they may relieve and save them from dying of starvation.'

Wednesday 7 July. Memorial of John Lavelle to Lord Lieutenant   *Ballycastle*
'One James Price broke into his house last April and stole out of it a stone   CSORP I.7871
and a quarter of meal and bread. Price was indicted to take his trial at the
Swinford Quarter Sessions in April last. Michael Lally, police constable stationed at Ballycastle in said county, arrested the offender and after a relapse of 12 hours enlarged him. Memorialist is a very poor man and prays the Lord Lieutenant will consider the matter, as memorialist was put to considerable expense in getting informations signed against the said Price. Price is now dead about six weeks and the robbery was committed early in April last.'
Mick Lally, constable to sub-inspector, Ballina, 10 July, re above:
'3 April last I arrested James Price who was at the time so weak I much feared he would die in the guardroom that night. Next day he was brought before Mr Fausset? JP, who at once ordered Price to be set at liberty and sent Mr Chambers with him to the soup kitchen with orders to put him on the list for soup to keep him from starving. Price being so weak at the time, he died in a few weeks ... Price was a small boy of about thirteen years of age.'

Friday 9 July. Francis Breaky to Poor Law Commission   *Boyle*
'The Board sent for several persons in town to induce them to contract for a   CSORP O.8010
month or three, but they refused ... I have as much food as will last until
Tuesday ... I would have been without fuel for the last fortnight, had I not got two poor men to give me 200 boxes of turf at 9d. a box, on the faith of being paid this day ... I cannot leave the door scarce for them.'
Extract from Guardians' minutes
'The Board observes with pain and great alarm that some doubt is expressed of the intention of the government to continue assistance. The Board is totally and absolutely out of its power to provide for the daily expenses of the workhouse ... The supplies for the last fortnight were obtained by two of the Guardians, relying on the faith of the weekly advances ... the unparalleled distresses and difficulties in which the whole country is involved, rendering the collection of any tax at the present moment almost an impossibility ...

There is difficulty in finding sufficiently solvent collectors ... The only alternative is that of discharging at an early date every inmate of the institution.'
12 July. Francis Breaky to Poor Law Commission
'Only one Guardian lives in town and one within a few miles of it ... The town is crowded to excess with the poor everyday receiving outdoor relief and it will be awful if the 635 I have here are obliged to turn out, many of whom, poor things, are not able to leave their beds ... I see no alternative unless in mercy you come to my relief ... If we had one fortnight over, we would have a considerable sum of our rates. Mr Elwood is the collector for Boyle and three or four other divisions. What on earth shall I do on Wednesday? To let those poor things, whom I have watched over so long with so much anxiety, go out, will indeed be painful; and what is to become of those who are laid on beds of fever and sickness? Some of these poor creatures this day heard in some way that they were to be turned out on Wednesday and the scene was truly afflicting, such weeping and "Oh, what will become of us and our poor children?" Unless you kindly send me glad tidings by Wednesday morning's post, the poor creatures must either go out or starve within ... I never despaired before. I do now, for the country about here is in a most awful state of distress, fever and sickness.'

Glannamadda
CSORP H.8009

Monday 12 July. John H. Sullivan, medical officer, to Lord Lieutenant
'Fever is this moment at its height. One poor wretch in this village was ten days past in low typhus and not a being would venture inside the door she is in but myself.'

Ballaghaderreen
CSORP W.7991

Monday 12 July. John O'Grady and John Neilan, surveyors and levellers, to Lord Lieutenant
'They were employed under the Board of Works under Mark McGarry, then engineer to the Board in this district, at 5 shillings a day, from 28 May to 18 June inclusive. McGarry promised on 18 June they would be paid on 27 June at the latest but they have not yet received remuneration. They applied to Mr Brett but he has only evasively replied to them, with a seeming disposition to captiously wheedle them.'
Report of H. Brett, Castlebar, 22 July re above:
'The writers were not employed by my direction or with my consent, neither was I aware of their being engaged. McGarry, who was assistant engineer, could not give a satisfactory account of their employment. I asked the parties to furnish detailed diaries of the services rendered ... They gave me evasive and unsatisfactory replies. The assistant himself should have done the work and in one week and not three weeks.'

Monday 12 July. Report of Richard Bourke

Ballina
CSORP O.8095

'I visited the workhouse this day and minutely inspected it throughout, making myself acquainted as far as possible by this means, with the condition of the inmates, and I also examined several officers of the establishment … I found the house in a state of excellent order, the appartments perfectly clean and ventilated, the paupers decently dressed, and such of them as were not under medical treatment, or recovering from it, healthy in appearance. I also observed the same amongst the children in the schools. But among the convalescent patients, I observed very few indeed approaching to a state of recovery, whilst the proportion which they bore to those under active medical treatment was larger than is usually the case. This I have no reason to doubt is to be attibuted to want of nourishment and the evidence of the doctors and nurses confirm this opinion. By these it will appear that for 24 hours patients under medical treatment or in a convalescent state have been kept without any description of food whatever, and that even when procured, it was often insufficient in quantity and not suited to their condition. Upon examining the nurses and comparing their evidence with the diet book kept in the hospital, I found that stimulants ordered for fever patients and nourishment ordered during recovery from fever or dysentery, had not been given, and it is manifest that without these recovery must be uncertain and tedious. In point of fact, that tho' deaths have not been frequent, relapses are daily taking place, and the appearance of the sick is strong evidence to show that they have not been supported as their necessities required … It further appears from the evidence that the healthy portion of the inmates of this workhouse have suffered much privation from diminished quantity of food, and irregularity in its supply, but it does not appear to me that this has in any way affected their health, or entailed more than temporary inconvenience and suffering.

It does not appear to me that there has as yet been any deficiency in the attendance upon the paupers. The number of paid nurses and other servants is, I think, sufficient, and as far as I can judge they have performed their duties well. But they are considerably in arrear of their salaries, and as their duties are severe and dangerous, it is not likely they will long continue to discharge them unless regularly paid. An example of this occurred today in the resignation of the head nurse …

In practice, the whole weight of anxiety and responsibility occasioned by the want of funds, and the difficulty of obtaining supplies for the workhouse, has fallen upon the master, an officer who appears to me to have discharged his duties with great zeal and attention. The money which has procured the paupers their daily food has in many cases been advanced out of his pocket, and the chairman of the Board appears to me the only member who has in any degree shared the responsibility, or by personal interference endeavoured to mitigate the extent of the evil.

After closing my enquiry at the workhouse, I attended the Board of Guardians, and represented to them in the strongest manner the grave responsibility they had incurred by their delay in putting the rate in collection which had been agreed to on 8 February. I urged upon them the duty of forthwith performing their part and doing all in their power as a Board to alleviate the sufferings of the poor ... I succeeded on a division in getting the warrants signed for all the electoral divisions, except two ...

The Guardians have thus perhaps done all that as a public body could be expected of them, but the present difficulties in the workhouse still continue. There is no money in hands and no food in store, and 755 paupers in the house. The provision for breakfast this day was one hundred weight of meal paid for by the master himself, and he has no prospect of obtaining their dinner in any other manner.

If any of the present rate is collected (which I think is doubtful ...)I fear in the interval before the first lodgement there must be very great suffering amongst the inmates of the workhouse and perhaps consequences fatal to the lives of some ... There is at present an execution in the house at suit of one of the contractors, and some portion of the new rate, if paid in, would probably be appropriated to liquidate this debt.

Evidence given and signed by Thomas Hart, master of the workhouse since its first opening: 'Considerable difficulty has been found within the last three months in procuring supplies generally for the use of the inmates of the workhouse. The ordinary diet is as follows for adults: Breakfast – 8 oz of meal made into stirabout and half a pint of new milk. Dinner – 12 oz of white bread three times a week, with a quart of soup, made of meat stock, seasoned and thickened. On the other four days – 8 oz meal made into stirabout with half a pint of new milk or one pint of buttermilk. The dietary has been observed up to about two months back, when the first difficulties arose. The contractors then declined to continue the supplies ... Represented the matter to the Board upon every Board day. Meal and bread have since been frequently procured on the master's sole responsibility. By this means he has secured to the adult inmates daily the stipulated allowance of meal. But the bread has been irregularly given. These two solely were supplied on credit by the contractors with the guarantee of the master and the amount paid to them on receipt of the occasional remittances from the P. L. Commissioners. Great delays and hardship has been entailed on the inmates. Upon one occasion, Monday the 5th inst., there was no meal or food of any kind in the house. I advanced £5 of my own money, which I gave to the clerk which he laid out in meal and I gave the paupers their breakfast. They got it between

10 and 11 o clock. The usual hour is 9. At noon the Board met and I represented the matter. The chairman said he would leave an order on the contractor. When the Board broke up, I went to the store for the meal but was
refused. Late in the day I sent again and obtained 17 cwt at 8 o'clock in the
evening. The paupers got their dinner of stirabout at 10 o'clock. The amount
for this has been paid out of the last £100 forwarded by the Commissioners.
This morning (12 July) I purchased from my own funds 1 cwt of oatmeal for
the paupers' breakfast. There is not anything in hands or in the house for dinner, nor do I know how it is to be obtained.

On one occasion there was no bread to be procured for 24 hours and consequently no food given to the sick paupers, many of whom required nourishment. The sick paupers are kept on bread diet with the addition of such articles as the doctor's diet book may order.

On Saturday night last at 10 o'clock I waited on the chairman who himself
gave £5 worth of bread for the use of the paupers. Without this authority we
would not have obtained it.

*Evidence given and signed by Catherine Kellet, head nurse tender in charge of
the infirmary.* 'Is aware of the orders given by the physician amd apothecary.
In many cases when such articles as porter, meat and milk were ordered for
patients, they did not receive it or get it very regularly. The paupers under my
charge have been for 24 hours without food. On this day week they received
a small quantity of Flummery (made of the husks of oats) in the forenoon
and nothing again until the following day at noon, when such as were
allowed it obtained 6 oz of bread. Is of opinion that the irregularity in supply and the actual want of many articles has in many cases delayed recovery
and in some produced relapses.'

Anne Gibbons, nurse: 'In attendance on patients in dysentery and other complaints in the body of the house.' *Corroborates Mrs Kellet to a certain extent
but was nervous and not much to be got from her.*

*Evidence given and signed by James McNair, apothecary more than six months
to this workhouse.* 'The course of business is for the physician to enter in his
book the articles whether of medicine or food required. In the case of food
the apothecary enters the articles required in a Diet Book which is handed to
the master and the articles required are by him given out to the nurses of the
different wards.

The wine when ordered medicinally is given to the apothecary and by him
given, in the quantities ordered, to the nurses. During the last five or six
months the order for wine has not been complied with upon six occasions
but not oftener.'

*Evidence given and signed by Mark Henry Devlin, surgeon, attending medical
man since 19 April last.* 'Fever and dysentery existed in the house more so than

at present ... There has been considerable difficulty in procuring for convalescent patients the articles of nourishment which their condition required, such as broth, meat, wine or porter. Has entered these articles in his prescription book from whence the apothecary marks them in his book which was sent to the master. But on enquiry of the hospital nurses, found that what was ordered has not been procured.

Attributes many of the relapses in fever cases to the absence of these articles. One death of a patient in dysentery believes to have happened for want of food. The delay in the supply of necessary articles extended to one or two days sometimes. At this moment there is a great occasion for broth and no means of procuring it.

There is at present sick the following numbers: fever, 114, dysentery, 106, other diseases, 113, total, 333. The hospital in the workhouse is calculated to hold about 100 persons. That number is now exceeded by 14. Fever patients are kept in the hospital as much as possible but it is insufficient for their accommodation and some of the convalescent patients have to placed in the front building. The safety of the inmates of the workhouse imperatively demands the shed to be got ready as soon as possible for the accommodation of patients.'

CSORP 0.8150   *13 July. Thomas Hart, master, to Edward Howley*
'Thanks for leaving the order with Mr Gahagan for 20 cwt of meal ... We are terribly situated as regards the sick. We have not 1 lb of bread to give them or the means to procure it as the last £5 worth you got from Mrs Daly is gone. The promptitude of the Poor Law Commission sending funds alone can save the lives of over 300 sick persons. Your absence is a loss to me on this trying occasion as I have no other resource to fall back on.'
Howley left the above note in the Poor Law Commission office on 16 July.

CSORP 0.8271   *15 July. Report of Richard Bourke*
'Any attempt at the present time to collect even the moderate rate imposed by the Board of Guardians must end in disappointment ... Three classes who pay rates, landed proprietors, occupiers of land and owners or occupiers of house property. A landed proprietor in this county is under peculiar difficulties. His property is infinitely subdivided ... The majority of occupiers are valued under £5 p.a. ... A large portion of the rate is thrown on the proprietor ... A number of farms are abandoned by the occupiers ... A huge extent of arable land is left uncultivated ... By the non-payment of rents, the proprietor's means of paying rates are reduced ... The barony cess collectors for Tyrawley and Gallen have great difficulty in collecting the Grand Jury cess from occupiers. It is necessary to employ a large force of police to assist and protect them. This means it would be impossible to collect rates. The owners of house property in towns like Ballina, Killala and Crossmolina would

most likely pay the rates demanded, even though much poverty exists among the small traders. Mr Joyner (manager of the Provincial Bank, Ballina), is of the opinion that the present resources of the principal rate-payers would not enable them at this moment to meet the demand.'

Monday 12 July. Ulic Burke MD to Bewley and Pim, acknowledging £5 to assist the sick poor (See Appendix 6V)

Swinford
SFFP 2/506/21

'The mode in which I find that rice can be administered most beneficially to the poor is by giving them a small quantity at a time (1lb or to a large family 2lbs) and directing them to boil it in a large quantity of water for one hour or two. This forms a very light complaceous drink which when flavoured with a litle sugar is most grateful to the sick and particularly beneficial to the convalescent and to the children, the great majority of whom have not a single drop of milk to dilute the dry food with which they are now being supplied. Should you approve of this mode of distributing it I should cheerfully dispose of any quantity you may give me.'

Draft reply, 14 July: 'Send an order on Ballina for a quarter ton of rice and 3 bags of biscuit.'

Monday 12 July. Henry Joseph McCarrick to Society of Friends (See Appendix 6B)

Aclare
SFFP 2/506/21

'The relief committee appointed for this electoral division often allow their depots which amount to three to run short of meal for two, three or four days in the week. On these days the disappointed peasantry flock about my house … Almost the entire of the applicants I know to be without provisions at home or the means of purchasing them …

P.S. The last Indian meal which I received from the government stores was commencing to malt, being in large lumps, which were sour or indeed not very well liked by the peasantry. It is reported that at present mallets must be employed to break it before it leaves the sacks.'

Draft reply, 14 July: 'Order on Sligo for half ton of Indian meal and a quarter ton of rice to assist persons who do not receive relief under the Act.'

Tuesday 13 July. Richard Keane to Poor Law Commission

Castlerea
CSORP O.8042

'If you do not continue the advances for a little longer, the house must be closed, as the former contractors will not give any more supplies without ready money. In fact they are unable to do so. Several struggling tradesmen have sent us clothing within the last few days on the promise that they will be paid in a few days.'

Tuesday 13 July. Bishop Laurence O'Donnell to Cardinal Franzoni, acknowledging the receipt of £50 sterling.

Galway
SC IRLANDA
vol 29, f.194r

Ballaghaderreen
ibid, f.200

Friday 16 July. Bishop Patrick McNicholas of Achonry to Cardinal Franzoni, acknowledging the receipt of £50 sterling for the relief of the poor of Achonry

Sligo
CSORP Z.8139

Friday 16 July. Petition of Widow Mary O'Brine, Rusheen, near Sligo town, to Lord Lieutenant

'Petitioner's cow was stolen by person or persons unknown, of the value of £15 sterling. The cow was found by Sergeant Hamilton, killed on the mountain of Killery, Co Sligo, and most part of the flesh carried away and there were two heifer calves contained within her, she being a few days of calving when stolen. She is a poor, desolate and distressed widow, having four orphans to support, without any friend or relations to look to them and since the occurence took place, they are almost in a state of starvation, as the cow so stolen was their only support by selling her milk. She has no means whatever to purchase another cow and begs to be paid a compensation to enable her and her helpless orphans to get over the difficulties she has to contend with in those miserable times.'

T. N. Redington to Mrs Mary O'Brine, 19 July:

'The circumstances to which you refer give you no claim whatever upon the government.'

Achonry
SFFP 2/506/21

Friday 16 July. Dean Hoare to Society of Friends (See Appendix 6A)

'I received 1 ton of rice, 1 ton of Indian meal and 5 bags of biscuit. I left for distribution by my curate (Tubbercurry) 2 bags of rice, 2 bags of meal and 3 bags of biscuit … Each day I have had a boiler which contains 60 gallons cooked thus, 4 stone of Indian meal to 2 stone of rice. 60 gallons distributed daily, given out at the rate of half a gallon daily to each family … The distributon of the food cooked has been of great benefit in this neighbourhood … The boiler kept daily in operation has been of great benefit in checking sickness … This part of the district is more free from sickness than other less favoured parts. As all my supplies will be exhausted in about 10 or 12 days, I shall be thankful for an additional supply.

Draft reply, 21 July: 'Order half ton of rice, half ton of Indian meal and 5 bags of biscuit for the sick, convalescent, infirm and young children.'

Tyrawley
CSORP Z.8304

Saturday 17 July. John Gardiner, inspector of drainage, to Richard Griffith

'The weather has been very favourable and the grain crop generally has improved very much this week. I heard this day of two instances of disease in potatoes, such as last year but I have not yet seen any such.'

Frenchpark, Richard Irwin, inspector of drainage, to Richard Griffith

'Crops of every description are most promising in their appearance and in every part of the county there is a prospect of an early and abundant harvest.'

Monday 19 July. Abby Fleming to Society of Friends (See Appendix 6)   *Keash*
'I have just distributed the last of the liberal grant of meal and rice so kindly   SFFP 2/506/21
made me … It has enabled me to relieve 87 destitute families, whose aggre-
gate number amount to 609 persons, besides 94 destitute strangers …
Dysentery has disappeared but fever is on the increase to an alarming extent
… In most cases it assumes a most virulent character. The destitution around
is now as great as ever, the government relief having partially ceased and will
entirely on the 15th of next month and no other relief available.'
Draft reply, 24 July: 'Order on Sligo ½ ton of rice for distribution to the sick,
convalescent and young children.'

Tuesday 20 July. Richard Griffith to T. N. Redington, enclosing extracts of reports   *Crops*
of 27 inspectors of drainage from 19 counties   CSORP Z.8307
'Potatoes in a precarious state … The matter will be decided within the next
month … One-sixth of the usual extent planted … Considerable number of
green crops, consisting of turnips, carrots, parsnips, peas, beans and mangold
vorstoyle? … Oats, wheat, barley, bere and rye is greater than usual. The general deficiency of food to meet the wants of the lower orders will not be considerable, except in the western and south-western counties, where the population is great in proportion to the extent of cereal crops sown, and where
heretofore the potato has been the sole food of the people. One acre of potatoes produces as much human sustenance as three acres of oats. Less than
100,000 acres of potatoes planted in the 10 western counties and probably
not half the crop will come to maturity.'

Tuesday 20 July. Denis Tighe PP to Bewley and Pim (See Appendix 6C)   *Ballaghaderreen*
'This is the most trying month they have to endure, and as fever is fearfully   SFFP 2/506/21
spreading among us, the poor are in the greatest distress. We owe you gentlemen a great deal for all you have done for us. I trust this is the last appeal
I will be obliged to make as the prospects of the coming harvest are as
promising as we could desire.'
Draft reply, 24 July: 'Order on Sligo ½ ton of rice and ½ ton of barley meal.'

Friday 23 July. Extract from Guardians' minutes   *Boyle*
'Its credit being not only wholly exhausted but the most importunate   CSORP O.8500
demands are made by the contractors for the payment of the large sums due
to them.
Resolved: That the deplorable circumstances of this Union be again laid
before the Poor Law Commissioners and that discharging the destitute
inmates of the house appears inevitable.'

Tyrawley
CSORP Z.8567

Saturday 24 July. Report of John Gardiner, inspector of drainage in Co Mayo
'The general appearance of the crops is encouraging. Barley and wheat look very well. The oats are rather short owing to the late sowing. The turnips are most flourishing ... Instances of the potato disease are not to be met with. The works continue to progress rapidly and satisfactorily and are being brought as fast as circumstances admit to a conclusion.'

Castlebar
CSORP H.8474

Sunday 25 July. G. V. Jackson to T. N. Redington re Castlebar Assizes
'Mr White sent to distribute turnip seed was attacked at Castlebar and died of fever ... The matron of the gaol is reported dead of fever. One of the medical gentlemen resident in the town is dead from fever. Great alarm prevails as to this state of things in connection with the approaching assizes. No jurors will have courage under pain of any penalty to attend the assizes if some measures are not taken to meet this fearful calamity. Could the Board of Health take any steps as regards the courthouse and that would tend to allay the public alarm. The gaol is so crowded I greatly fear for the consequences.'
Board of Health to T. N. Redington, 9 August, re above:
'The Board suggests whitewashing, ventilating and sprinkling with chloride of lime the courthouse ... Regarding the gaol, it suggests the separating of the sick from the healthy.'

Ballisodare
CSORP I.8866

Monday 26 July. Pat Flaherty to Lord Lieutenant
'About 12 o'clock on the night of 30 June he was arrested and taken off his bed in Ballisodare on the suspicion of sheep-stealing. He was sent to prison where he remained three days, when he was liberated by the constable. He asked the constable to pay him his wages and the constable said, "I'll pay you no wages. Go to Mr Cooper's head steward." He is a labouring man working in a public mill in the town of Collooney at the rate of 1s. 2d. a day and his reason for not lodging in Collooney is that his aunt lives in Ballisodare, having a commodious house. He requests the Lord Lieutenant to order an investigation into his case as he not only lost his time in gaol but his character, what is more invaluable, altho' holding but the humble rank of a labourer in society.'
J. McVeigh, constable, Ballisodare, to H. B. Pilkington, sub-inspector, Sligo, 2 August, re same:
'On 30 June received information from Mathew Walsh, Bresuge, that a sheep was given in charge to his boy from the fair of Tubberscanavan and ordered to be left at James Morrison's of Ballisodare. While on his way, he found the sheep to be the property of E. J. Cooper of Markrea Castle and that the sheep was stolen and would be called for that night. He immediately deposited the

sheep in the pound ... and kept watch on Morrison's house. About 12 o'clock, seeing a light in the house, he found two men, John Davy and Pat Flaherty. On getting no satisfactory answers, he arrested them and brought them to the barrack. Next day he brought them before Gowan Gilmore JP who committed them to gaol. Afterwards Davy confessed himself guilty.'

Tuesday 27 July. J. A. Holmes to Bewley and Pim (See Appendix 6M)   *Coolavin*
'I distributed your kind grant of 1 ton of rice and 1 ton of Indian meal. The   SFFP 2/506/21
rice was of the greatest possible service, so many poor people are ill of fever.
There is still much distress and will be for three weeks more. Much of it arises
from the relief commissioners having ordered a reduction among the persons
getting outdoor relief.'
Draft reply, 31 July: 'Order a ton of rice for the relief of the sick, convalescent
and young children.'

Tuesday 27 July. Capt Burmester, Boyle, to William Stanley   *Kilfree*
Thomas Quinn of Cloonlaugh came this morning and informed me that   CSORP Z.9992
James Cavanagh, store-keeper of the Kilfree electoral division, brought a
quantity of provisions of the Kilfree Relief Committee to sell at Boyle market ... I had Cavanagh arrested and Davis, sub-inspector of police sent
Cavanagh with an escort to Mullaghroe where the Kilfree Relief Committee
were assembled. Quinn and the carman who had brought the stores to Boyle
were examined It was proved that Cavanagh at daylight yesterday morning
took about 5 cwt of Indian meal from the Cloonlaugh depot and brought it
to Boyle, where he sold 1 cwt to the carman. Mr Holmes JP has remanded
him for a week. The store at Cloonlaugh is in the premises of Rev C.
Cosgrave PP of Killaraght, and Cavanagh is a brother-in-law to Cosgrave. I
bring this circumstance to your notice, in order that such a flagrant act may
not by any accident be allowed to escape punishment.'
15 September. Same to Relief Commissioners
'It is of consequence that Cavanagh should not be allowed to escape with
impunity. A similar case took place recently when a man named Irwin stole
Board of Works' property and escaped punishment because he had charge of
the stores. Cavanagh has employed the same solicitor as Irwin who was successfully defended in that as store keeper his offence only amounted to a
breach of trust and not theft.'
Burmester enclosed a letter he received from J. A. Holmes:
'Cavanagh was committed by me to Sligo gaol to await trial at the Quarter
Sessions at Ballymote on 9 October ... I think it would be very desirable that
the Relief Commissioners should employ counsel to prevent the ends of justice being defeated.'

CSORP Z.11321   *5 November. Charles O'Hara, Quarter Sessions Crown solicitor, to Relief Commission*
'I prepared an indictment for larceny ... at the last Quarter Sessions at Ballymote against James Cavanagh which was ignored. I procured a copy of the informations and personally examined the witnesses. I could not have done more.'

CSORP Z.739   *15 December. James Cavanagh, farmer, Cloonloo, to Lord Lieutenant*
'Upwards of 4 cwt of Indian meal belonging to him is most unjustly detained and withheld from him, in the police barrack, Boyle, by the chief officer, Mr Davis ... He (Cavanagh) brought the meal to Boyle for the purpose of disposing of same ... He was falsely charged with having embezzled same ... He is a very poor man and himself and his family are very much distressed by the withholding of so much necessary food, during the present time of deaths by starvation and hunger in this neighbourhood.'

CSORP A.739   *12 January 1848. Joseph A. Holmes JP to the Under-Secretary*
'About August last Cavanagh was employed by the Relief Committee of Kilfree as their depot store-keeper to distribute meal to paupers ... He had filled the situation for a short time when he was brought before me on suspicion of embezzling a quantity of meal to sell in Boyle. I examined the carrier who was employed by the committee to take meal from the central depot at Mullaghroe to Cloonlargh. He swore that about 4am Cavanagh brought him into his house and emptied 4 cwt of meal out of the committee bags into sheets, took the meal with Cavanagh into Boyle. The poor people heard of this and gave information to the police who arrested him. He was sent to stand trial at Ballymote where the bills were ignored. The inspecting officer to the Relief Committee ordered the prosecution to be carried on and the Relief Committee dismissed Cavanagh. Cavanagh has frequently applied to me for an order for the meal which I declined giving.'

Belmullet
SFFP 2/506/21   *Friday 30 July. Lt Cary to Society of Friends*
'They are reducing the relief lists under the late Act. I must confess I am utterly unable to understand either the policy, justice or humanity of this proceeding but so it is and its consequences will be fatal to the peace of this part of the country as well as to the lives of the people.'

Tyrawley
CSORP Z.8746   *Saturday 31 July. Report of John Gardiner*
'The grain crops are arriving fast at maturity and have improved very much lately. In only two instances have I observed disease in potatoes and these cases are by no means as evident as last year.'

Saturday 31 July. William Evans, secretary, Upper Canada Farming Society, to Edward Bullen, secretary, Royal Agricultural Improvement Society of Ireland

Montreal
CSORP 0.8807

'It is impossible to employ terms that would correctly convey to you the amount of suffering and death that has been the fate of the wretched people from their landing in Canada. The great majority of them on arriving are utterly unfit for any labour and only subjects for the hospitals. On landing they appear crippled in their limbs, and altogether so debilitated that they are unable to help themselves in any way. The most healthy portion of them appears to be unequal to even the most moderate labours. Were you to see these poor people as I do every day, many of them without any shelter except the fences, exposed in their unhealthy state to a burning sun, that has ranged from about 100° in the shade, for more than a week, and 140° in the sun, you would understand their sufferings. I believe all that is possible is done for them here, but preparation for the reception of tens of thousands of diseased emigrants was never contemplated, and it is no trifling difficulty to provide for such additions as we see land at Montreal every morning from the steam roads, frequently two or three thousand in a day. I cannot answer which state these poor people were in when they left home; but if you were to judge of their state by seeing them here on arrival, we must certainly conclude they were only food for the deep or for our burial grounds on their landing. I also beg to state that many of them who have been sent over by their landlords assert that they were promised money here on arriving, which has never been received by them since. I must now conclude and not shock you with any more horrors.'

Saturday 31 July. Amount of money distributed in Ireland by the Congregation of Propaganda since 31 April 1847

Rome
SC IRLANDA
vol 29, ff.224r 225r
226r

'In the province of Tuam, £750 was distributed as follows: Tuam, two remittances for £100 each, Elphin, two remittances for £100 and £50, Killala, same for £50 each, Achonry, same for £50 each, Galway same for £50 each, Kilfenora, one for £50, Clonfert, one for £50.
The province of Cashel received £779 14s., of Dublin, £400 and of Armagh, £863 14s. The total for the whole country came to £2,792 14s. 4d.'

Saturday 31 July. Elizabeth Holmes to Society of Friends (See Appendices 6C&M)

Ballaghaderreen
SFFP 2/506/21

'I send an account of the manner in which their grant of rice to Clogher school of 16 June has been distributed. There are now in attendance at the school 220 children. From the difficulty of feeding such a number, we have sometimes thought of reducing it but know not which child to begin with. They are fed six days in the week and the quantity of rice cooked for them each day is about five and a half stones. This might seem a large supply but in many cases they have very little support beside, and we have instances of the younger ones fainting from taking their food too quickly after a long fast.'

Draft reply, 4 August: 'Send an order on Sligo for ½ ton rice, ½ ton Indian meal and 5 bags of biscuit for the school.'

Autumn 1847

Partial Failure and 'Souperism'

Reports of the state of the potato crop varied. On 3 August C. G Otway, while reporting his first instance of disease in Ballina, declared: 'I never saw finer new potatoes at this time of the year in the market, as I saw within the last week at Sligo, Castlebar, Ballina and here (Swinford) today.' A month later, Denis Phelan reported: 'From Castlebar to Westport only three potato fields looked promising.' Even though the potato blight was on a far smaller scale than in the previous year, the actual yield was disappointing. It was estimated by some observers that only only one-sixth of the normal acreage was planted.

Isolated instances of proselytism occurred. Fr James MacDonagh complained to Rome about the activities of the Anabaptists and Presbyterians in his remote parish on the Atlantic seaboard. 'They have established schools in every quarter of the parish where they were giving a paltry subsistence to the Catholic children, who were first obliged to renounce their former faith before they got a morsel from them.' Emily and Rebecca Irwin had set up a Bible school on their demesne in the neighbourhood of Boyle. Up to recently their accommodation was sufficient 'but the troubles of the last year have wrought a wonderful change.' They asked the Society of Friends for a grant to help them expand the building to accommodate the greatly increased numbers of pupils. The Quakers turned down their appeal. These were exceptional cases. In most areas priests and ministers cooperated amicably and effectively in their untiring efforts to alleviate the distress of their parishioners.

Swinford
CSORP O.8813

Wednesday 3 August. C. G. Otway to Poor Law Commission
'I visited a potato field belonging to Dr Atkinson, Ballina ... The stalks were large and strong, with a light yellowish appearance and a slight sprinkling of black leaves ... Under the leaves were withered, crushed and in many cases black ... I dug some in different parts of the field ... The tubers were more or less diseased as the disease of last year. The potatoes were large and remarkably prolific. This was the first instance I saw of diseased potatoes this year. Coming from Ballina here (Swinford) today I remarked that the potato stalks had got a kind of autumnal hint, too early, but I did not see or hear of any distinct development of the disease. I never saw finer new potatoes at this time of the year in the market, as I saw within the last week at Sligo, Castlebar, Ballina and here (Swinford) today, selling at from 13d. to 9d. and 10d. a stone.'

Westport
CSORP O.9122

Thursday 4 August. C. G. Otway to Poor Law Commission, recommending the dissolution of the Westport Board of Guardians for dereliction of duty
'I arrived today at Westport from Swinford ... I met the master and clerk on the road, who told me that there was no meeting because of the assizes in Castlebar and that they were going up and down thro' the town looking for food on credit from the shopkeepers ... It was a most striking instance of dereliction of duty on the part of the Guardians ... The food for the previous week or two had been provided by the bounty of Lord Sligo ... There were 540 inmates, 106 of them with fever ... There were three Guardians living in the town, Mr Bland, Mr Graham and Dr Burke, who were not Grand Jurors.'
Poor Law Commission to clerk of the Union, 10 August, informing him of the dissolution of Westport Board of Guardians.

Kilkelly
SFFP 2/506/21

Monday 9 August. Edward P. MacDonnell to Society of Friends (See Appendix 6P)
'I beg on the part of the parish to return you my best thanks for your offer of rice ... If you could afford us a boiler it would be of the greatest possible service. It would be more preferable to get an order on Ballina ... The poor are in a most dreadful state. The parents of several families having gone to England and left the unfortunate children without any means whatever.'
Draft reply, 14 August: 'Send him a boiler for 50 or 80 gallons and an order on Gallaghers of Ballina for half ton of rice and 5 casks of Indian meal.'

Bunninadden
DP 7774

Thursday 12 August. Rev J. Garrett, chairman of Kilturra Relief Committee, to T. N. Redington
'This electoral division extends into a portion of Co Mayo, is the exclusive property of absentee landlords, has a thickly planted body of paupers, ten-

antry and others living in it, totally neglected by their natural protectors, and consequently when called upon to reduce the numbers on the ration lists, we find it a most painful task, since no relief from any part of the crop in the ground is yet available. Indeed, a large proportion of the soil is uncultivated, thrown up to the bailiffs, for the landlords are far away and the wretched population left to subsist solely on the rations. By the good management of this committee and the assistance of Capt Burmester, we have had few blank days as to our stores, but when this relief stops, we tremble for the fearful shock to this most miserable district. Scarcely any potatoes are to be seen in Kilturra electoral division.'

14 August. Rev J. Garrett, chairman of Kilshalvey Relief Committee, to T. N.   DP 7775
Redington

'The gigantic labour attendant upon the chairmanship of these several electoral divisions, which devolved upon me, in consequence of the non-residence of the landed proprietors, has in no instance been more perplexing than in this electoral division. My respected friend, Revd Edward Powell, was ordered for his health to the sea in June. He had been chairman and since his departure, the meetings were very irregular. At length I found it necessary to rescue the poor from starvation by taking the management and having found the electoral division deeply in debt to a provision merchant, have only this day been able to pay all the demands of that humane individual, and nearly the whole of the arrears to the staff, carriers etc, but to reduce the rations on the list formed no pleasing addition to our work ... There is much fever ... No relief from potatoes and no other crop within a month of affording relief. We have unhappily experienced some sad interruptions in our supplies, owing to the departure of our first chairman.'

27 August. Capt Burmester to Rev J. Garrett   DP 7927

'Your list for the electoral division of Kilshalvey has been reduced in accordance with the orders of the Commissioners from 1,000 to 134, the number of persons of the 1st class on the relief list and if any expense is incurred for more than that number, it will be at the private charge of the committee.

Your estimate is also reduced from £99 8s. 7d. to £15 18.s 1d. and you will have the goodness to reduce from this date the number of your depots. No payment will be sanctioned for more than one depot. You must therefore reduce the depot clerks and assistants to all above that number.

In consequence of the irregular way in which the accounts of the Kilshalvey Committee were kept, I will not sanction the arrear of wages due to the clerk.

28 August. Rev J. Garrett to Capt Burmester

'I ... am quite shocked at the sudden reduction you have felt it your duty to make. In one sweep you have reduced 1,000 rations to 134 which will throw a multitude of poor families into not only destitution, but multiply deaths by starvation. I can't agree with you in your construction of the letters which you did me the honour to read for me. The original lists of helpless poor selected for insertion in that part of our ration lists allotted for that class, merely set forth a few old infirm persons, fit objects at that moment for the workhouse, but since that list was prepared a total change has taken place in the condition of many of the families then classed among the able-bodied. Fever and dysentery have carried off the heads of families in great numbers and the strongest young men, in many cases who were the chief support of their families, either fled to America or to England to escape the contagion and left behind them feeble children and old women quite unable to labour, now fit subjects for the helpless list. But you have cut off the supplies of these wretches. Many farms held by those who were able-bodied in May last are now wasted in consequence of the deaths alluded to and the hovels are still inhabited by the surviving portion of the original inmates, and no food or crop of any sort is within the reach of these wretches. They have been existing on the rations and now must starve. In the committees of Kilshalvey and Kilturra, I have laboured to reduce the numbers gradually until I brought them to the lowest possible standard that they could bear without starvation, but you have now thrown them off one fortnight before the new intended system of relief is in operation and a month before any corn crop in these districts can be fit for food, even in the hands of those who still retain the farms. I would hope, Sir, that you would reconsider the instructions of the Commissioners and not limit the relief for the next fortnight to those few you have found in the original helpless poor lists. It is quite plain from letters I have received from the authorities that the reduction was meant to be gradual and the relief was not to be confined to the small number you have selected. It is a most painful duty that we all have to discharge, but we should clearly understand the instructions of the government before we take upon ourselves to cast into starvation thousands of poor feeble families just recovering from fever and without a morsel of food. You forget that in the electoral divisions of Kilshalvey and Kilturra there is not a single resident landed proprietor. In these the unfortunate inhabitants have no protector near to look after them and that if they are not sustained by the system of relief hitherto afforded till the new poor law is in operation, they will starve in hundreds to death. None can so well know their real condition as those who are doomed to live among them and I can't help pressing upon you the absolute necessity that you shall forward my estimate for a thousand rations for each of these electoral divisions for the next fortnight and grant me supplies to that amount for the miserable creatures who are on our ration lists. It may not be any guide to you, Sir, but I do assure you the view you have taken of your orders is quite different from that of other finance committees and inspecting officers and I am satisfied that you will regret that you have thus abruptly sent so many into starvation to whom extended relief for another fortnight was actually granted by the government.'

3 September. Capt Burmester to Relief Commission   DP 7914

'The population of Kilturra electoral division is 2,613; the number of rations estimated by J. Garrett for the present fortnight was 1,087. I reduced the number to 173. The population of Kilshalvey is 3,272, the estimated daily rations, 1,000. I reduced this to 134. The Committee of Kilturra and Kilshalvey will meet on Tuesday next to close their accounts.'

Friday 13 August. Rev J. Garrett, chairman of the Relief Committee of Drumfin,   *Ballymote*
to T. N. Redington   DP 7776

'This division is inhabited by a dense body of miserably poor cottiers, who have no present employment, many of them in fever and feeble from the effects of dysentery and not being blessed with a resident gentry to give employment or support, are thrown upon this committee for rations to keep them from starving. By the benevolent exertions of Capt Gilbert, the government inspecting officer, and the indefatigable labours of the Sligo Finance Committee, the arrangements for the supply of rations have been most effective, and no interruptions been permitted, but if the supplies now stop, deaths from starvation will multiply daily.'

Sunday 15 August. Patrick McGowan, Culur, near Louisbourg, to Lord Lieutenant   *Louisburgh*

'Petitioner served nine years and nine-twelfths in the Continental War and   CSORP Z.9035
was wounded at the battle of Tullevary, in the left hand, by which he is rendered unable to labour. He has a small pension of 6d *per diem* … He was forced to seclude himself from the human race to the mountainous confines of the west of Mayo, his pay not fit to support him in any other place. Distress crept in by the failure of the crops, of which he shared his fate, and left him totally destitute. Fever set into his family and the rations were not appropriate so that he is in destitution and much more, his family lying in fever, which causes his destruction unless looked upon. His creed also, as a Protestant, impedes his relief in this bigotted place.'

Lord Lieutenant to McGowan, 17 August:

'There are no funds at his disposal for this purpose.'

Monday 16 August. Bishop of Sarfina and Berinora to Propaganda, enclosing a   *Italy*
donation for the relief of the poor Irish.   SC IRLANDA
vol 29, f.253r

18 August. Chancellor of the Bishop of Chur to Propaganda, forwarding 7,000   *Switzerland*
French francs collected in the diocese for the relief of the poor Irish.

Co Roscommon
CSORP O.29108

Tuesday 17 August. Report of Thomas Derinsky RM re potatoes
'The disease has reappeared in this neighbourhood in a most decided and unquestionable form. I inspected a large crop in Lord Crofton's at Moat Park ... Half of them are destroyed. The blight was first observed on last Tuesday the 10th inst. ... In two or three days it increased considerably and has since increased very rapidly ... I have inspected very minutely the crops of several farmers and cannot discover any symptoms of the disease. On the contrary they appear generally to be most luxuriant and the produce unusually abundant ... The blight of last year took place a month earlier and was universal and simultaneous ... Those brought to market are generally dry, firm and well-flavoured.'

Broadhaven
OP 21/444

Thursday 19 August. Commander of Neptune, revenue cruiser, to Inspector General
'When on my passage to Dunkeehan, I observed at 10 pm (then about one mile to the eastward of the Stags of Broadhaven), six boats well-manned pull across the vessel's bows ... apparently with the intention of boarding. Having asked them what they required, their reply was meal or biscuit ... I immediately had a few rounds of musket ball cartridge fired over their heads, which had the desired effect of dispersing them and the lawless ruffians rowed for the shore as quick as they could.'

Castlebar
CSORP O.9345

Saturday 21 August. Robert Lecky, Arthur Thomas and William Carey to Poor Law Commission
'The great majority of all classes have experienced a sad and trying reverse by the calamity of last year and it will require a long series of prosperous harvests to restore the people to anything like their former reported condition ... Its population was immediately prostrated; the claims of the landlords were but partially discharged and, as the necessity of acquiring the means of purchasing food continued to press, the cattle, horses, sheep, pigs and even the fowl were brought to market and sold for whatever they would bring and hence the almost utter deficiency of stock on the smaller holdings.'

Sligo to Castlerea
CSORP O.9311

Saturday 21 August. Report of Denis Whelan
'The extent of land sown with potatoes is very limited with the exception of a few miles around Sligo, Boyle and Castlerea ... I saw a diseased potato field near Boyle town and near Frenchpark two fields diseased and I heard that a considerable number of fields there were also diseased. The oat crop is average or above average ... A large proportion of arable land from Frenchpark to Castlerea is unsown ... The quantity of food sown is insufficient to feed the population. The condition of the people is yet pretty good; there is not much appearance of actual destitution.'

22 August. R. M. Whelan RM to T. N. Redington   *Sligo*
'The continued and rapid decay of the potato crop in the counties of Sligo   OP 21/22733
and Mayo, having created great sensation amongst all classes, it has lately
become a subject of discussion with the labouring population, how they can
coerce the magistrates and cess-payers to apply for additional grants of
money for public works, in order to give more general employment and it
has been estimated that public meetings of the lower and working classes will
be assembled in different parts of the county of Sligo … Should such public
meetings take place of large bodies of people, will it be desirable that any military or police force attend at such meetings?'

Monday 23 August. William Dawson, coast guard, Belmullet, to the Inspector   *Belmullet*
General   OP 21/448
'The brig *Camilla* of Whitehaven, laden with sugar and rum from Demerara,
bound to Greenock, anchored off Blacksod quay at night from stress of the
weather … The system of piracy has so degraded the habits of the people,
that it matters little what the cargo consists of. No vessel approaching this
coast is safe from plunder.'

Monday 23 August. Bishop Patrick McNicholas of Achonry to Cardinal Franzoni,   *Ballaghaderreen*
acknowledging the receipt of £50 sterling for the relief of the poor of Achonry.   SC IRLANDA
vol 29, ff.271r 272r

Tuesday 24 August. Archbishop of Leucosia, major chaplain of Naples, to Cardinal   *Naples*
Franzoni, enclosing 1,700 Neapolitan ducats for the relief of the poor Irish.   ibid, f.279
24 August. Archbishop of Florence to Cardinal Franzoni, enclosing the sum of
£12,247 /5 /4 (Tuscan lire), comprising £8,987 /5 /4 from the diocese of Florence,   *Florence*
£460 from the city of Prato and £2800 from the vicar-general of Pistoja, for the   ibid, f.283rv
relief of the poor Irish.

Wednesday 25 August. Petition of Michael Gordon, Andrew Giblon and Michael   *Ballaghaderreen*
McNamara to Lord Lieutenant   CSORP M.9296
'On 15 August the 19th Regiment of Foot were marching from Boyle to
Castlebar and were billeted at Ballaghaderreen. A report prevailed that the
troops were infected with fever, such as were billeted on the aforementioned,
holding a house of entertainment. They refused but offered instead to take the
healthy. They were summoned at Ballaghaderreen and fined £2 which they are
unable to pay in these melancholy and starving times. Captain Kelly, police
officer for 13 years in the town, can certify that they never before refused a bil-
let. A man named Rush, who took one of the sick soldiers, died himself of
fever four days later. The case against a fourth man, Patrick Kirrane, was dismissed as he was working in the fields and it was his wife who refused.'

Draft reply: 'The Lord Lieutenant has no authority to interfere and their application should be made to the Secretary of War.'

Collooney
CSORP z.9368

Thursday 26 August. Memorial of Thomas Smith, Templehouse to Lord Lieutenant 'On 21 June he was going to the fair at Ardnaglass and met Paul Dyer and Martin McQuinny driving a cow to the fair to sell. Dyer said he would take £5 15s for the cow which he later reduced to £4 15s. He was surprised to see the cow milked and suspected she was stolen and took the two men prisoner. He asked George McMunn to help but he said it was a bad country and he was afraid to interfere. Dyer ran away. He (Smith) drew a knife and with a good deal of trouble marched McQuinny to Tanrego police station and handed him over to Sergeant Simpson. He made a statement to Capt King and McQuinny was committed to Sligo gaol to stand trial. Paul Dyer was taken the same day by Constable Daly. He gave evidence against both of them and they were sentenced to twelve months with hard labour. Later in Pound Street, he (Smith) was struck by a man with a whip. Constable Daly told him his life was in danger. He attempted to go home and was attacked by three men and a woman with stones. Finaly he was escorted by a policeman for seven English miles. The cow belonged to Widow Bridget Kilmartin who had seven orphan children and she had not another cow in the world. He applied numerous times for the money he spent in car hire to and from Sligo and in lodgings in Sligo for the trial. He had a bakery business and had to go to Sligo for flour. This was now too dangerous and he lost the bakery business.' *He asks the Lord Lieutenant to get him into the London or Dublin police.* 'I am only 25 years of age and I am six feet in height and I don't think there is a more active man in either forces.'

Ballina
SC IRLANDA
vol 29, f.293rv

Monday 30 August. Bishop Thomas Feeney of Killala to Cardinal Franzoni, acknowledging the receipt of £100 sterling.

Fermo, Italy
ibid, f.297r

Thursday 2 September. Cardinal da Angelis, Archbishop of Fermo, to Cardinal Franzoni, enclosing 680 scudi collected in the archdiocese for the relief of the poor Irish.

Mayo
CSORP o.9666

Saturday 4 September. Report of Denis Phelan, Poor Law inspector, on the potato crop
'From Castlebar to Westport only three potato fields looked promising. From Westport to Ballinrobe patches, not fields, were more numerous but the extent was inconsiderable. There is not enough potatoes or oats to feed the population for six months … The condition of the people since April and May is much improved. Then an immense number appeared to be starved;

now, altho' generally the peasantry and working people look thin and care-worn, they do not appear to be suffering from want of food to such an extent as they did before. The same applies to the towns of Castlebar and Westport. But in the lines of roads throughout, a considerable number of persons, boys and girls and children particularly, present the most wretched appearance; many nearly naked and evidently insufficiently fed. When the rations are discontinued a considerable number will be unable to subsist without food, money or employment.'

Monday 6 September. Abby Fleming to Bewley and Pim (See Appendix 6O)   *Keash*
'I have again to return you my warmest thanks for another grant for the sick   SFFP 2/506/21
poor in my neighbourhood ... I should like it to consist of equal parts of
meal and rice as I generally distribute it in a mixed state.'
Draft reply, 8 September: 'Send order on Sligo for a quarter ton of rice, a quarter ton of Indian meal and 3 bags of biscuit.'

Sunday 12 September. Estimate for Kilshalvey Relief Committee for fortnight   *Bunninadden*
ending today   DP 7297

> Destitute, 134 multiplied by 14 = 1,876 at 1½d., £11 14s. 6d.
> Thomas Irwin, clerk, £1 16s.
> John Anderson, depot, 18s.
> John Clinton, assistant, 10s.
> Carriage of meal from commissary store, 19s. 7½d.
> Total, £16 0s. 2d.

14 September. Rev J. Garrett to Society of Friends (See Appendix 6I)   *Kilturra &*
'As a great many poor people are relapsing into fever and dysentery, your   *Kilshalvey*
promised grants to the electoral divisions of Kilturra and Kilshalvey cannot   SFFP 2/506/21
come too soon ... Your former supplies did a vast deal of good among the
sick and destitute in these several electoral divisions but now that rations are
stopped I must fear great numbers will starve to death, since there are hundreds quite unable to labour.'
Draft reply, 18 September: 'Send order for half ton of rice and 3 bags of biscuit
... He is at liberty to allocate this according to his own judgement.'

Tuesday 14 September. Finance Committee of Swinford Union (G. V. Jackson,   *Swinford*
chairman, Francis R. O'Grady, Edward Deane and Charles Strickland), to Lord   CSORP Z.9934
Lieutenant
'We ... cannot allow our duties under the temporary Relief Act to come to a
close without expressing to your Excellency how deeply we are sensible of the
enormous efforts that have been made to save life and relieve human suffering in this Union, as well as in the country generally.

We are at a loss to say whether an offering of our gratitude is most called for by the unexampled benevolence of the generous English people, the charitable exertions of the Society of Friends, the aid and sympathy of distant communities, or the many and various measures of the government.

As to the latter channel of assistance, altho' opinions vary as to the direction given to the relief measures of the government, we feel there cannot be any second opinion as to the motives by which these measures were dictated, the object at which they were aimed and their surpassing magnitude by which thousands of lives were saved in this Union alone.

The value of these combined agencies of relief to us are largely enhanced by the painful retrospect the past year presents to our view, as well as the horrors we have ourselves witnessed. In this Union the prejudices of the population to the poorhouse were so deep and inveterate, that the house was a long time open before one pauper could be induced to enter it. Famine, however, came on with such unrelenting severity that in a short time the house was filled with the number (700) it was intended for. On the dreadful 10th of November 120 were admitted beyond the regulated number, hundreds were refused admission for want of room. Some unhappy beings perished on the high roads and in the fields. Influenced by terror and dismay, leaving entire districts almost deserted, the better class of farmers in numbers sold their property at any sacrifice and took flight for America, and the humbler classes left the country in masses hoping to find a happier doom in any other region. This awful state of things continued in the winter and spring in a greater or lesser degree. In this Union 367 persons died in the poorhouse; the master of the house also died. In one adjoining Union, Ballina, 200 were admitted to the house beyond the number it was built for; hundreds were refused admission for want of room and 1,138 died in the house. The medical officer of the house was also carried off. In another adjoining Union, Ballinrobe, all the officers of the house were swept away and 254 inmates of the house perished.

Our best acknowledgements are due to the Relief Committees in the various electoral divisions for the assistance they rendered us, and it only remains for us to look back with admiration and gratitude on the manner in which Captain Wellesley RN discharged his duties as government inspector of the Union. Placed as a stranger in an extensive Union, without the advantage of a resident gentry to assist him, he promptly made himself master of the actual state of the population. He constantly attended the meetings of the Board of Guardians and of the relief committees, and he constantly visited the food depots in the different parishes of the Union. He carried out the law in our opinion with great credit to the government, and marked advantage to the Union, and we feel a pleasure in knowing that he takes leave of us, carrying

with him the cordial wishes of all classes for his future welfare and happiness.'
14 September. Resolution of Swinford Board of Guardians:
'The public mind is agitated as to the demands made for the repayments of
the advances … The government should make the fullest enquiry into the
fearful operation of famine and pestilence in this Union and the present
capacity of the rate-payers to meet heavy demands … They seek time to
recover from the shock society in its every relation has received … as not to
overwhelm and crush the struggling industry of the country, at present sunk
to the lowest point of depression by a natural calamity which has not any parallel in history and which has fallen with its worst severity on this and on the
adjoining Unions.'

*Wednesday 15 September. Bishop George Browne to Cardinal Franzoni, acknowl-
edging the receipt of £50 sterling for the relief of the poor in his diocese.*

Elphin
SC IRLANDA
vol 29, f.324

Thursday 16 September. Fr Bernard McGauran to Archbishop of Quebec
'We have nine ships including three disembarking their passengers today and
there are quite a few cases of smallpox. The number of deaths is approximately the same. *(On each day from 14 till 20 September McGauran buried
from eight to fifteen persons.)* … These last days, I fell victim to an attack of
dysentery, but, with the help of God, I have recovered from it and I am perfectly well.'

Grosse Ile
Grosse Isle p. 292

*Friday 17 September. Arthur Gore to Sir William Somerville, enclosing a resolu-
tion of Ballina Relief Committee, adopted at a meeting, Thursday 9 September*
'As the number of the able-bodied poor is very large and as many of them
cannot find employment, there is a necessity of giving employment by the
completion of the unfinished roads, as otherwise the number of applicants
for relief will be so great that the Guardians will be unable to relieve but a
small number of the entire.
The number of persons relieved each day under the temporary Relief Act:
Kilgarvan electoral division, 2,400; Ballina electoral division, 3,546; Ardnaree
electoral division, 5,394; Backs electoral division, 4,412.
Unless this is done forthwith, I fear much this district will ere long be
plunged into anarchy and become a scene of plunder and starvation, as the
whole income of the Union will not support all those who will demand it …
The potato crop is not a 20th of what it used to be … a great part of the district being entirely uncultivated.'

Ballina
CSORP Z.10147

Friday 17 September. Miss Perceval to Society of Friends
'The poor in this neighbourhood are in such a wretched state from want of

Templehouse
SFFP 2/506/34

clothing … Many of them will perish from cold during the approaching winter … Having heard of the liberal grants of clothing made by the benevolent Society of Friends, Miss Perceval has been induced to apply for assistance.'

Swinford
SFFP 2/506/21

Saturday 18 September. Capt George Wellesley to Society of Friends (See Appendix 6V)
'The writer of the enclosed (Mr Bolingbroke) is a gentleman residing on his own property in the parish of Meelick and who will faithfully administer any grants confided to his care … There are no resident clergy in the parish … It would be as well to place it at the disposal jointly of Mr O'Malley and Mr Bolingbroke as between them all may have their wants attended to … I take this opportunity of returning my best thanks to your Committee for the liberal aid that has been afforded on various occasions to this Union … I quite agree with the conclusion come to by your Committee that relief in nourishing food for the convalescent is much better than medicine.'
Draft reply, 23 September: 'Send Capt. Wellesley an order for 1 ton of rice.'

Castlebar
CSORP O.10334

Monday 20 September.
'From the wan countenances and wasted figures of most of the applicants, considerable distress may be supposed to pervade the country. Still there is such an inherent dislike to the confinement, restraint and order of a well regulated workhouse, that except from dire necessity, the bulk of the mature population will not seek a refuge in it … In the Castlebar and Westport houses fever has nearly disappeared … The majority of the country is poor, unimproved and badly cultivated, the rural inhabitants to all appearances badly provided for and unprepared to meet the difficulties of an impending scarcity … There are vast tracts of the northern and southern parts of the Union nearly naked of either stock or crops … It will be hard for them to surmount the pressure of next year … A great loss has been sustained by the ravages of the storm of Wednesday and Thursday last on the standing crops. Either from ignorant prejudice or inertness, the farmers left their crops of wheat and oats uncut long after the proper time.'

Ballaghaderreen
SFFP 2/506/21

Tuesday 21 September. Elizabeth Holmes to Society of Friends (See Appendix 6C)
'Our school now contains 220 children. The Committee's last grant to it was on the 4th of last month, all of which is now exhausted by our still continuing to give each child in attendance one meal per day and which, from the public relief having entirely ceased, is now in many cases as much required by the children as it was at any time during the summer … If your Committee could see our poor children at their one comfortable meal of warm rice they would not, if in their power, allow it to cease for some time

longer. The harvest here is late, oats has in very few cases as yet been reaped and of potatoes there were very few planted.'
Draft reply, 25 September: 'Send order for half ton of Indian meal, quarter ton of rice and 3 bags of biscuit.'

Wednesday 22 September. Bishop Patrick McNicholas of Achonry to Cardinal Franzoni, acknowledging receipt of £100 sterling for the relief of the poor in his diocese.

Ballaghaderreen
SC IRLANDA
vol 29, ff.135r 136v

Thursday 23 September. Report of the Relief Committee of Tubbercurry electoral division, 9 May to 12 September, signed by Dean Hoare, chairman

Tubbercurry
CSORP Z.10458

'This committee was first brought together on 27 March last ... On 29 March we proceeded to elect a chairman and treasurer and to appoint a clerk. We put in our first estimate on 19 April and commenced the distribution of rations on 15 May as soon as we had funds available.
In the interval between 19 April and 15 May we distributed provisions to the value of £70, being the amounts of grants from the British Association received through Captain Gilbert, the government inspector, for which we owe to that association our grateful thanks.
The total number of rations distributed amounted to 367,640 and the actual expenditure for provisions was £2,690, being at the rate of 1¾d. per ration. The total cost of the relief afforded ... was £2,872 of which £2,712 was expended on the poor directly (including £10 for coffins and £12 for lime for whitewashing) while the other expenses of salaries, wages, rent and fitting up of 4 depots, stationary and all incidentals did not exceed £160, being at the rate of 5½ per cent of the entire expenditure.
... Rations have been discontinued since the 12th inst. The probable number of daily rations required for the helpless poor will be about 600 ...
We cannot close this report without acknowledging the benefits derived to the poor of this extensive district, under the operations of the temporary Relief Act, by which effectual relief has been afforded and at a comparatively moderate cost ... Unless employment be provided for the able-bodied poor, we fear that the ensuing winter will prove a season of distress equal to that through which we have just passed.
In the absence of any reproductive employment within this district, the Committee suggests the expediency of completing the several roads remaining in an unfinished state in this barony. As the law now provides outdoor relief for the infirm, it would not be necessary again to resort to the expedient of giving labour tickets to this class of destitute persons; and the Committee would therefore propose that the roads should be completed by contractors, who should be bound to employ a certain number of able-bod-

ied labourers in proportion to the extent of each work. As the necessity for thus providing employment for the poor on their estates arises from the neglect of the landed proprietors in not availing themselves of the means offered by the Legislature (through the Draining and Landed property improvement Acts) of providing reproductive employment, the Committee suggests that the entire cost of completing the works commenced under the Labour Rate Act should in justice fall on those proprietors who refuse to avail themselves of the proffered aid of the government for employing the people and improving their own estates.

In conclusion we beg leave to express our sense of the indefatigable exertions of the Finance Committee and of the valuable services of the government inspector for the Union in assisting us to carry out the well advised arrangements of the relief Commissioners, whose regulations appear to us to have been admirably suited to carry into effect the benevolent intentions of the government for the alleviation of the distress of the people through the late season of pestilence and famine with which it was the will of Providence to visit this country.'

The above report was handed to Capt Gilbert at a meeting of the Tubbercurry Relief Committee on Thursday, 23 September

'On the motion of the Revd James Gallagher PP and seconded by John Brett PLG – *Resolved:* That the cordial thanks of this Committee are eminently due and hereby given to the Very Revd the Dean of Achonry JP for his unwearied and very efficient exertions as chairman of the Tubbercurry Relief Committee.'

Tuam
DDA MURRAY PAPERS

Monday 27 September. Archbishop MacHale to Archbishop Murray thanking him for £500 received for the province of Connacht
'This donation from Rome will inspire all to sympathise with the sufferings of the Pope and to pray for him. The Holy Father's letter was full of blessings for the sufferings of the poor of Ireland.'

Coolavin
SFFP 2/506/21

Monday 27 September. J. A. Holmes to Bewley and Pim (See Appendix 6)
'I shall feel very much obliged if you would give me another grant for the sick people in this district ... Distress is very great particularly among the paupers who are confined with fever etc and unable to be sent to the poorhouse.'
Draft reply, 29 September:
'Send order for half ton of Indian meal and a half ton of rice.'

Foxford
SFFP 2/506/21

Friday 1 October 1847. Rev G. H. Mostyn to Bewley and Pim (See Appendix 6N)
'I shall gladly accept any grant of rice or meal which the sick and infirm alone will get. I did not intend to feed the able-bodied ... but I was desirous to

have always on hands a trifle to meet what appeared to me absolute want.'
Draft reply, 6 October: 'Send an order for a quarter ton of rice and a quarter ton of Indian meal.'

Saturday 2 October. Henry O'Connor, Mayor of Sligo, to Lord Lieutenant
'Large masses of men of the labouring class have assembled in this town on last Wednesday and came to my home demanding employment or food as they were in a state of starvation ... With the co-operation of the resident magistrate I so far succeeded as to get them to disperse quietly by pledging myself that they should obtain employment on Monday next ... Large numbers will assemble in the town on the latter day and lest they should resort to violence on that occasion, I would suggest the propriety of sending into town some additional troops, as the present small force here is inadequate to overcome any attempt to commit outrage on the part of the people ... I shall do everything in my power to preserve the peace of the town at this important crisis.'

Sligo
OP 26/26555

Monday 4 October. H. B. Blake, sub-inspector, to Inspector General
'On yesterday 3 October about the hour of 12 o'clock, as a ship was passing Eagle Island about 6 miles at sea, she was boarded by 25 small boats, manned by countrymen who plundered her of over 30 tons of Indian meal consigned to the commissary here. The vessel was again boarded this morning and plundered of about 10 more tons of the meal. From the enquiries I have made I have every hope to be able to track out the plunderers.'

Belmullet
OP 21/473

Tuesday 5 October. Report of Henry Brett
'In the baronies of Erris, Burrishoole, Murrisk and portions of Tyrawley, Carra and Gallen, the quantity of food grown is altogether inadequate and in several portions of these districts, the crop is not sufficient to maintain the population for one month ... caused by the inability and neglect of the people to crop their lands. Turnips and other vegetables were sown ... but from want of weeding and thinning them, they are little better than a failure. The facilities for obtaining food from the seaports of Westport, Newport, Belmullet, Killala and Ballina are ample enough ... if the people had the means to purchase it. The facilities for providing employment of a useful and reproductive character are most abundant, enclosure and draining the vast tracts of waste land, the breaking up of patches for immediate reclamation, new fences and drains for existing holdings, the construction of lime kilns and burning lime to manure the lands. The most practicable is to complete the most important roads ... It is quite idle to expect that the distress can be provided by the rates, and little or no aid can be expected from charitable contributions.

Castlebar
CSORP W.13441

Several other parts of Co Mayo are also threatened with distress ... There is less to apprehend in the eastern section of the county, the crops are better. Potatoes have been more generally planted in the baronies of Costello, Gallen etc and the crop has been a good one. The potatoes are failing rapidly within the last fortnight and I have little doubt but that in a few weeks hence there will be great and urgent privations in numerous localities.'

Tubbercurry
CSORP Z.10458

Wednesday 6 October. Dean Hoare to Sir William Somerville
'There does not appear to be any intention on the part of the landed proprietors of this district to provide employment or in any other way to improve the condition of the poor. In the upper half barony of Leyny there are 30,000 people and 100,000 acres and no resident proprietor or agent of an estate. Unless employment be provided for the able-bodied, the condition of the poor during the ensuing winter will be even worse than it was last year. The unfinished roads could give ample employment between now and March when the spring work begins. At last Petty Sessions in Tubbercurry, having decreed several persons for the non-payment of rates, a very good effect was produced. There is now a disposition on the part of the farmers to pay the Poor rates. Several settled in court last Thursday. I had taken informations about a month since against four or five persons for a riot and rescue connected with the collector of the Poor rates and the trial will come on at the Quarter Sessions next week.'

Boyle
SFFP 2/506/21

Thursday 7 October. Emily and Rebecca Irwin to Society of Friends
'It is well known to all who have taken an interest in the moral and religious condition of Ireland, that the work of education has, in large districts of the country, hardly been commenced. Our school, within the demesne of Camlin, supported partly by the London Ladies Hibernian Schools Society and partly by private contributions, is the only school of any kind in a circle of miles around this, except the National Schools, and these are entirely under the superintendance and patronage of Roman Catholic priests and taught by Roman Catholic teachers. The Scriptures are completely excluded from these, for popery cannot tolerate the light of the truth as it is in Jesus, and even the secular instruction given in them is of a very inferior description. The teachers being all males nothing whatever is done in the way of instructing the girls in needlework, knitting, etc, so that they grow up ignorant of all those arts of industry and meekness that make the houses of the English lower classes so infintely superior to ours.
Hitherto the priests made so successful a resistance to our Bible training that our present school house was sufficiently large for all the children we could induce to attend. The district being one of the most popish in all Ireland,

every parent who had the hardihood to send his children did so in defiance of all the obstacles that Romish priests and popery could throw in his way and these are neither few nor easily surmounted.

But the troubles of the last year have wrought a wonderful change. The people have greatly lost faith in their own church and clergy and are now ready to receive sounder instruction for themselves and their children. Such has been the anxiety for admission to the school that we have taken in a considerably larger number than our school room would conveniently accommodate and we are daily under the painful necessity of rejecting fresh applications.

We know how ready popery will be to reassert its former influence over such as may outlive their hard times and are therefore all the more anxious to work while we have an open door. If the necessity was equally great before, the opportunity was certainly not so tempting. Consequently we have resolved to lay our case before some of our Christian friends, hoping for their cooperation in the work of collecting funds for the creation of a new house capable of containing both our male and female classes. A friend in England has kindly promised to pay the salary of a master for the boys' school if we could build a school house. The Belfast Ladies Committee sent us a teacher for an industrial school, which has been in active operation for upwards of two months and promises to do an incalulable amount of good in raising the degraded condition of our female population. Muslin sewing and knitting are the chief branches of industry taught. These we consider important, but we attach still greater importance to the moral and religious training which must always be kept in view as the great object to be aimed at. We hope draughting the bigger girls from our ordinary day school into this one when we shall have the house built, which will give us the desirable opportunity of having them longer under our eye.

We have got an estimate of the cost of such a building as would suit us and the sum of £200 would be necessary. Of that sum we have collected little more than a quarter but even with that and upon the faith of further success we have commenced the work. We may state that as one of the reasons for beginning with funds so far from adequate that the necessity for supplying employment for some of the poor people about us was urgent in the extreme. We have now 20 men employed, quarrying stones, carting, building etc amd thus earning the means of supporting their families and at the same time we trust raising a house where their children shall be taught to make themselves useful in their day and generation here and look forward with a good hope to the glories of a better state hereafter. We conclude with the earnest request that you will give us your aid in this good work.'

Note signed J. B. (Joseph Bewley):

'I have reason to believe that E. and R. Irwin are doing much good for the poor around them and deserve our encouragement. I would submit that a grant of food or money to purchase food might be made to them for the purpose of aiding their school operations, but at the same time they be informed that we have no funds applicable to the object of building school houses.'

9 October. E. and R. Irwin to Society of Friends re grant of 20 August for sick. convalescent and young children
'In addition we gave half a stone of boiled food daily to 40 families whom we knew to be quite destitute not having but one in a family of 9 or 10 earning at most but 8d a day for their support ... In our school there are 144 children on the daily roll. Of those on a average 100 are fed each morning ... 40 of the children are quite an infant class and there are 30 boys attending who are taught writing and arithmetic during the working hours, when the elder girls are all taught knitting and needlework.'

Grosse Ile
Grosse Isle p. 318

Tuesday 12 October. Fr Bernard McGauran to Archbishop of Quebec
'Three vessels arrived last night, but they had comparatively few sick on board. The death rate is quite high at present. These poor people, completely exhausted by a long sickness, cannot withstand the cold winds of our climate. Dr Douglas received orders yesterday to ship everybody on the island to Montreal immediately ... Tomorrow, he is embarking two hundred and thirty on the *Lady Colborne,* and among the whole number there are hardly two who are able to make it to the steamboat themselves.'

Ballaghaderreen
OP 26/268

Tuesday 12 October. Sworn statement of Mark McDonnell, acting as the agent for receiving rents on the lands of Maheraboy
'In attempting to drive and take away some cattle for the recovery of the said rents, I was assaulted, struck and put in terror of my life, by persons residing on the said lands.'

19 October. G. Knox RM to T. N. Redington
'I received a report from the sub-inspector in Ballaghaderreen that placards had been posted up in different parts of the county, announcing a meeting of the peasantry to take place in that town on Monday, 18 October, in order to petition parliament against the payment of the Poor rates ... Having ascertained that a party of the 79th Regiment had arrived in that town, I considered it unnecessary to order additional police.'

Aquino, Italy
SC IRLANDA
vol 29, f.361r

Tuesday 12 October. Bishop to Cardinal Franzoni, enclosing 88.80 scudi collected
'in this poor diocese of Aquino and Sora for the poor of Ireland.'

Thursday 14 October. James Higgins PP to Bewley and Pim (See Appendix 6Q)
'The timely and generous relief afforded by your humane and charitable body has rescued hundreds of suffering creatures from sickness, from distress and from death for which eternal glory and happiness be their crown and their reward ... While I can never duly appreciate the merits of your Society at home for their laudable exertions for the poor, I cannot but record my unqualified approbation of the members of that body in America for their large consignments occasionally remitted and entrusted to your hands for distribution ... Since the rations have ceased, dysentery and fever have set in here and have fearfully increased for the last 10 days. The rice at the Commissariat store at Ballina is not good ... People would prefer oatmeal.'
Draft reply, 20 October: 'Send an order for a quarter ton of Indian meal and a quarter ton of rice.'

Kilmactigue
SFFP 2/506/21

Sunday 17 October. Petition of Mark Groarke to Lord Lieutenant
'Petitioner is 54 years of age and destitute both of strength and the means to subsist. In June last I asked the parish priest for relief but was refused because I was two years absent, begging through the kingdom. But successively, providentially and miraculously, I underwent death so that I am at present more like a skeleton than a human being. Your Excellency, I hope, will give ear to my petition by commanding the Revd Mr Hamilton, Tubbercurry minister, to allow me such measure as may be given to any individual. If such a relief be granted,

Cloonacool
CSORP Z.10772

    To my grief the truth I do declare
    Nothing permanent in the European vale
    But north of Eden lies my native soil
    And when called to Sion there I will rejoice

    My begging state I firmly reject
    And that in my youth I arithmetic read
    The waste book journal and ledger rules,
    Mensuration and surveying too.'

T. N. Redington to Mark Groarke, 21 October: 'Your application for relief should be made to the Poor Law Guardians of the Union.'

Wednesday 20 October. John Bolingbroke, Oldcastle to Society of Friends (See Appendix 6U)
'I beg to tender you my most grateful thanks for your munificent donation of 5 cwt of rice placed at my disposal by Capt Wellesley ... The number of families receiving relief is limited to 56. Of these 24 are widows in the lowest state of destitution, in some instances recovering from fever to which their

Meelick
SFFP 2/506/21

husbands fell victim. The remainder, including disabled tradesmen and orphans, were selected with a most impartial and searching scrutiny and in no instance has more than 1 stone of rice been given in the day to any family. Distribution has been confined to twice or three times a week ... I would most earnestly pray a repetition of your bounty ... As want of covering is a cause of much suffering any donation in that shape would be of incalculable benefit.'
Draft reply, 23 October: 'Send order for 5 cwt of rice.'

Keash
SFFP 2/506/21

Thursday 21 October. Abby Fleming to Society of Friends (See Appendix 60)
'The female poor are equally badly off for employment, from their being unable to sow flax seed in the spring. The kindness of a friend has enabled me to purchase a little wool for employing them, which I am getting manufactured into stockings and flannel to be given gratuitous to the destitute and cheap to others.'
Draft reply, 27 October: 'Order on Sligo a quarter ton of Indian meal, a quarter ton of rice and remit £5 as some assistance towards her manufactory objects.'

Mayo
CSORP Z.10985

Sunday 24 October. Henry Brett, county surveyor, to Col Jones, Board of Works
'The state of matters is daily becoming more and more alarming ... In Erris the people are subsisting on turnip tops, cabbage and such garbage as they can procure ... Deaths from starvation are now almost as frequent in that locality as they were at any time last year ... The accounts from the other coast districts are of a very alarming nature. In the interior and eastern portions of the county, the pressure for food is not yet become very great, as the small patches of potatoes which are rapidly decaying and the turnips will supply food for some weeks to come. The poorhouses are now filled ... There is no doubt the distress is becoming very general in a little time. The measures very generally resorted to for the recovery of the rents, added to the great depression in the markets for produce of every kind ... From the restriction of credit by banks, the state of the farmers, middlemen and proprietors is most disheartening. All classes feel themselves on the verge of ruin ... No outrages of any moment ... In some localities there are thefts and there have been some nightly meetings but I believe they have ceased. Some attempts were made, and are still making, to get up meetings of large masses of people to put forward statements of their condition, but I believe the general feeling is opposite to any such demonstrations. There is much reason to expect a sad state of things in this unfortunate county during the ensuing season, and if timely measures be not adopted to crop the land next year, Mayo must become a desolate county.'

Tuesday 26 October. Robert Lecky and Arthur Thomas to Poor Law Commission
'Having experienced a most painful day on Saturday in being obliged to remain for many hours listening to the clamorous and pitiful applications for admission from a wretched mass of human misery which were congregated about the doors of the workhouse ... none were admitted ... Capt Carey is to describe to you what occurred and the perilous prospects of this country in the future ... There are no shirts or shifts for the creatures whose filthy condition rendered them doubly dangerous ... Our advertisement for supplies appeared to be treated with scorn, as not one tender was sent in ... Yesterday we waited on Revd Mr Stoney, who has a considerable number of poor persons employed manufacturing frieze and linen. We got a considerable quantity of these goods from him and put every female that could be spared in the workhouse making inside garments ... A new (rate) collector, W. Malley, was appointed ... to concentrate most urgently on the great and wealthy.'

Castlebar
CSORP O.11034

Tuesday 26 October. Resolution of extraordinary meeting of the Board of Guardians
'That if the cultivation of the soil be not associated with the relief of the poor during the present winter and the approaching spring, the present position of this Union, bad as it is, will be infinitely worse.'

Swinford
CSORP O.11208

Wednesday 27 October. Rev James T. MacDonagh to Cardinal Franzoni
'It is with profound humility I hasten to address you in order to offer you and holy Rome the tribute of my gratitude for the many favours you have conferred on me during my time in the Propaganda, and for your charitable exertions in relieving the wants of the starving Irish during this year of famine and pestilence. I must now endeavour to give you an account of my mission. I have been sent here by my bishop, Dr Feeney, in April last, and ever since I hope I have discharged my duty faithfully both to God and man. This mission is most arduous, owing to its extent and population. It is 15 miles from north to south and 6 from east to west. The inhabitants are computed to be about 10,000. So that my labour must be enormous, tho' aided most strenuously by the parish priest, the Revd Mr Hart, who is now in a very delicate state of health from over-exertions in relieving his fellow cratures *(sic)* both spiritual and temporal. This year we are reduced to the lowest ebb in consequence of the distress of our poor parishioners, whose voluntary contributions was the only means the priests had to support them. I am sorry to tell your Eminence that I cannot for want of means continue any longer on the mission. I must endeavour through your assistance to go on a foreign mission, where I can at least get bread to live on. I do assure you I was obliged to go to bed on several occasions during the last six months and could not

Ballycastle
SC IRLANDA
vol 29, ff.382rv
383r

afford myself a penny worth of bread after the labours of the day. The Anabaptists and Presbyterians are endeavouring to make inroads in this parish by availing themselves of the pressures of the times. They have established schools in every quarter of the parish, where they were giving a paltry subsistence to the Catholic children, who were first obliged to renounce their former faith before they got a morsel from them. We have through the grace of God and our exertions, eradicated their schools with the exception of two which we will soon exterminate. Had I but the means of subsisting, I would never feel fatigued in persecuting the enemies of our holy religion, who are going about, as St Peter says, 'like roaring lions seeking whom they may devour.' The souls of the Irish are as dear to God as the Indians or Americans, and surely the priests should stand firm and feed their flock, when the wolf is already among them; but what can we do? We cannot live on the winds and labour in the vineyard. There is not a more distressed parish in the diocese of Killala than this, owing to the enormous population who lived principally on potatoes and on fishing, not having sufficient land to support their families with corn. I hope your Eminence will consider my condition and send me some means of subsistence.

Wishing your Eminence health and a long life and reverently kissing the hem of your sacred purple.'

Attymass &
Kilgarvan
CSORP Z.11451

Saturday 30 October. Memorial of the inhabitants, signed by Charles Arkinson, chairman, and Bernard Egan PP, secretary

'These two parishes are situated at the foot of the Ox Mountains and consist principally of reclaimable bog and mountain with a small proportion of arable land. The two successive failures of the potato crop have reduced a large number of the inhabitants to an awful state of destitution being unable for want of seed to supply the deficiency of food thereby created, by the cultivation of other crops to support themselves and families. The small crop of potatoes planted in the present year in this district … has unfortunately been attacked with the disease which destroyed former crops and are not now available for food. It has been and is now admitted by several government officers and others employed under the Board of Works that this district is with scarcely an exception the most impoverished and destitute in the entire county of Mayo. They are most desirous to obtain employment to enable them to purchase food but unfortunately there is no employment in either public or private to be had in the district in which there is but one resident landed proprietor. There are in the district a number of unfinished public works, and some of them in a dangerous condition, which if put in operation would afford considerable employment and at the same time confer much benefit on this district and the public at large. Under such circumstances they humbly solicit your Excellency's consideration to their unhappy condition, and pray you will be pleased to direct that relief be afforded them either by employment on the public works already mentioned, or in such other manner as your Excellency may deem proper.'

2 November. Bernard Egan PP to Lord Lieutenant, enclosing memorial, 30 October   *Kilgarvan*
'As the Catholic rector of the parish of Kilgarvan, I have had abundant opportunities of ascertaining the amount of destitution with which its poor and patient inhabitants are afflicted and I can therefore bear my humble testimony to the truth of the statements contained in the memorial.'

T. N. Redington to Bernard Egan PP, 10 November:
'The Lord Lieutenant laments the distress existing within these two parishes but cannot hold out any hope that public works will be resumed.'

Saturday 30 October. Archbishop John MacHale to Cardinal Franzoni, acknowl-   *Tuam*
edging the receipt of £100 sterling for the relief of the poor of his diocese.   SC IRLANDA
vol 29, f.384rv

Sunday 31 October. Katherine Strickland to Bewley and Pim   *Loughglynn*
'We have provided according to your instructions to Joseph Allen 1,074 vests   SFFP 2/506/3
and 949 yards of flannel in 14 bales by John Shannon, carrier. They left here the 29th and will reach Dublin in about 6 days from that time. We trust they will be approved by you tho' we fear that tho' really warm and serviceable they will not be to appearance equal to their cost. We are making efforts to find sale for the stockings ... Begging to thank you for the assistance given in this business so kindly.'

Winter 1847-48

More Relief and the British Association

During the winter applications for relief rose dramatically. Extra workhouse accommodation had to be provided. Buildings were leased for this purpose in Ballina and Sligo and an auxiliary workhouse was opened in Belmullet. The numbers on outdoor relief were also soaring. In Ballina on 18 December there were no less than 2,000 applicants for relief. In mid-January there were 1,000 in the workhouse and 8,400 on outdoor relief and increasing hourly. At the same time in the Castlebar Union, 3,221 were placed on outdoor relief bringing the total to 11,358 or upwards of one-sixth of the Union.

These figures and much other information were provided in the weekly reports of the temporary Poor Law Inspectors. They had been recruited largely from the British army and some of them had seen service in India or in other colonies. One was appointed in each of the Unions to oversee the implementation of the Poor Law and the Relief Acts. They were mostly dedicated and meticulous and fearlessly impartial in the execution of their duties. Some, like Capt Broughton in Swinford paid the ultimate price, falling victim to typhus fever in the spring of 1848.

A new scheme was inaugurated by the British Association to relieve destitute children. This association had been established in London in January 1847 by wealthy English businessmen and merchants, including Baron de Rothschild. It raised approximately £470,000 of which Queen Victoria subscribed £2,000. A Polish nobleman, Count Strzelecki, was appointed its agent in Ireland. Strzelecki decided to use what funds remained to help schoolchildren in the west of Ireland. For this purpose he sought to procure lists of schools which in some places, like the electoral division of Killedan, 'sprang up like mushrooms'. In mid November it was hoped to feed daily 1,000 children in seven schools in Belmullet and at the same time the system began operating in the Sligo Union. By early January the British Association scheme was operating extensively. In the Castlebar Union 3,297 children in 25 schools were then receiving daily rations. 12,000 schoolchildren were receiving daily rations in the Ballina Union and 7,400 in Castlerea Union by the end of the winter. When the British Association wound up its activities in July 1848 it had expended over £78,000, feeding and clothing 200,000 schoolchildren.

Friday 5 November 1847. G. V. Jackson to Society of Friends   *Ballina*
'Last Monday we were obliged to refuse hundreds admission to the poor-   SFFP 2/506/21
house at Ballina for want of room. At every point now the eye rests upon
unhappy beings sinking from illness and want of food … I will provide a list
of names … who are dreadful objects and send it for examination … It is
always desirable to have a charity administered thro' an organ not having
local connections or interests of any kind.'

Tuesday 9 November. Robert Lecky, W. Carey, and Arthur Thomas, vice-Guardians,   *Castlebar*
to Poor Law Commission   CSORP DP 47
'Today we had a four-hour interview with the Earl of Lucan, whose manner
was most affable and conciliating … He said that every farthing of rate he
was liable to should be forthwith paid and he would instruct his agent, sub-
agent and every person in authority on his estate to give every assistence and
facilitate the collection in every way.'

Tuesday 9 November. Report of Edward Hunt, sub-inspector, Swinford   *Kilmactigue*
'On 6 August Owen Gallagher, Colrecol, Kilmactigue, stated that his heifer   CSORP I.11534
had been stolen a few days earlier and he discovered it in Kilkelly. He (Hunt)
sent two of the police to recover the heifer and bring it to Swinford. He
refused to deliver it to Gallagher as on the same day Peter Walsh called and
claimed that he had bought the heifer at a public fair from Bridget Conlon.
Gallager and Bridget Conlon were living together and Hunt suspected that
they had arranged, one to sell the cow and as soon as the cow was paid for,
the other would claim it was stolen. All the parties were sent to trial at the
Petty Sessions in Swinford … On 17 August it was decided that Gallagher
and Conlon had defrauded Walsh and the heifer was given to Walsh.'

Wednesday 10 November. R. Hamilton, Poor Law inspector, to William Stanley   *Belmullet*
'The Ballina Board of Guardians passed a resolution that £140 should be   CSORP O.11634
given to the Erris Committee to relieve those unfortunate creatures who had
been refused admittance to the Ballina workhouse last week and some of
whom had died of want on their return to Erris. They also stated that "not a
farthing of the rates collected in the other electoral divisions of Ballina Union
should be supplied to the support of the Erris poor". As Erris never has hitherto been able to take care of its own, I do not think it likely it will be able
to do so now when all classes are either starving or next door to it.'
13 November. W. Hamilton to William Stanley   *Ballina*
'I informed the Guardians of the illegality of their resolution refusing admit-   CSORP O.11845
tance into the workhouse to the Erris paupers. There was a great deal of violent opposition on the part of Mr Jones who threatened to bring the paupers

of his electoral division to fill the workhouse ... There is a large amount of rates due by the Guardians themselves.'

Binghamstown
CSORP O.11844

13 November. R. Hamilton, Belmullet, to William Stanley
'The poor really in a sad state, their only food bad turnips and their supply of them limited ... Many have nothing to subsist on but the roots of weeds. The British Association have placed a small quantity of provisions at my disposal ... I gave it out through the medium of clergymen principally to destitute females and children under a certain age ... I have established seven schools and hope to have 1,000 children on Monday next receiving daily rations ... There is no proprietor or person of any respectability who takes the least interest in the welfare of the unfortunate poor in this district.'

Ballina
CSORP O.11678

Wednesday 10 November. Report of W. Hamilton, Poor Law inspector
'There is a great want of clothing and bedding ... The master informed me that the infirmary has not been visited by the Guardians for a considerable time ... There were three children who suffered from dysentery, very little removed from skeletons. I never saw such dreadful objects in my life. Dr Devlin said he was afraid to order them any extra diet as he was found at fault by some of the Guardians on previous occasions. I ordered him to give them such nourishment and stimulants he considered necessary and not allow a person perish for want of proper medical treatment. One of the Guardians, Mr Knox, who visited the infirmary, was greatly shocked at the appearance of the patients ... Ten cases of fever broke out this week ... There are 1,000 inmates in the workhouse ... The Board of Guardians are to hire a store and remove there the school children, schoolmaster and mistress ... The majority of the Guardians are against supporting Erris. Mr Jones (a magistrate), declared that the people of his neighbourhood would not pay a farthing of the rates if the Erris people are to be supported. The well-disposed members, Col Jackson, Mr Symes and Mr Knox, will have a mess of destitution to provide for before long but their difficulties will be much increased by the opposition of the other members ... Self-exertion and co-operation among all classes alone can effectually meet the coming calamity and present starvation. Many gentlemen have done their duty and will do it again. But there are many who have done nothing. 65,000 rations were distributed daily in this Union (exclusive of Erris).'
11 November. The Tyrawley Herald
State of the workhouse: admitted during the week, 94; discharged, 35; sick, 90; died, 3; remaining, 999. Weekly cost of a pauper, 1s 3¼.'

Monday 15 November. Report of Harloe J. Phibbs, solicitor, to the Board of Guardians, on the proceedings against defaulting rate-payers
'I attended Tubbercurry Petty Sessions. Mr Knox and Dean Hoare presided. There were ten cases on the books. Half of them paid before the cases were heard and the remainder were decreed … I attended at Collooney. Mr Cogan was the second presiding magistrate and I obtained 12 decrees … On 13 November I attended Ballymote Petty Sessions. Capt Whelan, Mr Knox and Mr Gethen were the magistrates. There were 58 cases, 40 of which were decreed and the remainder settled … I wish to know if I have received the consent of the Commissioners to proceed against Henry Burrows of Greenville in the superior courts for the recovery of the rates due by him.'

Sligo
CSORP O.12169

Tuesday 16 November. Resolution of Swinford Board of Guardians
'That inasmuch as there is at present ample accommodation for the poor of this Union in the workhouse, we respectfully call on the Commissioners to apply to the Lord Lieutenant that orders may be issued to the constabulary to arrest all strolling beggars, as rate-payers are suffering heavily by their depredation and more especially being the main cause of desseminating disease through the country.'

Swinford
CSORP I.12251

Tuesday 16 November. Capt Gilbert to Poor Law Commission
'An immense number of persons were asembled at the poorhouse, clamouring for admission. Some of the inmates were discharged and placed on outdoor relief and 200 were admitted … I am procuring lists of schools etc required by Count Strzelecki for the British Relief Association, to feed and clothe destitute children … This system will commence in Sligo on Monday.'

Sligo
CSORP O.11941

Thursday 18 November. The Tyrawley Herald
'Sudden Death – Alleged Murder'
On last Monday evening a man named Browne died at Bonnifinglass, a place within four miles of this town (Ballina). The deceased attended a fair held there on that day and was engaged in a fight with some other persons. It is reported that he received a blow of a loaded whip on the head, but that he afterwards transacted business. In the course of the evening, after having drunk, it is said, pretty freely, he retired to bed and shortly after expired. An inquest will be held on the body this day.'

Bonnifinglass

Sunday 21 November. Report of Capt Farren, Poor Law inspector
'None of the large proprietors have yet paid the rate … There is another class who are inclined to conform to the law but unable to meet the whole of their liabilities at once. The small holders in rural districts have never paid poor

Castlebar
CSORP O.12548

rates ... Some are removing their produce to avoid seizure ... The liabilities of the Union amount to £4,740 15s. 5d. (exclusive of the sums owed to the government). Some creditors have threatened legal proceedings.

State of the workhouse: males over fifteen, 109; females over fifteen, 204; boys under fifteen, 172; girls under fifteen, 163; children under two, 27; total, 676. Fever cases, 32; other cases, 55; total sick, 87.

70 applicants were admitted and 34 discharged ... Distress in this Union will be very great ... Many families at present have no other subsistance than a small crop of turnips ... The British Association are feeding the children through the schools.'

Belmullet
CSORP 0.12134

Monday 22 November. R. Hamilton to William Stanley
'I have not heard of any deaths from starvation but I have no doubt many will take place before long, and it will not be within the power of the Poor Law to prevent it, as some of the most distressed in this district are precluded by law from obtaining relief and they seem determined if possible to hold on to their spot of land in the vain hope that the government will both feed them and crop their farms.'

Sligo
CSORP 0.12196

Wednesday 24 November. Report of Capt Gilbert
'130 old and infirm with their children were discharged and placed on out-door relief and replaced by 250 able-bodied. The house now contains 200 more than its accommodation level. The house was surrounded by several hundreds anxious for relief ... Contracts were issued for erecting sheds for the boys' and girls' schools and the present schoolrooms will be converted into dormitories. The Charter House is being repaired to house 350 orphans.'

Swinford
Correspondence p. 94

Wednesday 24 November. Captain Broughton to Poor Law Commission re the meeting of the Board of Guardians yesterday
'The attendance, owing, I presume, to the weather, which has been very severe, and the long distances the majority of the Guardians have to come, was very small: from these causes also, the desire to get away again was very manifest, and indeed, by four o'clock, when the meeting broke up, it had become almost dark.

I drew the attention of the Guardians to the disproportionate number of women and children with husbands and fathers in the house, to those without ...

In reference to the ... Vagrant Act, the chairman, who is also a member of the Gaol Committee, stated there was not room in the gaol, for the commitments already made for other crimes ...

The amount of money paid in by the collectors was only £25 ... They were

all cautioned that upon the next dereliction of duty, they would be summoned and fined; and also, that if they did not exert themselves more in collecting the rates, and make examples of some of the defaulters, they would
render themselves liable to be dismissed. The property of this Union is unfortunately situated. Upon obtaining a list of the highest rate-payers, I find there
are no less than six properties in Chancery, and out of a return of nearly 70
names, from 50 to 60 are non-resident; the tenantry proportionately neglected,
or I might say abandoned, for in few cases is the agent resident either ...
It will shortly, I fear, be necessary to consider the steps to be taken to meet
the numbers applying for relief.'
Reply to above, 26 November: ibid, p. 95
'As regards the number of women and children in the workhouse, the
Commissioners recommend that the wives of men who are not in the workhouse should be required to swear informations before the magistrates
against their husbands for desertion, with a view to proceedings being taken
under the Vagrant Act ... With regard to the punishment of vagrants ... they
presume that if any temporary place could be provided, to which paupers
could be committed and kept to hard labour, for only a day, as often as found
begging, the practice would be checked.'

Wednesday 24 November. Anonymous threatening letter to Dean Hoare   *Tubbercurry*
'Mr Dean, Molly McGuire wishes to let you know she still lives as the pro-   OP 26/292
tector of the injured and the exterminator of tyranny. She is in possession of
Roscommon and Leitrim and intends planting a colony in Sligo very shortly,
as you Mr Dean and other tyrants of your description will be brought to
account for your deeds and her old neighbour George Knox will not be forgotten. She wishes to know how you disposed of the many remittances you
got from charitable institutions to feed the poor and is it by charging two
shillings and six pence a perch for turnips to a starving people you intend disposing of said funds. There is another affair she is informed you busied yourself lately in but when she hears the particulars you shall hear from her again.
You are, Mr Dean, one of the chosen few in Sligo whose days are numbered.
Molly never takes a mean advantage without giving due notice, and the
exterminator of the tyrant Mahon* will dare anything.
By order of Molly McGuire
Headquarters, Strokestown Bawn.'
25 November. Report of G. Knox RM
'During the month of October last the relief officer for the district of
Tubbercurry was dismissed from his situation by the chairman and Poor Law

---

* Major Mahon of Strokestown House was murdered allegedly by members of the Molly
Maguires.

Guardians at Sligo, in consequence of his being a publican in the town of Tubbercurry. Another relief officer has been appointed to his situation, and the dismissed person of the name of McDermot and his wife have expressed themselves very badly towards the Very Revd the Dean of Achonry. It appears that this person was dismissed during the period the Dean was in Dublin and he imagines that it was by his influence that he was dismissed. And from the bad feeling existing towards him and the copies of the attached threatening letter, and also copy of a friend's letter, I would recommend that two police-men be at once directed to sleep at his gate house. In the meantime I shall make every exertion to obtain an information against McDermot for his expressions towards the Dean, and keep up a regular patrol about his house for his protection.'

25 November. John S. Stewart, sub-inspector, to George Knox RM, correct copy of note found stuck in the Dean's hayrick

'This is to warn your Riverances worship agin those Mcdirmotts who have a spite to your Honour about the afare of Henry Connor and ar Threatning vingeance.

Your Riverance would need to have the Polis to watch when driving the Roads.

McDirmotts tell over this town that you have taken the bread from them and yet all knows you to be the Best Gintleman and the best Frind to the poor but I fear to give my name for a Bloody Informer But your Riverance should Disposess these Mcdirmotts minds.'

op 26/307   *6 December. Dean Hoare to T. N. Redington*

'I fear that McDermot and his party will not believe my denial, or anyone else's, of having interfered about his appointment as relieving officer and he appears desperate in consequence of the general suspicion attached to him, which will render it impossible for him to obtain any other situation. Previous to the receipt of the threatening letter, every thing had been done to remove the impression from this man's mind. Capt Gilbert, the Poor Law inspector, to whose face and to his clerk, McDermot and his wife had used the most threatening language against Capt Gilbert and me, assured them that I had nothing to do in the matter. This was on 18 November. Having been informed of this circumstance, I wrote a note to the Poor Law Guardian to assure him that I had not interfered and he took pains to make it known, adding that he knew of his own knowledge that what I stated was the fact. This was on 20 November. On 22 November I went to Tubbercurry, to attend the meeting which I had appointed for the "Practical Instructor" to address the people. I was advised by a very respectable person to return early and with protection, in consequence of a conversation which he had over-heard between McDermot and others in the public house. I did return early, and by another road, but without protection. On 24 November I wrote to the parish priest of Tubbercurry, requesting him to disabuse the mind of McDermot, and again solemnly assuring him that, not being a P. L. Guardian, I had not interfered in the matter. This letter was shown by Rev Mr McHugh to McDermot the same day. On the following day, I received, while presiding at the Petty Sessions, the threatening letter, and within two hours after my steward sent me the warning notice which was found in my haggard, after I had left home. Notwithstanding all that has been done, these people still suspect me and accuse me of having deprived them of their only means of support, (and they really have no other) and they still openly vow vengeance against me. Every one fears to come forward; but many give dark hints and warn me not to be without protection of the police. In addition to all I have stated, it is important to observe that McDermot is himself a native of Co Roscommon, and only left it about 8 years ago, having been two years in the *Hue & Cry*. His friends reside near Elphin, where the threatening letter was posted, altho' dated Strokestown. He denies to his Priest and to every one that he sent the letter, and if this be correct, it must have been written at Elphin or Strokestown, in consequence of his representations. Now if he should be convinced of the fact that I did not interfere as to his removal, it is not likely that he either would or could change the minds of his friends in Co Roscommon; and the fatal word may have been already given at Strokestown against me. Under all these circumstances, and others which I could mention, such as the report that I got … I consider it absolutely necessary for me to have the protection of the police on my premises by night. It is to be borne in mind that as a clergyman I stand specially in need of such protection, both at night and when on the roads, inasmuch I should consider it unbecoming my office to carry fire arms, and if I were compelled to use them in my own defence, it would doubtless cause an outcry, and would give the public an erroneous notion of my character and temper.

I am as far as possible removed from being an alarmist but I do feel that under present circumstances it would be madness in me to dispense with all necessary precautions for my safety. It is not attended with any addition of expense to the public, my having two of the police here at night, as I provide them with lodging, fuel and candles. Nor is it any inconvenience, but rather the contrary, as it affords a protection in a very remote neighbourhood. My house is situated, as respects police stations, about 2 miles from Chaffpool, about 4 miles from Tubbercurry, and about the same distance from Templehouse. I trust that under these circumstances, the protection which I seek may be continued to me at all events until after Christmas.

I need not say how much I approve of the government measures for the better protection of life and property. I particularly admire the wisdom of the novel features of the measure, of levying the extra expense of additional police etc immediately; and of calling on all persons to aid the authorities in pursuit of criminals; and of carrying out the law to its utmost rigour, against those who harbour and screen delinquents.'

Draft reply to above, 9 December:

'Immediate. Send to the county inspector who will grant until further orders the full protection of two policemen to live in the Revd Mr Hoare's house and to accompany him on his lawful business, without the usual charge prescribed by regulation.

Add and state that I have laid his letter before His Excellency who deeply regrets the fearful position in which he is placed and has desired I would assure him that especially in his position of a clergyman that he feels the claims he has upon the government for protection and – instructions have been given for – protection.'

9 December. £20 reward offered by George Knox RM for information on the person who sent a threatening notice to Dean Hoare. (See opposite).

Achonry
SFFP 2/506/22

Saturday 27 November. Dean Hoare to Bewley and Pim, enclosing an account of the distribution of the last grant with the names of 50 families served with gratuitous relief at the Deanery House by the Dean and his lady. Also from 150 to 160 pupils daily dined of it at the national schoolhouse at the Deanery. (See Appendices 1A & 6A)

Draft reply, 3 December:

'Send an order for ¼ ton rice, ½ ton Indian meal and 2 bags of biscuit.'

Swinford
Correspondence
pp. 95-6

Saturday 27 November. Captain Broughton to Poor Law Commission

'The weather this week has totally prevented my visiting the country portions of the Union. It has never ceased pouring since I last wrote to you; and has on some days prevented my getting as far as the workhouse … One of the collectors, in the execution of his duties, made a seizure of some cattle, when a rescue took place under rather serious circumstances … a sword-stick having been drawn and threats used. The parties were arrested and brought before the Petty Sessions Court yesterday, but the solicitor of the Union had the case postponed until the 17th proximo, in consequence of one of the principal witnesses being absent …

I have directed the collectors to proceed against the better class of rate-payers who either refused or neglected to pay the sums due by them. I regret to find such men as Lord Lucan, Lord Claremorris, Sir Roger Palmer and others among the defaulters … When they find proceedings have been commenced, they will spare me the painful necessity of having their property

£20
REWARD.

WHEREAS, a Rockite Notice bearing the *Elphin* Post mark, was recently sent to the *Very Rev. Dean Hoare*, of *Achonry*, threatening him :

I HEREBY OFFER A REWARD OF

TWENTY POUNDS

To any Person who shall, within Six Months from the date hereof, give such information as shall lead to the Arrest of the Person or Persons concerned in writing or sending the Notice in question.   Payable on conviction.

GEORGE KNOX,

Resident Magistrate.

Tubbercurry, 9th December, 1847.

42,638--G.

seized, and that it will duly operate on the other classes who as yet have not settled their rates ...

I have been employed chiefly in investigating cases in the workhouse, and have sifted out many who ought never to have been admitted. In one case, a woman and her child have been in since October, her husband living at Foxford in the Union at the time ... One man, this week returned from England, called at the house and took away two children (the one six and the other three years old); his wife, it appears, had died in his absence and the children were put into the house. I have ordered him to be applied to for their cost of maintenance, and in case of refusal to have him summoned.'

Reply to above, 1 December:

'The Commissioners approve the course which you are taking, of scrutinising the relief lists; but they do not think that legal proceedings against the parties liable for the support of such inmates, with a view to the recovery of the cost of relief afforded, will be successful ...'

Castlebar
CSORP O.12400

Sunday 28 November. Report of Capt Farren

'Rates collected, £146 10s. 2¾d., uncollected, £9,430 15s. 2d. ... The collector, James Malley was struck with stones and hunted out of the village of Kilmullagh in the electoral division of Addergoole.

State of the workhouse: males over fifteen, 118; females over fifteen, *205;* boys under fifteen, 172; girls under fifteen, 168; children under two, 27; total, 690. Fever cases, 34; other cases, 53. There were 222 applicants, 58 of them with fever. 95 were relieved, 47 of whom were admitted to the workhouse, and the remaining 48 placed on outdoor relief. 27 were discharged from the workhouse ... The nursery is very small and crowded as also the women's day room. The appearance of the children is not satisfactory ... More heat is required in the schoolroom.'

Castlerea
CSORP O.12546

Sunday 28 November. James Auchmuty to Poor Law Commission

'I had my first meeting with the Board yesterday ... They are a most refractory set with the exception of Mr Hills and Mr Strickland. I found the master and the matron most attentive and the upper part of the workhouse very clean, the yards in a shocking state of dirt, the windows broken ... The paupers can get over the walls as they please ... Most of the children are in rags, many of the men without shirts, and not the half of them in workhouse dress. Yesterday some of the paupers did not get their breakfast till half-past one for want of tins. There are five girls sleeping in some beds and four boys in others. There is no room to class the children from the crowded state of the house. All the sewers about the house are choked up ... No paupers admitted yesterday.'

Wednesday 1 December 1847. Patrick Durcan PP to T. N. Redington

Collooney
CSORP Z.12384

'Capt Gilbert, inspecting officer of the Sligo Poor Law Union, informed me more than a fortnight ago that the government would give one meal and clothing to the destitute children in all the schools and requested the number of destitute children in the different schools in my parish. I sent him the number and asked him today how soon they would get the promised relief. He replied that he got no order from the government. I request you to order Capt Gilbert to take immediate steps to relieve these poor starving children.'
T. N. Redington to Patrick Durcan:
'The relief is not being afforded by the government but by the British Relief Association.'

Wednesday 1 December. Report of Capt Gilbert

Sligo
CSORP O.12566

'200 applicants admitted to the workhouse … £800 rates collected but some of the highest rate-payers are refusing to pay theirs … Mr Holmes requests placing the schools of the Coolavin and Kilfree electoral divisions of the Boyle Union under my supervision … I meet with great difficulties in the want of zeal and co-operation on the parts of the resident gentlemen and clergymen, who should be foremost in offering their assistance for the relief of the destitute. In this town, where at the national schools upwards of 400 of the poorest children attend, the priest and teacher refuse to allow them to make use of the food cooked and given them gratuitously. They refused in the first instance on the grounds of not wasting the children's time, while at the other poor schools, the system is entirely carried out without injury to the studies of the children and to their material benefit. When suffered to overcome this difficulty by feeding the children after school hours, or for the last half hour, the clergyman stated that he would not allow his school to be turned into a soup kitchen. I have reported the circumstance to the agent of the British Relief Association and requested instructions.'

Wednesday 1 December. Capt Broughton to Poor Law Commission

Swinford
Correspondence
pp. 96-7

'The meeting that took place yesterday of the Board of Guardians for this Union was better attended than any previously held since my arrival at this place …
The case of the master of the workhouse was again brought before the meeting … I was called upon for an opinion of him since I joined the Union, and having found him intoxicated yesterday on visiting the workhouse, I strongly urged his removal at once. I understand he is an unfortunate man who, having inherited a nice little property, has managed to muddle it all away, and he is nearly connected with many members of the Board of Guardians, who naturally … would screen him. Still I feel from the situation he holds as mas-

ter of the house, the total destruction of all moral example he sets the inmates, renders it imperative he should be at once removed ...

The case also of the schoolmistress was brought again before the Guardians. From what I have seen she seems a respectable nice young woman, desirous of doing her duty, taking pains with the children, and if one may judge from her letter to the Board of Guardians, of superior education. I have also observed a kindliness of manner to the unfortunate children not to be over-looked ...

The admission of several paupers took place; amongst others ... was a woman and her family of four or five children. She had formerly belonged to this Union. She had, however, been 12 years absent in England and had only returned to this country three months. She was refused admission.'

Reply to above, 3 December: 'As regards the master of the workhouse ... the Commissioners will issue an order under seal for his dismissal, unless he immediately quits the workhouse.'

Foxford &
Killasser
SFFP 2/506/22

Thursday 2 December. Rev G. H. Mostyn to Bewley and Pim
'On the fair day of Foxford I sent a message to Mrs Rowley by Mr Geo. Cuffe of Killasser, requesting of her to wait on me. My object was that I might read in her presence the correspondence of her brother (in her name for the most part) with the Society of Friends. The letter of the 19 November is a curious document. It strikes me her brother James is the writer of it, altho' she says "I git one of my ouldest scolars to rite my words." Mary Rowley does not write herself. James Rowley does. He is a man of mind, self-taught but reaps the fruit of his infirmity, God forbid I should judge him. I saw Mary on 28 October and asked to see the boiler etc. James had the key of the barn and was away some two miles. She was after fever and very weak. I observed some very poor children about her wretched hovel on that day, especially a naked girl, apparently idiotic. It may be she does not know what was written in her name by her brother James and I would still humbly suggest that no money or bread stuffs be sent to Cartron West, till she goes over in my presence the letters you have sent me.

I would however recommend that a small grant of meal and rice be given to Mr Geo Cuffe, Killasser, who is Mr Gore's bailiff, and who will give it to such persons in Cartron as I shall select, lest any should perish from hunger. He lives within an English mile of Cartron. I live seven.

I now wish to acquaint the Society that the British Association, thro' their agent, Capt Broughton R. E., stationed at Swinford, are about to feed and clothe all children in the existing schools, from 6 to 14 years old in the Union of Swinford. This takes in Killasser (Mary Rowley's parish) and the parish of Toomore where I reside. Now it so happens from the poverty of this parish, from the non-residence of the rector etc, that there is no Scriptural school. There are two national schools (which upon principle I cannot patronise) but there is no school where the child must (as all teaching must be compulsory) read and commit to memory the Word of God. I ask your Society to place at my disposal such funds and food as will pay for a school house and school master for six months by way of experiment. The house and master could not cost more (for that period) than £15 and the Commissariat store in Ballina could supply me with a month's supply of meal for 50 scholars (all my school would consist of) at a pound of meal daily. My only desire is to teach the Word of God and as I can now procure a good master I trust the Friends will support me.

Your last grant of 2 bags of meal and a quarter ton of rice, dated 6 October, is now out. I gave it to the sick and infirm chiefly. There is now some pressure, as the relieving officer has not commenced his operations as yet in this parish. I would want a supply of meal and rice.'

Draft reply, 24 December: 'Order on Ballina a half ton of Indian meal, 3 bags of biscuit and a quarter ton of rice. He could place under the care of Geo Cuffe of Killasser such part of the grant as he might think right. Re school, no funds applicable for such an object. If the school were established we should be willing to grant some food for its support.'

Friday, 3 December. Extract from Guardians' minutes   *Boyle*
'In consequence of the hostile opposition encountered by Mr Elwood (rate CSORP O.12543
collector) in the Ballinamona electoral division, whereby his life and those of thirty armed police were placed in imminent danger, we beg the Commissioners would be pleased to recommend to the government that a sufficient military force be ordered to be in readiness to protect him, when he next proceeds to distrain ...'

Saturday 4 December. W. Hamilton to William Stanley   *Ballina*
'At the weekly meeting of the Board of Guardians there was a great deal of CSORP O.13361
talking and a great deal of important business left undone ... Today, I hired a store for 50 guineas p.a. capable of containing 300 paupers, who will be removed to it today from the workhouse ... There is very great destitution among certain classes. It is by no means general and there is a considerable portion of the population who may safely be left to their own resources for some months. There are others subsisting almost exclusively on turnips, the remaining portion subsisting either by plunder or begging ... Belmullet district ... number of applicants for relief increased from 600 to 1,100 ... Two-thirds of the population will shortly be applicants for relief and the remaining one-third are without either the means or the inclination to assist them.'

CSORP O.12545

5 December. Same to same

'300 paupers were moved today from the workhouse to the store ... 1,698 persons had to be provided for in the workhouse. The applicants are in the most miserable and filthy state ... There is neither bedding nor clothing for 600 ... Unless the Board meet more frequently and give more time to business, it is impossible that they can carry on the business of this large Union properly.'

CSORP O.12709

7 December. Same to same

'There were 11 cases of fever since yesterday ... The Guardians meet once a week and four or five hours are frittered away in discussing subjects ... Others of vital importance are put off until late in the day and generally either hurried over or altogether neglected. They have allowed destitution to get ahead of them ... I have witnessed much want and much imposition in Ireland but I never saw anything like the state of the unfortunate persons who are entreating indoor relief, in fact any protection from hunger and the inclemency of the season ... The relief afforded has been merely shelter and food ... No clothing ... no bedding and infection staring them in the face.'

Castlebar

CSORP O.13377

Sunday 5 December. Capt Farren to Poor Law Commission

'The tide of destitution may now be fairly considered to have set in ... A progressive and considerable increase has taken place in the numbers on the outdoor relief lists. On 13 November, 7 were discharged from the workhouse to outdoor relief, on 20 November, 34, on 27 November, 75, on 4 December, 341. Hitherto this form of relief was confined to the infirm, widows with two or more children and cases of fever. We are looking for extra relieving officers (there are 5 at present).

State of the workhouse: males over fifteen, 121; females over fifteen, 209; boys under fifteen, 172; girls under fifteen, 168; children under two, 26; total, 696. Fever cases, 25; other cases, 49, applicants, 364; admissions, 23; discharged from workhouse, 14.

School hours were changed, allowing longer periods of relaxation and exercise, and better ventilation of the schoolrooms. There has been a change of diet, substituting bread for the meal of stirabout once a day ... I have enforced a system of general responsibility from the master and matron down to the orderly men and women of each room.'

Sligo

Recipe circulated to the workhouses

Monday 6 December. Poor Law Commission to Capt Gilbert, enclosing a report from Mr Hancock, Poor Law inspector, Limerick, on the mode of baking Indian corn meal bread

'The work is performed by females from sixteen to twenty years of age, with one or two steady elderly women to teach them. This bread does not come

INDIAN CORN MEAL BREAD.

LIMERICK WORKHOUSE,
27th November, 1847.

SIR,

I have the honor to report the particulars regarding Hot Plates in this Workhouse, for Baking Bread.

Hot Plates (made of metal) 18 feet long, 3 feet 2 inches wide, and 1 inch thick, erected in Mill-house, to the back of the Kitchen flues, which flues are found to answer to the Kitchen and Bake-house.

Cost of erection, including all expenses, about £21 10s. 0d.

The Plates are in use here about 18 months, and required but very little repair; they were well set with large fire-blocks.

The Bread is made of Indian Corn Meal, by the Female Paupers, like griddle cake; there is nothing mixed with the Meal, save a little hot water to work it up; the Baking employs 14 Paupers daily.

The allowance of Meal made into Bread for Dinner is—

Men, ... 12 ounces.
Women, ... 8 ,,
Children, ... 8 ,, including luncheon.

The Bread for Men is made into cakes of 24 oz., or 1½lb., for Women and Children, into cakes of 16 oz. or 1lb.; immediately after the cake is worked up, and before placing it in the Plate, it is partly cut into two even parts, so that each Inmate receives their quantity by itself.

The numbers in the Workhouse supplied yesterday for Dinner with Indian Corn Meal Bread were—

284 Men.
476 Women.
680 Children.
———
1440

The Guardians do not allow this Bread for the sick, aged and infirm, or children under 5 years.

The Plates are capable of baking for 2000 daily, but at present we do not require for more than 1440.

The Contract price for Indian Corn Meal is £9 12s. 6d. per ton, or a small fraction more than 1d. per lb.

12 ounces of good Indian Corn Meal properly baked on this plan, will produce 1 lb. of Bread, at a cost, including fuel and salt, of less than 1d. per lb.

The Contract for Bread at present is 7d. for the 4lb. loaf.

I have the honor to be,
Sir,
Your very obedient servant,
D. O'CONNOR, *Clerk Union.*

To
W. J. HANCOCK, Esq.

to more than the former price of potatoes ... The health of the inmates appears more satisfactory.'

Achonry
SFFP 2/506/22

Monday 6 December. Catherine Rice to Bewley and Pim (See Appendix 6A)
'I disposed of it to a very numerous circle of extremely destitute beings ... according to the numbers of their familes, from 14lbs to 7lbs and 3 lbs at intervals of 8 and 10 days ... I also cooked a portion of it every day which I gave to persons out of employment and unable to procure a single meal in the day ... The workhouses are filled to suffocation and those not getting admittance are endeavouring to drag out a miserable existence from no other food than the garbage they can pick up in the turnip fields ... I know about very helpless families who are in the most wretched state of want and are at this inclement season without the comfort of any clothing better than tattered rags from the fact of their being obliged to dispose of the few necessary articles they had to procure food.'
Draft reply, 11 December: 'Order ¼ ton Indian meal, ¼ ton rice and 2 bags of biscuit.'

Coolavin
CSORP H.12607

Wednesday 8 December. Howard O'Farrell MD, Boyle, certifies that the Coolavin temporary fever hospital cannot be closed without certain loss of life
'To expose precipitately, in this weather at this inclement season, such a number of miserable creatures without either clothing, food or shelter, must inevitably be attended with very serious consequences ... Many of the patients will not be in a state fit to discharge for at least three or four weeks ... This is an extensive, remote and miserable district of country ... At no period since the outbreak of this epidemic have we had so many applications for admission during the summer months and up to 29 September. In consequence of the system of outdoor relief, many stricken with disease remained in their own houses ... All seized with the epidemic rush for admission to the hospital, as by remaining in their own huts, death is inevitable, if not from disease, from starvation.'

Sligo
CSORP O.12730

Wednesday 8 December. Report of Capt Gilbert
'More than 200 were admitted ... In some divisions of the Union, the ablebodied class are very destitute and without relief cannot subsist much longer. This want of food and employment may account in some degree for the increasing disturbance in this hitherto peaceable Union. There are few gentlemen throughout it who have not received threatening notices, and those who have distinguished themselves most by benevolence and attention to the wants of the poor during the late distress have been particularly marked out. The application of outdoor relief to the able-bodied may in some measure allay the evil and disaffected feeling at present prevailing amongst this class.'

Thursday 9 December. Capt Broughton to Poor Law Commissioners   *Swinford*
'The resignation of the master of the workhouse was accepted, and the porter   CSORP O.13271
intrusted to perform his duties, until a new master is appointed ... The
sealed order from the Commissioners, ordering no more than 750 persons to
be admitted into the Swinford Union workhouse, led to some discussion.
The fact of there being nearly 400 children included in the above number of
the present inmates, suggested the idea of having them removed to the new
shed which was built last year, but never occupied by fever patients ... These
sheds have not been covered with any material to keep out the weather, and
are altogether useless, on account of letting in the rain and weather at every
crevice ...

I wish to draw the attention of the Commissioners to the state of the officials
in this workhouse on my arrival. The master, who has just been got rid of, is
brother to the matron; the medical officer is brother-in-law to both; the
whole either cousins or connected with three or four of the Guardians. Now,
without wishing the least in the world to find any fault with the individuals,
the tendency of these connexionships is adverse to the proper working of the
system. It is obvious if any of these parties neglect their duties the other
would not be in a position to report faithfully any neglect; and it might be
worth the consideration of the Board, in any future appointments, to guard
against a system injurious to the pauper and detrimental to a fair working of
the Poor Law.'

Reply to above, 10 December: 'Near relationship between officers of a workhouse, who are intended to a certain extent to keep a check upon each other,
is not desirable.'

11 December. Capt Broughton to Poor Law Commission   CSORP O.13103
'I have now arranged to employ every man, young and old (capable of being
set to work) in the workhouse; and on Monday they will be in full employment.

A curious state of things occurs in the workhouse at this moment; on taking
the return of the inmates, out of 84 borne on the books as able-bodied there
are only 15 really able-bodied men, 24 who are only fit for breaking stones,
and 45, in fact, only children, who, by calling themselves 15, thought to avoid
school, and as the weather has been dreadfully severe, and very little outdoor
work capable of being done, preferred roasting themselves over the fire in the
men's wards to going to school; however, I have had them all sent into the
school-room.

Sixteen are in the infirmary or hospital, and 21 are either so infirm or bed-
ridden as to be unable to perform any work, and are, in fact, waiting their
time to die in the usual course of nature; making a total of adult males in the
house of only 60 ... The abstract of the state of the house at present would

be: adult males, 60; adult females, 176; girls, 204; infants, 25; and 251 boys, 45 of whom only are about 15 years old, the rest quite children. The knowledge that tools have been provided and work insisted on has already sent some out and deterred others from coming in … It is my intention to employ the 45 boys alluded to (as men) in breaking stones in a separate yard, when the weather permits, and they are not in school, and to propose to the Guardians to erect sheds, available either for work or play in bad weather.'

CSORP O.13416   *14 December. Same to same*

'I brought before the Board the necessity of at once entering into contracts for keeping the house in repair … The leakages in the roofs in various places are becoming very serious and require immediate looking after …

I was obliged to bring before the Board the conduct of the schoolmaster, Eugene McGuire, who, in passion, brutally assaulted a poor little child, only about seven years of age, leaving a cut extending from his eye to his mouth, and laying open his cheek. He has been forthwith dismissed … A person of the name of Kelly was recommended by the Board for the situation, who has been acting as assistant in the workhouse … I recommend his approval to be sent. Much dissatisfaction has been shown at being obliged to work, but by a little firmness this has been overcome; some have left rather than submit, which of course was not objected to.'

Ballina   *Saturday 11 December. R. Hamilton to William Stanley*

CSORP O.13170   'The auxiliary workhouse is almost immediately available in Binghamstown for almost 200 persons. It should be reserved exclusively for able-bodied men, those from a distance to have preference to accommodation to those from the locality, who should be fed and employed during the day and return home for the night. A school should be erected, a master and mistress appointed, the children fed and educated during the day and allowed home at night. Female adult paupers should be given a weekly supply of provisions … I find the greatest difficulty in briefing the applicants on the relieving officers' books before the committee of Guardians, in consequence of the crowd of people who collect round the door; and at the meeting last Wednesday, several hundreds thrust into the room, thereby putting a stop to all further business … There is scarcely any supply of provisions in the hands of the merchants.'

CSORP O.13358   *12 December. Same to same*

'Today, Sunday, I found 9 cases of fever had appeared since yesterday. There is no room in the fever hospital and the doctor could not separate them from the other inmates … There is no time to be lost in taking precautions to prevent a repetition of last year's disease. I ordered the discharge of some women and children and gave them outdoor allowance, a week's provisions if they had any place to go to. The numbers were thus reduced by about 300. The women and children in question had been in one of the fever sheds without bedding or any clothing but the filthy rags they came in, crowded together in a tainted atmosphere and liable to infection with being mixed up with half-cured fever cases … It would be inhuman to allow these poor persons perish from disease.'

Hamilton encloses a letter from Dr Devlin:
'There are 1,500 in a house built for 1,200 … Fever is very prevalent among the children … The most shocking fatal consequences will result from over-crowding … The entire house will be included in one terrific mass of disease.'

14 December. Same to same   CSORP O.13362
'The Board of Guardians have failed to carry out the Law effectually … The sooner paid Guardians are appointed the better. I ordered the removal of looms from one of the temporary fever sheds to increase the hospital accom-modation. It was countermanded by Capt Atkinson, one of the Guardians. Dr Devlin had to refuse to take 40 sick persons into the infirmary. It was resolved yesterday that food and one penny per head be given to 600 appli-cants to provide lodging for the night as they had come several miles and were in a state of the greatest destitution. The able-bodied were made to undergo the workhouse test, which in every case was most gladly accepted by the poor creatures … A week's supply of provisions was issued to the remain-der … A building was offered which could be made available for 600 child-ren for £100 or £130.'

Hamilton encloses Dr Devlin's letter:
'To keep the house in a healthy state, several hundreds of the present inmates ought to be removed.'

15 December. Same to same
'The Ballina Board of Guardians have allowed distress at this early period get ahead of them. I now see no alternative but outdoor relief in order to save life.'

22 December. William Stanley to clerk of Ballina Union
'Having considered the reports of their temporary inspectors, W. Hamilton, Ballina, and Richard Hamilton, Belmullet, the Commissioners have decided to dissolve the Ballina Board of Guardians and replace them with paid Guardians.'

Saturday 11 December. Capt Gilbert to Poor Law Commission, enclosing the pro-   *Sligo*
posed arrangement of relieving officers.   CSORP O.13424

Electoral division	Popl.	Relieving Officer	Salary
Collooney	4,798	Michael McDonnell	£45
Ballisodare &	4,419		
Coolaney	6,664	Richard Collins	£50

Electoral division	Popl.	Relieving Officer	Salary
Tubbercurry &	8,116		
Cloonacool	4,079	Henry Connor	£50
Ballymote &	4,811		
Cloonoghill	2,588	Thomas Allen	£50

Castlerea
CSORP 0.13105

Sunday 12 December. James Auchmuty to Poor Law Commission
'A number of the people in the workhouse are landholders. One person is a £10 freeholder. With a revision of the entire house I hope to reduce the numbers by 300 ... The present rate collectors should be changed. They will never do their duty, some from intimidations, others from being in the hands of the Guardians and magistrates. A person should be sent down to reside in the town to collect the entire rates of the Union ... This part of the country is in a very bad state, the magistrates are afraid to act ... In fact, no man's life is safe, that has any dealing with the country people.'

Castlebar
CSORP 0.13376

Sunday 12 December. Capt Farren to Poor Law Commission
'*State of the workhouse:* Males over fifteen, 122; females over fifteen, 206; boys under fifteen, 174; girls under fifteen, 165; children under two, 24; total, 691. Fever cases, 28; other cases, 60.
A crowd of applicants, destitute and misery-stricken, assembled at the workhouse door. There were 1,469 applicants on the relieving officers' books. 37 were admitted to the workhouse and 1,425 to outdoor relief. 38 (infirm and widows with children) were discharged and transferred to outdoor relief. 41 others were discharged on Monday with 6d. a week for lodgings. There are 2,000 receiving outdoor relief (from 472 to 1,919 in one week). Arrangements are being made for employing the able-bodied at stone-breaking. The county surveyor has a large supply of implements, hammers and crowbars, belonging to the public works which could be loaned to the vice-Guardians ... Assistants to the relieving officers have been appointed in each electoral division.'

CSORP 0.13309

13 December. Robert Lecky, Arthur Thomas and W. Carey to Poor Law Commission re appointment of another person to replace Mr Flanagan as master of the workhouse (his wife was matron)
'Ten assistant relieving officers were elected from 60 applicants at 10 shillings a week ... Mr Brett, county surveyor has 10,000 hammers with picks, wheelbarrows etc and suggests we apply to the Board of Works for the use of them.'

Tuesday 13 December. Rebecca Irwin, Camlin, to Society of Friends

Boyle
SFFP 2/506/22

'I write in great haste not to lose the post or I could give more in detail on account of a most cruel and unworthy attack made by the Roman Catholic priest of this parish on the 11th inst. on the little children of our school. He was on the road when they were dismissed watching for them, and using most violent language rode into the school grounds after them, using his whip upon all he could reach. I was in the school at the time and when they returned, crying "the priest, the priest", I went out, following him as he passed the door until he turned his horse again on the road to ride in and repeat the attack, had I not been there and had time to close the gate … None of the children were injured tho' one was thrown down by his horse. He has since said that it will not be his last visit. But the Lord, I trust, will still preserve us and the poor children from his fury.'

Draft reply, 15 December: 'We cannot countenance anything of a party or sectarian character and we consider the present time particularly unsuitable for any attempts at proselytising. Our funds have received subscriptions from all classes and from Roman Catholics to a considerable amount.'

Tuesday 13 December. Apostolic Delegate to the Cardinal Secretary of State
'I have received the collections (1,045 *scudi*) made by the various bishops of New Granada for the relief of the Irish. I will put it at the disposal of the nuncio in Paris to be given to some Irish bishops to be distributed amongst the most needy.'

Bogota, Colombia
SC IRLANDA
vol 29, f.670r

Thursday 15 December. James Auchmuty to Poor Law Commission
'Numbers of the most wretched creatures are brought to the workhouse door in fever. The Guardians from kind motives order them to be admitted. The doctor opposes it as much as possible on the grounds that there are too many in the hospital.'

Castlerea
CSORP O.2143

Thursday 15 December. Report of Capt Gilbert
'There are upwards of 1,400 in the house. Because of the wet weather during the week the sheds could not be completed. A large crowd of applicants were sent back and put on outdoor relief. The Mayor and clergy of Sligo requested the Guardians to relieve 1,500 able-bodied men in the town.
£1,228 rates collected last week. In some of the electoral divisions the military was required to protect the collector. I recommended to Colonel McArthur to apply for additional troops for the use of this Union … There is but a very small party quartered in the town and none in any part of the county.'

Sligo
CSORP O.13426

Saturday 17 December. Memorial of the Protestant inhabitants of Collooney and its vicinity, signed by W. N. Guinness, vicar of Ballisodare, chairman, to Lord Lieutenant
'We have observed with feelings of anxiety and alarm the evident existence of

Collooney
OP 26/338

a deep laid conspiracy against life and property throughout the country ... We have noticed a remarkable change in the bearing of the lower classes ... Threatening letters have been addressed to a number of the most benevolent and esteemed of the gentry and clergy of the Church of England ... and against the clergy of this parish. Terror and intimidation has been thus commenced. Violence and bloodshed may one day break forth ... (Protestants) purpose associating together at once for their mutual protection ... and in the prevention, repression and detection of crime.'

Keash
SFFP 2/506/22

Sunday 18 December. Abby Fleming to Society of Friends (See Appendix 6O)
'Never was relief more needed than the last, nor never were applications more numerous than at present ... The destitution is most heartrending in the extreme, the haggard, emaciated, miserable appearance of the applicants is truly appalling. Many hundreds of these are subsisting on turnips often uncooked.'
Draft reply, 22 December: 'Order in Sligo quarter ton of rice, quarter ton of Indian meal and 2 bags of biscuit.'

Ballina
CSORP 0.13106

Sunday 18 December. W. Hamilton to William Stanley
'The meeting yesterday was poorly attended because of the extreme severity of the weather ... There were no less than 2,000 applicants for relief, half of them extreme cases. To provide shelter from the weather the Guardians directed that the crowd be admitted into the dining hall and four days' provisions be issued to all with tickets from the relieving officers, but such was the dense mass of human beings, that the master, relieving officers and the inmates of the house found it impossible to keep any order ... Finally the police were sent for, and the scene of confusion can only be realised by those who witnessed it ... It was by the greatest good fortune that persons were not crushed to death ... This painful scene ended by the house being cleared: a few of the most destitute looking objects were ordered some relief for the night ... The real difficulties of the case are increased by the fact that it is not considered any crime by those who are not in want to take the bread out of the mouths of poor starving creatures. The Guardians are perfectly paralysed ... Many of them are comparatively speaking in great want; their properties lying waste and likely to remain so next year ... With whole tracts of country similarly circumstanced ... the prospect before them is not cheering ... There seems to be no limit to all this relief. It is only, therefore, from those men who look upon the salvation of human life as their first duty, that one meets with any disinterested co-operation ... It is only fair to those gentlemen, who are willing and anxious to carry out the law and overcome difficulties, that I should mention that all their exertions are counterbalanced by

the impossibility of finding in a Board of 66 members that unanimity which will insure for the law a firm and impartial administration.'

19 December. R. Hamilton to William Stanley   *Belmullet*
CSORP O.13312

'I am now returning to Erris with a cheque for £100 in my pocket, a portion of which is to pay the expenses incurred on the building, the remainder to provide for between 2,000 and 3,000 persons on the relieving officer's books. I have no staff on which I can place any confidence and as far as the committee of Guardians is concerned ... the only members who attended the meeting of the Board ... stated they would soon be applying for relief themselves.'

Sunday 18 December. Capt Broughton to Poor Law Commission   *Swinford*
CSORP O.13224

'It having been blowing a perfect hurricane the last three days, no one attended at the sub-committee of the workhouse ...

It appears to have been a system in this part of the world to collect rents, county rates and other fiscal dues, after certain fairs etc, a usage of so long standing as to have become almost law. The same view seems to have been applied to poor rates ... Most of the holdings are £4 annual value, and hence proceedings cannot be taken against the tenant until four months elapse, and another month's notice is given at the expiration ...

I have been lately much occupied again in endeavouring to organise the relief contemplated by the British Association through the existing schools; but really the state of things has become so monstrous, I have been obliged to refer to the Count Strzelecki for his views. For instance, in the electoral division of Killedan, where three schools were named to me by the inspector under the National Board, and containing on the 18th of last month, 56, 79 and 41 pupils respectively; a return has been sent to me of 17 schools with 2,138 children in this electoral division alone. They seem to have sprung up like mushrooms under the shower of relief to be afforded, whilst not one shilling is forthcoming for the purposes of management from any local source.'

Monday 19 December. Report of Capt Farren   *Castlebar*
CSORP O.13311

'*State of the workhouse:* males over fifteen, 105; females over fifteen, 181; boys under fifteen, 157; girls under fifteen, 153; children under two, 23; total, 619. Fever cases, 28; dysentery, 60; other cases, 12. There were 3,270 applicants for relief (a three-fold increase in the last seven days). 141 were admitted to the workhouse, 60 were discharged and 1,322 placed on outdoor relief.

Additional workhouse accommodation is needed. A universal feeling of hostility having arisen among the inhabitants of Castlebar against the appropriation of the house, for which the vice-Guardians were in treaty to such a purpose, legal proceedings have been threatened and a memorial forwarded to the lieutenant of the county for presentation to the Commissioners. This memorial has been returned by the Earl of Lucan and as the house is merely intended for the children, the vice-Guardians have determined upon taking possession.

The relief afforded by the British Association to the destitute children attending the schools is in operation in the town of Castlebar where 380 are fed daily. Arrangements have been made to extend the relief to the other electoral divisions.'

Boyle
CSORP W.13261

Tuesday 20 December. Memorial of Patrick Boyle to Lord Lieutenant
'He was employed as a quarry man on a new road from Boyle to Ballymote and on 27 October 1846, when preparing a blast, he lost his right eye and broke his right arm and suffered contraction of his fingers which rendered him unable to be of assistance to himself or his family, a wife and five desolate weak children. He lay upwards of 6 months in the greatest of torments and pains and since is able to creep about unable to work with his poor weak family in a state that words cannot express, their famishing starving situation was wholly depending on his daily work. He implores remuneration towards the support of himself and distressed starving little creatures.'
Reply to above, 26 December: 'Her Majesty's Treasury do not consider that persons who received injuries whilst employed in the public works have any claim upon the government.'

Swinford
Correspondence p. 101

Wednesday 21 December. Report of Capt Broughton
'The applications for admission into the workhouse today were very few, but the house being full, I brought before the Board the necessity of making room for them, and proposed ... that those women with families, who it is supposed to have their husbands in the country, should be discharged with a week's provisions to seek their husbands; the result has been the turning out (with rations) nearly 80 ... At the same time a list of them has been provided to each relieving officer, to scrutinise and make distinct inquiries as to their husbands being in the country, and holding land or otherwise.
The house in this way has been reduced below the complement allowed.'

Sligo
CSORP O.13427

Thursday 22 December. Report of Capt Gilbert
'The poorhouse was as usual surrounded by paupers, mostly able-bodied, who were exceedingly clamorous for relief. 542 were admitted which entirely filled the new sheds and other accommodation afforded by the removal of orphan children to the house provided for them. Fever and dysentery are on the increase ... Two additional fever sheds to be erected ... There is a laxity

among the Guardians, a few of whom only can be made to attend. Mr Wynne, chairman, Mr Wood and some others deserve the highest credit ... The meeting is held at 11 o'clock in the morning until 7 o'clock and later in the evening and frequently more than twice in the same week.'

23 December. Capt Gilbert to Poor Law Commission   CSORP O.1124

'I presided at the enquiry required by Mr Cormick, late schoolmaster of the workhouse, into charges preferred against him by a female pauper ... Although the evidence does not appear sufficient to criminate Cormick in a court of justice of having connexion with the girl, my opinion coincided with the Guardians' that he had taken most improper liberties with her.'

29 December. Report of Capt Gilbert

'There were two nights immediately following each other; on both times the parties met on the gangway; on the first night Cormick did not proceed to extremities, another girl being present. The succeeding night was that on which the charge of an attempt to violate the girl's person was founded ... The girl makes two charges on different nights and confounds them together in her evidence.'

Evidence of Mr Savage, master of the workhouse: 'I heard the report two or three days before I reported it to the Board of Guardians, 23 November 1847, from Mrs Savage, a rumour being through the house. I spoke to the girl, Catherine Kilmartin, who said that Cormick threw her down, uncovered his person and hers and had connexion with her.'

Evidence of Catherine Kilmartin: 'He did take up her clothes. They were about five or ten minutes on the ground ... I did not shout or say I would tell of him because I did not like to expose myself ...'

Questioned by Capt Gilbert:

'Did Cormick ever take improper liberties with you before these two nights?'
'Yes.'
'When?' 'In the wardmaster's room about three weeks before.'
'What brought you to the wardmaster's room?'
'I went in the morning to make his bed.'

Saturday 24 December. Richard Bourke, Poor Law inspector, to Commissariat   *Ballina*

'The Ballina Board retired today. The additional building at Ardnaree is not   CSORP O.13363
yet ready to receive paupers. The relieving officers' books had upwards of 5,000 applicants (exclusive of Binghamstown and Belmullet), a large majority requiring instantaneous relief. I ordered the relieving officers to continue provisional relief for one week and to obtain the necessary quantity of meal from the contractor in Ballina.'

Kilcolman
& Kilfree
SFFP 2/506/37

Sunday 25 December. Society of Friends clothes query completed and signed by J. A. Holmes

'About 500 needing clothes, flannel and cotton for the females and corduroy with shoes for the men ... He undertakes to pay for making them ... There is no other resident in the district but the applicant who takes an interest in these matters.'

Swinford
CSORP O.44425

Wednesday 28 December. Report of Capt Broughton

'The meeting of the Board of Guardians took place today and was fully attended ... I suggested at the last meeting the adoption of brown bread, or bread made from whole meal, in the workhouse in lieu of that made from the finest wheat flour ... The difference in price is from £18 to £10 per ton, and thus a great saving will be effected, whilst a more wholesome article is furnished. It has always appeared to me to be one of the many anomalies of this country, that one finds the poorest peasantry perhaps in Europe, feeding on bread made from the finest and most expensive material, and I do conceive that a great benefit would be derived to the community at large, by the general adoption of this brown bread ...

Out of the five candidates for the mastership of the workhouse, two were selected for competition, viz, Michael Henry, who obtained eight votes, and Martin Sheridan, who obtained five votes. The former was elected, subject to the approval of the Commissioners. I am bound to say that I do not consider either of the candidates, whether as regards position, education or local connection, calculated to make an efficient officer to the institution; the person selected is perfectly ignorant of his duties, was a Guardian to the Swinford electoral division, and resigned to enable his brother to occupy the situation of relieving officer, which he at present holds. If a retired sergeant of some regiment, accustomed to discipline and organisation, could be found sufficiently active and steady to fill these offices, I cannot but think great benefit would be derived to the institutions generally.

With regard to the memorial referred to me so numerously signed in this district, I do not consider it warranted by the circumstances of the Union. At present time much individual suffering may occur, but as yet we have not had recourse to outdoor relief, and the workhouse at this time is not full. It is remarkable that concurrent with this petition was an influx of paupers into the house, which crowded it a little for a few days, until the abuses I complained of were got rid of; and also that a verdict of a coroner's inquest was represented as finding a case from starvation to have occurred, which as far as I have as been yet able to make enquiry, was on the body of a stranger passing through, and who never made any application to any relieving officer or elsewhere, for assistance ... The rigid adherence to work as a test ... is operating most beneficially in its results, as the inmates are no longer allowed to sit idling over the fires …

Out of the persons sent out to seek their husbands … only three families returned this day.'

Reply to above, 8 January, 1848: 'The Commissioners have objected to the proposed appointment of Mr Henry and have recommended the Guardians to proceed to the election of another person to the office of workhouse master … Discharged non-commissioned officers of the army have been found in other Unions to make efficient masters of workhouses.'

28 December. Richard Bourke to Poor Law Commission, re death of Patrick Duffy, Ballinamore, in Killedan electoral division
CSORP O.13417

'The coroner, who is also a Guardian, returned a verdict at the inquest on 15 December, of death by destitution and starvation … The relieving officer, Joseph Jordan, swore before me that he attended on Thursdays, Fridays and Saturdays each week, both at the chapel and at Miss Cunniffe's house in Kiltimagh between 11 and 3 o'clock and that Duffy never applied to him for relief.

James Durkan, porter of the workhouse and acting master for the last week, swore before me that Duffy never applied for admission. "I have not had occasion to refuse any person who has applied for admission to this workhouse since I have been acting as master".'

Thursday 29 December. Roger Brennan ADM to Society of Friends' clothing department
Kilmactigue
SFFP 2/506/37

'This parish comprising a very extensive tract of mountainous district was at all times remarkable for the poverty and destitution of its inhabitants. It has suffered more from the potato blight than any other locality in this country … Since the cessation of the temporary relief act it has to subsist almost exclusively on turnips, even this is at present nearly exhausted … In many districts the old and young are literally naked, having neither shoes nor clothes.'

2 January. Society of Friends' clothes query signed by Em. Caulfield (See Appendix 6Q)

'There are 720 persons viz. 120 men, 120 women and 480 boys, girls and children of which 220 males and 260 females, needing clothes. Shoes are much needed as both men, boys and girls are barefoot and unable to stand outdoor work. Guernsey frocks, grey calico, blue print for girls and children. Flannel, barrogan, and cordury for trousers. Bed rugs, cotton sheets and blankets are much needed as many are obliged to lay on straw in their miserable clothes. Those who will act conjointly with her are Roger Brennan ADM, Rev A. K. Huston, rector, Hugh O'Hara, Mathew Ginty and Daniel O'Hara (tenants).

The applicant does not live in the district and was obliged to send this query to her agent to be filled.'
Draft reply: 'Grant no.1 sent by mistake to applicant's address (Armagh) and another grant no.1 to be made to Kilmactigue.'

Westport
CSORP A.21

Friday 30 December. Lord Sligo to T. N. Redington, seeking clarification on a point of law
'If a tenant offers possession to his landlord, agent or baillif, but such an offer is not accepted, is such a tenant barred from receiving outdoor relief? If the tenant offers possession of all except a quarter acre is he barred from relief? *Sligo cites the following case:* A tenant, named Woods, offered possession to O'Donel, baillif of the Earl of Lucan, who refused it. The relieving officer declared that Woods, being still in possession of more than a quarter acre, could not receive outdoor relief … Cases like these are most pressing and to postpone relief for a week might be a sentence of death. In the case of Woods, the distress was so urgent I suggested that he and his family be admitted to the workhouse.'
Reply to above, 5 January, 1848: 'The query was referred to the Law Adviser.'

Coolaney
SFFP 2/506/37

Saturday 1 January 1848. Society of Friends' clothes query completed and signed by Kate P. Thompson, Knockadoo House (See Appendix 61)
'There are about 300 persons needing clothes. Mens' shoes would be a great boon coming on spring. An equal number of mens' and womens' clothes are wanting. We will make the womens' clothes ourselves and will pay for the making of the shoes and menswear. I purpose to levy them as heretofore for the cost of making them. Miss Gray and Mrs O'Connor will act conjointly with her.'
Draft reply: 'Grant no.1.'

Tubbercurry
OP 26/16

Monday 3 January. Resolution of meeting of clergymen, gentry, farmers and others re statements in the public papers that the district is and has been for some time in a disturbed state, signed by James McHugh PP, chairman, James Gallagher PP, John O'Flynn PP, Curry; John Brennan CC, Curry, Thomas Judge CC, five Poor Law Guardians, and 29 others
'There is not the slightest ground for these unfounded statements … In no other locality in this country would the population remain quiescent under the very many privations and suffering they have and are still enduring from want, famine and disease.'

Shrule
SC IRLANDA
vol 29, ff.783rv 784r

Tuesday 4 January. Michael Phew PP to Cardinal Franzoni
'There is great distress, destitution and suffering through want of food in this

parish. The people here, to the amount of more than 10,000 human beings, are suffering the most appalling scenes of hunger. This day six of these poor people have died of starvation. There is fever and all other infirmities consequent on the want of sufficiency of food, very general among this, my poor and starving flock. The landlords in this parish, because they are not receiving their rents, have dispossessed a great number of families of their lands and have brought the sheriff to level their little houses, and these poor families are perishing of cold and hunger by the roadside. I cannot sufficiently describe to your Eminence the great and varied scenes of suffering that the poor here are patiently enduring, respectfully trusting that you Eminence will commiserate their wants by ordering a portion of any charities intended for the relief of Irish distress to be sent to this starving flock.'

Tuesday 4 January. Report of Capt Broughton
'I found the dairymaid feeding cows and pigs belonging to the matron, with an enormous pail of stirabout ... The matron is the sister-in-law or cousin to half the Board of Guardians.'

8 January. Poor Law Commission to Capt Broughton
'The Board of Guardians should at once take active steps to afford relief out of the workhouse and therefore to make room in the workhouse for any sudden pressure. The Board of Guardians should hire or rent a building for children or infirm persons ... Orders have been given for the dismissal of the matron.'

11 January. Report of Capt Broughton
'With some difficulty I attended today the Board of Guardians' meeting, still suffering from a severe attack of influenza ... The meeting did not take place till nearly 2 o'clock and was occupied until nearly 4 o'clock with discussion arising out of the Commissioners' dismissal of the matron. The meeting was unusually large ... expressly collected to resist the order for the election of a master. They stated that permission was given to the matron, when the inmates were on a potato dietary, to feed her pigs with the peelings and waste.'

Tuesday 4 January. Report of R. Hamilton
'On visiting the auxiliary workhouse at Binghamstown yesterday, I found the doors surrounded by several hundreds of the most miserable looking objects seeking admittance and stating that they had no place whatsoever to shelter them at night or a morsel of food of any description to eat. However, as the available portion of the building was quite inadequate to accommodate such a number of paupers, I had no alternative but to refuse taking them in ... It is absolutely requisite to provide indoor accommodation for nearly 1,000

Swinford
CSORP O.2192

CSORP O.2192

CSORP O.1070

Belmullet
CSORP O.1371

persons in the district ... There are upwards of 30 orphan children at present in the auxiliary workhouse, most of whom I sent there myself in order to prevent their dying on the roads for want of shelter. No other class of persons have been admitted, until a proper division is made to separate the males and females ... Fever has greatly increased in this district within the last few weeks.'

Sligo
CSORP O.1073

Wednesday 5 January. Report of Capt Gilbert
'The advertisement for a nurse has not been answered ... There is a daily increase of fever and dysentery ... Poor Law Commission should send down a nurse...'

CSORP O.1074

5 January. N. Furey to Capt Gilbert
'In Ballintogher electoral division the depot was broken into between 12 o'clock and one in the morning by an armed party of fellows, who took 12 cwt of meal. A search was made by the police and one suspect was arrested. A reward is to be offered and posted up by the police.'

Swinford
CSORP I.682

Thursday 6 January. Edward Hunt, sub-inspector, to Inspector General
'The Swinford poorhouse in my humble judgement is not capable of containing one-quarter of the destitute in this Union. So far from not having carried the Vagrant Act into force, I was recommended by some of the local magistrates not to send any more beggars to the county gaol, it being too full and fever prevailing to a great extent in it. No outrage by beggars or others has been reported to the police since the Vagrant Act became law.'

Ballaghaderreen

Thursday 6 January. Report in the Sligo Journal 14 January*
'*Taking a bull by the horns*'
'Mr Joseph Holmes is a resident proprietor in the county of Sligo, within a short distance of Ballaghaderreen. He is a magistrate and was made deputy lieutenant last summer, as a mark of the sense entertained by the authorities of his exertions on behalf of the poor during the late crisis.
Having received many friendly intimations, a short time since, that the parish priest, Mr Tighe, had made repeated attacks on him at the chapel, and that his life would be attempted by assassins who had arrived in the neighbourhood, he was prevailed on, by the entreaties of his friends, to leave the country for a short period till the passing of the late government measure, when he returned.
These facts coming to the knowledge of his brother, Alexander Erskine Holmes, who resides in England, the latter paid a hurried visit to this country. On Thursday last – old Christmas Day – he presented himself at the

Handbill from A. E. Holmes, London

chapel in Ballaghaderreen, and having asked and obtained permission from

* I am indebted to John C. McTernan for drawing my attention to this report.

TO THE

ROMAN CATHOLIC
INHABITANTS OF BALLAGHADERREEN,
And its Neighbourhood.

My Friends,

You remember that on the 6th of this Month, in the Chapel of Ballaghaderreen, I charged the Priest of your Parish, Mr. Tigue, with conduct abborrent to his Office as a Christian Minister.

I gave Mr. Tigue notice on the morning of that day that I would address you, and I refused to open my lips until he stood at my side at the Altar.   This you will allow, was fair, and open, and straightforward

I now hear that no sooner had I left the Country than he made an attack upon me at the Chapel, heaping upon me all kind of abuse, and, amongst other things, said, that I had called you Assassins and Murderers.

Some of you perhaps do not know the meaning of the word "Assassin!"   It means a man who will stab you as soon as your back is turned.

But base as an Assassin is, there is even a more degraded character than that,—a man who, without the courage to be an Assassin, will incite others to deeds of blood.

I never charged you with being Assassins.   I said that strangers had come into the Parish to commit murder; and we all know that the murders which now disgrace our Country are committed by strangers to the Districts where they are perpetrated.

That is what I said, and Mr. Tigue knows it is what I said; but it suits his purpose to put into my mouth words that I never uttered, that he may make dissession between you and me.   I have walked through the Parish alone at all hours and seasons, without even a switch in my hand.   Does that look as if I thought you Assassins?

If I thought you were Assassins, I should have asked for a guard of Policemen to attend me at the Chapel on the 6th of January.   Did I do so?   No.   And the orderly and peaceful conduct of most of you on that day, and generally, proves how little you have suffered by the bad example you have so long had before you.

One word more, and I have done.   The interruption I met with when I addressed you prevented my telling you that he who assumes the privilege of deciding who shall live and who shall die in his Parish, cannot evade the responsibility that attaches to it.   Let it be borne in mind, that when murder is committed, the Law makes no distinction between the head that counsels and the hand that is raised for the shedding of blood.

I remain,

Your sincere Friend,

A. E. HOLMES.

London, January, 1848.

the Rev Mr Tighe to address the congregation, a very numerous one, was accommodated with a place at the altar. He declined to address the people till Mr Tighe stood at his side; a second priest stood at his left. Mr Holmes, advancing to the front of the altar, addressed the congregation thus:

"My friends, Mr Tighe, your priest, has given me permission to address you from the altar, and I avail myself of it. I have travelled five hundred miles to say a few words to you – pray therefore, attend to me. You do not all know me but you know my brother, Mr Joseph Holmes. Is there amongst you a man who can say that my brother has ever done an unkind or an unjust act by him? Is there, I say? If there is, let him hold up his hand. Is there amongst you a man who can deny that for the last two years, my brother has been your slave? If there is, let him speak. – *(A pause)* – During the last two years, my brother has expended £20,000 in provisions, to keep down the markets here, that you and your children might not starve! He has daily for the last sixteen months fed 150 of your children at his schoolhouse. He has turned his house and offices into a provision store for your accommodation. Is there a man amongst you who can deny this? If there is, let him speak. And what is the return he has met with? Do you require to be told? Why, when he left home a month ago, it is common knowledge that the assassins, who were to murder him, had arrived in the parish and were harboured amongst you. There are those amongst you that know it – I can account for the presence of those miscreants. They were attracted hither by the inflammatory harangues of your priest here - *(pointing to Mr Tighe)* – I tell him so, to his face."

(Tremendous uproar in the chapel. Cries of 'turn him out, he is a liar'; a scene of great confusion, during which the curate in vain attempted to address and appease the people, followed. At length Mr Tighe succeeded, after many ineffectual efforts, in obtaining a hearing.)

Mr Tighe: "It is false that I made any attacks on Mr Holmes; there have been houses levelled in this parish, and poor wretches turned out, but I never attacked Mr Holmes."

Mr Holmes: "I know that you did, and I tell you at this altar to your face, and in the presence of your congregation, that it is your attacks on my brother from this spot that have brought these murderers to this parish."

(Here the uproar recommenced, and some of the more violent of the congregation appeared disposed to pass over the rails to the altar, the priests endeavouring to restrain them.)

Mr Holmes (advancing in front): "I am not afraid of you. I came here to tell you these truths alone, and am not to be deterred by five hundred of you."

Mr Tighe: "My friends, this is the house of God. Let us have no more of this. Mr Holmes has charged me with attacks on his brother, which I deny. If he has anything more to say, let him address you outside the chapel."

Mr Holmes, having declined any further address to the people, left the chapel surrounded by the people, who refrained from any act of personal violence, but saluted him with groans and execrations on his driving away.'

15 January. A. E. Holmes, 5 Chester Street, Grosvenor Place, London, to the editor of the Times

'... When I alleged my brother had expended £20,000 in keeping down the markets in his neighbourhood, I meant that he had imported into the district provisions to that amount (at great risk to himself from the rapid fluctuation of prices), which he disposed at first cost. His means, which consist of a fee-simple estate of 1,100 acres in the county of Sligo, would obviously not admit of his sacrificing so large a sum as that mentioned.'

20 January. D. Tighe PP to the editor of the Dublin Evening Post

'The report in the *Mail* of what occurred as regards Mr A. Holmes is substantially correct; but it does not give anything descriptive of the fury and passion of my assailant while attacking us. The report is defective in what I said, challenging proofs for the daring calumnies he gave expression to. The report also attributes language to me which I did not use; for instance, the words 'there have been houses levelled and poor wretches turned out,' were spoken by people in the crowd, alluding to the estate of Luny, the property of a Mr Waldron of Dublin, who 'cleared' this place in April last of nineteen families, consisting of 128 individuals, the most of whom are since dragging out a miserable existence. Mr Holmes is the agent, and it is to this the person who spoke alluded ...

It may, perhaps, be asked is there any difference of opinion between Mr Holmes and myself. I admit that there is – the greatest – but all on the score of religion. He resides in this parish since the death of his father, who purchased the little property of Clogher ... and since he came there has kept a Bible school for the accommodation of his Catholic neighbours – for be it remarked, this Mr Holmes is the first Protestant who settled down in this half-parish since the days of the "Reformation"...'

Monday 10 January. Vice-Guardians to Poor Law Commission

Castlebar
CSORP O.1048

'In the very limited intercourse we have had with the gentry of Mayo, we have found them kind, humane and affable, never shrinking from the tremendous abyss which appears to yawn before them; satisfied that the destitute should be supported, let the consequences to themselves be what they might ... Lord Oranmore on his Castlemagarret estate had 135 tenants paying under £10 rent ... Not more than 30 would be able to stand their ground and crop their land ... He intends to accept the surrender from the remainder and relet them their houses and a quarter acre of land to enable them to receive relief.'

Correspondence
pp. 436-7

11 January. Report of Capt Farren

'The amount of rate collected during the week was £163 9s. 2¾d. The total amount now obtained is £1,243 4s. 10¼d., leaving uncollected, £8,703 8s. 10d. In consequence of the receipts not keeping pace with the expenditure, the vice-Guardians found themselves yesterday in a difficult position: no funds being available to pay the contractors' bills, to two of whom about £440 was due for provisions supplied for outdoor relief ... It was at one time doubtful whether provisions would be forthcoming to feed the thousands already on the relief list, and the crowd of applicants then outside anxiously awaiting their turn to be called before the Board ... I explained to the contractors ... that all the powers placed in the hands of the vice-Guardians would be exerted to the utmost to enforce the payment of the rate. After some hesitation, the contractors consented to furnish a supply for another week ... The resident magistrate accompanies the collector tomorrow to the electoral divisions of Balla and Drum, to enforce the collection by seizing the property of wealthy ratepayers who have taken no notice of the collector's applications. To avoid all risk of opposition, a body of constabulary and a party of infantry with a few dragoons will be in attendance. These measures will break the spell of passive resistance, and bring in the rates more rapidly.

The number placed on the relief list on Saturday and Monday was 1,560. The number now receiving outdoor relief is 8,401. That the whole of these are actually in a starving condition may, I think, be doubted; and although the deep-rooted aversion of the peasantry to the workhouse, causing them almost to starve before they will enter it ... still the facts are sufficiently marked to give a colour to the supposition ... On the first day there were vacancies in the workhouse ... and numbers refused to enter the house ... As the parties appeared with their families and the relieving officer asserted their destitution, the vice-Guardians had no alternative but to afford outdoor relief ... The labour-test is applied as closely as possible to the able-bodied; 31 men were struck off the lists for non-attendance at the work, or for idleness during the week; their families thereby losing their rations.

The relief afforded by the British Association to the children attending the schools in the Union is now extensively in operation. 25 schools obtain relief and 3,297 received rations of rye-bread; and in some of the schools broth also, during the last week. The bread, when baked, costs three farthings per pound, and the broth twopence per gallon.'

Farren encloses a list of immediate lessors who have not paid their rates. At the top of the list was the Earl of Lucan, of Castlebar House and Latham House, Chertsey, England who owed £692 4s. 2½d.

Tuesday 11 January. Richard Hamilton to Poor Law Commission

Belmullet
CSORP O.1515

'We proceeded yesterday to the auxiliary workhouse at Binghamstown ... and having all the applicants for relief in the vicinity brought before us, after sitting until nearly dark and having only examined about 600, we were obliged to stop from the unruly disposition evinced by the paupers. At an early hour of the day we deemed it prudent to request the police officer would be good enough to send a few of his men for the preservation of order, who at that time had not arrived. Subsequently, four men were ordered down to guard the premises, and we requested the officer would direct them to remain that night and each night until an efficient staff arrived. We considered these precautions necessary in consequence of a number on the previous night having scaled the wall and made an attempt to enter the store room by placing a ladder to the window but were discovered before they effected entry ... The deplorable state of the people in the district, nine deaths from starvation having been reported on good authority to have occurred, and on coming under our personal observation, it was necessary to take the most prompt and decisive steps to prevent further loss of life.

Mr Bourke, the relieving officer for Belmullet, was charged with maladministration but refused to give up his books and went away declaiming before a mob of starving people that it was us who withheld provisions from them ... While this was going on there was a woman carrying a dead child and a man dying at the door ... We immediately proceeded to Drumkeehan, a distance of 17 miles, and made arrangements for dispensing relief in the northern and most distressed portion of Bourke's district, in order to prevent a repetition of the heartrending scenes which have occurred through the negligence of Mr Bourke. The coastguard said that Bourke only once visited the district ... Tomorrow we go to Bangor.'

Wednesday 12 January. Report of the vice-Guardians as to the collection of the rate

Ballina
Correspondence
pp. 81-4

'Magisterial summonses have not been hitherto effective, nor are they likely to be so, the magistrates being in the constant habit of postponing the sessions and thereby causing delay. We fear this is done intentionally, and are of opinion that the resident magistrate should be required to adjudicate at the next sessions ... The local magistrates are also ... in the habit of decreeing for a much less amount than what may be due, upon any trivial cause shown ... Two collectors reported this to us yesterday, they having lost seven weeks owing to postponements, having summoned defaulters for several hundred pounds. The amount paid in since we came, from 28 December to 11 January was £973.'

The vice-Guardians enclose a list of 130 defaulters, giving the amounts due and observations on each. Colonel Knox Gore, who was then resident at Kingstown,

near Dublin, owed £166. George Vaughan Jackson owed £93 19s. 61½d. He paid
£49 on account and promised the payment of balance as soon as possible. With
this arrangement the Guardians were satisfied, feeling from his explanation that
he was most willing to pay all and was prevented by his present inability. James
McNair, the apothecary to the workhouse, owed £7 15s. 9d., which was to be
retained from his salary.

Innishboffin
CSORP W.394

Thursday 13 January. Memorial of 28 islanders to Lord Lieutenant
'They are in great distress and want. They have no person to look to to assist
them as there is no person living on the island but Mr Henry Hildebrand,
Lord Sligo's agent. They are in debt to their landlord for over two years' rent
and he has assisted them for the last two years. But unfortunately the fishery
which was and is their only dependance was last year a total failure … And
if it is a failure again this year their fate will be a miserable one … as we are
only now dragging out a miserable existance waiting for it … Mr Hildebrand
has applied to the Board of Works for money to reclaim his land, but we have
never seen it yet or got any labour … We fear he is only filling us up with
false hopes to bring us to our fishery season, for if once our fishery commenced, we would try and be a burthen to nobody.'

Westport
CSORP A.709

Saturday 15 January. Lord Sligo to Lord Lieutenant
'Of the population of 68,000 in the Union, 1,000 are in the poorhouse and
8,400 on outdoor relief and the applicants are hourly increasing. Inspecting
officer Lynch estimates at 20,000 those who must soon receive relief but I
expect it to be double that number.'

Swinford
SFFP 2/506/37

Monday 17 January. Ulic Burke MD to Bewley and Pim (See Appendix 6V)
'I have been prevented by severe illness from acknowledging before this your
circular of the 17th of last month…The condition of the poor is beyond all
comparison considerably more deplorable than at this period of the past year
and our prospects are still more gloomy. There seems not the slightest chance
of any employment public or private and the measures adopted by the government will shortly reduce all classes to the same miserable level. The active
and unobstentatious benevolence of the Society of Friends has been under
Providence the means of saving hundreds from a premature grave in this part
of the country during the past calamitous season and I assure you that gratitude is but a poor expression of our feelings with regard to them.'
Society of Friends clothing query completed and signed by Ulic Burke
'There are 1,300 families in this district and certainly more than one-sixth of
the number are in the most destitute state with regard to clothing of every
description. Blankets and shoes are needed, flannel for women and some

warm clothing for children. Some members of the committee to undertake to pay for the making of 30 pairs of shoes and means will be found to have some more made. Mr Burke, Mrs Eames, Rev B. W. Eames, rector, Rev B. Durcan PP and Capt Broughton will act conjointly.
Draft reply: 'Grant no.1 adding 1 bundle of leather.'

Tuesday 18 January. Capt Broughton to Poor Law Commission   *Swinford*
'I am still suffering from the effects of influenza which has left me without a   CSORP O.2191
voice and with a most harassing cough.'

Wednesday 19 January. Report of Capt Farren   *Castlebar*
'About £400 has been collected during the week; this is the largest sum yet   *Correspondence*
obtained in any weekly period. On Wednesday the collector proceeded to the   *pp.* 439-440
electoral division of Balla, accompanied by the resident magistrate and parties
of constabulary, infantry and dragoons, for the purpose of distraining the lands
of several defaulting ratepayers. Some of the parties paid, but it was found necessary to bring to Castlebar 18 head of cattle, which were subsequently released
upon payment by the proprietors of the demands made upon them ...
On Saturday and Monday I attended meetings of the Board of vice-
Guardians ... *The following was the state of the workhouse:* men, 146; women,
224; boys under fifteen, 192; girls under fifteen, 78; infants, 27. *Auxiliary
workhouse:* women, 16; girls under fifteen, 98; total 781. Of the above there
were 36 fever cases and 71 other cases.
The pressure for outdoor relief still continues. The number on the application and report books amounted to nearly 4,000, of which 36 were admitted
to the workhouse and 3,221 placed on outdoor relief. The total now receiving
outdoor relief is 11,358, being upwards of one-sixth of the population of the
Union.
There can be little doubt of the fact that the whole of these persons are not
in a starving condition ... the assertion of the poor themselves (from whom
I can never obtain the names of the parties as they will not turn "informers"
as they call it) and the statement of persons of undoubted veracity, confirm
this. Indeed the majority of the lower orders seem to have lost all sense of self-
respect and the honest pride of independence ...
With much of shameless imposition is mixed up at the same time the direst
misery and destitution; the most harrowing scenes are witnessed in front of
the workhouse every Board-day. Crowds of squalid, wretched creatures,
wrapped in rags, the covering probably just snatched from the bed of fever,
rendering the air foetid with the poisonous emanations of disease, side by
side with the man who, not destitute, asserts his claim to relief with as much
energy as his starving neighbour ...

The relief officer in this town has resigned and only acts until another is appointed. He is followed by a crowd through the street, and when he unexpectedly visits a house to make his inquiry, his presence is known in a moment and he is surrounded by a clamorous crowd, thus setting all his attempts at investigation at defiance ... I have therefore suggested to the chairman of the Board, who at once adopted the proposal, to post up in the most conspicuous places in each electoral division, lists of the persons now receiving outdoor relief, showing their places of residence, number in family and number of rations received daily. Also to publish these lists in the local papers, accompanied by an appeal to magistrates, ratepayers and other well-disposed persons ... to afford the vice-Guardians all the information in their power regarding any cases ... of persons who have improperly obtained relief ... The dread of publicity will, it is hoped, then deter the non-destitute from making applications for relief.'

22 January. Poor Law Commission to Capt Farren
'The Commissioners recommend that the lists of persons receiving relief as paupers should be only posted, as publication in the newspapers would be attended with very great expense.'

Kilcolman, Ballaghaderreen
SFFP 2/506/37

Wednesday 19 January. Society of Friends clothes query completed and signed by J. A. Holmes
'There are 300 in need of clothes. Flannel, corduroy and calico are needed. Applicant undertakes to pay for the making of them. There is no one to act conjointly with him in their distribution.'
Draft reply: '2 pieces of flannel, 2 pieces of corduroy and 4 pieces of grey calico.'

Kilmactigue
SFFP 2/506/37

Thursday 20 January. Society of Friends clothes query completed and signed by Roger Brennan ADM (See Appendix 6Q)
'The application is made for Rhue, Tullanaglug, Tullymoy, Eskragh, Coolrecul, Knockshoney, Carraun, Gurterclin?, Annagh and Glenavoo in the parish of Kilmactigue. Guernsey frocks, grey calico, flannel, barragan, corduroy, bed rugs, cotton sheets, blankets and leather are needed. Rev Thomas Judge CC and Mr John Durcan will act conjointly with him.'
Draft reply: 'No grant – some assistance in clothing for this parish has been made through the hands of Em. Caulfield.'

Ballaghaderreen
CSORP O.2144

Friday 21 January. Sworn statement by Thomas Costello, Ballaghaderreen, poor rate collector, before C. O'Connell RM
'On 19 January I went to Tullaghan Rock in Ballaghaderreen electoral division and seized four head of horned cattle for the poor rates due ... I was forcibly and violently rescued of the said cattle and put in dread and terror

of my life by Patt Coleman and Michael Coleman, both of Frasnadiffa in said parish … and I saw a great number of persons coming and collecting from different parts and from the general objection of the country people to pay the poor rates and the threats and conduct of the said Patt and Michael Coleman and several others, I am in dread and terror of my life to attempt to enforce the poor rates now due in the said division and I am sure it would be useless for me to attempt it without good assistance and I therefore beg the protection of the law.'

Friday 21 January. Police report   *Tubbercurry*
'The relief depot at Piper's Hill was broken into and two sacks of Indian meal   OP 26/52
stolen … The meal was hidden under straw in the priest's garden. The following night the police set up watch on the homes of the suspects and saw them leave their houses and return with small bags of meal. In the morning they made a search and found a quantity of the meal in each of the premises.'
26 January. Report of Capt Gilbert
'The depot of Tubbercurry was broken into on 21 January and seven and a half cwt of meal taken. The police have arrested several persons on suspicion. One of them probably will turn evidence against the remainder and I hope the punishment inflicted on them will prevent such disgraceful outrages for the future.'

Saturday 22 January. Report of Richard Hamilton   *Belmullet*
'From the general emaciated appearance of the people, together with the hor-   CSORP O.2113
rifying sights coming under our immediate observation, we deem it absolutely necessary to make arrangements for affording relief on a more extended scale than heretofore and, as from experience we are quite convinced food can only with safety be given in a cooked form, we purpose erecting boilers in the most central parts of the two electoral divisions … There are at present 50 orphan children in the auxiliary workhouse and there are 17 cases of dysentery; this is to be principally attributed to the change of diet, after the privations these poor little creatures had previously undergone. The healthy children have been separated to a detached portion of the building and every precaution to check the progress of the disease has been made.
Unfortunately I have not been able to give Mr Waters much assistance during the last three days in consequence of a hurt I received in my knee, occasioned by an upset out of my gig when returning with him from a distant station late in the evening.'
Hamilton encloses a list of implements from the Board of Works for the purpose of able-bodied paupers in the district: handbarrows, 60, wheelbarrows, 60, hammers, 600, spades, 100, shovels, 50, picks, 20, planks, 50.

Sunday 23 January. Report of Capt Farren, enclosing a statement of the weekly expenditure for indoor and outdoor relief in the Castlebar Union.

'*Salaries:* three vice-Guardians, £8 1s. 7½d. weekly,

doctor, £60 p.a., £1 3s. weekly,

R.C. chaplain, £40 p.a., 15s. 4¾d. weekly,

Protestant chaplain, £20 p.a., 7s. 8½d. weekly,

master, £60 p.a., £1 3s. 10d. weekly,

matron, £30 p.a., 11s. 11d. weekly,

clerk of Union, £50 p.a., 19s. 2½d. weekly,

schoolmaster, £25 p.a., 9s. 7½d. weekly,

schoolmistress, £15 p.a., 5s. 9½d. weekly,

relieving officers, three at £50 p.a., £2 17s. 7½d. weekly,

ditto, two, £40 p.a., £1 10s. 9½d. weekly,

ditto, five, 15s. each weekly, £3 15s. 10.

superintendents of labour gangs at 10s. each, £5,

nurse-tender, £12 p.a. 4s. 7½d. weekly,

Total, £26 3s.

Rents: of site of workhouse, 13s. 5d.

of auxiliary workhouse, £1 8s. 10d.

Total, £2 2s. 3d.

Provisions: provisions and necessaries for workhouse, £64 19s. 1d.

Salaries and indoor relief, £93 4s. 4d.

Outdoor relief: total weekly expenditure for the nine electoral divisions of the Union (including Straide, £26 19s. 9¾d.) £323 15s. 7¾d.

Total weekly expenditure on indoor and outdoor relief amounts to £416 19s. 11¾d.

Monday 24 January. Society of Friends clothes query completed and signed by Anna C. Fleming (See Appendix 6C)

'The application is made for Abbeyville, Kingsfort and two other townlands. Above 100 are in need of clothes … Anything will be acceptable. The applicant will superintend the making of mens' clothes with the exception of shoes. Dorothea White will act conjointly with her.'

Draft reply: 'Grant no.1 omitting leather.'

Monday 24 January. Richard St George, vicar, to Ballina vice-Guardians

'… the awful state in which the poor of this extensive Union are placed by fever without any means of administering to their wants or giving them any relief or removing those in a state of fever from those who are yet unaffected. When the Relief Committee was in existence, I brought the subject before them. The only person who was willing to assist me or join in the application, was the Roman Catholic clergyman, Reverend Mr Costello. The consequence is that during the past 12 months, but more especially during the last 3 months, fever has been on the increase and much more malignant in its character than heretofore. Unless some means are afforded of giving relief and removing the infected, the whole population will be swept off.'

Monday 24 January. Resolution of magistrates and cesspayers
'That able-bodied paupers now on outdoor relief may be employed in such useful and necessary public works as the government inspecting officer and the county surveyor may point out, instead of stone-breaking as at present ordered by the Poor Law Commission.'
24 February. Poor law Commission to T. N. Redington
'The Commissioners are of the opinion that stone-breaking is better adapted than other kinds of employment to deter improper applicants from seeking to obtain relief from the poor rates, and as stone-breaking is more susceptible of precise measurement and thus is more easily superintended than ordinary public works, the Commissioners are desirous that the experiment of stone-breaking should be tried in the first instance in every Union wherein workhouse accommodation is insufficient ... They do not preclude themselves from entertaining a proposal at a more advanced season of the year for employing paupers mending roads.'

Castlebar
CSORP O.2376

Tuesday 24 January. Michael Kilty PP to Fr Synnott, Dublin thanking him for £15 for his starving parishioners
'This year is worse than last and the coming months will be fatal.'
26 January. Fr Timlin PP to Fr Synnott, Dublin (acting for Archbishop Murray), thanking him for £75 for famine relief
'At no time in the past two years has Mayo witnessed such distress. The workhouse is overcrowded and the procedure by which people are admitted so strict and vexatious that many perish of hunger. To gain admittance they must give up their cabins and patches of land. They are obliged to level their cabins which leaves them homeless and they make do with shelter in the ditches and die of hunger and exposure. I see this every hour of the day and with no prospect of redress ... I apologise for my tales of misery but I cannot suppress my feelings.'

Belmullet
DDA MURRAY PAPERS

Ballysokeary, Ballina

Friday 28 January. Report of James Auchmuty
'Patrick Giblin, one of the rate collectors, came to me this day with his face cut, in the most dreadful state. He has lodged information against the parties that assaulted him. He has been confined to bed since Monday ... John Byrne, another collector, was also assaulted, his coat torn off his back and

Castlerea
CSORP O.1476

much abused. He has also lodged information. Michael Connell, another collector, was knocked down with a stone when out collecting poor rates. He has lodged information also.'

Tubbercurry
CSORP Z.1440

Friday 28 January. Anonymous letter to Lord Lieutenant
'May it please your Excellency to listen to this petition ... has directly been creaved *(sic)* by upwards of one thousand persons requesting of me for to let your excellency know how the donations sent to them is plundered, such as soup houses by clergy ... All poor creatures thats most in its nessaty *(sic)* are not getting a morsel of this relief or any such but the followers and next door neighbours ... and their offspring and so on and in like manner ... To witness the daylight robbery of clergy, country buckeens, county surveyor, deputy county surveyor, the two most notorious robbers and the sons of bankrupts and murderers for the parish of Curry and Tubbercurry and unless your Honour be so pleased to appoint some just gentlemen to administer justice the poor is robbed by the works. There is two notorious vagabonds in this place, Luke Colleran of Curry and John Brett of Tubbercurry ... Any person these persons likes has employment to get their sons and their brothers and cousins, nephews, brother-in-laws and offsprings. May the Lord preserve your Excellency in prosperity and put a stop to this and be so pleased to put on it another mode and appoint police and parson to administer justice. These creatures are getting one thousand times more from the parson of justice than from the priest, for unless you belong to some hound of the priests, there is no sort of mercy to be found. This Brett has such a petrifarious scum belonging to him that the entire county is taken up by him and Luke Colleran. I am very much astonished that your Excellency would give any situation to these vagrants ... This Colleran is a brother-in-law of Priest Flynn's and one of the most earnest Repailers *(sic)*. Not a man bees working under him that must not give a shilling towards the Repeal. And the stones that are broken and quarried for the public works ... these two lads, Luke Colleran and John Brett, are road contractors. They will turn them stones out on these contract roads and that they are bound to do themselves and draw the wages in public works. So help me God, I witnessed this as been a steward myself some time on these roads. O good God and Redeemer of man, had you known the unjust robbery commetted *(sic)*, you would convert it to some other way...'

Ballina &
Belmullet
CSORP O.2325

Saturday 29 January. W. J. & R. Hamilton to Poor Law Commission
'Fever and dysentery continue to increase to an alarming degree. Mr Bingham, proprietor of the auxiliary workhouse in Binghamstown, and the person placed in temporary charge of the premises by the late Board of Guardians, pending the appointment of the necessary staff, died this morn-

ing of fever after a few days illness … It is exceedingly difficult to procure proper persons for subordinate situations in this Union, every candidate is so strongly recommended that strangers are apt to be misled.'

3 February. Poor Law Commission to Messrs Hamilton

'Recommends notice to be published in one of the Dublin morning newspapers as also in a weekly paper, when Union officers are required.'

Saturday 29 January. Report of Capt Broughton   *Swinford*

CSORP O.2379

'The schoolmaster Kelly has been taken with spotted scarlet fever of the most malignant kind and is not expected to live over this night; his assistant has also been taken ill … To check the contagion I have decided to have the whole house thoroughly white-washed by a tradesman and to order a list of essential medicines … In the absence of the master, matron or schoolmaster much responsibility devolves on myself … Fresh straw has been ordered for the beds which I hope to get, the ground being covered with snow.'

31 January. Reply of Poor Law Commission

'Commissioners have decided to issue an order authorising outdoor relief in the Swinford Union and are sending by the evening mail a cask of chloride of lime.'

They enclose the recommendations of the Board of Health:

'Chloride of lime should be supplied. The numbers in the workhouse should be reduced to a half for white-washing and ventilating. All bed clothes and dresses of those infected should be removed and at once plunged into boiling water. An examination should be made of all the inmates, particularly the children, at least every 24 hours. There should be no intercourse between the sick ward and other parts of the house.'

Spring 1848

Evictions, Rate Defaulters and Inquests

Evictions were becoming increasingly common. 80 families had been evicted from the estate of Mr Walsh at Mullaghroe in Erris during the last two months of the winter. In April evictions took place in two separate estates in Castlerea Union. 29 families, totalling 189 unfortunate creatures on the estate of Mr Farrell, had their houses levelled and 'were turned out on the wide world'. All three evicting landlords were rate defaulters.

Great difficulties were experienced in the collecting of rates which became a hazardous occupation for the collector. In February the military had to be called out to assist the collector in Ballisodare and Collooney. In the case of refusal to pay, seizures of cattle and other property were made, but often when these were later put up for auction no bidders could be found. Summonses were served on defaulters who included notables such as the Earl of Lucan who headed the list in the Castlebar Union, owing almost £700. These cases were frequently adjourned by magistrates who were themselves rate defaulters. Many ratepayers were unable to pay, being now virtually insolvent, not having received any rents for two years. Some defaulters, such as George Vaughan Jackson and Rev John Garrett, vicar of Emlefad, had made and were continuing to make heroic efforts at great personal cost to relieve the distress of their starving poor.

Inquests returning verdicts of death by starvation were reported weekly in the local newspapers. To the embarrassment of the government, whose relief measures were supposed to prevent such occurrences, these reports were regularly picked up by the Dublin papers. Poor Law inspectors were ordered to investigate the accuracy of such reports in their Unions. Some reports were not authenticated, such as the death of John Lyons who got drunk after selling a donkey at a fair and was found dead on the roadside on his way home. Many of the reports were substantiated. John Brennan in the Boyle Union had been refused relief by the Guardians as he possessed an acre and thus fell victim to the infamous Gregory Clause. It was the responsibility of the relieving officer to insure that the destitute received relief.

Tuesday 1 February 1848. Michael Muldowney CC to Society of Friends (See Appendix 6A)

'You have done an immensity by your charitable donations, may the Lord reward ye! I feel much obliged when you say you are inclined to send me some portion for the sick ... I am daily attending the sick beds (if I may call them beds), who have no means of subsistance save the paltry trifle, I who am without much means and some other charitable individual can afford them. In this inclement season of the year, they are returning from the work-house and have scarcely a covering on them or a place to shelter themselves unless they be admitted by some nearly equally indigent person.'

Draft reply, 12 February: 'Order on Sligo for ¼ ton of Indian meal and ¼ ton of rye.'

Achonry
SFFP 2/506/22

Wednesday 2 February. Archbishop to Cardinal Franzoni, enclosing 459.05 scudi Romani for the relief of the Irish.

Benevento, Italy
SC IRLANDA
vol 29

Wednesday 2 February. Report of Capt Farren

'I cannot report an improvement in the progress of the collection of the rate. The sum obtained during the week was only £41 4s. 2½d. The total amount now collected is £1,640 14s. 1¼d., leaving uncollected £8,306 8s. 9¾d.'

Farren encloses a list of 50 defaulters, with the Earl of Lucan heading the list, owing £692 4s. 2½d.

'... The collector attended at the Petty Sessions at Ballavary on 28 January and obtained 29 decrees against parties in the electoral divisions of Straide and Turlough, who were summoned for the non-payment of the rate ...

The pressure of destitution still continues. The number of applicants on the books of the relieving officers on Saturday and Monday amounted to 2,113, of which 13 were admitted to the workhouse and 1,416 were placed on out-door relief. 3 were discharged from the workhouse to outdoor relief. The total number now receiving outdoor relief is 13,114.

A considerable number of the able-bodied receiving outdoor relief have been struck out of the lists for idleness or non-attendance at the work depots. I vis-ited these depots during the week and at one ... found a considerable num-ber of men absent. On questioning the overseer, he stated "they had com-pleted their tasks" but on examining the heaps of stones broken, it did not appear that such was the case; moreover, his written instructions stated that the labourers must attend at work at eight in the morning and remain until four in the afternoon, allowing one hour for meals. I took his book and called the roll, when at least 50 men were found absent. I ordered their names to be handed to the relieving officer in order that their rations might be stopped ... The overseer was dismissed. It is exceedingly difficult to obtain overseers

Castlebar
CSORP O.2139

who will do their duty honestly and fearlessly. This is the second instance of an overseer being dismissed for neglect of duty and collusion of the labourers ... On the examination of the books, 140 labourers were struck off for idleness or absence from the work, by which they and their families, from 700 to 800 individuals, lost their rations ... The drainage of the Saleen Lakes near Castlebar, on the property of the Earl of Lucan, has been commenced and will afford employment to a considerable number of men. His Lordship affords employment to upwards of 300 men in this Union, in addition to the above ... There is ample room in this Union for the employment of the able-bodied poor in productive and remunerative works ... The inducements, however, held out by the Land Improvement Act and other Acts, have, with very little exception, not been taken advantage of. Indeed, there are but few proprietors who are in a position to do so ... so that the whole burden of the destitution is thrown upon the poor rates.'

Sligo
CSORP O.2345

Wednesday 2 February. Report of Capt Gilbert
'Great difficulty still exists in procuring carts for the conveyance of seized corn and at times it is totally impossible ... Regarding troops being stationed at Ballymote in order to help rate collectors, Sir Robert Gore Booth has offered to furnish proper barrack accommodation, provided the government will make it a permanent station.'

Ballina
CSORP O.2116

Friday 4 February. Vice-Guardians to the Commissioners
'We are most anxious to learn ... the manner in which you wish us to act under the following circumstances: Persons holding from one to five or more acres with a house make application to their landlord to take a surrender from them of the land, and at the same time refuse to give up the house; the landlords naturally refuse to accept such as a surrender, feeling that if they did so those persons might at any future time successfully claim the land again on the ground that that surrender, being only a portion of one certain letting, was not legal, and they at the same time warn us not to relieve such persons, they being still in possession. We have at all times given relief to destitute landholders who have *bona fide* endeavoured to act up to the spirit and meaning of the act of parliament ... Our difficulty is this – we wish to act humanely in not forcing people to part with their houses and become homeless ... and we feel if we act as humanity suggests, we would directly infringe an act, the provisions of which we were appointed to carry out.'
Reply to above, 7 February: 'The mere refusal of a landlord to accept a surrender of land does not disqualify a person, who has ceased to occupy more than a quarter of an acre of land, from receiving relief.'

Friday 4 February. Petition of James Touhy, Edmondstown, to Sir Robert Peel   *Ballaghaderreen*
CSORP W.1606
'Most Illustrious Sir, thro' you as the most gifted, most devoted and straight-
forward champion of the British Senate, I would earnestly implore that, in
the multitude of your great humanity, you would be graciously pleased to
interpose your clemency in my behalf to call the attention of the present
Secretary of Ireland or some other of Her Majesty's present government, why
my claim on the Board of Works of Ireland was never attended to … In
February 1847 I received an order to make 100 box barrows for the Board of
Works, six of which I then delivered, six more finished and the materials for
the remainder prepared. The six barrows delivered by order of the engineer
in charge, Mr Mark McGarry, the price agreed upon for the six barrows was
10s. 6d. each, amounting to £3 3s. and of the said amount, I have never
received one penny … and being out of my money 12 months, I earnestly
solicit your merciful interposition in my behalf.'

16 February. Board of Works' officer's report on claim of James Touhy   CSORP W.2493
'I called on James Touhy to produce an order for the implements in question
which he failed to do. I then brought him to Ballaghaderreen for the purpose
of pointing out to me the barrows alleged to have been made by him, in order
to see whether they were the same as those supplied by others and to enable
me to value them. He altogether refused to point them out in the store or to
take any trouble to satisfy me that his claim was a just one and I am fully persuaded there is some fraud mixed up with this claim.'

Sunday 6 February. Lieutenant Hamilton to the Commissioners   *Ballina
& Erris*
Correspondence
pp. 90-1
'I think the interior economy of the workhouse is gradually improving …
The schools appear to be well managed and the infirmary, considering its
crowded state, is very clean and regular. The mortality has been trifling; only
two deaths last week out of between 1,500 and 1,600 inmates … Mr
McNulty, the clerk, has recovered from fever and resumes his duties …
Several of the relieving officers (especially Mr John Palmer) are doing their
duty well; others I have little or no confidence in; but in the absence of any
proofs of the neglect of the interests of the poor … and owing to the very
great unwillingness of the latter class to give any information worth having,
we must only make the best of them until they commit themselves …
The Society of Friends have authorised me, in conjunction with Rev Mr
Lees, to take some lands which Colonel Vaughan Jackson and Mr Orme have
placed at their disposal rent free. The Agricultural Society have directed Mr
Martin, the practical agriculturalist, to render us every assistance …
The British Association are giving relief to 12,000 children daily at the
schools in my district. This great boon has been most thankfully received by
persons of all religious persuasions; and taking everything into consideration,

the experiment has succeeded beyond my most sanguine expectations ...

The condition of the poor in Erris is very frightful. I accompanied Mr Richard Hamilton through parts of the electoral division of Binghamstown. We witnessed the ruins of Mullaghroe, once a village on the estate of Mr Walsh of Castle Hill. This gentleman is a defaulter of poor rate to the amount of £63 16s. 1d. ... legal proceedings have been taken against him. 80 families had been ejected within the last two months by Mr Walsh, their houses destroyed, and the unfortunate outcasts left to seek shelter where they could find it. I rode through the ruins to try if there were any human beings to be found but I only saw one family. I inquired what had become of the other inhabitants and was informed that some were in their graves, others under the ditches, others begging shelter from house to house, and plundering whatever they could lay hands on ...

Several (I wish I could say all) of the landlords have acted with the greatest forbearance and liberality. I may mention the Earl of Arran, Colonel Wingfield, Colonel Vaughan Jackson, Mr Orme and others ... I am not aware Mr Walsh has been worse treated by his tenantry than other landlords have been; I presume he has, for I never before saw such wholesale desolation, and I hope I never may again. I am in daily correspondence with Mr Richard Hamilton; in one of his last letters he says, "I visited Mullaghroe again today in order to make some provision for the people turned out of it. I saw worse sights than the Geraghtys; it was neither more nor less than horrible." The Geraghtys were a wretched family we visited at Farrane, where we found the father lying dead, and the mother and five children huddled together on the floor, all bowed down by disease ...

P.S. Mr Walsh is pulling down houses in the electoral division of Crossmolina; his tenantry are all through the miserable town, which is full of fever.'

9 February. Reply to above: 'The Commissioners do not wish in any way to impede the benevolent exertions of the Society of Friends, for whom the Commissioners entertain the highest respect ... For general reason of policy ... they are desirous that you should not associate yourself with the proposed project of employing people on the lands of the Society of Friends.'

Report of Arthur Barrington, Ballina, to the Society of Friends, n.d. February:
'An agreement was entered into with Colonel George Vaughan Jackson of Carramore near Ballina and several other proprietors under which 900 statute acres were given to us, free of rents and poor rate for one year. We undertook to pay the county cess; to provide the labour, manure and seed; and to give up the land when the crops had been disposed of ... The cultivation was entirely by spade labour and employment was given for many weeks to upwards of 1,000 persons ... The crops consisted chiefly of turnips

and other green crops and 70 acres of flax … The wages were calculated by task work but as the persons employed were very generally chosen among those whose strength had been greatly reduced by previous starvation, the rates of payment were necessarily considerably higher …'

Tuesday 8 February. James Higgins PP to Society of Friends (See Appendix 6J)

Charlestown
SFFP 2/506/22

'On 20 November 1847 you kindly placed in my hands ½ ton of rice and ½ ton of meal for the poor of Kilmactigue parish, which you kindly allowed me allocate to my present parish (Kilbeagh) in Mayo and a small portion in Co Sligo viz. the small post town of Bellahy where I reside. From the constant use of turnips as the only food, dysentery has lately much increased and assumed the form of an epidemic. To 23 families afflicted with this wasting disease, I have administered ½ stone weekly for three weeks … The poor have not even turnips now and cannot be induced to take refuge in the workhouse lest they lose forever the possession of their wretched hovel and one or two acres of land. The poor here are nearly in a state of actual nakedness.'
Draft reply, 28 February: 'Order at Castlerea ½ ton of Indian meal and ½ ton of rye.'

Thursday 10 February. Memorial of Patrick Dougherty, Clooncara, to Lord Lieutenant

Ballaghaderreen
CSORP A.1691

'Patt Duffy of Clooncara and his two sons were at a dance in Clooncara and began to quarrel with his son. As the latter was going out Duffy's sons took two stones to strike the Doughertys. A few neighbours interfered and sent the Duffys home. About one and a half hours later, Duffy returned with four sons and four neighbours, armed with large sticks, a milk grissit or candlepan, used for making rush candles, an iron tongs and large pot stick, and attacked Dougherty's son. They then struck Dougherty with the iron tongs, knocked him down with a stone and struck him while down until he became insensible. When he recovered, he found that the parties were sent off by some of the dance people and the next morning Dougherty discovered that £2 17s. 6d. was missing from his pocket. On 27 December he went to Ballaghaderreen and got informations drawn up against the Duffys. On 28 December he met Charles Strickland who could not find ink to sign the informations. The Duffys were summoned to appear in court on 3 January and the court adjourned until 10 January as there was no magistrate. Finally, the case was heard on 7 February when Mr Strickland was away from home and Patt Duffy and his son were fined five shillings each and costs. On the same day, Michael Ryan was find £2 and costs, Thomas Kenny, 10s. and costs, Bryan Touhy, 10s. and costs, Owen Mulligan, £3 and costs, William Corcoran, 10s. and costs, all for assaults generally committed in public houses, where the quarrel arose from drinking whiskey, while nine men had come a distance of a mile and attacked the Doughertys. He is miserably poor, having nothing in the world but a small horse and cart, by which he supported himself by bringing meal and salt from Sligo, generally going for a load once a week. He has not gone since as he is very unwell and implores the Lord Lieutenant to order another trial when Mr Strickland comes home.'

Reply to above, 12 February: 'The Lord Lieutenant has no authority to order the rehearing of a case upon which the magistrates have already adjudicated.'

Kilmactranny
CSORP O.3845

Friday 11 February. Report of Capt Wynne
'Many townlands present a singularly wretched aspect in consequence of the number of ruined cabins, but on investigation I found that the late inhabitants had either gone to Scotland, America or the workhouse. A large proportion also had died during the past year. The consequence is that the demand for relief is at present comparatively small. The late inmates of these ruined cabins appeared to have been more kindly treated in the Boyle Union than in this.'

Tuam
DDA MURRAY PAPERS

Friday 11 February. Archbishop MacHale to Archbishop Murray thanking him for £250 for the poor of the province of Tuam
'I am consoled that good foreigners are full of mercy for the Irish poor, to whom their rulers are so utterly indifferent.'

Coolavin
SFFP 2/506/22

Saturday 12 February. Elizabeth Holmes, Clogher to Society of Friends re the last grant of Indian meal, rice and biscuit to her brother (See Appendix 6M)
'The meal was given mostly to the families of those who were ill, the biscuit was given to those recovering from sickness and the rice has been given partly cooked but some not cooked … The water it was boiled in was taken as a nourishing drink by fever patients of whom many still remain … Your last grant to our school could not be supplied by the government stores at Sligo … We got but 1 cwt and in place of the rest, 7 bags of rye meal. This mixed with Indian meal has made most excellent bread … It has hitherto fed 140 children. Our school now contains 300 pupils but more than 100 of these can support themselves by their own industry and some do not, from their parents' circumstances, require any assistance. For the 140 who need food we still have enough of your last grant to supply them for ten days, giving each child 1lb of bread in the day. 70 of these poor little ones are placed for assistance on the books of the British Association, but for the remaining 70 we must still look to the kindness of others … No outdoor relief has as yet been granted to this district and we have found in some cases, the industry of the children in the school has been the means of keeping a few families out of the poorhouse.'

Draft reply, 16 December: 'Order in Sligo ¼ ton of Indian meal, ¼ ton of rye, ¼ ton of rice and 2 bags of biscuit for the support of the school.'

Sunday 13 February. Report of James Auchmuty   *Castlerea*
'I have been employed the most part of last week for the British Association.   CSORP O.2102
I have 7,400 children in daily attendance at the schools receiving weekly
51,919 rations. There will be a further increase this week. I am afraid that
there will be great abuse as I find it impossible to visit all the schools.
Two boys were brought before the stipendary magistrate for stealing two
workhouse tubs but the prosecution failed. The Guardians turned them out
of the house.
Yesterday Capt Gray, a magistrate, was summoned for poor rates. Last week
he promised to pay but yesterday had a barrister employed to defend him.
The collector swore that he offered a bribe of £2 not to proceed against him.
After a long trial I had him decreed yesterday … Mr O'Connell, the
stipendary magistrate, goes tomorrow to Frenchpark with the military and
police to assist the rate collector.'
29 February. Capt Gray, Seafield, to Francis W. Brady, Court of Chancery 'I have
now fully answered those very serious charges against my character, both as
a magistrate and a gentleman, and I should hope that those charges having
been thus publicly made by a gentleman filling a very prominent government
official situation, that he will be called to prove the truth of these charges or
that he do retract them through the same channel they were conveyed against
me.'

Monday 14 February. Catherine Rice to Society of Friends (See Appendix 6A)   *Achonry*
'I have given to the heads of 70 families a weekly supply … I have also   SFFP 2/506/22
cooked a portion for those unable to do so themselves … There is scarcely a
house free from sickness. Fever is again set in with more violence.'
Draft reply, 18 December: 'Order in Sligo ¼ ton of rice, ¼ ton of Indian meal,
¼ ton of barley and 2 bags of biscuit.'

Wednesday 16 February. Report of Capt Gilbert   *Sligo*
'Yesterday 129 able-bodied paupers and their families were admitted to the   CSORP O.3195
workhouse. A few widows and children were put on outdoor relief. There
were 17 deaths since the last report, all young people under fourteen, chiefly
from dysentery and measles. There were 26 new cases of fever and 43 of
dysentery …
There is a repeated refusal of several parties to pay rates and the military had
to protect one of the rate collectors. They went yesterday to Ballisodare and

today to Collooney ... If troops were quartered at Ballymote they could be used. There are no troops quartered in the whole county except at Sligo. It is impossible for them to go beyond a day's march from their barracks as there is no accommodation for them (particularly for the cavalry) in any of the villages ... Six policemen with the collector would have the same effect ...

There is little preparation by the farmers for the ensuing crops. There are still extensive haggards of corn perceptible in every electoral division. The small tenants complain that they have not the means of preparing their ground, nor corn to sow. If the government would provide the corn for their land, it would be occupied, otherwise it will remain a complete waste ... of many thousands of acres. Potatoes are now getting scarce in the markets. Those who have them and can live without disposing them, are hoarding them for planting in the spring ... Markets are merely supplied by small farmers who are obliged to sell for subsistence. The potatoes planted in the autumn and those that are now in the pits are totally free from the late disease.'

Gilbert encloses a list of the six largest ratepayer defaulters in each electoral division, which included Rev John Garrett, Ballymote, who owed the highest amount, £47 16s. 9d.

Boyle Union
CSORP O.2566

Friday 18 February. Sworn statement of Bartly Drury re the deaths of Widow Kearns and her child and Mary Canery

'I knew the Widow Kearns. She had a child with her about three or four years of age. About two days before I saw her dead, she came to my house and asked me for lodging. I told her I had cattle in my outhouse but I went to Mary Canery and got her lodging there. She then took her in. Mary Canery was an old woman about 70 years of age. Her house was a small one but waterproof, at least one end of it. Mary Canery never applied that I knew to the workhouse for admission. She tried to get her bit and sup from the neighbours for charity's sake some days before her death. I told her that she ought to go to Capt Lloyd, the Guardian of the district, and apply to him for admission and she said she would but did not. There was a rumour in the county that the outdoor relief was going to commence and she wasted away from day to day waiting for it. The evening she died, I am told that she got some meal from the priest or some good neighbour and it was the opinion of the neighbours that she ate too much of it, her constitution broke down with distress and hunger.

The Widow Kearns was a woman who latterly was travelling begging about the country ... I heard she had been in the workhouse and had left it and the neighbours had but little compassion on her because she did not stop in it.

As to Mary Canery, I do not think that she made any application to the workhouse. She used to say that she had made application but I think it was merely an excuse to pacify the neighbours who were rather tired of supporting her. She used to get relief from the Misses Elwood but latterly she was not able to move and walk so far.

I did not see the widow and her child the day before she died but a neighbour told me that she saw them all three alive the evening before I saw them dead. I found them all dead in the evening when I went in. I went there in consequence of a report I heard that they were all dead. When I saw they were all dead, the woman who first went in said that she found the old woman dead but that the woman Kearns and her child were then alive. The widow was gasping then and said that the old woman had died in the course of the night and attributed her illness to the food she had eaten that day. She asked for something to eat for herself. It was brought to her by the neighbours but she was not able to eat it. She and the child died in the course of the following day. They were all very much emaciated and worn.'

Statement of Dr Burrowes:
'I did not make any post-mortem examination but am of the opinion that they died from destitution and want. I formed that opinion as much from the appearance of the hut in which they lived as from that of the bodies. Widow Kearns and her child were very much emaciated, the old woman not so much so. She lay with her head almost in the ashes of the fire. The weather was very cold and severe at the time and may no doubt have contributed to their death. The widow and her child had hardly any covering whatever upon them and the slight covering they had consisted of their rags.'

Monday 21 February. G. V. Jackson to Society of Friends   *Swinford*
'My recollection is that Capt Wellesley thought highly of Rev J. Higgins   SFFP 2/506/22
(Kilbeagh) and found him estimable … The schoolmaster's death on today of spotted fever, and Capt Broughton taking the same disease in the poorhouse, causes great terror and we try to unload the house rather than fill it just now … Capt Broughton has had a good night and is better today but he still has three medical men in attendance.'

Wednesday 23 February. G. Knox RM to T. N. Redington   *Ballaghaderreen*
'A most desperate case of murder had occurred on Sunday night, 20 February,   OP 21/75
within six miles from this town … It is an alleged case of house-breaking by the Molly Maguires. One man is killed and another in a hopeless way.'
Patrick Callaghan and John Touhy, Derrynabrock, Kilbeagh parish (Charlestown),   OP 21/83
were murdered by Peter, James & Pat Costello who were condemned to transportation for life.

Emigrants
CSORP Z.2387

Thursday 24 February. John McArdell, North Strand, Dublin, to Lord Lieutenant

'Emigrants in general of the lower orders are open to many impositions when about to embark from this port or Liverpool or perhaps other ports, also by a class of low persons called flag or street-agents, who are employed by the ships' offices. These poor people, who are perfect strangers, are met upon the way towards the offices and coaxed into such offices as those street-agents are employed in, where they are charged rates of passage money, according to their ignorance or anxiety to proceed with the first ship. Those street-agents then bring their dupes to such shops to buy sea stores etc as they (street-agents) will be allowed a large discount for buying at ... They bring those creatures to their own houses to lodge ... I have voyaged several times to and from America and frequently noticed emigrants' stores to be of the worst description and in prices and quantity most shameful ... As a result some of these poor people have no money upon landing.'

Castlebar
CSORP O.2624

Tuesday 29 February. Report of Capt Farren

'The collector has been pursuing a more vigorous course and during the week made seizures of property for poor rates in the electoral division of Ballyhean and Straide. On Friday he was supported in this duty by detachments of cavalry and infantry. After the cattle had been seized, some of the parties paid the rate. In other cases the cattle and property have not been released and when put up for auction, no bidders could be found. The collector's bailiff therefore bought them in and they are on the collector's lands. There is a determination on the part of the public not to purchase in poor rate cases in order that the law may be defeated and the local papers sympathise in the feeling and add to it by sending reporters to publish all particulars of these auctions.'

Templehouse
SFFP 2/506/35

Tuesday 29 February. Rev Henry Perceval to Society of Friends

'Several of the children are confined to bed in consequence of being entirely destitute of clothing, all that the parents can procure being required for their support. He has already twice received assistance from the Society of Friends, first a grant of £20 and afterwards a supply of food and now seeks a grant of clothes.'

Ballina
Transactions
pp. 210-11

Thursday 2 March. Report of Richard D. Webb to the Society of Friends

'I met with George Vaughan Jackson of Carramore, who brought me round the experimental farm which the committee has formed on his lands. Here, I was gratified to see ... upwards of 200 persons at full work, on fair country wages ... No effort that is being made by the committee ... appears more likely to benefit a large number of the destitute than this ... The chief diffi-culty in this part of Ireland is that of finding trustworthy persons to oversee and conduct operations of this kind ... Half of the complaints one hears arise from what the people call "favour and faction"; from the tendency to gratify the love of petty patronage or from the malice arising from old grudges or the desire to serve one's own friends or one's own tenants. The spirit of "a lit-tle brief authority" bristles up in great vigour in most of the small officials.'

Friday 3 March. James Henry PP to Society of Friends (See Appendix 61)   *Bunninadden*
'I beg to solicit from your benevolent Society some relief for the poor of the   SFFP 2/506/22
electoral division of Cloonoghill, very many of whom are suffering from sick-ness and hunger. Three men and many children have died of actual starva-tion within the last few days. The remains of two of those creatures were buried even without a coffin.'
13 March. Capt Gilbert to Society of Friends
'I beg to assure you that I have a very excellent opinion of Mr Henry but must express very great surprise at the contents of his letter ... If there is such distress as he states, I have not heard of it because the relieving officer under me in that electoral division is giving relief to all who apply to him and there are not many from that electoral division in the poorhouse at present ... Should there be any sick, I feel confident, if Mr Henry was entrusted to dis-tribute to their wants from your very benevolent Society, you could not place it in better hands.'
23 March. James Henry PP to Society of Friends
'The relief solicited at your hands is for the electoral division of Kilturra in the Boyle Union where deaths are now of daily occurence from starvation. As the poor have neither milk or any drink but water, I don't think that biscuit would suit them as food.'
Draft reply, 31 March: 'Order on Sligo ¼ ton of rice, ¼ ton of Indian meal, ¼ ton of rye and 2 bags of biscuit.'

Friday 3 March. John Bolingbroke to Society of Friends (See Appendices 1K&6U)   *Meelick*
'The barley meal ordered was short of weight 47½lbs, of which circumstance   SFFP 2/506/22
I acquainted the officer in charge of the depot, who replied that he was not in charge at the time of issue, that his storekeeper assured him the two bags containing meal were issued in the same state as when received by him, namely of 280lbs. I again wrote to say, if he wished to investigate the matter, the carrier and my steward are prepared to prove my complain ... At no period of last year was there greater individual want, in most cases attended by dysentery and fever, the former proving very fatal.'
Draft reply, 9 March: 'Order in Ballina ¼ ton of Indian meal, ¼ ton of rye, ¼ ton of rice and 3 bags of biscuit.'

Emigrants
CSORP O.2807

Tuesday 7 March. Circular letter from Poor Law Commission to Poor Law inspectors, enclosing a letter from the Commissioners of Colonial Lands and Emigration, 17 February 1848, proposing to send 4,000 female orphans to New South Wales, South Australia and the Cape of Good Hope this year.
'Emigrant ships will be sent every month from Plymouth. The females should be provided with six shifts, six pairs of stockings, two pairs of shoes, two flannel petticoats and two gowns.'
Enclosed the daily diet on the voyage which included a half pound of beef or pork each day.

Castlebar
CSORP O.2905

Wednesday 8 March. Observations of Capt Farren on a report in Dublin Evening Post
'I visited Islandeady electoral division on 23 February and examined Michael Kane in whose house the deceased Michael Stanton lodged ... Stanton received relief during the summer ... He and his wife got the fever during the harvest. When he got a little better he forsook his wife, who was supported by her brother (Kane) until she died in harvest time. After Christmas Stanton came back, was weak, looked badly and had a great cough. He went begging about the country, received outdoor relief about the middle of January and the weekly allowance he received for himself and his child was 14lbs of meal. On the Thursday before he died he received 14lbs of meal and left his home on Sunday saying he would go and get a little help for himself along with his meal, and on the succeeding Friday the child came back and said that his father was dead upon the roadside ... The child did not appear to be above nine years.'

CSORP O.3056

9 March. Poor Law Commission to T. N. Redington re reports in the Dublin Evening Post (citing the Mayo Telegraph) of deaths from starvation
'Martin Connolly (who was reported as remaining unburied for seven days for want of a coffin) died of fever. He was registered in the Balla electoral division. The Guardians cannot supply coffins for those who die outside the workhouse. Dominick Moran of Bunbee registered on 13 January but did not appear. He applied again and was ordered relief on 5 February. Pat Mullen of Bunbee (reported as twice supplied with food but a skeleton before he got it) was ordered outdoor relief on 15 January. Mary Thomas of Cregg in the same parish (reported as twice supplied with food) obtained outdoor relief. She died of fever. Bryan and Mary Solan (reported as dying from starvation) were returned for relief on 17 January but did not attend work and were struck off. When the relieving officer heard that Solan and his family were in fever, he sent meal to them. Solan and one of his daughters died on 6 February. The other daughter was living at the date of the inquiry.'

Wednesday 8 March. James Auchmuty, to Poor Law Commission re deaths of Daniel Connor and John Lyons

Castlerea
CSORP O.2782

'Connor was a strolling beggar, supposed to come from Tipperary. He certainly died from want. He never made any application to the relieving officer.

John Lyons went to the fair of Costello and sold a donkey. He got drunk on his way home and was found dead on the roadside. He was not on the relieving officer's books as he was a holder of five acres of land.'

Week ending Saturday 11 March. Number of paupers who received indoor and outdoor relief in Sligo Union (from Sligo Journal, 17 March)

Sligo

Electoral Division	Indoor	Outdoor
Ballisodare	84	45
Ballymote	79	482
Coolaney	34	474
Collooney	64	431
Cloonoghill	4	268
Cloonacool	32	290
Tubbercurry	77	417

Monday 13 March. E. J. Howley to T. N. Redington

Ballina
CSORP A.2839

'A very large and significant popular demonstration will take place in Ballina on Friday next and that it is likely the public peace may be endangered unless precautionary measures be adopted … As a magistrate of considerable experience and as a resident gentleman of influence I offer to act with Mr Cruise RM on this occasion.'

Monday 13 March. James Higgins PP to Bewley and Pim

Charlestown
CSORP 2/506/35

'The constant demand for food for the last three years and particularly this year has completely exhausted their means and within that time has left nothing to apply to procure clothing … They are now in a state of perfect and absolute nakedness, so much so that two-thirds of the poor creatures must decline coming into public for want of more covering and that in a village the same cloak or coat is used by ten or twelve persons on the same day to bring home a few quarts of meal from the market for their sustenance. On the part of those naked wretches, I do most earnestly beseech a share in your charity of clothing. This parish comprises 9,000 or 10,000, all small farmers, needy and naked.'

Draft reply, 16 March: 'The Committee is painfully sensible of the extreme distress of the poor for want of clothing but the means at their disposal for this object are too limited to admit of any large distribution and the quantity already granted to various districts in the west of Ireland is considerable in proportion to other parts of Ireland, that they are not prepared at present to go further.'

James Higgins PP to Society of Friends, 22 March:
'I freely admit the extraordinary charity and zeal of your good Committee both in food and clothing grants but I don't know of any clothes given in this parish or neighbourhood. I therefore beg to be excused for renewing and pressing my suit.'

Bunninadden
OP 21/106

Wednesday 15 March. Report of John S. Stewart, sub-inspector
'On 13 March an inquest was held on the body of Bryan Flanagan of Bunninadden, at Ogham in the parish of Achonry, who was found insensible at the end of a man's house, named Thomas Leonard, who brought him in but he expired about an hour afterwards. The verdict was "death by want and destitution". Leonard, into whose house he was brought, is a man in extreme want himself, holding two or three acres of land, although his family are walking skeletons, rather than go into the poorhouse.'

Emigration

Friday 17 March. The Sligo Journal
'The following ships will sail from Sligo for St Johns, New Brunswick:
    The Exchange, 28 March 1848
    Rebecca, 8 April 1848
    For Quebec:
    The Hibernia, 8 April 1848
    Columba, 12 April 1848
    Horatio, 20 April 1848
    Harriet, 28 April 1848

Ballina
CSORP Z.3741

Monday 20 March. Petition of Phelim O'Hara, Curremla, to Lord Lieutenant
'I have taken the oath of allegiance in the reign of George IV and to his ears *(sic)* forever. I am so reduced in circumstances that I was not able to meet my landlord, William Ormsby Esq., with his rent as usual at November last. He seized all my oats and took it from me and left me without one pound of human food for six in family, but living on turnips ever since and, to grow in my misery, we have them exhausted. I applied for the relief and would get none until I would give up the pocession *(sic)* of my little farm to my landlord, which I hold by lease of lives. I offered to surrender it on condition to compensate me for my improvement on the land those 40 years and besides. I have a cluster of threes *(sic)* to suit a gentleman's seat, which I reared from the seedling. He refused to allow me any compensation. I think it a heartbreak to surrender the pocession *(sic)* to him and be turned out like a criminal … I and my family are in a state of starvation, between my landlord and

AMERICA !

FOR

NEW YORK.

Direct from Limerick,
ON OR ABOUT 20th OCTOBER, NEXT,

WIND AND WEATHER PERMITTING,

THE SPLENDID FIRST CLASS FAST SAILING FULL RIGGED UNITED STATES SHIP,

"JOSEPH MEIGS,"

DANIEL H. WOOD, COMMANDER.

355 TONS REGISTER, 600 TONS BURTHEN,

This truly magnificent American Ship is now at the Quay discharging grain from New York, (which Port she belongs to,) and is engaged to leave here for home at the advertized time. She will be found on inspection one of the finest Vessels that ever conveyed Passengers from this port ; and the accommodation she offers is of a superior style, such as, a well arranged First Cabin, for select Parties, an excellent intermediate one, and extensive decks, permanently laid, giving considerably more height than required by law, 70lbs. of Bread Stuffs and 10lbs. of Beef will be put on Board for each Passenger, and Capt. WOOD, who is well experienced in the trade will have every comfort afforded those sailing with him during the voyage. Early application to secure berths is absolutely necessary to the Agents,

RYAN, BROTHERS & CO.
Ship, Insurance & General Agents, Howley's-quay, Limerick.

J .W. HOGAN, Printer, Town-hall, Limerick

the relieving officer of the district that I live in ... I hope that you will reward my allegiance to the Crown as a loyal subject, by extending aid towards the cultivation of my little farm.'

Ballina
csorp o.3432

Monday 20 March. Report of W. Hamilton
'On my return from Erris last week, I found everything much in the same state as when I left Ballina. I was, however, struck with the improved appearance of the people generally. I think that, considering the prevalence of fever and dysentery, they look wonderfully well.

The workhouse is clean and healthy – the mortality in the infirmary is very much less than might be expected – last week there were only four deaths.'

Hamilton annexes some communications on the progress made in farming operations compared with this time last year.

Extract from letter of William Orme of Owenmore: 'From the continued severity of the weather, little has yet been done ... The worn out state of the land generally, the impoverished condition of the landlords, and their consequent inability to procure seed or manure in sufficient quantity, forbid the hope that the land thus occupied can yield anything like an average crop ... There is, however, another class of landholders even less likely to crop their lands fully ... a large number of the landed proprietors whose estates have been deserted and are now wholly or in great part waste. This is the natural consequence of the immense emigration and mortality of last year ... The quantity of land in this state ... I compute at least one third of the land of this barony.'

Extract of a letter of Colonel Vaughan Jackson: 'The population appear disposed to make every exertion in the matter. I think every man that possibly can will make a sowing.'

Extract of a letter of John Symes, agent to the Earl of Arran: 'There will be a considerable deficiency in the quantity of land sown with barley and oats as compared with 1846 and 1847 ... A great majority of persons receiving outdoor relief, who have such holdings, are not in a position to sow, not having means, money or seed ... There will be a considerable increase over the last two years both in the potato and turnip crop ... The inclemency of the weather for the last three weeks with constant rain, has stopped the digging and ploughing of the lands ... and will cause the spring works to be very backwards.'

Extract of a letter of Henry Brett, county surveyor: 'In most parts of Mayo great efforts will be made to put down a crop, but there are districts, such as Erris, Achill, the Islands and parts of Tyrawley and Gallen etc, that must of necessity lie waste.'

Extract of letter of Thomas Howley: 'Such of the tenantry as are engaged in the cultivation of their lands are doing so in a more painstaking and workman-like manner than heretofore, and altho' a smaller breadth of land may be cultivated this season, that owing to the good advice and example of the Society of Friends, a more than usually productive crop may be expected.'

Extract of a letter of Mr Martin, practical instructor: 'The deficiency will be in a great measure lessened in this locality by the kind exertions of the Society of Friends … Their example of deep cultivation is followed by the small farmers in each locality where the Society are carrying on their useful operations.'

Extract of a letter of Peter Hopkins, extensive farmer in Tireragh: 'Emigration is more the topic of the day in this locality, but not more than one to every ten or fifteen will be able to go out compare to last year for want of means. Very many who could have gone last year could not attempt it this year.'

Tuesday 21 March. Capt Gilbert to Poor Law Commission re the death of one Niland reported to have died of starvation

Collooney
CSORP O.3517

'He and his wife were on the relieving officer's books for the Collooney electoral district. He was about 70 years of age, totally blind and very deaf. About ten days or a fortnight before his death, his wife left him and went off with another man and has not since been heard of. The man certainly did not die of want or from cold and exposure but in all probability from his loss of sight fell into a ditch where he was found dead, about twelve hours after he had been seen in his usual health.'

Observation on above, 30 March: 'It was not known that his wife had left him or that he required assistance, until after his death. He received meal always and part of it was found in his cabin after he had died.'

Wednesday 22 March. Sworn deposition of John McEvoy, assistant relieving officer, re the death of Anne Currith, reported to have died of starvation

Ballycastle
CSORP O.3454

'On 16 February Michael Currith, her husband, asked for relief for himself, his wife, Anne, and his son, Patrick. He gave them 21lbs of meal provisionally and this was continued up to the present. He met Michael Currith some days after his wife's death on the night of 20 March, who told him that his wife left him to go begging. She was subject to fits of epilepsy and, when attacked, if not taken care of, was liable to be suffocated.'

Wednesday 22 March. John P. Waters, vice-Guardian, Ballina, to William Stanley

Binghamstown
CSORP O.3540

'On 20 March the poor rate collector, John Cosgrave, went to Binghamstown to serve a summons on Denis Bingham Esq., a magistrate, for £120 18s. 2d. due by him. He was met by a number of men and women who struck him several times and from the excitement he was compelled to make his escape.'

Ballinrobe
CSORP 0.3624

Saturday 25 March. Dr Dempster's report
'At Kilmaine Petty Sessions, Mr Farragher, the relieving officer, was accused of having used light weights and a false balance in the distribution of the meal to the poor of that electoral division … The suspension of the relieving officer still continues.'

Ballymote
OP 26/112

Saturday 25 March. Rev J. Garrett to the Under Secretary
'Every individual farmer possessing substance in this country is quite ready to support the government and highly approves the arrest of incendiaries who are endeavouring to excite the starving peasantry to rebellion. The priests have ordered that no signatures to this effect should be sent forward but still now they are obliged to confine their opposition to the one grievance, 'the want of food or employment'. Upon this they harp every day and it is impossible to foresee what mischief may be done in an outbreak by starving wretches, driven to distraction by want of food and raiment for themselves and their children. I firmly believe that no religious or political hostility now endangers the peace of this county. Destitution and want of employment are the ready tools with which the base hope to excite insurrection, and the quarter acre test, the most lamentable bar to relief in the poorhouses, is a sad grievance. If the government would make a grant for giving employment to the able-bodied, to be paid in food and not in money, there is no doubt that the great multitude would be grateful and peaceable as well as loyal, and life and property be secured. The poor rate so deeply affects the farmers that they cannot now pay labourers and the work is done by horses and farm servants.'

SFFP 2/506/22

25 March. Same to Society of Friends (See Appendix 6F)
'Your last grant of rice and meal is finished and many lives were saved by it, tho' it would extend to but few compared with the great multitude who require relief … The poorhouses of Boyle and Sligo are but rude hospitals whence dead bodies are daily carried forth in great numbers and even so are full while vast numbers in vain apply for admission and the state of the wretched creatures who go many miles for admittance is deplorable, ending frequently in the death of the disappointed applicants, before they can reach their miserable abode. Your Society have done much in relieving the destitute, clothing the naked, healing the sick and rescuing multitudes from death … No district in Ireland is more in need of your continued bounty.'
Draft reply, 31 March: 'Order on Sligo ¼ ton of rice, ¼ ton of Indian meal, ¼ ton of rye and 2 bags of biscuit.'

Saturday 25 March. Petition of Eneas Collins, Mullenmadogue, to Lord Lieutenant   *Bellaghy*
'On 2 November in the town of Bellaghy, a man of the name of Groarke   CSORP A.3357
made an attack on me and beat me severely. The police came, seased *(sic)* him
or else he would have killed me there. The sergeant sumond *(sic)* me to the
Petty Sessions of Tubbercurry and got him indited *(sic)* to the Quarter
Sessions of Ballymote and got him in preason *(sic)* for one mont *(sic)* in Sligo.
After he came out, he is ever sense *(sic)* after me and said to me and every
person that he meets, that he will have my life … On Thursday last in the
town of Swinford, and I coming home from the market, he came across me
and thought to complate *(sic)* his promise, only that two or three friends
saved me. I have been a very poor man and has a weak family and no money
to defre *(sic)* any expense by law, and so I hope your Lordship will order the
fellow to keep the peas *(sic)*.'

Saturday 25 March. Eleanor MacDonnell, Doocastle to Society of Friends (See   *Bunninadden*
Appendix 61)   SFFP 2/506/22
'I ask you to call the attention of the Committee to this parish and extend
their charity to assist our poor people who are daily expiring around us …
The people are not blessed with a resident gentry. With the exception of my
own family, there is not a gentleman's family resident in the parish … Our
worthy parish priest, the Revd James Henry is using every exertion within his
power but alas what can be done. Without funds our feeble efforts are of little avail. Aid us or we perish.'
Draft reply, 7 April: 'Order on Sligo ¼ ton of Indian meal, ¼ ton of rye, ¼
ton of rice and 3 bags of biscuit.'

Sunday 26 March. Charles Dillon, relieving officer, to James Auchmuty   *Ballaghaderreen*
'James Moran was registered on my application book on 3 January last and   CSORP O.3888
did not apply to me. He died on 28 February. I at the time announced his
death to you and stated that the verdict was starvation. His sister died on 11
February and in the same hut. Why was not an inquest held? Perhaps they
died of fever. I think that James Moran could procure as much as would support nature at the season of the year that he died or that he would have
applied to me who was constantly in Ballaghaderreen within 500 or 600
yards of the hut he died in.'
27 March. James Auchmuty to Poor Law Commission
'He died previous to outdoor relief being given out in this Union. From
inquiries I made from the police, he was turned out of his holding and died
in a hut. He never made application to the workhouse to be admitted.'
7 April. Observations of James Auchmuty
'James Moran had a cabin from Patt Philips, an under tenant to a Mrs

Cogan. He gave a few days work yearly for the cabin. It fell to the ground. He built a hut in which he died.'

Castlebar
CSORP 0.4717

Monday 27 March. Vice-Guardians' report
'The rate collector has lodged £130 since the last report. He was delayed in the enforcing of payment, without the protection of the civil powers. Last Thursday he attended the Petty Sessions at Castlebar, to which he had several persons summoned. The magistrate, Dr Dillon, adjourned the court as there was only one magistrate present … As a result rates will be lost as the parties were carrying away their property.'

Ballina
SFFP 2/506/22

Monday 27 March. G. V. Jackson to Society of Friends
'The Poor Law meets starvation as now administered here but the allowance of food is very small and in cases of illness not equal to restore health. I received a parcel of clothes which I am preparing to issue.'

Sligo
CSORP 0.4843

Tuesday 28 March. Board of Guardians to Col McGregor, Inspector General
'There is a difficulty experienced by the magistrates in carrying out the provisions of the Vagrant Act, from the want of the co-operation of the constabulary. This Union (tho' there is plenty of accommodation in the workhouse for the reception of paupers) is nevertheless crowded with vagrants from other Unions, which evil cannot be checked without the vigilant and active co-operation of the constabulary force. The Board of Guardians wishes the Inspector General to order the constabulary to arrest all vagrants and beggars and carry them to the nearest magistrate.'

Ballymote
SFFP 2/506/35

Sunday 2 April 1848. Rev J. Garrett to Society of Friends, thanking them for the order for provisions received yesterday at the government stores (See Appendix 6F)
'I hope that you will extend to my wretched people of this union of five parishes a grant of clothing. The state of nakedness in which I daily meet the destitute inhabitants is among the many fearful consequences of an absentee proprietary. Indeed no stranger can possibly imagine the pains with which a minister is obliged to refuse the working classes some covering for their children and women and many able-bodied men would go off to England to seek employment if they had working garments to appear in.'

SFFP 2/506/37

5 April. Society of Friends clothing query completed and signed by Rev J. Garrett
'Quite impossible for the labouring classes to clothe themselves and their children … They are in rags and in many multiplied cases have not bed clothes … Bed clothes are needed and working suits of barragan for men and boys and druggets for the women and girls with flannel for petticoats. Shoes are a luxury which few can procure. It will be difficult to sell to the most des-

titute who have not employment and not even food. Shoemakers can be paid for their labour from the proceeds of the sale of clothing generally. The excessive poor rate has put a great bar to private subscriptions. Mrs Gethen of Earlsfield, Mrs Garrett, Mrs Knott of Rathofield, Mrs Fleming of Abbeyville and Mrs Trumble of Kilmorgan will act conjointly with him in the distribution of the clothes.'
Draft reply, 19 April: 'Grant no.1.'

Tuesday 4 April. Colonial Office to William Somerville, enclosing a letter from Sir Robert Gore Booth, defending himself against some unfavourable remarks made in Canada about his emigrants

Emigration
CSORP Z.3673

'I asked the government to give a grant of waste land in Canada and I would send out an agent with the emigrants and keep them at my own expense until they could shift for themselves. I got no reply and could only let all those who chose to go, shift for themselves. They did so. The industrious are getting on well, the idle and lazy not better than they would anywhere else. Many died, having the seeds of disease in their constitutions ere they sailed, from the want of proper attendance and judicious arrangements at the quarantine station.'

Wednesday 5 April. James Dempster MD to William Stanley re the reported death from starvation of John Kibbin

Ballinrobe
CSORP O.3654

'Kibbin died on 17 March. He was from the neighbourhood of the town of Galway and was a man possessed of money which he lent out to the poor people at usurious interest and had arrived in Ballinrobe Union two or three days previously on his periodical journeys to collect his interest. He was a miser and denied himself the necessaries of life, which he was well able to afford, and well known to the inhabitants of the neighbourhood (Maam in Joyce Country).'

Saturday 8 April. Sworn deposition of Patrick Martin, relieving officer for the Rockingham and Ardcarn district, re the reported death from starvation of John Brennan of Kilfaughan

Boyle Union
CSORP O.3768

'On 19 February Brennan applied for relief but he was refused by the Board of Guardians as he possessed an acre of ground. His widow, Mary Brennan, has since been receiving 10lbs of meal weekly for herself and her four children.'

8 April. Report of Owen LLoyd, Poor Law inspector, on Edward Henry, Boyle, who was found dead on the roadside on 9 March 'from want of nourishment and excessive cold', as recorded by the inquest

CSORP O.3994

'Henry had been a dissolute character, cast off by his friends and so addicted to pilfering no one would admit him into his house. He did not apply to the relieving officer, though he had been an inmate of the workhouse for nearly a month in 1846.'

Sworn statement of Patrick Regan, lodging home keeper:

'Edward Henry lived with him as a servant and labourer for a couple of years previous to November last and he parted with him for leading an irregular life. He was in his house the night preceding the morning he was found dead. There were two of the revenue police in the house also, one of whom remarked, "that man won't live further than morning".'

Castlerea
CSORP O.4060

Sunday 9 April. Report of James Auchmuty

'I went this week to see a property near this belonging to a Mr Bushy (Busley?), who is a defaulter of poor rates. I never witnessed such a scene ... The sheriff turned out under an *Habere,* 27 families on the estate, allowing 7 to each family, throws 189 unfortunate creatures on the poor rates. All the houses are levelled and the poor creatures turned out on the wide world. I am told that two years' rent was the most they owed and some of them only owed a year's rent.'

Ballisodare
CSORP I.4629

Sunday 9 April. Report of Capt Gilbert on the death of a beggar at Ballisodare

'The deceased was a beggar from Co Mayo and wholly unknown in this Union ... So long as beggars from adjoining Unions, who whether refused relief or otherwise, stray into this and the constabulary here neglect to perform their duty by the Vagrant Act, deaths may occur from starvation.'

13 April. Observations of W. Hamilton, Ballina

'I will visit the district tomorrow and inquire from the relieving officer ... The Ballina Union is just as much subject to wandering beggars as other Unions ... However much our relieving officers may err in other matters, they know their duty too well to refuse immediate relief to any urgent case, no matter whence it comes, until they can make enquiries and have the order of the vice-Guardians respecting it.'

18 April. Report of W. Hamilton

'I enquired from Mr Ray, relieving officer of the Easkey and Dromore West divisions, whether he ever refused to take the proper notice of all applications for relief. He positively denies ever having done so.'

Claremorris
CSORP A.3714

Sunday 9 April. James Fahey, 'lover of justice', to Lord Lieutenant re

'one of the most barbarous and inhumane acts committed by the bailiffs of Pat. C. Lynch Esq of Clogher House, Co Mayo. The poor man bought the tenant right for £9 at a yearly rent of £3. Nine months after, the bailiffs of Lynch, without any notice, seized the poor man's cows, value £6. They returned in 20 days and seized the bed and bedding clothing and furniture and taking the blanket that the child was rolled in the cradle, throwing the child on the floor. The unfortunate family remained in this situation for three weeks. The monsters again returned, throwing down the house and burying the unfortunate family in the ruins. The poor man brought a civil bill action for £20. The assistant barrister, Michael O'Shaughnessy, gave him £16 damages … The case was tried at the Claremorris Sessions. If your Lordship will investigate the case you'll find the facts as I state, by applying to the barrister for his report.'

Wednesday 12 April. Report of Capt Farren *Castlebar*
'On Thursday 30 March at Castlebar Petty Sessions a charge was brought   CSORP O.4018
against a contractor for using light weights in distributing provisions to destitute persons receiving outdoor relief … The contractor is of course not now employed by the vice-Guardians but it is most desirable that the penalties of the law should be enforced to deter others from a like proceeding.'

Wednesday 12 April. James Browne PP to Lord Lieutenant *Ballintubber*
'Michael Igoe was recommended by me to the relieving officer, Stephen   CSORP O.4777
Bourke. His name was placed on the relief list and he got at length some meal. The bailiff of the property on which he lived interfered in the meantime to have the relief discontinued and accordingly the poor man was struck off the relief … I wrote to the relieving officer but in vain. I wrote again and again, stating that he tendered possession of his holding. Finally, I requested the relieving officer to have the kindness to say in reply to a sealed letter from me, upon what authority did he withhold from a starving man who tendered possession of his holding in order to obtain relief. To this last letter from me there was no reply … At the persuasion of some humane neighbours who heard of the sufferings of this poor but once comfortable and virtuous man, I laid his case before the Guardians on Saturday last. And in my presence the relieving officer was ordered to give him at once provisional relief until his case would be further enquired into. On my return home yesterday from a distant portion of my parish, I found the poor man at my door, nearly dead. In my absence from the locality there was no one to give him a morsel of food. And hence poor Igoe has been from Saturday to Tuesday night with his whole family without food. The relieving officer in question is a Mr Bourke who held the situation of master of the poorhouse at one time but was dismissed … on account of charges brought against him by the Guardians … As acting chairman of the Ballintubber Relief Committee, I was connected with their officers in the application of relief … and I can refer to my respected friend, Count Strzelecki, for my humble exertions to give local effect in my

relation as a pastor, to every measure for the relief of the people for the last two years.'

17 April. Report of Capt Farren

'Michael Igoe, aged 60, his wife Dorah, aged 50, Michael, 14, Tom, 13, Patrick, 17, and John, 15. Igoe was entered for relief on 11 March and they received weekly 42lbs of meal until 8 April. The relief was suspended when the landlord sent a message to the relieving officer that Igoe was in possession of land. The Board of Guardians offered him the workhouse but he would not go.'

DDA MURRAY PAPERS

19 April. James Browne PP to Archbishop of Dublin thanking him for £15

'Ballintubber is gone – alas! my fine, virtuous holy people have been starved to death. The landlords of all sects and creeds conspired for their extinction – the Catholic landlords the most cruelly disposed. We are ourselves reduced to the level of our people; how inscrutable the design of heaven.'

Swinford
CSORP O.4351

Thursday 13 April. Report in Saunder's News Letter (see also Freeman's Journal, 13 April)

'*Death from Hunger*'

On Wednesday last a poor woman and her infant were found dead in a tenantless house within a mile from Swinford, their names unknown. An inquest was held on the bodies when a verdict of death from starvation was returned.'

Extract from Guardians' minutes, 15 April:

'The case of a woman and child who died of starvation within a mile and a half of Swinford is a gross fabrication. It appears a woman in the town of Swinford was found dead, the child alive. The sub-inspector sent the child to the workhouse, where it now is and taken good care of. An inquest was held on the woman and the verdict was "died from disease and cold".'

17 April. Mr Gibbon's observations

'There was an inquest yesterday on the body of Sibby Horan who died in this town on the morning of 6 April. She appears to have died of dysentery and want. Her name appears on the relieving officer's book on 24 March but she does not appear to have had any relief from the Union or from the relieving officer by way of provisional relief or otherwise. I did not hear of her till after her death on 6 April. She had a child which I have had taken to the poorhouse. The child is in a miserable state. It was necessary to send it at once to the infirmary. It has been stated that the relieving officer was aware that the deceased was in an extreme destitute state and should consequently have relieved her. I should therefore feel obliged by being forwarded the copy of the inquest in order that the charge may be inquired into. The relieving officer states that he called her before the Board on 24 March but that she did not appear. He admits that he was aware that she was very destitute and had not relieved her. There appears from his statement a great want of humanity on his part and it is desirable that the case be examined into on oath.'

15 April. Extract from Guardians' minutes:

'When the relieving officer brought the case to the notice of the Board of Guardians and stated the relief he had afforded, the Board of Guardians ordered the relief to be continued. The house in which the woman and her daughter took shelter appears from the report of the relieving officer not unroofed, the end inhabited by them being covered … a hole that a person would fit through at the other end. The Board of Guardians believes that death was caused either by the inclemency of the weather or by the destitution she must have suffered previous to her having come into this Union, as she was relieved on 5 April and her application to the relieving officer was only made on 4 April. And she being merely a stranger passing through the country, could not have been known to the relieving officer. Having got a stone of meal, she hoped to be enabled to reach her home. The Board of Guardians has no confidence in the verdicts of juries in what they call starvation deaths on coroner's inquests. They are generally for the purpose of taxing the county and so satisfied were the Grand Jury at the last assizes, they refused paying for them.'

Thursday 13 April. Report of James Auchmuty   *Castlerea*
'There has been twenty families turned off the estate of Mr Farrell near this   CSORP O.4059
town under an *Habere*. He is a defaulter of poor rates and is returned to our
solicitor to be proceeded against in the superior courts.'

Thursday 13 April. Society of Friends clothing query completed and signed by Wm   *Kilmactigue*
Fetherstone (See Appendix 6Q)   SFFP 2/506/37
'Clothes are needed for about 100 children of both sexes from one to fourteen years old, in the townlands of Culdaly, Letterbrone, Belclare, Claddagh and Stonepark. Grey calico, blueprint, flannel and corduroy are needed. I do not look for anything but the materials for childrens' clothes. They are in many instances nearly naked. There is not one person for whom clothing is required able to pay one penny to buy them. I will undertake to pay for the making of the clothes. Revd Arthur Huston, rector of Kilmactigue, his wife, and Rev Thomas Judge CC will act conjointly with me in the distribution.'
Draft reply, 24 April: 'Grant 3 pieces of grey calico, 3 pieces of blueprint, 1 piece of flannel and 1 piece of corduroy.'

Saturday 15 April. Report of W. Hamilton   *Ballina*
'The weather has been very unfavourable … A large quantity of potatoes has   CSORP O.4272

been planted with every prospect of success, but I do hope the bitter experience of the past two years will have a salutary effect, and that no persons will plant more than they can afford to lose, without bringing them to the brink of starvation ... There is not at present that cause for depression which appears to pervade all classes ... It is impossible to foresee the effect of the system of unroofing cabins, which if carried much further, will render all attempts at providing workhouse accommodation, as a test for the able-bodied, utterly hopeless.'

Islandeady
CSORP O.4578

Sunday 16 April. Petition of John McIntire, Carnacoole, to Lord Lieutenant
'Petitioner has four in family in the act of starvation. I was getting two stone of meal until I was sent off the relief list five weeks ago without cause. Thomas Phellin, my steward, if called upon, can certify that I attended my work regularly. Even John Conner, the schoolmaster, who is teaching school under the British Association, would not allow my children to this school get the bread. I have neither house or land, meal or malt?, nothing but the daylight, glory be to God in his mercy towards us. I beseech your Excellency to direct forthwith to order my children on the school, one of them 10 years old and the other, 12 years old, and order those who has money in the bank and also those who has cows and value land and give the poor who has neither, the preference. Also Edmond Moran of Derrycouse has six in family and was getting 9 stone of meal. He was curtailed this three weeks past. He petitioned the vice-Guardians and spoke to Capt Farren, inspector. They would neither hear his complaint or redress his grievances. Thomas McManmon, relieving officer, said in the presence of Ulick Walsh, tailor of Derrycouse, that it was a mistake. No matter, petitioners are suffering the severest pangs of hunger without pity from those who are paid to ameliorate their wants. Petitioners beseeches, craves, and implores your powerful and humane Excellency to take their case into your kind consideration, by forthwith directing this petition to some person who will inquire into our distress and (not) to allow your petitioners to die with hunger without a hearing. One word from your Excellency will leave your petitioners on the land of the living, until God is pleased to take us out of this with sickness and old age. Save us from hunger and starvation and petitioners will incessantly pray.'
Capt Farren's observations: 'John McIntyre was cancelled on 18 March, having only two children dependant on him. He was offered a ticket for the workhouse but would not accept it. He occupies about a rood of land, has an ass and sells turf. Edmond Moran has six in family, two children only are dependant on him. Moran, his wife and two children were accordingly cancelled on 18 March and relief was continued to the other two children. The relieving officer offered the rest of the family a ticket for the workhouse but they did not accept it.'

Monday 17 April. Eugene Coyne PP to Archbishop of Dublin thanking him for £15 sent

Ballyhaunis
DDA MURRAY PAPERS

'If the Central Committee could be got to believe that hundreds will die of starvation unless quickly relieved I am sure they would send funds, if any remain. My parish is the worst off of any. My people have no landlords or anyone to do anything for them except myself. The lands are in chancery and the landlords in some safe hiding place. On my visits I find the people lying on their beds with hunger, fever and dysentery – the result of unwholesome food. If you were to see my house surrounded every day with starving countenances you would pity me and them.'

Friday 21 April. F. Gibbons, Poor Law inspector, to William Stanley re the death of Sibby Conway

Swinford
CSORP O.4351

'It appears that Mr Henry, the relieving officer, offered indoor relief to the deceased, believing that she would not accept it and that she was not destitute. The case appears doubtful but I cannot establish that the relieving officer was aware that she was ill until the day previous to her death. She and another girl lived together and a day or two previous to her death they were turned out of the hut in which they lived by the proprietor principally, as I am informed, on account of their immoral character.'

21 April. William Henry, relieving officer, to F. Gibbons

'I offered her indoor relief from the conviction that she was not destitute … which she obstinately refused to accept. She did not even appear the day of the meeting, when called, being fully cognisant of the decision the Guardians, who knew her, would come to on her case.'

Saturday 22 April. Extract from Guardians' minutes re death of James Forrester

Boyle
CSORP O.4713

'He was 16 years old and was not included in the class entitled to relief … He came once to the workhouse for admission but found no vacancy. On 31 March he received outdoor relief, although not strictly entitled to it; he received 7lbs of meal on 8 April, the day being one of extreme severity, and is reported to have fallen on his way home with the meal in his possession.'

Monday 24 April. Police report

Ballymote
OP 26/143

'A Frenchman was arrested in Ballymote … He was drinking at the priest's house which was watched by the sub-inspector and the head constable … They heard noises inside the house as if persons were thumping the table in revelry and one person exclaimed he was the man to lead them on. The priest was Rev McNicholas CC who had been in France.'

Erris
CSORP A.4250

Monday 24 April. Daniel Lynch RM to T. N. Redington
'In Erris a few days ago I was glad to see the people there show such an inclination to till their ground. Several of them told me that they would have to
discontinue as the outdoor relief was withheld from them by absenting themselves from breaking stones. In this remote and distressed area the poor people should get relief for a fortnight or ten days while they put down their
crops.'

Castlebar
CSORP O.4253

Tuesday 25 April. Extract from vice-Guardians' report
'The rate collector reported yesterday having collected during the week £170
4s. 6d. On that day he made a distress on the cattle of Mr Browne JP of
Rehins near Castlebar and that, when in the act of driving away the cattle,
Mr Browne refused to allow the field gates to be unlocked and defied the collector to force the gates ... He eventually came away without the cattle and
reported the case to us ... We recommended him to return and drive away
the cattle. It appears to us that Mr Malley's (collector) ignorance or timidity
is no apology for Mr Browne's conduct. Such an example by a magistrate and
a county gentleman is most pernicious.'
*W. M. Browne to T. N. Redington denying that he violently resisted the rate col-
lector, 3 May.*
Observations of Mr Bourke, Poor Law inspector:
'On the point of bad example, Mr Browne's conduct is just as well known to
ratepayers in general and just as likely to be imitated, as if a hundred people
were looking on when the events occurred.'

Kiltimagh
SFFP 2/506/22

Tuesday 25 April. Daniel Mullarkey PP to Society of Friends (See Appendix 6S)
'There are numerous instances of your liberal and enlightened generosity
towards the relief of the poor and destitute of this country ... Fever is rapidly
increasing in this parish ... Scarcely a day passes when I do not witness with
regret from five to six funerals.'
Draft reply, 9 May: 'Send an order for ½ ton of Indian meal, ½ ton of rye and
½ ton of rice.'

SFFP 2/506/34

*29 April. Daniel Mullarkey PP and Michael Wm Henry MD (Kiltimagh and
Bohola dispensary) to Wm Todhunter, Society of Friends*
'There are more than 400 families in this parish who have cultivated their
holdings to a limited extent, which deprived them of the necessaries of life ...
It is frightful to witness the numbers daily dying from fever and dysentery
ensuing from insufficiency of food and clothing. Measles and chincough are
prevalent and in this season more than usually fatal. We solicit your Society
will order some oats and potatoes for seed and also meal and rice for those
suffering from disease.'

1 May. G. V. Jackson to Society of Friends   SFFP 2/506/22
'Killedan is a poor electoral division with a great population, no employment
and no resident gentry. All over the Swinford Union enormous efforts are
being made to crop the land and the poor almost starve themselves to put in
a crop. Their holding land by law excludes the industrious strugglers from
Poor Law relief … There is among this class great suffering and they are alone
sustained by the enormous relief given to the children by the British
Association. Regarding Rev Mullarkey, I consider a grant of meal and some
rice could be safely confided to his care … The class who have cropped the
land deserve peculiar sympathy. If they go to the poorhouse and surrender
their lands, the crops are likely to be lost.'

Thursday 27 April. Petition of John Mooney to Lord Lieutenant   *Turlough*
'Petitioner was on his way to a shoemaker's house on 18 April and passed by   CSORP A.4475
an illicit stillhouse in the parish. He went in with intent to light his pipe and
have a smoke. When in a minute or two subsequently a party of the revenue
police came in, commanded by their chief officer, a Mr Clendenning. He was
arrested on the spot, together with James Moran, owner of the stillhouse. He
is quite innocent and has also a poor most helpless family, eight in number;
which depends merely on his daily labour and has no other means whatever
to subsist on.'

Friday 28 April. Extract from Guardians' minutes re the deaths of Bridget   *Boyle*
Coleman and Mary Moran   CSORP O.4740
'Bridget Coleman never applied to the relieving officer or Board of Guardians.
She procured food by begging and did not die of immediate starvation. She
had for four months exposed herself publicly to excite commiseration and for
some time resided near the workhouse. She was a professional beggar.
Mary Moran, Rockingham electoral division, had possession of two acres of
land and would not give them up. She was offered relief on condition of so
doing but declined. She died of absolute want.'

Summer 1848

Cropping the Land

Due to the partial success of the potato crop in the autumn of 1847, extraordinary efforts were made in spring and early summer to crop the land. From Castlebar it was reported in May that 'hope in the future has superceded the apathy and despair which at this period last year existed in the Union.' In some parts of the Castlebar Union the quantity of potatoes sown was nearly as great as in ordinary years, in others, three-quarters or more than a half.

The cropping was done largely by smallholders, having two to six acres of land and at enormous cost and risk to themselves and their families. In Ballina many of them had to part with everything they possessed. and were facing three to four months with nothing to subsist on. Even in ordinary years these were known as the 'hungry months'. 'Three-quarters of the entire population are now reduced to utter destitution,' Bernard Durcan, parish priest of Swinford, informed the Lord Lieutenant in mid-May. They were excluded from relief under the Poor Law by the Gregory clause. The Protestant curate of Achonry solicited a food grant from the Society of Friends specifically for such smallholders.

Now that they had cropped their lands, they would rather risk starvation than give up their little holdings to qualify for relief. Some of them paid the ultimate price. Pat Thornton of Aughagower held one acre which he had planted with potatoes. Eventually he decided to give up his holding and seek relief for the survival of himself and his family. On his way to the relieving officer, his wife and one of his children died. Reporting the incident from Westport, Mr Bourke added: 'This is by no means a solitary instance of death from starvation proceeding from the disinclination to part with land.'

Others were not given the choice of surrendering their lands. On 14 June the sheriff, with a strong force of police, arrived in the townland of Treenagleragh in Kiltimagh to evict 33 families, tenants of the Earl of Lucan. Those unfortunate persons had their lands well cropped and some had their rents paid or owed merely a half years' arrears. Their parish priest brought the eviction to the notice of the *Freeman's Journal* and as a result the Lord Lieutenant had the incident investigated and concluded that although Lucan's evictions were harsh, they would in the long term help to reduce poverty by encouraging more capital investment in the land.

Monday 1 May 1848. Board of Health to T. N. Redington   *Sligo*
'Judging from information received ... from official returns of the hospital   CSORP H.4397
cases returned by the Sligo Board of Health, it is nearly certain that fever does
not prevail in that district beyond its ordinary frequency. Sligo Board of
Health should send in its closing account and be dissolved with the closure
of the hospitals at Collooney, Coolaney etc, and the patients to be transferred
to the Poor Law Guardians.'

Tuesday 2 May. Richard Hamilton to Capt Neill, 40th Regiment   *Belmullet*
'The rate collector in this district has reported to me that cattle he had under   CSORP O.5464
seizure have been rescued no less than three times within the last few days, at
one of which rescues both Mr Waters, the resident vice-Guardian here, and
myself were present, when a crowd of several hundred persons attacked us
with sticks and stones and eventually succeeded in bringing away the cattle
in triumph.'

Tuesday 2 May. Resolution of the Board of Guardians   *Swinford*
'That the exertions being made all over the Union to crop the land is most   CSORP O.4921
gratifying to us, as well as the cheerfulness with which the rate is being paid,
the ratepayers expressing their anxiety to pay, as their children are being fed
by the British Association.'

Wednesday 3 May. Abby Fleming to Society of Friends (See Appendix 6Q)   *Keash*
'The small sum, £1 11s. 9d., was all that I received or could dispose of. The   SFFP 2/506/35
rest of your kind grant I was obliged to give gratuitously, so great was the destitution of the locality ... The most dire distress still prevails and hundreds
will die. There is the greatest possible need of clothing.'

Thursday 4 May. Petition of Michael Godfrey to Lord Lieutenant   *Castlebar*
'I retired from the constabulary in 1843 ... I tried everything to procure some   CSORP I.4806
employment but failed owing to not being a favourite of the Roman Catholic
hierarchy, with one of whom I had an altercation which led to a prosecution,
in the discharge of a public duty, and whose influence appears so powerfully
on the minds of the people in this part of the country at present that if I
apply for any public situation I am sure to meet with a signal defeat, through
their opposition and influence.'
*Godfrey asks for his reappointment in the constabulary or a free passage to British
America.*

Friday 5 May. Fitzgerald Higgins JP to sub-inspector, Westport   *Westport*
'It is reported that the master of the workhouse has been attacked and that   CSORP I.4599

riot and disorder by an outbreak of the paupers had taken place. Six police sub-constables and one constable should be sent to protect the master and restore order.'

Co Sligo
CSORP H.4598

Friday 5 May. Dr Burton's report to Board of Health

'With regard to the general character of disease thro' the Union of Sligo, their inspector states that since the month of March it has assumed a somewhat more malignant and fatal character, that complication of diarrhoea and dysentery have become very general and that fever and dysentery did not seem to shew a tendancy to subside below a standard apparently reached some months since ... Collooney, Ballisodare and four other electoral divisions appear to be comparatively free from fever, the inhabitants applying early for hospital relief, which they obtain at Sligo or Collooney. It appears to be very much on the decline in the town of Sligo ... Coolavin fever hospital has been closed since 31 January ... Notwithstanding repeated and urgent remonstrances to Boyle Board of Guardians, the Coolavin district still remains without either hospital or dispensary relief ... In Cloonacool electoral division the amount of disease is considerable ... I visited several cases of fever, one of which had just died, 12 miles from a hospital ... In Tubbercurry electoral division there is a considerable amount of disease; in the parish of Achonry three families in fever were visited and a hospital is much needed for this and Cloonacool electoral division and would be best situated at Tubbercurry ... Dispensary attendance very inefficient, the dispensary physician not visiting outcases in his district ... In the village of Bunninadden, Cloonoghill electoral division, I saw eight families lying ill of fever. In the mountain tracts of this division fever is very prevalent ... Dispensary attendance very defective, the medical attendant residing at Sligo, a distance of 11 or 12 miles ... Ballymote electoral division is suffering less than other electoral divisions, the patients obtaining admission into hospitals in Sligo and Collooney. The dispensary, from the failure of subscriptions, has closed. Dr Lougheed has done duty gratuitously for some time but does not visit and has not visited for a long time any case of fever and thus the actual amount of disease is in doubt ... In Coolaney on 14 March nearly every bed was occupied by two patients suffering principally under dysenteric affection. The hospital is only capable of accommodating 18 beds ... There were crowded into it, on 26 October 1847, 67 patients and the number for many weeks was never less at any time than 50 patients, the average number in the hospital during its whole time of operation being 49 in 18 beds ... Increased accommodation is required ... Dispensary attendance is very inefficient ... There are 80 to 100 daily applicants for relief. Two thirds suffer bowel complaints ... Medicine is given only once a week except in bad cases when it is given on each dispensary day.'

Monday 8 May. Society of Friends clothes query completed and signed by Denis Tighe PP (See Appendix 6C)

'The population is 12,000, most of them in need of clothes. Corduroys and friezes are needed for the men and flannels for women. The tailors and shoe-makers are all idle. Other grants received from the Society of Friends included 2 tons of rice and Mr Forster gave Charles Strickland £10 and other grants since.'

Draft reply, 12 May: '1 piece of flannel, 1 piece of calico, 1 piece of corduroy, ½ piece of check and 50 garments.'

Ballaghaderreen

Monday 8 May. Statement of Mr Bourke re death of Mary Thornton and her son

'Pat Thornton, the father, held an acre of land in Aughagower electoral division and had planted it with potatoes. Though in deep distress he had never applied for relief, being unwilling to part with his land. At length, on the day before his wife's death, he resolved on applying for relief. He deserted his holding and set out to seek the relieving officer. On his way his wife and one child died from exhaustion and want. The moment the relieving officer heard of it, he went out to the family, gave the survivors provisional relief and visited his house … This is by no means a solitary instance of death from starvation proceeding from the disinclination to part with land.'

Westport
CSORP O.4800

Monday 8 May. Richard D. Webb to the Society of Friends

'I called at Carramore, the residence of George Vaughan Jackson, a gentle-man who has devoted himself with great energy to the alleviation of the prevalent distress. He travels upwards of 100 miles per week while attending three relief committees in various parts of the country.'

Ballina
Transactions p. 198

Wednesday 10 May. Rev J. Garrett to Society of Friends (See Appendix 6F)

'After waiting in vain to hear of the arrival of a bale of clothing for this district which was to have been delivered a fortnight ago at Mr Judge's in Boyle, I went there yesterday and could not hear anything about it.'

Draft reply, 12 May: 'I have seen the person who lifted the bale on yesterday. He says it is at home by this time.'

15 May. Garrett to Society of Friends

'The bale of clothing for this district has at length arrived, valued at £13 7s. 4d. I would be glad to have the particular value of each item that I may know what to demand in disposing of the articles.'

Ballymote
SFFP 2/506/35

Wednesday 10 May. Vice-Guardians' report

'Destitution is on the increase owing to the want of employment, particularly among the able-bodied class, and we see no prospect of it decreasing before

Castlebar
CSORP O.4902

harvest. We are still greatly in want of implements to keep them employed as we have no order from the Board of Works, though applications have been made for them.'

Ballina
CSORP O.4900

Thursday 11 May. Report of W. Hamilton
'Only one thirteenth of the land under crops in the Ballina Union last year. In the Swinford Union, one eighth, Westport, one twentieth, Castlebar, one eighth, Ballinrobe, one eighth, and Sligo, one fifth … All accounts agree that the people are now making the most unusual efforts to crop their lands, so much so that numbers of them are parting with everything they possess. How they purpose subsisting for the next three or four months is a question which, I fear, many of them cannot answer.'

Achonry
SFFP 2/506/22

Thursday 11 May. Michael Muldowney CC to Society of Friends (See Appendix 6A)
'On the part of this flock, 60 of whom you have saved from actual starvation, I thank you mostly kindly. May God in his mercy aid and assist ye for your kind exertions in the cause of suffering humanity, is the daily prayer of those wretched beings whom you have saved from a premature grave. Those 60 are miserable creatures, some of whom have a small portion of land and others none. Some were stretched for ten days in miserable hovels, who after recovering a little strength went the distance of fourteen miles to the workhouse, were sent back again to get outdoor relief but were refused. In fact they abhor the workhouse as a place of immediate dissolution.'
Draft reply, 19 May: 'Order on Sligo ¼ ton of rye meal and ¼ ton of Indian meal.'

Meelick
SFFP 2/506/22

Friday 12 May. John Bolingbroke to Society of Friends (See Appendix 6U)
'The number of heads of families relieved by meal to 30 March was 17 and of dependants 80. From 30 March to 18 April food was distributed in a cooked state, when 45 families containing 205 persons received assistance daily but from want of a proper boiler or one sufficiently large, this mode of relief was only continued for the consumption of some parsnips and turnips that proved a plentiful and, as I was assured by Dr Gawley, a wholesome addition … I was obliged to trust the distribution of the green crop seed to a person of whose honesty I am fully satisfied … I am not the less grateful for your generous sympathy for the poor in sending such a liberal supply of seeds.'
Draft reply, 20 May: 'Order at Ballina ¼ ton of rice, ¼ ton of Indian meal, ¼ ton of rye and 2 bags of biscuit.'

Monday 15 May. Bernard Durcan PP to Lord Lieutenant, enclosing an address from the united parishes of Kilconduff and Meelick, asking for relief for the destitute smallholders

'The population of the parishes is 2,000 families or 11,000 persons, mostly small occupiers of 3 to 6 acres of inferior quality, raising oats to pay the landlords' rents and potatoes for food. Potatoes being almost totally wanting this year because of the very limited extent sown … their scanty resources are now completely exhausted. The partial success of the potato last year inspired such hope that they made every possible effort this year to sow a large crop. To do so they disposed of every property they possessed and have no means of support until harvest … Three-quarters of the entire population are now reduced to utter destitution. They are excluded from relief under the Poor Law by the quarter acre clause. There are no resident proprietors, no class of farmers. Not a single landlord availed himself of the Land Improvement Act … A great portion will perish before harvest unless relief be given. Fever is fearfully increasing, deaths from want and disease are very frequent.'

21 May. Poor Law Commission to T. N. Redington, giving a summary of the report of Capt Hanley, Poor Law inspector, Swinford

'The contents of the memorial as regards the small holders of land were true; and they are generally speaking in great distress … Having exhausted all their efforts and all their means in cultivating their farms of from two to five acres, they are now in many instances driven to the necessity of surrendering all to their landlord to qualify them to apply at the workhouse for relief … The favourable appearance of the crops, the hopes … in the success of the potato, and the painful struggle before surrendering all, has delayed this last resource in some cases till too late. According to the last return received from Swinford Union, there were 10,792 in the receipt of outdoor relief and 548 in the poorhouse. Relief is likewise afforded to the children in the schools under the agency of the British Association.'

18 May. Memorial of magistrates, cesspayers, clergymen and ratepayers of the barony of Gallen to Lord Lieutenant, re the poor holding small quantities of land

'Nothing has been done to ameliorate their condition … There are no greater objects to be found in any part of the globe than the wretched holders of small portions of land, a class who have expended the last resource they could by any means command in putting down their crops so as to have some provision for the ensuing season. They are now in a most deplorable state … Hundreds will perish through hunger, it not being in the power of the Board of Guardians to afford them any assistance, they holding above a quarter acre of land. We most earnestly implore your Excellency to devise some way to assist those wretched objects which can easily be done by directing some of the public works commenced last season completed … We greatly fear they will be obliged to part (with) the holdings they expended their all in endeavouring to till and thus become burdens to the county when, were some small assistance promptly given, will enable them to become useful members of society ... The poor and industrious should not be allowed to perish thro' want, when by the law of the land we are compelled to support the indolent.'

Costello barony
SFFP 2/506/37

Tuesday 16 May. Katherine Strickland, Loughglynn to Society of Friends, requesting some clothes for the destitute poor in the neighbourhood of Loughglynn and the barony of Costello (See Appendix 6T)
'If anything could be given in the way of bed clothes for those sick of fever, it would tend to spread the check of that disease amongst the lower classes, who suffer very severely for the want of additional bed clothes to separate the healthy from the sick members of the family.'
Draft reply, 30 May: 'Grant 50 rugs and 2 pieces of calico.'

Achonry
SFFP 2/506/23

Wednesday 17 May. Rev W. R. Hiffernan, curate, to Society of Friends
'I am induced to solicit a grant of food chiefly for persons living in a state of destitution, yet not objects for the workhouse or entitled to outdoor relief as having small portions of land. I beg to refer you to the Dean of Achonry residing at 6 Lower Merrion St, whose place I at present occupy.'

Straide

Friday 19 May. Report in Freeman's Journal
'Deaths from Starvation'
'Steadily but fearfully is hunger performing its work of human destruction. With a cheap loaf and markets glutted to overflowing with provisions, our fellow beings are permitted to drop, one by one, into untimely graves. The deaths of thousands may be laid very justly at the doors of relieving officers, and yet there are not legislative enactments by which to punish them; for if there be found persons sufficiently humane to charge them with neglect, there are either charges preferred against the exposer of villainy, or the relieving officer snuggles out of the affair because the dead victims can tell no tales. The following case occurred in this Union (Castlebar), and a summary of the evidence will throw some light on the disgraceful fact. The inquest was held before Richard O'Grady, coroner, on the body of Patrick Gallagher of Templemore.
Bryan Dunlevy stated that deceased slept in his brother's house the night before he died, and was speaking to him; deceased told him that he was not getting the relief because he would not go to break stones, and he was too weak to do so; he was begging about the neighbourhood; appeared to be in a weak state but did not complain of illness; after he left his brother's house, saw him dead outside a door in the village.
Martin Mallee, who was formerly relieving officer for the electoral division

of Straide, having resigned in favour of his brother, stated that he knew deceased, who was on his relief list and gave him relief regularly until 25 March last; he had no house or land; he was healthy and able-bodied up to that time and as such was disentitled to outdoor relief and the Castlebar Guardians took his name off the list; he refused indoor relief and afterwards applied for outdoor relief, but witness stated he could give him nothing but indoor relief, which he again refused; there were few who were more destitute, a fitter object for relief.

Our correspondent who favoured us with the above, writes that the police were so satisfied of the culpability of the relieving officers that they charged them as accessories to the poor man's death in their requisition to the coroner. We must say that the conduct pursued in this case is not isolated or confined to the district of Straide.'

30 May. Observations of Capt Farren

'Martin Mallee, the late relieving officer … and his brother who succeeded him … are both ill of fever… Patrick Gallagher, widower of Knockageerane, and his son, Thomas, were ruled for relief by the vice-Guardians on 7 February, 14lbs daily and that both were cancelled on 25 March … single able-bodied men and married men having only 2 children dependant upon them were excluded from out-door relief … Yesterday I proceeded to Foxford and took down the statement of sub-constable John Quinlan who was present at the inquest. I annex his statement … "The inquest was held on the 9th instant. Two evidences were examined in the case, who proved that he slept in one of their houses and got something to eat that night, that he said he was not getting relief, that he left the house the next morning and lingered about the village until he died that day. Martin and Edward Mallee, two brothers, were examined … Martin Mallee stated that he had given the man relief for some time and was struck off the books by order of the Board of vice-Guardians at Castlebar as he was an able-bodied man and had only one child … but that he would give him a note for relief in the workhouse. The man refused it and said he would rather beg than go in. The jury gave a verdict to the following effect: 'that deceased came to his death on Saturday last, 6 May, in the townland of Ballinaculla … from the effects of destitution chiefly caused by his refusing to comply with the rules laid down by law to afford him indoor or outdoor relief by labour …' No charge was brought against the relieving officer and it was stated by the coroner that the relieving officer had performed his duty."'

Friday 19 May. Rev Edward Powell to Bewley and Pim

'I tried it (rice) in the district of Coolavin and the people are now habituated to the economical method of preparing the rice and meal to make it go to

Coolavin

SFFP 2/506/18

the utmost extent and I am so well acquainted with the persons in absolute destitution that no abuse or imposition can arise by distributing food in an uncooked state. However, if it is your particular wish to have the relief administered in a cooked state I will not object.'

Kilmactigue
SFFP 2/506/36

Friday 19 May. Completed Society of Friends clothes query (See Appendix 6Q)
'There are private individuals in a starving state who make all these articles in the best manner. Shoemakers and tailors are in very great distress not getting any work since this famine has set in. The majority of the females can do plain needlework very well and also knit stockings. Previous grants included £5 from Mr Forster for the relief of the sick poor, 2 bags of rice, £1 towards maintenance of a foundling and also 100 yards of domestic flannel.'
Draft reply, 19 May: 'Grant 32 yards of frieze, 32 yards of barragan, 20 Guernsey frocks, 2 pieces of calico, 100 assorted articles and 1 bundle of leather.'

Castlebar
CSORP O.5361

Saturday 20 May. Report of Capt Farren
'Activity in agricultural operations still continues in the district. Potatoes for seed and seed for green crops are sought for with much avidity. Rev Mr Stoney, rector of Castlebar, has obtained a supply of turnip seed from the Society of Friends, which he is selling at a reduced price to the poor and

Revds Curley, Geraghty and McGuinness, Catholic curates, Castlebar, have obtained a loan of £400 to purchase seed and issue it as a loan. The holders of lands are making the most satisfactory exertions to crop their lands and hope in the future has superseded the apathy and despair which at this period last year existed in the Union. The cottiers, and those who depended in former years upon the conacre system for support, are exceptions to the general activity. They are a numerous class. The clergymen of all persuasions are indefatigable in their exertions to stimulate the people to crop their lands.'

Saturday 20 May. W. D. Spratt and Henry Noone, vice-Guardians, to W. Stanley re the deaths of Simon Finn and Patrick Morahan

Boyle
CSORP O.5212

'The verdict of the jury at the inquest of Simon Finn (Frain?), Kilfree, was "died of cold and destitution". James Ekins, relieving officer of Coolavin and Kilfree, stated that Finn lived within a quarter of a statute mile of Ekin's office at Mullaghroe but never applied to him for relief.'

12 June. Sworn statement of Betty, widow of Simon 'He was rather foolish some time before he died. It was said that he died about 3 miles from her house. He was brought back a corpse. He left her on Sunday evening and was brought back on Monday evening. He was very pleasant and danced going out. Before he went away on Sunday, she boiled something she does not recollect, and he got a pint of it. Her husband held land. They say it was about a half an acre. She never asked for relief from the relieving officer previous to her husband's death. She heard her husband say that he had himself applied. She heard before her husband's death that she could not get relief unless she gave up the land. She is now getting relief. She has not given up her land. She does not know what her husband died of unless it was hunger and want.'

12 June. Sworn statement of James Ekins, relieving officer: 'He applied once not in the office. I then gave him a few pence, knowing that he could not have relief because he had land. He was a madman.

The verdict at the inquest on Patrick Morahan was "died from extreme destitution". He had for many days an allowance of only 10lbs of Indian meal for himself, his wife and five children, aged 15, 14, 8, 4 & 3. The relieving officer stated that he applied to the former Board of Guardians for an increase in this allowance and was refused ... The relief administered to Patrick Morahan was very inadequate for the support of himself and his family and if the full amount of relief to which the deceased man was entitled had been administered, his death would not have ensued, as it did, from starvation.'

7 June. Report of S. Woulfe Flanagan to Poor Law Commission: 'Since 23 March, Patrick Morahan, his wife and four children from 14 to 3 years old, received 10lbs of Indian meal per week, about 1½lbs per day for six persons. It is a mockery to call such an allowance relief. The unfortunate man, about a fortnight before his death, left home and rambled about the country seek-ing for that sustenance which he could not otherwise procure and leaving his wife and children in receipt of the miserable pittance doled out to them under the name of relief. The day before his death he returned home in a state of weakness and debility and died, I can have no doubt, from actual starvation. His wife died a few days after himself. The relieving officer asked the Board of Guardians for an increased allowance but they refused. Notwithstanding, he gave them 18lbs which the vice-Guardians have since increased to 20lbs. Although his wife died of fever, there can be little doubt that her illness must have been very much aggravated, if not originally caused, by want of sufficient nourishment.'

Tubbercurry
Transactions p.456

Monday 22 May. Extract from letters of correspondents to Society of Friends
'The Poor Law relief system has come into operation. But alas it proves of no service to the many poor families who are struggling to retain their little patches of ground and who, having expended all in sowing their land, are now absolutely starving and have no prospect of relief until the crop of this year is fit for use.'

Sligo
CSORP 0.5225

Tuesday 23 May. Report of Capt Gilbert
'Patrick Somers, 60 years old, had been labouring under dysentery two months before his death. He subsisted by selling turf but, as the weather had been continually wet for some days together, he was temporarily prevented from supporting himself in that way; when going to Sligo on 6 May, accom-panied by his wife, his weakened state and the want of sufficient nourish-ment for 36 hours, caused his death on the road. The man had one and a quarter acres of land and was thereby disqualified to receive relief under the act; but neither he nor his wife had ever applied to the relieving officer or for admission to the workhouse. The doctor's opinion was that he died from pro-tracted dysentery and not from want of food, as he had never applied for such to the authorities or to his neighbours, which a man in a starving state would do most undoubtedly.'

Foxford
SFFP 2/506/23

Tuesday 23 May. Rev G. H. Mostyn to Bewley and Pim (See Appendix 6N)
'I am just out of meal and rice ... There is a good deal of sickness just now, measles, fever etc and some absolute want among poor, decent housekeepers. I wrote some time since to Mr Todhunter for turnip seed but he never answered my letter.'
Draft reply, 27 May: 'Order on Ballina for ¼ ton of rice, ¼ ton of Indian meal and ¼ ton of rye.'

Wednesday 24 May. Extract from letters of correspondents to the Society of Friends
'The destitution has never been so great in this neighbourhood as at present, owing to the want of employment; and the greater number having from a half to two acres of unproductive land, are shut out from poorhouse relief. There are above 40 families circumstanced in this way and it has required my most strenuous efforts to prevent many of them from dying of starvation.'

Ballymote
Transactions p.456

Thursday 25 May. Elizabeth Holmes, Clogher to Bewley and Pim
'I enclose the manner in which two grants of clothing made to my brother for the poor of this place have been disposed of ... Some articles have been given *gratis* but mostly to those who lost their parents or persons recovering from fever and dysentery. The price of those sold amounts to £9 2s. 3d.'

Coolavin
SFFP 2/506/35

Friday 26 May. Rev J. Hamilton, incumbent, to the Under Secretary
'... the frightful state this town and locality are in from swarms of vagrants and strolling beggars who, coming down upon us from the county Mayo, spread like locusts over the entire country, carrying disease and death along with them. So numerous and annoying are these swarms of vagrants that I for one would prefer residing in some penal settlement, if by so doing I could escape from this terrible nuisance. Is it not enough that we have a heavy rate to pay? If the poor rate is not enough, but has to be doubled, only save us for mercy's sake from the vagrants. I am told that a Vagrant Act has been passed. Why, I most respectfully inquire, is it not enforced? What are the police about? The present state of affairs is disgraceful, that unfortunate house-holders and farmers should have to submit to a double fleecing, 1d. by the poor rate and 2s. by the hordes of vagrants pouncing upon them and their substance.'
31 May. T. N. Redington to Rev Hamilton: 'Any person may enforce the Vagrant Act by delivering offenders against its provisions to the constabulary to be brought before a magistrate.'

Tubbercurry
CSORP A.5365

Saturday 27 May. Report of Capt Hanley to William Stanley
'The carriers bringing the week's supply of meal for the division of Bohola from the contractor's store at Ballina, were attacked yesterday about four miles from this town, by a numerous party, and their loading, two tons of meal, forcibly taken from them. The police having arrested several, charged them with the offence, the case was fully inquired into this day at the Petty Sessions at Foxford, where I attended and four of the party were identified and committed for trial to Castlebar gaol ... From the state of this district, without an escort, no carrier is safe in conveying provisions.'
Capt Hanley encloses the sworn statements of the carriers, Pat Naughton of

Swinford
CSORP O.5423

Listrisnane and Thomas Browne of Bohola, taken before the magistrates, G. Vaughan Jackson and John Symes in Foxford.

'Pat Naughton stated that on Friday, 26 May, he was proceeding on the road between Foxford and Swinford with his horse and cart laden with Indian meal (1 ton weight), that about 200 persons assembled and carried off said load with other meal, with which he was accompanied … That a person named Thomas Hannen (and who he now identifies) was one of the persons who first came up to his cart and took hold of his beast and stopped him, and took and assisted different other persons to take away the said meal, and further identified a person, named Thomas Quinn, as being one of the party aforesaid. Informant further said that in the forcing off of the meal, he received three or four blows of stones and was stabbed with a knife.

Thomas Browne stated … that he also had a horse and cart laden with Indian meal … was at the aforesaid time and place attacked by different persons and the said meal carried off forcibly … He now identifies a person named Catherine Quinn as being one of the persons and also a person named Thomas Quinn. Pat Naughton found a bag with some meal in the house of Thomas Reynolds.'

Ballina
CSORP O.5539

Saturday 27 May. Report of W. Hamilton

'1,834 acres of potatoes were planted in the Union last year and four times that planted this year … With the exception of potatoes, generally speaking every other species of crop is unusually backward for even this most backward Union … The agricultural operations carried on by the Society of Friends are most interesting … The instruction afforded through their agency by the practical instructor will prove of lasting benefit … The poor labourers who have been employed by them (nearly all of whom are in occupation of land), will know how to make better use of the seed which has been given to them … The Society of Friends have, in addition to many other charitable and considerate acts, recently distributed large quantities of turnip, carrot, parsnip, onion and flax seed in every electoral division in the Union. I have paid upwards of £2,000 in money wages, a considerable portion of which has been spent by the recipients in purchasing seeds, especially potatoes.'

Bonniconlon
SFFP 2/506/23

Monday 29 May. Rev Mr Lees, Ballina to Bewley and Pim enclosing 'a list of the distribution of the last grant of meal and rice your Society made through me to Mr O'Dowda … I should feel obliged by your giving another grant, say of 2½ cwt of meal rye and 2 cwt of rice.' *(See Appendices 1E & 6H)*

Draft reply, 2 June: 'Order as above.'

Monday 29 May. Meeting of a committee of local Guardians re charges in a letter   Bohola
printed in the Weekly Register, 17 May   CSORP 0.5650
Present: Capt Hanley, government inspector, and Poor Law Guardians, Bernard
McManus, Edward P. McDonnell, James Jordan & Charles McManus
'The circumstance of each case of death stated to have occurred from want through gross neglect on the part of the Board and its officers were duly and patiently investigated, and after hearing the evidence in some cases of the parties themselves, who were stated to have been the victims, in others of the parents of such parties, and in the remainder, of the immediate friends and neighbours of the deceased, who were fully acquainted with the facts, the result proved to be as follows:

No. 1. Daniel Flanery stated to have died from want: This man held about four acres of land and consequently could get no relief from Union rates.

No. 2. John Golding and four children stated to have died from same cause: This family were in receipt of outdoor relief from 25 March: only two of the children died, and from fever.

No. 3. Mrs Fahy, stated to have died on her return from the workhouse where she was denied relief on account of having three roods of land: It does not appear that this woman was ever an inmate of the workhouse. Her name does not appear on the register or application and report books.

No. 4. Three children of Thomas Higgins stated to have died from real want: This family was receiving outdoor relief regularly and since 15 February only one child died – was in a decline and delicate from birth, as proved by the father.

No. 5. Four children of Patrick Higgins to have died from same cause: This family also receiving from time of application, three weeks before child's death, outdoor relief. Only one child, aged 5, died from chincough.

No. 6. Thomas Davis stated to have died from want and to have been buried without a coffin: This man was receiving outdoor relief for four weeks at least before he died. His age he gave to the relieving officer as 80, although he did not appear to him to be more than 60 – was placed on the outdoor relief, from his apparent poverty and his stating his great age, without being required personally at the Board.

No. 7. James Clerke, also to have died from want and to have been buried coffin-less: This person was never an inmate of the workhouse. His name does not appear on the register, or application and report books, never having applied to the relieving officer.

No. 8. Mark McToody of Garame and four children died from same cause: This family was in possession of four acres of land. Mark McToody himself had been in bad health for the year previous to his death, and died of decay – only two of his children died, and from chincough.

No. 9. Widow Conlon to have died from same cause: This woman was getting outdoor relief for herself and family. She was seventy years of age.

No. 10. Widow Tiernan and two children to have died from same cause: Was receiving outdoor relief for herself and family – only one of her children died – and from fever.

No. 11. Widow McNicholas and two daughters to have died from want: Were receiving outdoor relief, all three died from fever.

No. 12. Two children of Thomas Noon, to have died from want: This family receiving outdoor relief – all alive and well.

No. 13. Three children of Thomas Byrne to have died from same cause: This family receiving outdoor relief – all are alive – but in fever.

No. 14. wife of James King and three children, two of whom were buried coffin-less, to have died from same cause: This family on first making application for relief was admitted into the workhouse. Having refused, however, to put on the workhouse uniform, was put out. Took fever and were in consequence put on outdoor relief and a doctor sent especially to see the members of it, who had instructions to give them anything necessary. Only two children died and from fever.

No. 15. Bridget (mistaken for Honour) Lynch to have left the workhouse in a raging fever and to have died from want: Had been in the workhouse, but the medical officer positively denies she had any appearance of fever on leaving it, nor was she under medical treatment for it. She died from fever.

No. 16. Bridget Carney and five children and James Heston to have died from same cause: Bridget Carney was getting outdoor relief from commencement. Died from fever. James Heston holds five acres of land and has a cow; consequently could get no relief for himself or family. The five children died from fever.

No. 17. Two children of Honoria Browne (intended for Bridget Hines) died from want: This family was receiving outdoor relief – only one child died and from fever.

No. 18. Honour Connell (or otherwise Honour Browne) and four children, to have died from want: This family on making application for relief was admitted into the workhouse – was afterwards put on the outdoor relief – only two of the children died and from fever.

No. 19. Patrick Flanigan and daughter to have died from same cause: This family was receiving outdoor relief and the two persons in question died from fever. It was afterwards discovered that the servant who was in attendance on the sick family had been making away surreptitiously with the meal allowed by the Union.

The scale of rations for outdoor relief in Swinford Union is:
>   Adults over 15 years of age, 7lbs of Indian meal weekly
>   Children from 9 to 15 years, 6lbs
>   Children from 5 to 9 years, 5lbs
>   Children under 5 years, 3½lbs

… Not the slightest particle of blame can be by any possibility attached to either the Board of Guardians or their relieving officers. In all the cases of destitution … it was distinctly proved that they did not arise from either neglect or want of humanity on the part of those whose duty was to relieve distress, wherever the Law would admit. But if cases of great hardship arose (such as families possessed of small holdings of land above the statute rood, to cultivate which they had sacrificed their all and left themselves a prey to want and destitution being reduced to a state of actual starvation … Such cases are most numerous in this Union) the Board of Guardians or their relieving officers can not or ought not to be blamed for that which it is totally out of their power to prevent or remedy. If blame is to be attached, it should be to the defects in the Law, and not to those who are merely administrators of it.'

31 May. Observations of Capt Hanley: 'I was present at the inquiry at Bohola, which was attended … by the Revd gentleman who had vouched for the authenticity of the newspaper statement.'

Wednesday 31 May. Sworn statement of Patrick Keane, clerk of the Union
'Thomas Jordan, relieving officer for Castlerea electoral division, was handed a cheque for £60 by the vice-Guardians on 12 May, for the purpose of relieving the destitute poor of this electoral division and he was unable to account for £39 11s. 11d., which he has embezzled and fraudulently misapplied.'

Castlerea
CSORP 0.6175

Friday 2 June 1848. Rev Hugh Conway, secretary, Ballina and Ardnaree Relief Committee, to W. Hamilton
'The funds at the disposal of the committee have been employed since Monday last in giving relief to the poor in and about Ballina and Ardnaree … Last January the committeee purchased about five tons of flax from farmers. 100 women were employed daily for more than two months, scutching and dressing at 4½d. a day. The scutched flax was sent to Belfast and sold and millspun yarn taken in exchange. A small weaving factory was set up where weavers were trained in the use of the fly shuttle. Then they go to their own houses and are provided with work by the committee. 50 are now employed at 8d. a day. The committee hopes to employ 50 more and only those who could not otherwise support themselves. The committee are anxious to prevent the demoralisation naturally resulting from a system of gratuitous relief

Ballina
CSORP 0.5860

and wishing to establish in its place the principle of self-reliance … give a stimulus to employment in the culture of flax in this district and might induce capitalists to invest money here in the erection of buildings and machinery for spinning flax and bleaching linens.'

Keash
CSORP 0.5729

Friday 2 June. Report of Edward Wynne on death of Bridget Brennan, Templevanny
'I examined on oath the relieving officer, Francis Soden and witnesses, Patt Connelly, Mark Walsh and Patt Mullaney, who reside in the village. Deceased returned from England about the middle of April and arrived at Templevanny on 28 April, as she herself stated, wishing to die in her native place and to be buried in the old churchyard of Templevanny. She was between 70 and 80 years old, and though strong and able to walk, she exhibited symptoms of disease, which alarmed the neighbours and prevented them from giving her lodging in their dwelling houses. On 28 April she applied to the relieving officer and received a ticket for the workhouse, which was found on her person after her death … She did not go but took up her abode in an empty house, the property of the witness, Patt Connelly. For the three first days she appeared about the villages in the neighbourhood apparently strong. On the fourth day she was unable to move and in a stupor from which she did not recover and on the sixth day she was found dead … She was supplied with a sufficient quantity of food, but it was oatmeal in an uncooked state, while she had no means of cooking it, nor was she able to cook it if she had the means, for the last three days of her life. It is probable that paralysis was the immediate cause of death … The relieving officer was laid up with fever at the time, and when he gave her the ticket for the workhouse … she was a proper subject for outdoor relief … An impression prevails very generally amongst relieving officers that if they can show that they have offered the workhouse to an applicant for relief, they are thereby exonerated from all responsibility, no matter how urgent the case may have been … I think many of the worst cases I have investigated, have ensued from this cause; a ticket to the workhouse is the least troublesome mode of getting rid of the importunity of the applicants. William Fairbanks, relieving officer during the illness of Soden, never heard of the case until after her death.'

Shrule
SC IRLANDA
vol 29, ff.783rv,
784rv

Sunday 4 June. Michael Phew PP to Cardinal Franzoni
'There is great distress, destitution and suffering thro' want of food in this parish. People here, to the amount of more than 10,000 human beings, are suffering the most appalling scenes of hunger. This day six of the poor people have died of starvation. There is fever and all other infirmities of body, consequent on the want of sufficiency of food, very general among this my poor starving flock. The landlords in this parish, because they are not receiv-

ing their rents, have dispossessed a great number of families of their lands and have brought the sheriff to level their little houses, and these poor families are perishing of cold and hunger by the roadside … Respectfully trusting that your Eminence will commiserate their want by ordering a portion of any charities intended for the relief of Irish distress, to be sent to this starving flock.'

Cardinal Franzoni sent £30 sterling.

7 July. Michael Phew PP to Mgr Alexander Barnabo, acknowledging receipt of subscription from Cardinal Franzoni: ibid, ff.816rv, 817rv

'I and the poor people are most grateful for these benefactions. The poverty and destitution here is great in the extreme. There are great numbers of them dying for want of food … There are many of the deceased buried without any coffin, but a little straw tied about them. The people very generally look pale and emaciated because they have not half enough to eat. They are notwithstanding very religious and patient in their suffering. I hope you will be pleased to present their wants and privations to those in Rome who are charitable … and save them from dying of starvation.'

Tuesday 6 June. Report in Mayo Constitution, 6 June and Freeman's Journal, 9 June, re the death of Thomas White of Knocklogh *Castlebar* CSORP O.6136
'Poor Law Cruelty'
'… With indifference to human suffering or life the Poor Law continues to be administered in this Union … This is but one case of the gross neglect and savage indifference which these gentlemen, "starving officers", are guilty of.'
13 June. Relieving officer, Michael Sheridan's sworn statement on above: 'Thomas White had six acres, part mountain and part bog and part arable, a milch cow, two heifers, an ass and had sown half an acre of oats, half an acre of potatoes, a rood of turnips and 400 to 500 cabbages. This morning I met the widow and her son, William, in the main street of Castlebar, on their way to the fair of Turlough with two heifers to sell there.'

Wednesday 7 June. Rev J. Garrett to Society of Friends *Ballymote* SFFP 2/506/35
'There was a great many miserable wretches now sick and in utter destitution and tho' your last grant was instrumental in saving many lives, it is now finished and I would supplicate most earnestly for a further grant.'

Wednesday 7 June. Thomas Costello CC to Lord Lieutenant *Balla* CSORP O.5866
'Not one sod of turf in this district and the surrounding neighbourhood is cut as yet; all the poor people are employed in stone-breaking. I hope your Excellency will see the necessity of allowing the people one month at least to cut turf to guard against the inclemency of the ensuing winter.'

14 June. Reply of Poor Law Commission:
'They cannot authorise the vice-Guardians to give outdoor relief to able-bodied persons cutting turf, as such an arrangement would be at variance with the principles on which alone the Law can be administered.'

Cong
CSORP 0.6134

Saturday 10 June. Richard Waldron PP to Lord Lieutenant
'If the class of small farmers in this parish, who have cropped their lands and who up to this lived on their own resources, are not relieved for the next two months up to 15 August, they will be obliged to give up their holdings and we will have them as recipients of charity to add to that already too numerous a class, but if relieved for the two months they will be independent. The present appearance of the crops is cheering ...'

Achonry
SFFP 2/506/23

Sunday 11 June. Catherine Rice to Society of Friends seeking another grant of food (See Appendix 6A)
Draft reply, 16 July: 'Order on Sligo for ¼ ton of Indian meal and ¼ ton of rice.'
1 June. Rev W. R. Hiffernan, curate, to Society of Friends (See Appendix 1N & 6W)
'I relieved upwards of 40 families, besides 70 distressed individuals who were in a sickly and starving condition for a period of six weeks.'
Draft reply, 15 July: 'Order on Sligo ¼ ton of Indian meal, 2 bags of biscuit and ¼ ton of rice.'

Kiltimagh
SFFP 2/506/23

Monday 12 June. Rev Brownslow Lynch, curate, to Society of Friends (See Appendix 6S)
'The number of persons relieved amounted to 1,100 persons, comprising 201 families. It is all given away this day.'
Bewley and Pim to Rev Lynch re above, 17 June: 'More economy should have been used in the distribution of their last grant ... It should have lasted a longer time. The Committee feel much commiseration for the painful circumstances under which many of the small farmers are placed ... but it is beyond their means for efficient relief by any distribution of food but the assistance they now afford to the sick.'
24 June. Same to same: 'The number of sick, convalescent and young children, amounting to 1,100 persons relieved for the period of 15 days by their grant of 17 cwt in all of meal, rice and biscuit, which you perceive does not afford ½lb per day to each person ... Cases of dysentery and fever are very numerous here and the former is increasing in the parish.'
Draft reply, 3 July: 'Order for ¼ ton of rice, ¼ ton of Indian meal and ¼ ton of rye.'

G. V. Jackson to Society of Friends: 'The distress in Killedan is greater than in any other part of the Swinford Union … there is a great deal of fever and childrens' diseases prevalent all over the Swinford Union just now.'

Thursday 15 June. Report of Capt Hanley

'A very painful case of eviction took place yesterday at Treenagleragh, the property of Lord Lucan, in this Union. 23 families (106 individuals) were dispossessed and their houses razed to the ground; the scene as described to me was truly heartrending; those unfortunate persons had their lands well cropped and in may instances the rent paid.'

26 June. G. Annewall Lewis, Whitehall, to T. N. Redington

'Sir George Grey wishes to know whether this statement (Capt Hanley's report) has been brought under the notice of the Lord Lieutenant and whether to call for a special inquiry … It is desirable that the reason should be ascertained for a proceeding which, independently of its apparent harshness towards the parties, must have the effect of throwing a heavy burden on the poor rates.'

22 June. Daniel Mullarkey PP to the editor of Freeman's Journal

'Extermination in Mayo'

'On the 14th instant, the sheriff with a strong force of the police, arrived in the townland of Treenagleragh, parish of Killedan, county Mayo, with strict orders from the landlord, Lord Lucan, to execute the law by evicting the poor inhabitants. The townland is now made the theatre of many a melancholy and heartrending scene. The whole townland, I may say, presents the appearance of a battlefield the day after the fight – nothing to be seen but the shattered ruins of what were so lately the abodes of men. No less than thirty-three families, numbering in all one hundred and forty-five human beings, have been thrown on the world. It would be impossible for me, Sir, to give you a full and fair description of the wretched and deplorable condition of these unfortunate creatures, stretched along ditches and hedges – many of them children and decrepit old parents – falling victims to cold and hunger and destitution.

I send you a list of those evicted'. *(See Appendix 1J)*

29 July. Daniel Mullarkey PP to Wm. Todhunter, Society of Friends, acknowledging the grant of 5 May of ½ ton of Indian meal, ½ ton of rye, ½ ton of rice and 2 bags of biscuit (See Appendix 6S)

'I have given ever since partial relief to at least 200 families and I am sure numbers of them would meet a premature grave were it not for the relief afforded them … I never had more applicants for relief in consequence of the tyranny and oppression of Lord Lucan, a landed proprietor of this parish, who lately evicted 36 families numbering 150 individuals, stretched along

Kiltimagh
CSORP O.6588

SFFP 2/506/23

ditches and hedges, not even allowed to touch one leaf of their own cabbages or stand on the land of their forefathers. These unfortunate creatures are daily falling victims to hunger, cold and destitution.'

Draft reply, 3 August: 'Order for ½ ton of Indian meal and ¼ ton of rice.'

Ballycastle
DDA MURRAY PAPERS

Monday 19 June. Martin Hart PP to Archbishop of Dublin seeking relief for his parishioners 'to counteract the proselytisers who have come from the Belfast societies and are very active for over a year in my area and are also buying up land to found a colony. They have abundant money and offer money and meal on Sundays, but, so far, thank God, no perverts.'

Swinford
SFFP 2/507/3

Tuesday 20 June. G. V. Jackson to William Todhunter
'Whispers prevail too as to the potato disease re-appearing. God forbid this and I cannot have it to be an authentic source as a general principle. Partial failures traceable to bad seed are found ... The demoralisation of the people is awful, rich and poor thinking they must be fed and they refuse the work-house and labour tests. It will take a long time to heal the terrible evils entailed by the famine.'

Westport
CSORP Z.6187

Thursday 22 June. Petition of James Tully, Castlebar gaol, to Lord Lieutenant
'Petitioner is a cartwright by trade and went to America to better his condi-tion. Before going he earned 60 guineas and lodged it in the Bank of Ireland, Westport, to bring his wife, one child and his brother to America. After com-ing home he met some friends and drank whiskey at Westport quay. Under the influence of whiskey he went to Westport House and told one of the maids there that he would shoot Mr Hildebrand, if he had been there. He was arrested on the information of the maid.'

On the bottom: 'I have no disposition to prosecute the memorialist.'

Achonry
SFFP 2/506/23

Thursday 29 June. Michael Muldowney CC to Society of Friends (See Appendix 6A)
'I have distributed to 60 persons, mostly all in fever or dysentery, the former in a convalescent state ... There are many families who have exhausted their means to crop their little holdings now reduced to the greatest want and have no relief to get unless they give up their sowing, so dearly earned. Alas! a piti-ful sentence to go to the workhouse. I know six families, about 25 persons in fever, who got nothing to relieve them these ten days past, save what I had to give them out of the never to be forgotten grant your benevolent institution gave me.'

Draft reply, 15 July: 'Order on Sligo for ¼ ton of rye meal, ¼ ton of Indian meal and ¼ ton of rice.'

SFFP 2/506/18

12 July. Dean Hoare to Bewley and Pim re Revd Mr Muldowney: 'I do not know the party myself. I know that distress prevails in that part of the country and sickness and I should suppose a small grant might be usefully entrusted to the applicant. The Roman Catholic clergyman of Tubbercurry is Revd Mr McHugh.'

Saturday 1 July 1848. Count Strzelecki to T. N. Redington
'The fund of the Association is now exhausted. It was given to the most dis-tressed districts since last October. The money spent exceeded £138,680. Rationing and clothing destitute children in the schools, £78,662 0s. 17d. The total amount expended was £217,343 8s. It contributed towards the mainten-ance of 300,000 paupers as also to afford during last winter food to 200,000 children ... I wish to acknowledge the valuable assistance and co-operation received from the temporary Poor Law inspectors, to whose zeal, anxiety and honourable exertions I attribute mainly the extent and degree of relief, which it was the good fortune of the Association to afford to the poor of Ireland.'

British Association
CSORP Z.6450

Sunday 2 July. Report of Capt Farren
'The agricultural prospects of the Union continue to be satisfactory. In some parts ... the quantity of potatoes sown is nearly as great as in ordinary years, in others three-quarters and rather more than a half ... The appearance of the crop is at present very healthy and it may be expected that the early potatoes will be fit for food in the middle of August ... and generally available in the middle of September ... The progress which green cropping has made, though still rudely conducted, is surprising; previous to the last season the turnip was unknown or rather not understood by the peasantry and now they are most eager to plant it ... They seem to be well impressed with its advan-tages for their cattle etc. Indeed, many of the poorest existed on it themselves at the commencement of the winter. This season it has been sown twice and even thrice, previous settings having been destroyed by the fly. They also seem determined never to rely so completely upon the potato again, although they still fondly hope that this treacherous plant will again flourish ... The turnips will feed the cattle and the potato will be reserved for human food ... Looking to the future the pressure on the Poor Laws will be greater than in former times, as the class, which existed by the potato raised by the conacre system, not having the mode of support and the demand for labour in this district being trifling and totally inadequate to meet the case, this class must seek relief in charity, emigration, or by application to the relieving officer.'

Castlebar
CSORP Z.6687

Saturday 8 July. J. A. Holmes to Bewley and Pim (See Appendix 6M)
'In my sister's, Miss E. Holme's, absence, I am induced to make another application for a grant to Clogher school ... We gave daily food to 70 chil-

Coolavin
SFFP 2/506/23

dren out of 250 attending daily. I hope this will be the last application I will
have to make as from the prospect of the potatoes here, I hope they will in
another month be sufficiently forward to be used.'
Draft reply, 15 July: 'Order on Sligo for ¼ ton of rye meal, ¼ ton of Indian
meal, 3 bags of biscuit and ½ ton of rice.'

Keash

SFFP 2/506/23

Monday 10 July. Abby Fleming to Society of Friends (See Appendix 60)
'Your last grant has enabled me to relieve 40 to 50 persons daily … There are
only very few cases of fever. Dysentery still prevails but not to such extent as
it had done last year. Measles and smallpox are raging to an alarming extent
in this district. Those diseases are taking their rounds through each family …
The crops are at present very promising.'
Draft reply, 15 July: 'Order on Sligo ¼ ton of Indian meal, ¼ ton of barley, 2
bags of biscuit and ¼ ton of rice.'

SFFP 2/506/18

18 July. Abby Fleming to Society of Friends: 'I have gratefully to acknowledge
how very thankful I feel for the liberal and timely grant made to me for the
poor in this district.'

Sligo

SFFP 2/506/23

Tuesday 11 July. Capt. Gilbert to Society of Friends
'In my tour of inspection within the last few days, I have been very much
grieved to see the extreme state of want amongst some of the lowest classes
… At this moment fever and dysentery are prevalent and unhappily, another
miserable and fatal disease is attacking the children. Measles are raging in
every village.'

Mayo

CSORP Z.6686

Tuesday 11 July. John S. Bindon, sub-inspector, to Inspector General
'There are some statements circulating that a disease in the potato crop has
been observed. I … have seen in fields the stalks partially infected with black
streaks … but not to any great extent, supposed to have been caused by
recent lightening, and in other fields the stalks look most healthy and luxuriant. There is a large quantity sown in this district and much less wheat than
usual.'

Westport

CSORP I.6966

*Tuesday 11 July. Report of Denis Walsh, sub-inspector, to James O'Connor, county
inspector*
'I attended the fair of Aughnagower with my party on 24 June. I returned in
the evening and about the hour of 9 o'clock in the evening went on patrol
duty with the men … It being a holiday, several large bonfires were lighted
through the town, together with persons returning from the fair. There was
a great number of petty rows during the night which I had dispersed.
Between the hours of 12 and 1 o'clock as we were passing Bridge St, we heard

a cry of murder opposite Capt Bew's house and hurried on as quick as possible and found three persons there fighting, one of them on the ground crying out most piteously for help. I at once ordered them to be brought to the barrack for being drunk and disorderly.'

12 November. Sub-inspector to Inspector General, regarding a letter of Dean Bourke, 6 November

'The Revd Gentleman has been greatly misinformed. Tis true there were some petty brawls as is usual on fair nights which myself and party suppressed, but there has been no bloodshed except in the case of the unfortunate Mary Scanlan stabbed without any quarrelling whatever. It was the work of a moment and I had the man who did it arrested and sent to jail. This is the only case of homicide which has occurred in this town these four years past. Had Dean Bourke spoken to his curate, Rev O'Dowd, he could have informed him that the police had done their duty on the night referred to, for he met the patrol quashing the disturbance and advised them to arrest a few persons who were inclined to quarrel. The police continued to patrol the streets until five o'clock in the morning ... Rev Mr O'Dowd has often assisted the police in suppressing riots ... Having been the whole of Sunday night last through bogs etc in pursuit of Scott for the homicide alluded to ... I got a severe cold for which I had to blister my chest ...'

Wednesday 12 July. Rev John Hamilton to Society of Friends (See Appendix 6W)   *Tubbercurry*
'A considerable number of poor creatures have been assisted. I endeavoured   SFFP 2/506/23
to confine the distribution to the sick and infirm but found it morally impossible to do so on account of the extreme misery and famine-stricken appearance of some of the applicants ... The distribution was made by tickets which were all issued by myself and in no instance was relief granted to a person who was not in a starving condition.'

Draft reply, 13 July: 'Order on Sligo for ½ ton of Indian meal, ½ ton of rye meal, 2 bags of biscuit and ½ ton of rice.'

15 July. Rev John Hamilton to Society of Friends: 'I have yours of the 13th inst.   SFFP 2/506/18
in which you have sent orders for 1 ton of meal, ½ ton of rice and 5 bags of biscuit to be distributed to the convalescent and young children only : I have no doubt that this present supply will carry them through the present season of distress and into the harvest.'

Thursday 13 July. E. Waldron PP and P. Conway CC to Lord Lieutenant   *Ballinrobe*
'There is a report currently circulating here that a boy was murdered some   CSORP A.11841
time since by the master, William Murphy, and having heard there would be an investigation into the matter yesterday, we went to the poorhouse with the father of the murdered boy and with many witnesses. As soon as we arrived

at the gate, Murphy, seeing one of the witnesses, assaulted him, took him by the collar and though he was asked as a favour by one of the clergymen to admit him, still he persevered in the assault. The people then became indignant when they saw the maltreatment and insult of their clergy (which by the way is no unusual thing in this Union by Poor Law officials). We, to our great surprise, were told by the Guardians and the brainless inspector that there was no idea of holding an investigation. Now we, expecting no courtesy or redress from the present Poor Law Commissioners, demand on the part of the public, an investigation in the courthouse of this town as to the fact of the murder, the drunkenness of the schoolmaster, and the assault as committed yesterday by Murphy and his associates in the poorhouse.'

15 July. Statements of Mary Loftus, Mary Naughton and Mary McGovern before Geoffrey Martyn JP on the death of Patt McGovern: 'Mary McGovern said she had been in Ballinrobe poorhouse for the last five weeks, where her son, Patt, was also. Bridget Burke told her that her son was sick in hospital. On the following day, Catherine Fry told her that her son was beaten by the master in the hall of the workhouse.

Mary Naughton of Knockae was an inmate of the workhouse for about six weeks. Three days before she left the workhouse, she saw William Murphy, master of the workhouse, beat with kicks on the back and on the head a boy of about 11 or 12 years of age. He knocked him violently against a table in the hall. Honor Comer was present and cried out that the boy was murdered and she carried the boy out of the hall. Next day she went to the dead house and saw the boy lying dead with a small handkerchief tied across his nose. Mary Loftus and Mary Mullowney were also present when the boy was beaten and heard his name was Patt McGovern.

Mary Loftus was present in the hall and saw Murphy lash a boy with a lash and when he had beaten the boy for a considerable time with the lash, he struck said boy repeatedly with his fist and when the boy attempted to get away, Murphy caught him by the head and dashed him with violence against a table in the hall. The following day she heard the boy was dead and that his name was Patt McGovern.'

CSORP A.7923   *15 July. Memorial of Protestants and Catholics to Lord Lieutenant:*
'Memorialists request a public inquiry into the fact that the town of Ballinrobe was placed in a state of siege for several hours last Thursday, 13 July, to the great terror and alarm of her Majesty's loyal and peaceable subjects, to the infringement of their civil rights and the violation of their private properties. That a full public inquiry be held into the mode in which the Poor Law has been administered for the last twelve months, into the conduct of the officials in the workhouse and the outdoor relief, that there be a rigid scrutiny of the mode of treating the paupers, the beating and maltreating of

them, the drunkenness and general conduct of the officials of the workhouse and rumours of a murder or murders said to be committed within that establishment.'

16 July. Report of Charles Arabin JP to the Under Secretary:

'The parish priest had published in his chapel on the previous Sunday that an inquiry into these rumours, (that two boys had been beaten by the master, causing their deaths), was to be held at the poorhouse on Thursday 13 July. Rev P. Conway proceeded to the poorhouse accompanied by a number of persons, whom he brought as witnesses. Conway was admitted within the gate and to the boardroom but his followers were not ... Some attempted to force an entry ... A scuffle ensued, stones were thrown on both sides and a report that the priest was killed was circulated in the town. An immense mob collected about the poorhouse and on the road leading to the poorhouse in a state of great violence and excitement and endeavoured to force their way into the poorhouse. James Cuffe JP of Creagh was in the boardroom and sent a requisition for the military and police. The military promptly arrived and soon cleared the space about the poorhouse and Mr Cuffe, finding the road to the town occupied by a violent and excited mob, read the riot act and after a little time directed the military to disperse the mob. This act seems to have excited the anger of the shopkeepers and the respectable inhabitants of the town. Many of them have stated to me that the military used unnecessary violence, that although it was quite right to disperse the crowd about the poorhouse, yet the town was perfectly quiet and no necessity whatever existed for the interference of the military ... It is a most unfortunate event and has disturbed the good feeling and harmony that previously existed in this town. A large meeting was held about 7 o'clock yesterday evening ... for the purpose of petitioning the Lord Lieutenant to grant an investigation. Previous to that meeting I was asked to assist Geoffry Martyn JP of Curraghmore to take informations against William Murphy, master of the poorhouse, for causing the death of a boy named Patt McGovern by beating and ill-using him. Mr Martyn had taken the informations before I met him at the house and in the presence of Revds Conway and Waldron and had signed a warrant to arrest and have him amenable at the Ballinrobe Petty Sessions next Monday ... on which day, I am credibly informed, a large number of persons are to assemble in this town, particularly from Partry, the former residence of Rev P. Conway, for the purpose of holding a meeting in respect of this unfortunate event.'

18 July. Report of Charles Arabin JP to Under Secretary:

'Yesterday at the Petty Sessions in Ballinrobe charges were pressed against the master of the workouse of beating cruelly a boy in the workhouse, from the effects of which he subsequently died. There was an unusual attendance of magistrates on this occasion. Several Roman Catholic clergy attended as also a large number of neighbouring gentry and inhabitants. The excitement and interest was considerable. After a very protracted inquiry, the magistrates decided … on committing the master to abide his trial at the next assizes at Castlebar … He has been consequently committed to the county gaol at Castlebar.'

20 July. Statement of Mary Thornton, Lough Mask, Kilmaine: 'Her child, Peggy Thornton, admitted to Ballinrobe workhouse, four weeks before 1 May, was about 11 years old. Two or three weeks before Michaelmas, she was in the nursery with her child when the master, William Murphy, gave the child a kick and a fist and threw her on the ground. He then told Big Mary (one of the paupers) to take the child to the hospital. The master then took hold of herself, shook and kicked her and locked her up in the black hole. Two hours later, he came with a woman and told her that her little girl wanted her. She then went to the hospital where she found her child dead and believes she died from the effects of said beating.'

Statement of Ellen O'Malley, Cooleloughane, Rabeen parish: 'She was a nurse in the hospital of Ballinrobe workhouse and was present in September 1847 when William Murphy beat Peggy Thornton. She (O'Malley) called out for mercy and was told to mind her own business. She went back to the hospital and was there when Big Mary arrived with Peggy who was in convulsions. She died about two hours later from the effects of the beating.'

Kilfree
CSORP A.6764

Sunday 16 July. Winifrid Finn, Doonwest, to Lord Lieutenant
'Petitioner on 29 June was returning from Ballymote market and met Pat Doddy of Doonwest. He did there and then violently drag and knock her down and robbed her of her mantle and four shillings. She went to J. A. Holmes, magistrate, made a statement against Doddy and had him arrested. Doddy was later discharged because she would not swear she saw his hand in her pocket.'

CSORP A.6935

19 July. J. A. Holmes to T. N. Redington: 'She swore information before me that he had robbed her of a cloak and four shillings. I issued a warrant for his apprehension and on his being brought before me, Finn refused to swear he had stolen four shillings from her as she had done before. The cloak was proved to have been previously sold by Doddy or his wife to Finn and never paid for. I declined sending Doddy to trial as no conviction could take place on the evidence, but desired Finn, if she could procure better proof, to attend the next Petty Sessions.'

Swinford
CSORP O.6818

Tuesday 18 July. Board of Guardians to Lord Lieutenant
'Deeply sensible of the enormous drain that the Irish famine has been upon

The Boardroom
of the Swinford
Workhouse

the industry and resource of the Empire, we were unwilling, until the last extremity forced us to it, to solicit further aid from the government.

Our numbers on the rates were at or under some 10,000 persons out of a population of 73,000, and there being every disposition to pay the Poor Rate in the Union, and no opposition to it, and the rate coming in pretty fairly each week considering the desolation caused by the famine, we were carrying out the law in the Union upon safe and solvent grounds, when the construction given to the law as appeared by the Commissioners' letter of 23 May, legalising relief to the families of occupiers of land, suddenly caused an enormous accession of applicants for relief; altho' the Guardians sat almost every day, and altho' every exertion that could be made to carry the law out fairly was made, still the number getting relief ere long more than doubled and in this way the Board of Guardians incurred an enormous debt to the house of Messrs Gallagher for meal supplies for the poor of the Union …

Messrs Gallagher, thro' all the painful stages of the famine, have freely assisted us to save life, and on more than one occasion they were … instrumental in saving hundreds from inevitable death … We owe a sum that must cause them very serious inconvenience at a time of such pressing pecuniary difficulty. And we seek the favour of Your Excellency's obtaining for us a loan from the Lords of the Treasury … to enable us to keep faith with our contractor.'

CSORP O.7165   *28 July. Poor Law Commission to T. N. Redington:*
'The numbers receiving outdoor relief in the Union on 8 July, 24,518, increasing from 2,532 on 25 February ... The Poor Law Commission cannot accept the Board of Guardians' statement that it was on safe and solvent grounds before the extension of relief to starving families occupying more than a quarter acre of land.'

CSORP Z.7308   *29 July. Board of Guardians to Lord Lieutenant*
'We ... being deeply sensible of the kindness of Her Majety's government ... for their late munificent donation of £2,000 ... We beg leave most respectfully to submit our opinions ... as to the necessity of providing some measure for the effectual relief of that portion of the poor, whose privations will receive no alleviation from the abundant harvest, which a kind Providence, as far as we can foresee, is about in his mercy to bestow ... owing to their inability to cultivate the soil in the last spring ... who, without some such interference on their account, must ever remain the victims of hopeless and irretrievable destitution.'

Meelick   *Tuesday 18 July. John Bolingbroke to Society of Friends (See Appendix 1K & 6U)*
SFFP 2/506/23   'I have been obliged to stop (the distribution) on Friday last unless you come forward once more and I trust it will be the last time there will be any necessity for so doing ... The green crops, I am happy to say, are now doing well.'
Draft reply, 20 July: 'Order on Ballina for ¼ ton of rice and ½ ton of Indian meal.'

SFFP 2/506/18   *John Bolingbroke to Society of Friends, 25 July acknowledging their generous grant as above.*

Achonry   *Thursday 20 July. Catherine Rice to Society of Friends (See Appendix 6):*
SFFP 2/506/23   'I have been enabled to administer relief to upwards of 30 families.'
Draft reply, 21 July: 'Order on Sligo for ¼ ton of rice and ¼ ton of Indian meal.'

SFFP 2/506/18   *27 July. Catherine Rice to Society of Friends:* 'The order to the Commissariat office, Sligo has been returned to me as their provision is all issued. I hope your benevolent Society will consider the deplorable state of the poor and allow them the meal thro' some other channel. I do not know what will become of us under the present state of affairs, the relief depots for outdoor relief all about being closed. So it is a melancholy prospect for those who would not be relieved until they gave up their holdings of land. They have now neither relief meal to get nor the prospect of a potato garden to look forward to.'

Kiltimagh   *Monday 24 July. Rev Brownslow Lynch to Society of Friends*
SFFP 2/506/23   'Your donation relieved 170 families, comprising 900 individuals ... I am sat-

isfied that many here have been saved from a premature end.'
Draft reply, 27 July: 'Write to G. V. Jackson with an order on Gallaghers for 2 tons of Indian meal and 1 ton of rice to be allocated for the Union of Swinford.'

Monday 24 July. Petition of six fishermen to Lord Lieutenant
Names: Michael Weir, John Wall, James Rooeen, John Rooeen, John Rooeen Jr, William Weir.

Easkey
CSORP W.6936

'The poor petitioners have carried on the salmon fishery at the bar of Easkey river during the last thirty years, whereby the public were benefited in a considerable degree. On 20th instant they put out in their boats and dropped their nets and when in the act of hauling in, the sea rose in its fury from a sudden terrific wind, so as they were necessitated to abandon the nets and fish, and make to the shore with all expedition. By this means they lost their nets, valued at about £16 sterling, by which they and their families are out of employment in the present most alarming times and if Your Excellency do not interpose on the present occasion, their destitution will be considerably aggravated. They are informed the Fishery Board grants pecuniary assistance to fishermen at reaonable interest to purchase fishing tackle etc etc. They hope Your Excellency will be considerate in their regard by lending them the price of a net and if Your Excellency do not consider that the case lies within your own jurisdiction, that their petition, it is hoped, will be transmitted to the Fishery Board for consideration. Petitioners repose an entire confidence in the integrity and humane disposition of Your Excellency and with such opinions and fond hopes, petitioners will always pray.'
Reply of T. N. Redington: 'It appears the Commissioners of Fishery have no funds whatever available for the purpose of assisting fishermen to purchase tackle and nets etc.'

Thursday 27 July. Rev J. Garrett to Society of Friends

Ballymote
SFFP 2/506/35

'On the return of my daughter who has been the principal agent in the distribution of the clothing, I shall fill and forward the account you require. Some who promised to pay for clothes granted to enable them to earn wages, have not yet been able to pay.'

Saturday 29 July. Police report on 'seditious remarks' of Rev Pat McNicholas CC

Ballymote
OP 26/226

'On the evening of 28 July a large number of persons, about 50 or upwards, were collected together opposite the lodgings of Rev McNicholas CC ... The priest was encouraging the assembly in an inflamatory manner and speaking against the government ... Sub-Constable Jackson was pointed out as a government spy and should be removed by force, saying that he was a blackguard and a ruffian. First Constable Patrick Curley who arrived at the scene reported: "I have to add that the Revd gentleman was under the influence of liquor and that not much heed was paid to his discourse."'

13 August. Rev J. Garrett to the Under Secretary

'The county being perfectly quiet, the Lord Lieutenant should refrain from taking steps to punish the Revd Mr McNicholas for a seditious speech from his window ... The speech was made when the young priest was after dinner and excited by too free indulgence, after a drive from Sligo with a friend, and I believe was a great penitent next day. He is a nephew of the Bishop of Achonry, who is always a man of peace and I have no doubt he will exercise his episcopal authority to silence this youthful agitator upon political subjects in future.'

Outdoor Relief

Monday 31 July (See Appendix 7)

Ballina, 42,364; Castlebar, 26,041; Swinford, 23,369; Boyle, 15,532; Castlerea, 19,378; Sligo, 9,872.

Autumn 1848

Total Failure Again and Female Orphan Emigrants

Early in August the Society of Friends were informed from Boyle and Castlebar that blight had appeared extensively in these Unions. 'The potato crop is universally blighted' was the report on Co Mayo. A month later it was reported from Castlerea that 'the late crop is completely gone'. The failure of the potato crop was as total as in 1846. 'Great as their sufferings have been for the last three years', the parish priest of Shrule wrote to Rome, 'their sufferings for the want of food this year will be awful in the extreme.'

The numbers of those entering the workhouse rose spectacularly. From just over 700 in Swinford at the end of July, the total reached over 1,900 by the end of October. Of these over 1,100 were children under the age of fifteen. Similar increases were recorded in the workhouses in Ballina, Boyle, Castlebar, Castlerea and Sligo.

In 1848 a scheme was inaugurated to send female orphans, aged between 14 and 18, selected from the various workhouses, to Australia. Their passage was paid by the Colonial Lands and Emigration Commissioners while their outfit and conveyance to the port of embarkation was funded by their own Union. They were taken by steamboat from Dublin and Cork to London and Plymouth where two depots had been established for their reception. Here they were identified and underwent a medical examination. Their outfits were examined and they and their clothes cleaned before embarkation for Australia. The voyage lasted from 90 to 100 days.

203 such orphans arrived in Sydney at the beginning of October. Among them was a group from Belfast of low moral character who behaved badly on the voyage, earning for the whole group the reputation of being 'a rough lot'. However, good accounts were received from the employers of the first girls who became servants and afterwards there was a great demand for them. By the beginning of September, 25 orphans had been sent from Ballina and 40 from Sligo. By late 1849 the total number sent was 4,175 of which the number from Ballina was 87, Ballinrobe 25, Boyle 51, Castlebar 15, Castlerea 20, Sligo 68, and Westport 10.

Achonry
SFFP 2/506/18

Tuesday 2 August. Michael Muldowney CC to Society of Friends (See Appendix 6A)

'I have been absent for a few days and I have not received your kind order until last Sunday and on application to the Commissariat store, there are no supplies. May I therefore beg you change the order or give it on some other stores.'

8 August. Same to same: 'I have received your kind letter of 3rd inst. for ¼ ton of Indian meal and ¼ ton of rye. I could find no rye in Sligo. Instead I took ½ ton of Indian meal as I consider it better food.'

17 August. Same to same acknowledging receipt of £4 10s. and enclosing an invoice from Peter O'Connor, merchant, Sligo for 9 cwt of 'the best American kiln dried maize meal'.

Boyle
SFFP 2/506/18

Friday 4 August. Edward Wynne to Bewley and Pim

'Very serious loss in the potato crop by blight is now discernible in a greater or less degree in this Union.'

Castlebar, 4 August. Capt Farren to Society of Friends

'I regret to say that the potato blight has appeared extensively in this Union and in some instances the plants have been severely injured.'

Aclare
SFFP 2/506/18

Friday 4 August. William Fetherstone to Society of Friends

'It was only last week I was able to go to the neighbourhood of Aclare to distribute the clothing, as I have been suffering for a long time from acute sciatica. I send you a list as nearly correct as I could make it. The total cost of making is correct, as also the number in each family, as given to me by the resident clergy of the parish. It was no easy task to distribute these from the immense crowd which assembled when they heard of the distribution ... No person got an article who had one penny to pay, except the first four names on the list. All the others reside in the parish of Kilmactigue. The Revd A. K. Huston was present at the distribution. I paid for the making myself and the work was of great use in this neighbourhood. My wife cut out all the articles except the corduroys which were made by a starving tailor.'

Kiltimagh
SFFP 2/506/18

Monday 7 August. Rev Brownslow Lynch to Society of Friends

'I forwarded your order for ½ ton of rice and ½ ton of Indian meal ... He stated he had no meal of either kind. Biscuits are of course not so economical nor last as long as meal ... Destitution and illness from fever and dysentery are very general in this district ... The destitution is caused by every tenth head of family being put off the outdoor relief, which is done without any selection whatever but as they occur on the list.'

Tuesday 8 August. Patt McGowan, Balliniland, to Lord Lieutenant
'Petitioner has been a contractor on several roads in this county and during
the last three years he has been expending his own property on the repairs of
same and a part of the work which should have been certified two years ago,
has now been discharged by the county surveyor, which amount the treasurer of the Grand Jury refuses to pay.'

Foxford
CSORP W.7587

11 August. Anthony Connor, on behalf of 162 road contractors, to Lord Lieutenant
'Petitioners have learned with dismay from the treasurer of the county that
there are no funds to pay them … Lord Lieutenant should direct the treasurer to pay them the sums now due and thus rescue themselves and their
families from the horrors of destitution which awaits them if their just claims
are not paid.'

Castlebar
CSORP W.7905

14 August. Henry Brett, county surveyor, to Lord Lieutenant
'There was a deficiency of £6,242 8s. 5d. at the last assizes between the various
claims and the present available assets to meet them. Almost the entire of the
contractors are destitute persons, quite unable to meet the payments due by
them to labourers and others employed in the execution of works, and on
every principle of charity and humanity, it is hoped the Treasury will sanction them being paid.
I have within a recent period visited most parts of the county … The
prospects for the ensuing season are of the most gloomy description: the
potato crop is universally blighted. The corn crop is very indifferent, owing
to the exhaustion of the land by successive grain crops and the diminished
quantity of land sown this year, and the general resources of the county are
such as must lead to consequences fatal to all classes in that unfortunate district.'

CSORP W.7905

15 August. John McTigue to Lord Lieutenant
'Petitioner was a contractor on a portion of the mailcoach road, which he
faithfully fulfilled to the satisfaction of Henry Brett, county surveyor. His
funds and all available means were exhausted in providing labour and materials for the said road. Upwards of £70 are now due. By the decision of the
Grand Jury the money has been detained up to the present. He is a poor
industrious man having the support of a wife and ten children, who are now
utterly ruined and in a state bordering on starvation. Their potato crop having failed, he is now unable to procure food for them.'

CSORP W.7883

15 August. John Collins, contractor, to Lord Lieutenant
'I, as well as every contractor, was obliged to wait at considerable expense till
the last day of the assizes for Co Mayo at Castlebar and was then told that
there were no funds. Some of the unfortunate contractors were so exhausted
from hunger and want, they fainted on the green opposite the court, others
were obliged to pawn their clothes for support to save life.'

Claremorris
CSORP W.7933

Swinford
CSORP Z.8049

Tuesday 15 August. Board of Guardians to Lord Lieutenant
'With the alarming condition of the potato crop, it is utterly impossible to meet the growing exigencies of the destitute from our ordinary resources ... Some system of public works should be instituted ... to prevent the calamitous consequences ... if we be left to our own unaided exertions at this awful crisis.'

Westport
CSORP M.8087

15 August. Commander of H.M.S. Avon, to Rear-Admiral Mackay
'I arrived at Westport on the morning of 15 August. I enquired into the state of the crops. I found from my own observation the potatoes to be all more or less diseased but the grain crops look remarkably well ... On 16 August I arrived in Clifden. The only outcry is 'What is to become of the poor?' The potatoes here as well as along the coast are getting very diseased and it is feared that without assistance from the government, the poor will all be starved.'

Dublin
CSORP Z.7962

17 August. Poor Law Commission to T. N. Redington
'There is no part of Ireland in which the potato disease has not appeared. The intensity and extent of the disease vary in different Unions and even in different electoral divisions of the same Union. In some Unions the leaf has been affected, in other the tubers have been attacked, while in some divisions the tubers have become half black and unfit for human food.'

Ballinrobe
CSORP Z.8193

19 August. Report of John S. Bindon, sub-inspector
'The stalks of all the crops are in a state of decay and the leaves black. I have had some of the stalks of a late sowing dug up. The potatoes are small and a great portion of them rotten with a most offensive smell.'

Shrule
SC IRLANDA
vol 29, f.854rv

24 August. Michael Phew PP to Mgr Alexander Barnabo, Rome
'The condition of the Irish this year with regard to food will be lamentable. The potato crop ... is blighted, almost totally destroyed in my opinion. Great as their sufferings have been for the last three years, their sufferings for the want of food this year will be awful in the extreme. Unless the government do something extraordinary in the way of relieving them, two-thirds of the population will die of famine. May God in his infinite mercy succour and comfort them.'

Tubbercurry
CSORP Z.838

26 August. Report of George Knox RM
'One-third of the crop is gone and unfit for any kind of use. The extent sown is so very great that, unless the remainder of the crop entirely fails, there will be a large quantity of potatoes. The oat crop in the Sligo portion of this district is the finest I can recollect.'

Loughglynn
SFFP 2/506/34

Monday 28 August. Charles Strickland to Society of Friends (See Appendix 6T)
'I have not yet given out but very few of the blankets and rugs you were so good as to let me have. I have been reserving them except in very bad cases

until the winter months when the want of such relief in cases of sickness is so very much more severely felt.'

Tuesday 29 August. Kate P. Thompson to Society of Friends (See Appendix 6L)   *Coolaney*
'With most heartful thanks from our poor people and myself for the last   SFFP 2/506/18
grant entrusted to my care … It was given to those people who we saw by
honest industry were struggling to keep their lands and who without such aid
must with their families have been reduced to beggary. 600 were relieved
every week for five weeks … for their every penny was put to sow their produce. May the Lord bless their industry! I lament to say that the renewed disease in the potato crop is beyond all doubt … The late crop, I fear, will be
useless. May the Lord give you wisdom to devise some plan to aid our people, for the struggle is not yet over. Through me they beg to offer you their
tears of gratitude.'

Tuesday 29 August. Report of the resident magistrate   *Sligo*
'The potato blight continues slowly to progress, the stalks are fading but the   CSORP Z.8433
tubers as yet not much injured. The late crops are destroyed generally but in
most cases the setting of seeds took place at an earlier period than usual. Most
farmers had pulled up the potato tops to prevent the disease communicating
to the tubers and when this course has been adopted, the small farmer continued to send in unusual quantities to market.'
31 August. Report of John Andrew Kirwan RM   *Boyle*
'The potato disease is rapidly progressing. At least one-eighth of this crop is   CSORP 8503
now destroyed and the weather continues very unfavourable to it.'
5 September. Report of the Resident Magistrate   *Castlerea*
'The disease in the potato crop in my district has increased to such an extent   CSORP Z.8666
that the late crop is completely gone and only half of the early crop is fit for
food.'

Saturday 9 September. Mayor to T. N. Redington   *Sligo*
'An American ship came to this port and her crew, Americans, deserted her,   CSORP A.8985
took their sea chests out of the ship in defiance of their captain. The captain
complained to the consul who ordered the sailors to go on board their ship,
which they refused to do. The American consul then applied to me as Mayor
but I do not know to what extent the civil power is justified in assisting a foreign consul.'
Reply, 18 September: 'There does not appear to be any law on this subject.'

Ballinrobe
CSORP H.92452

Saturday 9 September. Rev James Anderson, vicar of Ballinrobe, to Under Secretary
'A case of asiatic cholera has appeared in Ballinrobe workhouse. Harrison is the man's name. Dr Twiss showed me the case and stated that it is as well-defined a case as he ever saw. The man is ill since the night before last and is of course in a most dangerous state of collapse, his arms and hands as blue as indigo ... In the event of a further case appearing the proper steps should be taken to ensure as far as possible the safety of the town.'

Castlebar
CSORP A.8838

Saturday 11 September. James Wynn to Lord Lieutenant
'In the winter of 1846 two young boys, Patt and Michael Finan, were employed by the Board of Works to break stones by piece-work, not by him who was engineer and overseer, but by Hugh Hannick. The mother of the boys summoned him to appear before John Symes JP for the wages of the boys but the jury dismissed the case and exonerated him. He was summoned again by the mother to Ballina Petty Sessions, which again dismissed the case. Summoned a third time, he was convicted behind his back and a warrant against his goods and chattels is now in the hands of the constabulary.' *Wynn requests the Lord Lieutenant to order a re-hearing.*

Swinford
CSORP W.8929

Tuesday 12 September. Board of Guardians to Lord Lieutenant
'... our surprise and regret at the appointment of a second county surveyor to Mayo at a moment when the ratepayers are undergoing the worst severities from the visitation of God and are quite unable to bear even the present pressure of taxation, much less any increase to it, and on the part of the Union and all classes in it, we request Your Excellency to postpone this appointment for the present.' (*See Appendix 1M*)

Ballinrobe
CSORP C.11841

Wednesday 13 September. Courtney Kenny JP to T. N. Redington
'I trust I shall be excused in expressing an anxious hope that at the next meeting of parliament the Irish Poor Law will be revised so as to render the law a benefit and a blessing to the country, instead of being, as it now is, the ruin of Ireland, serving none but the innumerable paid officials, demoralising the people, encouraging idleness, the promoter of every evil habit, crushing industry, perpetuating poverty, destroying the industrial resources of the country and rapidly confiscating every man's property.'

Swinford
CSORP Z.9284

Saturday 16 September. Report of Capt Hanley on potato crop
'The disease is rapidly progressing and is as bad as it was in 1846. Of 46 Irish perches on the workhouse site, the yeild was only 2 cwt of sound potatoes.'

Saturday 16 September. James Gallagher, Hawksford, to Pat Dougherty, Hawksford

'I hereby give you notice that I require you to deliver up to me on Thursday 25 September, the quiet and peaceable possession … of the house situate at Hawksford, parish of Kilcolman, which you hold as tenant from week to week and at will and that in default of your so doing I will proceed against you for the recovery of the possession of said house … Take notice that I do this day distrain your goods and chattels for the sum of one? pound sterling, being the amount of 52 weeks rent owed to me as your landlord … The particulars of the above distrain are as follows: one frieze yarn, one loom and warping bars, one box, one spinning wheel, three stools and a creel, a quantity of woollen yarn, two reeds, two saucepans, one pot, one bowl, one pair of stockings.'

25 September. Patrick Dougherty to Lord Lieutenant:

'He was an under tenant for two and a half years and was a weaver by trade. On 16 September a party came to his house, viz. his landlord, James Gallagher, and his assistants, Pat McDonogh, Martin Regan, Martin Gallagher and John Frain … and by force and violence broke his loom and took same with sundry articles. He requests the Lord Lieutenant for justice and immediate relief as some Indian meal, the support of the sick in his family, was taken away. The parties were summoned to the Petty Sessions but there was no magistrate.'

4 October. George Knox RM to T. N. Redington:

'I did not hear his case at Ballaghaderreen Petty Sessions as I was engaged in enforcing Poor Rates at Doocastle on that day. I have given him a fresh summons for Saturday 7 October and his case will be heard on that day.'

Thursday 21 September. George Knox RM to Capt Wynne, Poor Law Inspector, Boyle

'The small force of my district are completely exhausted and fatigued, watching your hay at Doocastle since Monday and falling asleep on the roadsides from hunger and fatigue, some of them being 20 hours on duty … Unless you either remove the hay early this day, or dispose of it in some manner, I must permit the police to return to their stations, as in fact their lives would be in danger from what they are suffering were they to remain longer in their present position, and besides, the stations of the district are stript of men and the entire duty of it neglected since Monday … Unless you come out and make some immediate arrangements, I must withdraw the men, both for the safety of my district and of their own health.'

22 September. Capt Wynne to Poor Law Commission:

'I only required a patrol of police for the purpose of protecting our keepers. I have employed every carrier I could induce to take service in order to relieve

Ballaghaderreen
CSORP A.9304

Tubbercurry
CSORP O.9258

the police as soon as possible from their duties. I have made every exertion in my power to prevent the law being defeated and to set a salutary example. Yet failure and the most injurious consequences as regards the future collection of the rates must follow the withdrawal of protection, before the entire of the property shall have been carried away. About 25 tons have been already brought to Boyle.'

23 September. Poor Law Commission to T. N. Redington:
'The hay referred to therein has been seized for non-payment of Poor Rate on the property of Joseph Myles MacDonnell of Doocastle and the Commissioners have reason to apprehend that if the collector should be baffled in his efforts to enforce payment in that quarter, the effect on the general collection of that rate in that portion of the Union in which Mr McDonnell resides will be most injurious.'

Claremorris
CSORP A.9335

Monday 25 September. Michael O'Shaughnessy JP to T. N. Redington, outlining the case of James Fahy, evicted by William Bourke and Pat Meeny, bailiffs of the landlord, Pat. C. Lynch, Clogher House
'The plaintiff claimed £10 for the loss and injury sustained by him in consequence of the defendants pulling down his house and £10 for the seizure and carrying off of his crops ... The rent was £3 a year and was not more than due when the crops were seized and subsequently the furniture, every article of which was removed. Plaintiff had a wife and infant children. They were stripped of everything ... The object of Mr Lynch was to get possession of the house, which was near his own residence, to throw it down. While plaintiff's wife and children were in the house and refusing to leave it, the defendants and several others, the servants of Mr Lynch, tumbled down the house and thus expelled them. I gave a decree for £14 and £6, the value of the crops. In my judgement, I publicly characterised it as a most unjust and cruel proceeding.'

Mayo
& Sligo
Transactions p.421

Wednesday 27 September. Report of James Perry and Edward Barrington to Society of Friends
'We went on 18 September and for the ensuing four days visited, with the exception of the farms in the Attymass district ... all the farms under cultivation for the Committee in the counties of Mayo and Sligo, amounting to 30 and comprised within an area 14 miles long and 12 miles broad.'

Keash
SFFP 2/506/18

Wednesday 4 October 1848. James Fleming, Abbeyville, to Bewley and Pim
'Having seen an advertisement in the papers stating that the Society of Friends had in contemplation the project for establishing model farms through Ireland ... I should with pleasure accommodate you with land for

that purpose on moderate terms in this locality, on which there is a roomy comfortable dwelling-house and offices. I could accommodate you with any quantity of land from ten to sixty acres.'

Friday 6 October. Houston Steward to Commissioners of Customs

Blacksod
CSORP O.10166

'I have visited the north-west of Ireland and inspected with much care and consideration that part of the coast where the acts of piratical plunder were committed previous to the middle of the month of October last year … The arrangements and disposition of the coast guard on shore and the emirgers? afloat, which were then determined upon, have been most effectual, not one single act of piracy having taken place since the emirgers took up positions on the coast and the three boat crews were stationed at the point of Blacksod Bay, on the island of Iniskea and at Port na Franck. The boat crew on the island of Iniskea in particular is most important, as being advanced in front of the other parts of the coast, from which the plunderers were in the habit of issuing … If the inhabitants of this part of Ireland can be induced voluntarily to forsake their habits of plundering … it will be necessary to maintain a boat crew on this island and at Blacksod for years to come.'

Saturday 7 October. Henry G. Douglas MD to Colonial Secretary, announcing the arrival in Sydney of 203 Irish female orphans

Sydney
CSORP O.4203

'… Some of them were early abandoned to the unrestrained gratification of their desires and some boast of the prolific issue of their vices … About 56, known as the 'Belfast girls', were not landed in Sydney, as it would assuredly lead to their final ruin. They were sent into the interior where there is a great demand for servants and have all but one obtained situations. Of the others, they were all rapidly hired and most of them by persons resident in Sydney or its immediate neighbourhood.'

Evidence of Dr Douglas before the Orphan Immigration Committee, 12 October:

'There were 40 or 50 who have been by their own admission of the lowest class of society at home … They have frequently charged each other with being public women and two or three have even gone so far as to state that they have given disease to various persons … They used the most abominable language and actually fought with each other. On Friday 16 June, about 1pm I was called by one of the girls to quell a fight below. I found two fighting, one armed with a fork, with which she threatened to take the life of the other. I ordered her immediately to be placed on the poop; this led to an absolute revolt amongst the Belfast girls who demanded her release. This I refused and they threatened to rise en masse (the Belfasters) and release her. The captain assisted me and the row was quelled. The girl remained on the poop alone. In an hour I spoke to her and on her expressing her sorrow in tears, I told her to go below, which so soon as the Belfasters saw her, they cheered. I immediately ordered the girl back and explained to her fellows that I would not permit the slightest manifestation of approval or disapproval of my conduct. I therefore ordered her back for which they have only to thank themselves. They were cowed and in less than half an hour, I sent the culprit back to her dinner.'

Dublin
CSORP Z.9861

Wednesday 11 October. Resolution of the Irish Catholic bishops
'That we contemplate with grief, anxiety and alarm the impending famine and the miseries which another year of destitution must necessarily entail on an already impoverished people, many of whom will inevitably perish, if some general and comprehensive measures for their relief be not adopted without delay … We implore the government to take all such other steps as the alarming condition of the country demands, to employ for the immediate relief of the poor all the resources at its disposal … A notice has been given of a parliamentary motion regarding state provision for the Catholic clergy of Ireland. We deprecate such a proceeding. That having shared in the prosperity of their faithful flocks, the clergy of Ireland are willing to share in their privations and are determined to resist a measure calculated to sever the people from their pastors.'

Straide
CSORP O.9887

Tuesday 17 October. James McNulty NT, Straide National School, to Lord Lieutenant
'This school is in constant operation for the last nine years, during which time the attendance of the pupils has been pretty fair and also paid the trifling salary charged to them till this present time, and now that the attendance of pupils, together with the refusal of salary, is totally declined, owing to the badness of the times and particularly the poor of this parish are almost starved from hunger, which renders them incapable of sending their children to school or paying the salary or schooling, makes me suggest to your Lordship, if there be not provision afforded to them and the salary increased by the Commissioners of National Education to exempt the poor from any salary from themselves to the teacher, I rest in doubt this school will be shut up.'

Keash
SFFP 2/506/18

Saturday 28 October. Abby Fleming, Abbeyville, to Society of Friends
'Unless timely relief be afforded hundreds will die of starvation in this neighbourhood … I could not give you an adequate idea of the appalling misery that exists but it far exceeds other years. For their resources are all exhausted and the failure of the potato this season has given a fatal blow to their prospects. Many of the poor householders so let their beds and furniture to enable them to purchase seed which is now gone.'

Winter 1848-49

The War of the Rates

The government decided after the disastrous harvest of 1848 that any relief provided would be the responsibility of local taxation and the rates were to be the main means of financing it. Many of the ratepayers were themselves in financial difficulties and were facing ruin on account of the rates. 'So oppressive is the poor rate,' Rev John Garrett told the Society of Friends, 'that a host of the better sort of farmers are daily emigrating to America.' If Garrett, who was himself a rate defaulter, had not his clerical duties to discharge, he would have emigrated with them. The vice-Guardians in Ballina believed that striking a new rate in the Union would cause many of the farming class to sell their property and emigrate. Richard Bourke, the Poor Law inspector, stated that this taxation has brought all classes to the verge of ruin and queried whether the experiment of making property support poverty should be continued in the west of Ireland. 'I have no doubt whatsoever,' he declared, 'that such an experiment must ultimately fail and I therefore think it would be most cruel to persevere in it.'

But the government did persevere in it and a virtual war broke out between the ratepayers and the collectors. In Keash a crowd of 50 to 60, armed with sticks and stones, threatened the life of the collector early in November, if he proceeded. The collector in Loughglynn and Frenchpark had to be escorted with a force of cavalry and infantry, amounting to 360 men as well as 100 policemen. Early in January a virtual battle took place in Coolavin when the collector and his men were attacked and severely beaten. It was deemed advisable to desist. Summonses were issued, but the summons-server was unable to serve them, being met by large mobs. Such violent incidents continued during the spring and summer of 1849.

Ballaghaderreen
SFFP 2/506/34

Thursday 2 November 1848. J. A. Holmes to Bewley and Pim
'I feel much obliged by your remembrance of me in your grant of clothing. It will be very acceptable indeed, as there are but too many objects of it.'

Ballymote
SFFP 2/506/34

Friday 3 November. Rev J. Garrett to Bewley and Pim
'Since our correspondance commenced, death and disease have been busy in our family. Our son and our daughter died and another son lay in fever for several days and is only now well ... You may be assured that to the poor miserable widows and orphans any surplus has been given ... I gave no clothes that were not made up.'
5 November. Same to same: 'Our peasantry never were in a more lamentable state both as to food and raiment ... The potatoes are already nearly finished. There is no employment for the labouring classes and so oppressive is the poor rate that a host of the better sort of farmers are daily emigrating to America. The poorhouse will be soon filled and the outdoor relief swamp the landlords who would in other days give labour and clothing.'

Swinford
SFFP 2/506/18

Wednesday 8 November. G. V. Jackson to Society of Friends
'I hope a market is open at Swinford poorhouse for the purchasing of some of your crops. Yesterday I was there and the Poor Law Temporary inspector, Bourke, and the medical officer authorised me with the Board to send a ton of carrots, a ton of parsnips and a ton of swede to make a beginning. The medical officer recommends the use of these vegetables for health and the Guardians desire to have vegetable soup substituted for milk which is both scarce and dear. The existence of these crops in the country at this dreadful time is quite a blessing. I hope the Ballina Guardians will follow our example.'

Westport
CSORP O.11072

Thursday 9 November. Memorial of landed proprietors, clergy, gentry and inhabitants of the Union to Lord Lieutenant
'A more terrible famine than any we had to contend with, even during the last three years of suffering, is now imminent and is already staring us in the face ... The potato crop has proved almost a total failure ... Without food of any sort, with rags scarcely sufficient for decency and yet, in this sad and sickening plight, numbers are being daily legally banished from their wretched cabins to live or die as the case may be without anyone to care for them.'

Kiltimagh
SFFP 2/506/18

Thursday 16 November. Rev Brownslow Lynch to Society of Friends
'No part of their last grant to the Union of Swinford has been received by me for distribution in the parish of Killedan. I wrote to Col. Jackson and Capt Hanley ... The former stated that this food issue is thro' the relieving officer in the electoral division and to apply to him ... The relieving officer is strictly

enjoined to allow relief to none but the destitute. The relief afforded by your Society extends to the sick poor, convalescents and young children ... Your Society's grant of biscuit and rice has relieved 206 families, averaging in family five souls, commencing 28 July and lasted four weeks from that date.'

Friday 17 November. John Duffy, Uggool, to Lord Lieutenant   *Kilmovee*
'Petitioner is a poor man with a family of four. He has no land or mains *(sic)*   CSORP O.10759
to support them (except by) making some oaten meal and retailing it again.
In June last he brought some meal to sell at Ballaghaderreen market. David
Keys, inspector of weights, Castlebar, took his weights to have them stamped
and had him summoned. He was fined the enormous sum of £2 3s. 6d. On
16 November Keys took his only one cow and has her in the pound at
Ballaghaderreen and she is to be sold by auction on Tuesday next to the
destruction of himself and his family. Petitioner asks Your Excellency to order
Capt Kelly, sub-inspector of police, to liberate his cow and order an investigation of his case at the Petty Sessions in Ballaghaderreen.'

Monday 20 November. John P. Waters and P. Comen, vice-Guardians, to Poor   *Ballina*
Law Commission   CSORP O.11964
'We owe at this moment nearly £13,000 ... and obliged to pay cash for every
article. Two contractors, Mr Gallagher and William Malley, have started legal
proceedings to recover £5,346 ... Striking a new rate would tend to cause
many of the farming class to sell off their property and emigrate.'
Observations of Mr R. Bourke re above, asking 'whether the experiment of
making property support poverty is to be continued in the west of Ireland. I
have no doubt whatsoever such an experiment must ultimately fail and I
therefore think it would be most cruel to persevere in it ... This taxation has
brought all classes to the verge of ruin. Another rate would have the effect of
banishing every solvent tenant from the Union and completely ruining the
majority of proprietors.'

Tuesday 21 November. Bishop T. Murphy, chairman, Children Apprenticeship   *Adelaide*
Board, to Colonial Secretary   CSORP O.3081
'219 females orphans arrived on 23 October on the *Roman Emperor.* All of
them, except one who is sick, have found a situation. Unfavourable reports
were circulated about them as being insubordinate during the voyage and as
being an inferior class of their kind and one newspaper described them as 'a
rough lot'. Five members of the Board visited the ship on arrival and were
well satisfied with the appearance of the orphans. They were clean and orderly
and did credit to the surgeon and matron in charge. The emigrants are as useful a class as could have been sent to this colony ... The orphans should be

sent out between 1 June and 31 October to be gradually prepared for the effects of the hot weather ... Three instances occurred in which the Board removed girls from their situations, five in which the girls and their mistresses did not agree, and several others may possibly happen ...

The wages are as follows:

14 - 15 years, £5 p.a.

15 - 16 years, £6 p.a.

16 - 17 years, £7 10s. p.a.

17 - 18 years, £9 p.a.

18 - 19 years, £10 p.a.'

CSORP O.3081   *29 November. H. E. F. Young to Earl Grey*

'On 24 October I reported the arrival of the ship, *Roman Emperor,* with Irish orphan emigrant girls, without any deaths after a voyage of 91 days ... 14 days after the arrival, not one orphan was unemployed. The Children Apprenticeship Board recommends 300 to 400 young females to be sent to the colony during the year ... The early and satisfactory disposal of the Irish orphan girls is the more gratifying, as that desirable result was endangered by unfair reports of the character and discription of these emigrants which came from England and at first prevented the colonists from engaging the girls, until the first 20 who entered into service conducted themselves so creditably as to create a feeling as much in favour of the emigrants as it had been before adverse.'

Keash   *Wednesday 22 November. Sworn statement of Richard Fleming, poor rate collector*
OP 21/473   *of Toomour electoral division*

'... having been threatened in a very violent manner by a large crowd of persons at Templevanny and Brogher, 50 to 60 in number, armed with sticks and stones, on 1 November, not to attempt to collect or destrain for the rates, that they would take his life.'

Ballina   *Thursday 23 November. A. J. Campbell, Melrose, to Poor Law Commission*
CSORP O.11306   'I propose to take a farm of 100 acres in Ballinglass and to bring over a Scottish agriculturalist to manage it, who shall employ several labourers and train active young persons as agricultural scholars ... It will greatly benefit the surrounding population ... by introducing a better method of cultivating the soil to put the poor people beyond the reach of a continually recurring famine ... There is such a panic here about the ruinous nature of the Irish Poor Law.'

Castlerea   *Thursday 23 November. James Auchmuty to Poor Law Commission*
CSORP O.11113   'On Monday, 20 November, accompanied by the resident magistrate with a

force of cavalry and infantry, comprising 360 men together with 100 police
to protect the Poor Rate collector in distraining for rates due in the electoral
divisions of Loughglynn and Frenchpark, I had procured by great exertions
10 horses and carts from Roscommon, a distance of 18 miles ... We met no
opposition and found the houses closed up and the cattle in every case locked
up. When the collector proceeded to fill on the carts the corn he had distrained, in most cases they then came forward and paid the amount and in
all other cases they gave cattle for sufficient value sooner than let the corn be
removed. I brought 20 paupers from the workhouse to assist in loading the
carts. They performed the duty most willingly ... The large force we had ...
put an end to the decided opposition we experienced on a former occasion
... I hope that such a display will not be necessary on any future occasion.'

7 December. Report of James Auchmuty
'I went to Ballaghaderreen and on Monday, Tuesday and Wednesday, accompanied by Mr O'Connell RM, with 100 infantry and 100 police and 20 soldiers of the Scotch Greys. We commenced to enforce the rates in the electoral division of Artagh; only for the large force we had, we would have met
with the most determined opposition. In all cases the people had their houses
closed up and not a head of cattle to be seen. The only thing we had to distrain was their oats. The moment the collector commenced to remove their
crops, they paid in almost every instance. The last two days we were out, the
people had their corn removed into their houses. We had nothing to distrain
but straw. On Wednesday the people pulled down the bridge of
Carnacrewan. After some trouble we got the carts over ... The troops were
out each day from 9 o'clock in the morning till night. From what they suffered from bad weather the resident magistrate thought it prudent not to
proceed to other electoral divisions until next week.'

Thursday 23 November. Report of vice-Guardians   Westport

CSORP O.10999

'It is painful to contemplate the melancholy prospects of the approaching
winter in this Union, which we fear will far exceed in destitution any that
preceded it ... The mortality in the workhouse amounted to 20 in two weeks
... 16 of these were children, the majority of whom had been recently admitted, some of them affected by disease and others much reduced in strength
by want of nourishing food and sufficient clothing.'

Monday 4 December. Number of female orphans, aged 14 to 18 years, sent to   Emigration
South Australia from workhouses
'Boyle, 30; Castlerea, 20.
The total number to be sent out is 2,500. 1,233 remain from 42 other Unions.
200 will be selected from 10 Unions for the next ship due to sail on 1 March

1849 and a vessel will be sent out at least once a month until the 2,500 shall have been sent out.'

Ballavary
CSORP A.11610

Thursday 14 December. Patrick Kelly to Lord Lieutenant
'Petitioner was summoned to the Petty Sessions of Ballavary as he was found fishing with a candle and a spear in the river of Balinscana on the night of 17 November. He was find £2 and seeks a fresh trial as he has a long helpless family and never was known to fish this twenty years back.'

Templehouse
SFFP 2/506/34

Monday 18 December. Miss Perceval to Society of Friends
'The district around Templehouse is inhabited by numbers of the very poorest clas who are totally unable to purchase clothes … I am induced at Capt. Gilbert's suggestion to apply to the Society of Friends in the hope of their sending here a grant of clothes.'

Ballymote
SFFP 2/506/34

Tuesday 19 December. Rev J. Garrett to Bewley and Pim
'I am almost the only resident gentleman in the barony of Corran and the six electoral divisions around me are nearly in the same state. I called on a gentleman on Monday last, whose estate ought to produce £1,000 a year, and he is unable to pay the poor rate and apprehensive of arrest if he goes outside his door. The workhouses are full and outdoor relief, in a shamefully small form of ration, is doled out to creatures who walk many miles for it and are often sadly disappointed. But sickness and death surround me and if I had not clerical duties to discharge, I would emigrate with the body of my best conditioned parishioners, who are gradually leaving Ireland. If your most benevolent Society can spare me a grant of provision and clothing at this most inclement season, it will help save the lives of some who are sick, weak and naked.'

Killasser
OP 21/521

Wednesday 20 December. Police report
'Michael Monaghan, a poor labourer, was assaulted by Bridget Ginty, alias McNulty, when returning from a wake on 11 December. About 1 o'clock in the morning Monaghan went into the house of Martin McNulty to inquire after his step-brother, Pat McNulty, whom he heard was drinking in the house, and on entering the door, Bridget Ginty hit him a blow on the head with a loy … She fled to Aslington where her husband is labouring. Michael Monaghan died on 20 December from the effects of the blow. The jury returned a verdict of wilful murder and a warrant was issued for her arrest.'

Monday 25 December. Thomas Thompson, sub-inspector, to Inspector General
'On Sunday morning, 24 December, at 10 o'clock, as J. Delaney, J. Cordukes, J. Wilson and H. Caldwell were returning home, they heard some women crying in a house and at the same time they met the Revd O'Neill, one of the Catholic curates, accompanied by a person named McLoughlin, who is his clerk or sexton. Delaney inquired of them what was the matter and the latter replied that they had been whipping the girls in that house. Delaney then said that it was most shameful and unmanly conduct or words to that effect. A scuffle then ensued between McLoughlin and Delaney, upon which O'Neill came up and knocked down Delaney with a loaded weapon, broke three of his teeth and gave him two or three cuts on the hands. He also knocked down Cordukes and gave him a most severe cut on the cheek. Wilson and Caldwell were also knocked down and received cuts on their hands. I believe those parties were to some extent intoxicated upon the occasion. The mayor was at once called upon and he has taken bail for Mr O'Neill's appearance. No investigation has as yet taken place owing, I believe, to Delaney and Cordukes being unable to leave their houses. Mr O'Neill, I believe, escaped unhurt on this occasion. He has been in the habit for some months past of going through the streets at night and visiting houses of bad repute and whipping any unfortunate females he may meet. He has assaulted many of them very severely. He has also placed some of them in a house in which he supports them. He was thus employed when this occurrence took place which has caused a great deal of excitement and angry feeling, particularly among the lower classes, who appear very much incensed against the parties in question. Mr O'Neill's removal would appear to be very desirable. All the reputable inhabitants appear to disapprove of the means he is adopting to reform the unfortunate females.'

5 January. Same to same: 'The case was investigated by the magistrates at the Petty Sessions here on yesterday … There was very great excitement and angry feeling exhibited by the people who assembled in and about the courthouse and indeed in all parts of the town. Messrs Delaney and Cordukes had to be escorted to their houses by a large force of police, who had much difficulty in protecting them from the violence of the people who followed them through the town, hooting and shouting at them. Several small stones were thrown at them which struck some of the police but did not injure any of them. The professional person employed by Delaney was also struck with a stone when leaving the courthouse. I had him escorted safely out of town.'

28 January 1849. Memorial of Alderman Cordukes, John Delany, merchant, Henry Caldwell and William Wilson to Lord Lieutenant regarding the assault by Rev James O'Neill on Christmas Eve as they were returning from the house of a friend where they had been passing the evening.

Sligo
CSORP A.517

CSORP A.985

CSORP A.2852   *3 February. Martin Dillon Manning JP to Court of Chancery*
'The meeting in the parish chapel on Sunday 21 January 1849, where he acted as chairman, was for the sole purpose of according their approval of the exertions of the Revd James O'Neill in the cause of morality and good order and to rescue his character from the very unfounded and slanderous attacks which appeared in the Sligo, Dublin and several London newspapers ... Mr O'Neill briefly described the very immoral condition of the town before he commenced his exertions to promote morality and good order and for that purpose he established a Magdalen asylum at his sole expense to shelter and reclaim the victims of vice and seduction, and in consequence of which a subscription was then commenced at the said meeting to aid these laudable exertions and for that purpose solely ... It is not true that the collection was made for the purpose of defraying the expenses of the forthcoming trial.'

CSORP A.2852   *5 February. Henry O'Connor JP to Court of Chancery:*
'The meeting of 21 January was held for the purpose of approving of the conduct of Rev James O'Neill in establishing and supporting at his own expense for several months an asylum for the reception of females of abandoned character whom he reclaimed from vice ... Subscriptions were raised to support the Magdalen asylum which the Revd Mr O'Neill had founded here and in which at his own expense he up to that had supported and kept employed upwards of 20 unfortunate females whom he succeeded in reclaiming from the abandoned life they previously led ... Rev Mr O'Neill distinctly swore that he did not lift a hand until he was seized by the throat by Alderman Cordukes.'

CSORP A.2852   *13 February. Court of Chancery to M. D. Manning JP, re the resolution passed at the meeting of 21 January, proposed by Henry O'Connor JP and seconded by James Tighe*
'That whilst we cannot find words to express our regret and astonishment that persons have been found in our town so forgetful of the respect due to a clergyman as to make an unprovoked assault on the Revd Mr O'Neill for the purpose of deterring him from his most laudable mission, we must also thus publicly express our surprise and indignation at the calumnies on the conduct of the Reverend gentleman, so industriously circulated by the press of a faction either not knowing or culpably concealing the true particulars of the case.'
'The Lord Chancellor desires an explanation as to why Manning, as one of the magistrates before whom informations were taken, took part as chairman of the meeting.'

CSORP A.2852   *21 February. Henry O'Connor to Court of Chancery*
'At the meeting of 21 January it was communicated that a conspiracy was known to exist for a considerable time for the purpose of waylaying and assaulting the Revd Mr O'Neill whenever he appeared in the streets at night

IMPORTANT
Public Meeting.

Rev. J. O'NEIL

The Inhabitants of Sligo,
AND ITS VICINITY,

Being anxious to record their approval of the
exertions of the Rev. J. O'NEIL, in the cause
of Morality and Good Order,

A Public Meeting
WILL BE HELD FOR THAT PURPOSE,
IN THE

Chapel Yard,
ON SUNDAY NEXT,
THE 21st INST.,
At Two o'clock precisely.

Sligo, 19th January, 1849.

Gibson, Printer, Sligo.

Poster for the meeting
of 21st January

or endeavoured to dissuade young females of abandoned character from a life
of prostitution and that young men were to be armed and dressed up in
female attire for the purpose of engaging his attention while others were to
collect round to waylay and beat him … We did express disapproval that a
portion of the public press should, by representing the conduct of an individual, seek to slander the Roman Catholic priesthood as a body.'
*SligoJournal, 9 March. Report of the trial, the Queen v. Rev James O'Neill. 7
March**

'Mr Keogh, prosecuting counsel, addressed the jury. "Is it to be said that the
follower of Him whose feet were washed by the sinful and erring daughter of
Eve, is to stand with lacerating whip over the disfigured form of woman –
miserable victims of man's caprice – poor sufferers and receivers of His commiseration? Can the spirit of manhood tolerate the affliction of a dastard torture upon their writhing forms? I trust a voice would go from this jury box

* I am indebted to John C. McTernan for this item.

proclaiming to the world, that the highest bishop in the land shall not dare with impunity to strike the meanest prostitute or to violate those laws which in protecting we protect ourselves …"

The jury retired and in a few minutes returned a verict of guilty of common assault …

Alderman Cordukes said that he believed he had the concurrence of Mr Delaney in saying that he hoped his Lordship would pass but a nominal sentence. Judge Baron Lefroy said he felt the greatest difficulty in yielding to the wishes of the prosecutor and that he would take till tomorrow to consider. … The Revd James O'Neill was then bound to appear at nine o'clock to receive sentence on the following morning.

This morning (9 March) at nine o'clock the judge took his seat and after hearing what the prisoner O'Neill had to say, sentenced him to nine months imprisonment, saying, if the indictment had been properly framed, he would have been compelled to transport him.'

3 April. Court of Chancery to M. D. Manning:

'The proceedings have now terminated in the trial and conviction at the late assizes of the Revd Mr O'Neill, for the assault on Alderman Cordukes and the sentence of imprisonment thereupon pronounced by the court. From the verdict of the jury, as well as the evidence given on that occasion, there was no colour of just foundation of the allegation contained in the resolution of the meeting of 21 January that an unprovoked assault had been made on the Revd Mr O'Neill.'

Swinford
CSORP 0.12240

Tuesday 26 December, Board of Guardians to Lord Lieutenant

'We humbly beg that Your Excellency may be pleased to direct that the collection of the Labour Rate in this Union may be postponed some time longer in the hope that our resources may be recruited and we may be thus enabled to discharge this equitable demand without adding to the sufferings of the locality, even now under the greatest pressure and embarrassment. Whatever decision Your Excellency may be pleased to come to on this subject, we shall ever entertain the most lively feelings of gratitude for the favours we have already received at the hands of Your Excellency.'

Tubbercurry
CSORP 0.497

Tuesday 26 December. Declaration of Robert Navin, relieving officer, re death of Ann Kearns

'I visited Ann Kearns who lay sick of fever and gave her provisional relief on 18 November, where she lay in Cloonaraher and at the same time proffered her a cart to carry her to the fever hospital. She refused doing so. I sent a boy to request of her to go. She refused secondly. She died some time after and had two shillings in the hands of Michael Gormanly, which was expended on

her burial. I provided a coffin for her; her death was not reported to me until the evening before the inquest was held on her.'
Extract from Guardians' minutes:
'The poor woman had in the hands of a friend two shillings, still remaining of a sum of £2 received some time back on being turned out of her holding. She was a married woman but her husband was not living with her.'

Thursday 28 December. Memorial of ratepayers of Coolavin, signed by Patrick Lynch JP, Peter Brennan PP and 248 others, to Lord Lieutenant
'On account of the present most distressed situation of this district, it will be impossible for them to pay the rates about to be collected … Had they the means to meet those demands at present, they should never make this application … They will be hereafter most willing to meet those demands aided by Providence.'

Gurteen
CSORP A.96

Saturday 30 December. Patrick McHale PP to Lord Lieutenant
'The alarming state of the physical and social condition of this parish from the progressive tide of destitution, forces me to direct your attention again and again to the sufferings of the people for whom I am interested as a pastor … Though dark the picture then, it is much darker and more gloomy at present. The constitution of man is not framed to resist the violence of hunger, without the shelter of a roof, or raiment for the body to bear against the cold and pelting of the storm. Hundreds and hundreds of individuals and families in this electoral division are thrown on the world's wild waste, unheeded and unrelieved, who have no employment, no quarter acre, no house, no clothes to protect them from the inclemency of the weather, nothing under heaven save the light of day and water … Is a person under 14, or in other words able-bodied, under such circumstances to get relief or be neglected as an improper object? I don't see why the life of a widow or orphan is preferable or of more value to Queen or country than the life of an able-bodied person.'

Miltown
CSORP O.551

7 January. Report of Capt Farren:
'The object of Revd McHale is to obtain more extensive outdoor relief in Addergoole electoral division … A stream of able-bodied persons from every electoral division is constantly passing through the workhouse and numbers of the same class ruled on board-days for admission to the workhouse, do not avail themselves of the relief afforded therein, the assistance desired by those persons, and indeed the majority of applicants of all kinds, being outdoor relief and not an asylum in the workhouse.'

CSORP O.557

Kilmaine
DDA MURRAY PAPERS

Sunday 31 December. Edward Waldron PP to Archbishop of Dublin
'On Christmas Eve the sherriff, with horse and foot soldiers, police and a posse of well-paid men came to evict 48 poor tenants and levelled their houses. These people are now wandering about the roads. There is no room for them in the workhouse and they sleep in places not fit for pigs. It is terrible to see how men are treated by their fellow-men.'

Erris
CSORP 0.440

Tuesday 3 January 1849. Report of R. Hamilton
'The collection (of rates) hitherto has been very unsatisfactory ... principally by the inability of the ratepayers to pay their rates ... I applied to the vice-Guardians (Ballina) for clothing and various articles which are indispensably necessary for the Erris auxiliary workhouse, but their finances are in such an embarrassed state and they are so completely solvent, I fear they will not be able to forward the articles required ... The expenses of the district amount to £200 weekly and everything will shortly come to a standstill unless funds can be provided.'

Coolavin
CSORP 0.747

Sunday 8 January. Capt Wynne, Boyle, to W. Stanley
'A considerable force of military and police under the direction of Mr Knox RM assembled on yesterday morning at 10 o'clock in the electoral division of Coolavin for the purpose of affording protection to the collector in the execution of his duties. Mr Hall accompanied by 25 men arrived in the district at an early hour in the morning, taking with them carts and carriers to remove corn and other property which might be distrained during the day. The moment Mr Hall and his men were discovered, the whistle was raised and large crowds assembled from the surrounding hills. About 8 o'clock Mr Hall and his men were attacked and severely beaten. Mr Hall was able to reach the police barrack not far distant. The police at once accompanied him to where the assault had taken place and succeeded in arresting two of the assailants. During Mr Hall's absence, the carmen had been attacked and beaten and could not be induced to proceed further. At this period a most determined effort was made to rescue the prisoners when Mr Knox arrived with the military and, not without some difficulty, secured the prisoners and marched them into Ballaghaderreen, where informations were lodged by the collector and the prisoners bound to appear at the next Quarter Sessions to take their trial. From the determination of the mob to resist to the uttermost and the insufficiency of the force present to effect the purpose for which they were assembled, without having recourse to the use of their firelocks, as also from the absence of the means of carrying away any distress which might be made, it was deemed advisable to relinquish further proceedings on the occasion and withdraw the force, a proceeding against which I should have

strongly protested, had I been present, but the necessity of writing a report before I left Boyle and 13 miles over the worst road in the country, necessarily delayed my arrival till after this step had been decided on and put into execution. I fear the consequences will greatly increase the difficulty of putting down the combination which exists in that district, as everywhere the people claimed a victory over the law and stated to me their determination to persevere to the uttermost in the course they had adopted. I think nevertheless, if we could procure carts that could be depended on, that the next time the result would be more satisfactory. With regard to the proceedings against the parties engaged in the previous assault on the collector and his men, summonses were issued but the summons-server was unable to serve them, being met by large mobs and obliged to return. The summonses however have been handed to the police. Several of the collector's men have been severely injured and I fear can scarcely be induced to enter his service again. He himself has escaped tolerably well and acted on the occasion with great firmness. Before another day can be named it will be necessary to secure the services of carriers as otherwise the proceedings must be futile.'

Sunday 8 January. C. J. Latrobe to Colonial Secretary, Sydney
'Upon the arrival of the vessel *Lady Kennaway* ... all unauthorised communication with the vessel was prohibited. The married emigrants were landed at once and sent into the immigrant depot in order to facilitate their entering into engagements without delay. The orphan girls were detained on board for four days in order that when landed they might be fully prepared for immediate service if called for ... The following day the Board having met, the orphans were all formally inspected and divided into two classes ... The older girls were allowed to enter into engagements in the ordinary manner, on suitable application being received. The younger were allowed to hire under a condition that a regular act of apprenticeship should be entered into ... In a few days the whole number was satisfactorily disposed of ... Very general approbation has been expressed with their character and capabilities.'

Port Phillip
CSORP O.7152

Monday 16 January. Deposition of Michael McDonnell, relieving officer, re death of Bridget Doyle
'She was an illegimate child living with her mother, who is, as he believes, a wandering beggar. He was never applied to by deceased Bridget Doyle or her mother for outdoor or indoor relief or any person on their behalf.'

Collooney
CSORP O.1809

Wednesday 18 January, meeting of the Catholic clergy
'The vast majority of people waste away with hunger, cold and destitution ... The manner in which those called 'able-bodied poor' are treated is cruel and unmerciful beyond description.'

Castlebar
CSORP Z.972

Ballintubber
CSORP O.1361

Wednesday 18 January. Threatening notice served on James O'Brien, relieving officer

'James O'Brien parish officer in Ballintubber I notice you by these few lines to change your way with the poor of that parish and to give them relief as they are entitled to get and immediately to do so or if not by the Holy Mass Book the first opportunity that will be got of you at your house, Ballintubber, Castlerea, Roscommon or any other place I meet you, I will give you Major Mahon's* breakfast to keep you from future hunger. So if you put us to it, this oath will be performed by one or more of us.'

Castlebar
CSORP O.773

Tuesday 24 January. Report of Capt. Farren

'Weekly rate collected, £455 3s. 1½d. which exceeds by more than £150 the highest amount ever collected in one week. 1,062 applicants for relief, 157 admitted to the workhouse, 287 placed on outdoor relief, 618 rejected or did not appear, 157 discharged from the workhouse. Total on outdoor relief, 8,601.

A revision of outdoor relief lists was completed for all the electoral divisions. Advertisements were placed in the local newspapers giving the place, date, day, and hour of the meetings of ratepayers in each electoral division and notices were posted in the electoral divisions. Lists of persons receiving relief were printed and distributed and people were asked to give information on abuses. This duty has been a very laborious one to the vice-Guardians, and the close confined places in which the meetings were held – many of them were cabins – added to the proximity of the crowd of destitute creatures, recipients of relief, numbers clad in rags and covered with bed quilts and blankets, taken probably from a bed of disease, made it doubly difficult. ... Attempts at imposition and simulated circumstances of distress are so cleverly contrived and mixed up with cases of such extreme destitution, that the relieving officers cannot in all cases detect them ... The number of persons objected to by the ratepayers being trifling (372 only) when it is considered that since 29 September 1848, a period of little more than three months, there were 17,873 applicants for relief.'

Capt. Farren gives details of a meeting held in Straide electoral division on 8 November 1848 attended by 12 ratepayers. 131 were struck off the outdoor relief list which totalled 711.

* Major Mahon of Strokestown House was allegedly murdered by the Molly Maguires in 1847.

Spring 1849

Increase in Mortality and Cholera

Mortality in 1849 reached a new peak. There were more deaths in Connacht that year than in either 1847 or 1848. It was estimated that almost 45,000 deaths occurred, some 2,000 more than was estimated for 1847. In the Ballinrobe workhouse there were 27 deaths during the week ending 3 March and this had risen to 42 by the end of the month and 52 by mid-April. 336 deaths were reported in the Ballinasloe workhouse early in May. Cholera made its appearance in the western Unions in March. It reached Ireland from Britain and was first detected in the seaports. Westport was particularly affected. By early July the workhouse there reported 80 deaths during the previous week, over half of which were from cholera.

The Gregory Clause continued to take its toll among the small landholders. 'Very many of them are clinging with desperation to their tenements,' it was reported from Swinford in April. Some, like Pat Roache of Straide, clung on just too long.

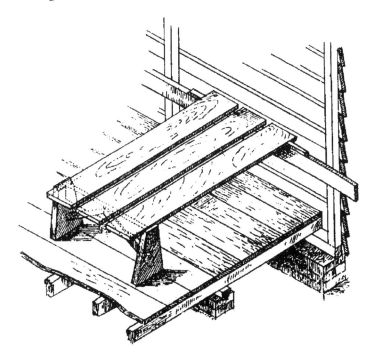

A workhouse bed

Ballinrobe
CSORP A.1119

Friday 2 February 1849. John M. Sheridan to Lord Lieutenant
'I visited Ballinrobe workhouse and found in the storeroom all the measures and a weighing machine incorrect. A half-pint measure, used in issuing rations to the paupers, is short of the quantity it should contain. The gallon measure used to receive the milk from the contractors is nearly a naggin or a gill too large and as the daily supply is over 400 gallons, the contractor is at a daily loss of about 50 gallon.'

CSORP A.2467
21 March. Poor Law Commission to T. N. Redington:
'A charge was made at the Petty Sessions against the vice-Guardians and master of the Ballinrobe workhouse, of using false weights and measures.'

Castlebar
CSORP O.1762

Wednesday 7 February. John Hogan to Frederick Cavendish published in the Connaught Ranger
'On Sunday last, while walking up Gallowshill in this town, my feelings were appealed to on behalf of a poor family (Michael Mullany's), four in number, actually dying of starvation within a few acres of the so-called workhouse …
I entered the miserable hut and on the cold earth on a handful of old straw I found two children lying, the mother also sick, but struggling to sit up, watching by her children … I supplied them with the price of food for that day and the next. The poor father with tears in his eyes declared to me they had not tasted food since the previous Friday morning, save one halfpenny worth of raw turnips.
I asked him why he had not been relieved by the vice-Guardians. He said he knew not. He attended the meetings of the Board on the two previous Thursdays and on the latter day was ordered off, being 'an able-bodied man'. Why, the father, wife and two children would not, I am sure, weigh ten stone … I purpose calling upon the relieving officer to bring them again before the Board on next review day, when, if not passed by the Gods of the Star Chamber, I shall have their Mightinesses summoned before the magistrates to account for why they would starve this family to death.'

Castlerea
CSORP Z.1325

Monday 12 February. Memorial of Hugh Flannery to Lord Lieutenant
'I served 8 years and 90 days in the 88th Regiment and was present at all the campaigns and engagements that my regiment was in during the late Peninsular War, which was 10 general engagements and 12 skirmages *(sic)* and am at present a parish charge without the benefit of a pension or any other means to support nature … My parents being dead and having no property, I was obliged to work journey work at the weaving trade until I lost the use of two fingers of the left hand 8 years ago and was begging since.'

CSORP O.2258
Vice Guardians to Poor Law Commission, 27 February:
'Flannery's wife is in the habit of going about the country as a fortune-teller and in that way earns a considerable amount.'

Thursday 15 February. Memorial of merchants and traders to Lord Lieutenant
'The Union owes them a total of £10,198 10s. 10d.
Hugh Gallagher & Son, £1,400, W. Mally jr, £4,176 12s. 3d., Geo. S. Mally, £1,218, John McAndrew, £2,695 13s. 5d., James Duffy, £273 17s. 8d., Robt G. Baxter, £94 7s. 6d., Messrs Mally & West, £340.
Poor Law Commission to T. N. Redington, enclosing memorial of Hearne & Joynt, Ballina merchants, complaining that they are owed £2,883 9s. 7d. out of a total of £4,720 10s. 1d., for Indian meal supplied to Ballina Union from 30 September to 31 December 1848 at £11 a ton. The Poor Law Commission considers that there are many cases in which the parties, who have contracted in some distressed Unions, have much more to complain of than Messrs Hearne & Joynt.

Ballina
CSORP O.1457

Tuesday 20 February. Report of Capt Farren on rate collection
'The opposition is passive in its nature, the people are most civil when the cattle are safely housed and the doors shut … No sooner does the collector arrive, than as by magic people are seen on all the heights and his approach is thus telegraphed from village to village, so that, save when those rated are really honest and inclined to pay, the collector's time and money are quite lost … Local magistrates are unwilling to act … In nearly every electoral division rescues of what was seized for the rate have taken place and the offenders remain unpunished … Much of the land is waste and many have not the means of discharging their liabilities.'
27 February. Report of Richard Bourke, Poor Law inspector:
'The resistance to the payment of rates shown by several proprietors of high position, and the strong feeling of opposition to the Poor Law manifested by the higher classes, have undoubtedly a powerful influence upon the farmers and encourages them in the opposition they are naturally but too well inclined to offer to the collector of any tax … On my way from Castlebar yesterday morning, I passed one of the collectors accompanied by his bailiffs and escorted by police, and in a very short time afterwards, I was overtaken by a person driving in a gig at a violent pace and accompanied by two servants, one armed with a double-barrelled gun. This person moves in a respectable class of life and his residence is situated a short distance from the roadside … As I was passing it, I observed the farm servants and others driving their master's stock into the farm offices where they were safely under lock and key upon the arrival of the collector.'

Castlebar
CSORP O.1763

CSORP O.1959

Thursday 22 February. Sworn evidence before Capt Hamilton
'Eleanor Ruane was an inmate of Ballina workhouse before 10 June 1848 when she was placed on the outdoor relief list for Kilgarvan electoral division and continued to receive it until 12 August 1848 when outdoor relief to per-

Bonniconlon
CSORP O.1689

sons of her class was stopped. On 29 September she again applied and received a ticket for the workhouse which she declined. In October, four or five weeks before her death, her sister stated that she applied again. She died on 9 January 1849. Rev Bernard Egan stated at the inquest that on that day he sent a note to William Crean, relieving officer, stating that there was an urgent necessity for immediate relief but, because of some differences Crean had with Egan, he refused to receive his communication and no relief was given.'

Poor Law Commission to vice-Guardians:
'They consider this act of the relieving officer extremely reprehensible, as whatever were his personal feelings, he was bound in duty to receive and give attention to a letter from a clergyman addressed to him as relieving officer. They suggest that the vice-Guardians dismiss Crean.'

Ballina
CSORP O.2061

Monday 26 February. Report of Capt Hamilton
'I never remember to have seen so many beggars in Ballina as there are at present and so many wretched looking people wandering about the Union, begging and plundering. They do not generally belong to this Union. They have probably come here on account of the allowances to paupers being better, I believe, than in either the Sligo or Westport Unions. They are generally offered relief in the workhouse but prefer begging. The police do not interfere, as far as I can see, in the slightest degree to check the nuisance.
R. Bourke's observation: 'The Vagrant Act cannot be enforced in the west of Ireland without increasing the gaol accommodation three or four-fold. Petty crime is fearfully on the increase.'

Swinford
CSORP A.2190

Monday 12 March 1849. Memorial of Eleanor Byrne to Lord Lieutenant
'Her husband John a yearly tenant had been summoned to make him give up possession, before Mr Knox and Mr O'Malley who sat on the bench in this town. They done (*sic*) me the greatest injustice. They issued an order to the police who brook (*sic*) in my door forcibly and illegally threw myself and my effects on the street in the absence of my husband. My landlord being a man in business keeps a book account with one of the said magistrates ... I am lead (*sic*) to understand, that was his inducement to act illegal and contrary to law.'

CSORP A.2638

16 March. Edward Deane JP to T. N. Redington
'Michael Durkan was charged on 26 January last by Charles Todd Gilmore, excise officer, with carrying a tub containing pot ale out of a house, where the private making of illicit whiskey was carrying on. Defendant's solicitor, Charles Bourke Jordan, contended that the defendant could not be convicted under the act. The magistrates sought the advise of the Law Advisor and received an opinion in favour of the accused and dismissed the case.'

Saturday 17 March. Investigation of the death of Charles Durkan, Carnaghlough
'He was admitted to the workhouse on 8 February. Mr Ward, agent to Mr Thompson, stated that Durkan had land. Durkan was discharged from the workhouse on 14 February. He applied for relief but was refused until he showed a certificate that he had given up his land. On 28 February he gave up the land, was given 14lbs of meal and died the following day.'

Bonniconlon
CSORP O.2937

Sunday 18 March. Inquest on Thomas Hopkins, Cloonieron, presided by Richard O'Grady, coroner of Co Mayo
Evidence of Bridget Hopkins: 'Thomas Hopkins was my husband. He died on the night of Sunday last in his own house … he was complaining of a pain in his heart for about three weeks before his death but used to be up every day and about the street and used to go to the neighbours' houses and continued to do so until Wednesday last, two days before his death. He was complaining of weakness for the last three months but more particularly for the last three weeks before his death. I heard him say that his weakness was caused by insufficiency of food. Deceased and I had five children living with us, making in all between deceased and myself a family of seven. We had no land, only the cabin we live in. We had no tillage the last year, nor any other earthly means of support, except what we got by the relief meal. Deceased and I and all our family were in the Swinford workhouse for a week last year and for a fortnight this year. The last time we were there, we were discharged on outdoor relief and we were getting 2 stone of meal in the week, after we were so discharged, from Redmond Costello, the relieving officer. When I was getting 2 stone of meal in the week there was no allowance for my two eldest daughters, not being allowed as adults by the Board, but at a later period they were allowed and after we got 3 stone of meal in the week for about four or five weeks. The relieving officer, not having got the necessary supplies, I got in one week but 2 stone of meal and the week before the deceased's death, we got but 1 stone, in consequence, as I was informed, of the meal being robbed off the carts in coming to the relief stores. The deceased, myself and the children were weak from hunger, while we were curtailed in the meal as aforesaid, but we never had any cause for complaint against Redmond Costello, relieving officer, for he always gave us what we were entitled to. The Wednesday week before deceased's death, he, deceased, left his own house about dinnertime, to go to the market of Bellaghy to buy ½ stone of meal, that he had got the price of from Hugh Regan of Uggool. He, deceased, went only 40 or 50 perches from his house when he returned in a weaker state than when he left the house and he told me that he met something strange, having some appearance of a human being, which he believed to be Death, and which desired him to return home and that he had not long to live. In my

Kilmovee
CSORP O.3141

opinion, the want of sufficient food was the cause of his death.'
Evidence of Andrew Dillon MD: 'I have examined the body of the deceased
... From the appearance, I am of the opinion that his death was caused by
want of sufficient food.'

Lahardane,
Ballina
CSORP O.3581

Tuesday 20 March. Inquest on the death of Anthony Moffitt, Culnakillen on 5 March
Evidence of Ellen Moffitt: 'On the Tuesday and Monday neither my husband
nor myself had any food whatever. It was the same on the Sunday. On
Wednesday I went to Lahardane to Mrs Bourke to see whether I could get
meal on credit until such time as I could get the price of it, but she had it not
in the house but gave me a quart of meal. I made gruel of it and my husband,
myself and my family partook of it. We had no other food on that day. On
the Thursday there was no food of any kind in my house. Neither myself nor
my husband nor my children had any food on that day. Mary, my daughter,
19 years old went out and endeavoured to get 6d. for a gown of hers, but
nobody would purchase it. On Friday I got a stone of meal from the relieving officer early in the morning ... I owed 2 quarts of meal to Kitty McNulty
and I went and paid it. The moment I brought home the meal I made it into
two meals for my family on the Friday and the rest into one meal on the
Saturday. On Saturday I made this into gruel and my husband and family
partook of it. This was breakfast time. Neither my husband or my family had
anything more that day. On Sunday, the day before my husband died, he had
no sustenance and myself and my family had nothing except some nettles
which I boiled.'

Ballinrobe
CSORP A.2966

Saturday 24 March. Report of Mr Lucas, Poor Law inspector
'The master reported at a meeting of the vice Guardians on Thursday last
that a pauper boy, named Edward Murphy, had been arrested by the police
at Hollymount for having absconded with Union clothing but the magistrates at Ballinrobe Petty Sessions on 19 March refused to punish him and
sent him back to the workhouse ... As the practice of absconding with Union
clothing is carried to an alarming extent in the Ballinrobe Union, the refusal
of the magistrates to convict in the case in question will most assuredly tend
to increase this description of robbery.'

CSORP A.2966

9 April. Statement of Ballinrobe magistrates:
'At the Petty Sessions held on 19 March a boy, Edward Murphy, was convicted
on a charge of absconding from the Ballinrobe workhouse with the Union
clothes. The boy appeared so extremely destitute and so very sickly, the magistrates feared he would not survive transmission from here to Castlebar if
committed and they then directed him to be brought to the workhouse with
a written request that he might be admitted.

The magistrates have convicted and punished in several instances for this offence and abstained in doing so in this solely from the miserable and sickly appearance of the accused.'

Monday 26 March. Thomas Gallogly, governor of Mayo Prison, to T. N. Redington   *Castlebar*
'Eight convicts made their escape from this gaol at about 3 o'clock this morn-   CSORP G.2599
ing. They effected their purpose by breaking the locks of their cells, making a rope of their bed ticks and by placing a form against the outward wall. Had not one of the party succeeded in concealing himself from the turnkey and thus avoided being locked up, the parties could not possibly have left the prison, the cooperation of a person outside the cell being indispensable. That great neglect of duty is attachable to the turnkey already alluded to is unquestionable, and I have to add that on being made aware of the unfortunate circumstance, I had a diligent search made. Notice was given to the police and mounted men despatched to Westport (from which district four of the convicts had been committed) and to Belcarra and I am now about going to the High Sheriff of the county with a view to reporting on and requesting an immediate inquiry into all the circumstances of this case.'

Monday 26 March. Memorial of Michael Keane, Shroove, to Lord Lieutenant   *Coolavin*
'On 22 March William Hall, Poor Rate collector of Coolavin electoral divi-   CSORP A.2590
sion, accompanied by the military and constabulary and George Knox RM made a seizure of his cattle … The rates chargeable against him had been previously paid by his landlord, J. A. Holmes, his valuation being under £4. His sons refused to allow their property to be illegally taken away by a parcel of fellows, in number about ten or twelve. A riot commenced and he and his children were beaten by Hall's assistants in a most brutal and savage manner. They were arrested, conveyed to Ballaghaderreen and kept there in their gore of blood that night and part of the next day. They were obliged to find bail to abide their trial at the quarter sessions of Ballymote.'
31 March. George Knox RM to T. N. Redington: CSORP A.3184
'On 22 March I proceeded with a military force thro' a mountain road as far as was practicable for them to advance, but Mr Hall, the rate collector, requiring to go to a holding about a half mile in the mountain, I gave him Sub Inspector Galway and twenty of the police force to protect him. In about an hour he returned with six prisoners and stated to me, that Mr Hall's assistants, seeing some country people running off with cattle, ran after them and in doing so advanced a short distance from the police: that he followed them as quickly as possible and on coming up found Michael Keane and his two sons and the other prisoners engaged with Mr Hall's men and, that only he arrived so quickly, he believed there would have been murder. I then, in the

presence of Col Tennant and Sir G. Hawpen of the Scots Greys and the other officers, confronted Mr Hall's men with the prisoners and their statement was that the prisoners, having shut up the cattle in their houses, then followed them with loaded sticks, stones and pitchforks and identified Pat Scanlan and John Keane as the persons who stabbed two of them in the body (which wounds they showed us at the time) and persisted in beating them until the arrival of the police saved them ... They took the names of four of the prisoners for summonses and liberated them and they brought the other two who used the pitchforks to Ballaghaderreen, where they were kept for the night in the police barracks ... I bailed them to the Quarter Sessions of Ballymote. Regarding Keane's memorial, Mr Holmes is the instigator of the entire matter and that memorial was written by his clerk ... I have never had to bring the military to any part of the district but among his tenants.'

4 April. Same to same:
'William Hall has resigned his situation as collector for the Coolavin district and is now the 4th collector who has ineffectually endeavoured to perfect the collection of the rates in that locality during the last twelve months.'

CSORP A.3681   *2 May. Same to same:*
'The case of Michael Keane and others against William Hall, Poor Rate collector of Coolavin and the case of Hall against Keane for assault were adjourned at Mullaghroe Petty Sessions yesterday.'

Costello barony
CSORP W.2589   *Wednesday 28 March. Memorial of the contractors of the public works in the barony of Costello to Lord Lieutenant*
Patrick Dougherty, Ballaghaderreen, Luke Colleran, James Fallon, Pat McGowan, Philip O'Brien, John Mulligan, Pat Rogers, James Gordon, Garret C. Dalton
'They have completed their several contracts and to complete the contracts, most of them raised money on bills in the local banks. Non-payment by the treasurer will be the consequent ruin of themselves and their families.'

Cholera
CSORP O.8338   *Monday 2 April 1849. Poor Law Commission to Sir G. Trevelyan*
'Cholera has appeared in some Unions. Can funds be advanced to distressed Unions be used for treating victims? ... Cholera is a particularly painful disease and intense suffering may be experienced by cholera patients if they are not promptly and effectually treated.'
26 May. £100 to Ballina Union and £50 to Castlebar for cholera treatment.
26 June. Cholera has broken out in Westport workhouse in a more virulent form than in the town of Westport.
4 July. £50 to Castlebar Union for cholera treatment.

Monday 16 April. Archbishop MacHale to Freeman's Journal   *Kilmaine*
'Of those numberless victims, of the most unchristian policy that ever yet   CSORP O.4024
emanated from the councils of any state that are now strewing the public
ways, I met one last evening near the little town of Kilmaine, on my way
from Ballinrobe, stretched lifeless on the side of the road, who often applied
but applied in vain, until, according to the testimony of two skeletons in
whom life but yet remained, he sunk and expired without even the shelter of
a cabin.'

Wednesday 18 April. James Nolan to T. N. Redington   *Roscommon*
'...the crowded state of the prison, in consequence of their being at present   CSORP G.7057
53 convicts confined in it, which, with the numbers committed from the sev-
eral workhouses, renders the prison incapable of accommodating half that
number. Fever and dysentery have now set in and it is of the utmost importance that the convicts should be removed as soon as possible.'

Wednesday 18 April. Capt. Whelan RM to T. N. Redington, re case of John Casey   *Coolavin*
against Mr Hall, rate collector   CSORP A.3215
'Hall's assistants had broken the lock off a dwelling house and forced open
the door. Then entering, they carried away the furniture and sold them in the
town of Ballaghaderreen. The case was returned for trial at the Quarter
Sessions of Ballymote. Casey's solicitor stated that the Poor Rate collector had
no authority to break into dwelling houses.'

Thursday 19 April. Memorial of Board of Guardians to Lord Lieutenant   *Swinford*
'Possessors of small farms are suffering the greatest, the most unprecedented   CSORP Z.3292
privations ... Very many of them are clinging with desperation to their tenements.' *(see photocopy)*

Friday, 20 April. Inquest on Dominick Hughes, Belgarrow   *Foxford*
Evidence of James Hughes, son of deceased: 'He died on Wednesday last 18   CSORP O.3727
April. He was near sixty years of age when he died. It was in a waste house
on the lands of Belgarrow, where he and his family got into for shelter about
a fortnight before his death. Deceased had five children, including himself
and his wife, making in all a family of seven. Deceased had no land for the
last three years, nor any other earthly means of support, but as deceased,
myself and two other brothers of mine got an odd day of employment and
that very seldom, at two pence a day and diet. My deceased father and his
three sons were able to work, if we had food and employment but we had
neither. Deceased and his family were often without any food to live on but
as they used to get in rooting the potato soil after the potatoes being dug

about the neighbourhood. One of my brothers had more frequent employment than the rest of us at twopence a day and for the last fortnight he had three pence per day. This earning at this wage was the chief means of support deceased and the rest of the family had. Deceased and two of the youngest of his children were in the Swinford workhouse for four or five days last year and he and all of his family, except one of his sons, were in the workhouse this year for a fortnight and three days. They left the workhouse on each of the occasions of their own free will, they being in bad health while in the workhouse, as being exhausted from hunger and weakness before they went into it. Their bad state of health in the workhouse was the cause of their leaving it. Deceased nor any of his family did not apply to the relieving officer for any relief since they left the workhouse, though in a starving state. Deceased was sick from dysentery for a week before his death. He was three days the week before his death without a morsel of food to eat except about a pint of barley meal gruel. The entire of the family, seven in number, had but two quarts of barley meal to live on the week deceased died. If deceased had food he was able to consume it but he had not. The want of food was the cause of his death. He was every day crying out for food and that he was dying with hunger. My mother is now lying in her bed, and got the last rites of the Church on yesterday, from hunger and starvation and the rest of the family are nearly as bad as she is as the jury may see by myself and two brothers now present at this inquest. He did not apply to the relieving officer since we left the workhouse until yesterday after my father died. When he was informed of our state he sent us a stone of meal, being all the food we had for the last week.'

Evidence of Michael Coghlan, relieving officer of Toomore electoral division: 'I visited the house in which he and his family were and I found them in a most deplorable state for want of clothing, food or fire.'

Evidence of Eccles Gawley MD: 'From the emaciated appearance of the body ... death must have been caused from want of sufficient nourishment.'

Verdict: 'That the deceased, Dominick Hughes, came to his death from extreme destitution and starvation, caused by his having left the Swinford workhouse of his own free will and refusing to comply with the rules laid down by the law, in submitting to the workhouse test, together with the want of employment in this country to enable himself and his able-bodied sons to earn means for their support, and to our certain knowledge there are numerous families in a similar state of destitution in this parish, living on seaweed, nettles and water cresses, in preference to giving up their little holdings of land to entitle them to Poor Law relief.'

27 April. Capt Hanley to Poor Law Commission:

'Hughes and family were in the workhouse from 1 to 20 March ... They discharged themselves and took up their residence in a wretched hovel on the lands of Belgarrow, living in the utmost misery … A coffin was sought for him. The relieving officer visited the cabin and found the rest of the family in a deplorable state, lying on straw without fire or covering, but their daily rags.'

Sligo, Saturday 21 April. Report of Capt Gilbert

Currhowna

CSORP O.3693

'Farrell McGloin left Sligo workhouse on Good Friday, 6 April, travelled about 5 miles when he reached the place of his death. His legs and feet were much swollen and he appeared in ill-health and much debilitated. He was placed in the chapel by the wayside on some straw. He received no food and from his weakness, want of nourishment and cold of the chapel, without adequate covering, he was discovered dead the following morning. He had applied to a person near the chapel to give him shelter in his house, but having stated that he came from the workhouse and appearing so seriously ill, he was refused admittance, fearing he might introduce fever amongst a numerous family of children … He died in the chapel of Currhowna.'

Monday 23 April. Vice-Guardians to Poor Law Commission

Castlerea

CSORP O.4033

'Mary King was single, a cripple and aged 65 years and is said to have been in the habit of occasionally begging through the country. After the inquest was held, the Revd Mr Coyne, Roman Catholic clergyman, caused a collection to be made and handed five shillings to two persons, Michael Hestor and Richard McNulty, to have the body interred. They, however, came to the relieving officer of Ballindine and obtained a coffin. It is supposed they have converted the money to their own use.'

Castlerea
workhouse

Turlough
CSORP O.3845

Saturday 28 April. Capt Farren's report on death of Michael Roche
Evidence of Bryan Moran, bailiff of the Earl of Lucan: 'Roche was a tenant of Lord Lucan's in a joint lease and had at least two acres and was in arrears of rent three half gales. About 10 days before he died, Moran impounded a horse for the rent. Roche and his two sons were in England during the last harvest and his two sons are there now.'
Evidence of John Moran, relieving officer: 'Roche applied for relief three weeks before he died. I told him to surrender his land. I did not see him again until the day before he died, when I was told to go and see him as he was in a dying state. It was the priest and others who informed me of this. I went to his house and found him not able to move. I said I could give him some tea and bread but they told me he could not use it. In the course of the day I caused some warm milk to be sent to him. He died shortly after.'
Surgeon Barrett stated that he died of starvation as there was nothing but fluid in his stomach.

Ballina
CSORP O.3576

Saturday 28 April. Report of Richard Bourke.
'There appears to be now some signs of improvement and that the alarm and despondency which has heretofore paralysed almost all exertion, seems to be giving way to a feeling of hope ... Strenuous exertions are being made by all classes to draw out the resources of the soil. More land has been sown with corn than during the past year and a very considerably larger quantity of potatoes has been planted at this early season ... and calculating upon a certain amount of turnips and other green crops being sown at a later period ... The effect will undoubtedly be felt by the labouring classes whose assistance will be required to carry on the work which has now been commenced.'

Straide
CSORP O.3844

Monday 30 April. Report of Capt Farren on the death of Patt Roache of Knocknakillew
'On 19 March John Gordon, Rathslevin, Bohola, bailiff to Colonel McAlpine, stated on oath that Roache could not have been less than 50 years old and he had several children grown up. He held land in Ballinaculla under Colonel McAlpine, in a joint lease by 28 persons originally, but divided into 10 parts last spring, each having about 12 or 13 acres, and Roache held one part. Gordon offered 10s. to Roache and the other tenants to give up possession but they would not altho' they owed 5 years rent.'
Michael Shanly, Poor Rate collector, Straide electoral division, stated: 'On 2 March I was proceeding to my district to collect rates and when I got to the place where the party of paupers were working between Ballavary and Turlough, I was informed that a man was lying by the roadside in a dying state. I went to the spot and found a man as described with two boys with

him. I could not procure a barrow at the nearest house and therefore sent to the working party and had one brought with some of the men. I desired the men to take the man I found by the roadside and had him conveyed to the house formerly occupied by the late Revd Paul McGrail PP. I there caused Mrs Sweeny, the wife of the owner, to prepare some tea and biscuit for the man, which I saw done, and Mrs Sweeny took it to where the man was. I also left three shillings in money with Mrs Sweeny and desired her to let him want for nothing … As an officer of the Union, I considered it right to afford relief, the relieving officer not being present.'

The verdict of the jury at the inquest was 'died of starvation'.

Summer 1849

Smallholders and Evictions

Famine continued to gnaw its way upwards through the social classes. By now the cottier class had been largely decimated and it was now the turn of the smallholders to suffer the greatest privations. As in the previous year, they made heroic efforts to crop their lands. An Ulster traveller noticed in Mayo the incredible amount of land sown with potatoes and commented: 'The man who stakes his all on the last throw of the dice, is not gambling for a more fearful stake than are these poor men, who are risking their existence and that of their families, on the next potato crop.' In June it was reported from Ballina that they were now 'reduced to an extreme point of distress'. Both Charles Strickland and J. A. Holmes appealed to the Society of Friends for a grant specifically to help this class and were duly accorded it.

Evictions continued to be carried out and those on the estates of Sir Roger Palmer in the Ballina Union were described as 'without parallel as regards the numbers evicted'. As regards cruelty they were also without parallel as many of the victims were sick families with young children lying on straw, when the roofs were stripped from their cabins. Sir Roger Palmer was an absentee landlord living in luxury. He was also a rate defaulter. He used the government grants to carry out drainage on his estates which were intended to give employment to the destitute but instead he employed comfortable farmers with good-sized holdings. Richard Bourke commented that the employment of such farmers was to insure the payment of their rents to him.

Cholera continued its ravages in the western unions. The medical officer in Crossmolina was struck down with the disease in mid-August and when attempts were made to set up a hospital there to deal with cases, the inhabitants were so alarmed they resorted to violence to foil the authorities. At the same time the number of deaths from cholera in Sligo workhouse peaked at 55 out of a total of 67.

Friday 4 May 1849. Capt Hamilton's report on the death of Thomas Murray, Tooreen.
'Thomas Murray, aged 24, and his wife, aged 24, were admitted to the workhouse on 8 November 1847. Thomas left on 8 June 1848. On 30 April 1849
Mr Duncan, vice-Guardian, saw him at Crossmolina, was much struck by his
miserable appearance and ordered him 7lbs of meal weekly … If this poor
man had remained in the workhouse, he would have been now alive … He
was found dead in a field near his own place on Tuesday morning and, as represented by the person who found him, with some of the meal in his mouth
and the remainder strewed around him.'

Monday 7 May. Memorial of William McAdam to Lord Lieutenant   *Castlebar*
'As a very humble individual, ranked among the class of small farmers in   CSORP G.3085
Ireland, I beg leave to lay my grievance before your Lordship … I have supplied the Mayo Prison with coal and straw for the last 18 months without
receiving a shilling … Now, my Lord, if this be the case, it is a great grievance to poor men, who have invested all their capital in this way, trying to
make out an honest livelihood and one who has paid all demands up to this
time. The destructive pauper, the midnight robber and assassin, the outcast
and the reprobate, are all taken care of through the generosity of the greatest
government on earth and is it possible that this very same government will
not do something for the struggling or the upright. It may be stated that the
county cess cannot be collected. If a government investigation was to take
place publicly and the High Constables were to post lists of their defaulters on
the different churches and chapels, it would throw some light on the matter
and render a service to the government and this most unfortunate country.'
24 May. J. Hamilton to T. N. Redington   CSORP G.4428
'Castlebar gaol is threatened with famine. The food contractors declare their
inability to supply any longer … Cholera has within the last four or five days
made its appearance in the prison and should there be a failure in the supply
of provisions for even 24 hours, the consequences may be fearful … I request
permission to hire two houses for the lodging of females and juvenile prisoners, in order that a portion of the prison may be allocated to the temporary lodgement of cholera cases … This would relieve the prison of about 100
prisoners, which at present contains 329 above its number.'

Wednesday 9 May. Memorial of Patt Feenaughty to Lord Lieutenant   *Ballinrobe*
'Petitioner was sentenced to 12 months hard labour, which he diligently per-   CSORP G.4096
formed and is now at freedom … He daily and every day during his confinement, went through his degrees of punishment and all the idle hours he
could spare, he was continually employed in the capacity of a tailor, in making, altering and mending clothes for six of the turnkeys and spent many a

night with candlelight to satisfy the said turnkeys. Each and every of the persons he wrought for, promised ample payment when he would be discharged.'

20 May. Report of Thomas Gallogly, prison governor:

'Feenaughty was committed to the prison in a state of nakedness. The clothing he had on was obliged to be burned and the prison dress was given to him. He did some little repairs for some of the turnkeys but of so trifling a kind, that when offered payment, he positively refused. He is now in Galway gaol charged with cattle stealing.'

Shrule
CSORP O.4233

Monday 14 May. John F. Lynch, relieving officer, to Wm Lucas, Poor Law inspector

'William Langan was arrested for having previously deserted his wife and family and was taken before Charles Kirwan of Dalgan on the morning after, 28 April, by the police, but Mr Kirwan said he would not like to act summarily in the case and ordered me to have him summoned before the magistrates at Kilmaine Petty Sessions, but before he could be summoned he left again for England.'

14 May. Wm Lucas to Poor Law Commission:

'The crime of desertion is increasing in this Union. I have instructed the relieving officers to prosecute in every instance.'

Foxford
CSORP A.8682

Monday 21 May. M. A. Little, Ballina to Sir W. Somerville

'I am the agent to the Moy fishery. The attendance of magistrates at Foxford Sessions was never good and since the death of Colonel George V. Jackson has become much worse. Our fishery has deteriorated considerably, owing to the increase of poaching ... We were obliged to employ a much larger staff to try to prevent it ... We were obliged to summon the same parties three or four times, due to the non-attendance of the magistrates. We request a resident magistrate in Ballina who can attend Foxford, Swinford, Ballaghaderreen and Tubbercurry.'

Castlebar
CSORP Z.5157

Thursday 24 May. Resolution of a public meeting

'That the condition of hundreds of families in these parishes – Castlebar, Ballyhean and Breaffy – are now on the very brink of death and who cannot obtain relief, except on the condition of surrendering both their tillage and holdings, with the heartrending certainty of never again enjoying them ... We have a most solemn duty to unite and make a last great and generous effort to preserve the lives of this meritorious class.'

Friday 1 June 1849. Meeting of the landed proprietors and farmers to Lord Lieutenant   *Ballina*
'We have accurate knowledge of the circumstances of the small occupiers of   CSORP W.4813
land and labourers and we perceive with the deepest pain the present condition of this class of our fellow creatures, who having exhausted all their means
cultivating and sowing their small portions, are now reduced to an extreme
point of distress. They have no alternative to save themselves from death but
that of accepting the degrading relief afforded from the Poor Rate, surrendering their land and abandoning all prospect of reward for their painful
struggles ... We have exerted ourselves to the utmost in providing for the
employment of the poor on our properties and farms ... No available extent
of private employment can sufficiently meet the present evil ... We are most
unwilling to see them sink to the level of paupers.'
They ask the Lord Lieutenant for the establishment for public works.

Monday 11 June. Colonial Lands and Emigration Office to Lord Lieutenant   *Emigration*
'Commissioners collect the emigrant Irish orphan females for each ship   CSORP O.4674
before they embark for identification, medical examination, examination of
outfit etc and for cleansing of themselves and their clothes. For this purpose
two depots were established, one in London and one in Plymouth. The ships
used are of a particular class found almost exclusively in the ports of London
and Liverpool. The Commissioners have a contract with steamboat compa-
nies at Dublin and Cork for conveying Irish emigrants to Plymouth. No
additional expense is entailed by the emigrants. The whole expense is borne
by the colonies and not by the country.'

Saturday 23 June. Arrest warrant signed by James Dillon JP   *Ballyhaunis*
'For John Mullany of Ballyhaunis who deserted his apprenticeship on 22 June   CSORP I.8168
and feloniously did steal a shoe.'
> "These are therefore in Her Majesty's name strictly commanding and
> requiring you and every of you respectively on receipt hereof, to appre-
> hend the said John Mullany ... and bring him before me or some other
> of Her Majesty's justices of the peace ... to be further dealt with accord-
> ing to the law and for so doing, this shall be your sufficient warrant."
'Mullany absconded from his master, Patrick Fitzmaurice, carpenter, he
being an indentured apprentice ... He is described as 19 years old, 5ft 7ins,
slender, swarthy, dark hair black eyes, large nose, with a cap, black frieze coat,
corduroy trousers, black cloth vest and from Haglehill. He is suposed to be
on his way to Liverpool where his father resides at no 48 Portland St.'
Memorial of Patrick Fitzmaurice to Lord Lieutenant:
'He had an apprentice boy, John Mullany, who was bound to him for 5½ years
to learn his art as a carpenter. He served three years and absconded taking a

part of his property ... He supported the said apprentice for three years of famine and when he knew some trade, he left him to the great loss of petitioner.'

Loughglynn
CSORP O.7396

Tuesday 26 June. Statement of Joseph Gethen, rate collector
'I went to Aghalow with my men, some of whom I had provided with guns and bayonets, more with the view of intimidating these rebellious persons and to check their opposition than for any other purpose and on my arrival at this townland, my approach being quickly announced by the continued shouting of the inhabitants, I was instantly surrounded by at least 200 or 300 persons, consisting of men, women, boys and girls with stones in their hands, and attacking my men and me, pursued us, flinging an incessant shower of stones on our persons, and thereby inflicting many wounds on the hands and bodies of my men. Myself on the occasion was struck repeatedly and tumbled over a ditch in the townland. Strange to say, all this occurred quite convenient to the police barrack at Loughglynn and the police looking on did not offer us the slightest assistance.'

New York
CSORP O.7187

Saturday 7 July. Father Matthew to New York Herald regarding his British government pension of £300 p.a.
'I assure you that nothing but the overwhelming necessities of my position could induce me to accept any pecuniary aid from the British government ... Nor need I assure you that I cannot so far forget the duty I owe to humanity to identify myself even in thought with the workings of that heartless and unchristian policy, which consigns thousands of brave and virtuous Irishmen to starvation, disease and premature death ... I would consider it the happiest epoch of my life if I would be enabled to resign this paltry stipend and once more move amongst my beloved countrymen, free, untrammelled and independant.'

Galway
CSORP A.6421

Saturday 7 July. Adverisement in The Galway Vindicator
'The splendid new ship, *Sea Bird,* of Galway, J. McDonagh, Master, 100 tons, will sail for New York on or about 7 August (weather permitting) ... This truly lucky vessel landed her passengers, all in good health, this season after a most agreeable passage of 20 days ... We are now discharging from on board the *Sea Bird* 700 tons of yellow Indian corn which we offer for sale on moderate terms.'

Mayo
CSORP A.6421

Saturday 7 July. Notes on the state of Connaught by John Lamb in The Galway Vindicator
'Mayo. It is incredible the breath of land that is under potatoes. The man

who stakes his all on the last throw of the dice, is not gambling for a more fearful stake than are these poor men, who are risking their existence and that of their families, on the next potato crop; if it fail, it will be the death warrant to thousands, who as it is, are more like walking spectres than human beings. It was very painful to me to see decent-looking women and girls, wading through drains and ditches, gathering young nettles, young docks and any other wild green plant that was not actually poisonous, for the purpose of boiling to eat ... They use anything that is possible for filling up. The last shift for them is to give up the bit of land and go into the poorhouse. The potatoes everywhere look healthy and well so far; many persons were quite alarmed by observing withered leaves but it was only the effect of frost or a cold east wind ... There are several Scotch agriculturalists who have taken farms in the West and are mostly doing well. In Mayo and Roscommon the strong men of the country were assembling in gangs to walk across Ireland, pass into England to labour in the hay and corn harvests, where they work exceedingly hard at task work, and return home with their little savings in time to cut their own harvest.'

Monday 9 July. Memorial of Denis Brogan, Largan(more), to Lord Lieutenant   *Killasser*
'Petitioner is a poor industrious man with a large family of eight souls   CSORP A.6327
depending on him for support and since the awful calamity set in, which has reduced this unhappy country to its present wretched and destitute state, had no means of support for them but a small mill, termed in this country a "gig mill", which he succeeding in erecting on a small mountain stream in an isolated portion of the country. That being a poor ignorant uneducated man, he suffered this mill to ground a few stones of grain of a distressed and starving neighbour, contrary to the law in such cases and the stream on which his mill is erected, being a tributary of the river Moy, where an extensive salmon fishery is established, the proprietors of which caused him to be summoned to the Petty Sessions of Foxford, for a breach of the laws which protect the inland fisheries of Ireland and was there fined the penalty of £1 or one month's imprisonment. Under the circumstances a distraint warrant was issued and a cow, the only four-footed beast belonging to this miserable family, was seized and canted for the sum of 15s. 6d., depriving this unfortunate family of the last resource of sustaining the load of a precarious and wretched existence ... He would gladly avail himself of the act passed for the relief of the destitute of Ireland but that in the hope of an abundant harvest, he wishes to cling to that spot, where his ancestors lived for ages back ... He humbly implores that your Excellency will be graciously pleased to direct a remittance of the aforesaid sentence.'
Draft reply, 11 July: 'His Excellency possesses no control over penalties imposed for the violation of fishery laws.'

Loughglynn
SFFP 2/506/23

Thursday 12 July. Charles Strickland to Bewley and Pim (See Appendix 6T)
'The persons now in the greatest distress are the poor but small landholders who have suffered sorely in sowing a crop and have in very many instances left themselves completely destitute and are now more dead than alive … Relief should be given in food only, from 1 to 2 stones of meal weekly to families who are not receiving poor law relief and who have their lands cropped … The poor landholders with a good crop sown is by far the most deserving object of relief and at present far the most distressed class … I have already given out 6 tons of meal as a mere temporary relief in one district … I have not thrown a house or turned out a tenant from Lord Dillon's estate in all these distressed years. A few have given up their land but are left in their houses.' *Draft reply, 20 July:* 'Remit £30.'

Coolavin
SFFP 2/506/23

Tuesday 24 July. J. A. Holmes to Samuel Darton, Society of Friends (See Appendix 6M)
'Please return my thanks to the relief Committee for their very liberal donation of £30 … I perfectly agree with them in the necessity of persons getting relief giving some return in the way of labour … I have a very great interest in Claremorris, having the management of a very large estate including all the town … I employ 150 labourers there.'
28 July. Same to same:
'With regard to the grant of £30 given to me for this district (Coolavin), I have had during this week 43 heads of families at work on their own farms under an intelligent person appointed by me. This week's work was this day inspected. They did it most cheerfully and willingly … 43 families have been supplied with enough provisions for next week's consumption. I purchased 3 tons of Indian meal in Sligo, as I thought it better to supply them with provisions than money.'

Killala diocese
SC IRLANDA
vol 29, f.212r

Wednesday 25 July. Bishop Thomas Feeney's Relatio Status to Rome.
'Before the famine which devoured the people the lay souls of all this diocese were about 131,000, of which 28% were non-Catholic. Of this almost half vanished through famine, disease, emigration and death. In the town of Ballina before the famine there were about 7,012 lay souls, of which almost 15% were non-Catholic but now from the same causes this number is hugely diminished.'

Meelick
SFFP 2/506/23

Sunday 29 July. John Bolingbroke to Society of Friends. (See Appendix 6U)
'I fully agree with your Committee that merely gratuitous aid is most injudicious and relief administered in the way you point out is sure to be productive.'

2 August. Same to same: 'I will give 20 acres of land, free from rent or taxes, and capable of producing grain and green crops at a moderate outlay. The people can be employed under the superintendance of the Practical instructor or any person you may appoint. I will contribute half the – required for the same and leave the entire crop at your disposal.'

Draft reply, 4 August: 'Remit £30 and inform him that the Committee accepts his proposal to allot 20 acres of land for cultivation by spade.'

Monday 30 July. Dean Hoare to Bewley and Pim   *Achonry*
'I shall most gladly cooperate with your Committee in relieving the distress   SFFP 2/506/23
of the poor small farmers in this neighbourhood in the way suggested in your
circular and which appears to me the best way of giving effectual relief without demoralising the recipients of your bounty.'

Autumn and Winter 1849

The End of the Blight and the Growth of Emigration

The harvest of 1849 was mostly healthy, with only isolated instances of potato blight. The same was true of the potato harvest of 1850. Favourable reports were received from Co Mayo, where many of the distressed unions were situated, for the first time since 1845. However the average crop yields still tended to fall below their pre-Famine level but in many places the Famine could be said to be 'over'. A new spirit of optimism could be detected, possibly reflected in renewed poteen-making in places like Kilmactigue. It is also reflected in the relative scarcity of archival documentation.

The enduring legacy of the Famine was emigration. An average of about 200,000 people emigrated during the years 1847, 1848 and 1849. By 1851 that figure had reached over 250,000 and it peaked in 1852, long after the potato blight had disappeared, at almost 370,000. In the following twenty years a further two million emigrated and in the sixty years after that an additional six million left. By then the great Irish diaspora was a feature of the modern western world.

Ballina
CSORP A.8427

Tuesday 7 August 1849. Sworn evidence of William Keane, Ballinclecka, Lackan
'He remembers the day on which he was put out of his house ... A notice
was left at the house in which he resided some weeks before the last Quarter
Sessions at Ballina. He does not know what was in the notice. On the day the
sub-sheriff came to the lands of Burnhill, he and four of his children were
lying sick in the same bed. Two men came into the house and wanted him
and his children to get out of their bed, as the house was to be thrown down.
The men then commenced removing the chest, pot, plates and dresser from
his house. They then desired him a second time to get out of bed and that he
would be given a house to go into. He said that he would remain where he
was until he died. Some men then got on top of the house and commenced
pulling it down while he was lying in bed. The children were shivering with
fright and got up and sat under an old wall but he remained a short time in
the bed, while they were pulling off the roof. He distinctly saw the sky thro'
the roof. Mr Palmer, the relieving officer, came in and begged him to get up
and leave the house and he at last made an effort. If he had remained he
would have been killed. He and his children were then permitted to enter
another house next door. He was suffering from passing blood ... He was on
the working party but was unable to continue. He was told that every sick
person would be provided with another house but he preferred his own house
to any other man's house. He made no complaint to anyone, nor did he hear
anything of this investigation, until warned to appear before Capt Hamilton.
He knew there was an act of parliament which allowed the houses of the poor
to be thrown down, but never heard of any act for the protection of the poor.
He knows nothing about acts of parliament.'
Sworn evidence of Michael Kennedy of Corbat-Park: 'He resided there for the
last 15 years. He was a tenant of Mr Thomas Palmer of Summerhill, who held
the lands from Sir Roger Palmer. He built the house which he resided in. He
has five children, three at service in Killala for their bit. One of them has £2
a year besides. The rest have nothing. He has two children living with him.
He is in receipt of outdoor relief and is on the infirm list. On the day the
sheriff came to his house he was in bed. He was desired to leave his bed as
the house was to be thrown down. He got up and went to the house he was
desired to go to but was refused admission. He then went back to his own
house which had been thrown down in the meantime and he put up a hut
inside the ruins where he has resided ever since with his two children.'
Sworn evidence of William Palmer, relieving officer: 'I accompanied the under
sheriff on the day on which he was evicting from Sir Roger Palmer's estate at
Burnhill ... Two men were ordered to the roof to pull the thatch off. He saw
two on each side of the roof. They took off some of the thatch and the scraws
while Keane was lying in his bed. He begged Keane to leave but he said he

was unable to do so. In his absence, Keane got up and went to another house belonging to Owen McDonnell and had nothing on him at the time but a shirt. The house was completely unroofed. There were fifteen houses unroofed on that day viz, John Toro's, Patrick McLean's, Honor Toro's, Martin Kearney's, Sarah Magee's, James O'Neill's, John Kearney's, Catherine Langan's, John Kelly's, Michael Langan's, Anne Langan's, Patrick Carroll's and William Keane's ... Keane's children were in a very miserable state ... When he next saw Keane, he was standing on a heap of straw in his shirt in McDonnell's house.'

CSORP A.9901   *Report of Capt Hamilton:* 'The principal feature in this Union during the last fortnight has been the wholesale evictions which have taken place. In almost every instance the houses of the persons evicted have been unroofed and in a few cases, which have come under my notice, there appears to have been much cruelty evinced towards persons who were suffering from disease ... I had frequently seen the family of William Keane, my attention having been first attracted by their very emaciated appearance ... I have given them since 7 July three shillings a week out of some private funds ... No words of mine can convey any adequate idea of the state in which I found these people ... Public opinion can alone have any salutary effect in such matters and from the numerous visits which have been made by the many strangers visiting the Union, to the localities in which these evictions have taken place, I have no doubt that sooner or later, the matter will be subjected to that tribunal ... On 9 July I brought Sir Roger Palmer's evictions before the vice-Guardians and sent a letter to Palmer requesting the payment of Poor Rates due by him. I got no reply. I sought to take proceedings against him in the court but this is now not necessary as Palmer's agent yesterday agreed to pay the balance due forthwith. Regarding the eviction of William Keane, no steps have as yet been taken for the prosecution of Sir Roger Palmer but if the Poor Law Commission agrees, there is ample time to take proceedings ... With respect to the evictions from the estates of Sir Roger Palmer in this Union, they are without parallel as regards the numbers evicted and I do believe that in no evictions which have as yet occurred in Ireland, could more be said on both sides of the question. On the one hand, misery and helplessness in their worst possible forms, aggravated by neglect (it is notorious that there is not a more neglected property in the Ballina Union than Sir Roger Palmer's), and on the other hand, the grossest possible provocation that a landlord could meet with.'

CSORP O.7444   *11 August. Vice-Guardians, Ballina to Capt Hamilton regarding the class of persons employed on Sir Roger Palmer's estate at drainage works, the cost of which is defrayed by a government loan.*

'They are with one exception, comfortable farmers, having good-sized hold-

ings and cattle, in some cases having money and in others, being single men or men without families. It appears that no farmer has been employed who has not paid his rent and that persons are allowed to send their hired servant, whom they have engaged for their food only, and receive the wages of such servants. It is quite clear that the farmers who are on the works have no need of employment to provide present subsistance.'
Observation of Richard Bourke: 'A vast number of good labourers are procurable in the Ballina Union, who without employment must enter the workhouse ... The employment of farmers is, in other words, the payment of the landlord's rent.'

Friday 11 August. Report of Capt Hamilton   *Crossmolina*
'On Wednesday 8 August a messenger arrived in Ballina with the intelligence   CSORP 0.7635
that Dr McNair, medical officer, was seriously ill of cholera ... Without a
moment's delay another medical officer was despatched to Crossmolina to
perform Dr McNair's duties. On Friday 10 August Mr Duncan and I visited
Crossmolina to see whether any further steps were necessary. We inspected
all the persons in the fever hospital but it did not appear to us that the state
of these persons would admit of their being put out. We then proceeded to
visit the persons stated to be suffering from cholera. There were only four
cases in the town ... Two of them were lying in a miserable cabin, on straw,
without any bed clothes whatever. Their names were Cawley (Cowley?) and
they are since both dead ... A necessity might arise for opening a hospital.
The miserable state of the town seemed to call for some provision of the
kind, notwithstanding that the feelings of several of the inhabitants were
much opposed to any building in the town being devoted to cholera purposes. Crossmolina does not afford many buildings much better than mud
cabins ... At length it occurred to me that the courthouse might be procured.
We arranged with the proprietor of the courthouse in a few minutes, procured a carpenter etc and arranged that if any fresh cases should occur, they
should at once be removed to the building. We directed that the Cowleys be
removed there immediately. Arrangements were made for nurses, bedding etc
and we returned to Ballina. On Saturday 11 August a report reached the vice-
Guardians that on the previous night a large mob had assembled at
Crossmolina, and had thrown the bedding out into the street, that the police
had been called to render assistance but had refused to interfere. I immediately proceeded to Crossmolina where a large mob gathered round me and
swore that they would never allow a hospital to be opened in the town, and
that they would do all kinds of mischief if I persisted ... The bedding was
brought back to the courthouse. I addressed the mob and told them that neither the vice-Guardians nor myself had any desire to open the building

unnecessarily ... Two of the patients that I had seen on the previous day, (viz. the Cowleys), had since died and as there were no new cases, I would defer opening the hospital, unless a further necessity should arise ... On Tuesday night I received a note from the medical officer, in which he stated that the magistrates objected to give up the courthouse ... The vice-Guardians signified their approval of another house being taken. On Wednesday 15 August I went to Crossmolina and was informed that upon attempting to move the bedding, a mob assembled and effectually resisted such a step, not withstanding that the police were looking on. It was rather late and much too wet to move the patients when I arrived at Crossmolina. Therefore I arranged to be present on the following morning. On going to Crossmolina yesterday morning, I found a very violent mob awaiting my arrival. The moment the bedding appeared it was the signal for an attack. I therefore sent for a magistrate and for the police and before a half an hour I had the building occupied with six patients. Once occupied, it was safe and the mob fled. Two of the poor persons who were removed to it were the Widow Quinn and her daughter ... I visited the cabin in which they were lying. The cabin was about 10 by 5½ft. There were three decided cases of cholera on the floor, besides four children who were lying with them. One of the cases was beyond all hope. She and her mother died in about two hours afterwards ... Two persons, named West and Keane, the former a blacksmith, were the most conspicuous on Wednesday last in kicking and throwing about the beds. They shall both be prosecuted under the Nuisances' Act. I do not understand why the police did not interfere. I think their conduct should be inquired into.'

Ballina
CSORP O.7794

Monday 20 August. Mark O'Rorke, pauper, to Lord Lieutenant
'A few weeks ago Jerry Lonagan, an overseer in the workhouse, had made a malicious attack on a pauper of the name Melody, used him to such severity that he died ... The like attack had been made by Lonagan against another pauper, Anthony O'Dowd, stuck him with a stroke of a brush under the eye, which caused him to fall to the ground and lay sprawling, but Lonagan supposed him to be scheeming, struck three times with a water bucket to hurry him away but to no purpose. His mouth began to froth, had to be carried on a man's back to the infirmary and in two days time died. Whereas on the 15th day of this present month as I, Mark O'Rourke, presented a resolution to Capt Hamilton in hopes to obtain a larger portion of diet for myself and fellow paupers, that Lonagan, on my return to the workhouse, asked where I was, I told him the truth and when he found an opportunity he confined me to the black hole, until it came to the governor's ears who set me at liberty and whereas on the 17th day of August I had been an eye-witness of a sack full of bread, rotten and blue mould, about 4 cwt had been scattered outside

the yard, which ought to have been given to the paupers that were half-starved. The valediction inflicted on the poor here is more than I can call to mind to state. People from fifty to seventy years did not get the heat of a fire for these eight weeks, dying supposed by the cholera. But I own the cholera to be large enough in Ballina. I hope your Excellency will not suffer your poor subjects to be tortured any longer.'

25 September. Report of Capt Hamilton:

'O'Rorke is the same man who wrote last month that he had lost his wife and family by cholera in Glasgow, while they were then inmates of the work-house. Regarding Melody, he entered the workhouse on 26 June, went to the infirmary on 21 July and died on 5 August. The master of the workhouse never heard of ill-treatment. Regarding O'Dowd, Lonagan threw a bucket of water on him to relieve him as he was suffering from a fit of epilepsy. O'Rorke was confined for leaving his work and going to Capt Hamilton without a pass. O'Rorke has deserted from the workhouse, leaving his wife and children.'

Saturday 25 August. Sworn statement of Mary Gilboy to Richard Bourke, Poor Law inspector

Ballina
CSORP I.7811

'Before I entered the workhouse, I lived in Ballysokeary. My father and I and my five sisters came into the workhouse about five and a half years ago. I have been ever since in the workhouse, employed in the matron's kitchen. I am now with child. Upon my oath, the father of the child is Patrick Synott. About the month of February he had connexion with me. One evening about 5 o'clock, before dark, just about the time when people would stop work, and after attending the master and matron at dinner, I proceeded to the room over the boardroom to look for my clothes. I intended to leave the house. I had not asked for my discharge but I was in hopes of getting out with my sisters on outdoor relief. I went up to the store by myself. The door was open. There were four women and the porter, Patrick Synott, in the room. I remained for about an hour looking for my clothes. At the end of that time the women went away. Patrick Synott remained behind them. It had then become dark. There was no candle in the room … about ten minutes after they went away, he shut the door. He took hold of me and offered me money. I refused and he had connexion with me against my will. He kept me there some time afterwards. I screamed and resisted. I believed there were some people in the boardroom or clerk's room. But I cannot say whether they must have heard me if I cried out loud. I never told anyone of this at the time. About three or four days after, the porter, Patrick Synott, came to me in the master's room and offered me if I would go down again with him to the clothes store, he would either give me money or marry me. I went with him.

Interior of a
workhouse

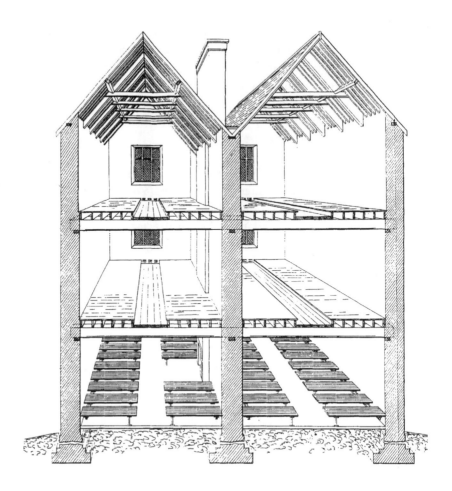

This was late in the evening. I had intercourse with him two or three times afterwards. I never told my sisters anything about this. I know a man, named Thomas Mullen. Upon my oath, he is not the father of my child, nor had he ever connexion with me.'

28 August. Richard Bourke to Poor Law Commission:

'I attended in the boardroom on Saturday 25 August. Patrick Synott (now a sub-constable in Co Meath) did not appear … I proceeded to take depositions from the young woman. I see no reason to doubt its general accuracy. From its tenor it seems clear that Mary Gilboy was a consenting party to the criminal connexion between herself and Patrick Synott and that in all probability she was influenced in her conduct by a promise of marriage on his part. In all other respects, except as relates to this transaction, the girl has borne a good character and appears respectable.'

16 August. Constabulary Office, Dublin Castle to Co Meath:
'The Commandant is requested to direct sub-constable Synott to proceed to
Ballina, where he should arrive on the morning of the 18th inst, as charges to
be preferred against him are to be investigated on that date by the Poor Law
inspector, Mr Bourke.'

17 August. Sub-constable Patrick Synott to Dublin Castle:
'It would be out of my power to attend, it being 108 miles from where I am
stationed. I could not under any circumstances be there sooner than Sunday
19 August. I would much rather that the inspector-general would grant me
leave to tender my resignation, than to give the Guardians or Capt Hamilton
the satisfaction of bringing me to Ballina for the alleged crime that I have
been accused of, for which I have been as innocent of as the child unborn.
The inspector-general may dispose of the case as he thinks fit. I request that
he shall allow me to resign for the purpose of enlisting.'

Note, 28 August:
'At the expiration of the notices required by law, the sub-constable may withdraw from the force.'

Monday 10 September. Memorial of Roger Malony, Kilmorgan to Lord Lieutenant   *Ballymote*
'He is a landholder and a ratepayer. He wishes to complain about the unmer-   CSORP O.10444
ciful, relentless conduct of the collector, Thomas Charlton ... There are
numbers of his wealthy favourites of whom he never asks a farthing till the
eleventh hour, while he goads and persecutes the poor man ... Charlton is a
man of very peculiar cast and disposition, such as are sufficient to disqualify
him from the responsible office he holds ... His demeanour towards poor
humble creatures is highly imperious and brutal; he is naturally a hippish,
excentrick and splenetick character, who renders himself disagreeable to all
classes in the discharge of his duty.'

Saturday 29 September. Sub-inspectors Michael Maher and Michael Purtill to   *Killala*
sub-inspector W. J. Fox, Ballina   CSORP I.8649
'We were on town duty on the 18th inst. and about the hour of 1 am, we
heard great noise and saw a light in the house of Thomas Townly, publican
of the town. We knocked at the shop door several times and were told to go
around to the kitchen door. We told them that it was the police and that we
would not go around. Thomas Townly came out. Sub-Constable Purtill
asked him why he had such noise in his house at so late an hour. He, Townly,
said it was a private party, and told Sub-Constable Purtill "to go and be
damned". Sub-Constable said to Townly, "Do not make use of that expression again. Go into your house and allow no more noise." We continued to
patrol the town and in about a quarter of an hour on our returning to the

barrack, we overtook Thomas Bourke, who asked was it we who knocked at Townly's door and Sub-Inspector Maher said it was. He then said we had no right to knock. I (Maher) said I did not think they were inside, that we thought it was people fighting. On coming a few paces further, I met Walter Bourke, William Walker and Thomas Meehan. Walter Bourke said to sub-Constable Purtill, "You, fellow, you had no right to knock where we were." On hearing him call Sub-Constable Purtill "a fellow", I said: "Bourke, what do you say to Purtill? You shall not abuse him. I will be accountable for any-thing he does." He, Walter Bourke, called him a ruffian and said I had no right to speak. He continued abusing me. His brother, Thomas, called sub-Constable Purtill and I, rascals several times. We told them to go off the street. Sub-Constable Purtill told them if they did not conduct themselves and not be abusing us, he would bring them to the barrack. Thomas Bourke then struck Purtill a box of his clenched fist in the eye, which swelled it severely. Purtill took hold of Thomas Bourke. William Walker at the same time caught hold of sub-Constable Purtill and Walter Bourke violently took hold of me and endeavoured to drag me. Thomas Bourke made his escape and ran to the barrack and stated to acting Constable Martin that the two men on town duty were drunk and assaulted them. We immediately came into the barrack before Head-Constable Abbott, acting Constable Martin, and several of the sub-constables. Head-Constable Abbott seeing that we were perfectly sober and not drunk as the Bourkes had stated, and on hear-ing both complaints told Mr Bourke to go home until morning. On the next morning we had summonses served on Thomas and Walter Bourke for assaulting Constables Maher and Purtill in the discharge of their duty on that night. In the course of three or four days the Bourkes had us served with summonses for assault and abusive language. 28th inst. being Petty Sessions day, the magistrates present were John Parkins and Robert Kirkwood. John Parkins being chairman, on hearing the whole case and both sides, asked Robert Kirkwood for his opinion, which he gave in favour of the Bourkes and against the police, in which opinion the chairman did not concur. Robert Kirkwood JP is married to the defendant's sister and from the feeling he evinced towards the police during the whole course of the trial, we much prefer a stranger magistrate to preside, as it is adjourned until 18 October. We hope the Inspector-General will be pleased to investigate the case.'

30 September. Sub-Inspector Fox to Inspector-General:
'I suggest the necessity of two resident magistrates being sent to Killala on next Petty Sessions day ... The Mr Bourkes alluded to are the sons of Mr Palmer Bourke of Killala, a magistrate.'

Saturday 29 September. Report of Frederick Barry, district engineer

'The labourers at first believed they were working by contract and not by day work. At the end of the fortnight when pay day came round, idlers earned 7d. a day and the good ones, 1s. 3d. At the end of the third fortnight a combination was evidently entered into by most of the labourers to try and force us to give them day work, as they thought by doing little or nothing, we would be afraid to return their names at a rate of wages below the usual rate given by the farmers etc. I only gave what they earned, in one case only, 1¼d. Last Tuesday I rode out and visited every gang and stated that I would stop the works if on the next pay day good wages were not made by each of them. I am confident the average wages next pay day will be the highest since the commencement.'

Balla
CSORP W.8472

Monday 1 October 1849. Society of Friends, extract of letters from correspondents

'Regarding the grant of £30 last August, it was divided amongst 26 individuals representing inclusive of their families 164 persons. The largest sum was £2 10s. to a family of 14; the smallest sum 10s. ... The recipients of these grants are most thankful. All were above the class of paupers and many of them had never applied for or received any relief but all were sorely pressed and to each the relief was most opportune.'

Achonry
Transactions p. 457

Thursday 8 November 1849. Whitehall to T. N. Redington enclosing

'An order of Her Majesty in council, dated 6th instant, for a form of prayer and thanksgiving to Almighty God for his mercy in having abated the cholera, to be prepared and used in all churches and chapels on Thursday the 15th instant, which Her Majesty has by her royal proclamation appointed to be observed as a day of general thanksgiving.'

London
CSORP O.9559

Monday 19 November. G. Knox RM and Richard Gethen JP to T. N. Redington

'Honor Conlon being arrested where illicit malt was found and brought before Richard Gethen JP on the following morning and was bailed to the next Petty Sessions here, when on the clearest testimony she was convicted by us and fined in the mitigated penalty of £6 or 3 months imprisonment.'

7 November. Memorial of Bryan Conlon, Flagfield, Ballyfarnan, to Lord Lieutenant:

'Petitioner is a poor man renting 6 acres of land. Sooner than see his aged wife (now upwards of sixty years) go to prison, he paid the money, all the money he possesses on earth, all the money he had for rent and poor rate and the only means he had at his advanced period of life to keep himself from penury and want.'

Ballymote
CSORP A.9901

Kilmactigue

CSORP A.10100

Saturday 24 November. Sworn statement

'Matthew Farmer, Swinford, saith he is a sergeant of the 33rd party of the revenue police and that on 22 November he was on duty under the command of Lt Todd Gilmore in the townland of Belclare in the parish of Kilmactigue ... Lt Gilmore ordered the informant with Privates Christopher Tumath, Edward Faughnan, John Jennings and Thomas Kelly to search the townland of Culdaly, also in the parish of Kilmactigue and to meet him, the said Lt Gilmore at the mill of Belclare. That the informant and the said four privates seized a quantity of illicit malt in the said townland of Culdaly and that while they were conveying the said malt on a horse and an ass towards the said mill of Belclare, the country people commenced to assemble at the sound of horns on the adjoining rising ground. That in consequence of the informant being told by the aforesaid Private Jennings, that the mob so assembled had in Irish called out to rescue the malt, the informant directed his said party to load and fix bayonets and desired the mob there assembled and still closing in, to keep back, for that if they attempted a rescue, he would fire. That upon informant and his said party arriving at the village of Letterbrone in said parish, the said mob so assembled then and there cried out that now was the time to murder the robbers, meaning thereby the said revenue party, and that thereupon the said mob, now numbering about 40 or 50 persons, poured in a shower of stones on informant and his said party and then and there attempted to disarm Privates Tumath and Kelly. When the mob were repulsed by said party with the bayonets and that informant fired a signal shot for Lt Gilmore to come to his assistance and that informant, finding he could no longer hold the said seizure, gave it up and ordered his men to run. Informant and his said party were pursued by the said mob (which had now increased to about 60 or 70 persons) for upwards of half a mile, and who called out to murder the robbers and continued to throw stones and close in on informant and his said party and that thereupon informant was compelled, in defence of the lives of informant and his said men, to order them, the said party, to fire a few shots to frighten them (the mob) and keep them off, so that they, the informant and his men, might escape with their lives and that thereupon some shots were fired by informant's men towards the said mob, after which informant and his said party ran away and were no longer pursued by the said mob ... That the two men that he now identifies in the police barrack at Aclare and who give their names as John Walsh and John Meyer, were of the mob who assaulted and obstructed the said revenue party and informant, while in the execution of their duty as aforesaid.'

23 November. G. Knox to T. N. Redington:

'An affray took place on yesterday, 22nd inst. between the party of the revenue police, stationed at Swinford, and the peasantry at the townland of

Letterbrone in the parish of Kilmactigue. I proceeded at 7am this morning to the scene of the outrage, accompanied by Mr Jones (the nearest local magistrate), and we have been engaged all day investigating the matter. There are three prisoners in custody for the attack and I have kept two of them in the police barrack here for further examination. The investigation will be continued and the third prisoner was so badly wounded in the hand, that I had to send him to Sligo. Up to this period of the evidence, it appears that a sergeant and four privates of the revenue detached on duty, had made a seizure of illicit malt and were rescued of same by a large mob of persons, were then attacked with stones and had to fire in self-defence. This is their statement. We are to hear the evidence on the part of the prisoners tomorrow.'

24 November. Same to same:
'The investigation has terminated here this day in open court and the residing magistrates, Messrs Jones, Fetherstone and myself, unanimously decided on taking informations against three of the parties concerned in the attack on the police and have bailed them to stand their trials at the next General Assizes of Sligo, themselves in £200 each, and solvent securities in £100 each according to the Act.'

Monday 26 November. Report of Poor Law Inspector Otway regarding the death of Hugh Gallagher, a poor boy in the Sligo Union
Sligo
CSORP O.10012

'The relieving officer gave him a ticket for the workhouse and offered to procure a cart to carry him but his mother delayed until too late. The relieving officer visited the boy and his mother in the house where they were lodging. When the people of the house feared he would die in it, they turned him and his mother out. The mother applied to the relieving officer but before her return, the boy had expired.'

Tuesday 8 December. Poor Law Commission to Sir William Somerville
Ballina
CSORP O.10485

'For two years, ending on 29 September 1849, payments were made to merchants by the Ballina Union as follows: George Malley, £16,513 18s. 8d., William Malley, £14,867 19s. 9d., Charles Malley, £6,108 17s. 9d. Total, £37,490 16s. 1d. Those merchants summoned the vice-Guardians for the sums that remained unpaid: W. Malley, £4,175 12s. 3½d., G. Malley, £950, C. Malley, £40.

They seized and sold all the moveable property in the Ballina, Ardnaree and Belmullet workhouses. Capt Hamilton attended the sale with a sum given him by Mr Gurney and Sir Edward Buxton to buy back what might be best calculated to prevent loss of life. He branded it with Mr Gurney's name to prevent the Malleys' reseizure.'

Dublin
CSORP H.10821

Saturday 18 December. Board of Health to Sir W. Somerville
'Smallpox of a malignant type has made its appearance and appears to be spreading throughout the country ... Out of 2,049 electoral divisions or less than half Ireland, contracts for vaccination were taken in only 989 ... The spreading of smallpox is still further promoted by the people encouraging quacks, 'inoculators' as they are termed, who spread the disease by inoculating with smallpox, to which the people will naturally resort to, when cowpock inoculation is not readily available ... Smallpox is an epidemic perhaps more to be dreaded both in its immediate and secondary effects, than either fever or cholera.'

Appendix 1: Names

Names as spelt in originals; x denotes illiterates

Achonry, 27 November 1847. List of the sick families who received Society of Friends' food from Dean Hoare and his lady.
Widow Conlon, 5, John Moran, 6, Thos Moran, 11, James Muloy, 7, William Irwin, 10, Richard Garner, 6, Catherine Shannon, 10, Martin Benson, 5, Thos Henery, 5, Bartly Gaffiny, 7, Widow Burke, 8, Widow Digenane, 5, Patt Melmour, 4, Widow McHugh, 6, Widow Healy, 4, Patt Hunt, 1, Martin Brenan, 4, William Armstrong, 3, James Hammend, 6, Widow D. Hunt, 6, Anthony Hunt, 7, Francis Mannion, 5, Andrew Hart, 6, Widow Conlon, 7, Michael May, 7, Owen Killoran, 7, Martin May, 3, Peter Bereen, 2, John Barclay, 4, George Brett, 7, Manis Moran, 5, James Flin, 7, Patt May, 1, Widow Waters, 4, Widow O'Hara, 6, Michael Scally, 5, Patt Bereen, 5, Peter Henery, 4, Francis McDonough, 7, Widow McDonough, 3, James Finan, 5, Martin Carroll, 6, Margaret Davy, 1, George Powell, 4, Francis Ferguson, 2, Mary Cuffe, 1, Nathy O'Donnell, 2, Magaret Feely, 3, Bess Armstrong, 4, James Reynolds, 5.

A: Achonry

Ballaghaderreen, 30 May 1847. Memorial of labourers and tenants to Lord Lieutenant.
Signatories: Pat Grady, Roger Grady, Michael Connor, Owen Flannery, Michael Higgins (all of Toobracken), Francis Roddy, Laughlin Touhy, Michael Moran, James Roddy, (all of Cloonlumney), David Morrisroe (Toobracken).

B: Ballaghaderreen

Ballisodare, 30 September 1846. Memorial of labourers to Lord Lieutenant.
Patt (2), James, Stephen, John (2), Denis Burns, Dominick Benson, Patt Treacy?, Thomas Gafney, Owen Minan?, Patt Finaghty, William O'Donelly, Patt Gilgan, James Lynch, Michael, John (3), Patt (2), Martin, Bryan, Bartly, & Thomas Hart, William Simpson, John & Patt Carroll, Barry Cousco?, Daniel & Michael White, James & Stephen McFadden, Michael McDonogh, Hugh Savage, James Grey, Terry Foly, Charles & John Brett, James & Thomas Sweeny, John Mathews, Robert Gallbuto?, Patt Carter, Barry McCan, James Gallagher, Michael & Edward Donelly, Thomas Hunt, John Waters, John & Thomas McCoy.

C: Ballisodare

Bohola, 12 November 1846. Memorial signed by 13 inhabitants of the parish of Bohola to the Lord Lieutenant.
Edward Deane JP, Thomas McNicholas PP, John Connolly, Henry Jordan, Patrick Hurst, Andrew McEvoy, Joseph Jordan, P. J. O'Connor CC, James English, Thomas Mullany, John Fahy, Patt Walsh, & Patt Ruane.

D: Bohola

E: Bonniconlon

Bonniconlon, 20 May 1848. List of families who received Society of Friends' food from Mr O'Dowda.

Heads of families	Age	lbs of meal per week	Rice per week
Anthony Buslawn	40	5 for 9 weeks	1 for 8 weeks
Dependants: Nancy, wife 38; Patt, 17; Mary, 15; Biddy, 12; Sally, 9			
James Rowan	38	2 for 9 weeks	1 for 8 weeks
Dependants: Biddy, wife 36			
Nelly Kerigan	41	3 for 9 weeks	1 for 8 weeks
Dependants: Charles, son 23; — 20			
Michael Loftus		6 for 9 weeks	1 for 8 weeks
Dependants: Mary, wife, 51; John, 27; Anne, 24; Mary, 20; Peggy, 16; Neddy, 14; Michael, 10			
Mary Kilroy, widow	72	2 for 9 weeks	1 for 8 weeks
Dependants: Kitty, 28			
Anthony Kilroy	48	5 for 9 weeks	
Dependants: Biddy, wife, 46; Mary, 20; Biddy, 18; Anthony, 16;Kitty, 14;Michael, 10			
Sibby Philbin	40	1 for 9 weeks	1 for 8 weeks
Nelly Mullin	60	2 for 9 weeks	1 for 8 weeks
Dependants: Thos, son, 22			
Daniel McNulty	45	3 for 9 weeks	
Dependants: Mary, 16; Daniel, 12			
— Rowane	38	3 for 9 weeks	
Dependants: Mary, wife, 38; Patt, 12; Mary, 8			
Widow Rowane	65	1 for 9 weeks	
Anthony Dowd	63	5 for 9 weeks	1 for 8 weeks
Dependants: Mary, wife, 62; Anthony, 25; Mary, 22; Martin, 16; John, 12			
William Jordan	37	3 for 9 weeks	
Dependants: Biddy, wife, 36; Mary, 10; James, 8			
Anne Mullarkey	40	2 for 9 weeks	
Dependants: Anne, 26			
Catherine Kilroy	35	1 for 9 weeks	
Richard Walsh	59	4 for 9 weeks	1 for 8 weeks
Dependants: Biddy, wife, 58; Anthony, 18; Biddy, 16; Kitty, 14			
— Kenady	44	5 for 9 weeks	
Dependants: Mary, wife, 45; Martin, 16; John, 14; Mary, 12; Biddy, 11			
Michael Clerk	52	1 for 9 weeks	
Widow Kelly	80	1 for 9 weeks	
Charles McAndrew	73	2 for 9 weeks	
Dependants: Biddy, wife, 65			
Sally Thomas	74	1 for 9 weeks	
Patt Igo	62	1 for 9 weeks	
Thomas Kinsey	72	1 for 9 weeks	1 for 8 weeks
Martin McLoughlin			1 for 8 weeks
Mary Kennedy			1 for 8 weeks
Biddy Kilroy			1 for 8 weeks
Widow Cabry			1 for 8 weeks

F: Bunninadden

Bunninadden, 14 June 1846. Inhabitants of Cloonoghill, Kilturra and Kilshalvey.
James Henry PP, John Finn CC, B.McGetrick, Thomas O'Connor, Peter Brenan, Patt
Durkan, James Truman?, Henry Boyle, Patt Gallagher, Pat O'Brien, Thomas Scanlon, Hugh
Gildea, Ambrose Cunningham, Michael Mahan, Patt Hannan, Michael Cauley, Frank
McGown, James Wynne, Thomas Marren, Owen Roddy, Thomas Marren, Michael
McGlone, Pat Devit, Michael McDonnell, Thomas McHugh, Pat Davy, Luke Mullany,
Peter Henry, Patt Cryan, James Gardner, Simon Gallerher.

G: Foxford

Foxford, 18 July 1846. Residents of the town.
Sylvester Sheil, John McGloin, John McCarrick, Samuel Stroggen, Mark Carroll, Pat Davis,
Joseph Atkinson, Pat Sheil, Pat Corly, James Coleman, Eccles Gauly MD, J. Fitzgerald, Pat
Coghlan, W.Lundy, Patt McGowan, Farrell Higgins.

23 January 1847. Memorial of the inhabitants of Foxford to the Lord-Lieutenant.
Signatories: John Corley PP, Pat Corby, Nathan Lundy, provision merchant, John
McCarrick, merchant, Eccles Gawly MD, William Lundy, Timothy Deane, Patrick
Coghlan, Robert Neal, merchant, John Gaughan, shopkeeper, Patt Conwell, shopkeeper,
Thomas Neafsy, carrier, Andrew Gallagher, shopkeeper, Mark Carroll, publican, Martin
Howley, Patt Mulhearn, publican, Samuel Stroggen, churchwarden, John McPuir?, national
teacher, John McIvor, national attendant, John Nyland, Michael Coghlan, William
Stroggen, Pat Deaves, provision merchant, Patrick Higgins, James? Thomas, Patrick Carroll,
carrier, Thomas Neafsy, Widow Fox, shopkeeper, Charles Simpson, Patrick Coleman, baker,
John McGloin, provision merchant.

H: Keash

Keash, 10 August 1846. Inhabitants of Drumrat and Kilshalvey to Lord Lieutenant.
James O'Hara PP, Richard Gorman, John Gorman, Thomas Higgins, Dudly O'Gara, John
Keelty, Peter Karny, Patt Keaveny, Patt Downs, Darby x Brehony, Bryan x Davey, John x
Dyre, Michael x Davey, Patt x Gallagher, – x Dougherty, Michael x Battle, Mark x Battle,
Bartly x Padden, Pat x Nary, Andrew x O'Doud, Bartly x McGowan, John x Kevany,
Mathew x Kilmartin, Thomas x Conlon, John Kelly, Mathew x Golden, Thos x Golden,
Martin McCormick, Patt x Conlon, John x Keelty, Michael x Davy, Thos x O'Doud, James
x Hart, Pat x Heaver, Neil x Rafferty, James x Cryan, Martin Gallagher, John x Hannon,
Luke x McGowan, Thady x Heaver, John x McCarrick, Pat x Kilday, James x Hannan,
Michael x Rafferty, Pat x McGowan, Michee Hart, Pat x Hart, Manise Rafferty, James
Rafferty, Pat x Dyer, Patt x Mury, James Galeher, Patt x Walsh, Martin Gallaugher, Patt
Gallaugher John Nerny, James Scanlon, Dominick x Breheny, James Bowls, Pat Devine,
John x Walsh, James x Hart, Darby x Millouney, James x Scanlon, Pat x Rafferty, Mathew x
Killoran, Michee x Killoran, John x Gauly, Pat x Killoran, Hugh x Tahany, Maurice
Hannan, John x Devine, Pat x Qunann, James x Caesy, Myles x Coyne, Andrew x Murry,
Mark x Kevany, James x Soden, Martin x Soden, Thos x Soden, Michael x Scanlon, Michael
x O'Connor, John x Conway, Patt x Duffy, Thos x Hanly, Thos Rafferty, John Taylor, Pat
Kelly, Pat Breheny, Michael x Cain, James x McGowan, Pat x McGowan, Michael Walsh,
Andrew Walsh, Michael x Coleman, Pat x Coleman, John x Cryan, John x Smith, John x
Smith, Michael x Conlon, Pat x Costelloe, Peter x Costelloe, John x Costelloe, Dominick x
Dolan, John x Dolan, Michael x Dolan, Mark x Cain, Dominick Keany, Thos x Dyer,
Bartly x McGowan, Thos x Kevany, Andrew x Crofton, Thos x Crofton, Henry x Crofton,
Edward x Crofton, Pat x Conlon, John x Foly, Mark x Foly, James x Foly, James x Mulligan,
John x Mulligan, James x Caesy, James x Neephin?, Bartly Breheny, John McManamay,
Dominick Breheny, Bartly Dyer, Owen Mulligan, Myles Brannen, Philip Breheny, Farrel
Cawley, Peter Cawley, Patt Breheny, Peter Dyer, Patt Breheny, Ned Kilgarriff, Michael

Kilgarriff, James Kevill, James Davey, Mick Forry, John Gallaher, Malachy Riduan?, Martin Doud, James McGowan, Patt McGettrick, John Sheridan, Michael Tansy, Charles Dyer, Thos Corcran, John Corcran, Dominick x Brenan, Bartholomew x Kevil, Thos x McManamy, Michael x McManamy, Patt x McManamy, John x Dowd, James x Doud Sr, Laurence x Keelty, James x Keelty, John Horan, Thos O'Gara, Michael x Killoran, Peter x Keelty, John x Keelty, Michael x Keelty, John Conlon, James Doud Jr, James Conlon, Patt Duffy, John x Duffy, Patt x Dyer, Michael x Kenny, Dominick x Leydon, Darby x Mullony, Mark x Leydon, Bartholomew x McGowan, John x Walsh, Peter Leydon, Thos Henry, Thos x Bowels, James x Hanan, Thos x Davy, Thos x Henery, Patt x Kevil, John x Dyer, Michael x Dyer, Martin x Walsh, John x Dyer, James x McGloin, Thos x Dyer, James x Dyer, James Duffy, Michael Gilmartin, James x Nerny, Michael x Carny, Michael Gallagher, John Henry, Maurice Hanan, John Hannan, Bryan Dyer, Patt x McGettrick, James x McGowan, John x Dowd, James Rushy, Bartholomew Mcgowan Jr, Laur Quigly, John Judge, Edward Rafferty, Wm Rafferty, Patt Meighan, James Cryan, Michael Cryan, Peter Meighan, John McGowan, Michael Davy, Michael Shiel, Owen Tansy, Dominick Dyer, John McDonagh, John Higgans, Michael McCarrick, Patt McCarrick, Patt Rafferty, Patt Bowls, Peter Dyer, James O'Gara, Patt Killorn, Owen x McCue, Denis Fogarty, Patt Mcgowan Jr, Patt Brenan, Patt Murry, Thos O'Dowd, Mathew O'Dowd, John O'Dowd, James O'Dowd, Patt O'Dowd, Dominick Kevil, Mark Killoran, John x Killorin, Anthony x Killorin, Thos x Dyer, James x Gormuly, Patt x Gormuly, John x Hanan, Patt x Hanan, James Scanlon, Patt Mulligan, Gilbert x Derigg, John x Derigg, John x Sheeran, Michael x Killorn, Dominick Healy, Thos Healy, Michael O'Connor, Martin Healy, Dominick McManamy, Andrew Gilaspy, Michael Gilaspy, Peter Kevil, Patt Gordon, Patt Dyer, Patt Keelty, Luke Keelty, Bartholomew McGowan, Michael McKeon, James Conlon, Patt Breheny, Patt Doyle, Michael Doyle, Andrew Doyle, John Gildea, John Cain, Peter Higgans, James Shannon, Peter Redican, James Dyer, Peter Doyle, Dominick Dyer, Thos Redican, Andrew Murry, Farrel O'Hara, Michael Conway, Michael Bowels, Mark Meighan,Patt Meighan, Thos Keelty, Mark Kielty, Mathew McCormick, Michael Caen, Francis Dyer, John Gallagher, Thos Cauly, Thos Judge, John Cauly, Michael Cain, John Meighan, Patt Callaghan, Michael Mulligan, Martin Dyer, James x Dyer, James x McGloin, Wm x McGloin, Michael McGloin, Patt x McGloin, Bartholomew x Donoghue, Thos x Denison, Michael x O'Dowd, John x Brenan, Peter Murry, Dominick x Dolan, Patt x Dolan, John x Dolan, Patt x Murry, Edward x Murry, John Cain, Mathew Cain, James Cain, Michael x Keaveny, Peter x Keaveny John x McKeon, Patt x Gilldea, Hugh x Gilldea, Thady x Heven, Patt x Heven, John x Heven, Andrew x Hanan, Patt x Gallagher, John x Walsh, Martin x Walsh, James x Walsh, John x Callaghan, Michael x Callaghan, Patt x Callaghan, John x Kelly, Patt x Cauly, James x Cauly, John x Keelty, Dominick x Keelty, Michael x Dyer, James x Rafferty, Bernard x Shanon, George x Cain, Thos x Coyne, Patt O'Gara, John x Killorn, Luke Golden, Patt Duffy, Patt x Murry, John x Keelty.

8 August 1846. Names to a memorial.
Francis Soden, Andrew Nealon, Hugh Bannon?, Patrick Cryan, John x Cryan, Walter Henery, Patt x Lydon, James x McGowan, John Henery, Patt Cryan, John x Mulvanny, Thomas x Mulvanny, John Henery, Luke x McGowan, Michael x McGowan, Mathew x Cryan, Michael Maddin, James x Cryan, Denis x Cryan, Edward Wynne, Patt x Kilmartin, Roger x Cryan, Michael Grey, Patt x Higgins, Thomas Higgins, Patt Henery, James x Cryan, John x Forry, Peter x Higgins, John Forry, Darby x Brehony, Patt Candon, Daniel Brehony, James Sweeny, Bryan x Brehony, John Sweeny, John x Clarke, John x Wynne, Thomas Keville, Peter McManamy, James Killoran, John Clerk, John Forry, Patt Dyre, John Cryan, John Cryan Sr, John Foly, Thomas Walsh, James Brehony, Luke O'Donnell, Widow Nealon,

Edward Kennedy, Philip Forry, Bartholomew x Wynne, Philip Mannion, Thomas Jordan,
Bryan Dodd, John x Brehony, John Quenane, Bryan Spellman, Michael Quenane,
Dominick Tahony, Bartholomew Morrisroe, Michael Clarke, John Clarke, James Clarke,
Martin x Phillips, Pat x Tahony, Barth. Taheny, James Cryan, Andrew Cryan, Martin Cryan,
James Cryan, James Cryan jr, James Cosgriff, Andrew Clerk, Patt Cryan, Roger Cryan,
Martin Mullin, James Cryan, Patt Snee, John Cryan, Michael Cryan, James Kielty, Patt
Cryan, Patt Foody, John McDonogh, Thos. McLoughlin, Thomas x Flanagan, John Cryan,
John O'Gara, Michael Conlon, Patt Henry, James Harmon, Patt Garvan, Dominick Clerk,
Daniel Cryan, Martin Nealin, Patt McGowan, Patt O'Gara, Michael Keveny, Michael Dyre,
Mathew Cryan, Martin Clarke, Andrew O'Connor, Michael McGragh, Dominick Cryan,
James Kerican, John Keasy, Michael Toolan, Michael McGowan, John x Tahony, Patt x
Mullany, Patt x Walsh, Patt x Donoher, Patt x Mannan, John O'Connor, Patt Connolly, Patt
x Connor, Patt Mullin, James O'Connor, Mark x Walsh, Patt Cowey, Mark x Dyer, Thos
Gaffney, Maurice Hannan, Thos. Kevil, Patt x Horan, Patt Dolan, Michael x McGarry, Patt
Fory, John Digenan, Mark Kerins, John x Langton, Patt x Langton, Michael x Horan,
Dominick x Costello, Peter x Egan, John x Scanlon, Edwd x Scanlon, Hugh x Cox, James
McDonough, Owen Drury, Peter x Hannan, Thos. x McGowan, Andrew Scanlon, Patt x
Dyar, Peter x Feeny, Darby x Fory, Bryan x Taghran, Widow x Cryan, Patt Kerans, James x
Battle, Edward x Crofton, John Crofton, Thos. x Henery, Michael Farrell, Andrew x
Donogher, Patt x Garvan, Batholomew Regan, Laurence x Regan, John x Regan, Andrew x
Regan, Patt Smith, Richard x Smith, Mathew x Cryan, Thomas x Cryan, Laurence x
McDonogh, Michael x Regan, Pat x Mulvanny, Michael x Conlon, Thomas x Hensy, Thos x
McCormick, Michael x Henery, Michael x Cryan, Thos x Dyer, Cormick x Gray, Widow x
Drury, Pat x Garvin, James x Fitspatrick, James x Cryan,, Pat x Cryan, Patt Gray, Thos. x
Cryan, James x Dyer, Pat x Scanlon, Michael Gray, Edward Quigley, Widow x Lavin, John x
Lavin, Owen x Lavin, John Quigley, Michael x Quigley, Edward x Quigley, John Garvin,
James Brehony, Patt x Brehony, Pat x Judge, Pat x Deavy, John x Brehony, Martin x
Brehony, Michael x Cryan, Pat x Gaffeny, James x Cryan, Thady x Mullin, Bartly x Dyer,
Michael Flanagan, Thos. Cryan, John x Dodd, Michael x Dyer, Widow x Dyer, Michael
Fitspatrick, Mathew x Lavin, James x Dolan, Michael Benson, Owen Handberry, Thos.
Walsh, John x Carrell, Bryan x Tansy, Peter x Langton, Maurice x Hannen, Pat x McKeon,
Thos. Dogher, Michael Nangle, Bartly Padon, Bartly Cryan, Pat McNiff, Pat x Horan, Pat x
Digenan, Patt Caesy, Thomas Flagherty, Martin x Cryan, Pat x Lavin, James x Lavin, Peter
Keveny, Laurence Doud, James Snee, Thomas Scanlon, John Tahany, Mathew Battle, John x
Hannan, Edward Gaffeny, Michael Mainon, Mark x Gray, Dominick Tahany, James x
Candon, Philip McGarry, Thomas Higgins, John Langan, Patt Forry, John Hannon, Widow
x Cryan, Bryan x Bryan, John McGloughlin, John Feely, James Spellman, John Walsh,
Dedly O'Gara, Ned x Gaffeny, Patt Kevill, Michael x Dyer, Bryan Higgin, Patt Duffy, John
Colman, Michael Scanlon, James x Hannan, John Young, Martin Nealon, Thos. Walsh,
Andrew Walsh, John x Caesy, Laurence x Lavin, James Duffy, Mark Kevany, Martin Clark,
James Henery, John x Cryan, John Lavin, Maurice Hannan, Mathew Gaffany, James Duffy,
James McManus, John McManus, Martin x Kielty, Andrew x Breheny, Patt x Breheny,
Michael x Breheny, Thomas Casey, Michael Underwood, James x Breheny, John x Kaviny,
Patt x Sheeran, Patt O'Connor, Thomas O'Connor, Michael Breheny, Walter Henery,
Bartholomew Tighe, Martin Tighe, Andrew Tighe, Patt Walsh, James Laven, Patt Kaveny,
Peter Kaveny, Michael White, Patt White, Owen x Nerheny, Patt x Mullin, Michael x
Hannan, James Hannan, James Noon, Michael Flynn. Michael Henery, Patt x Mullin,
Daniel White, Patt Gaffeny, Bartholomew Gaffiny, John Cain, Thomas Cain, Patt x Cain,
Patt McDonough, Michael x McDonagh, Patt x Cain, Michael x Ward, John x Cain,
Michael x Kenny, Patt x Ward, James x McDonough, Laurence x McDonough, Widow x

Breheny, Michael x Seal, Michael x Drury, James x Davey, Bryan Nangle, Francis Walsh, Thomas Walsh, John Casey, John Walsh, Mark x Connelly, Larry x Conelly, Michael x Connelly, Thomas Nangle, Patt x Scanlon, Patt Nangle, Michael McManus, Thomas McManus, James x Scanlon, John x Scanlon, Thos Scanlon, Bryan Keaveny, John x Keaveny, Patt x Keaveny, Patt Hannon, Michael Kielty, Michael McDonagh, , John Coyne, Patt Donougher, Thos x Laven, Peter Langan, Patt Laven, Patt Conlon, Bryan Tansy, Michael Devine, Robert Parkes, F. Stephen Devine, F. Maurice Devine, Michael x Hannon, Laurence O'Doud, Bryan McDermott, Michael Qunane, Patt Cunnane, John McDonagh, Andrew Hannon, Bryan x Kielty, Mathew Kielty, Mathias O'Connor, Thos. O'Connor, John O'Connor, Laurence O'Connor, James O'Connor, Michael Breheny, James Breheny, Martin Breheny, Mark Breheny.

14 May 1847. Petition of 477 able-bodied men of Toomour, above seventeen and under fifty years, to Toomour Relief Committee.

Dominick Clarke, John Hannan, Martin Nealon, Patt Cryan, Thomas Flanagan, Hugh Hannan, James O'Connor, Mathew Tuohy, Luke O'Donnell, Patt Nangle, Patt Drury, Patt Cryan, John Garven, Patt McGowan, Andrew Nealon, Andrew O'Connor, Patt O'Gara, John Dood, Andrew Clarke, Mark Keaveny, Patt Cryan, Patt Snee, Patt Kerane, James Battle, Patt Cryan, Thomas Cryan, John O'Gara, John Scanlon, Jack Scanlon, Thomas Scanlon, Farrel Conlon, Michael McGarry, Patt Conlon, John Foly, Patt Lidan, Patt McGarry, James Henery, Patt Devine, Richard McKinsy, Thomas Kevill, Edward Winn, Patt Killmartin, John Clarke, James Clarke. John Forry, John Cryan, Peter Kevill, Michael Gray, Patt Higgins, Thomas Higgins, John Clarke, Peter Higgins, Martin Clarke, John Forry, Patt Forry, John Winn, Bartholomew Kevill, Thomas Kevill, Philip Forry, John McDonough, Michael Conlon, Philip Mannion, James Sweeny, John Sweeny, Bryan Breheny, Daniel Breheny, Thomas Henery, Patt Candon, Darby Breheny, Bryan Dood, James Cryan, John Mullvany, Mathew Cryan, Michael Madden, James Cryan, Thomas Cryan, Roger Cryan, Michael Lidon, John McGloughlin, James Kielty, John Cryan, Henry Morrisroe, James Morrisroe, Patt Connolly, Patt O'Connor, Michael Horan, Martin Mallen, Bartly Cryan, John Cryan, Michael Flanagan, Neddy Crofton, Patt Walsh, John O'Connor, Patt Donoghue, Patt Hannan, Mark Kerans, Dominick Tahany, Patt Culkerin, Michael O'Donnell, Maurice Hannan, Thomas Walsh, Patt Donoghue, John Crofton, Mark Gray, Patt Cryan, James Cryan Sr, James Cryan Jr, Patt Cryan Sr, Patt Cryan Jr, Patt Cryan red, John Killoran, John Laven, Thomas Walsh, Patt Walsh, James Breheny, Michael Langan, John Hannan, Patt Hannan, Patt Mullen, John O'Gara, John Casey, Patt Casey, Thomas Walsh, Henry Morrisroe, James Henery, Thady Mullen, Michael Walsh, Patt Hannan, Thos Keaveny, Dominick Cryan, Andrew Donogher, John McDonough, John Cunnan, Patt Farrell, Michael Cunnan, Bryan Spelman, John Laven, Patt Laven, Mathew Laven, James Laven, Michael Cryan, James Garvy, John Cryan, Mathew Cryan, Patt Clarke, James Feehily, Andy Scanlon, James McDonough, Michael Gaffeny, Patt Taheran, Andy Scanlon Sr, Martin Cryan, James Cryan, Maurice Hannan, James Breheny, John Regan, Michael Regan, Thomas Sweeny, Patt Walsh Sr, Patt Clarke, Patt O'Gara Jr, John Langan, Patt Langan, James Laven, John Breheny, Thos Scanlon, Bryan Horan, Michael Hevers, Michael Keraghan, Oliver Fitzwilliams, Patt Breheny, Martin Breheny, Michael McCormick, Martin Keelty, Dominick O'Connor, Michael Cryan, Thos. Dyer, Michael Cryan, Dominick Scanlon, Mick Lavin, Michael Scanlon, Michael Gray, Patt Garvin, Michael Fitzpatrick, Thady Mullin, John Horan, Philip Forry, Michael McCormick, Hugh Scanlon, Luke Scanlon, Morris Scanlon, Andy Nealon, Michael Breheny, John Keilty, Tom Keilty, Francis Walsh, Larry Regan, James Deavey, Michael Smith, Dan Breheny, Patt Cryan, Michael Battle, Dick Smith, Michael Henery, Patt Langan, Martin Cryan, Patt Gaffeny, Mathew

Gaffeny, Patt Mullin, Patt McHugh, Dominick Morrisroe, Henry Morrisroe, Mick Killoran, James Cryan, Bryan Nangle, Thos. Deavey, Thos. McDonagh, Thos. Nangle, Martin McCormick, Patt Duffy, John Duffy, Patt Murry, Patt Gormelly, Patt Smith, Michael Regan, Dudly Gray, Thos. Golden, Luke Golden, Patt Hannan, James Conlan, Mick Killeen, Thos Horan, Mathew Cryan, Patt Higgins, Patt Duffy, Thos. Henery, Patt Dolan, Martin McGowan, Thos McGowan, Patt McGowan, James Doud, Michael Higgins, Michael Hart, Bryan Keveny, Patt Keveny, Patt Walsh, Michael Casey?, Andy Walsh, Patt Duleavy, Patt Scanlon, John Scanlon, James Conlon, Patt Regan, Michael Regan, Thos. Walsh, John O'Connor, John Henery, James Conlon, John Ginley, Mick Snee, Tim Keelty, Peter Cryan, James Doud, Patt Keelty, Thos Conlon, Michael Battle, James Killoran, Andy McDonagh, Andy Breheny, Michael Breheny, John Casey, Michael Cryan, John Lavin, John Hevers, John Smith, Thos Doud, Andy Breheny, Andy Donaher, Morris Hannon, Patt Breheny, Patt Keveny, Michael Underwood, Patt Sheran, John Sheran, Michael Keveny, Patt Sheran Sr, John Keveny, Larry Breheny, Frank Keveny, Patt Breheny, Bryan Keelty, Michael Keveny, Mathew Keelty, Martin Keelty, Thos. Keveny, James Breheny, Thos Breheny, John Keelty, Andy Keasey, Michael Breheny, James Deavey, John Gaffeny, Mick Ward, Hugh Ward, Paddy Breheny, Patt McDonagh, Thos Callon, Martin Scanlon, Larry Scanlon, James Scanlon, Owen Scanlon, John Scanlon, Andy Keelty, Barry Keelty, John Devins, Thos Hart, Michael Devine, Patt Hart, James O'Connor, Larry Connor, James McManis, James Trumble, John Conlon, Thos McGarry, John Sesnon, John Walsh, Patt Hart, James Brehuny, Morris Hannon, Robin Fitzwilliam, Michael Hannon, Patt Hannon, Patt Cunnane, Ned Gaffeny, Michael Conlon, John Quigly, Michael Quigly, John McManamy, Mark Keelty, Michael Killashy, Andy Killashy, Patt Connelly, Mathew O'Connor, Thos O'Connor, James O'Connor, Michael O'Gara, Thos Hunt, Patt Cawly, James McCormick, Andy Donaher, Patt O'Connor, Dominick O'Connor, James McManus, Michael Keelty, Michael Drury, Bartly Cryan, Bartly Deavy, Martin Kenny, Dominick O'Connor, Thos Gordon, James Cryan, Bartly Dyer, Thos Dyer, Michael Duig, Mathew Killoran, Larry McDonagh, Peter Costelloe, James O'Gara, Michael Killoran, John Killoran, Bartly Hannon, Hugh Killoran, John Hannon, Owen Mulligan, John Cryan, Bartly Horan, Thomas Conlon, Edward Kilgarif, Michael Deavy, James Deavy, Patt Dyer, Charles Dyer, Bartly Kevil, Bryan Horan, Thos Deavy, James Deavy, Patt Dyer, James Cawley, Mick Walsh, John Cullen, James Conlon, John Tolin, Michael Keelty, Patt Kildea, Patt Casey, Martin Cryan, James Cryan Sr, Patt Cain, Mark Cain, Frank Cainy, Patt Caney, Patt Caney Jr, Dominick Caney, Philip Scanlon, Martin Connelly, Michael Horan, Patt Brennan, Michael Langan, James Cryan D, Tom Sherlock, Patt Lang, Patt Regan, Roger Vallentine, James Vallentine, Roger Kelly, Patt Brenan, Michael Breheny, Andy Breheny, Owen McHugh, Patt Kenny, James Hannen, John Hannen, Patt O'Gara, Peter Hannen, Owen Drury, John O'Connor, Thos Gaffeny, Patt Horan, James O'Gara, Mick McCormick, Michael Shiel, Thos McManis, John Donagher, Dominick Leydan, Patt Cunane, Dominick Costello, James Costello, Patt Lavin, Dominick Crofton, Mark Grey, Thos McGowan, Patt McGowan, Thos. Gaffeny, Thos McDonogh, John Healy, Thos McDonogh Jr, Darby Cawley, James McDonogh, Peter Costello, John Langan, Patt Conry, Patt O'Connor, Mathew Harte, Thos Cryan, Peter Feeny, John Feeny, James Lavin, Patt Horan Sr, Michael Horan Jr, James Connaghton, Patt Cryan, Ned Gaffeny, Michael Dyer, Luke Scanlon, Farrel McKenzie, Michael Grey, Andrew Dyer, Michael Rafferty, Patt Keelty, Thos Cryan, Thos Henery, Peter McGlinn, John McGlinn, Gilbert Derrigg.

Kilfree (Coolavin), 28 April 1846. Declaration to J. A. Holmes

I: Kilfree

Thomas x Duffy of Kilmore for self & 6 in family, Arthur? x Connor, Kilmore, for self & 4 in family, John x Higinn, do, for self & 4 in family, David x Henry, do, for self & 5 in family,

Mary x O'Gara, do, for self & 7 in family, Betty x Williams, do, & 2 in family, Widow x –, do, & 2 in family, Peggy x McDonagh, do, & 3 in family, Michael x Henry, do, & 1 in family, Widow x Henry, do, & 3 in family, Mary x Cunningham, do, for self & 5 in family, Widow x Geoghan?, do, for self & 4 in family, Martin x Geoghan?, do, for self & 5 in family, John x Geoghan?, do, for self & 3 in family, Michael x Sherlock, Kilmore, 4 in family, James x Gilchrist, do, 3 in family, Widow x Gilgarriff, do, 3 in family, Larry x Gilgarriff, do, 4 in family, Luke x McDonagh, do, 5 in family, Michael x Mattimo, Ragwood, 1 in family, Michael x Mullowny, Cullard, 5 in family, Patrick x Regan, –, 4 in family, Widow x Henry, Doon, 2 in family, Mary x Hannan, Annaghmore, 3 in family, Dominick x Lynch, Ragwood, 4 in family, Mathew x Leydan, Cuipruglish, 4 in family, Dominick x Mattimo, Ragwood, 2 in family, Daniel x Murphy, Mullaghroe, 4 in family, Martin x Callaghan, Moygara, 6 in family, Dominick x Lavan, Carn, 8 in family, Pat x Dyer, Kilfree, 6 in family, Francis? x Kilmartin, do, 4 in family, Luke x Dochery, Ragwood, 5 in family, Thos x O'Hara, Carn, 6 in family, Michael x Kilmartin, Ragwood, 3 in family, – x Brennan, Cloonlaheen, 3 in family, Bryan x Duffy, Cloontycarn, 6 in family, Pat x Hestin?, Kilfree, 3 in family, Pat x Sherlock, Doon West, 1 in family, Andy x Connor, Calteraun, 3 in family, Martin x Haran, Mt Irwin, 5 in family, Nelly x McDonagh, Calteraun, 5 in family, Biddy Dowd, Kilfree, 4 in family, Mary x Cravin, Carn, 2 in family, Mary x –, Knocknaskeagh, 3 in family, Darby x Redican, Ragwood, 4 in family, James x Brennan, Moydough, 3 in family, Andy x Killoran, Cloontycarn, 1 in family, Pat x Coffey, Mt. Irwin, 6 in family, Michael x Power Jr, Doon east, 7 in family, Francis x Gardiner, Culcashel, 3 in family, Thos x Dyer, Dumhilloch, 7 in family, Mathew x Walsh, Sragh, 4 in family, Thos x Mulligan, Culcashel, 3 in family, Michael x Flanagan, Knocknashammer, 1 in family, Francis x Carroll, Culcashel, 5 in family, Farrell x Hestin, Calteraun, 4 in family, Thos x Sherlock, Annaghmore, 4 in family, Francis x Grady, Annaghmore, 8 in family, Michael x McDermot, Drumleisna?, 7 in family, Bartly x Irwin, Calteraun, Owen x McDermotroe, Carns, 6 in family, – x McCoy, Lisballely, 3 in family, Pat x Neilan, Doon east, 6 in family, Widow x Farrell, Carn, 5 in family, Martin x McDermot, Cloontycarn, no family, Francis x Comer, Lishcashena?, 1 in family, Larry x McGarry, Cloonlaheen, 4 in family, James x Smith, Calteraun, 7 in family, Michael x Coleman, Rathmadder, 6 in family, Sally x Callaghan, Gortygara, no family, Dominick x Cawley, Ragwood, 5 in family, Pat x Killoran, Cloontycarn, 7 in family, Widow x Mcdonnell, Gurteen, 1 in family, Francis x O'Hara, Culmillin, 5 in family, Con x Muluony, Mullaghroe, 6 in family, Widow x Leonard, Gurteen, 1 in family, Pat x Flanagan, Leitrim, 1 in family, Thos x Taylor, Sragh, 6 in family, Thos x Ganly, Calteraun, 7 in family, Thos x McDermot, do, 6 in family, Widow x Meehan, Ragwood, 2 in family, Widow x Smith, Carn, 4 in family, Widow x Roche, Ragwood, 3 in family, Larry x Cuilpruglish, 2 in family, Widow x Salmon, Mweelroe, 3 in family, Francis x Casy, Kilfree, 2 in family, James x Casy, Esker, no family, Thady x McCarrick, Ragwood, no family, Pat x O'Neill, Doon, no family, Mathew x Roddy, Mt Irwin, 1 in family, Pat x Dodd, Doonwest, 4 in family, Pat x Walsh, Cloonlaheen, 1 in family, Thos. x Callaghan, Moydough, 4 in family, Thos x Carney, Doon east, 3 in family, Nabby x Farrell, Esker, 1 in family, Widow x Harne?, Kilfree, 1 in family, Francis x Irwin, Kilfree, 4 in family, Nancy x Gara, Ragwood, 1 in family, Widow x Mulony, Cloontycarn, 1 in family, Widow x O'Donnell, Lisballely, 4 in family, Widow x Cains, do, 1 in family, Francis x Fitzpatrick, Mt Irwin, 4 in family, Mathew x Killoran, Culcashel, 3 in family, Pat x Cawley, do, 9 in family, James x Carroll, do, 4 in family, Kitty x Dyers, Knocknasheagh, 3 in family, Pat x Mullany, Cloonanure, 5 in family, Widow x Madden, Cloonsillagh, 1 in family, Francis x Smith, Ragwood, 5 in family, James x McLaughlin, Saiveynane?, 6 in family, Darby x Cryan, Sragh, 9 in family, Michael x Casy, Doobally, 7 in family, John x Fesnan?, Annaghmore, 4 in family, Denis x Connor, Leitrim, 7 in family, Michael x Conway, Kuldina?, 7 in family, Widow x Mullough , Cairn, 4 in family,

Pat x Grey, Mahanagh, 3 in family, Pat x Rodgers, do, 7 in family, Connor x Tansy, Mahanagh, 6 in family, Francis x Moran, Coolcashel, 2 in family, Myles x Golden, Doon east, 2 in family, Pat x –, Calteraun, 4 in family, Michael x Gaffny, Clooniren?, 1 in family, Widow x Henry, Doon west, 3 in family, Widow x Foody, Mahanagh, no family, Francis x Sherlock, –, 5 in family, Martin x Coghlan, Cloontycarn, 3 in family, Francis x Benane?, Moydough, 3 in family, Sally x Oats, Mahanagh, 5 in family, Robin x King, do, 6 in family, Francis x Irwin, Moygara, 3 in family, Pat x Sharkit, Cuilpruglish, 3 in family, Widow x Connor, Ragwood, 6 in family, Peggy x Dyer, Calteraun, 1 in family, Peter x Kaveny, Mweelroe, 1 in family, James x Casy, Leitrim, 4 in family, Pat x Henry, –, 3 in family.

Kiltimagh, 11 October 1846. Memorial signed by inhabitants of Killedan parish to Lord Lieutenant.   *J Kiltimagh*

Peter Walsh, James & Denis Bayan, Matt Grogan, James x Lavan, Patt x Walsh, Walter Brennen, Patt Cunnane, Bryan Reilly, John Brennen, Bryan & James Murtagh, Mathew Corraggan, Patt Mullaney, Patt Walsh, Henry Carroll, Owen Furrey, Michael Egan, Owen Laven, James Brennan, Pat Kelly, Andrew Carney, John Benson, Patt Mulloy, Patt Costello, Thomas Gill, Daniel Dunleavy, Pat Hany, Pat Ivers, John Benson, Martin, Pat & Michael Rooney, Thomas & John Brown, John Benson, James Walsh, Thomas Brenan, Michael Kelly, Mark Gormley, James Benson, John Rooney, Henry Walsh, James Laven, John Carroll, Thomas Ivers, Patt McKellester, John Ford, Arthur McGlaghlin, Edmond Browne, Pat Solon, Michael Solon, Andrew Walsh, – Walsh, Thos Gannon, Wm Canavan, Michael Solon, Luke Keveny, – Solon, Patrick Gunenghna? Michael McDonagh, James Cunnigham, Dominick Branan, Michael Carroll, Jas. Foy, Martin Moram, Alexander Dunlavy, Bridget Murtaugh, James Carroll, Pat Brennan, Thady Brennan, George McGlaughlin, Martin Brennan, John Walsh, Daniel Carroll, Martin Langan, Thomas Brennan, Andrew Mullanny, Thos Ansborough, John O Bryone, Tarry Lydon, Pat McAlister, James Ivers, James Foly, James Walsh, Thomas Brennan, Ternessa? Murtagh, James Conlon, Pat Byrne, Joseph Stanton, Pat Conlon, James Hyland, Martin O'Brion, Michael Kelly, Thos Hunt, Michael McClune, Thos Nun?, Matt Walsh, Kitty Walsh, David Walsh, Pat Walsh, Nancy Brennan, Mark Hyland, Michael Conlon, Michael McGreal, Pat Lavin, John McDonnagh, Martin Lavin, Pat McGreal, Pat Ruane, Thos Carroll, Martin Lavin, Owen Lavin, John Lavin, Michael Connell, Michael Cunningham, Murth Gavin, Augustine Ford, John Connor, Mark Gilligan, Charles Kilgallen, James Kilgallen, Thomas Hyland, Frank ?, Bridget Hyland, Richard Walsh, Thomas Brennan, Michael Brennan, Pat Walsh, Thos Gill, Thomas O'Byrne, Michael Reily, Hugh Ford, Robert Carr, Anthony Browne, Richard Righerton, William Byrne, Pat Byrne, Pat Creaton, Mark Mallee, Patrick McElin, Martin McElin, John Carrol, William Royan, Patrick Brennan, Michael Carroll, John Kilroy, Michael Walsh, Patrick Walsh, Andrew Carney, Anthony Carney, Thomas Cavena, Roger Carr, John Neary, John Reilly, William Gerraghty, Anthony Lavin, Patrick Reilly, Patrick MacGuinn, Patrick Conlon, Jas Brennan, Patrick Brennan, Patrick Byrne, Jas Brennan, Thomas Brennan, Walter Shannon, Thomas Doyle, Thomas Carroll, Thomas Brennan, Michael Walsh, Patrick Walsh, Jas Walsh, Michael Ford, Pat Leech, Thomas Ford, Martin Walsh, Martin Gill, James Dwyre, Martin Lyndon, James Ford, Thomas Gill, Patrick Higgins, John Higgins, John Lydon, Thomas Cavanagh, John Carroll, Martin Carroll, James Walsh, Thomas Walsh, Patrick Carroll, Luke Mullanney, Pat Mullanney, Patrick Carroll Jnr, Patrick McElinn, Michael Royan, James Laven, Margaret Walsh, Daniel Duddy, Thomas Mulligan, Patrick Halligan, Patrick Duddy, Patrick Moran, Hugh Halligan, Martin Ruane, Neddy Ruane, Michael Reagan, Tom Walsh, Thomas McElin, Mick Walsh, Billy Walsh, Martin Regan, Mick Commins, Patrick?, Michael Gallaher, Peter Ferock, Hugh Carr, Anthony Carr, Patrick Carr, Ann Carr, Bee Feely, John Murtagh, James Murtagh, Patrick Murtagh, Martin

Carroll, Bryan Lavin, Patrick Lavin, Thomas Lavin, James McNicholas, Patrick Heally,
Edmond Sheridan, John McGinnis, Michael Taffe, Margret Sheridan, Billy Sheridan, Mary
Sheridan, Patrick Taffe, Elenor Walsh, James Cunnigam, John Brennan, John Cunnigam,
Patrick Solan, John Solan, Michael McNicholas, Thomas McGloughlin, James Murtagh,
Larry Murtagh, John Murtagh, Thomas Walsh, Nicholas Walsh, Thomas Gill, Martin Gill,
John Gill, John Brennan, Thomas Brennan, John Walsh, Matthew Walsh, James Walsh,
Larry Lavin, John Reilly, Patrick Kelly, James Hyland, Thomas Brennan, Andrew Gallagher,
James Lydon, John McDonough, Thomas Reilly, Patrick Cunnigan, James Henry, James
Gallagher, John Gallagher, John Flinn, James Mooney, Patrick Walsh, Anthony Flinn,
Thomas Murphy, Larry Murphy, Catherine Walsh, Patt Gill, James Kiggans, Michael
Moran, James Egan, Patrick Stanton, Patrick Egan, Thomas Browne, James Hyland, John
Egan, Patrick Brennan, James Brown, Dominick Deary, John Deary, Thomas Walsh, Patrick
Ivers, Bridget Ivers, Thos Ivers, James Tunney, John Costello, John Connor, Patrick
McNicholas, Mark Murtagh, William Costello, Michael Muldowney, John –, Albert
McHugh, James Kilgallen, Thomas Murtaugh, Jas Brennan, William Canan, Patrick
Browne, Bernard Haughey, Matthew Carrigan, John Lavin, Patrick O'Byrne, Matthew
Gorman, Thos O'Byrne, Patrick Brennan, Martin O'Byrne, Anthony Canan, William
McHugh, James McHugh, Francis McHugh, Patrick Langan, Patrick Carney, Edward
Gallaher, William Carney, Michael Cavanagh, James Murtagh, Patrick Feeley, Thomas
Walsh, Michael Walsh, James Devine, Edmond Walsh, Patrick McNicholas, Thady
Cavanagh, Michael Lavin, Patrick Costello, William Costello, Peter Costello, Edmond
Lavin, Michael Feely, Edmond English, James English, Michael English, Martin Lavan,
Francis Gormily, James Gormily, Thomas Walsh, Patrick Walsh, James Doyle, Anthony
Doyle, Michael Doyle, Ferral Cunnane, Constantine Cunnane, – Currane, Luke Laven,
Mark Laven, John McDonagh, Patrick Lally, Patrick Lally Jnr, Anthony Hughes, Michael
Hughes, Timothy Gunnigan, Patrick Begly, Patrick Kilgallen, Patrick Brennan, William
Royne, Patrick Hyland, Michael O'Byrne, Peter Laven, Thady Brennan, James Kilgallen,
Mark Hyland, Patrick Walsh, Patrick McNicholas, William Ford, Anthony Jordan, Michael
McNicholas, Pat Munhinna?, James Munhinna?, Thomas Byrne, John Byrne, Thos Clarke,
Andrew Clarke, Pat Mullany, Thos Mullany, Thos Egan, Edmond Jennings, Thomas
Jennings, James Reilly, James Reilly, Michael Costello, Pat Jennings, Peter Jennings, Michael
McGreal, Patrick McGreal, Thomas McGreal, John Gill, – Gill, Martin Gill, Michael Gill,
Matthew Caulfield, Thomas Flanery, Thomas Carravagh?, John Carravagh?, John Moran,
Thomas Moran, Patrick Moran, John Benson, John Gill, John Carrol, Michael Conilan,
Michael Browne, James Browne, Michael Hyland, Michael Weldon, Michael Benson,
Patrick McNicholas, Stephen McNicholas, David Mullen, Peter Griffin, John N. Griffin,
James Benson, Thos Benson, Thomas Hyland, Matthew Gill, Pat Mullaney, Dominick
Mullaney, Owen Walsh, Edmond Brown, Edmond Ivers, Patrick Ivers, John M. Ivers, Bryan
Nyland, Patrick O'Byrne, John Ford, James Cannen, Patrick Caulfield, James Double, John
Brennan, Anthony Lavin, Edmond Lavin, John Mooney, Luke Walsh, Betty O'Donnell,
John Brennan, Thomas Crean, Thos Walsh, John Ford, Hugh Conlon, Martin Walsh,
Martin Coan, Michael Carroll, Michael Roughneen, James Solon, John Ryan, Thomas
Brannan, Patrick Byrne, Thomas Lydan, Dominick Byrne, Anthony Canivan, Patrick
McGrath, James McNicholas, Martin Egan, John Saleen?, Thomas Carroll, Mark Carroll,
Bryan Lavin, Henry Higgins, Bryan Lavin, Catherine Byrne, Thomas Walsh, Nancy
Mullany, Patrick McLoughlin, Michael Dealy, Pat Cormican?, David Walsh, Mary Doyle,
Alfy Canavan, James Canavan, Andrew Walsh, Patrick Quinn, Nancy Doyle, Thomas
Brennan, James Walsh, David Walsh, Patrick Walsh, Martin Hyland, John Connor, Ellen
Connor, Anthony Gill, Mary Gill, Bridget Mullany, Thos Lavin, James Murtagh, John
Cunnane, Cormack Brennan, John Brannan, Mark Lavin, Phelim Brennan, Martin

Murtagh, Mark Gormally, Patrick Mullany, Nancy Doyle, Bridget Murtagh, Michael
Carroll, Catherine Rooney, Michael Rowley, Andrew Ford, John Ruane, Michael Ruane, Pat
Ruane, Saby Roach, Anthony Faughy?, Bridget Guiness?, Thomas McDonough, John
McDonough, Bridget Lavin, Michael Cunningham, Bryan Lavin, Bridget Murtagh, James
Munninha, Patrick O'Byrne, Matthew Brennan, Bryan Lavin, John Walsh, James Walsh,
James Connolly, John Connolly, Owen Lavin, Margaret Dunlany?, Bridget Dunlany?, Mary
Dunlany?, Nancy Dunlany?, Thomas Dunlany?, Bridget Burke, Sally Devine?, – Hyland,
Thomas Byrne, John Byrne, Patrick Carroll, Thomas Brennan, Patt Byrne, Jas Byrne,
Matthew Brennan, William Ford, Thomas Byrne, – Greeney, Dominick Mullany, – Feely,
Jas Muldowney, John Gahagan, Owen Brennan, Thomas Brennan, Thomas Roach,
Catherine Creaton, Bartly Walsh, Elenor Lavin, James McNicholas, John McNicholas,
Owen Brennan,Thomas Walsh,Thomas Carney, Dominick Devany, John Feeley, Phelim
Brennan, Jas McManus, Michael Morrisroe, James Morrisroe, Michael Kiggans, Patrick
Kiggans, Dominick Mullany, John McDonagh, Patrick Cuff, James Lyden, Michael Walsh,
Mary O'Bryne, Peter Walsh, Patrick Brennan, Martin Brennan, Thomas Langan, Patt
Walsh, John Murtaugh, James Murtaugh, John Murtaugh, Michael McHlus?, Patt Lavin,
James Lavin, Thomas Lavin, Thomas Walsh, Luke Murtagh, Mick Carroll, Thadeus Walsh,
John Walsh, James Walsh, John Carroll, Bridget Murtagh, Peter Lavin.

14 June 1848. 33 families in Treenagleragh evicted by Lord Lucan.
Pat Jennings, 5 in family, half year's rent due; John Hyland, 3, do; Thomas Hyland, 2, do;
Mark Hyland, 2, do; John Hyland, 4, do; James Jennings, 5, do; Thos Jennings, 5, do;
Pat Hyland, 4, do; John Jennings, 0, do; Anne Hyland, 4, no rent due; Peter Carolan, 4,
one year's rent due; James Carolan, 5, do; Pat Carolan, 4, do; Widow McNicholas, 6, do;
Widow Carolan, 5, do; Widow Walsh, 3, none; Thos Jennings, 6, one year; Edward
Jennings, 4, do; Edward Jennings, Jr, 3, do; Widow O'Neill, 1, do; Pat McNicholas, 7, do;
Geofry Gibbins, 6, do; P. J. McNicholas, 4, do; Widow McNicholas, 5, do; Pat Gallagher, 7,
do; Pat Lanan, 4, do; Widow Kilgallin, 2, do; A. Durkan, 6, do; Pat Kilgallin, 6, do; James
Kilgallin, 6, do; Pat Byrne, 7, do; Michael Byrne, 6, do; Widow Mallee, 1, none.
Total evicted: 145.

*Meelick, 11 January 1848. List of families who received Society of Friends' rice from John
Bolingbroke.*

K: Meelick

Name	No.	lbs	Observations
Michael Reilly	7	22	Wife died of fever 2 December: 3 still sick
Edmond Flynn	5	22	Edmond & son died: remainder convalescent
Bridget Ginty	1	23	sickly and destitute
Sarah Reilly	1	22	Old, sickly and destitute
Patrick Lyons	7	22	Patrick died: wife and 2 children ill of fever
James Lyons	7	21	whole family unwell
Bridget Farrell	1	23	old, sickly and destitute
Widow O'Donnel	1	23	do
Patrick Clarke	5	23	do
John Clarke	4	15	John & wife in fever
Bridget Fleming	1	19	old, sickly and destitute
Patrick Gallagher	6	23	do
Widow Dunbar	8	15	old do
Widow Laffy	5	15	convalescent from fever

Name	No.	lbs	Observations
Thomas Stanton	9	21	do
William McNulty	11	15	do
James &			
Michael Stanton	2	15	orphans
Thomas Dacy	9	15	sick
James Conwell	3	11	died 22 November
Patrick Conwell	6	21	sick and destitute
Widow McDermot	1	23	old sick and destitute
James Clarke	7	10	old destitute: gone into the workhouse
Sibby Sheeran	1	23	do
Widow Kenny	1	12	died
Widow Conwell	1	18	old and destitute
Bridget Philbin	5	15	ill of fever: deserted by her husband
Michael McNulty	1	2	disabled
George O'Neill	9	15	whole family sickly
James Jordan	8	22	do
Thomas Clarke	5	15	dysentery
Widow Doyle	1	23	old, sickly and destitute
James Moran	2	21	disabled tradesman
James Loftus	1	24	crippled
John Clarke	8	15	ill of fever
Patrick Durkan	7	15	do
Widow Horkan	1	7	sickly
John Brady	7	3	ill of fever: wife died 3 December
Patrick Lamb	5	21	Patrick disabled: wife deranged
Bridget Hannon	6	17	sickly and blind
Widow O'Hara	1	16	old, sickly and destitute.
Thady Delany	6	6	sickly and destitute
Thomas Laffy	9	13	ill of fever
David Laffy	6	17	do: son died 2 November
Widow Loftus	5	23	sickly and destitute
Widow Laffy	1	14	do
Martin Mullowny	11	15	fever and dysentery
Widow Durkan	1	14	dysentery
Widow Lamb	2	21	old and infirm
John Rock	1	18	do
Nelly & Nancy Durkan	2	18	orphans
Nelly Murphy	1	22	old, sickly and destitute
Patrick Ruane	2	1	
William Tolan	7	14	disabled and destitute
Widow Stanton	6	13	sickly, do
May Stanton	7	13	children unwell
Elinor O'Donnell	1	2	sick
Widow Sheeran	1	13	old, sickly and destitute
Thomas Foster	8	11	ill of fever
Widow Dempsey	1	16	old, sickly and crippled
Widow Kenny	5	11	do and destitute
Owen Kain	2	10	sickly tradesman

Name	No.	lbs	Observations
Mary Meehan	4	9	do, destitute: deserted by husband
Michael Flynn	6	9	sick
Andrew McGowan	5	18	fever
John Kelly	5	9	do
Dermot Gallagher	7	4	sick
Edward Gallagher	1	1	do
James Coghlan	13	7	sickly and destitute
Honor Mulligan	1	11	old, sick and destitute
Catherine & Mary Ormsby	2	5	orphans
Edward O'Donnell	4	6	sick
Neal O'Donnell	2	6	do
Patrick Laffy	4	5	fever
Martin McGeever	6	1	child sick
John Mullowny	6	8	fever
James Mulroy	5	10	wife and children sick
John Ruddy	7	1	child sick
Michael Murphy	11	6	fever
George Mahern	5	1	child ill of dysentery
Widow McGeever	3	9	fever
Patrick Gallagher	1	1	sick
Patrick Gibbons	5	1	child sick
John Mulloy	7	1	family in fever

Meelick, 3 March 1848. List of the families who received the Society of Friends' food from John Bolingbroke.

Name	No.	Meal	Rice
Widow Flynn	3	35 lbs	
Widow Ginty	1	20	
Widow Reilly	1	20	2
Widow Lyons	4	35	4
Widow Hand	1	22	
Widow O'Donnell	1	34	8
Patrick Clarke	5	31	½
Michael Reilly	6	35	
Patrick M.Gallagher	6	3½	12
Widow Dunbar	8	3½	12
Widow Gallagher	8	3½	
Patrick Davet	6	35	2
Thomas Stanton	9	3½	10
Anthony Doyle	11	3½	10
Widow Stanton	6	3½	10
Widow Kenny	5	3½	10
Widow McDermot	1	24½	
Widow Loftus	5	23	
George O'Neill	9	35	
Michael Flynn	5	35	2
Thomas Kelly	6	37	9
Widow Doyle	1	20	11

Name	No.	Meal	Rice
James Moran	2	20	11
Owen Kean	2	20	
James Jordan	7	28	2
William Tolan	7	35	3
Nelly Durkan	1	16	
Nancy Durkan	1	16	
Widow Sheeran	1	20	2
James Bury	6	35	12
Patrick Row Gallagher	7	35	
James Loftus	8	35	11
William McNulty	11	3½	2
Thomas Foster	8	17½	4
Martin Doyle	7	3½	12
Widow Durkan	2	20	
Honor Mulligan	1	2	10
Widow Mary Golden	3	20	
Michael McNulty	4	33½	
Patrick Gibbons	4	35	
John Rock	1	18	
Widow Laffy	3	18	3
Widow O'Hara	1	2	
James Lyons	7	31½	8
Mary Stanton	7	3½	8
Neal O'Donnell	2	20	
Thomas Clarke	5	35	
Patrick Brady	4	2	
Anthony Dacy	7	3½	4
James Mulroy	5		8
Patrick Walsh	8	35	2
Nelly Murphy	3	3½	2
Michael Murphy	10	3½	13
Mary Mulloy	1	12	
Bridget Fleming	1	21	4
Widow Conwell	5	33½	
Winny Kenny	1	17	
Nancy Kenny	1	17	
Edward O'Donnell	4	20	
Patrick Conwell	6	33½	2
Bridget Hannon	6	20	
Bridget McGloin	5	20	
Patrick Lamb	5	24½	11
Widow Lamb	2	20	
James Clarke	7	24½	8
John McNulty	4	24½	
Mary Meehon	4	31½	
John Mulloy	7	21	
Anthony O'Neill	4		14
Patrick Bartly	5	31½	

Name	No.	Meal	Rice
Patrick Durkan	7	3½	
Patrick Foster	6	28	
John Gallagher	3	19½	
Sibina Mulloy	6	28	
Honor Mulligan	2	16	
Mary Devine	3	16	
Mary O'Neill	1	8	
Mary Mulloy	2	10	
Widow Burke	4	28	
Margaret Foy		16	
Margaret Gallagher	6	17½	8
Dominick Browne	7	10½	
James McHugh	1	1	
Widow Harkan	1		14
Patrick Mulloy	3		2
George Matern	6		6
Patrick Murphy	6		7
Martin Farrell	2		6
Thady Mullowney	6		4
John Doyle	3		2
May Ruddy	1		2
Patrick McDonagh	6		4
Patrick Groarke	6		7
Thomas Gallagher	5		8
Patrick Gallagher	6		7
Martin Reilly	4		13
Anthony McNulty	6		11
Michael Browne	5		12
Monoghan Oyan?	1		1
Thomas Ormsby	6		12
Patrick Solon	6		10
Patrick Ruane	2		10
John Kelly	5		12
Widow Honor Laffy	5		8
Thomas Mulroy	8		10
Widow Kilgallin	4		13
David Laffy	5		10
Patrick D. Gallagher	3		6
John Clarke	4		10
Honor Clarke	4		6
John O'Neill	5		6
Mathew Muldowney	6		8
Widow Murphy	1		12

Straide, 24 February 1847. Memorial of housekeepers and widows to Lord Lieutenant.   *L: Straide*
Straide: Widow Mulroy, 3 in family attending school and not able to work; Widow Stephens, 2; Pat Tunny, 3; Michael Foxe, 3; John Tunny, 3.
Ballylahan: Widow Craby, 3; Widow Kelly, 2; Martin Higgins, 3; Widow Croneen, 3.

Ballinakellue: Peter Cafferty, 3; Owen Mulroy, 1; Widow McHale, 1; Martin Roach, 2; Widow Mullahy, 2; Michael McHugh, 2; Michael Raney, 2.
Lyonsfield: Widow Walsh, 2; Pat Devaney, 1; Pat Walsh, 2.
Fencefield: Ins McNicholas, 3; Js Sweeny, 3; Richard Howard, 3; Anthony Foxe, 1.
Knockogorrane: Widow Foxe, 1; Michael Stephens, 3; Pat Mulroy, 3; Dominick Stephens, 1.
Lianageeha?: Widow Gallagher, 1; Thomas Durkan, 1; Thomas Murphy, 3; Michael Murphy, 4.
Straide Road: Jno Mulroy, 3; Thomas Mulroy, 4; Michael Murphy, 1.
Ardcloon: Jno Donleavy, 2; Js McDonnell, 2; Thomas Mulroy, 2; Jno Stephens, 2.
Ummoon: Widow T. Porter, 2; Widow H. Porter, 3; Widow McCarrick, 1; Jas Kelly, 3; Pat Gordon, 2; Bryan McGreal, 2.
Cloonconlonbane: Martin Ruane, 2; Widow Mulroy, 2; Nicholas King, 2; Thomas Walsh, 2; Jas Foy, 2.
Total: 107.
P.S. The reply to this will be returned with as little delay as possible in care of Rev John McHugh PP Templemore.

M: Swinford   *Swinford (Kilconduff and Meelick), 27 January 1846. Board of Guardians:* George J.O'Malley, George Rutledge, Francis R.O'Grady, Patrick W.Kelly, Patrick Durkan, Austen Mullarkey, John Durkan, Edward P.McDonnell, James Horkan, Daniel Keane. *Also present:* Charles Strickland, David Rutledge, Rev John Coleman PP Swinford, Rev Patrick Spelman CC Swinford, Edward Bollingbrooke, Luke D.Fitzgerald
2 September 1846. Signatories to a memorial to Lord Lieutenant.
Bernard Durcan PP, James Devine CC, P. Spelman CC, and B. W. Eames, vicar, James Harkan (2), Ulic Burke MD, – D. FitzGerald MRCSRI, John Mulligan & Co, Edward O'Donnell, Pat W. Kelly, Peter & Michael Cawley, Michael, Pat, Patt, Charles, Anthony, John (2), James (3) Durkan, Charles Carroll, Francis Davis?, Patrick Horkan, John & Michael Moloney, Daniel Henegan, Michael William Henry MRCI, William Mulligan, James P. O'Dowd MD MRCSI, Michael Mellet, James Bourke?, Pat Corley, Patt & Michael Henry, Joseph Kelly, Patt & Henry Hurst, Edward Carney, Edward Neilan, James & Martin O'Doude, Thomas, John & Patt Connor, Patt Kelly, Martin McDonagh, William J. Fleming, George Harkan, Martin Sheridan, Michael Howley, Mark Henry, Douglas Kelly MD, Neal Tolan, Thomas Groarke, Patt Stanton, John Gannon, Dominick, John & Martin Mulloy, Patt Cunniffe, Patt Moore, Michael Harkan, Patt Halligan, Phelim Campbell, Thomas Conmy, Patt & Thomas Gallagher, John, Patt & Anthony Kelly, Thomas Harkan, Thomas McClure, Anthony Granen, Michael Lamb, William & Coll Devitt, James Stanton, Michael Kelly, R. Doyle, Coll Gordan, R. Jordan, Thomas Horkan, Dominick Coleman, Dan O'Brien, Charles O'Connell, P. Spelman CC, Christopher Moore, James O'Brien, William Murphy.
13 September 1846. Memorial to Lord Lieutenant signed by:
Bernard Durcan PP, Patrick Spelman CC, James Devine CC, B. W. Eames, vicar, Patrick & John Halligan, John Mulligan & Co, merchant, Ulic Burke MD, James Harkan, Mathew Coleman, Anthony Moran, Michael (2), James (3), Andrew, and John Durkan, Michael, Mark & Patrick Henry, Peter Cawley, William Mulligan, Thomas & John O'Connor, P. Burne, Patrick Corley, Laurence Feeny, Patrick Cuddy, James Brabazon, John Dodd, Daniel McLean, John & Patrick (2) Kelly, Patt Callaghan, John & Charles Carroll, Bryan & Austin Brennan, Anthony & Michael Conmee, Martin Dougherty, Phelim Campbell, Patrick Feely, Patrick Cunniffe, Patrick Horkan, Michael Howley, Thomas Groarke, Patrick Kelly, Anthony Fahey, John Varelly?, John Kyle, William Fleming, Dudly Nully?, & Anthony Dunlevy.

17 September 1846. Magistrates and cess-payers.
George Vaughan Jackson, chairman. *Magistrates:* Colonel Knox Gore, William Orme, Captain Fitzmaurice, Thomas Ormsby, W.J Bourke, Edward Deane, George Ormsby, Edward Orme, Francis C. McDonnell, Francis R.O'Grady, Isidore Blake.
Cess-payers: George Fenton, A. Ormsby, Neal Dempsey, James O'Dowd, Patt Peyton, Patt Davis, Wellington Stroggen, George Cuffe, James Walsh, John Beckett, Michael Dempsey, George Horkan.

23 May 1848. Clergymen and other inhabitants of the united parishes of Kilconduff and Meelick (Swinford) to Lord Lieutenant.
B. W. Eames, vicar of Kilconduff, B. Durcan PP, James Hurst CC, Pat Durkan PLG, Peter Harkan PLG, Patrick Horkan PLG, Luke D. Fitzgerald, surgeon, Edward L. Clarke MD, Michael Wm Henry MD, Ulic Burke MD, Edward Hunt, sub-inspector, Thos Mulligan, John Doyle, Ch O'Connell, – F. Robinson, Peter Cawley, Michael Cawley, Eugene McGuire, William Mahon, Wm Henry, Michael Roach, James Burns, Joseph Burke, Pat Durkan, Pat Henry, shopkeeper, James Durkan, Michael Harkan, John Kyle, shopkeeper, Pat Corley, hotel keeper, Michael Mahony, John Mulligan & Co, William Mulligan, John Groarke, Thos Groarke, shopkeeper, Michael Coleman, Mathew Coleman, John Coleman, Mark Henry, Patrick Halligan, Pat O'Connor, Neil Tolan, Peter Stephens, James Burke, Michael Henry, Anthony Conlon, Martin Conwell, Pat Conwell, John Dougherty, John Berry, Pat Berry, Martin Gallagher, Thomas Gallagher, Daniel Murry, John Nolan, Michael Ryan, John Martin, Pat Neafsey, Michael Neafsey, Michael Mulligan, Michael Briane, John Thompson, Pat Thompson, John Kevlehan, Hugh Doyle, Denis Gallagher, Pat Gavan, Bryan Mulloy, Stephen Walsh, Michael Gallagher, Pat Brennan, John Murray, John Lally, Thos Walsh, Daniel McLean, John Gannon, John Mulloy, James Sheridan, Thomas Horkan, James Horkan, Pat McNulty, Daniel Hinigan, Anthony Horan, Stephen Connor, Thomas Stanton, Bryan Callaghan, John Connor, Michael Horkan, William Fleming, Martin Doyle, Pat Gallagher, Walter McNicholas, Thady Conlon, James Callaghan, Patrick (illegible), Edward Keelan, Arthur Collins, John Pidgeon, Martin Devany, Michael Judge, Pat Cunniff, Bryan McNulty, Michael Conwell, John Dogherty, Bryan McNulty, Joseph Gallagher, Laurence Feeny, Patrick Stanton, John Henry, Martin McHugh, John Halligan, Mark Horan, John Durkan, James Clarke, John Frain, James Doyle, Anthony Durkan, Michael Durkan, Peter Groarty, James White, Michael McManus, John Lally.

12 September 1848. Swinford Board of Guardians to Lord Lieutenant. Signatories:
G. Vaughan Jackson, chairman, Richard O'Grady, James Beytagh, Patrick Durkan, Peter Horkan, Pat Peyton, Pat Horkan, Luke Colleran, Bernard Colleran, Peter Colleran, Patrick Touhy, James Dillon, Francis O'Grady, Charles B. Jordan, solicitor to the board.

Tubbercurry, 18 September 1846. Memorial to Lord Lieutenant of the inhabitants of Tubbercurry, Carrentubber, Ballyara, Tullacusheen, Clooneen, Sessua Common, Tullavella, Frenchford, Mullaun, Cloonacool. Sessua Garry, Sessua Kilroy.

N: Tubbercurry

Rev Michael Cawley, James Wynne, James Dony?, Thomas Askin, Margaret McNuly, Catherine Doyle, Danniel Madden, Patt Wynne, Mary Battle, Edward Gallagher, John McCan?, Bartholomew x O'Hara, Roger McNulty, Martin x O'Hara, James Clarke, Bryan x Rogers, Patrick x Dyre, Mathew x Gallagher, Patt Connell, Roger x Battle, P. McDyre, Anthony Glynsk, Mark Nylon, James Cunleen, Bartholomew x Quinn, Mathew x McIntyre, John Doherty, James x Gallagher, John Killoran, Richard Armstrong, Miles x Sweeny, Phelim x Kilday, Martin x Calvey, Patt x Armstrong, Necros x Brannan, Thomas Gynard, Thomas Armstrong, Patt Bradley, James Wynne, John Walker, Thomas x Gallagher, Thomas

Gannon, Patrick Gallagher, Patrick Calvy, James Armstrong, Patt McIntyre, Philip Kennedy, Mathew Scanlan, Thomas Sweeny, Thomas Nealon, Patt Wynne, Andrew Mullarkey, Martin Killmore, Thomas x Henry, Patt Wynne, Robert Wynne, Thomas Caverty, Dominick Wynne, Andrew Geinty, Thomas Kennedy, Denis Wynne, Roger O'Connor, John O'Connor, Michael Devany, Bartly Ginty, Luke Brennan, James Henry, Robt Collens, James Gallagher, Patt Smith, Peter Finnen, Jack Mullarkey, John Kilday, Owen Sweeny, John Gallagher, Edward Gallagher Jr, Thomas Sweeny, Michael Kilday, Patrick Brannen, John Davies, Thomas McGlen, John Brennan, John Loftus, Owen Ganty, Edward x Wynne, Dominick x Wynne, Thomas Sweeny, Edward Henry, Daniel Preston, Patt Feely, Patt Garachy, Owen Johnston, Patt Battle, Owen Higgins, James Woods, Patt Gallagher, Morgan Brenan, Thomas Rennels?, Dan Calleary, Michael Colgan, John Mullarky, Michael Madden, Patrick Colleary, Patt Mullarkey, James Sweeny, Patt McIntyre, James Mullarkey, Thomas Lang, Thomas Gulden, Hugh O'Donnell, Dominick Flynn?, John McGawran, James Mitchel, Michael Armstrong, Dominick Henry, Patrick Connolly, Dominick Wynne, John Callaghan, Michael Gallagher, Thomas Gildea, Michael Mulhatton?, John Devine, Patt Gildea, Luke Ginty, Denis Mullarkey, Patt Mullarkey, Patt Carrane, Thomas Wynne, Patt Dooney, John Dooney, Michael Battle, James Meredith, Peter Henry, James Henry, Paul x Kivlighan, Patt x O'Donnell, Michael x O'Donnell, John x O'Donnell, James Glinsky, Francis Mullarkey, James Dooney, John Gethens, James Carrane, Daniel Lynch, Francis Lynch, Gilbert Cowan, Luke Armstrong, Martin Preston, Patt Preston, James Haran, Peter McEvan, James Henry, Daniel Wynne, Gerry Meredith, John Meredith, Francis Rogers, John Rogers, Edward Johnston, Michael Gallagher, Patt Lagan?, Patt Feely, Darby Regan?, Patt Tarpy?, Farel O'Garry, John Gallagher, John Hury, Michael Madden, Michal Gethens, John Ginty, John Quin, Pat McEvan, Dominick Brennan, John x Smith, Anthony Gallagher, Michael Gallagher, John Sweeny, Phelim Marren, Martin Durcan, John Rogers, John White, Thomas Sweeny, Patrick Irwin?, Joseph Henry, Robert O'Boyle, Michael McHugh, Patt Clark, James Clark, Patt Armstrong, Luke Dyre, Michael McHugh, William Finn, John Calvey, Daniel Calvey, Hugh O'Donnell, John McIntyre, John McGlone, John Price, Andy Price, Francis Rogers, Noell McCoy, John McKensie, Patt McCarrick, John McIntire, John Wynne, James Goldrick, John & James Mullarky, Denis Wynn, Patt Henigan, James, John & Patt Carrane, James Sr & James Farrell, James McVann Sr & Jr, Patt, Owen, Jack, & Patt Sr Mullarkey, John Hinighan, Patt Neary, Patt & Tom Gallagher, Ned Colgan, Tom Hanen?, Andrew Neary, Michael O'Brynn, James, Owen & John Gallagher, Francis O'Hara, James Mitchel, Mathew Meridith, Brian Wynne, Dominick, Thomas & Patt Wynne, Patt Walsh, Thomas & Patt Mullarky, Michael Layng, John Brett, Thos Tighe, Patrick Gallagher, Morgan Feely, John Curneen, Andrew Donleavy, Michael Tedurvy?, Patrick Dwyer, Martin Spelman, Denis Gallagher, John Gallagher, John Burke, Patrick Marron, Thomas x Powell, Thomas x Stenson, Philip x Murphy, Peter x McGarry?, John x Henery, Owen x Walsh, Michael x Gallaher, James x Scanlon, John x Gaffney, Michael x Durkan, Michael Gallagher, Patrick McGloin, John Connelly, James Haran, John x Nealan?, John x Smith, James x Phillips, James x McGowan, Charles x Cuff, James x Healy, Patrick x Stenson, Bryan x Sweeney, Pat x Kirrane, John x Durkan, Michael x Lynan?, Thomas x Golden, Patrick McGetrick, John x Byrne, William Keenan?, John Keenan, Richard x Golden, John x Brennan, Hugh x McGannon, Owen x McGannon, Michael x McGannon, Thomas x McGannon, Martin x Doyle, Pat x Carroll, Thomas x Carroll, Martin x Carroll, Thomas x Murray, Pat x Scanlon, Anthony x Feely, Thomas B. Durcan Sr, John x Brennan, Pat x Byrne, William x McEnally, Pat x McEnally, Thomas x McEnally, John x Narree, Michael x Walker, John x Murphy, James x Spelman, Thomas x Taaffe?, Bartly x Spelman, Patrick Moffatt, Pat x Sweeney, Pat x Gibson?, Thadie x Murtagh, – Walsh, John x Egan, Thomas x Brett, Michael x Moffett, Peter x Davy, Michael x Healy, Thomas x Connolly, Martin x Scanlon, Thomas x Brennan, Thomas x Murphy, Michael x Murtagh, Laurence x Kilcoyne, John x Cauly, Laurence x Dwyer, John x Stuart, Thomas Keenan, John Murtagh, John Henry, John x Connolly, Pat x Scanlon, Denis x Higgins, Michael x Snee, Thomas x Morrisey, Pat x Brennan, Thomas x Brennan, Peter x Brennan, John Gallagher, William Keenan, Joseph x Hynes, James x Burke, Michael x Feely, John x Callahan, Patrick x Burke, Martin x Henry, Luke O'Brien, Patrick O'Brien, Thomas x Ross, James x Burke, John x Leonard, John x Connell, Patrick x Henry, Patrick x Gaffney, Bryan x Sweeney, Patrick x Kildea, John x Brennan, Patrick x Doddy, James x Burke, Jr, Walter x Burke, Patrick x Healy, Luke x Walsh, William Mullarky, Martin x McHugh, Martin x Doyle, John x Ganly, Mike x Nicholson, Molly x Durkan, Mary x McFadden, Michael Connelly, Michael O'Brien, Patrick Kennedy, James x Sweeney, William x Ruane, Pat x Connolly, John x McGloin, Thos x Durkan, Edward x Dorean, John x Dowd, Laurence x Durcan, Pat x Kennedy, Owen x Redican, Michael x Lacy, Michael x Collins, Thos Walker, Daniel Feely, John x Devine, Pat x McGloin, John x Doherty, Pat x Brennan, Jas x Spelman, Jas x Moffatt, Michael x Davy, Michael x Byrne, Phelim x McMarron, Michael x May, Thos x Brennan, John x Marron, John x Killoran, John Breheny, Patrick McGowan, William Miller, Luke x Connell, Patrick x Connell, Michael Connell, John x Hynes, James x Hynes, William x Cosgrave, Thomas x Collins, James x Higgins, John x Gilligan, Pat x Higgins, John x Brennan, Michael x Ready?, James Rogers, Thomas Brennan, Owen x Ginty, Andrew x Quinn, Martin x Brennan, Anthony x Mullane, Pat x Collins, Daniel x Snee, Martin x Brennan, Francis x Marren, Jas x Wynn, Jas x McGannon, Roger x Getting, Michael x Moryson, John Dyer, Patrick Quinn, Pat x Ginty, Pat x Feely, Thadeus x Carobine, Mark x Connolly, Thomas x Connolly, John x Connolly, William Miller, Michael x Killoran, Denis x Brennan, Matthew x Brennan, John x Brennan, Michael x Nicholson, Patrick x Nicholson, Michael x Carroll, John x Higgins, Michael x Cunnane, Thomas x Doudican, Christopher x Doudican, Martin x Gallagher, Thomas x Gallagher, Pat x Gallagher, John x Gallagher, Pat x McGannon, Thomas x McGannon, John x Trumble, John x O'Hara, John x O'Hara, John x Mecack?, Matthew x Connor, Pat x Hellis, J. x Walker, Frank x Manning, Thomas x Brett, John x Cunnane, Pat x Cunnane, Jas x Murray, Bartholomew x Henry, John x Walker, Michael x Walker, John x May, Luke x Feely, John x Hellis, Thadie x Cealus?, Murtagh x Heally, William Walker, John Cosgrove, Denis Wynne, Luke x Calalee?, Pat x Leonard, Ned x Kenedy, Pat x McGowan, Pat x Hunt, Mike x Hunt, John x Hunt, Mark x Feely, Michael x Brennan, Michael x Feely, John x Brennan, Bryan x Kenedy, John x Hara, Michael x Lockard, Pat x O'Brien, Thomas x Heally?, John x Phillips, Thomas x Nicholson, Bartly x Conway, Patrick x Gormely, Thomas x Marren, Mark Bourke, Martin x Hellis, Hugh x Gildea, Jas Connolly, Robert Walker, James Walker, Vincent x Durkan, Thomas Dorran.

n.d. 1848. List of those relieved by Rev John Hamilton from Society of Friends' food grant.
The Craven orphans, Ogham, 14 lbs of meal, James Armstron, Cloonerara, 7 lbs, Thos Black, Tubbercurry, 14 lbs, Mary Synott, do, 7 lbs, Alexander Gleany, Carraun, 14 lbs, John Callaghan, Carraun, 14 lbs, Mary Neill, Tubbercurry, 7 lbs, Geo West, do, 14 lbs, John Hynes, Rathmagimy, 14 lbs, Richard Craven, Ogham, 14 lbs, Widow Cassidy, Ogham, 7 lbs, Pat Devany, Carrowreagh Knox, 14 lbs, Chas West, Tubbertelly, 14 lbs, Orphan Calpine, Carrowreagh Knox, 14 lbs, Andrew Mosgrove, Tubbercurry, 14 lbs, Mathew McHugh, do, 14 lbs, Richard Whyte, Castleoye, 14 lbs, John Armstrong, Sessue, 14 lbs, James Philips, Tubbercurry, 14 lbs, Luke Kilmartin, Mucketta, 14 lbs, Mathew Meredith, Tubbercurry, 14 lbs, James Sheeran, do, 14 lbs, Honora Fahy, Rathscanlan, 14 lbs, Bridget Welsh (cripple), Tubbercurry, 7 lbs, Anne Kilmore, Rathscanlan, 14 lbs, Widow Roderick McKenzie, Tubbercurry, 14 lbs, Margaret Gildea, Tubbercurry, 14 lbs, Morgan Feely, do, 14 lbs, Orphan Caroline Montgomery, do 14 lbs, Widow Barry, do, 14 lbs, Michael Morrison, do, 14 lbs, Honora McDonagh, Tubbercurry, 14 lbs, Luke Welsh, Tubbercurry, 14 lbs, Thos

Murray, Ogham, 14 lbs, Honora Gormally, Streamstown, 14 lbs, Widow McGettrick, Carntubber, 14 lbs, Orphan Anne Henry, Rathscanlan, 14 lbs, Mary Casey, Carraun, 14 lbs, Mary Davey, Ogham, 14 lbs, Widow Millar, Carntubber, 14 lbs, Michael Gallagher, do, 14 lbs, Mary Henderson, Rathscanlan, 14 lbs, Mary Ross, Ogham, 14 lbs, John Golden, Rathscanlan, 14 lbs of biscuit, Henry Glenny, Carraun, 14 lbs, James Glenny, do, 14 lbs, William Goulden, Rathscanlan, 14 lbs of biscuit, David Ruane, Ballyaise, 14 lbs, Susan Glenny, Carraun, 14 lbs, William Craven, Ogham, 14 lbs of biscuit, Catherine Murtogh, Rathscanlan, 7 lbs, Orphans Healey, Tubbercurry, 7 lbs, Michael Timon, do, 7 lbs, Bessy Downs, do, 7 lbs, Widow Bridget Gorman, do, 7 lbs, Mary Farrell, Clooneen, 7 lbs, Anne Armstrong, Carraun, 7 lbs, Pat Scanlan, Carntubber, 7 lbs, John Durkan, Tubbercurry, 14 lbs, Orphans Trumble, Carraun, McSharry, Doomore, 14 lbs of biscuit, Widow Smith, Tubbercurry, 7 lbs, Peter McIntire, Doomore, 7 lbs, Thos Finigan, Doomore, 7 lbs, John McIntire, do, 14 lbs, Pat Finigan, do, 7 lbs, Mary Gallagher, do, 7 lbs, Geo West, Tubbercurry, 7 lbs, Richard Burns Golden, sick, Rathscanlan, 7 lbs of rice, Edward Meekings, sick fever, do, 7 do, Thos West, Tubbercurry, 14 do, Mary Black, sick in fever, do, 14 do, Anne Glenny, sick in fever, Carraun, 14 do, Dominick Feely, wife sick, Tubbercurry, 7 do, Orphan Eliza Reardon, do, 14 do,, Widow Gibson, Ballyara, 7 do, Widow Mary Byrne, Tubbercurry, 7 do, Chas Dwyer, do, 14 do, James Brennan, sick, do, 14 do, Mary McDermott, do, 7 do, Thady Tiernan, sick in fever, do, 7 do, Widow Armstrong, Castleoye, 14 do, Hesther O'Malley, Tubbercurry, 7 do, Widow Robt Burns, Ogham, 14 do, Widow Thos McKim, Mucketta, 14 do, Widow Mary Allen, Ogham, 14 do, Geo Smith, sick in fever, Derreens, 14 do, Widow Ino Golden, do, Rathscanlan, 7 do, Rickard Golden, do, do, 14 do, Thos Costelloe, do, Ballyaise, 7 do, Widow Benson, Tubbercurry, 7 do, Orphans Henry, sick, do, 14 do, , Widow Cassidy, Ogham, 7 do, Orphans Craven (both parents died in fever), do, 14 do, Anne Ginty, Kilcummin, 7 do, Geo West, family sick, Tubbercurry, 14 do, Widow Margaret Walton, do, 7 do, Bridget Quin, Tullycusheen, 7 do, Orphan Mary O'Connor, do, 7 do, Widow Preston or Henry, Castleloye, 7 do, James Philips (10 in family), Tubbercurry, 7 do, Anne Neill (family ill), do, 14 do, Thos Killoran, Mullaghanarry, 14 do, Rebecca Glenny (10 in family: all in fever), Carraun, 14 do, Alexander Glenny, do, 14 do, Thos Dolphin, Carrowreagh Knox, 14 do, Orphan Catherine Callaghan, Powellsboro, 7 do, Edward Golden, sick, Mucketta, 14 do, Susan Black, Tubbercurry, 14 do, Edward Meekings, sick, Rathscanlan, 7 do, Richard Golden, sick, do, 7 do, Widow Golden (recovering from fever), do, 7 do, Alexander Glenny, do, Carraun, 14 do, Thos Craven, do, Ogham, 7 do, Andrew Mosgrove, Tubbercurry, 7 do, Thos West, in fever, Tubbercurry, 14 do, Chas. West, Tubbertelly, 14 do, Winifrid Brennan, Carrowreagh Cooper, 21 lbs of meal, Pat Kilmartin, do, 17½ do, Mick Kilmartin, do, 17½ do, Owen Durkan, Tubbercurry, 17½ do, Thos Whyte, do, 14 do, Pat Scanlan, do, 21 do, Widow Gilroy, Carrowreagh Cooper, 17½ do, Mary Connor, do, 7 do, James Morrison, do, 17½ do, Widow Kilmartin, do, 14 do, Thos Spelman, do, 14 do, Mathew Kilmartin, do, 7 do, Robert Morrison, do, 17½, Betty Scanlan, Tubbercurry, 14 do, Widow Bourck, do, 7 do, Mary Kilmore, do, 14 do, Anne Leonard, do, 7 do, John Walsh, Carrowreagh, 17½ do, widow McGuinn, 17½ do, Thos Durkan, do, 7 do, John Haran, Tubberscardan, 7 do, Mary Magher, do, 3½ do, James Redican. do, 7 do, Lackey Grogan, do, 7 do,Widow Marren, do, 7 do, Catherine Davey, do, 7 do, Catherine Kilmartin, do, 14 do, Michael Scully, do, 7 do, John Boland, do, 7 do, Luke Kilmartin, do, 14 do, James Gannon, do, 3½ do, Widow Gilgan, Carntubber, 7 do, James Cunneen, do, 7 do, Thos Ross, Ogham, 14 do, Mary Davey, do, 3½, Owen Tanzey, Tubbertelly, 7 do, Patt Mannion, do, 3½ do, Eleanor Kilmore, do, 7 do, James Williams, do, 28 do, Chas West (10 in family), do, 42 do, Thos Reynolds, do, 7 do, Abraham Allen, do, 21 do, Bridget Allen, do, 14 do, Mary Durkan, do, 14 do, Atty May, do, 7 do, Eleanor Alcock, do, 7 do, Margaret Doran, do, 7 do, Bridget Durkan, do, 7 do.

Appendix 2: Relief Committees

Ballaghaderreen Relief Committee, 24 August 1846
Members: Charles Strickland, chairman, J. A. Holmes, John Coghlan PP, Denis Tighe PP, D. Mo-? PP, Michael Mulowny CC, Ambrose McTucker, J. P. Dalton, Thomas Philips, Anthony McDonnell.

A: Ballaghaderreen

Bunninadden Relief Committee, 8 February 1847
James Henry PP, Arthur Stanley, Barth. McGettrick, Thomas Irwin, Thomas O'Connor, Thomas Rice.

B: Bunninadden

Corran Relief Committee, 13 August 1846
Present: Richard Gethen, chairman, William Phibbs, James Fleming, Alexander Crichton, James Knott, John Trimble, John McDonough, Bartly McGetrick, Philip Gormley, James O'Hara PP, James Henry PP, James Higgins CC, Rev James Fleming, Presbyterian minister, John McManamny, Arthur Hanly, George McElroy, William Shaw.
21 August 1846
Present: Richard Gethen, chairman, Alexander Crichton JP, Dr Logheed, James Knott, James Fleming, Philip Gormley, Arthur Stanley, J. Finn PP, Bernard O'Kane PP, James O'Hara PP, J. McManamny, Bartly McGetrick, Sam Gilmore, J. McDonagh, William Shaw, J.Taylor, J. Henry PP.

C: Corran

Costello Relief Committee, 7 October 1846
J. A. Holmes JP, Rev J. Seymore JP, vicar of Castlemore, Denis Tighe PP Ballaghaderreen, Charles Strickland JP, chairman, Thomas Philips JP, Cloonmore House, John Coghlan PP Kilmovee, and William McHugh PP.

D: Costello

Gallen and Costello Relief Committee, 26 May 1846
Members: George Vaughan Jackson, Edward Deane JP, Robert Orme JP, William Orme JP, Francis R. O'Grady JP, George J. O'Malley JP, George Rutledge JP, James Dillon JP, Charles Strickland JP. *Poor Law Guardians:* Edward P McDonnell, James Beytagh, Richard O'Grady, John Bollinbrooke, James Jordan, Patrick W. Kelly, Oliver Dalton, Luke Colleran, Patrick Durkan, Michael Henry, Daniel Keane. *Priests:* Denis Tighe PP, Patrick O'Grady PP, Patrick Duffy PP, Thadeus Mullany PP, Denis O'Kane PP, William McHugh PP, John McHugh PP, Bernard Durcan PP, John Corley PP, Bernard Egan PP, Michael O'Flynn PP, Thomas McNicholas PP, James Devine CC, Patrick Spelman CC, Michael Muldowney CC, John Brennan CC, Patrick Groarke CC. *Ministers:* Rev Mr Mostyn, Rev Mr Seymour, Rev Mr Eames. Richard Kyle, clerk of the Board of Guardians, was made clerk of the Relief Committee.
9 June 1846
Present: G. V. Jackson, chairman, Edward Deane JP, Francis R. O'Grady JP, Charles Strickland JP, John O'Grady, Richard O'Grady, John Bollingbrooke, Thadeus O'Douda, Daniel Keane, Patrick Durkan, John Corley PP, Bernard Egan PP, William McHugh PP,

E: Gallen & Costello

John McHugh PP, Denis O'Kane PP, Michael O'Flynn PP, Michael Muldowney CC, Patrick Spelman CC, Patrick Groarke CC.

7 July 1846
Present: G. V. Jackson, chairman, Edward Deane JP, Charles Strickland JP, Francis R.O'Grady JP, Oliver C. Jackson PLG, Edward P. McDonnell PLG, John O'Grady PLG, Richard O'Grady PLG, James Jordan PLG, Patrick W. Kelly PLG, Daniel Keane PLG, Pat Durkan PLG, Thadeus O'Dowda PLG, L. D. Fitzgerald MD, Ulic Burke MD, Capt Gordon OPW, Henry Brett, county surveyor, B. W. Eames, vicar, Bernard Durcan PP, Bernard Egan PP, Michael O'Flynn PP, John McNulty PP, Thomas McNicholas PP, John McHugh PP, William McHugh PP, James Brennan CC, Pat Hyland CC, Pat Groarke CC.

14 July 1846
Present: G. V. Jackson, chairman, Edward Deane, Francis R.O'Grady, Charles Strickland. *PLGs:* Oliver C. Jackson, Edward P. McDonnell, Thadeus O'Dowda, James Jordan, Pat Touhey, Pat Durkan, Daniel Keane, Luke Colleran, Patrick W. Kelly, Oliver Dalton. *Priests:* Bernard Egan PP, Bernard Durcan PP, Michael O'Flynn PP, John McNulty PP, Thomas McNicholas PP, John McHugh PP, Pat Spelman CC, James Devine CC, Pat Groarke CC, McNicholas CC, – Prendergast CC, John Brennan CC, John Hyland CC, Capt Gordon OPW, Henry Brett, county surveyor.

28 July 1846
Present: G. V. Jackson, chairman, Edward Deane JP, Francis R.O'Grady JP, Charles Strickland JP. *PLGs:* James Jordan, Pat Touhey, Pat Durkan, Luke Colleran, Daniel Keane, Michael Henry. *Priests:* Bernard Durcan PP, Bernard Egan PP, John McNulty PP, John McHugh PP, Paul McGreal PP, John O'Connor CC, Patrick Spelman CC. Mr McManus, assistant county surveyor.

26 August 1846
Signatories: G. V. Jackson, chairman, Charles Strickland JP, Thomas Philips, Bernard Durcan PP, John Coghlan PP Kilmovee, James Jordan, Thomas Ormsby JP, John Brennan CC, J. Seymore, vicar, Patrick Spelman CC, Geoff Mostyn, Protestant curate, Paul MacGreal PP Turlough, Thomas McNicholas PP Bohola, James Devine CC, Michael Mulowny CC, Michael O'Flynn PP, Bernard Egan PP, Thadeus O'Dowda, Anthony McDonnell, John McHugh PP, D. Mc –? CC, James Beytagh, Edward P. McDonnell, Edward Deane, Daniel Keane, Michael Henry, Pat Durkan, Patrick W. Kelly.

13 October 1846
Present: George Vaughan Jackson, chairman, Edward Deane JP, Francis R. O'Grady JP, Edward P. McDonnell PLG, Richard O'Grady, PLG, Patt Durkan PLG, Patt W. Kelly PLG, Daniel Keane PLG, Peter Colleran PLG, Revd Mr Coghlan PP, Revd Mr Egan PP, Revd Mr O'Flynn PP, Revd Mr McNicholas PP, Revd B. W. Eames, vicar, Revd Mr Mostyn, Protestant curate, Revd Mr Spelman CC, Revd Mr Muldowny CC.

F: Foxford

Foxford Relief Committee, 19 February 1847
Members: G. V. Jackson, chairman, Bernard Egan, PP Kilgarvan, Michael O'Flynn PP Attymass, John Corley PP Toomore, Thomas McNulty PP Killasser, J. Fitzgerald, G. H. Mostyn, Protestant curate, Foxford.

G: Kilkelly

Kilkelly Relief Committee, 3 February 1847
Richard O'Grady, John Coghlan PP Kilmovee, Michael Muldowny CC, Edward McDonnell.

8 February 1847
Francis R. O'Grady, chairman, John Coghlan PP, John O'Grady PLG, Michael Muldowny CC, Patrick Groarke CC.

Swinford Relief Committee
Edward Deane JP, chairman, Bernard Durcan PP, B. W. Eames, vicar, Patrick Spelman CC, Thomas McNicholas PP Bohola, Daniel Mullarkey, PP Killedan, Edward Hunt, sub-inspector.

H: Swinford

Upper Leyny, 16 October 1846
John Armstrong, chairman, Edward Hoare, dean & vice-chairman, John Grey, PLG, Cloonacool, Daniel Mullarky, PP Kilmactigue, Rev John Hamilton, perpetual curate, Tubbercurry, John Flynn, PP Curry, James McHugh, PP Cloonacool, James Gallagher, PP Achonry, F. G. Jones, Banada Abbey, John Stewart, sub-inspector, Tubbercurry, John Brett, PLG Tubbercurry, Luke Colleran, PLG, Curry, John Durcan, PLG, Kilmactigue.
15 March 1847
Signatories: Edward N. Hoare, chairman, James McHugh PP, John Flynn PP, James Higgins PP, Luke Colleran, John Grey, Thomas McManus, Frederick G. Jones, Banada, Rev John Hamilton.

I: Upper Leyny

Tirerrill Relief Committee, 24 October 1846, which included the parishes of Killery, Kilross, Ballysumahon, Ballisodare & Ballinakill
Members: E. J. Cooper, chairman, John Ormsby, vice-chairman, Rev. E. A. Lucas, secretary, Rev Patrick Durcan, Edward L. Neynoe JP, Rev William McGuinness, Rev Luke Cullenan, Rev John O'Farrell, Charles O'Hara, chairman of the Poor Law Union, John Grant, constabulary officer, Captain Gilbert, Nicholson O'Fury, Thomas Irwin, Samuel Williams, John Lougheed, Thomas Phibbs.

J: Tirerrill

Appendix 3: Subscription Lists

A: Coolaney

Coolaney, 26 March 1847
Subscribers: Charles K. O'Hara, £20, E. J. Cooper, £10, Archdeacon Verschoyle, £10, Charles Langley, £10, William Phibbs, £2, Rev A. K. Huston, £1, Rev Mr Hurst PP, £1, James Kelly MD, £1, Mr Thompson, £1, Harloe Phibbs, £1, Messrs Fut? & Co, English agents to the O'Hara accountants, £10. Government grant, £69.

B: Coolavin

Coolavin, 5 August 1846
J. A. Holmes, £20, Charles J.Willermot JP, – , Rev. G. Powell, Vicar of Kilfree, £10, Rev Peter Brennan PP Kilfree, £10, Rev M. Coghlan CC Kilfree, £3, Rev C. Cosgrove, Killaraght, £1, Mr Costello PLG, £1, Mr Powell PLG, –, Mr Baker, £5, Mr Sherlock, –, P. Whelan RM, –, George Lynch?, £5.
10 August 1846
Calcutta Relief Committee, £30, Lord Lorton, £30, Lord de Freyne, £10, Patrick Lynch, £10, Patrick Owen Cogan, £3.
17 March 1847
Relief Association, 16 Upper Sackville St, £20, Central Relief Association of Ireland, £20, Society of Friends, £20, 'Guernsey Friends', £5, John Stuart?, Castlerea, £10, Rev P. Brennan PP, £1, James Powell, £1, M. Callaghan, £1, A. Baker, £1, Rev E. Powell, £1, Mr Bellet, Dublin, £8, Mrs Neix?, Lydenham, Kent, £1, Miss Stellican, Clifton, £3 10s., Mrs Ball, Granby Place, Dublin, £2, Mrs Day, Clifton, £5, Mrs Rawdon Briggs, Stakefields, £13 17s. 6d., Mr Bewley, Booterstown, £3, A. G. Holmes, London, £5, Mrs A. G. Holmes, London, £5, Rev J. Hensman, Clifton, £10, Ladies Relief Association, Dublin, £30, Mr Caulfield, Bath, £3 3s., Mrs Nahab, Blackrock, £1, Rev J. Seymour, Ballaghaderreen, £2, Mrs G. Holmes, £1 10s., Mr Webb, London, £5, Miss Kelly, Dublin, £6, friends in Dorsetshire, £20, Mr J. Holmes, £2.

C: Corran

Corran, 23 July 1846
Viscount Lorton (for specified road), £150, Col Perceval, £25, Harloe Phibbs, £10, William Phibbs, Seafield, £20, Richard Gethen, £10, Henry Irwin, Dabari?, £5, Robert Orme, Gortnerabay, £5, – –, £5, The Widow Phibbs, £3, James Knott, £2, Rev James O'Hara, Keash, £3, Rev James Henry, Bunninadden, £3, Rev James Fleming, Presbyterian minister, £1, Philip Gormley, £2, Bartly McGettrick, £1, Mr & Mrs Shaw, £1.
30 July 1846
Additional subscriptions: Sir Alexander Crichton, £10, John Wynne, Hazelwood, £5, Jemmet Duke, Willowbrook, £3, Bernard O'Kane PP Ballymote, £3, Rev John Garrett, £1, Rev James Higgins CC, £1.
13 August 1846
William Phibbs, £5, Alexander Crichton, £10, Major Charles Parke, £3; Dean Hoare, £2, John Trimble, £1, John McManamny, £1.
28 August 1846
Lord Lorton, £10, Alexander Crichton, £10, Jemmet Duke, £10, William Phibbs, £5, Rev

Mr Hearn, £3, Mr Wood of Elmville?, £2, Major Parke, £3, John McManamny, £1, John Trumble, £1.

18 September 1846

William Phibbs, £25, Lord Lorton, £10, Sir Alex Crichton, £20, Richard Gethen, £10, Henry Irwin, £5, Jemmet Duke, £13, widow of Richard Phibbs, £3, Rev James O'Hara PP, £3, Rev James Henry PP, £3, Alex Crichton, £3, John Wynne, £5, Edward J.Cooper, £10, Major Parke, £3, Rev Bernard O'Kane PP, £3, James Knott, £2, P. Gormley, £3, Rev Mr Kearn, £2, Mrs Wood, £2, Rev Dean Hoare, £2, James Fleming, £1, Major Phipps, £1, Revd J.Garrett, £1, Har Phibbs, £1, Bartly McGetrick, £1, William Shaw, £1, Rev James Higgins CC, £1, John MacManann, £1, John Trumble, £1, Laurence Gillmore, £1, Rev James Fleming, Presbyterian minister, £1, Rev Mr Finn CC, £1.

23 October 1846

Robert Orme (2nd sub), £5, Jemmet Duke, £5, P. Gormley, £1, Edward Tigue, £1, Abraham Motherwell, £1, Hartstongue Robinson, £1, William Callaghan, £1, Robert L. Morrison, £1, John Gillmore, £1, Rev John Garrett Jr, £10, Henry Baker Irwin, £1, Bartly O'Brien, 10s., Miss Irwin, 7s. 6d., Bartly Dodhill, 10s., Bartly Coghlan, 5s., Francis Morgan, 5s., Edward O'Brien, 5s. 6d., Barry Flinn, 2s. 6d., Jack Dyer, 5s., Patt Flanagan, 2s. 6d., Michael Brehony, 2s. 6d., John Flinn, 1s. 6d., George McElney, 5s.

29 January 1847

Rev John Garrett of Hull, £10, Wm Phibbs, £1, Jemmet Duke, £2, Major Parkes, £2, Lord Lorton, £2, Major Orme, £2, Sir Alexander Crichton, £10, Wm Flood?, £2, Society of Friends, £20, Irish Famine Fund through Bishop of Tuam, £9, John Wynne, £5, Lady Norbery, £6. Government grant, £120.

20 February 1847

Subscribers: Rev William Pollock, St Helen's, England, £20, Thomas Aubertin, Cambridge, £6 6s., Irish Association, College Green, Dublin, £50, Dr Logheed, Ballymote, £2, James Fleming, Abbeyville, £1, Robert Morrison, £1. Government grant, £30.

2 March 1847

Society of Friends, £20, Thomas Aubertin, £5 13s 6d.

Lower Leyny, 21 August 1846   *D: Lower Leyny*

C. K. O'Hara, £100, Colonel Perceval, not at home, has given much employment to his own tenants, E. J. Cooper, has only one townland in the district and will employ his own, Lord Lorton, same, do, William Phibbs, £5, takes care of his own, Harloe Phibbs, £1, Meredith Thompson, £3, employs his own, Charles Thompson, offers £25 to be expended on a road through his own ground, Charles Langly, no answer, absentee, John Wynne, £5, only one townland, J. P. Somers MP, £10, absentee, Colonel Kirkwood, no answer, absentee, Edward Irwin one townland, do, John Armstrong, same, very active in adjoining district, Colonel Irwin, no answer, one townland, Owen Lloyd, no reply, absentee, Dr W. McManus, no reply, James Dodwell, no reply, Archdeacon Verschoyle, £30, rector of Killoran, Rev Mr Hurst, £3, RC clergyman, Killoran, Henry Burrows, £1, respectable farmer, J. Simpson, £1, respectable farmer.

25 September 1846

C. K. O'Hara, chairman, £100, Archdeacon Verschoyle & Killoran parish, £30, Dean Durcan PP Ballisodare, £5, Rev. W. Hurst PP Killoran, £3, William Ormsby Gore MP, £10, Charles Langley, £10, John P. Somers, £10, W. Phibbs, £5, H. Phibbs, £1, M. Thompson, £3, Henry Burrowes, £1, J. Simpson, £1.

Upper Leyny, 8 June 1846   *E: Upper Leyny*

John Armstrong, £30, William Phibbs, £20, Mrs R. P. Irwin, £10, The O'Conor Don, £1,

A. Caulfield, £5, Adam –, £5, Richard Irwin, £3, – Irwin, £2, Mrs Luke Irwin, £3, Dean of Achonry, £3, Rev J. McHugh, £3, Roger D. Robinson, £2, M. McHugh, £3, Richard Phibbs, £3, Mr Treacy, Carnalack, £3, Sir Roger Palmer, £20.

15 July 1846

Subscribers: John Armstrong, £30, Lr Phibbs, £20, The O'Conor Don MP, £10, Mrs Irwin, £3, Richard Phibbs, £3, John Irwin, £3, Richard Irwin, £3, Hon A. Caulfield, £5, Mr Irwin, £10, A. D. Robinson, £2, James McHugh PP, £3, Dean of Achonry, £3, James Gray, £3, James McHugh, £3, Henry Irwin, £10, Adam Robinson, £5, Mrs? Phibbs, £5, Sir Roger Palmer, £30, Samuel Robinson, £3, James A. Knox, £25, D. Mullarkey PP, £3, J. Flynn PP, £3, John Brett, £3, Hugh Gray, £4, Rev. J. Hamilton, £2, Ed. Ormsby Gore MP, £10, J. Gallagher PP, £3, Col. Kirkwood, £5, James McManus, £3, Daniel Jones, £10, Col. Irwin, £5, Harloe Phibbs, £3, Tubbercurry Loan Fund, £12.

Non-subscribors: E. J. Cooper, James Knott, Robert Young, Col Wingfield (contributed £10 on 16 July), Martin Cooper, Countess of Norbery, Connell O'Beirne, W. Meredith, Denis O'Connor, Robert Digby, Major Brownhead, John F. Knox, – Nolan, E. J. Nolan, James Lord?, David A. Farrell, Edward Nicholson, R. C. Walker, John Ffolliott MP, F. French.

15 December 1846

Colonel Wingfield, £10, the late John Armstrong, £20, E. J. Cooper, £10, – Phibbs, £10, E. J. Nolan, £5, Colonel Irwin, £5.

9 January 1847

Society of Friends, £20, Irish Relief Association, £10 (as well as a boiler), 'Guernsey Friends', £5.

4 February 1847

Society of Friends, £20, same, second donation, £20, Deputy Commissary-General Dobree from Guernsey Friends, £5. Richard Phibbs, £5.

20 February 1847

Subscribers: Mrs Armstrong (for Chaffpool), £50, Charles K. O'Hara, £10, Colonel Kirkwood, £8, Mr Phibbs, £5, R. P. Irwin, £1, Hon Mr Caulfield (for Kilmactigue), £3, Major Brossehead, £1, Dean of Achonry, £2, two Sligo friends of Rev M. McHugh, £10, Rt Rev Dr McNicholas by Rev John Flynn, £6, Lady Norbury, £10, an English friend by Dean of Achonry, £3.

10 March 1847

Messrs Bewley & Pim of Society of Friends, £20, Harloe Phibbs, £1, friend by same, 5s., Dowager Lady de Saumerez (by Deputy Commissary General Dobree), £10, Mr Sheils, Liverpool, £10, Rt Rev Dr McNicholas by Rev James Higgins for Kilmactigue, £15, same by Rev J. McHugh PP for Tubbercurry, a Dublin friend by Rev J. McHugh for Tubbercurry, £10, Mr Jones for Banada Abbey estate, £30, W. Forster by ditto for ditto, £5.

20 March 1847

Subscription list: Sir Roger Palmer, £20, George Knox RM, £3, a friend by Dean of Achonry, £5, Rt Rev Dr McNicholas by Rev J. Flynn PP, £5, same by Rev James Gallagher PP, £5, a friend by Miss Jones, £3, same by Frederick Jones, £1, Rev A. Minchin for Irish Relief Association, £10, Generai Central Relief Association, £100, J. Standish Haly from British Relief Association (provisions), £65, Count P. de Strzelecki, £35.

F: Gallen &
Costello

Gallen and Costello, 26 June 1846

George Vaughan Jackson, £20, Sir Roger Palmcr, £25, John Bollingbrooke, £10, Francis R. O'Grady, £5, Anthony Ormsby, £5, William Orme, £5, William James Brabazon, £5, Thadeus O'Dowda, £5, Bernard Egan PP, £5, Walter Eakins for minor Rowne, £3.

9 July 1846

Colonel Knox Gore, £5, Robert Orme, £10, George H. Moore, £50, Mrs Louisa Moore, £20.

31 July 1846
Lord Viscount Dillon, £100, Costello barony subscription, £40, Francis R. O'Grady (2nd subscription), £5, James Cuffe, £3, Valentine O'Connor Blake, £2.
9 August 1846
Colonel McAlpine, £10, James Darcy, £5, Townsend Kirkwood, £5, Lord Dillon (2nd subscription), £8, G. V. Jackson (2nd subscription), £5, Sir Compton Dombelle?, £10, Rev F. Rutledge, £2.

Ballaghaderreen Relief Committee, 15 February 1847   G: Ballaghaderreen
Subscribers: British Relief Association, South Sea House, £25, Central Relief Association to Rev D. Tighe, £75, Society of Friends (part of £100), £10, Lord Dillon, £30, Mr Waldron Esq, £5, Mr Cogan, £1, Costello minors by Mr Holmes, £15, Denis Tighe PP, £1, Andrew Dillon MD, £1, Charles Strickland, £2.
15 March 1847
Subscribers: 18 February, General Central Relief Committee, Dublin, £75, 19 February, Sam Gurney, London, £10, 23 February, British Relief Association per Commissioner Amas Lister, Westport, £50, 15 March, Rt Rev Dr Briggs, York per Most Rev Dr McHale, £15, an order of a ton of rice from the Society of Friends per Jonathan Pim, £25, Society of Friends, £80, Lord Dillon, £290.

Bohola Relief Committee, 29 December 1846   H: Bohola
Edward Deane, £10, Charles McManus, £5, John Touhy, £5, Philip Taaffe, £3, Dominick Jordan, £3, Thomas McNicholas PP, £3, Patrick O'Connor CC, £3, Patrick Hurst, £1. Government grant, £32.

Foxford, 18 July 1846   I: Foxford
Rev. Mr Corley, £3, John Bollingbrooke, £3, John McCarrick, treasurer, £2, John McGloin, £2, Geo V. Jackson, £1, Edward Deane, £2, Patrick Corly, £1, Sylvester Sheil, £1, Pat Davis, £1, Rev Mr Hyland, £1, Mr Lundy, £1, John Fitzgerald, £1, Dr Gauly, 10s., Joseph Atkinson, 10s., Mathew Sheil, 7s. 6d., Pat Coghlan, 5s., James Coleman, 5s., Samuel Stroggen, 5s., Farrell Higgins, 5s., Pat McGowan, 5s., Mark Carroll, 5s.
14 August 1846
John Fitzgerald, £2 10s., Hugh Shields, 5s., Pat Horkan, 10s., Mat Shiel, £1, John Eliot, 5s., Sylvester Shiel, 10s.

Kilkelly, 26 March 1847   J: Kilkelly
Subscribers: Right Rev Dr McNicholas, £10, Rt Rev Dr ?, £20, Rt Rev Dr Briggs, £10, Henry Romarne?, London, £120, William Jones, London, £15, Francis R. O'Grady, £10, Rev John Coghlan, £5, William -earnon?, £5, Miss Widguard, £5, Society of Friends, £22, General Central Relief Association, £20, British Association, £60, Dr O'Grady, Lamanska, £5, Rev Dr Drum, £15. Government grant, £220.

Swinford, 7 April 1846   K: Swinford
Mr Ormsby Gore, £10, Revd Mr O'Rourke, £3, James Darcy, £3
2 November 1846
Subscriptions: Rev B. Durcan PP, £5, Rev P. Spelman CC, £3, Rev W. Devine CC, £4 10s., Dr Burke, £3, Dr Fitzgerald, £1, P. Prendergast, £5, P. Durcan, £3, James Horkan, £5, M. Mellet, treasurer, £3, P. Henry, £3, P. Corley, £1, P. Cawley, £1, A. – ?, £1, Edward Hurst, £1, P. Cunniffe, £2, Richard Kyle, £3. Recommended grant £48.

10 November 1846
Oliver C. Jackson, £7, G. V. Jackson, £5, Rev B. Eames, vicar of Kilconduff, £2, P. Kelly, £1.
26 December 1846
Rev Charles Twistleton, £10, F. Blake Knox, £5, Rutledge Watson, £2. Government grant, £17.
23 January 1847
Capt Stirling, £2, donors unknown per G. V. Jackson, £20, Lord Lieutenant, £50. Government grant, £100.
19 February 1847
Swinford Poor Relief Committee Soup Kitchen Fund, £175, General Central Committee for all Ireland, £70, Society of Friends, £30, Swinford Meal Fund, £50, B. Durcan PP, £15, Captain Perceval per G. V. Jackson, £10.

L: Templehouse

Templehouse Relief Committee, 12 March 1847
My daughters & small subscriptions, £32, collected by Mr A. Perceval, £36, collected by myself, £35, Smith & Payne's Bank, £22, John Abel Smith, £20, Mr Attwood, £20, Lady Arbuthnot, £10, Mr and Mrs Annesley, £10, Mr Venables, £10, Mr P. Perceval, £10, Mr Magan and Patrick Bark, £10, Mr V. Corrie, £10, Miss Bethune, £5 7s., Miss Maran, £5.

M: Tirerrill

Tirerrill Relief Committee, 17 September 1846
E. J. Cooper, £50, Mrs O'Gore, £10, Wm Weir, £10, C. W. Cooper, £10, Rev W. French, £5, W. Phibbs, £5, K. D. Lloyd, £1, John Ormsby, £10, John Ffolliott, £5, E. Frazer, £2, N. O. Fury, £2, Sir G. King, £10, Rev R. Cage, £2, John Grant, £2 12s, Thos Irwin, £3, Rev E. A. Lucas, £2, Rev D. Durcan, £2, John Gethen, £5, Rev L. Cultenan, £2, John Duke, £2, B. O. Cogan, £5, John Wynne, £5, Michael Kough, £10, Rev Barry Phibbs, £5, Rev E. Feeny, £2, Thomas Phibbs, £1, Rev E. Elwood, £1, Roger Duke, £5, Charles Langley, £10, Earl of Zetland, £30.

Appendix 4: Public Works

Coolavin 5 November 1846
OPW recommended £4,500 for 16 works: 1. Complete new road from Drumrock to Carrowntemple, £100. 2. Complete the road leading from Ballymote to Ballaghaderreen into Townybrack, £100. 3. New road from Ballaghaderreen through the lands of Lesserlough, £80. 4. Complete new road from Boyle to the fort at Clooncunny through Ardsoran, £100. 5. Widen & fence the present road from Boyle to Ballina and make a portion of new road between Knockranna and Gurteen, £500. 6. Make a new road from Mullaghroe to the mearing of Co Roscommon, £500. 7. Make a new road 1,150 perches from Ballaghaderreen to Boyle between the crossroads in Monasterevan and Mullaghroe, £700. 8. Make 36 perches of new road to connect the road now in progress in Co Roscommon, £40. 9. Make & repair 580 perches of road from Ballaghaderreen to Boyle between Townymuckla and the ford of Clooncunny, £400. 18. Repair 690 perches of road leading from the Boyle road in Knocknashammer to the mearing of the county at Culmore, £300. 22. Make 670 perches of road from Boyle to Frenchpark 670 perches through Ardsoran and Killaraght to Thomas Cregg's house, £500. 33. Make a new road, 1,035 perches from Boyle to Tubbercurry and build 5 bridges, commencing at the mearing of Co Roscommon and ending at Drumlusta on the road from Ballaghaderreen to Ballymote, £500. 25. Make 200 perches of new road from Boyle to Tubbercurry commencing at the mearing of the barony at Ardrahon and ending at the forge at Gounoris, £200. 29. 60 perches of new road being a continuation of that leading from Doon to Carrowntemple church, £60. 30. Make 16 perches of new road being a continuation of that leading from Boyle to Ballina in the townland of Cappanagh, £20. 32. Make a new road from Ballaghaderreen to Boyle commencing at Redwood and ending at Moygara, £400.
OPW recommended one additional work, making 828 perches of new road from Ballaghaderreen to Bunninadden, commencing at Carrowntemple and ending at the crossroads at Ballygalder.

Corran, 8 October 1846
OPW recomended £798 to make a new road, 633 perches long from the road from Ballymote to Tubbercurry at Woodhill to Ballinaleck.
2 November 1846
OPW recommended £300 for making a new road from the mailcoach road at Drumfin to Branchfield, between the turn to Riverstown and the road at Branchfield.
7 January 1847
OPW recommended 34 works amounting to £7,796 17s 6d: 1. New road 420 perches from the mearing of the barony at Currodory West to new road on townland of Carrowcrory, £450. 2. New road 520 perches in townlands of Derrygolagh and Meenmore from the termination of the Linagh (Liskeagh?) road to the present Battlefield and Boyle road, £400. 3. New road 380 perches from Ballymote and Boyle new road in Carrowcunny to the mearing of the barony in townland of Tully, £400. 5. New road 400 perches from Farranmaurice to the mearing of the barony at Linagower (Lismagore?), £400. 7. Completing the cutting of

429

the hill on the townland of Ballincarrow on the road from Ballymote to Castlebaldwin, £200. 8. Complete cutting of the hill in Camross on road from Ballymote to Coolaney, £150. 9. Complete cutting of Drumfin hill on road from Ballymote to Drumfin, £120. 10. Complete cutting Ballybrennan hill on road from Ballymote to Tubbercurry, £200. 11. New road from Ballymote to Boyle to avoid the hill of Emlefad, £400. 12. Completing new road from Ballymote to Collooney, £200. 13. Complete new road at Clooncunny, £100. 14. New road to avoid the hill in townland of Knocknagee, £240. 15. Complete new road from Branchfield to Knockadalteen, £240. 16. New road from Ballymote to Drumfin between Curnmean and Cloonlurg, £400. 17. New road from Bunninadden to the ford of Moyrush, £500. 18. Widening road from Tubbercurry to Boyle between the mearing of Coolavin and Peter Gannon's forge, £40. 19. Completing road from Ardree to the bridge at Knockbrack, £300. 20. Repair 500 perches of road from crossroads at Cloonkeary to Greyfort, £125. 21. Widen & improve road from Ballymote to Tubbercurry on townland of Oldrock, £57 10s. 22. New road from the Eel weir at Carrowreagh and Oldrock, £16 17s 6d. 24. Cut hill on townland of Cloonagh and repair road from Keash chapel to the new road of Knockacommon, £80. 25. Finish the improvement of the road from Rathmullin bridge to Coolavin, £200. 26. Finish the new road from Templehouse to Oldrock, £200. 28. New road from the crossroads at Drumrolla to the Boyle road at Tawnalion, £500. 29. Complete the new road from Boyle to Tubbercurry thro' Knockalass and Quarryfield, £300. 30. New road through the townlands of Cledda, Roscrib, Sacalla commencing at Knocknawhishogue and terminating at Cloonoghill, £400. 33. Cut the hill at Quarryfield at Pat Marren's on the road from Ballymote to Tubbercurry, £300. 35. A continuation of the Knockadalteen road from the present terminus to the new road from Ballymote to Sligo, £300. 37. New road from Kilmorgan to new road from Ballymote to Drumfin, £300. 39. Cut a hill on Drumcormick and widen and fence the road from Ballymote to Castlebaldwin, £60. 40. 700 perches of fencing between the Bough? road at the bridge of Riversdale, £87 10s. 41. Widening the road from the mailcoach road at the Stage to the mearing of the barony of Tirerrill, £80. 43. Cut the hill on the lands of Cloonkeary on the road from Tubbercurry to Collooney, £100. 45. Widen and improve the entrance to Ballymote at the chapel, £30.

16 February 1847

OPW recommended new road from James Flanagan's house at Knockgranna to the mearing of the barony of Costello, £300.

19 February 1847

New road 1,261 perches from Ballymote to the townland of Clooncunny between Millstreet and Cloonlurg.

23 February 1847

New road from Ballymote to Ballaghaderreen between Woodhill to Lissananny Beg, £400.

1 March 1847

New road 986 perches from Tubbercurry to Boyle between Ballyvally East and the crossroads in Knockranna.

C: Costello   *Costello, 7 October 1846*

OPW recommended £21,899 for 80 public works out of 132 applied for amounting to £40,007: 1. Improving the road from Ballaghaderreen to Boyle, £200. 2. Making 119 perches of road from Greenwood to Knock, £700. 3. Making 713 perches of new road from Coolicaha to Cloongonnagh, £400. 4. Lowering the hills on the road from Cloughwoly to Cartron, £90. 5. Lowering the hills on road from Urlaur to Kilmovee road from Bellaghy to Ballyhaunis, £150. 6. Lowering the hills at Brackloon on road from Ballyhaunis to Loughlynn, £50. 7. Lowering the hills at Coolnafarna & Scregg on road from Ballyhaunis to Ballaghaderreen, £40. 8. Improving the road from Ballaghaderreen to Kilkelly, £500. 9.

Improving the road from Ballaghaderreen to Doocastle, £800. 10. Making 600 perches of road from Eden to Bruff, £600. 11. Making 200 perches of new road from Cloonfallagh to Caher, £200. 12. Making 1000 perches of new road & improving 1480 perches of the present road from Ballaghaderreen to Kilkelly, £1500, modification, £500. 13. Making 660 perches of new road & improving 330 perches of road from the county boundary at Cloonfaghtren to Cloonlarhin, £760. 15. 370 perches of new road from Cloonlaurhin to Co Sligo at Lugacashel, £500, modification, £250. 16. 2,500 perches of road from Uggool to Killaturly, £2,500, modification, £600. 17. 700 perches of road from Barnacooga to Glentauran on road from Loughglyn to Swinford, £700. 18. Improving 2,000 perches of road from Kilkelly to Bellaghy, £1,000. 20. 800 perches of new road from Tunnagh to Bellaghy, £800. 21. 320 perches of new road from Slateford to Kilnock, £300. 22. 600 perches of new road from Ballaghaderreen to Clare, £600, modification, £200. 23. 140 perches of new road & improving 490 perches of the present road from Belesker to Cloonbook & Redhill, £630. 24. 320 perches of new road from Redhill to Tubrahan, £300. 25. 1,600 perches of road from Ballyhaunis to Castlebar, £1,500. 26. 900 perches of new road from Clare to Roscommon, £900. 27. 700 perches of new road from Ballyhaunis to Ballinlough, £500. 28. 400 perches of new road from Ballyveel to Cronane, £400. 29. 1,000 perches of road from Kilkelly to Urlaur, £750. 30. 600 perches of new road from Coolnaha to Mountainincommon, £650. 31. 1,500 perches of new road from Ballyhaunis to Swinford & Ballinacostello, £1,500, modification, £500. 32. Completing 300 perches of new road from Sragh to Baroe, £200. 33. Completing 1,400 perches of new road from Kiltybo to Crossard, £700, modification, £350. 34. Improving 1,000 perches of the road from Baroe to Derymacarthoo, £500. 35. 1,200 perches of road from Boherboe to Clonmeen, £1,200. 36. 360 perches of road from Kiltimagh to Ballyhaunis, £250. 39. Repairing 650 perches of the road from Knock to Aughauine, £300, modification, £50. 44. Building a wall round the burial ground of Kildana, £80. 48. Making a new road from Ballyhaunis to Kilkelly, £270. 50. New road from Ballaghaderreen to Loughglynn, £50. 54. 262 perches of new road from Ballyhaunis to Swinford, £162. 56. Building 20 perches of a wall round the graveyard at Ballyhaunis, £20. 68. Repairing 93 perches of road from Lung to Banada, £46. 69. Remaking and repairing 340 perches of the road from Doogery to Ballymote, £136. 70. Repairing 150 perches of new road from Frenchpark to Ballymote, £75. 71. Repairing 204 perches from Bellaghy to Boyle between the crossroads at Clonmeen and Lanagan, £82. 72. Repairing 135 perches of road from Ballaghaderreen to Tubbercuury, £54. 75. 67 perches of new road from the Doocastle road at Flughena to the quarry at Flughena, £34. 78. Lowering 3 hills and widening the road from Ballyhaunis to Tuam on the townland of Hollywell, £30. 81. 236 perches of new road from Ballaghaderreen to Sligo, £177. 84. 1,000 perches of new road from Bogtiduff to Carracastle, £600. 85. 380 perches of new road from Bogtiduff to Clooniron, £200. 89. Lower 4 hills on the road from Kiltimagh to Ballyhaunis, £60. 90. Widen and deepen 500 perches of drains along the road from Castlebar to Tubbercurry, £13. 92. Lower 3 hills on the road from Ballaghaderreen to Kilkelly, £100. 93. Lower 2 hills at – and Doogha, £30. 100. Repair 100 perches of road from Kilkelly to Bellaghy, £50. 103. New road from Ballaghaderreen to Bellaghy, £45. 106. 100 perches of new road from Kiliune to the road at Kilkelly, £30. 108. 1300 perches of road from Swinford to Castlerea, £600. 109. Complete the cuttings at Carrowreagh, £20. 110. Complete the cut at Carrownedin and Tulrahair, £50. 111. Complete the cut at Lurga on the road from Ballyhaunis to Bellaghy, £20. 112. Complete the cut at Drimbane, £150. 113. Complete the cuttings at Tunnagh on the road from Castlerea to Sligo, £25. 114. Complete the cuttings at Bruff, £170. 115. Complete the cuttings at Faulsullis, £100. 116. Complete the cuttings at Bekin and Lisaniskea, £150. 117. Complete the cuttings at the chapel of Bekin, £100. 118. Complete the cuttings at Kilkelly, £125. 119. Complete the cuttings on the road from Ballyhaunis to Ballaghaderreen. 120. Complete the cuttings at Brackloghboy, £150. 121. Complete the cuttings at Scregg?, £60. 122. Complete the cuttings at Friarshill and Castlerune, £130. 123. Complete the cuttings at Glenvallyure, £50. 124. Complete the cuttings at Crossard, £40. 125. Complete the cuttings at Swordshill, £60. 126. Complete the cuttings at Clooncana, £15. 129. Lower the hills at Craggahduff on the road from Ballaghaderreen to Boyle, £100. 130. Repair 770 perches of the mailcoach road from Ballaghaderreen to Lung, £100. 131. Repair 934 perches of the mailcoach road from Bellaghy to Lugahill, £100. 132. Scour 1,000 perches of drains along the road from Cloonrow to Glentarane, £20.

19 November 1846

OPW to T. N. Redington recommending 19 additional works to the extent of £4,507: 19. 900 perches of new road from Ballyhaunis to Bellaghy near the mailcoach road at Tavina & Lurga & the schoolhouse at Tavrane, £900, modification, £600. 41. 230 perches of new road from Ballyhaunis to Dunmore between Framere and Kilmaine, £120. 46. Lower the hills on the road from Loughglynn to Swinford on the townlands of Cullagh, Kildinane, Clooniron, Canalarky and Carracastle, £800, modification, £600. 47. 150 perches of new road from Ballyhadrum to Tubbercurry, £75. 53. 400 perches of new road from the schoolhouse at Tavrane to the old chapel of Glann, £400. 58. 350 perches of new road from Clare to Ballyhaunis between Bekin and Hollywell, £200. 60. 320 perches of new road from Swinford to Ballaghaderreen Copplecurragh & Cloonrune, £300. 63. 246 perches of new road from Ballaghaderreen to Swinford between Tample & Cloonrune, £200. 64. 440 perches of new road from Ballaghaderreen to Lowpark between Carracastle and Lehanoney?, £250. 67. 160 perches of new road from the mailcoach road at Ammer? to the Aughalusha road, £100. 74. Make & fence 480 perches of new road from Boyle to Swinford between Gawlane & the bridge of Roosky, £480. 76. 614 perches of new road from Kilkelly to Kiltimagh between the bridge of Rhun & the crossroads at Woodfield, £307. 86. To make, form & flag 300 perches of footpaths along the main streets of Ballaghaderreen, £200. 95. New road from Loughglynn to Bellaghy between Castlemine road & Kill, £30. 98. Repair 80 perches of a bridle road from Castlerea to Kilmore, £20. 101. Lower a hill on the road from Ballaghaderreen to Drumnacasson? at Thos McDermott's, £100. 104. Make & repair 702 perches of the road from Ballaghaderreen to Kilkely and Boghtiduffy, £350. 105. 150 perches of a new road at Castlemore near Barnaboy?, £75. 107. 250 perches of new road Coolaghtane thro' Baloughsen? & Doogerry to meet the main line, £100.

8 December 1846

OPW recommended 10 additional works amounting to £1,505: 14. 340 perches of new road from the county boundary at Kilmore to Flughena, £300. 15. 570 perches of new road from Cloonlaurshin to Co Sligo at Lugacashel, from Cloonlaurshin to Tavrane to the county boundary at Lymehill, £250. 49. 180 perches of new road from Ballyhaunis to Ballaghaderreen in the townland of Tullaganny, £200. 55. New road from Ballyhaunis to Bellaghy between Raith & Glan chapel, £200. 57. 300 perches of new road from Ballaghaderreen to Bellaghy between the churchyard of Kilmore and Uggool, £190. 73. 60 perches of new road through Cloonmeen in Clonted to connect the Islandmore road with the Clonted road, £30. 77. Repair 300 perches of the road from Kilcolman to Bellaghy between the mearing of Saxony and Anthony Fergus's, £175. 79. 96 perches of new road from Bellaghy to Ballyhaunis between Widow Haran's and Bellaghy, £50. 83. 46 perches of new road from Carracastle to Kilbeagh between Martin Mulligan's and Edward Doonan's at Bracklogh, £30. 87. Repair the road & lower the hills at Urlaur and Cloonrair on the road from Castlebar to Bellaghy, £80.

Gallen, 24 July 1846

1. Improving the road from Swinford to Kiltimagh by making a new line of road to avoid
the hill at Globe, £600. 2. Making a road from the chapel of Attymass to the public road at
Roosky, £300. 3. Making a road through the townlands of Kilgarvan & Bonniconlon, £350.
4. Improving the road from Bohola to Ballylahan, by making a new road to avoid
Ballylahan hill, £150. 5. Improving the road from Carrowleckeen to Straide by cutting hills
at Grallagh, Ashbrook & Carrowleckeen, £50. 6. Completing two short portions of new
road in the townlands of Froes? & Knocks, to finish the new line from Swinford to Aclare,
£100. 7. Improving the road from Ballavary to Foxford by making a new line of road
between Foxford & the Deerpark and cutting hills at Knockagunane, £600.

3 October 1846

OPW recommended £12,538 18s 4d for the following public works: 1. Improving the road
from Swinford to Ballyvary & lowering hills on said road, £605. 2. Improving the road from
Swinford to Clare, £1226. 3. Completing the road from Foxford to Ballavary between the
town of Foxford & Ballavary, £700. 4. Completing the cutting of the hills at Grallagh &
Carraleckeen on the road from Castlebar to Swinford, £50. 5. Lowering the hills & filling
the hollows on the entire line from Ballylahan to the cross roads at Barleyhill, together with
completing the cuts, £100. 6. Completing the road from Swinford to Aclare, £90. 7.
Making 870 perches new road from Mr Nicholson's house at Clunmeanan? to Knocks,
£860. 9. Making 320 perches of new road from Castlebar to Tubbercurry, £320. 10.
Making 500 perches of new road from Crosmolin to Swinford between the chapel of
Meelick & the bridge of Esker, £500. 11. Making 320 perches new road in continuation of
the line now in progress from the chapel of Attymass to Franvebee?, £320. 12. Making 600
perches of new road from Ballymount to Glenree, £600. 13. Making some new portions &
repairing the remainder of the road from Foxford to Aclare, £200. 14. Making 800 perches
of new road from Kiltimagh to Ballyhaunis, £800. 15. Making 700 perches of new road
from Balla to Ballavary, £700. 17. Making 150 perches of new road from Ballina to Aclare,
£150. 18. Making 300 perches of new road from Tubbercurry to Castlebar, £300. 19.
Making 400 perches of new road from Foxford to Kilkelly, £350. 20. Making 320 perches
of new road from Swinford to Kilkelly, £300. 25. Making 400 perches of new road from
Swinford to Lavy? between Kilmone & Tumdeish, £300. 26. Lowering 2 hills at
Cullenatraghta & Newcastle on the road from Kilkelly to Foxford, £100. 27. Lowering 2
hills at Laghtadurkan on road from Castlebar to Aclare, £70. 28. Lowering 4 hills at
Brackloon & Midfield on road from Kinaff to Kilkelly, £100. 29. Lowering 5 hills on the
road from Swinford to Ballyhaunis between Curryane & Kiltibo, £100. 30. Lowering 3 hills
& improving the road generally, on the road from Ballina to Tubbercurry, £150. 33.
Lowering 4 hills on the road from Foxford to Balla, between Strand & Carrowleckeen, £80.
34. Lowering 4 hills on the road from Swinford to Cressy?, £160. 35. Making 400 perches
of new road from Balla to Foxford, £150. 36. Making 200 perches of new road from
Ballavary to Crossmolina, £50. 40. Making 200 perches of new road from Kiltimagh to
Ballygarvy, £100 10s. 41. Gravelling 100 perches of road from Foxford to Castlebar, £50.
42. Making 182 perches of new road from Swinford to Castlebar, £50. 44. Widening &
improving 160 perches of road from Foxford to Ballina, £15. 45. Making 253 perches of
new road from Kiltimagh to Castlebar, £88 13s. 4d. 46. Repairing 30 perches of the back
lanes & streets of Swinford from the Courthouse to Mulligans & from Curry's to Rev Mr
Eame's gate, £40. 47. Making 50 perches of sewer & pave the channels from the National
School House to the sewer already made at T. Groarke's new house in Swinford, £60. 49.
Repairing 356 perches of road from Swinford to the Strand between the mail coach road at
Liseraghtish & Pullagherra, £53. 50. Making 216 perches of fences along the new road from
Swinford to Aclare between the rivulet at Cloongullaun & the river Moy. £12. 51. Making a

new line of road from Swinford to Banada, between the mail coach road at Cloonlara & Michael Horkan's, £14. 52. Gravelling 100 perches of road between the rivulet at Cloongullane & the river Moy., £21. 53. Filling a hollow & building 2 gullets at the bridge of Pullogh on road from Kiltimagh to Ballavary, £40. 54. Making 250 perches of new road from Swinford to Ballina, £250. 55. Making 760 perches of new road from Kilkelly to Foxford between the mail coach road at Sussregh? & the Cloonfinish road, £456. 56. Lowering the hills & widening the road from Castlebar to Aclare, £200. 57. Repairing 100 perches of road from Kiltimagh to Castlebar, £25. 58. Making 64 perches of road from Foxford to Bellaghy, £20. 59. Repairing & widening 150 perches of road from Foxford to Balla, £18 15s. 60. Lowering the hills, widening & improving the road from Castlebar to Aclare, £200. 61. Making 364 perches of new road from Kilkelly to Foxford, £200. 62. Repairing 300 perches of new road from Foxford to Aclare, £150. Making 60 perches of new road from Castlebar to Kilkelly, £15. 67. Making 30 perches new road & complete the bridge of Rathreedane on road from Bonniconlon to Easky, £50. 69. Lowering 4 hills and filling the hollows at Althinea on road from Castlebar to Longford, £160. 70. Making 20 perches new road from Clare to Kiltimagh, £25. 73. Making 200 perches new road from Foxford to Castlebar, £50. 74. Finishing 300 perches new road from Attymass to Rooskey, £330 8s. 75. Finishing 460 perches new road from Kilgarvan to Bonniconlon, £414.

4 November 1846
OPW recommended 7 works out of 73 applied for, amounting to £1,201 out of £16,980 3s. 4d. applied for: 1. Making 400 perches of new road to avoid the hills at Kilduff on road from Castlebar to Tubbercurry, £300. 2. Making 350 perches of new road and repairing and improving the present road from Kiltimagh to Castlebar, between Cragga and Bohola, £300. 3. Making 800 perches of new road from Ballina to Tubbercurry, between Lough Talt and Cloonkellane, £300. 4. Making 223 perches of new road from Balla to Foxford, between Martin MacHale's and Robert Stewart's, £67. 5. Making 220 perches of new road from Castlebar to Kiltimagh, between the crossroads at Cara to Knocksorkan, £55. 6. Making 262 perches of new road from Kiltimagh to Foxford, between Loughaula and the mill of Lismurrane, £131. 7. Making 320 perches of new road from Castlebar to Kiltimagh, between Pat Kearn's house and the Cragga road.

12 November 1846
OPW to T. N. Redington, recommending two works out of 75 applied for, to the extent of £310 out of £17,724 applied for: 1. Lowering four hills on the road from Foxford to Balla, between Shanaghee & Ballinamore, £250. 2. Lowering two hills at Cloonmore, or make a new road to avoid them, on the road from Kiltimagh to Clare, £60.

23 November 1846
OPW to T. N. Redington, recommending two works to the extent of £124 5s.: 1. Repairing 226 perchs of the road from Bohola to Kilkelly, between the Widow Doyle's in Carracanada & Pat Jordan's, £10. 2. Repairing 410 perches of road from Kiltimagh to Castlebar, between the double gullet at Trianacleragh & Mr Colgan's at Brackly, £104 5s.

12 January 1847
OPW recommended 41 works amounting to 6,568 17s.: 5. 300 perches of road from Morgan Kilbrides to Clonkeelan, £200. 10. Improve 340 perches of road from Moorbrock to Carrowkesoble, £150. 6. Improve road from Bonnycinton to Rathreedane, £100. 11. 212 perches of new road from Tranvebee to Cunviver, £200. 13. New road from Binniafinglass? to Derryvicknell, £100. 15. 250 perches of new road from Dovehall to Loughmuck, £100. 16. Improve 500 perches of road from Killduff to Ballylahan, £150. 17. Improve 500 perches of road from Irishtown to Killmore, £100. 18. Complete road from Craggagh to Killmore, £100. 20. Improve road from hill to Cregnafield road, £100. 21. Improve road from Moorbrock to Callow, £100. 22. Improve road & build footbridge over river at Moorbrock

on road from Moorbrock to Foxford, £150. 23. Improve road from Moorbrock to Rooskey, £100. 25. Improve road from river Moy at Pulnagnora to Toomore, £100. 30. Improve 300 perches of road from river Moy to Dromedy, £200. 27. Improve 300 perches of road from Killduff to Drumeanis?, £450. 32. Fence & gravel 300 perches of road from Carralean to county bounds, £200. 36. Improve road from Cullen to Callow, £200. 37. Improve road from Carton to Glenduff, £200. 40. Make road from Tumgeish to Lisloghnish, £50. 41. Make 600 perches of new road from Killanogh to Foxford, £292 10s. 42. Make 600 perches of road from mail road to Meelick chapel, £195. 43. Lower hill & improve road from Scarnageeragh to Lisheraghty, £195. 49. Make new road from Cloongouna to Poulnagouna, £97 10s. 50. Funds for stonebreakers, £35. 52. Make new road from Killonagh to Foxford, £450. 54. Make road from Balluhler to Treebnabantey, £150. 53. Make road from Garrowhill. Raheen, £200. 56. Lower hill at Carragola, finish cuts at Ballylahan, £100. 57. Make road from Kilmagh to Foxford, £50. 59. Make road from Bohola to Althnica, £150. 60. For stonebreakers, £45 1s. 75. Make 200 perches of road from Armstrongs road to Balla & Oxford road, £100. 76. Make 500 perches of road from Annahill to Kinaffe, £300. 77. Make 500 perches of road from Kiltobo bridge to mill of Glosch?, £300. 81, Repair 600 perches of road from Kiltimagh to Ballyhaunis, £100. 82. Repair road from Kiltimagh to Ballyhaunis, £100. 84. Repair road filling over bridge of Poullagh, £50. 85. For breaking stones, £50 16s. 88. Make 700 perches of road from Pullagh road to Chancery, £400. 89. Make road from Pullagh road to Moy to Cloongee, £150.

13 January 1847
OPW recommended 21 works amounting to £3887 15s: 19. Improve road from Peter Murphy's to the hill of Kilmore, £100. 24. Improve & extend the road from Glenduff to Cullane, £100. 44. 200 perches of new road from Ballinvoher to the new road in progress at Cloonagalloon, £97 10s. 45. Repair 200 perches of new road from Culleens to Clooninshin, £48 15s. 47. Lower hills & improve the road from Ballymiles to Scarnageeragh, £195. 48. New road from Doherty's at Carrabaun to the boundary at Castles, £97 10s. 65. New road from Bohola to Carrinteeane, £250. 80. 2,750 perches of new road from Loughglynn to Kiltimagh between Kincun & Gorvelbee, £304. 97. New road from the old bridge of Chancery to Keelogues, £300. 100. Lower the hills & improve road Ballavary to Ballylahan, £250. 103. Lower the hills & improve the road from Dara? to Carraleckeen, £250. 110. Make 1,200 perches of road from Swinford to Kilkelly between Swinford & barony boundary, £500. 111. Make 1,100 perches of road from Kinaff to Faheens, £300. 112. Make 300 perches of road from the mailcoach road at Cloonlara to Lisderloraghane, £150. 113. Lower the hills & make 300 perches of road from Swinford to Ballyhaunis between Swinford and Kiltibo, £200. 114 Lower the hills on the road from Kinaff to Tullinahoo, £100. 115. Lower the hills on the road from Swinford to Cloonfinish, £150. 116. 600 perches of new road from Swinford to Ballaghaderreen between Howley's forge & barony boundary, £300. 117. Repair 100 perches of road from Swinford to Cloongullane. 118. For breaking stones, £115. 119. Repair the road from Tullinahoo to Liscottle by D. Durkan's.

16 February 1847
OPW recommended 21 works amounting to £2,701: 1. 50 perches of new road from Roosky to Bonnyacton, £200. 4. 600 perches of new road from Foxford to Tubbercurry between Kilgarvin and the White stream, £200. 7. New road from Lisarmore to Sallymount, £100. 12. Improve and alter the road from Mullahawney to Bunnacurry and Bunnafinglass, £150. 29. Level, gravel and fence 300 perches of road from the chapel of Boolaghee to Fross chapel, £150. 33. New road from the south of Carraleamhey to the south of the village and on to the new road through Major Gore's property, £50. 34. 530 perches of new road from the old road at Killasser to Glenduff, £200. 35. Widen and improve 100 perches of road from Cullen to Glenduff, £150. 38. Improve road from Callow to Cullinaghten, £100. 39.

Improve the road from the government's road at Davis's to Orlaque, £71 16s. 58. New road from Ballyglass to Derryahore, £100. 62. Repair the road from Carragowan to Carraghell, £50. 72. Make 300 perches of new road from the new road from Kiltimagh to Ballavary between Byrne's forge and Cungerry, £100. 86. Improve the road at Langan, £30. 87. Lower the hill and improve the road at Derryvaghey, £100. 91. Widen and improve the road from Ballinstand to Ballyloshen, £100. 92. New road from Straide to Redhill and improve and extend the present road, £300. 93. Lower the hills on the Springhill road, £100. 94. 250 perches of road from Tawnaghmore near Balla to Craggagh, £200. 95. Improve the road at Taunaghbey? road from Balla to Minglla?, £100. 102. Road from Aughalusk to Cortoon, £150.

E: Leyny

Leyny, 7 October 1846
OPW recommended £6,126 5s. for the following public works: 1. Making a new road 68 perches long & widen & fence 72 perches & cut the hills & fill the hollows on the road from Tubbercurry to Collooney, £1,120. 2. Making a new line of road from Ballina to Tubbercurry, £200. 3. Making a new road 800 perches long, leading from Aclare to new road from Ballina to Boyle.
21 October 1846
OPW recommended £1,271 for making a new road, 1,271 perches long, leading from Banada to Cully, commencing at Banada and ending on the road from Curry to Swinford.
7 November 1846
OPW to T. N. Redington, recommending two works in the barony of Leyny to the extent of £385 12s.: 1. Making a new road 480 perches long, leading from Tubbercurry to Ballaghaderreen, between Moylough and the mearing of Co Mayo, £300. 2. Making a new road 361 perches long, leading from the circuit road from Sligo to Castlebar to the eel-weir at Grayfort through the townlands of Rinbane & Carrowrile, £85 12s.
21 November 1846
OPW to T. N. Redington, recommending three works to the extent of £570 in the barony of Leyny: 1. Repairing 76 perches of road from Ballinacarrow bridge to Michael Henry's house, £10. 2. Cutting down a hill on the road from Sligo to Tubbercurry, between John Coan's house & John Corkran's, £60. 3. Making a new road, 1295 perches, leading from Tubbercurry to Dromore West, between Tubbercurry & Sessua Common, £1000.
26 January 1847
OPW recommended 25 works amounting to £3,725: 1. Finish the road from Major O'Hara's by Court Abbey, £150. 2. Cutting the hills at Moylough & Powelsboro, £60. 3. Cutting the hills at Achonry, £150. 4. Cutting the hills on road from Sligo to Castlebar, £40. 5. Cutting the hills at Bunnacranagh & Sandyhill, £80. 6. Finish the road from Tubbercurry to Coolaney, £200. 7. Finish the road from Moylough to Co Mayo mearing, £200. 8. Finish the road at Longhill from Coolaney to Cloonacool, £60. 9. Finish the road from Ballina to Boyle, £60. 10. Finish the road from Aclare to Mullany's Cross, £150. 11. Finish the road from Bellaghy to Cully, £80. 12. Finish the road at Carane, £100. 13. Finish the road from the circuit road and Grayfort, £200. 14. Finish the road from Curry to Swinford, £140. 23. Finish the road from Meemlough to Glan, £150. 24. Finish the road from Sligo to Ballina and Coolaney, £100. 25. Finish cutting hill at Rathgran, £20. 26. Finish the footpath in Coolaney, £20. 27. Finish the road between Rathgran & Killoran church, £140. 29. Widen and fence 456½ perches of road between Somuton? & Templehouse, £200. 17. Make a new road from Rue to Ballyara, £200. 18. Make a new road from Cloonacool to Mullany's Cross to avoid the hill at Mullawn, £250. 20. Make a new road from Curry to Carrownagopple, £450. 21. Improve the road from Carrowilkeen to Drumina, £300. 22. Make £350 perches of new road from Drumina to Sessua, £225.

6 February 1847
OPW recommended new road from Kilmactigue to Garterslim?, £300.
9 February 1847
OPW recommended additional works: 1. Widen 180 perches on the lands of Killamanagh between Paul Corkran's house and the Coolaney river at Anaghbeg ford, £63. 2. 547 perches of new road from Coolaney to Ballina. 3. 480 perches of new road from Carrownagopple to Drimina, £300. 4. New road from Ballyglass to Carrane, £300.
27 February 1847
OPW recommended: 1. Make a double gullet on the road from Sligo to Ballina by the back strand between the chapel of Binbrownagh and the strand, £10. 2. Repair and improve 360 perches of road commencing at Luke Ginty's at Poo? and ending on the road from Tubbercurry to Ballina at Pat Mullarkey's at Ballyara, £204. 3. Improve the mailcoach road from Sligo to Ballina, £200. 4. Lower and reform 100 perches of the streets of Coolaney.
19 April 1847
OPW recommended the completion of 22 works (many already mentioned) amounting to £9,233, as well as the following: 3. Complete the new road from Aclare to Drumartin, £900. 5. Complete the cutting of the hills on road from Tubbercurry to Ballymote between Tubbercurry and Leitrim, £200. 19. Complete the bridge over the river Moy at Kilcummin, £40. 22. Complete new road from Shancough to Lisserlough, £150. 28. Complete the road between the old church of Killoran and Michael Gannon's house, £250. 29. Complete the road from Charles Graham's house to the old church at Killoran, £300. 30. Complete the road from Coolaney on lands of Glan, £300. Complete the road from Templehouse to the old church at Killoran, £550. 32. Complete the road from the crossroads at Miss Jones's bridge to Major O'Hara's road at Gortakeeran, £1,000. 33. Complete the mailcoach road from Sligo to Ballina at Stonehall and the Ox mountains of Glan, £600. 35. Complete the new road leading from the new road at Meemlough to the road from Ballymote to Coolaney at Rathbarron church, £325.

Employment on Public Works 1846-7
Returns showing the daily average number of persons employed on the roads.

Barony & county	able-bodied	infirm	women	boys
Week ending Saturday 26 December 1846:				
Costello	4,371	3	264	109
Gallen	2,769	17	369	169
Total: Mayo	18,321	129	1,218,	842
Coolavin	1,208	11	304	237
Corran	1,559	37	357	255
Leyny	2,739	47	282	337
Total: Sligo	10,720	68	1,189	1,324
Week ending Saturday 9 January 1847:				
Costello	4,613	6	499	246
Gallen	3,349	7	453	186
Total: Mayo	29,558	198	2,149	1,513
Coolavin	1,369	7	430	302
Corran	1,505	36	480	274
Leyny	2,970	22	352	367

Barony & county	able-bodied	infirm	women	boys
Week ending Saturday 23 January:				
Costello	7,002	17	744	344
Gallen	1,885	9	374	173
Total: Mayo	36,931	275	2,575	2,179
Coolavin	1,486	9	522	330
Corran	1,841	49	725	431
Leyny	3,689	23	546	508
Total - Sligo	14,035	211	2,442	2,012.
Week ending Saturday 6 February:				
Costello	7,160	12	707	411
Gallen	4,296	20	990	478
Total: Mayo	39,366	271	3,745	2,877
Coolavin	1,469	1	557	354
Corran	2,109	51	929	548
Leyny	4,214	30	949	596
Total: Sligo	14,783	292	3,259	2,720
Week ending Saturday 20 February:				
Costello	8,701	45	1,357	674
Gallen	5,373	21	1,176	573
Total: Mayo	48,398	472	5,650	4,006
Coolavin	1,542	1	595	353
Corran	2,026	74	1,031	563
Leyny	4,420	37	978	600
Total: Sligo	15,696	304	3,751	2,719
Week ending Saturday 27 February:				
Costello	4,886	10	938	466
Gallen	5,597	29	1,244	564
Total: Mayo	46,497	459	5,757	3,332
Coolavin	1,423	2	651	414
Corran	2,432	66	1,250	678
Leyny	5,821	33	959	589
Total: Sligo	16,742	362	4,290	3,410
Week ending Saturday 13 March				
Costello	9,275	256	1,799	1,069
Gallen	5,502	23	1,406	693
Total: Mayo	49,425	532	7,001	4,936
Coolavin	1,192	9	840	495
Corran	1,975	69	1,241	642
Leyny	5,230	44	1,674	940
Total: Sligo	15,970	311	5,711	766

Barony & county	able-bodied	infirm	women	boys
Week ending Saturday 20 March:				
Costello	8,382	18	1,659	982
Gallen	4,744	24	1,402	728
Total: Mayo	46,215	590	6,761	4,722
Coolavin	1,008	7	945	558
Corran	1,583	79	1,180	634
Leyny	5,184	52	2,132	1,035
Total: Sligo	15,925	337	6,762	4,479
Week ending Saturday 3 April:				
Costello	6,616	15	2,279	890
Gallen	4,267	14	1,389	617
Total: Mayo	34,538	326	9,147	3,938
Coolavin	723	6	842	489
Corran	1,698	83	1,020	779
Leyny	3,867	55	1,871	923
Total: Sligo	11,763	315	5,070	3,920
Week ending Saturday 10 April:				
Costello	5,620	13	1,185	774
Gallen	3,868	16	1,325	609
Total: Mayo	33,004	243	5,486	4,104
Coolavin	644	6	855	501
Corran	1,256	58	483	566
Leyny	2,859	27	1,622	732
Total: Sligo	2,070	286	4,304	3,597
Week ending Saturday 17 April:				
Costello	4,529	32	1,089	599
Gallen	3,706	14	1,338	619
Total: Mayo	29,956	238	5,308	3,603
Coolavin	631	6	903	521
Corran	1,181	56	677	523
Leyny	1,639	16	906	443
Total: Sligo	8,635	242	3,859	3,351
Week ending Saturday 24 April:				
Costello	5,834	22	1,323	819
Gallen	4,189	14	1,505	723
Total: Mayo	32,204	252	5,543	3,853
Coolavin	942	7	436	368
Corran	1,529	60	535	629
Leyny	1,056	9	296	191
Total: Sligo	8,260	225	2,422	2,806

Barony & county	able-bodied	infirm	women	boys
Week ending Saturday 1 May:				
Costello	5,262	31	991	538
Gallen	1,299	2	71	24
Total: Mayo	25,741	160	4,188	3,902
Coolavin	1,069	8	282	253
Corran	1,412	35	317	420
Leyny	1,094	8	243	207
Total: Sligo	8,179	177	1,745	2,259
Week ending Saturday 8 May:				
Costello	426	-	60	55
Gallen	1,441	-	29	16
Total: Mayo	8,780	14	285	237
Coolavin	940	-	-	-
Corran	810	-	-	-
Leyny	1,182	4	3	16
Total: Sligo	6,055	8	86	159
Week ending Saturday 15 May:				
Costello	2,131	5	214	95
Gallen	470	-	-	-
Total: Mayo	11,517	41	348	165
Coolavin	970	-	-	-
Corran	824	-	-	-
Leyny	984	2	2	3
Total: Sligo	5,812	11	16	103
Week ending Saturday 22 May:				
Costello	3,405	17	218	122
Gallen	1,660	-	-	-
Total: Mayo	14,168	31	358	232
Coolavin	994	-	-	-
Corran	594	-	-	-
Leyny	103	-	-	-
Total: Sligo	3,256	9	7	45
Eeek ending Saturday 29 May:				
Costello	1,909	-	235	182
Gallen	1,769	-	1	-
Total: Mayo	10,429	16	326	247
Coolavin	1,007	-	-	-
Corran	393	-	-	-
Leyny	10	-	-	-
Total: Sligo	2,578	-	7	36

Barony & county	able-bodied	infirm	women	boys
Week ending Saturday 5 June:				
Costello	1,229	-	131	124
Gallen	1,321	-	17	21
Total: Mayo	5,644	-	157	145
Coolavin	1,032	-	-	-
Corran	358	-	-	-
Total: Sligo	1,900	-	-	25
Week ending Saturday 12 June:				
Costello	-	-	-	-
Gallen	599	-	19	9
Total: Mayo	699	-	19	9
Coolavin	80	-	-	-
Corran	225	-	-	-
Leyny	23	-	-	-
Total: Sligo	798	-	4	34
Week ending Saturday 7 August:				
Costello	161	-	-	-
Gallen	113	-	-	-
Total: Mayo	998			
Week ending Saturday 14 August:				
Costello	147			
Gallen	124			
Total: Mayo	843			

Appendix 5: Workhouses

Returns of the average number of inmates, fever, other diseases and deaths:

	Union	Inmates	Fever	Other Diseases	Deaths
1846	*Week ending Saturday 21 November 1846:*				
	Swinford	757			
	Week ending Saturday 12 December:				
	Ballina	1,162			
	Castlebar	132			
	Swinford	720			
	Boyle	560			
	Castlerea	979			
	Sligo	1,119			
	Week ending Saturday 19 December:				
	Ballina	1,151			
	Castlebar	131			
	Swinford	722			
	Boyle	635			
	Castlerea	1,010			
	Sligo	1,122			
1847	*Week ending Saturday 9 January 1847:*				
	Ballina	1,029			
	Castlebar	123			
	Swinford	693	8		
	Boyle	635			
	Castlerea	1,048	4		
	Sligo	1,129			
	Week ending Saturday, 16 January:				
	Ballina	1,218			16
	Castlebar	112			9
	Swinford	693	9		2
	Boyle	696			16
	Castlerea	1,088	5		14
	Sligo	1,129			26
	Week ending Saturday 6 February:				
	Ballina	1,218			19
	Castlebar	107			2
	Swinford	668	13		8
	Boyle	697			24
	Castlerea	1,148	65		25
	Sligo	1,047			18

Union	Inmates	Fever	Other Diseases	Deaths
Week ending Saturday 20 February				*1847*
Ballina	1,221	16		35
Castlebar	247			2
Swinford	543	18		9
Boyle	696			26
Castlerea	1,128	120		48
Sligo	978	208		28
Week ending Saturday, 27 February:				
Ballina	1,196	41		43
Castlebar	295			3
Swinford	553	19		3
Boyle	699			34
Castlerea	1,147	80		52
Sligo	961	200		21
Week ending Saturday 6 March:				
Ballina	1,177	67		47
Castlebar	348			3
Swinford	595	18		10
Boyle	700			19
Castlerea	1,092	110		69
Sligo	946	182		28
Week ending Saturday, 20 March:				
Ballina	1,038	156	294	46
Castlebar	390		57	2
Swinford	568	23	113	11
Boyle	705	204	204	24
Castlerea	1,095	125	342	38
Sligo	915	17	427	6
Week ending Saturday 3 April:				
Ballina	929	224	426	87
Castlebar	405		66	7
Swinford	480	26	125	20
Boyle	667		202	33
Castlerea	796	256	540	42
Sligo	852		392	10
Week ending Saturday 10 April:				
Ballina	812	230	320	55.
Castlebar	100		53	1
Swinford	455	27	129	19
Boyle	670		292	34
Castlerea	1,034	152	337	46
Sligo	850	80	104	10
Week ending Saturday 17 April:				
Ballina	768	190	281	65
Castlebar	357		64	8
Swinford	428	25	134	20
Boyle	697		215	29
Castlerea	988	146	368	57
Sligo	872	80	170	6

1847

Union	Inmates	Fever	Other Diseases	Deaths
Week ending Saturday 24 April:				
Ballina	723	96	249	47
Castlebar	299	58	63	8
Swinford	398	26	137	32
Boyle	690	215	215	39
Castlerea	1,039	180	290	47
Sligo	912	0	56	6
Week ending Saturday 1 May:				
Ballina	704	81	194	50
Castlebar	265		65	14
Swinford	330	16	118	36
Boyle	691		217	34
Castlerea	1,003	200	296	46
Sligo	923	40	209	11

Week ending Saturday 8 May, Only average number of inmates are available:
Ballina, 742; Castlebar, 234; Swinford, 306; Boyle, 694; Castlerea, 810; Sligo,930.
Week ending Saturday 15 May:
Ballina, 781; Castlebar, 225; Swinford, 304; Boyle, 699; Castlerea, 786; Sligo, 934.
Week ending Saturday, 22 May:
Ballina, 869; Castlebar, 258; Swinford, 311; Boyle, 700; Castlerea, 758; Sligo, 963.
Week ending Saturday, 29 May::
Ballina, 904; Castlebar, 303; Swinford, 343; Boyle, 699; Castlerea, 758; Sligo, 979.
Week ending Saturday 5 June:
Ballina, 907; Castlebar, 331; Swinford, 368; Boyle, 695; Castlerea, 760; Sligo, 973.
Week ending Saturday 12 June:
Ballina, 890; Castlebar, 364; Swinford, 382; Boyle, 697; Castlerea, 781; Sligo, 969.
Week ending Saturday 19 June:
Ballina, 878, Castlebar, 366, Swinford, 392, Boyle, 676, Castlerea, 787, Sligo, 987.
Week ending Saturday 26 June:
Ballina, 857, Castlebar, 375, Swinford, 397, Boyle, 656, Castlerea, 814, Sligo, 997.
Week ending Saturday 10 July:
Ballina, 755, Castlebar, 352, Swinford, 431, Boyle, 635, Castlerea, 897, Sligo, 1,058.
Week ending Saturday 17 July:
Ballina, 729, Castlebar, 361, Swinford, 390, Boyle, 607, Castlerea, 893, Sligo, 1,022.
Week ending Saturday 24 July:
Ballina, 665, Castlebar, 365, Swinford, 397, Boyle, 505, Castlerea, 890, Sligo, 1,033.
Week ending Saturday 31 July:
Ballina, 623, Castlebar, 373, Swinford, 83, Boyle, 459, Castlerea, 928, Sligo, 1,022.

Union	Total	Men	Women	Children	Fever	Other Diseases	Deaths
Week ending Saturday 2 October:							
Ballina	595	36	47	347	-	57	-
Swinford	307	22	43	171	5	4	2
Sligo	1,090	48	198	578	60	122	3
Week ending Saturday 9 October:							
Ballina	699	49	55	393	-	71	-
Swinford	334	26	55	180	4	46	1

Union	Total	Men	Women	Children	Fever	Other Diseases	Deaths	
Week ending Saturday 16 October:								*1847*
Ballina	797	45	68	432	7	-	3	
Swinford	355	27	58	193	4	48	1	
Sligo	1,194	51	213	669	65	110	3	
Week ending Saturday 23 October:								
Ballina	888	64	72	475	-	87	4	
Swinford	408	44	65	215	6	54	1	
Sligo	1,205	52	205	662	60	141	2	
Week ending Saturday 30 October:								
Ballina	943	69	78	500	-	36	3	
Swinford	420	42	69	226	7	48	-	
Sligo	1,220	56	206	656	50	160	3	
Week ending Saturday 6 November:								
Ballina	999					99	3	
Swinford	457	45	72	249	9	54	1	
Sligo	1,163	43	198	618	60	156	5	
Week ending Saturday 20 November:								
Ballina	1,125	78	94	545	16	140	2	
Swinford	534	57	101	325	12	56	1	
Sligo	1,241	71	215	683	62	172	6	
Week ending Saturday 27 November:								
Ballina	1,209	93	120	576	22	143	3	
Swinford	630	69	113	335	14	65	-	
Sligo	1,292	113	216	680	63	181	1	
Week ending Saturday 4 December:								
Swinford	630	82	105	362	12	71	-	
Week ending Saturday 11 December:								
Ballina	1,721	108	157	775	40	146	3	
Castlebar	695	29	95	321	28	60	7	
Swinford	731	84	125	394	18	72	1	
Boyle	700	58	141	360	-	120	4	
Castlerea	1,364	120	189	662	146	91	3	
Sligo	1,298	109	217	673	54	207	9	

Week ending Saturday 26 February 1848. Totals only available: *1848*
Castlebar, 747, Swinford, 789, Boyle, 752, Castlerea, 1,050, Sligo, 1,701.
Week ending Saturday 4 March:
Ballina, 1,267, Castlebar, 780, Swinford, 1,067, Boyle, 751, Castlerea, 1,063, Sligo, 1,693.
Week ending Saturday 11 March:
Ballina, 1,107, Castlebar, 859, Swinford, 1,042, Castlerea, 1,017, Sligo, 1,720.
Week ending Saturday 25 March:
Ballina, 1,367, Swinford, 405, Castlerea, 1,078, Sligo, 1,712.

1848	Union	Total	Men	Women	Children	Fever	Other Diseases	Deaths
Week ending Saturday 8 April:								
	Ballina	1,394	165	196	518	42	228	42
	Castlebar	771	no return					
	Swinford	395	no return					
	Boyle	774	74	120	309	-	209	21
	Castlerea	1,071	117	263	502	55	104	6
	Sligo	1,662	167	383	669	-	438	17
Week ending Saturday 15 April:								
	Ballina	1,322	143	183	504	42	210	5
	Castlebar	no return						
	Swinford	413	no return					
	Boyle	-	75	127	303	-	226	20
	Castlerea	1,107	127	262	490	55	104	3
	Sligo	-	168	389	672	-	413	17
Week ending Saturday 22 Apri:								
	Ballina	1,267	138	171	489	42	228	4
	Castlebar	no return						
	Swinford	446	33	93	187	14	110	5
	Boyle	727	80	116	280	-	224	15
	Castlerea	1,065	133	282	481	33	113	3
	Sligo	1,708	192	405	669	-	442	20
Week ending Saturday 29 April:								
	Ballina	1,267	146	179	495	44	214	3
	Castlebar	no return						
	Swinford	515	42	124	239	10	91	3
	Boyle	?	82	122	277	-	265	12
	Castlerea	1,063	no return					
	Sligo	1,690	173	398	658	-	461	21
Week ending Saturday 6 May:								
	Ballina	1,339	147	186	535	40	208	3
	Castlebar	no return						
	Swinford	513	46	116	237	11	94	4
	Boyle	742	86	120	254	-	255	7
	Castlerea	1,040	110	252	535	44	100	-
	Sligo	1,702	172	403	666	-	461	14
Week ending Saturday 13 May:								
	Ballina	1,477	161	206	598	41	214	4
	Castlebar	?	180	192	333	13	54	7
	Swinford	548	57	126	243	8	98	2
	Boyle	774	94	128	285	-	236	9
	Castlerea	1,037	no return					
	Sligo	1,751	181	435	738	-	397	9
Week ending Saturday 20 May:								
	Ballina	1,480	165	215	507	33	217	3
	Castlebar	747	164	185	309	18	65	10
	Swinford	597	74	143	260	8	98	4
	Boyle	no return						

Union	Total	Men	Women	Children	Fever	Other Diseases	Deaths	1848
Castlerea	no return							
Sligo	1,784	180	442	759	-	403	8	
Week ending Saturday 27 May:								
Ballina	1,477	169	207	577	35	224	4	
Castlebar	753	157	191	307	21	71	8	
Swinford	691	89	185	317	5	84	1	
Boyle	774	111	134	292	-	210	8	
Castlerea	1,066	123	201	506	48	186	6	
Sligo	1,867	185	460	806	50	366	13	
Week ending Saturday 3 June:								
Ballina	1,505	194	275	592	35	253	4	
Castlebar	826	179	219	320	25	75	12	
Swinford	699	93	174	320	4	98	2	
Boyle	765	110	127	260	-	234	14	
Castlerea	1,214	151	331	557	55	120	3	
Sligo	1,961	237	484	894	47	299	9	
Week ending Saturday 10 June:								
Ballina	1,619	203	265	669	34	258	2	
Castlebar	874	201	265	348	22	60	9	
Swinford	827	112	230	389	4	73	5	
Boyle	no return							
Castlerea	1,253	219	475	581	65	112	3	
Sligo	1,912	219	475	839	50	329	5	
Week ending Saturday 17 June:								
Ballina	1,703	206	285	716	31	244	8	
Castlebar	835	195	222	332	22	56	6	
Swinford	1,136	148	341	552	3	77	-	
Boyle	798	106	156	306	-	197	14	
Castlerea	1,239	161	330	563	65	120	3	
Sligo	2,027	247	497	905	43	314	14	
Week ending Saturday 24 June:								
Ballina	1,643	191	292	702	26	240	2	
Castlebar	806	195	207	313	26	57	8	
Swinford	906	166	285	436	5	79	1	
Boyle	776	105	140	296	-	203	5	
Castlerea	1,307	177	355	575	74	126	4	
Sligo	2,020	263	488	912	43	314	14	
Week ending Saturday 1 July:								
Ballina	1,699	197	317	726	19	220	2	
Castlebar	809	183	211	322	31	54	4	
Swinford	914	161	263	396	4	79	1	
Boyle	no return							
Castlerea	1,319	182	373	562	85	117	3	
Sligo	1,995	273	484	853	41	304	16	

1848	Union	Total	Men	Women	Children	Fever	Other Diseases	Deaths
Week ending Saturday 8 July:								
	Ballina	1,702	201	315	729	20	217	2
	Castlebar	864	197	229	345	32	52	5
	Swinford	933	125	174	339	5	78	-
	Boyle	801	112	171	296	-	192	7
	Castlerea	1,360	267	393	591	75	94	1
	Sligo	1,959	282	481	853	41	318	14
Week ending Saturday 15 July:								
	Ballina	1,589	214	308	667	24	186	4
	Castlebar	895	202	241	343	25	55	-
	Swinford	726	120	183	340	4	68	2
	Boyle	828	120	170	322	-	186	7
	Castlerea	1,423	222	439	583	69	110	5
	Sligo	2,013	306	518	891	26	272	11
Week ending Saturday 22 July:								
	Ballina	1,487	207	298	614	24	181	6
	Castlebar	963	207	329	344	17	50	1
	Swinford	708	117	158	335	-	89	1
	Boyle	844	119	179	368	-	159	4
	Castlerea	1,389	233	429	499	56	172	-
	Sligo	2,041	301	515	912	31	202	7
Week ending Saturday 29 July:								
	Ballina	1,451	209	291	615	20	158	3
	Castlebar	924	191	308	331	21	66	-
	Swinford	713	117	161	346	-	78	3
	Boyle	no return						
	Castlerea	1,390	227	432	511	47	173	4
	Sligo	1,961	292	495	877	35	262	7
Week ending Saturday 5 August:								
	Ballina	1,324	206	275	564	21	150	5
	Castlebar	927	199	308	334	15	62	2
	Swinford	707	120	150	349	3	80	2
	Boyle	no return						
	Castlerea	1,336	210	379	533	49	165	8
	Sligo	1,882	255	478	851	24	274	9
Week ending Saturday 12 August:								
	Ballina	1,315	203	277	568	17	147	2
	Castlebar	994	213	308	384	18	62	2
	Swinford	734	120	164	372	5	68	1
	Boyle	789	116	175	360	-	111	6
	Castlerea	1,336	209	390	546	37	122	3
	Sligo	1,779	246	440	791	29	265	6
Week ending Saturday 19 August:								
	Ballina	1,884	no return					
	Castlebar	1,037	209	326	407	13	63	2
	Swinford	722	115	148	377	5	71	1
	Boyle	748	94	159	361	-	107	2

Union	Total	Men	Women	Children	Fever	Other Diseases	Deaths	1848
Castlerea	1,228	196	390	546	37	122	3	
Sligo	1,691	222	419	766	23	261	5	
Week ending Saturday 26 August:								
Ballina	1,937	293	489	730	19	178	2	
Castlebar	1,037	214	323	426	15	50	2	
Swinford	902	134	182	494	5	82	2	
Boyle	810	no return						
Castlerea	1,217	196	376	525	26	94	3	
Sligo	1,601	207	370	760	18	238	7	
Week ending Saturday 2 September:								
Ballina	1,811	273	461	695	13	171	7	
Castlebar	no return							
Swinford	1,142	143	254	646	5	88	-	
Boyle	907	114	200	478	-	84	4	
Castlerea	1,343	221	409	593	17	103	3	
Sligo	*1,633*	*176*	*385*	*799*	*19*	*254*	*4*	
Week ending Saturday 9 September:								
Ballina	1,866	293	559	742	13	154	3	
Castlebar	955	no return						
Swinford	1,342	164	303	788	6	74	-	
Boyle	no return							
Castlerea	1,474	236	430	701	17	90	2	
Sligo	1,612	161	378	803	16	254	4	
Week ending Saturday 16 September:								
Ballina	1,785	268	537	712	13	173	2	
Castlebar	985	no return						
Swinford	1,395	171	330	824	5	60	-	
Boyle	780	no return						
Castlerea	1,410	236	416	657	14	85	3	
Sligo	1,503	133	347	766	23	234	4	
Week ending Saturday 23 September:								
Ballina	1,773	268	543	764	10	189	1	
Castlebar	1,062	no return						
Swinford	1,465	168	331	977	6	76	2	
Boyle	no return							
Castlerea	1,454	230	433	677	21	93	1	
Sligo	1,602	147	387	821	18	229	4	
Week ending Saturday 30 September:								
Ballina	no return							
Castlebar	1,017	206	315	421	17	40	3	
Swinford	1,463	175	332	883	13	69	1	
Boyle	no return							
Castlerea	1,603	235	450	767	21	93	1	
Sligo	1,659	152	411	855	11	230	5	
Week ending Saturday 7 October:								
Ballina	no return							
Castlebar	1,009	232	299	411	14	45	1	

1848	Union	Total	Men	Women	Children	Fever	Other Diseases	Deaths
	Swinford	1,431	174	326	841	15	70	-
	Boyle	826	no return					
	Castlerea	1,858	258	511	918	32	139	2
	Sligo	1,690	154	432	863	15	226	3

Week ending Saturday 14 October:

	Ballina	no return						
	Castlebar	1,067	243	308	433	22	50	-
	Swinford	1,696	204	407	991	15	72	-
	Boyle	886	91	214	459	-	85	3
	Castlerea	2,425	330	651	1,260	39	145	1
	Sligo	1,775	170	460	906	10	226	4

Week ending Saturday 21 October:

	Ballina	no return						
	Castlebar	1,019	194	291	425	31	63	4
	Swinford	1,770	217	446	1,026	22	52	4
	Boyle	no return						
	Castlerea	2,370	290	591	1,286	33	170	6
	Sligo	1,864	186	493	931	18	236	5

Week ending Saturday 28 October:

	Ballina	2,721	407	726	1,255	8	269	2
	Castlebar	1,058	197	294	461	27	62	-
	Swinford	1,928	228	501	1,104	22	67	4
	Boyle	no return						
	Castlerea	no return						
	Sligo	1,964	208	501	996	21	238	6

Week ending Saturday 4 November:

	Ballina	2,781	437	738	1,284	8	344	4
	Castlebar	1,112	201	300	487	35	88	3
	Swinford	1,918	225	506	1,092	27	63	6
	Boyle	922	104	220	447	-	111	3
	Castlerea	2,884	no return					
	Sligo	2,053	225	527	1,027	29	245	8

Week ending, Saturday 11 November:

	Ballina	2,841	449	764	1,294	8	318	18
	Castlebar	1,121	203	301	476	35	88	3
	Swinford	2,041	237	540	1,155	32	77	12
	Boyle	934	no return					
	Castlerea	3,009	388	761	1,600	58	202	4
	Sligo	2,214	262	592	1,082	31	247	7

Week ending 18 November, totals only available:
Ballina, 2,814, Swinford, 1,730, Castlerea, 3,294, Sligo, 2,324.
Week ending 25 November:
Ballina, 2,987, Swinford, 2,327, Sligo, 2,437.
Week ending 2 December:
Ballina, 2,950, Castlebar, 1,403, Swinfod, 2,001, Castlerea, 2,894, Sligo, 2,632.

Week ending 9 December:
Ballina, 2,990, Castlebar, 1,541, Swinford, 2,025, Boyle, 988, Castlerea, 3,356, Sligo, 2,766.
Week ending 16 December:
Ballina, 2,969, Castlebar, 1,541, Swinford, 1,730, Boyle, 1,004, Castlerea, no return, Sligo, 2,860.
Week ending 23 December:
Ballina, 2,803, Swinford, 1,780, Boyle, 940, Sligo, 2,822.
Week ending 30 December:
Ballina, 2,681, Swinford, 1,859, Castlerea, 2,630, Sligo, 2,959.

Deaths

Union	Total	Fever	Dysentery	Other causes
Week ending 3 March 1849				
Ballinrobe	27	2	20	5
Castlerea	24	16	3	5
Sligo	22	2	15	5
Westport	33	5	24	4
10 March:				
Ballinrobe	24	5	12	7
Castlerea	34	18	12	4
Westport	30	2	20	8
Ballinrobe	19	2	9	8
Castlerea	24	11	11	2
Westport	26	4	19	3
24 March:				
Ballinrobe	42	1	33	8
Sligo	27	2	15	10
Westport	28	5	21	2
31 March:				
Ballinrobe	41	5	23	13
Westport	35	2	27	6
14 April:				
Ballinrobe	52	7	45	
12 May:				
Ballinrobe	32	1	24	7
Westport	47	2	30	15
Ballinasloe	336			
26 May:				
Ballinrobe	19	2	12	5
Boyle	18	1	3	14
Westport	88	8	50	30
Ballinasloe	101			
16 June:				
Ballinrobe	62	7	25	28 (2 cholera)
Westport	26	2	9	15 (11 cholera)
23 June				
Ballinrobe	35	9	19	7
Westport	15	1	9	5

1849	Union	Total	Fever	Dysentery	Other causes
30 June:					
	Ballinrobe	35	9	11	15 (9 cholera)
	Castlerea	25	6	6	6 (3 cholera)
2 July:					
	Ballinrobe	14	3	10	1
	Castlebar	15			
	Westport	80	1	28	80 (42 cholera)
7 July:					
	Ballinrobe	32	5	16	11 (5 cholera)
	Castlerea	26	6	2	18 (11 cholera)
14 July:					
	Ballinrobe	41	4	26	11 (9 cholera)
	Castlerea	20	5	6	15 (9 cholera)
28 July:					
	Ballinrobe	19	5	13	1
	Castlerea	17	5	1	10 (9 cholera)
11 August:					
	Ballinrobe	16	6	8	2
	Castlerea	16	5	3	8 (4 cholera)
18 August:					
	Ballinrobe	19	9	8	1 (1 cholera)
	Sligo	67	-	10	57 (55 cholera)
25 August:					
	Sligo	44	1	7	36 (23 cholera)
1 September:					
	Sligo	24	11	6	7
15 September:					
	Boyle	8	2	6	
13 October:					
	Boyle	7	4	3	

Appendix 6: Society of Friends' Grants

Achonry (see also Tubbercurry), 28 December 1846. £20. 22 February. £20 (3rd donation).   *A*
9 April 1847. 4 tons of rice. n.d. 1847. 1 ton of rice, 1 ton of Indian meal and 5 bags of
biscuit. 21 July 1847. ½ ton of rice, ½ ton of Indian meal and 5 bags of biscuit. 15
September 1847. ½ ton of rice and 5 bags of biscuit. 3 December 1847. ¼ ton of rice, ½
ton of Indian meal and 2 bags of biscuit. 11 December 1847 (per Catherine Rice). ¼ ton of
Indian meal, ¼ ton of rice and 2 bags of biscuit. 12 February 1848 (per Michael
Muldowney CC). ¼ ton of Indian meal and ¼ ton of rye. 18 February 1848 (per Catherine
Rice). ¼ ton of rice, ¼ ton of Indian meal, ¼ ton of barley and 2 bags of biscuit. 21 April
1848 (per Catherine Rice). ¼ ton of Indian meal, ¼ ton of rice and ¼ ton of rye. 16 June
1848 (per Catherine Rice). ¼ ton of Indian meal and ¼ ton of rice. 15 July 1848 (per Rev
W. R. Hiffernan). ¼ ton of Indian meal, ¼ ton of rice and 2 bags of biscuit. 15 July 1848
(per Michael Muldowney CC). ¼ ton of rye meal, ¼ ton of Indian meal and ¼ ton of rice.
21 July 1848 (per Catherine Rice). ¼ ton of rice and ¼ ton of Indian meal. n.d. August
1849. £30.

Aclare (see also Kilmactigue), 8 March 1847. £10. 10 April 1847. 1 ton of rice. 21 April   *B*
1847. ½ ton of Indian meal. 14 July 1847. ½ ton of Indian meal and ¼ ton of rice.

Ballaghaderreen (see also Loughglynn), 4 March 1847. 1 ton of rice. 3 April 1847. 1 bag of   *C*
rice and 5 stones of oaten meal. 14 April 1847. 1 ton of rice. 12 May 1847. 10 sacks of
Indian meal and 10 sacks of barley meal. (Kilcolman), 21 June 1847. 1 ton of Indian meal
and 5 bags of biscuit. (Kilcolman) 13 June 1847. Clothing grant: 1 piece of flannel, 1 piece
of calico, 1 piece of blueprint, 1 piece of corduroy, 1 piece of B. worsted, 1 piece of B. cotton. 21 June 1847. ½ ton of rice and 5 bags of biscuit. 23 June 1847. 3 tons of Indian meal
and ½ ton of wheaten meal. 8 July 1847. ½ ton of barley meal and ½ ton of wheaten meal.
24 July 1847. ½ ton of rice and ½ ton of barley meal. 12 May 1848 (per Denis Tighe
PP).Clothing grant: 1 piece of flannel, 1 piece of calico, 1 piece of corduroy, ½ piece of
check and 50 garments.

Ballinacarrow, 9 February 1847. £20.   *D*

Ballisodare, 9 February 1847. 1 boiler.   *E*

Ballymote, 25 February 1847. £20 (2nd donation). 9 April 1847. ½ ton of rice and 6 bar-   *F*
rels of Indian meal. 31 May 1847. ½ ton of rice. 27 October 1847. ¼ ton of rice and ¼ ton
of Indian meal. 20 December 1847. ¼ ton of Indian meal, ¼ ton of rice and 3 bags of biscuit. 31 March 1848. ¼ ton of rice. ¼ ton of Indian meal, ¼ ton of rye and 2 bags of biscuit. 19 April 1848. Clothing grant: no.1 (value £13 7s 4d).

Bohola, 31 May 1847. ½ ton of meal and 5 cwt of rice.   *G*

H   Bonniconlon, 21 March 1848 (per Mr O'Dowda) food grant. 2 June 1848. 2½ cwt of meal rye and 2 cwt of rice.

I   Bunninadden, 26 May 1847. ¼ ton of Indian meal and ¼ ton of rye. 18 September 1847. ½ ton of rice, and 3 bags of biscuit. 19 December 1847 (Kilshalvey). Clothing grant: 40 garments, 20 Guernsey frocks, 20 rugs, 20 pairs of sheets and 1 pair of blankets. 31 March 1848 (per James Henry PP). ¼ ton of rice, ¼ ton of Indian meal, ¼ ton of rye and 2 bags of biscuit. 7 April 1848 (per Eleanor MacDonnell). ¼ ton of Indian meal, ¼ ton of rye, ¼ ton of rice and 3 bags of biscuit. n.d. July 1848 (per Elizabeth MacDonnell). Food grant.

J   Charlestown, 31 March 1847. 5 barrels of Indian meal. 28 February 1848. ½ ton of Indian meal and ½ ton of rye.

K   Collooney, 8 March 1847. £20.

L   Coolaney, 12 February 1847. £30. 10 November 1847. ¼ ton of Indian meal and 2 bags of biscuit. 1 January 1848 (per Kate P. Thompson). Clothing grant: grant no.1. 22 March 1848. Clothing grant: 2 pieces of calico, 1 piece of flannel, 20 rugs and 20 pairs of sheets.

M   Coolavin, 2 February 1847. £20. 13 February 1847. Clothing grant. 20 February 1847. £20. 23 March 1847. 1 ton of rice (£28 19s 9d) and £10. 10 April 1847. 1 ton of rice. 16 June 1847. 1 ton of rice. 5 July 1847. ½ ton of wheaten meal, 1 ton of rice, and 5 bags of biscuit. 31 July 1847. 1 ton of rice. 4 August 1847 (Clogher school). ½ ton of rice, ½ ton of Indian meal and 5 bags of biscuit. 25 September 1847 (Clogher school). ½ ton of Indian meal, ¼ ton of rice and 3 bags of biscuit. 29 September 1847. ½ ton of Indian meal and ½ ton of rice. 7 February 1848. Bale of clothes. 16 February 1848 (Clogher school). ¼ ton of Indian meal, ¼ ton of rye, ¼ ton of rice and 2 bags of biscuit. 15 July 1848 (Clogher school). ¼ ton of rye meal, ¼ ton of Indean meal, ½ ton of rice and 3 bags of biscuit. 24 July 1849. £30.

N   Foxford, 18 March 1847. Clothing grant: 80 garments and 1 piece of calico. 20 March 1847. 10 barrels of Indian meal, 10 bags of peas, ½ ton of biscuit (value £46). 14 April 1847. 10 barrels of Indian meal and ½ ton of biscuit. 21 April 1847. 10 barrels of Indian meal. 12 May 1847 (per G. V. Jackson). 8 sacks of Indian meal and 20 bags of biscuit. 6 October 1847. ¼ ton of rice and ¼ ton of Indian meal. 24 December 1847 (part for Killasser). ½ ton of Indian meal, ¼ ton of rice and 3 bags of biscuit. 27 May 1848 (per Rev G. Mostyn). ¼ ton of rice, ¼ ton of Indian meal and ¼ ton of rye.

O   Keash, 23 June 1847. ½ ton of Indian meal and ¼ ton of rice. 24 July 1847. ½ ton of rice. 8 September 1847. ¼ ton of rice, ¼ ton of Indian meal and 3 bags of biscuit. 27 October 1847. ¼ ton of Indian meal, ¼ ton of rice and £5. 22 December 1847. ¼ ton of rice, ¼ ton of Indian meal and 2 bags of biscuit. 24 January 1848. Clothing grant: no.1 omitting leather. 15 July 1848. ¼ ton of Indian meal, ¼ ton of barley, ¼ ton of rice and 2 bags of biscuit.

P   Kilkelly, 26 April 1847. 8 sacks of Indian meal. 14 August 1847. A boiler for 50 or 80 gallons, ½ ton of rice and 5 casks of Indian meal.

Q   Kilmactigue (see also Aclare), 28 December 1846. £20. 8 February 1847. £20. 7 April 1847. 1 ton of rice. 20 October 1847. ¼ ton of Indian meal and ¼ ton of rice. 2 January

1848. Clothing grant: no.1. 4 March 1848 (per W. Fetherstone). Clothing grant: 3 pieces of calico, 3 pieces of blueprint, 1 piece of flannel and 1 piece of corduroy. 24 April 1848 (per Wm Fetherstone). Clothing grant: 3 pieces of grey calico, 3 pieces of blueprint, 1 piece of flannel and 1 piece of corduroy. 19 May 1848. Clothing grant: 32 yards of frieze, 32 yards of barragan, 20 Guersey frocks, 2 pieces of calico, 100 assorted articles and 1 bundle of leather.

Kilmovee, 26 February 1847. ½ ton of rice.   *R*

Kiltimagh, 9 May 1848. (per Daniel Mullarkey PP) ½ ton of Indian meal, ½ ton of rye and   *S*
½ ton of rice and 2 bags of biscuit. n.d. June 1848 (per Rev Brownslow Lynch). 17 cwt of
meal rice and biscuit. 3 July 1848 (per Rev Brownslow Lynch). ¼ ton of rice, ¼ ton of
Indian meal and ¼ ton of rye. 3 August 1848 (per Daniel Mullarkey PP). ½ ton of Indian
meal and ¼ ton of rice.

Loughglynn, n.d. £100. 1 February 1847. 1 ton of rice for immediate distribution. C.   *T*
Strickland proposes to have boilers ferried by canal to Longford, 1 of 130 gallons, 1 of 100
gallons and 1 of 70 gallons. 16 February 1847. 1 ton of rice. 16 May 1848 (per Katherine
Strickland). Clothing grant: 50 rugs and 2 pieces of calico. 12 July 1849. £30.

Meelick, 23 September 1847. 1 ton of rice. 14 January 1848. ¼ ton of Indian meal, ¼ ton   *U*
of barley meal, ¼ ton of rice and 3 bags of biscuit. 9 March 1848. ¼ ton of Indian meal, ¼
ton of rye, ¼ ton of rice and 3 bags of biscuit. 20 May 1848. ¼ ton of rice, ¼ ton of Indian
meal, ¼ ton of rye and 2 bags of biscuit. 20 July 1848. ¼ ton of rice and ½ ton of Indian
meal. 4 August 1849. £30.

Swinford, 16 February 1847. £30. 18 March 1847. 1 ton of meal. 20 March 1847.   *V*
Clothing grant: 100 articles, 1 piece of calico and 1 piece of flannel. 10 barrels of Indian
meal, 10 bags of peas, ½ ton of biscuit (value £46). 21 June 1847. ½ ton of rice, ½ ton of
Indian meal and 5 bags of biscuit. 9 July 1847. £5. 14 July 1847. ¼ ton of rice and 3 bags
of biscuit. 17 January 1848. Clothing grant. no.1 adding a bundle of leather.

Tubbercurry, n.d. 1847. ¼ ton of Indian meal, ¼ ton of rye meal, ¼ ton of rice and 2 bags *W*
of biscuit. 13 July 1848 (per Rev John Hamilton). ½ ton of Indian meal, ½ ton of rye meal,
½ ton of rice and 2 bags of biscuit.

Appendix 7: Outdoor Relief

Total numbers on outdoor relief during 1848:

31 July 1848:
Ballina, 42,364, Castlebar, 26,041, Swinford, 23,369, Boyle, 15,532, Castlerea, 19,378, Sligo, 9,872.
Saturday 19 August:
Ballina, 29,015; Castlebar, 21,676; Swinford, 4,125; Boyle, 6,040; Castlerea, 14,807; Sligo, 6,023.
Saturday 26 August:
Ballina, 23,063; Castlebar, 16,401; Swinford, 1,701; Boyle, 4,820; Castlerea, 12,525; Sligo, 4,808.
Saturday 16 September:
Ballina, 24,620; Castlebar, 7,650; Swinford, 1,776; Boyle, 2,085: Castlerea, 9,963; Sligo, 1,835.
Saturday 7 October:
Ballina, 10,653; Castlebar, 8,584; Swinford, 2,117; Boyle, 960; Castlerea, 5,053; Sligo, 354.
Saturday 14 October:
Ballina, 12,792; Castlebar, 9,799; Swinford, 2,115; Boyle, 31; Castlerea, 4,304; Sligo, 864.
Saturday 21 October:
Ballina, 12,365; Castlebar, 9,605; Swinford, 2,171; Boyle, 83; Castlerea, 2,971; Sligo, 897.
Ballina, 12,271, Castlebar, 8,744, Swinford, 2,198, Boyle, 692, Castlerea, 2,655, Sligo, 937.
Saturday 11 November:
Ballina, 12,672; Castlebar, 8,686; Swinford, 2,309; Boyle, 1,304; Castlerea, 2,705; Sligo, 930.
Saturday 18 November:
Ballina, 12,954, Castlebar, 8,244, Swinford, 2,695, Boyle, 2,110, Castlerea, 1,348, Sligo, 930.
Saturday 2 December:
Ballina, 13,970, Castlebar, 7,980, Swinford, 3,333, Boyle, 4,532, Castlerea, 3,104, Sligo, 994.
Saturday 9 December:
Ballina, 14,467, Castlebar, 6,186, Swinford, 3,856, Boyle, 5,401, Castlerea, 3,168, Sligo, 1,022.
Saturday 16 December:
Ballina, 15,227, Castlebar, 8,253, Swinford, 5,168, Boyle, 6,391, Castlerea, 3,319, Sligo, 1,175.

Appendix 8:
Passengers on ships from Sligo to New York

Taken from Glazier, Ira A., ed., *Famine Immigrants*

Name	Age	Sex	Occupation	Name	Age	Sex	Occupation
				Mary (D)	06	F	Unknown
				Martin (S)	02	M	Unknown
Ship: Richard-Watson, 05 January 1847				Laden, Bgt	17	F	Unknown
Tighe, M.	26	M	Labourer	Owens, P.	22	M	Labourer
Ann (W)	26	F	Wife	Mgt. (W)	25	F	Wife
John (S)	01	M	Child	Biddy (D)	02	F	Child
Begly, A.	26	M	Farmer	Rourke, D.	18	M	Labourer
Anne	26	F	Unknown	Dyer, Bdgt.	28	F	Unknown
O Beirne, H.	20	M	Farmer	Mullery, Bdgt.	18	F	Unknown
Bdgt.	00	F	Unknown	Hart, P.	21	M	Labourer
Coleman, Ann	19	F	Unknown	Parsons, J.	20	M	Labourer
Scanlan, P.	50	M	Farmer	Mary	23	F	Unknown
Magt (W)	50	F	Unknown	McSunnas, Bdgt.	19	F	Unknown
Mary (D)	22	F	Unknown	Shannon, Honor	28	F	Unknown
Ann (D)	20	F	Unknown	Drury, P.	30	M	Labourer
Pat (S)	18	M	Farmer	Allse (W)		F	Wife
Cath. (D)	16	F	Unknown	Peter (S)	01	M	Child
Mgt. (D)	14	F	Unknown	Gallagher, P.	24	M	Farmer
Biddy (D)	12	F	Unknown	Cath.	29	F	Unknown
Julia (D)	10	F	Unknown	Ian	20	M	Labourer
Wm. (S)	08	M	Child	Neilan, Cath.	16	F	Unknown
McGowan, M.	45	M	Labourer	Mary	18	F	Unknown
Mary (W)	35	F	Wife	Gaffrey, Mich.	34	M	Labourer
Ellen (D)	12	F	Unknown	Ellen (W)	25	F	Wife
Winnfred (D)	03	F	Child	Mary (D)	01	F	Child
Mary (D)	02	F	Child	Middleden, R.	25	M	Farmer
Geever, P.	32	M	Labourer	Mary-A.	22	F	Unknown
Cath.	26	F	Unknown	Loftus, D.	25	M	Farmer
Cath.	19	F	Unknown	Jane	24	F	Unknown
Torny, Mary	20	F	Unknown	Harn, A.	22	M	Farmer
Connell, M.	21	M	Labourer	Loftus, O.	30	M	Farmer
McHugh, T.	37	M	Labourer	Pat	25	M	Farmer
M. (W)	36	F	Wife	Anthy.	27	M	Farmer
Wm. (S)	09	M	Child	Carnan, P.	45	M	Farmer
Bgt (D)	07	F	Child	Davey, P.	44	M	Farmer
M. (D)	05	F	Child	Mary (W)	50	F	Wife
Thos. (S)	3	M	Child	Jno. (S)	26	M	Farmer
Scanlan, O.	30	M	Labourer	Cath. (D)	20	F	Unknown
Ann (W)	30	F	Wife	Andr. (S)	19	M	None
Madvia (D)	10	F	Unknown				

Name	Age	Sex	Occupation	Name	Age	Sex	Occupation
Bgt. (D)	17	F	Unknown	Mary (D)	07	F	Child
Mary (D)	14	F	Unknown	Christian (S)	04	M	Child
Michl. (S)	12	M	Unknown	Barclay, Ellen	20	F	None
Sarah (D)	10	F	Unknown	Ann	19	F	None
Arthur (S)	08	M	Child	McWilliams, Sarah	18	F	None
McDonough, F.	35	M	Farmer	Doulins, Margaret	18	F	None
Mary	35	F	Unknown	Cunningham, Wm.	24	M	Labourer
Thos.	35	M	Farmer	James	26	M	Labourer
Frank	13	M	None	McCabe, Matthew	25	M	Labourer
Martin	11	M	None	Cunningham, Sarah	22	F	None
Bdgt.	07	F	Child	Danly, Margaret	23	F	None
Jno.	05	M	Child	Susan	17	F	None
Pat	03	M	Child	Hanly, Delia	21	F	None
Jno.	02	M	Child	Wilson, Jacob	25	M	Farmer
Cath.	01	F	Child	Slavin, Margaret	21	F	None
Burrows, A.	28	M	Labourer	McQuide, Hugh	40	M	Farmer
Ann (W)	28	F	Wife	Biddy (W)	40	F	None
Wm. (S)	09	M	Child	Thomas (S)	15	M	None
Thos. (S)	07	M	Child	Sarah (D)	12	F	None
Jas. (S)	05	M	Child	Rosanna (D)	10	F	None
Danl. (S)	03	M	Child	Bridget (D)	08	F	Child
Jno. (S)	01	M	Child	Maria (D)	05	F	Child
Parker, T.	52	M	Farmer	Terrance	22	M	Stone Mason
Ware, Bdgt.	20	F	Unknown	Isabel	20	F	None
McHugh, Mary	20	F	Unknown	O Donnell, John	21	M	Labourer
Glenn, Elizbt.	02	F	Child	McKenna, Hugh	22	M	Labourer
Fdck.	29	M	Labourer	McGuy, Ellen	23	F	None
Louise	21	F	Unknown	Sheridan, Pat	25	M	Labourer
Fdck.	02	M	Child	Macisessony, Rose	17	F	None
Frns.	03	M	Child	Merston, Bridget	17	F	None
Maria	22	F	Unknown	Roaden, Mary	18	F	None
London, A.	32	M	Unknown	McGuin, Thomas	22	M	Labourer
Chuty	43	F	Unknown	Bliggen, James	21	M	Labourer
Rarin, J.	38	M	Labourer	Smith, John	29	M	Farmer
Kelso, J.	24	M	Labourer	Brady, Eliza	19	F	None
Viebis, Fdck.	25	M	Labourer	Kelly, Martin	36	M	Labourer
Robins, J.	28	M	Labourer	Hyde, Ellen	18	F	None
Mitney, Danl.	27	M	Labourer	Waters, Alway	34	M	None
Kain, Mike	24	M	Labourer	William	02	M	Child
Higgins, Bridget	25	F	None	Higgin, Mike	30	M	Labourer
McQuill, Mike	32	M	Labourer	Mary (W)	28	F	None
Ann (W)	32	F	None	Lettitia (D)	04	F	Child
Mike (S)	01	M	Child	John (S)	02	M	Child
Clinton, Lawrence	55	M	Labourer	Murphy, Mike	58	M	Labourer
Mary (W)	40	F	None	Johanna	16	F	None
Lawrence (S)	12	M	None	Kate	14	F	None
Hugh (S)	12	M	None	McGuin, Kate	19	F	None
William (S)	09	M	Child	Biddy	17	F	None

Name	Age	Sex	Occupation
Costlan, Thos.	29	M	None
Bridget (W)	28	F	None
Ellen (D)	06	F	Child
Maria (D)	05	F	Child
Barbara (D)	03	F	Child
Gordon, James	30	M	Labourer
McCabe, Mary	24	F	None
McCrunnan, Mary	19	F	None
Dennison, John	30	M	Labourer
McAwinry, Ann	27	F	None
Gogerty, George	26	M	Labourer
Daily, Pat	30	M	Labourer
Dawby, Margaret	22	F	None
Susan	16	F	None
Cummins, Sarah	19	F	None
Faiver, Terrance	30	M	None
Betty (W)	30	F	None
Owen (S)	06	M	Child
Elizabeth (D)	04	F	Child
Mary (D)	01	F	Child
(Died-At-Sea)			
Mickleman, Mary	22	F	None
McConnocky, Mary	12	F	None
Renalds, Pat	24	M	Labourer
Mary	24	F	None
Kelly, Jane	20	F	None
McQuade, Antony	22	M	Labourer
McGivern, Rose	15	F	None
Walsh, Thos.	30	M	Labourer
Nancy	22	F	None
Duffie, Margaret	20	F	None
Stevens, J.W.	27	M	Gentleman

Ship: F. Matthews, 27 February 1847

Name	Age	Sex	Occupation
Patterson, Samuel	25	M	Clerk
Bride, Ann	20	F	Servant
Leonard, Mary	23	F	Servant
Haily, John	56	M	Farmer
John-Jr. (S)	25	M	Farmer
Bridget (D)	22	F	Unknown
Susan (W)	50	F	Unknown
Susan (D)	20	F	Unknown
Finn, Patrick	32	M	Farmer
Patrick Jr (S)	02	M	Child
Mary (W)	28	F	Unknown
Ann (D)	04	F	Child

Name	Age	Sex	Occupation
Finley, Bart.	65	M	Farmer
Bart-Jr.	20	M	Farmer
Honor (W)	65	F	Unknown
Honor (D)	18	F	Unknown
Thomas (S)	10	M	Unknown
Brodin, John	19	M	Tailor
McDonald, Thos.	22	M	Labourer
Kelly, Hugh	22	M	Tailor
Fox, Michael	25	M	Labourer
Moran, Michael	20	M	Labourer
Ann	22	F	Unknown
Conway, Bart.	38	M	Labourer
Ann (W)	22	F	Unknown
Ann (D)	01	F	Child
Bart Jr. (S)	07	M	Child
O Goren, Bridget	18	F	Servant
Sittle, Charles	24	M	Cooper
Kelly, James	35	M	Labourer

Ship: Imperial, 14 April 1847

Name	Age	Sex	Occupation
Thompson, William	41	M	Labourer
Nancy (W)	45	F	Unknown
John (S)	18	M	Labourer
Bridget (D)	19	F	Unknown
Mary (D)	14	F	Unknown
James (S)	22	M	Labourer
Gallagher, James	28	M	Labourer
Gorman, John	21	M	Labourer
Kenny, James	35	M	Labourer
McGettrick, John	20	M	Labourer
Danagher, Michael	26	M	Labourer
Gorman, John	21	M	Labourer
Fanny	18	F	Unknown
Mulhern, Ellen	18	F	Unknown
Dunn, Patrick	19	M	Labourer
Ward, James	19	M	Labourer
Devany, Nancy	19	F	Unknown
Grimes, James	36	M	Labourer
Cunlisk, James	18	M	Labourer
Murray, Dan	21	M	Labourer
Gillen, Dominick	21	M	Labourer
Finnegan, John	20	M	Labourer
Waters, James	22	M	Labourer
Michael	18	M	Labourer
Patrick	16	M	Labourer
Henry	14	M	Labourer
Cath.	11	F	Unknown

Name	Age	Sex	Occupation
Dillon, Daniel	22	M	Labourer
Rooney, Francis	20	M	Labourer
Mary (W)	22	F	Wife
Kate (D)	01	F	Child
Devany, Michael	34	M	Labourer
Mary (D)	15	F	Unknown
Michael (S)	14	M	Labourer
Alice (D)	10	F	Unknown
Loftus, Michael	30	M	Labourer
Mary	35	F	Unknown
Mary	20	F	Unknown
Kate (D)	10	F	Unknown
Frank (S)	10	M	Labourer
Malany, Owen	50	M	Labourer
James	18	M	Labourer
Barrett, John	45	M	Labourer
Walter (S)	20	M	Labourer
Catharine (D)	15	F	Unknown
James (S)	13	M	Labourer
Lochlin, John	22	M	Labourer
Matthew	20	M	Labourer
John	20	M	Labourer
Hillis, Michael	25	M	Labourer
Mary	20	F	Unknown
Finnegan, James	22	M	Labourer
Hanly, Bele	20	F	Unknown
Hatley, Andrew	16	M	Labourer
Mary	09	F	Child
John	14	M	Labourer
Mary (M)	51	F	Unknown
Finnegan, Thomas	21	M	Labourer
Nancy	19	F	Unknown
James	14	M	Labourer
Michael	14	M	Labourer
Moffit, John	10	M	Labourer
Margt.	21	F	Unknown
Kate	23	F	Unknown
Dunn, Hugh	18	M	Labourer
Kearny, Stephen	22	M	Labourer
May	23	F	Unknown
Cullen, Owen	48	M	Labourer
Honor	13	F	Unknown
Mary	26	F	Unknown
Ellen	08	F	Child
Kelly, Biddy	43	F	Unknown
John (S)	03	M	Child
Bartholomew (S)	08	M	Child
Smith, Kate	21	F	Unknown

Name	Age	Sex	Occupation
Finnegan, Henry	22	M	Labourer
Feeny, Mary	23	F	Unknown
McCoul, Ann	15	F	Unknown
Kelly, Ann	18	F	Unknown
Maguirk, Teresa	19	F	Unknown
Finnegan, Matthew (Born-At-Sea)	00	M	Infant
Coyne, Bridget	24	F	Unknown

Ship: Dromahair, 25 May 1847

Name	Age	Sex	Occupation
Nesson, Honor	21	F	Labourer
Cauly, Thomas	21	M	Unknown
Nicholson, Patt.	24	M	Unknown
Clark, Jane	56	F	Unknown
Gildea, Thos.	36	M	Unknown
Gannon, Patt.	25	M	Unknown
Rose (W)	30	F	Wife
Mary (D)	03	F	Child
May, Francis	23	M	Unknown
Patt. (B)	18	M	Unknown
Mary (M)	56	F	Unknown
McNulty, Honor	20	F	Unknown
Johnson, Bridget	21	F	Unknown
Patt.	22	M	Unknown
Ann	22	F	Unknown
Bessey	00	F	Infant
William	23	M	Unknown
Bryan	24	M	Unknown
Brien, Patt.	21	M	Unknown
Waters, Stephen	25	M	Unknown
Fallon, Anne	25	F	Unknown
Walters, Roger	24	M	Unknown
John	22	M	Unknown
Byrnes, John	24	M	Unknown
Eleanor (W)	22	M	Unknown
Thomas	15	M	None
Bridget (D)	.03	F	Infant
Thomas (S)	.02	M	Infant
Gilmartin, Thos.	29	M	Unknown
James (P)	62	M	Unknown
Bridget (T)	20	F	Unknown
Mary (M)	50	F	Unknown
Sibly (T)	16	F	Unknown
Sally (T)	14	F	Unknown
Kitty (T)	12	F	Unknown
Winney (T)	10	F	Unknown

Name	Age	Sex	Occupation
Mary (T)	18	F	Unknown
Nancy (T)	11	F	Servant
Feeney, John	48	M	Servant
Gildea, Michl.	25	M	Servant
Jordan, Maria	20	F	Servant
Catherine	18	F	Servant
Preston, Thomas	30	M	Labourer
Mary	20	F	Unknown
Paddon, Sarah	56	F	Unknown
McTernan, Danl.	30	M	Unknown
Hart, Catherine	24	F	Unknown
Scanlon, Ann	20	F	Unknown
Peter	23	M	Unknown
Ward, Mary	22	F	Unknown
Smyth, Owen	26	M	Unknown
Martin, Francis	25	M	Unknown
Eleanor	25	F	Unknown
Cogan, Mary	16	F	Unknown
Dowd, Michael	44	M	Unknown
Mary (W)	30	F	Unknown
Anne-Jane (D)	11	F	Servant
Matilda (D)	09	F	Child
John (S)	07	M	Child
Thomas (S)	05	M	Child
Laing, Michael	22	M	Unknown
Mary	19	F	Unknown
Winnifred (M)	48	F	Unknown
Thomas, Philip	24	M	Unknown
Kilvlagann, James	25	M	Unknown
Mary (W)	20	F	Wife
Catherine (D)	03	F	Child
Patt. (S)	01	M	Child
McGetrick, Bridget	30	F	Unknown
Regan, Timothy	20	M	Farmer
Loftus, Peter	30	M	Unknown
Cogan, Seamus	35	M	Unknown
Margaret (W)	22	F	Unknown
John (S)	03	M	Child
Clancey, James	30	M	Unknown
Golden, William	60	M	Unknown
Mary (W)	55	F	Unknown
Martin (S)	26	M	Unknown
Mary (D)	24	F	Unknown
Patt. (S)	25	M	Unknown
Martin (S)	22	M	Unknown
Peter (S)	27	M	Unknown
Margt. (D)	18	F	Unknown
James (S)	15	M	Unknown

Name	Age	Sex	Occupation
Eleanor (D)	13	F	Unknown
Anne (D)	12	F	Unknown
Bridget (D)	24	F	Unknown
Gallagher, Jas.	22	M	Unknown
McTernan, John	28	M	Unknown
Nicholson, Wm.	26	M	Unknown
McHugh, Danl.	25	M	Unknown
Mary	24	F	Unknown
Hart, Peter	24	M	Unknown
Cogan, Daniel	25	M	Unknown
Maria	19	F	Unknown
Waters, Patrick	19	M	Unknown
Mullony, James	28	M	Unknown
Libby	25	F	Unknown
Geraghty, Corns.	24	M	Unknown
Margt.	26	F	Unknown
Gillen, Francis	28	M	Unknown
Kivlaghen, Thady	60	M	Unknown
Mary (D)	22	F	Unknown
Cathe. (D)	16	F	Unknown
John (S)	24	M	Unknown
Jordan, John	56	M	Unknown
Edward (S)	22	M	Unknown
James (S)	19	M	Labourer
Thomas (S)	15	M	Unknown
Feeny, Honor	48	F	Unknown
Patt. (S)	18	M	Unknown
John (S)	16	M	Unknown
Cathe.(D)	14	F	Unknown
Mary (D)	12	F	Unknown
Bryan (S)	09	M	Child
Cecilia (D)	08	F	Child
Biddy (D)	05	F	Child
Hatley, Patt.	26	M	Unknown
Rose (W)	24	F	Unknown
Cathe. (D)	01	F	Child
Winney (D)	01	F	Child
Boyle, Margaret	26	F	Unknown
Nancey	24	F	Unknown
Conlon, Anne	24	F	Unknown
Brennan, Walter	24	M	Unknown
Gildea, Betty	22	F	Unknown
Sarah (D)	03	F	Child
Kelly, Owen	30	M	Unknown
Honor (W)	21	F	Unknown
Patrick (S)	02	M	Child
Mary-Ann (D)	01	F	Child
Gilmer, Hugh	26	M	Unknown

Name	Age	Sex	Occupation
Duffy, Danl.	40	M	Unknown
Duffy, Margt. (W)	30	F	Unknown
Mary (D)	10	F	Child
Margt. (D)	08	F	Child
Honor (D)	06	F	Child
Cathe. (D)	04	F	Child
Bridget (D)	01	F	Child
Michael (B)	35	M	Farmer
Rose (L)	26	F	Unknown
Owen (N)	11	M	Unknown
Peter (N)	09	M	Child
Michl. (N)	04	M	Child
Thos. (N)	06	M	Child
Rose (N)	01	F	Child
Kilvihan, Peter	22	M	Unknown
Nancy	21	F	Unknown
McGloin, Martin	50	M	Unknown
Michl.	20	M	Unknown

Ship: Sarah-Boyde, 10 June 1847

Name	Age	Sex	Occupation
Golden, Pat	20	M	Farmer
McMurray, Pat	40	M	Farmer
Pat (S)	19	M	Farmer
Higgins, John	23	M	Farmer
Barthy	22	M	Farmer
Michael	60	M	Farmer
Mary	60	F	None
Cathe.	28	F	None
Mary	25	F	None
Margt.	20	F	None
Clabby, Mary	22	F	None
Ann	20	F	None
Eleanor	10	F	None
Dunn, Michael	30	M	Farmer
Bridget (W)	30	F	None
Pat (S)	05	M	Child
Barthy. (S)	03	M	Child
Bridget (D)	02	F	Child
Mary (D)	.09	F	Infant
Higgins, Honor	15	F	None
Ann	13	F	None
McIntyre, Thos.	20	M	Labourer
John	25	M	Labourer
Kate	15	F	None
Derry, Mary	25	F	None
Hister, Pat	45	M	Labourer
Pat (S)	20	M	Labourer

Name	Age	Sex	Occupation
Thos. (S)	18	M	Labourer
Mary (W)	40	F	None
Bridget (D)	10	F	None
Carl, Pat	30	M	Labourer
Heveron, Owen	60	M	Labourer
Pat (S)	30	M	Labourer
John (S)	28	M	Labourer
Winne. (S)	20	M	Labourer
Bridget (W)	60	F	None
Mary (D)	20	F	None
Bridget (D)	25	F	None
Brown, Mary	23	F	None
Finegan, Michael	53	M	Labourer
Fineron, Pat	20	M	Labourer
Conway, Anthony	35	M	Labourer
Celia (W)	30	F	None
Pat (S)	01	M	Child
O'Connor, Mary	47	F	None
Bridget (D)	22	F	Nonw
Ellen (D)	16	F	None
Hugh (S)	12	M	Labourer
Finnegan, Thos.	20	M	Labourer
Flately, Andw.	40	M	Labourer
Martin, Owen	35	M	Labourer
Dondicon, Bridget	50	F	None
Martin, Ann	20	F	None
Burns, Honor	18	F	None
McDermot, John	30	M	Labourer
Bridget	30	F	None
Kelly, Pat	30	M	Labourer
Jordan, Pat	32	M	Labourer
Nancy	35	F	None
Ellis, Cathe.	22	F	None
Jordan, Pat	.06	M	Infant
O Bryan, Betsey	18	F	None
Hart, Martin	32	M	Labourer
Dyer, Pat	35	M	Labourer
Carlson, John	25	M	Labourer
Feeny, Pat	25	M	Labourer
Jordan, Andw.	25	M	Labourer
Mary (M)	57	F	None
Bridget	22	M	None
Gillen, John	25	M	Labourer
Rooney, Neal	25	M	Labourer
Waters, Michael	25	M	Labourer
Wood, Henry	25	M	Labourer
Waters, Michael	25	M	Labourer
High, Mary	22	F	None

Name	Age	Sex	Occupation
Bagley, Mary	22	F	None
Gannon, Cathe.	20	F	None
John	22	M	Labourer
Ann	18	F	None
Larvin, Danl.	22	M	Labourer
Flinn, Ninles.	20	M	Labourer
Matamo, Mary	17	F	None
Flinn, Bridget	21	F	None
Carley, Michael	21	M	Mechanic
Davy, Pat	21	M	Mechanic
McGarighlan, Darly	20	M	Mechanic
McLaughlin, Pat	20	M	Mechanic
Correy, Pat	45	M	Mechanic
Celia (D)	17	F	None
Jones, Luke	28	M	Mechanic
Ford, Thos.	20	M	Mechanic
McLaughlin, John	21	M	Mechanic
Ann	23	F	None
McParthin, Owen	21	M	Mechanic
McGoldrick, Pat	24	M	Mechanic
McDermot, Pat	26	M	Mechanic
Gilmartin, Ed.	25	M	Mechanic
Mary	20	F	None
Comer, Michael	57	M	Mechanic
Sarville, Michael	23	M	Mechanic
Kelley, Anthy.	20	M	Mechanic
Sarville, Bridget	18	F	None
Hoine, Anthy.	28	M	Mechanic
Michl.	25	M	Mechanic
Bridget	29	F	None
Margt.	29	F	None
Mary	25	F	None
Preston, Michael	50	M	Mechanic
Thos. (S)	20	M	Mechanic
Mary (W)	50	F	None
Bridget (D)	18	F	None
Mary (D)	17	F	None
Sarah (D)	16	F	None
Margt. (D)	14		None
Conway, John	25	M	Mechanic
Wm.	20	M	Mechanic
Jas.	35	M	Mechanic
Mary	60	F	None
Nancy	23	F	None
Cormick, Thos.	25	M	Mechanic
May	22	F	None
May, James	30	M	Mechanic
Nancy (W)	24	F	None

Name	Age	Sex	Occupation
James (S)	07	M	Child
Morrican, Pat	60	M	Labourer
John (S)	20	M	Labourer
James (S)	15	M	Labourer
Bridget (D)	20	F	None
Mary (D)	18	F	None
Duffy, John	40	M	Labourer
Pat	17	M	Labourer
Bridget	50	F	None
Ann	20	F	None
Ellen	15	F	None

Ship: Dewdrop, 13 July 1847

Name	Age	Sex	Occupation
McGowan, Pat	20	M	Labourer
Rooney, Ann	20	F	None
Byrne, Jno.	34	M	Labourer
Rooney, Thos.	24	M	Labourer
Mich.	21	M	Labourer
Joy, Jno.	17	M	Labourer
Callergan, Cath.	16	F	None
Egan, Thos.	28	M	Labourer
Bridget	20	F	None
Foley, Chas.	17	M	Labourer
Mary	19	F	None
Flannigan, Mary	13	F	None
Dacy, Jno.	38	M	Labourer
Mary	17	F	None
Jno.	13	M	Labourer
Boyle, Wm.	21	M	Labourer
Carty, Patt.	30	M	Labourer
Bridget	32	F	None
Quinn, Dennis	23	M	Labourer
Eleanor	19	F	None
Connelly, Patt.	19	M	Labourer
Moran, Jno.	21	M	Labourer
Thos.	18	M	Labourer
Gallagher, Cath.	18	F	None
Margt.	15	F	None
Bridget	18	F	None
Rock, Timothey	30	M	Labourer
Nelson, Jno.	18	M	Labourer
Hon.	18	F	None
Munn, Bridget	23	F	None
Rooney, Mich.	25	M	Labourer
Finon, Chas.	28	M	Labourer
Finegan, Luke	30	M	Labourer
Wm.	14	M	Labourer

Name	Age	Sex	Occupation
Mullen, Anthony	18	M	Labourer
Eleanor	35	F	None
Timon, Mary	13	F	None
Mullen, Dord.	16	F	None
Boland, Pat	10	M	None
Mich.	07	M	Child
Murray, Thady	23	M	Labourer
Higgins, James	60	M	Labourer
Nancey	17	F	None
Nancey	50	F	None
Peter	20	M	Labourer
Jordan, Jas.	20	M	Labourer
Gilgan, Dennis	23	M	Labourer
Morrow, Peter	25	M	Labourer
Mich.	20	M	Labourer
Jno.	27	M	Labourer
Darby	17	M	Labourer
Ann	19	F	None
Lacken, Ellen	16	F	None
Hart, Ann	21	F	None
Slatty, Jno.	25	M	Labourer
Thomas, Bridget	23	F	None
Dunn, Andrew	26	M	Labourer
Walsh, Mich.	26	M	Labourer
Ann	20	F	None
McGowan, Mary	19	F	None
King, Darby	26	M	Labourer
McGrath, James	20	M	Labourer
McEwan, Mich.	16	M	Labourer
Biddy	18	F	None
Feeny, John	45	M	Labourer
Jas.	15	M	Labourer
Mary	10	F	None
Kerr, Bridget	18	F	None
Hart, Peter	20	M	Labourer
Reily, Edwd.	18	M	Labourer
David	20	M	Labourer
Mulvey, Jno.	22	M	Labourer
Benj.	20	M	Labourer
Ann	18	F	None
Flanagan, Cath.	16	F	None
McGowan, Dom.	23	M	Labourer
Dunn, Luke	22	M	Labourer
Rush, Patt	22	M	Labourer
Rogers, Jas.	25	M	Labourer
Gilpatrick, Mary	24		None
Cunningham, Cath.	20	F	None
Flynn, Patt	23	M	Labourer

Name	Age	Sex	Occupation
Mary	19	F	None
Margt.	17	F	None
Durken, Mich.	18	M	Labourer
Sweeny, Thos.	22	M	Labourer
Edwd.	24	M	Labourer
O Donnell, Mich.	22	M	Labourer
Carty, Cath.	16	F	None
Mattins, Patt	24	M	Labourer
Eleanor	20	F	None
Dunne, Jno.	26	M	Labourer

Ship: Sarah-Brown, 26 July 1847

Name	Age	Sex	Occupation
Dwyer, M.	50	F	Unknown
M.	20	F	Unknown
Campbell, A.	18	F	Unknown
A.	16	F	Unknown
Falcon, A.	23	F	Unknown
Cambry, M.	20	F	Unknown
Maloney, J.	25	M	Merchant
M.	20	F	Unknown
Falcon, P.	45	M	None
Bolton, B.	21	M	None
Bushe, E.	16	F	Unknown
Bourke, C.	22	F	Unknown
Waldron, W.J.	28	M	Farmer
E. (W)	20	F	Unknown
M (D)	.03	F	Infant
Davis, E.	20	F	Unknown
Grogan, L.	39	M	Farmer
B.	30	F	Unknown
Cribbon, M.	18	F	Unknown
Folland, W.	35	M	Farmer
B.	20	F	Unknown
C.	18	F	Unknown
Ellis, H.	18	F	Unknown
Henry, B.	22	F	Unknown
Dyer, C.	20	F	Unknown
Collins, M.	20	F	Unknown

Ship: Adario, 16 September 1847

Name	Age	Sex	Occupation
Quinan, Bryan	20	M	Labourer
Kaveny, Mary	22	F	Spinster
Quinan, Eleanor	49	F	Spinster
Michael (S)		M	Farmer
James (S)	05	M	Child
Ormsby, Mary	14	F	Spinster

Name	Age	Sex	Occupation
Missett, Robert	42	M	Carpenter
Mullaney, James	25	M	Tailor
Padden, Mary	17	F	Spinster
McGloin, Patt	23	M	Labourer
Eleanor	19	F	Spinster
Tansy, John	20	M	Labourer
Duffy, Margt.	17	F	Spinster
Tansy, Mary	19	F	Spinster
Jennings, Honor	21	F	Spinster
Malachy	17	M	None
McAndrew, Anne	41	F	Spinster
Michael (S)	19	M	None
Bridget (D)	13	F	None
Hale, Barny	20	F	Spinster
Fury, Andrew	24	M	H & I kpr
Duffy, Patt.	30	M	Labourer
Bridget	30	F	Matron
Hogan, Michael	12	M	None
Tiernan, Besy	24	F	Spinster
McGuire, Winefred	20	F	Spinster
Vennard, Esther	47	F	Spinster
Heron, Ellen	30	F	Spinster
Breadin, Mary	23	F	Spinster
Curran, Margt.	28	F	Wife
John (S)	04	M	Child
William (S)	03	M	Child
Brennan, Anne	18	F	Spinster
Heally, David	42	M	Merchant
Mary (D)	16	F	Spinster
Ferguson, Bridget	25	F	Spinster
Feeny, Michael	17	M	Labourer
John	20	M	Labourer
Murrae, Mathew	30	M	Labourer
Biddy	20	F	Spinster
Costello, Michael	14	M	None
Cooney, Michael	30	M	Labourer
Mooney, Anne	19	F	Spinster
Lang, Patrick	32	M	Labourer
Erdis, Samuel	22	M	Farmer
Jane (W)	19	F	Wife
Kilmartin, Martin	30	M	Teacher
Meaney, Patt.	29	M	Wheelwright
Taylor, John	40	M	Tailor
Shulthiess, Gottfried	23	M	Clock Maker
Gillon, James	28	M	Labourer
Catherine	31	F	Matron
Costello, Maria	12	F	None

Name	Age	Sex	Occupation
Devany, Mick	30	M	Labourer
Missett, John	16	M	None
Heal, Patt.	16	M	None
Shaw, Eliza-Jane	20	F	None
Feeny, Michael	30	M	Labourer
Mary (W)	30	F	None
Devaney, Anne	28	F	Spinster
Goldrick, Owen	17	M	None
Cowan, Thomas	25	M	Bootmaker

Ship: British-Queen, 29 June 1848

Name	Age	Sex	Occupation
Colleary, Pat.	23	M	Labourer
Andrew	20	M	Labourer
Johnston, Ellen	19	F	Spinster
Thomas	20	M	labourer
Sweeney, Biddy	24	F	Spinster
Mary	03	F	Child
John	04	M	Child
Daley, Pat.	17	M	Labourer
Mary	14	F	Spinster
Rooney, James	20	M	Labourer
Anne	28	F	Spinster
Shumms, Mary	24	F	Spinster
Anne	18	F	Spinster
McFadden, John	50	M	Labourer
Fetanagun, Mich.	50	M	Labourer
Cullen, Charles	22	M	Farmer
James	22	M	Labourer
Kelloran, Mich.	19	M	Labourer
Davy, Thomas	30	M	Labourer
Flynn, Mich.	22	M	Labourer
Scanlon, James	25	M	Labourer
Brennan, James	45	M	Shopkeeper
Bridget (W)	45	F	Wife
Fitzpatrick, Bess	30	F	Spinster
Brennan, Bess	16	F	Spinster
Mary	14	F	Spinster
James	10	M	Child
Honor	03	F	Child
Magloin, Mary	15	F	Spinster
Devany, Mary	.06	F	Infant
Magowen, Biddy	22	F	Spinster
Foley, Mary	20	F	Spinster
Berne, Mich.	24	M	Labourer
James	25	M	Labourer
Cath.	25	F	Spinster
Judy	59	F	Spinster

Name	Age	Sex	Occupation	Name	Age	Sex	Occupation
Colleary, Anne	20	F	Spinster	Mattimore, Mick	28	M	Sawer
Kilhy, Biddy	24	F	Spinster	Laeken, Mick	23	M	Labourer
Kerrigan, John	20	M	Labourer	Ellen	30	F	Spinster
Biddy	24	F	Spinster	Tanrey, John	30	M	Labourer
Burke, Cath.	18	F	Spinster	Ternpany, John	20	M	Labourer
Hannan, Bessey	21	F	Spinster	Egan, Pat	25	M	Labourer
McDermott, Mich.	19	M	Labourer	McNultay, Pat.	24	M	Labourer
Mell, Dan.	35	M	Labourer	Dogan, Pat.	20	M	Labourer
Jane	24	F	Spinster	Mary	18	F	Spinster
Dowdion, Hannah	19	F	Spinster	Anne	16	F	Spinster
Scanlon, Mich.	19	M	Labourer	McSweeney, Terrence	14	M	Labourer
Sily, John	15	M	Labourer	Morison, Martin	30	M	Labourer
Hart, Anne	30	F	Spinster	Rose	25	F	Spinster
Avent, Joseph	20	M	None	Conlan, Mary	20	F	Spinster
James	20	M	None	Donohue, Owen	50	M	Labourer
Gallagher, John	21	M	Labourer	Rose	48	F	Matron
Cath.	10	F	Child	Mary	18	F	Spinster
Roony, James	21	M	Labourer	Biddy	16	F	Spinster
Reed, Margt.	20	F	Spinster	James	12	M	Child
Murphey, Pat.	21	M	Labourer	Nancy	06	F	Child
Cath.	15	F	Spinster	O'Hara, Ellen	18	F	Spinster
Judy	17	F	Spinster	Smith, Mary	21	F	Spinster
Spence, Mary	18	F	Spinster	Dooney, Mary	20	F	Spinster
Farrell, Bridget	20	F	Spinster	Filbin, Anthony	24	M	Labourer
Alice	12	F	Spinster	Andrew	24	M	Labourer
Mary	40	F	Spinster	Kilcauly, Martin	22	M	Labourer
Walsh, Sarah	20	F	Spinster	Anne	20	F	Spinster
Sabrina	22	F	Spinster	Shannon, Pat.	17	M	Labourer
Kaverny, Cath.	22	F	Spinster	Bergen, John	26	M	Labourer
Maguire, Mich.	28	M	Labourer	Courterey, Margt.	20	F	Spinster
Weir, Peggy	24	F	Spinster	Killiha, John	14	M	Labourer
McDonnell, Alice	24	F	Spinster	James	16	M	Labourer
McGowan, James	26	M	Labourer	Hunt, Cath.	40	F	Spinster
Biddy (W)	24	F	Wife	Bessy	40	F	Spinster
Pat. (S)	03	M	Child	Eliza-Anne	14	F	Spinster
Carroll, Mary	14	F	Spinster	Emily	10	F	Spinster
Farry, Mich.	22	M	Labourer	Dalton, Margt.	30	F	Spinster
James	20	M	Labourer	Brennan, Margt.	22	F	Spinster
Brennan, Anne	24	F	Spinster	Anne	20	F	Spinster
McGowan, James	26	M	Labourer	McHugh, John	25	M	Labourer
Waters, Biddy	26	F	Spinster	Dixon, James	23	M	Labourer
Bral, Anne	24	F	Spinster	Ellen	20	F	Spinster
Quinn, John	17	M	Labourer	McQuinn, Mich.	47	M	Labourer
Foley, James	26	M	Labourer	McGrath, Jane	46	F	Matron
Mary	21	F	Spinster	Mary	48	F	Spinster
Dyer, Bessy	20	F	Spinster	Margt.	16	F	Spinster
McAndrew, Pat.	12	M	Child	Bridget	14	F	Spinster
Kerr, Robt.	24	M	Farmer	James	12	M	Child

Name	Age	Sex	Occupation
Cath	09	F	Child
Anne	07	F	Child
Kems, Pat.	30	M	Labourer
Conaghlin, Mary	24	F	Spinster
Grahem, James	25	M	Labourer
Kilbride, Owen	25	M	Labourer
Cath	24	F	Wife
Hannelly, Mary	40	F	Spinster
Pat.	20	M	Labourer
Cath.	17	F	Spinster
Thos.	10	M	Child
James	09	M	Child
McCann, Pat.	26	M	Labourer
Smith, Mark	25	M	Labourer
Margt.	20	F	Spinster
Roger	40	M	Labourer
Rogar, Owen	26	M	Labourer
Cavanagh, Biddy	16	F	Spinster
Hurt, Thomas	26	M	Labourer
Roony, Thomas	18	M	Labourer
McArdle, Maria	14	F	Spinster
Bessey	14	F	Spinster
Grilgen, Ellen	24	F	Spinster
McCloud, Mich.	30	M	Labourer
Boland, Susan	24	F	Spinster
Moffit, Margt.	50	F	Spinster
O'Hara, Bryan	30	M	Labourer
Rooney, Sarah	18	F	Spinster
Honan, James	20	M	Labourer
Dyer, Pat.	21	M	Labourer
Garney, Anne	20	F	Spinster
McGowan, Anne	24	F	Spinster
Bolunse, Pat.	50	M	Labourer
McHugh, Biddy	20	F	Spinster
Kern, Henry	35	M	Printer
Kerr, Ann	30	F	Wife
Mortyre (S)	.06	M	Infant
Smith, Sarah	22	F	Spinster
O'Malley, Mary	17	F	Spinster
Shea, Pat.	40	M	Labourer
Henry, Margt.	25	F	Spinster
Elliott, John	20	M	Farmer
Ellen	45	F	Spinster
Adam	50	M	Farmer
Dowd, Ellen	19	F	Spinster
McFeman, Hugh	40	M	Labourer
Water, Mary	20	F	Spinster
Cregg, Mary-Ann	21	F	Spinster

Name	Age	Sex	Occupation
Higgins, Mich.	23	M	Labourer
Davery, John	30	M	Labourer
Peggy	40	F	Spinster
O'Hara, James	30	M	Labourer
O'Connor, Luke	27	M	Labourer
Mart.	17	F	Spinster
O'Hara, Sarah	26	F	Spinster
Mullen, Mary	22	F	Spinster
Frizell, Wm.	25	M	Labourer
Fallow, Cath	20	F	Spinster
Gordon, Mary	26	F	Spinster
McHugh, Margt.	24	F	Spinster
McMonin, James	45	M	Labourer
McCormick, Biddy	20	F	Spinster
Campbell, Ellen	22	F	Spinster
Donohue, Pat.	24	M	Labourer
Farrell, John	22	M	Labourer
Begley, Thomas	27	M	Labourer
Mich.	26	M	Labourer
James	25	M	Labourer
Catharine	24	F	Spinster
Kerr, William	30	M	Farmer
Jane (W)	35	F	Wife
Nancy (D)	12	F	Child
Fanny (D)	08	F	Child
Eliza-Jane (D)	04	F	Child
Isabella (D)	02	F	Child
Wm. Rockfort (S)	01	M	Child
Favry, Bessy	21	F	None
Hart, Pat.	19	M	None
Cregg, Antery	20	M	Labourer

Ship: Archimedes, 13 July 1848

Name	Age	Sex	Occupation
Kerrigan, Bridget	24	F	Spinster
Cullen, Anne	25	F	Spinster
Flemming, Thady	30	M	Farmer
Winnyfred	24	F	Matron
Michael	.01	M	Infant
Rogers, Mary	21	F	Spinster
Caraway, Bernard	21	M	Farmer
Colville, William	28	M	Labourer
Roddy, Charles	21	M	Labourer
Forde, Peter	24	M	Labourer
Michl.	21	M	Labourer
Bridget	24	F	Spinster
McHugh, Patt.	21	M	Farmer
Bridget	18	F	Spinster

Name	Age	Sex	Occupation	Name	Age	Sex	Occupation
Flynne, Margaret	21	F	Spinster	Smith, Mary	23	F	Spinster
Cryan, Bridget	22	F	Wife	Rowen, Hannah	21	F	Spinster
Parke, Honor	27	F	Wife	Bolton, William	18	M	Accountant
Bridget (D)	06	F	Child	Anderson, Andrew	23	M	Farmer
Ellen (D)	01	F	Child	Johnstone, Anne	24	F	Seamstress
Cryan, Henry	22	M	Farmer	Murnaghan, James	21	M	Tailor
Henry, Catharine	21	F	Spinster	Minchan, Thomas	19	M	Labourer
McCarrick, James	20	M	Farmer	Killey, Catherine	21	F	Seamstress
Henry	18	M	Labourer	Shannon, Edward	19	M	Labourer
Meredith, Duke	17	M	Labourer	Fairbanks, John	20	M	Labourer
James	28	M	Labourer	Lunny, Hugh	34	M	Carter
Sweeny, Mary	20	F	Spinster	O'Connor, Sarah	24	F	Spinster
Lyans, Mary	20	F	Spinster	Crean, Mary	22	F	Spinster
Miles, Bridget	29	F	Wife	Drury, Betty	25	F	Spinster
Daniel	22	M	Labourer	Creighton, Michl.	21	M	Farmer
Murray, Patt.	28	M	Farmer	Drudge, Bridget	22	F	Spinster
Catherine	24	F	Spinster	O'Connor, John	21	M	Labourer
Hennigan, Daniel	24	M	Labourer	Keane, Patt.	29	M	Labourer
Nary, Mary	20	F	Spinster	Murphy, Thos.	21	M	Labourer
Walsh, Elizabeth	10	F	None	O'Donnell, Wm.	21	M	Labourer
Honor	06	F	Child	McDonnell, Mary	24	F	Labourer
Tucker, Patt	24	M	Farmer	Derrig, Andrew	23	M	Farmer
Cawley, Anne	21	F	Spinster	Rooney, Margaret	21	F	Spinster
William	20	M	Labourer	Gilgan, Patt.	22	M	Farmer
Fox, Rose	17	F	Spinster	Margaret	20	F	Spinster
Clinton, Marie	19	F	Spinster	Mary	11	F	None
Johnston, Susan	24	F	Spinster	Rooney, Daniel	21	M	Labourer
Allen, Bridget	24	F	Spinster	McKion, Bridget	22	F	Spinster
McGowan, Anne	25	F	Spinster	Gaughan, Anthony	21	M	Labourer
Mary	20	F	Spinster	Patt	20	M	Labourer
Hadan, James	20	M	Labourer	Hugh	18	M	Labourer
Sarah	09	F	Child	Casey, John	21	M	Labourer
Bridget	21	F	Spinster	Loftus, Martin	26	M	Carpenter
Catherine	20	F	Spinster	Ward, Rebecca	22	F	Spinster
Lunny, Mary	21	F	Spinster	McGourty, Hugh	23	M	Labourer
Moran, Patt	22	M	Labourer	Mary	20	F	Spinster
Bridget	18	F	Spinster	Walsh, Michl.	22	M	Labourer
Tahany, Catherine	21	F	Spinster	Hope, Anne	23	F	Spinster
Moran, Mary	22	F	Spinster	Foody, Ellen	22	F	Spinster
McKinney, Mary	21	F	Spinster	Mulligan, John	25	M	Shopman
Doherty, James	24	M	Hatter	Cavanagh, Patt	24	M	Farmer
Ownes, Charley	22	M	Farmer	Michell, James	26	M	Farmer
Flynne, Michael	20	M	Labourer	Atty	18	F	Spinster
Johnston, Eliza	24	F	Spinster	McGuire, Patt	20	M	Labourer
Hannah	20	F	Spinster	Reilly, Honor	21	F	Spinster
Kinney, Catherine	21	F	Spinster	Lavin, Thady	24	M	Labourer
Henry, Ellen	20	F	Spinster	O'Connor, Patt	22	M	Labourer
McKim, Mary	24	F	Spinster	Bouly, Mary	21	F	Spinster

Name	Age	Sex	Occupation	Name	Age	Sex	Occupation
Healy, Winny	21	F	Spinster	Anne	08	F	Child
Doyle, Andrew	20	M	Labourer	Honor	06	F	Child
Grourke, Bridget	18	F	Spinster	Patrick	04	M	Child
Darkin, Bridget	21	F	Spinster	Thomas	00	M	Infant
McDonough, Sarah	22	F	Spinster	Fitzzgerald, Lawrence	28	M	Farmer
Bolton, Beatrice-A	20	F	Unknown	Honor	22	F	Spinster
				McCann, Anne	38	F	Matron

Ship: Dromahair, 01 November 1848

Name	Age	Sex	Occupation	Name	Age	Sex	Occupation
				Mary-Ann	18	F	Spinster
Malley, Joseph	40	M	Labourer	Margt.	15	F	Spinster
Hargodon, Michl.	20	M	Labourer	Cath.	13	F	Unknown
Mary	18	F	Matron	Edwd.	10	M	Unknown
Clark, Anne	18	F	Spinster	William	08	M	Child
Harrison, Mary	26	F	Spinster	John	06	M	Infant
Lowe, Ellen	16	F	Spinster	Thomas	00	M	Infant
Goulding, Anne	19	F	Spinster	Gilgan, Ellen	18	F	Spinster
Fox, Bridget	22	F	Spinster	McAvoda, Bridget	20	F	Spinster
McPartland, Jane	20	F	Spinster	McHugh, John	25	M	Labourer
Garly, John	26	M	Labourer	McGloyn, Patk.	22	M	Labourer
Grevalt, Joseph	35	M	Cbtmkr	Ginty, Anne	22	F	Spinster
Jane	29	F	Matron	Brennan, Edwd.	24	M	Labourer
Elizabeth	10	F	Unknown	Partland, Cathn.	18	F	Spinster
Margaret	08	F	Child	Hannon, Sarah	13	F	Unknown
John	05	M	Child	McGrevy, Margt.	20	F	Spinster
Ginty, Ann	24	F	Matron	Hever, Cath.	18	F	Spinster
Mary	.10	F	Infant	Cunningham, Patrick	17	M	Labourer
Feeny, Brian	26	M	Labourer	Connor, Patrick	45	M	Farmer
Gillan, Michl.	20	M	Labourer	Irvin, Richard	24	M	Farmer
Hogan, Mary	26	F	Matron	Ellen	20	F	Matron
McCann, Thomas	38	M	Labourer	Carvey, John	40	M	Farmer
Gray, Honor	20	F	Spinster	Luke	10	M	Child
Beirne, Bryan	26	M	Labourer	John	08	M	Child
Commion, Ellen	25	F	Spinster	Patrick	06	M	Child
Righe, Mary	20	F	Spinster	Sheil, Michael	26	M	Farmer
Browne, Joseph	35	M	Gdnr	Anne	24	F	Matron
Kelly, Patrick	40	M	Farmer	Patrick	20	M	Farmer
Honor	38	F	Matron	Jane	22	F	Matron
Honor	13	F	Spinster	Clancy, Bridget	20	F	Unknown
Ellen	11	F	Unknown	Ready, Bridget	20	F	Spinster
Joyce, Eleanor	25	F	Spinster	Gliney, Thomas	22	M	Labourer
Minahan, Michl.	25	M	Labourer	Sadler, Anne	22	F	Spinster
Peter	24	M	Labourer	Gorman, Paul	38	M	Farmer
McDaniel, Cecily	18	F	Spinster	Conlan, Alice	18	F	Spinster
McKim, John	18	M	Painter	Gorman, Ellen	38	F	Matron
Carrolly, Sarah	20	F	Matron	Sarah	14	F	Unknown
Pendergast, Richd.	38	M	Farmer	Ellen	12	F	Unknown
Sarah	37	F	Matron	Bridget	08	F	Child
Mary	10	F	Unknown	James	06	M	Child
				Joseph	04	M	Child

Name	Age	Sex	Occupation	Name	Age	Sex	Occupation
Henry, Mary	26	F	Matron	John	02	M	Child
Cunningham, Mary	18	F	Spinster	Burke, Bridget	20	F	None
Henry, Bridgit	10	F	Unknown	Scanlon, John	40	M	None
Kelly, John	28	M	Labourer	Mary	40	F	None
Ellen	24	F	Spinster	Mary	40	F	None
Murty, Bridget	18	F	Spinster	Henry, James	18	M	None
Smith, Thomas	32	M	Labourer				
Harrison, John	24	M	Carpenter	*Ship: Glen,* 06 April 1849			
Aeneas	20	M	Farmer				
Clark, Patrick	30	M	Farmer	Haraghty, P.	40	M	Farmer
Kilbride, Michl.	20	M	Joiner	Connell, O.	24	M	Unknown
Roony, John	25	M	Labourer	Flynn, Bgt.	26	F	Unknown
Campbell, Francis	27	M	Carpenter	Barrett, P.	19	U	Unknown
Sweeney, Thomas	28	M	Farmer	Barnes, M.	28	U	Unknown
Betty	26	F	Matron	Gilmartin, J.	28	U	Unknown
Kerrigan, Patrick	24	M	Farmer	Cath.	01	F	Child
Campbell, Nancy	23	F	Matron	Ann	13	F	None
Poe, Isaac	21	M	Carpenter	Warren, J.	43	M	Unknown
Gallagher, Bridget	18	F	Spinster	Cath.	11	F	None
McClean, Honor	20	F	Spinster	Jane	09	F	Child
Loftus, Bridget	20	F	Spinster	Feeny, J.	30	M	Unknown
Lally, Honor	38	F	Spinster	Keegheam, J.	30	M	Unknown
Dunleavy, Margt.	22	F	Spinster	Rotchfort, Mgt.	23	F	None
Cain, Sarah	18	F	Spinster	Feely, My.	28	F	None
McAndrew, Rose	20	F	Spinster	Gleer, Ann-M.	30	F	None
McNally, Mary	38	F	Matron	Rover, Bessy	19	F	None
Cathe.	10	F	Spinster	Gilgan, L.	20	M	Unknown
Mary	08	F	Child	Green, T.	19	M	Unknown
Patrick	06	M	Child	McNiff, M.	22	M	Unknown
Cuff, Cathn.	30	F	Matron	Ann	19	F	Unknown
Molarky, Denis	10	M	Unknown	Monaghan, J.	20	M	Unknown
Murphy, Anthony	14	M	Labourer	Horan, T.	19	M	Unknown
Clark, John	26	M	Labourer	McMany, M.	22	M	Unknown
Lavelle, Patk.	24	M	Labourer	Peter	20	M	Unknown
Gallagher, Patk.	28	M	Labourer	Gilgan, P.	20	M	Unknown
Mullowny, Michl.	24	M	Labourer	Darcy, Cath.	20	F	None
Padden, Peter	20	M	Labourer	Hart, M.	23	M	Unknown
Reilly, Michl.	22	M	Labourer	Stephen, M.	23	M	Unknown
Babby	18	F	Spinster	Battle, Bessey	17	F	None
Tollett, Elizabeth	19	F	Spinster	My.	15	F	None
Lally, Bridget	36	F	Matron	Thos.	12	M	Unknown
Patrick	10	M	Unknown	John	16	M	Unknown
Fanny	08	F	Child	Hart, Mgt.	13	F	None
Kelly, Hugh	40	M	None	Cath.	11	F	None
Bridget	40	F	None	Domnick	09	M	Child
Gorman, Richd.	35	M	None	Ann	07	F	Child
Julia	30	F	None	Oats, P.	21	M	Unknown
Charles	05	M	Child	Wynn, My.	15	F	None

Name	Age	Sex	Occupation	Name	Age	Sex	Occupation
Lynn, Bgt.	17	F	None	Bgt.	11	F	None
Monaghan, Bgt.	26	F	None	Cassidy, B.	24	M	Unknown
Gallagher, J.	22	M	Unknown	Henger, Lucy	20	F	None
Bgt.	20	F	None	Cath.	23	F	None
Thos.	01	M	Child	Carey, D.	23	M	Unknown
McPadden, D.	22	M	Labourer	McGrath, M.	25	M	Unknown
Gallagher, My.	15	F	None	Moron, P.	20	M	Unknown
Clarke, Sah.	18	F	None	Judith	18	F	None
Scanlan, F.	28	M	Unknown	Gallagher, Elen	16	F	None
Slane, D.	17	M	Unknown	Mann, M.	01	F	None
Cath.	20	F	None	Mogan, Eleanor	30	F	Child
Eleanor	18	F	None	Kenny, J.	35	M	Unknown
Prolok–, Bgt.	47	F	None	O'Beirne, T.	24	M	Unknown
Anne	12	F	None	Bgt.	43	F	None
John	19	M	Unknown	Coare, P.	27	M	Unknown
Benent, P.	20	M	Unknown	My.	27	F	None
My.	24	F	None	Mich.	03	M	Child
Bgt.	18	F	None	McGrath, Bgt.	17	F	None
Thos.	02	M	Child	McGleen, W.	33	M	Unknown
McKee, W.	18	M	Unknown	Flynn, J.	28	M	Unknown
Cossan, Cath.	19	F	None	Bgt.	20	F	None
Smith, Bgt.	18	F	None	Bgt.	01	F	Child
Atkinson, Mgt.	20	F	None	McGleen, Rose	16	F	None
Coleman, Mgt.	15	F	None	Donlan, M.	19	M	Unknown
John	22	M	Unknown	Luke	18	M	Unknown
Walsh, B.	36	M	Unknown	Mgt.	17	F	None
Preston, J.	35	M	Unknown	Howe, R.	23	M	Unknown
Kenny, W.	17	M	Unknown	My.	23	F	None
Irwin, A.	25	M	Unknown	Wm.	01	M	Child
Savage, Rose	20	F	None	O'Hara, J.	24	M	Unknown
Roger	30	M	Unknown	Atkinson, J.	22	M	Unknown
Mullony, My.	30	F	None	Flynn, T.	20	M	Unknown
Cawly, M.	21	M	Unknown	Frances, Mgt.	25	F	None
Dempsey, M.	21	M	Unknown	Conlan, J.	30	M	Unknown
Pat	20	M	Unknown	Mgt.	25	F	None
Cawly, Bgt.	18	F	None	Black, J.	55	M	Unknown
Dempsey, My.	24	F	None	Jane	52	F	None
Melvin, T.	26	M	Unknown	R.	22	M	Labourer
Bgt.	26	F	None	Jane	18	F	None
Mich.	03	M	Child	Thos.	14	M	Unknown
My.	01	F	Child	Mgt.	10	F	None
Hill, C.	25	M	Unknown	Wm.	09	M	Child
Mgt.	18	F	None	Gustavus	07	M	Child
Feeney, Bgt.	24	F	None	John	20	M	Unknown
O'Hara, J.	40	M	Labourer	O'Brien, My.	20	F	None
Callen, J.	30	M	Labourer	Flynn, J.	34	M	Unknown
Gallagher, A.	35	M	Labourer	Ganty, P.	30	M	Unknown
My.	16	F	None	Fadden, J.	29	M	Unknown

Name	Age	Sex	Occupation
Emma	29	F	None
Henderson, J.	18	M	Unknown
Anna	15	F	None
Kelles, Cath.	20	F	Unknown
Smith, Sarah	14	F	Unknown

Ship: Dromahair, 25 April 1849

Name	Age	Sex	Occupation
Gilgan, Mary	45	F	Unknown
Bridget	17	F	Unknown
Matthew	14	M	Unknown
Scalley, Bernard	25	M	Unknown
O'Brien, James	40	M	Labourer
McCoy, Mary	22	F	Unknown
Sexton, Patrick	22	M	Labourer
Cathe.	17	F	Unknown
Kiolhan, Bridget	18	F	Unknown
Judge, John	30	M	Carpenter
Cathr.	30	F	Unknown
John	03	M	Child
Mary	00	F	Infant
Morain, John	30	M	Farmer
Bridget	20	F	Unknown
Mary	00	F	Infant
Waters, Mary	20	F	Unknown
Caveny, Mary	20	F	Unknown
Ellen	22	F	Unknown
Mighan, James	30	M	Farmer
McCormick, Bryan	22	M	Labourer
McCarroll, John	18	M	Labourer
Gillan, Cath.	20	F	Unknown
Eliza	17	F	Unknown
Fonley, Doley	25	M	Labourer
Campbell, Margt.	20	F	Unknown
Anne	00	F	Infant
Downes, Ellen	18	F	Unknown
Marahen, Timothy	30	M	Farmer
Mary	22	F	Unknown
Bridget	00	F	Infant
Reynolds, John	20	M	Unknown
Monahan, John	19	M	Farmer
McGowan, Thos.	40	M	Farmer
Edwd.	40	M	Farmer
Brehany, Thos.	30	M	Farmer
Bridget	30	F	Unknown
Crowin, Martin	23	M	Labourer
Grunning, George	20	M	Unknown
Conway, Mary	25	F	Unknown

Name	Age	Sex	Occupation
Judge, Edward	05	M	Child
Mehan, Darby	35	M	Labourer
Dowd, Mich.	50	M	Labourer
Anne	50	F	Unknown
Anne	23	F	Unknown
John	22	M	Labourer
Patrick	20	M	Labourer
Hugh	28	M	Labourer
Finnenn, James	26	M	Labourer
Bridget	24	F	Unknown
Anderson, Bridget	18	F	Unknown
Crown, Mary	26	F	Unknown
Anne	27	F	Unknown
Firnan, Thomas	22	M	Labourer
Mulherin, John	40	M	Farmer
Flanagan, Thomas	24	M	Farmer
Bridget	22	F	Unknown
Mary	04	F	Child
Catherine	02	F	Child
Bridget	00	F	Infant
Boland, John	20	M	Labourer
Tucker, Catherine	17	F	Unknown
Hopper, Cathe.	20	F	Unknown
Foley, Ellen	18	F	Unknown
McGarry, James	20	M	Labourer
Bridget	17	F	Unknown
McManus, James	20	M	Labourer
Fox, John	28	M	Labourer
McGuire, James	50	M	Farmer
McGuinness, John	20	M	Farmer
Sarah	16	F	Unknown
Rouse, Cath.	40	F	Unknown
Patrick	04	M	Child
McGovern, James	15	M	Labourer
Lynn, Michael	18	M	Labourer
Cullen, Lazarus	30	M	Labourer
Rorke, Patrick	30	M	Labourer
Kenny, Hugh	35	M	Upholsterer
Foy, Winifred	35	F	Unknown
Morahan, John	35	M	Labourer
Regan, Farrell	19	M	Labourer
Begly, James	63	M	Labourer
Mary	20	F	Unknown
Carthy, John	37	M	Surveyor
Mary	35	F	Unknown
John	00	M	Infant
Cooney, Ellen	20	F	Unknown
Higgins, Ann	20	F	Unknown

Name	Age	Sex	Occupation
Hughes, James	26	M	Farmer
Kelly, Charles	25	M	Labourer
Sarah	60	F	Unknown
Sarah	50	F	Unknown
Regan, Mary	08	F	Child
Dean, Bridget	20	F	Child
Melany, Hugh	35	M	Labourer
Mary	30	F	Unknown
Owen	13	M	Labourer
Hugh	08	M	Child
Healy, Marcus	21	M	Labourer
Levens, Patrick	23	M	Labourer
Bartley, Miles	40	M	Labourer
Bridget	35	F	Unknown
Patrick	09	M	Child
Michael	07	M	Child
Mary	00	F	Infant
Devany, John	23	M	Farmer
Fahy, John	28	M	Farmer
Mary	28	F	Unknown
Ann	00	F	Infant
Hunt, James	23	M	Labourer
Cathn.	21	F	Unknown
Tighe, Michael	53	M	Labourer
Cathn.	30	F	Unknown
Kelly	17	M	Unknown
John	12	M	Unknown
Winifred	13	F	Unknown
Dominick	06	M	Child
Bridget	03	F	Child
Michael	01	M	Child
(Died-At-Sea)			
McShaney, Mich.	20	M	Farmer
Conway, James	45	M	Farmer
Jane	40	F	Unknown
Patrick	22	M	Farmer
James	16	M	Labourer
Jane	15	F	Labourer
Mary	21	F	Labourer
Sarah	14	F	Unknown
John	12	M	Labourer
Cathn.	04	F	Child
Haran, Patrick	40	M	Farmer
Ann	35	F	Unknown
Patrick	12	M	Unknown
Mary	10	F	Unknown
Bridget	08	F	Child
Thomas	06	M	Child

Name	Age	Sex	Occupation
Margaret	04	F	Child
Hugh	00	M	Infant
(Died-At-Sea)			
McDonagh, Mary	30	F	Unknown
Brown, Margaret	25	F	Unknown
McYanaghan, Wm.	22	M	Merchant
Powell, Jane	36	F	Unknown
Mary	24	F	Unknown
Susan	27	F	Unknown
Julia	06	F	Child
Margt.	04	F	Child
Fanny	02	F	Child
Woodland, Isabella	22	F	Unknown
Duncan, Patrick	16	M	Farmer
Dolan, John	25	M	Farmer
Devany, Michl.	30	M	Farmer
Carroll, Jane	25	F	Farmer
Cascadden, John	20	M	Farmer
Mary-Anne	20	F	Unknown
Callaghan, Mary	20	F	Unknown
Laura	25	F	Unknown
O'Hara, John	30	M	Tailor
Dolan, Winifred	36	F	Unknown
Foley, Turner	20	M	Merchant
Kevins, Andrew	29	M	Unknown
Mooney, Patrick	35	M	Farmer

Ship: Linden, 04 May 1849

Name	Age	Sex	Occupation
Linet, Patk.	30	M	Labourer
Fury, Mary	18	F	Spinster
McDermott, Thos.	22	M	Labourer
Smyth, Mary-A	24	F	Spinster
Towly, John	25	M	Farmer
Conlan, Owen	30	M	Clerk
Michl.	18	M	Clerk
Gowan, Pat	26	M	Carter
Towly, Margt.	18	F	Spinster
Gilgin, Dennis	23	M	Labourer
McDermott, Cath.	19	F	Spinster
Ryan, Thady	24	M	Labourer
O'Connor, Mary	17	F	Spinster
Ferguson, Francis	25	M	Labourer
Murray, Winefred	18	F	Spinster
McGowan, Mary	19	F	Spinster
Gorman, Eliza	24	F	Wife
Conlan, Thos.	21	M	Clerk
O'Rorke, Patk.	22	M	Farmer

Name	Age	Sex	Occupation	Name	Age	Sex	Occupation
Misset, Robert	26	M	Labourer	Mary	33	F	Spinster
McDonnell, Anne	23	F	Spinster	Smyth, George	24	M	Farmer
Farvey, Margt.	25	F	Spinster	Rooney, Cormack	33	M	Farmer
Malone, Thos.	27	M	Clerk	Cogan, Anthony	25	M	Labourer
Flynn, Ann	17	F	Spinster	Feeney, Mary	23	F	Spinster
Smyth, Mary	28	F	Spinster	Reiley, Michl.	24	M	Labourer
McDermott, Mary	24	F	Spinster	Healey, Martin	30	M	Labourer
Malone, J.R.	02	M	Child	Durkin, Cath.	20	F	Spinster
Ellen	24	F	Matron	Margt.	00	F	Spinster
McGuire, John	29	M	Labourer	Bridget	26	F	Spinster
Margaret	26	F	Spinster	Anne	23	F	Spinster
Moore, Jas.	14	M	Farmer	Hugh	22	M	Farmer
Gerathy, Honora	24	F	Spinster	Gaffney, John	20	M	Labourer
Rooney, Luke	30	M	Labourer	McIlroy, Thos.	23	M	Labourer
Cafry, John	24	M	Labourer	Reiley, Bridget	22	F	Spinster
Doherty, Michl.	19	M	Dealer	McLaughlin, Thos.	24	M	Clerk
McCauley, Terence	25	M	Farmer	Mullarky, John	19	M	Clerk
Leonard, Dennis	26	M	Farmer	Rooney, Terence	22	M	Farmer
Connolly, John	40	M	Farmer	Mullarky, John	40	M	Doctor
Wm.	16	M	Farmer	Rooney, Mary	23	F	Spinster
McCawley, John	30	M	Farmer	Cath.	21	F	Spinster
Cath.	25	F	Matron	Laughlin, Mary	18	F	Spinster
Ann-J	00	F	Infant	Flynn, Wm.	36	M	Labourer
McBlannett, Sarah-A.	16	F	Spinster	Cath.	27	F	Spinster
Kerrigan, Owen	24	M	Farmer	Glancey, Roger	29	M	Farmer
Cath.	17	F	Wife	Flynn, Mary	22	F	Spinster
Gillaspie, Jas.	25	M	Farmer	Glancey, Ellen	24	F	Matron
Noble, Bridget	23	F	Matron	Clancy, Mary	21	F	None
Edwd.	10	M	Child	Conlan, Ann	20	F	Spinster
Mary	08	F	Child	Flynn, Cath.	00	F	Infant
Finegan, Darby	21	M	Farmer	Kelly, Michl.	25	M	Farmer
Golden, Bridget	20	F	Matron	Moran, Owen	30	M	Farmer
Mary	06	F	Child	Ellen	22	F	Farmer
Bessy	03	F	Child	Middleton, John	18	M	Unknown
Sarah	02	F	Child	Fenneran, Jas.	30	M	Farmer
Cath.	07	F	Child	Winefred (W)	28	F	Wife
Rooney, Mary	19	F	None	Jas. Clinton	25	M	Labourer
Michl.	21	M	Farmer	Farrell, John	28	M	Labourer
Peter	07	M	Child	Kerney, Andrew	27	M	Labourer
Larkin, John	20	M	Labourer	Susan	22	F	Wife
Patk.	18	M	Labourer	Patk.	24	M	Labourer
Spence, John	22	M	Labourer	McGavin, John	21	M	Labourer
Jane	20	F	Matron	O'Rourke, Terence	18	M	Labourer
Jane	00	F	Infant	Mary	20	F	Spinster
Dolan, Peter	32	M	Farmer	Ann	07	F	Child
Kilpatrick, John	24	M	Farmer	McDonough, Peter	45	M	Farmer
Fenton, Michl.	26	M	Labourer	Cath.	50	F	Matron
Burke, Cath.	24	F	Spinster	Bridget	14	F	Child

Name	Age	Sex	Occupation	Name	Age	Sex	Occupation
Cath.	07	F	Child	Clinton, Mary	25	F	Spinster
Mullany, Cath.	20	F	Spinster	McGowan, Mary	27	F	Spinster
McDonough, Bridget	41	F	Spinster	Pat	26	M	Farmer
Catton, Ann	36	F	Wife	Thornton, Thoms.	24	M	Farmer
Patk.	30	M	Farmer	Mary	23	F	Spinster
Cath.	07	F	Child	Nelly	20	F	Spinster
Kerr, Anthony	27	M	Farmer	Libby	25	F	Spinster
Cullen, Thos.	10	M	Child	Thoms.	00	M	Infant
James	07	M	Child	Sweeny, Martin	30	M	Labourer
McDonough, Mary	30	F	Matron	McHale, John	34	M	Labourer
Grady, Winefred	32	F	Spinster	Quinan, Pat	21	M	Labourer
Cosgrove, Mary	25	F	Matron	Cummings, Owen	30	M	Labourer
Mary	20	F	None	Anne	31	F	Spinster
Barth	07	M	Child	John	22	M	Labourer
Bridget	06	F	Child	Mary	24	F	Spinster
McDonough, Bridget	04	F	Spinster	Cartey, Michl.	21	M	Labourer
Mary	21	F	Spinster	Coggins, Patk.	27	M	Labourer
Kerr, Ann	30	F	Matron	Connaghton, Pat	28	M	Labourer
Ann	26	F	Matron	Connor, John	27	M	Labourer
Durken, Bridget	00	F	Infant	Biddy	00	F	Spinner
Kerr, Patrick	00	M	Infant	Charles	23	M	Labourer
Beaty, Robt.	18	M	Student	John	24	M	Labourer
Burke, John	26	M	Law Clerk	Mary	25	F	Spinster
				Pat	.07	M	Infant

Ship: Mozambique, 04 May 1849

Name	Age	Sex	Occupation	Name	Age	Sex	Occupation
				Welch, Thoms.	03	M	Child
Conway, John	20	M	Farmer	Grimes, Thoms.	31	M	Labourer
Pat	21	M	Farmer	Mary	31	F	Spinster
Cath.	19	F	Spinster	Cath.	.03	F	Infant
Barber, James	25	M	Labourer	U	.03	U	Infant
John	23	M	Labourer	Cunnane, Michl.	32	M	Labourer
Scully, Thady	24	F	Spinster	Padden, Magt.	29	F	Spinster
Anne	27	F	Spinster	Zuccan, Cath.	27	F	Spinster
Mary	.06	F	Infant	Lynch, Mary	4	F	Spinster
Regan, Thos.	25	M	Farmer	Naughton, Michl.	21	M	Labourer
Hinnigan, Marth.	24	M	Butcher	Tuffy, Dennis	24	M	Labourer
James	25	M	Farmer	Rooney, Bartley	27	M	Labourer
Michl.	21	M	Farmer	Feehly, Michl.	40	M	Labourer
Elenor	24	F	Spinster	Feckley, Elenor	41	F	Spinster
Bridgt.	30	F	Spinster	McDermot, Thaddy	28	M	Labourer
Honor	27	F	Spinster	Atkinson, Thoms.	27	M	Labourer
Owen	29	M	Farmer	Mary	24	F	Spinster
Cath.	23	F	Spinster	Robt.	28	M	Labourer
Brennan, Pat	20	M	Farmer	Cowley, Pat	.09	M	Infant
McGowan, Terence	21	M	Farmer	Bridget	25	F	Spinster
Owen	25	M	Farmer	Pat	23	M	Labourer
Ginhein, Magt.	23	F	Spinster	Carroll, Mary	25	F	Spinster
McGowan, Bartley	24	M	Farmer	Kean, Ellen	26	F	Spinster
				Fee, Jane	27	F	Spinster

Name	Age	Sex	Occupation	Name	Age	Sex	Occupation
Brown, Cath.	25	F	Spinster	Jane	18	F	Unknown
Fenarghty, Owen	24	M	Farmer	Mary	25	F	Spinster
Cath.	27	F	Spinster	Connolly, Owen	24	M	Farmer
Ellen	25	F	Spinster	Cath.	27	F	Spinster
William	10	M	Unknown	Boland, Thoms.	15	M	Unknown
Gordon, James	24	M	Farmer	Magt.	09	F	Child
May, John	31	M	Farmer	Jordan, Henry	21	M	Farmer
Grove, Thoms.	30	M	Farmer	Mitchel, Cath.	20	F	Spinster
Fanssell, Robt.	35	M	Farmer	Sheridan, Susan	24	F	Spinster
Bowels, Pat	35	M	Farmer	Wallace, Bridgt.	21	F	Spinster
Bowley, Cath.	34	F	Spinster	Camaron, Toms.	17	M	Farmer
Harrison, Rebecca	37	F	Spinster	Cath.	29	F	Spinster
James	27	M	Farmer	Flynn, Bridgt.	25	F	Spinster
Thomas	29	M	Farmer	Gollica, Patk.	24	M	Farmer
Robt.	31	M	Farmer	Patk.	43	M	Farmer
Rebecca-Jane	30	F	Spinster	Mailey, Patk.	25	M	Farmer
Foley, Bridgt.	34	F	Spinster	Boyd, James	19	M	Farmer
Smith, Winfred	25	M	Labourer	Bridgt.	19	F	Spinster
Linch, Bridgt.	27	F	Spinster	Thoms.	25	M	Labourer
Domnick	.08	M	Infant	Biddy	34	F	Spinster
Koheng, Thady	27	M	Labourer	Ann	.09	F	Infant
Kilculler, Michl.	25	M	Labourer	O'Counsell, Pat	27	M	Labourer
Cavanagh, Ann	45	F	Spinster	O'Connor, Ann	24	F	Spinster
Bridget	29	F	Spinster	Tenpany, Thoms.	29	M	Farmer
Kaheny, John	17	M	Labourer	Mary	30	F	Spinster
John	25	M	Labourer	Smith, Bernard	27	M	Farmer
Haticery, Hugh	19	M	Labourer	Hurt, William	29	M	Farmer
Kaheny, Letty	27	F	Spinster	Hart, Sally	21	F	Spinster
Gilgan, Domnick	27	M	Labourer	Margt.	15	F	Spinster
Smith, Wm.	18	M	Labourer	Rodger	19	M	Farmer
Fenarghty, Thomas	25	M	Labourer	Conners, Biddy	24	F	Wife
Cath.	24	F	Spinster	Peter	27	M	Farmer
Mary	27	F	Spinster	Hugh	29	M	Farmer
Doud, Winifred	30	F	Spinster	Cath.	23	F	Wife
Waters, Pat	31	M	Farmer	Curnan, Owen	24	M	Farmer
Mary	37	F	Spinster	Hugh	25	M	Farmer
Riely, Pat	29	M	Farmer	Mastinid, Pat	27	M	Farmer
Gillen, Mary	24	F	Spinster	Callaghan, John	29	M	Farmer
Henry, James	27	M	Farmer	Cath.	31	F	Wife
Kilcorn, Mary	19	F	Spinster	Giller, John	42	M	Farmer
Gannon, Thoms.	18	M	Farmer	Mullen, Susan	41	F	Spinster
Cath.	20	F	Spinster	Hurt, Mark	27	M	Farmer
Cath.	21	F	Spinster	Martin	49	M	Farmer
Pat	35	M	Labourer	Peary, Eliza	16	F	Unknown
Wynins, Pat	40	M	Labourer	Hinigan, John	25	M	Farmer
Margt.	41	F	Spinster	Johnston, Eliza	24	F	Spinster
Michl.	10	M	Unknown	Eliza	27	F	Wife
Coulter, William	19	M	Farmer	Gallagher, John	34	M	Farmer

Name	Age	Sex	Occupation
McDermot, Margt.	21	F	Spinster
McGowan, Margt.	23	F	Spinster
Thackerberry, Jane	18	F	Unknown
Keir, Ellen	20	F	Unknown

Ship: Mary, 07 June 1849

Name	Age	Sex	Occupation
Shaw, Wm.	22	M	Painter
O'Connor, Terence	24	M	Servant
Maquire, Pat	26	M	Labourer
Conlan, Mathew	50	M	Farmer
Catherine	52	F	Wife
Jas.	16	M	Farmer
Ward, Mary	15	F	Servant
Carley, Mary	23	F	Servant
Mortimer, Lizza	22	F	Servant
Goffeney, Jane	20	F	Servant
Toury, Pat	18	M	Labourer
Keegan, Catherine	14	F	Spinster
Atkinson, Thos.	30	M	Labourer
McGowan, Patt	23	M	Labourer
Lawrence	22	M	Labourer
Smith, Ann	21	F	Servant
Verdon, Biddy	35	F	Servant
Mulligan, Mary	35	F	Servant
M. Ann	07	F	Child
Heally, Mary	36	F	Servant
Allen, Eliza	20	F	Lady
Molloy, Pat	35	M	Farmer
Honor	20	F	Servant
Kennedy, Bridget	20	F	Spinster
Reed, Hester	18	F	Spinster
Jane	24	F	Spinster
Brady, Hugh	22	M	Clerk
Brenan, John	30	M	Labourer
Bridget	28	F	Servant
Ryan, Catherine	35	F	Servant
Bridget	27	F	Servant
McNalme, Honor	30	F	Servant
Gowman, Mary	29	F	Servant
Kearens, Bridget	25	F	Servant
Honor	19	F	Servant
Michael	18	M	Labourer
Meehan, Pat	22	M	Labourer
Frances	20	F	Servant
Jane	23	F	Servant
Keeny, Rose	28	F	Servant
Margaret	21	F	Servant

Name	Age	Sex	Occupation
McDermott, Edward	40	M	Labourer
Shannan, Jane	26	F	Servant
Scanlane, Ellen	30	F	Servant
Mulrony, Biddy	30	F	Servant
Darcy, Betty	25	F	Servant
Mary	27	F	Servant
Judge, Thos.	38	M	Labourer
Irwin, Ellen	40	F	Lady
Henry	20	M	Farmer
William	10	M	Farmer
Hannah	24	F	Lady
James	23	M	Farmer
Ann	19	F	Lady
Catherine	14	F	Lady
Judge, Michael	35	M	Labourer
Fallen, Margt.	30	F	Servant
McHugh, Neal	35	M	Servant
Carson, Jason	32	M	Servant
Catherine	28	F	Servant
Mary-Jane	07	F	Child
Carson, John	06	M	Child
Farley, John	18	M	Servant

Ship: British-Oak, 30 July 1849

Name	Age	Sex	Occupation
Fahany, Jno.	25	M	Farmer
Mary	25	F	Spinster
Killeon, Biddy	26	F	Spinster
Currad, Mary	18	F	Spinster
Fanzey, Bridget	17	F	Spinster
Tanzy, Mary	14	F	Spinster
Boyle, Susan	16	F	Spinster
Mullen, Mich.	35	M	Farmer
Bridget	28	F	Labourer
Jas.	06	M	Child
Regan, Jas.	30	M	Labourer
Ann	28	F	Spinster
Catherine	08	F	Child
Armstrong, Margt.	25	F	Spinster
Isabella	18	F	Spinster
McIntyre, Mary	17	F	Spinster
Ward, Barry	20	M	Labourer
Foley, Michl.	20	M	Labourer
Heally, Ellen	23	F	Spinster
Fee, Jane	30	F	Spinster
Shendan, Marg.	27	F	Spinster
Monaghan, Henry	28	M	Labourer
Wm.	30	M	Labourer

Name	Age	Sex	Occupation	Name	Age	Sex	Occupation
Burke, Nancy	19	F	Spinster	Burns, Richard	41	M	Farmer
Keary, Wm.	34	M	Tailor	Gibbon, Mary	22	F	Spinster
Mary-Ann	23	F	Wife	Kaveny, Dominick	34	M	Saddler
Gelman, Bessy	25	F	Spinster	Margt.	28	F	Wife
Binan, Mary	30	F	Spinster	McDonogh, Sarah	24	F	Spinster
Doherty, Pat	41	M	Labourer	McDermott, Mary	37	F	Spinster
Ann	35	F	Labourer	Lofters, Martin	41	M	Labourer
Milmore, Mary	29	F	Spinster	Cogan, Pat	28	M	Farmer
McCormack, Jas.	30	M	Labourer	Gillen, Margt.	39	F	Spinster
Foley, Thomas	21	M	Farmer	Feeny, Margt.	21	F	Spinster
Mary	60	F	Wife	Reed, Maria	30	F	Spinster
McGowan, Pat	21	M	Labourer	McCarthy, Catherine	30	F	Spinster
Bridget	31	F	Wife	Omelia, Rebecca	29	F	Spinster
Oates, Catherine	41	F	Spinster	Gorman, Sally	30	F	Spinster
Finan, Bridget	35	F	Spinster	Scott, Ann	20	F	Spinster
Kearens, Dominick	18	M	Labourer	Greaham, Ellen	25	F	Spinster
Harrison, Mich.	19	M	Unknown				
Brady, Henry	20	M	Labourer	*Ship: Linden,* 25 August 1849			
Flanagan, Edward	31	M	Labourer				
Ormsley, Mary-A.	37	F	Spinster	McGowan, Jean	19	F	Spinster
Hunt, Ann	44	F	Spinster	Ruane, Ann	24	F	Spinster
Patt	20	M	Unknown	McMord, Pat	18	M	Labourer
Ellen	17	F	Unknown	John	.02	M	Infant
Jas.	08	M	Child	Mary	22	F	Spinster
Mary	06	F	Child	Brenan, Mary	20	F	Spinster
Jno.	04	M	Child	Breheny, Mary	19	F	Spinster
McCann, Ann	23	F	Spinster	Hoy, Catheren	22	F	Spinster
Dolan, Pat	27	M	Butler	Boid, Rose-A	19	F	Spinster
Gorman, Pat	34	M	Labourer	Catherine	12	F	Spinster
Byrnes, Ellen-A.	29	F	Spinster	Oats, Pat	40	M	Labourer
Clifford, Bailard	30	M	Unknown	Walsh, Antony	40	M	Labourer
Corner, Roger	41	M	Labourer	Deram, Richard	50	M	Shopkeeper
McDongal, Pat	34	M	Labourer	McMord, Barney	25	M	Labourer
Smith, Wm.	27	M	Labourer	Mary	21	F	Spinster
Toffee, Catherine	34	F	Spinster	Palmor, Bridget	16	F	Spinster
Kelly, Jane	21	F	Spinster	Mary	18	F	Unknown
Rawlet, Pegg.	37	F	Spinster	Banks, John	25	M	Labourer
Fleming, Pat	42	M	Labourer	Gallagher, Catherine	20	F	Spinster
Connor, Jas.	21	M	Labourer	Black, James	25	M	Labourer
O'Connor, Ann	30	F	Spinster	Ellsa	23	F	Matron
Cunningham, Michl.	28	M	Labourer	Daniel	05	M	Child
Kilcullen, Rich.	26	M	Labourer	Mary L.	02	F	Child
Fee, Wm.	31	M	Labourer	William L.	.11	M	Infant
Kerr, Patt	40	M	Carpenter	Hanna	.01	F	Infant
Ann-Jane	37	F	Spinster	Barret, Mary	30	F	Matron
Hannah	16	F	Unknown	Honor	50	F	Matron
Killgallen, Ellen	24	F	Spinster	Bridget	03	F	Child
Lofters, Wm.	37	M	Unknown	Heggins, Bess	18	F	Spinster

Name	Age	Sex	Occupation	Name	Age	Sex	Occupation
Gahagan, Charles	14	M	Labourer	Healy, Mary	19	F	Spinster
Connel, Pat	05	M	Child	Flyn, Ann	06	F	Child
Michael	04	M	Child	O'Hara, Bridget	24	F	Spinster
Henry	.11	M	Infant	Elenor	16	F	Spinster
Devit, Pat	20	M	Labourer	Gilmartin, Daniel	56	M	Farmer
Margret	15	F	Spinster	Mary	21	F	Spinster
Sweeny, Bernard	18	M	Labourer	Bridget	19	F	Spinster
Heneghan, Michael	18	M	Labourer	Ann	13	F	None
McCerrick, Bridget	18	F	Spinster	Bradly, Mary	20	F	Spinster
Rilley, Jean	16	F	Spinster	Synn, Pat	29	M	Smith
Jean	19	F	Spinster	Mary (W)	29	F	None
Charles	24	M	Hatter	Winifred (D)	06	F	Child
Cryster, Margret	19	F	Spinster	Michael (S)	03	M	Child
Burne, Pat	17	M	Labourer	Bridget (D)	00	F	Unknown
Burk, Pat	55	M	Shopkeeper	Callaghan, Ann	15	F	Spinster
Mary-A.	54	F	Wife	Burk, Richard	37	M	Mason
Barret, Frances	20	M	Labourer	Bridget	22	F	Wife
Mary	14	F	Spinster	Margaret	.11	F	Infant
Langan, Michael	17	M	Labourer	Flyn, Pat	24	M	Clerk
Anderson, Bess	17	F	Spinster	McEntire, Owen	40	M	Labourer
Stephen	15	M	Labourer	Black, Thos.	24	M	Labourer
Dixon, Bridget	41	F	Matron	McGowan, Bridget	21	F	Spinster
Jas.	11	M	Unknown	Cavand, Honor	28	F	Spinster
Mary	09	F	Child	Cosgrove, Sarah	23	F	Spinster
Pat	07	M	Child	Belgy, Mary	02	F	Infant
Catherine	02	F	Child	Reed, George	19	M	Labourer
Thos.	01	M	Child	McGuire, Ann	25	F	Spinster
Gorman, Richard	16	M	Labourer	Thos.	21	M	Labourer
Connelly, Jean	13	F	Spinster	Pat	19	M	Labourer
Higgins, Ann	10	F	Spinster	Jas.	17	M	Labourer
Keaveny, Thos.	18	M	Labourer	Slevin, Mary	20	F	Spinster
Falk, Thos.	28	M	Shoemaker	Hughes, Mary	22	F	Spinster
O'Brian, John	20	M	Labourer	Pat	20	M	Unknown
Higgins, Michael	24	M	Labourer	Conlan, Ann	20	F	Spinster
McGuire, Hugh	25	M	Shopkeeper	Honor	22	F	Spinster
Catherine	25	F	Wife	Palmor, Margret	23	F	Spinster
Honor (D)	10	F	None	Black, Sarah	26	F	Spinster
Pat (S)	08	M	Child	Catherine (D)	10	F	None
Charles (S)	02	M	Child	Conlan, Frances	02	F	Child
Charles	22	M	Labourer	McLoughlin, Thos.	40	M	Labourer
Dinison, Barthly	30	M	Labourer	Gillon, Catherine	18	F	Spinster
Margaret	25	F	Matron	Connor, Bridget	12	F	Spinster
Ann (D)	03	F	Child	Ryan, Bridget	22	F	Spinster
Crean, Mary	40	F	Matron	Begling, Arthur	40	M	Labourer
Timlin, Charlet	20	F	Spinster	Feeny, Margaret	20	F	Spinster
Sayny, Celia	20	F	Spinster	Brown, Thomas	40	M	Labourer
Esibela	22	F	Spinster	Smith, Martin	22	M	Labourer
Evans, Maria	19	F	Spinster	Catherine	60	F	Matron

Name	Age	Sex	Occupation
Honor	20	F	Spinster
Grimes, Ann	20	F	Spinster
Henry, Andrew	33	M	Farmer
Carr, Robert	33	M	Carpenter
Irwin, Mary	23	F	Spinster
Dixon, Daniel	18	M	Labourer
Hunt, Winifred	50	F	Matron
Winifred (D)	12	F	None
Carmick, Edward	48	M	Unknown
Eleanor	40	F	Unknown
Bridget	08	F	Child
Mary A.	06	F	Child
Patk.	05	M	Child
John	.10	M	Infant
Edmond	.10	M	Infant
McLoughlin, Pat	19	M	Unknown
Maria	20	F	Unknown
Cormick, Mary	17	F	Unknown
Phibbs, Thos.	67	M	Unknown
Gahagan, Letty	30	F	Matron

Ship: Dromahair, 03 October 1849

Name	Age	Sex	Occupation
Beglane, Ann	22	F	Spinster
Drew, Jno.	50	M	Farmer
Ellen	30	F	Matron
McDermott, Bridget	18	F	Spinster
Jane	14	F	Spinster
Hargadon, Pat	22	M	Farmer
Haaly, Jno.	14	M	None
Thomas	50	M	Farmer
Quin, Bridget	16	F	Spinster
Down, Jas.	21	M	Spinner
O'Brien, Terence	21	M	Farmer
Cain, Margaret	19	F	Spinster
Quin, Margaret	16	F	Spinster
Ennig, Thomas	30	M	Farmer
Bessy	25	F	Wife
Downers, Margaret	30	F	Spinster
Walker, Mary	20	F	Spinster
Hart, Henry	22	M	Farmer
Stewart, Bridget	40	F	Matron
Shaw, Jas.	19	M	Servant
Killgallen, Mary	20	F	Spinster
Mahon, Bridget	13	F	Spinster
McMurray, Maria	18	F	Spinster
Feeney, Maria	08	F	Child
Jas.	06	M	Child

Name	Age	Sex	Occupation
McDonough, Jane	18	F	Spinster
Smith, Eliza	19	F	Spinster
Budery, Jno.	30	M	Farmer
McLoughlin, Catherine	18	F	Spinster
Budery, Ann	28	F	Wife
Jno.	00	M	Infant
Dolany, Mich.	18	M	Spinner
Catherine	16	F	Spinster
Hyland, Jane	18	F	Spinster
Flanagan, Ellen	25	F	Spinster
Laurean, Ellen	17	F	Spinster
Jenks, Jno.	09	M	Child
Rogers, Ellen	10	F	Unknown
Casey, Catherine	14	F	Spinster
Henry, Pat	35	M	Farmer
Mary	24	F	Spinster
Kilcullen, Mack	20	M	Farmer
Neary, Peter	16	M	Farmer
Early, Mary	17	F	Spinster
Jane	19	F	Spinster
Beglane, James	60	M	Farmer
Mary	26	F	Spinster
Laung, Mary	45	F	Matron
Trumble, Thomas	21	M	Yeoman
Sharkey, Jno.	21	M	Farmer
Walls, Jno.	18	M	Farmer
Galeck, Andrew	33	M	Farmer
Mary	25	F	Spinster
Mary	05	F	Child
William	.04	M	Infant
McDonough, U.	39	M	Farmer
Jno.	50	M	Farmer
Morgan	17	M	Farmer
Corcoran, M.	21	M	Farmer
Coyne, Jno.	26	M	Farmer
Curren, Bess	13	F	Unknown
Jno.	05	M	Child
Clark, Ann	19	F	Spinster
Winfred	21	F	Spinster
Cavanaugh, Thomas	15	M	Farmer
Tunney, Mary	08	F	Child
Dowans, Mary	18	F	Spinster
Sheridan, Ellen	19	F	Spinster
Burnett, Mary	18	F	Spinster
Reddican, Jno.	22	M	Labourer
Watson, William	14	M	Farmer
Gibbny, Jane	26	F	Spinster
Burk, Bridget	36	F	Matron

Name	Age	Sex	Occupation	Name	Age	Sex	Occupation
Jno.30		M	Yeoman	Doherty, Jane	20	F	Matron
Mary	17	F	Spinster	Eliza	00	F	Infant
Bessy	09	F	Child	Maguire, Matty	30	F	Matron
Mary	05	F	Child	Thomas	10	M	None
Nolan, Jno.	23	M	Farmer	Michael	08	M	Child
Phillips, Biddy	22	F	Spinster	Terence	04	M	Child
Carroll, Ann	19	F	Spinster	Garven, Pat	24	M	Farmer
Gallagher, Pat	24	M	Farmer	Cullen, Bridget	24	F	Spinster
Ann	20	F	Wife	Hope, Jno.	32	M	Farmer
Mary	20	F	Spinster	Middleton, Mary	40	F	Matron
Honora	20	F	Spinster	Jane	20	F	Spinster
Cawley, Mary	18	F	Spinster	Thomas	21	M	Farmer
Wiliam	20	M	Farmer	Clancey, Mary	19	F	Spinster
Catherine	16	F	Spinster	Biddy	17	F	Spinster
Taaffe, Alley	30	F	Matron	McGuire, Frank	21	M	Farmer
Jane	25	F	Spinster	Clenton, Honora	10	F	None
Neary, James	30	M	Unknown	Bernard	08	M	Child
Muchnug, Charlotte	50	F	Matron	Traverse, Catherine	20	F	Spinster
Charlotte	18	F	Spinster	Fahany, Catherine	19	F	Spinster
Gaddes, Ann	20	F	Spinster	Carr, Thomas	22	M	Farmer
Sweetmary, Mary	22	F	Spinster	Keegan, Catherine	20	F	Spinster
Burnett, Jane	18	F	Spinster	Conroy, Bridget	14	F	Spinster
Thehary, Ellen	18	F	Spinster	Peggy	10	F	Spinster
Mary	14	F	Spinster	Barney, Elizabeth	21	F	Spinster
Tunney, Catherine	12	F	Unknown	Walsh, Henry	09	M	Child
Goverany, Francis	36	M	Farmer	Smith, William	19	M	Labourer
Honora	32	F	Matron	Mehan, Peter	28	M	Labourer
Ann	17	F	Unknown	Foy, Winey	19	F	Spinster
Thomas	14	M	Unknown	Clanrey, Margaret	18	F	Spinster
McGee, Winfred	11	F	Unknown	Walter	12	M	Labourer
Hanney, Jno.	22	M	Farmer	Krolahin, Jas.	24	M	Block
Delishany, James	30	M	Shopkeeper				Maker
Healy, Ellen	30	F	Spinster	Gelhooly, Rose	23	F	Wife
Curran, Ann	10	F	Unknown	(Died-At-Sea)			
McKiny, Isaac	23	M	Unknown	Flyn, Catherine	.10	F	Infant
Johnston, William	18	M	Unknown	O'Connor, Dormas	22	F	Spinster
Parks, Thomas	23	M	Unknown	Mildorn, Margaret	19	F	Spinster
Gibbny, Louisa	43	F	Unknown	William	29	M	Mason
Michl.	17	M	Unknown	Krolahan, Maria	30	F	Matron
Jas.	13	M	Unknown	Jno.	10	M	None
Benjamin	11	M	Unknown	O'Hara, Mary	19	F	Spinster
				Campbell, James	30	M	Farmer

Ship: Sarah-Maria, 19 October 1849

Name	Age	Sex	Occupation	Name	Age	Sex	Occupation
				Flynn, James	20	M	Farmer
				Vernon, William	17	M	None
Gordon, Mary	30	F	Spinster	Callan, Henry	19	M	Labourer
Regan, Honora	19	F	Spinster	McNulty, Michael	70	M	Labourer
Gilhooley, Catherine	18	F	Spinster	Sweeney, Catherine	18	F	Spinster
Burnett, Jane	20	F	Spinster	Mary	17	F	Spinster

Name	Age	Sex	Occupation
Krolahan, Mary	28	F	Matron
Jane	00	F	Infant
Margaret	07	F	Child
Mary	05	F	Child
Fieny, Bridget	19	F	Spinster
Catherine	17	F	Spinster
Gilgan, Ann	19	F	Spinster
Hart, Michael	31	M	Farmer
Mehan, William	40	M	Farmer
Rorke, Beezy	20	F	Spinster
McNorra, Pat	21	M	Farmer
McGreeny, Jno.	20	M	Farmer
Margaret	19	F	Wife
Rooney, Thomas	38	M	Farmer
Jane	36	F	Wife
Joseph	.09	M	Infant
Catherine	05	F	Child
Simon	40	M	None
Reed, Jane	19	F	Wife
Thomas	10	M	None
Robt.	45	M	None
Joseph	28	M	None
Sarah	29	F	Wife
Cullen, Anthony	20	M	Farmer
James	19	M	Farmer
Carey, Charlotte	18	F	Spinster
Jane	19	F	Spinster
Cosgrove, Ann	17	F	Spinster

Ship: London, 22 April 1850

Name	Age	Sex	Occupation
Mitchel, Patrick	22	M	Farmer
Edward	20	M	Farmer
Armstrong, George	18	M	Farmer
Mary	12	F	Unknown
Bridget	09	F	Child
Cooney, Michael	26	M	Farmer
Feeney, Rose	20	F	Spinster
Kerns, Mary	18	F	Spinster
Hanghan, Bridget	22	F	Spinster
Kienan, Michael	30	M	Farmer
Meehan, Patrick	23	M	Servant
Clarke, Bridget	20	F	Servant
Fenarty, William	20	M	Labourer
Dunn, Mary	23	F	Spinster
Kelly, Mary	20	F	Servant
Cafferty, Michael	22	M	Farmer
Libby	50	F	Matron

Name	Age	Sex	Occupation
Mary	20	F	Spinster
Catherine	18	F	Spinster
Patrick	12	M	Unknown
Ferrins, James	30	M	Servant
Margaret	29	F	Matron
George	.01	M	Infant
Walker, Bridget	20	F	Matron
John	22	M	Teacher
George	.01	M	Infant
Fennigan, Jane	20	F	Spinster
McMorrow, Michael	30	M	Farmer
Meehan, Mary	20	F	Spinster
McHugh, Bridget	20	F	Spinster
Armstrong, Thomas	32	M	Labourer
Scanlan, John	35	M	Labourer
Laney, George	20	M	Servant
Downie, Jane	21	F	Matron
Kelly, Jane	24	F	Spinster
Smyth, Bernard	24	M	Farmer
Connelly, John	32	M	Labourer
Kilcullen, Thomas	25	M	Farmer
Mary	23	F	Matron
Gilgan, Hugh	20	M	Labourer
Burns, Martin	25	M	Farmer
Teirnan, Michael	24	M	Farmer
McGuire, Michael	36	M	Farmer
Parks, John	40	M	Farmer
McGowan, John	33	M	Farmer
Thomas	20	M	Farmer
Mearn, Patrick	25	M	Farmer
Teirnan, John	20	M	Farmer
Brennan, Catherine	20	F	Spinster
Doherty, Peter	18	M	Labourer
Downie, Francis	25	M	Farmer
Keeney, Francis	35	M	Farmer
Burns, Michael	25	M	Farmer
Keeney, William	14	M	Farmer
Connor, Eliza	16	F	Spinster
Hannan, Michael	22	M	Labourer
Mullany, Denis	24	M	Labourer
Kilcanley, Thomas	24	M	Labourer
Farny, Mary	35	F	Matron
John	13	M	Unknown
Conboy, Mary	20	F	Spinster
Power, Joseph	20	M	Shoemaker
Haddock, Jane	17	F	Spinster
Robert	14	M	Unknown
Murray, Cormac	40	M	Farmer

Name	Age	Sex	Occupation	Name	Age	Sex	Occupation
Mary	30	F	Matron	Stewart, George	17	M	Labourer
Mary	17	F	Spinster	Neilly, Ellen	20	F	Spinster
Finn, Anne	30	F	Matron	Harrison, Thomas	20	M	Labourer
Jane	13	F	Unknown	Loughlin, James	30	M	Labourer
White, Denis	20	M	Labourer	Golden, Honora	36	F	Matron
Devitt, Henry	19	M	Labourer	Mary	28	F	Matron
Gorman, James	30	M	Labourer	Catherine	08	F	Child
Flynne, John	19	M	Labourer	Patrick	06	M	Child
Healy, Thomas	18	M	Labourer	Owen	04	M	Child
Mary	17	F	Spinster	Cuman, Margaret	20	F	Spinster
McGown, Libby	20	F	Spinster	Kerranne, Thomas	34	M	Labourer
Hannon, Patrick	48	M	Farmer	Redhain, Thomas	18	M	Labourer
Scanlon, John	45	M	Farmer	Kilcullen, Bridget	30	F	Spinster
Gray, Bridget	22	F	Spinster	Roonane, Bridget	25	F	Matron
McSharry, Thomas	18	M	Labourer	Winifred	.01	F	Infant
Mary	16	F	Spinster	Meehan, Bridget	30	F	Matron
Margaret	13	F	Unknown	Patk.	05	M	Child
James	09	M	Child	Cogan, Jane	20	F	Unknown
Bridget	07	F	Child	McCauley, Anne	24	F	Unknown
Cooney, Michael	26	M	Labourer	Murn, Patrick	28	M	Unknown
Cooney, Patrick	19	M	Labourer	Brennan, Patrick	22	M	Unknown
Fowley, Michael	30	M	Labourer	James	20	M	Unknown
Mary	23	F	Matron	Wilson, James	18	M	Unknown
Scanlon, Bartley	34	M	Labourer	Kirkpatrick, John	00	M	Captain
Mary	32	F	Matron	Gillan, John	00	M	First Mate
Martin	.01	M	Infant	McGanran, Thomas	00	M	Second Mate
Johnston, Mary	33	F	Spinster	Barry, Andrew	00	M	Unknown
Coggins, John	18	M	Labourer	Hart, Bernard	00	M	Unknown
Patrick	02	M	Child	Gaten, Henry	00	M	Unknown
Mary	04	F	Child	Ward, Richard	00	M	Ck-Stwd
Gilgan, Terence	21	M	Labourer	Kirkpatrick, James	00	M	Unknown
Gray, Mary	20	F	Spinster	Davis, William	00	M	Unknown
Langan, Michael	30	M	Labourer	Gillan, Michael	00	M	Unknown
Mary	28	F	Matron	Fetherston, Barthlome	00	M	Apprentice
Scahill, Thomas	33	M	Labourer	Kenny, Patrick	00	M	Apprentice
Mary	30	F	Matron				
Ann	09	F	Child	*Ship: Dromahair*, 26 April 1850			
Sarah	06	F	Child				
Margaret	03	F	Child	Sheeran, Thomas	36	M	Labourer
Ellen	.01	F	Infant	Rorke, Hugh	19	M	Unknown
Caulfield, Martin	28	M	Labourer	Brennan, B.	23	M	Unknown
Eliza	26	F	Matron	Mary	19	F	Unknown
Martin	01	M	Child	Wynne, Ann	20	F	Unknown
Collery, Patrick	34	M	Labourer	Carvey, Jno.	26	M	Unknown
Collery, Edward	28	M	Labourer	Hugh	30	M	Unknown
Collery, John	19	M	Labourer	Jane	27	F	Unknown
Anne	18	F	Spinster	Margt.	24	F	Unknown
Collery, Jane	11	F	Spinster	McGowan, Ann	30	F	Unknown

Name	Age	Sex	Occupation	Name	Age	Sex	Occupation
Pat	35	M	Unknown	Carty, James	20	M	Unknown
Bessy	08	F	Child	Nicelson, Pat	20	M	Unknown
Maria	06	F	Child	O'Boyle, Bridget	25	F	Unknown
Kivehan, Pat	16	M	Unknown	Cassady, Jno.	40	M	Unknown
Healy, Owen	40	M	Unknown	Gibbin, Jno.	20	M	Unknown
Biddy	30	F	Unknown	Conlain, Pat	26	M	Unknown
Thomas	01	M	Child	Catharine	21	F	Unknown
Hargadon, Ann	20	F	Unknown	Rorke, Ann	16	F	Unknown
Deville, James	22	M	Unknown	Mitchell, Jno.	20	M	Unknown
Curnan, Winifred	17	F	Unknown	Biddy	18	F	Unknown
Michl.	15	M	Unknown	Jas.	03	M	Child
Kellelea, Bryan	23	M	Unknown	Morrison, Jas.	17	M	Unknown
Gaffany, Owen	38	M	Unknown	Cullen, Margt.	16	F	Unknown
Mary	28	F	Unknown	Conilan, Jon	21	M	Unknown
Ann	05	F	Child	Bridget	26	F	Unknown
Catherine	03	F	Child	Ann	14	F	Unknown
Mary	00	F	Infant	Mulligan, Winifred	18	F	Unknown
McLoughlin, Jno.	26	M	Unknown	Lavan, Bridget	15	F	Unknown
Jno.	06	M	Child	O'Hara, Ellen	22	F	Unknown
Catherine	03	F	Child	Murphy, Ellen	20	F	Unknown
McNiff, Hugh	20	M	Unknown	McLoughlin, Mary	19	F	Unknown
McLoughlin, Barbara	50	F	Unknown	Morrison, Richard	27	M	Unknown
James	16	M	Unknown	Mary-Ann	22	F	Unknown
Catherine	18	F	Unknown	Mary-Ann	00	F	Infant
McSereman, Bryant	25	M	Unknown	McCormack, Mary	18	F	Unknown
Alice	24	F	Unknown	Mullany, Mary	08	F	Child
McDermott, Kurney	40	U	Unknown	Lynch, Jane	20	F	Unknown
White, Jno.	22	M	Unknown	Simon, Mary	17	F	Unknown
McDermott, Thomas	24	M	Unknown	Gilhaly, Mary	22	F	Unknown
Carney, Honor	25	F	Unknown	McCaffrey, Peter	24	M	Unknown
Monaghan, Pat	30	M	Unknown	Catherine	16	F	Labourer
Gilmartin, Thomas	17	M	Unknown	McPartlane, Michl.	25	M	Unknown
Hinnegan, C.	30	U	Unknown	Ann	22	F	Unknown
Mullany, C.	30	U	Unknown	McCahal, Fanel	30	U	Unknown
Bridget	25	F	Labourer	Early, Catherine	24	F	Unknown
Mary	01	F	Child	Gilran, Michael	30	M	Unknown
Kelly, Pat	20	M	Unknown	Ann	27	F	Unknown
Welsh, Thomas	23	M	Unknown	Gallagher, James	28	M	Unknown
Hamilton, James	24	M	Unknown	Margt.	23	F	Unknown
May, Susan	18	F	Unknown	Pat	00	M	Infant
Nelson, Mary	20	F	Unknown	McNiff, Pat	26	M	Unknown
Burns, Catherine	28	F	Unknown	Kinny	24	U	Unknown
Devaney, Pat	20	M	Unknown	Catherine	00	F	Infant
O'Connor, Jno.	21	M	Unknown	Mac, Margaret	20	F	Unknown
Kilfeather, Mary	20	F	Unknown	Cunnisky, Jno.	28	M	Unknown
McHugh, Michl.	20	M	Unknown	Gilgan, Ann	24	F	Unknown
Coghlin, Catherine	25	F	Unknown	Ellen	20	F	Unknown
McGlin, Mary	23	F	Unknown	Kelly, Eleanor	18	F	Unknown

Name	Age	Sex	Occupation	Name	Age	Sex	Occupation
Eliza	00	F	Infant	Catherine	40	F	Unknown
Black, Thomas	22	M	Unknown	Thomas	16	M	Unknown
Farry, Jas.	60	M	Unknown	Jno.	14	M	Unknown
Bridget	49	F	Unknown	Mary	06	F	Child
Michl.	18	M	Unknown	Convey, Ellen	20	F	Unknown
McGowan, Pat	20	M	Unknown	Davey, Jno.	28	M	Unknown
Glove, Catherine	30	F	Unknown	Winefred	24	F	Unknown
Ford, Jno.	25	M	Unknown	McMorrow, Owen	20	M	Unknown
Scanlon, Andrew	26	M	Unknown	Ann	12	F	Unknown
Scanlon, Betty	24	F	Unknown	Bridget	14	F	Unknown
McPadden, Michl.	20	M	Unknown	Mullowney, Ann	20	F	Unknown
Kilroy, Bryan	32	M	Unknown	Campbell, Robt.	25	M	Unknown
McAvey, Jno.	24	M	Unknown	O'Brien, Denis	28	M	Unknown
Nangle, Jno.	40	M	Unknown	Kenigan, Pat	20	M	Unknown
Battle, Thomas	23	M	Unknown	McGown, Mary	25	F	Unknown
Gellan, Pat	18	M	Unknown	Nancy	25	F	Unknown
Ganley, Peter	17	M	Unknown	Elliot, Catherine	35	F	Unknown
Nangle, Ellen	20	F	Unknown	Alexander	16	M	Unknown
Rooney, Kenny	20	M	Unknown	Thomas	12	M	Unknown
Hart, Cicely	20	F	Unknown	McCalment, Thomas	25	M	Unknown
Tuney, Kinney	15	M	Unknown	White, Mary	20	F	Unknown
McPartlane, Bridget	17	F	Unknown	Callagher, Owen	26	M	Unknown
Ellen	15	F	Unknown	Dempsey, Peter	25	M	Unknown
McGowan, Michl.	20	M	Unknown	Jordan, Mary	22	F	Unknown
Peter	18	M	Unknown	Kelly, Bridget	20	F	Unknown
Chas.	18	M	Unknown	McGowan, Ann	17	F	Unknown
Keighron, Jno.	21	M	Labourer	Denis	13	M	Unknown
McGarry, Mary	20	F	Unknown	Alice	11	F	Unknown
McDermott, Bridget	50	F	Unknown	O'Connor, Margt.	30	F	Unknown
Buchard, Jno.	45	M	Unknown	McGarry, Margt.	27	F	Unknown
Ann	44	F	Unknown	Hirtle, Francis	18	M	Unknown
Eliza-Jane	14	F	Unknown	Gainn, William	23	M	Unknown
Rebecca	10	F	Unknown	Kilcullen, Geo.	21	M	Unknown
McCann, Thomas	21	M	Unknown	Ann	21	F	Unknown
McDermott, Bridget	14	F	Unknown	Honora	00	F	Infant
Clark, Mary	35	F	Unknown	Kelly, Michl.	30	M	Unknown
Burns, Pat	16	M	Unknown	Davey, Michl.	30	M	Unknown
McLoughlin, Mary	60	F	Unknown	Murphy, Thomas	14	M	Unknown
Harn, Mary	20	F	Unknown	Ellis, Thomas	23	M	Unknown
McLoughlin, Ann	20	F	Unknown	Bridget	21	F	Unknown
Mullany, Jno.	00	M	Infant	Catherine	26	F	Unknown
Henry, Thomas F.	14	M	Unknown	Middleton, John	21	M	Unknown
Pyne, William	15	M	Unknown	Longhead, Jane	20	F	Unknown
Grady, Jno.	23	M	Unknown	McLoughlin, Owen	30	M	Labourer
				Hartt, Martin	40	M	Unknown
				Catherine	40	F	Unknown
				Bessie	18	F	Unknown
McHugh, Jas.	50	M	Labourer	Gorman, Sarah	18	F	Unknown

Ship: Industry, 30 April 1850

Name	Age	Sex	Occupation	Name	Age	Sex	Occupation
Lackan, Hugh	30	M	Unknown	Donoher, Catherine	21	F	Unknown
McCeever, Pat	30	M	Unknown	Gwil, Jno.	22	M	Unknown
Hannah	28	F	Unknown	Cullen, Thomas	25	M	Unknown
Mulhouse, Ann	27	F	Unknown	Mick	23	M	Unknown
Grumes, Judy	24	F	Unknown	Fry, Margt.	17	F	Unknown
McNully, Bridget	18	F	Unknown	Feman, Jno.	30	M	Unknown
Bourke, Mathew	25	M	Unknown	Brien, Mary	23	F	Unknown
Maria	08	F	Child	Downs, Edward	20	M	Unknown
Donohy, Owen	52	M	Unknown	Nutty, Hugh	20	M	Unknown
Edward	20	M	Unknown	Mary	22	F	Unknown
O'Donnell, Roger	24	M	Unknown	Graham, Francis	38	M	Unknown
Daly, Pat	20	M	Unknown	Ganahan, Bridget	30	F	Unknown
Mulvaney, Mary	30	F	Unknown	Giblin, Henry	24	M	Unknown
Bridget	13	F	Unknown	Gillispie, Pat	21	M	Unknown
Patrick	10	M	Unknown	Hannigan, Pat	25	M	Unknown
Burns, Bridget	28	F	Unknown	Mulloy, Bridget	20	F	Unknown
Hart, Michl.	25	M	Unknown	McKane, Bessy	25	F	Unknown
McAnew, Bridget	20	F	Unknown	Brennan, Mary	02	F	Child
Kuane, Honora	30	F	Unknown	Roche, Thomas	28	M	Unknown
Catherine	23	F	Unknown	Hannow, Mary	20	F	Unknown
Mary	20	F	Unknown	Daly, Bridget	16	F	Unknown
Patrick	00	M	Infant	Darcy, Thady	20	M	Unknown
Savalle, Margt.	22	F	Unknown	Malcom, Martin	24	M	Unknown
Connelly, Alice	25	F	Unknown	Mary	23	F	Unknown
Cowley, William	50	M	Unknown	Cowley, Michael	24	M	Unknown
Bridget	40	F	Unknown	Walton, Thomas	20	M	Unknown
William	20	M	Unknown	Ann	16	F	Unknown
Margaret	16	F	Unknown	Jane	15	F	Unknown
Mary	14	F	Unknown	Lundy, Daniel	25	M	Unknown
Hart, Pat	20	M	Unknown	Doherty, Barbara	40	F	Unknown
Catherine	13	F	Unknown	Sarah	18	F	Unknown
Cavanagh, Chas.	30	M	Unknown	Moffitt, Sarah	18	F	Unknown
Ann	24	F	Unknown	Bartlett, Set-M	24	M	Unknown
Michl.	35	M	Unknown	Miller, Sarah	30	F	Unknown
Michl.	24	M	Unknown	Geo.	03	M	Child
Jordan, Mary	20	F	Unknown	McHugh, Bridget	30	F	Unknown
Kelly, Pat	25	M	Unknown				
Peter	28	M	Unknown				
Longhead, Ellen	21	F	Labourer				
Brennan, Bridget	19	F	Labourer				
McGown, Michl.	25	M	Labourer				
Quinn, Margt.	40	F	Unknown				
Michl.	12	M	Unknown				
Healy, Jno.	25	M	Unknown				
Honora	25	F	Unknown				
Ann	00	F	Infant				
Connell, Mary	30	F	Unknown				
Pat	10	M	Unknown				

Bibliography

ARCHIVAL SOURCES

Dublin Diocesan Archives (DDA)   *Ireland*
Murray Papers (calendared in *Archivium Hibernicum*, vol. XL, 1985)

National Archives, Dublin
Relief Commission Papers (RLFC)
RLFC 2/Z 1218, 1220, 1808, 2208, 2776, 3098, 3910, 5748, 13210, 13466, 14282,
14304, 14316, 14344, 14450, 14920, 15250, 15348, 15500, 15796, 16024, 16036,
16462, 16838, 16886, 17842.
RLFC 3/1/ 101, 112, 393, 404, 484, 489, 494, 537, 627, 724, 863, 924, 942, 974, 1181,
1190, 1616, 2057, 2467, 2510, 2678, 2870, 2916, 2989, 3088, 3169, 3181, 3225, 3271,
3288, 3436, 3437, 3464, 3525, 3527, 3585, 3586, 3602, 3634, 3666, 3727, 3747, 3929,
4061, 4132, 4143, 4162, 4165, 4212, 4223, 4306, 4319, 4329, 4387, 4396, 4398, 4407,
4432, 4484, 4520, 4549, 4667, 4677, 4707, 4737, 4751, 4831, 4890, 4910, 4922, 4929,
4940, 4982, 5080, 5084, 5091, 5163, 5184, 5195, 5203, 5228, 5272, 5273, 5277, 5389,
5396, 5412, 5428, 5434, 5426, 5463, 5492, 5502, 5553, 5561, 5580, 5863.
RLFC 3/2/21/ 23, 24, 25, 27, 37, 38, 39, 40, 42.
RLFC 3/2/26/ 1, 2, 3, 4, 15, 16, 17,18, 19, 20, 21, 22, 23, 24, 25, 26, 27, 29, 40, 42.
RLFC 4/21/ 31, 34, 35.
RLFC 4/26/ 08, 09, 10, 11, 12, 13, 14, 15, 16, 17, 18, 20, 21, 22, 33.
RLFC 5/21/ 2, 9.
RLFC 5/26/ 1, 2, 7.

Chief Secretary's Office Registered Papers (CSORP)
A. 21, 39, 96, 372, 517, 709, 739, 1584, 1691, 2190, 2467, 2590, 2612, 2638, 2839,
2852, 2966, 2986, 3184, 3215, 3357, 3584, 3714, 3762, 4475, 5365, 6327, 6421, 6764,
6935, 7923, 8427, 8682, 8838, 8985, 9304, 9335, 9508, 9542, 9901, 10100, 10278,
10412, 10652, 11514, 11610, 11841.
C. 299, 320, 11841.
F. 9132.
G. 2599, 3985, 4096, 4267, 4428, 7057, 7524, 11918, 16308.
H. 322, 782, 913, 1100, 1677, 1678, 1946, 2235, 2241, 2410, 2562, 2754, 2898, 2903,
2933, 3162, 3365, 3418, 3910, 3968, 4150, 4258, 4397, 4598, 4629, 4808, 5105, 5238,
5373, 5432, 5973, 6075, 6744, 6764, 6784, 6786, 6931, 7034, 7043, 7277, 7513, 7954,
7983, 8007, 8009, 8474, 8921, 10301, 10821, 11149, 12193, 12384, 12607, 12641,
92452.
I. 682, 1047, 1498, 3727, 4629, 4806, 4599, 6226, 6336, 6649, 6966, 7811, 7377, 7871,
8168, 8232, 8649, 8866, 8868, 10434, 11534, 12251, 13285.
M. 548, 3169, 4126, 8087, 8789, 9296.
O. 28, 85, 103, 176, 342, 345, 362, 497, 551, 567, 718, 719, 806, 862, 905, 987, 1048,
1070, 1073, 1074, 1075, 1122, 1123, 1124, 1140, 1182, 1191, 1207, 1231, 1323, 1341,

1371, 1373, 1411, 1457, 1476, 1515, 1557, 1607, 1667, 1689, 1696, 1733, 1761, 1762, 1763, 1810, 1863, 1879, 1880, 1908, 1923, 1959, 1977, 1987, 2061, 2098, 2102, 2112, 2113, 2115, 2116, 2137, 2138, 2139, 2140, 2141, 2142, 2143, 2144, 2145, 2151, 2187, 2188, 2191, 2192, 2230, 2232, 2295, 2325, 2345, 2376, 2379, 2566, 2624, 2782, 2783, 2807, 2835, 2842, 2881, 2905, 2937, 2969, 3141, 3054, 3055, 3056, 3081, 3195, 3196, 3272, 3419, 3432, 3454, 3475, 3496, 3517, 3540, 3576, 3581, 3610, 3624, 3654, 3655, 3693, 3728, 3768, 3844, 3845, 3891, 3895, 3888, 3941, 3949, 3994, 4018, 4024, 4033, 4059, 4060, 4097, 4151, 4173, 4203, 4233, 4253, 4272, 4275, 4348, 4350, 4351, 4352, 4377, 4383, 4520, 4537, 4576, 4578, 4658, 4674, 4713, 4717, 4729, 4740, 4777, 4800, 4807, 4843, 4864, 4900, 4902, 4921, 4959, 5019, 5044, 5076, 5078, 5102, 5159, 5208, 5212, 5225, 5252, 5256, 5298, 5303, 5361, 5422, 5423, 5424, 5464, 5501, 5521, 5527, 5539, 5580, 5636, 5650, 5658, 5729, 5792, 5859, 5860, 5863, 5866, 6040, 6088, 6091, 6134, 6136, 6150, 6175, 6405, 6417, 6528, 6588, 6673, 6723, 6808, 6816, 6818, 7065, 7187, 7192, 7278, 7352, 7371, 7396, 7444, 7464, 7495, 7498, 7635, 7660, 7706, 7708, 7758, 7792, 7794, 7814, 7844, 8010, 8011, 8042, 8095, 8129, 8150, 8161, 8172, 8173, 8250, 8271, 8338, 8395, 8459, 8472, 8500, 8562, 8579, 8616, 8669, 8683, 8807, 8813, 8867, 9061, 9112, 9122, 9245, 9258, 9285, 9311, 9345, 9461, 9558, 9559, 9573, 9666, 9759, 9775, 9807, 9887, 9928, 9847, 10012, 10086,10088, 10166, 10271, 10312, 10334, 10444, 10474, 10485, 10568, 10759, 10876, 10973, 10999, 11034, 11072, 11079, 11081, 11085, 11113, 11208, 11306, 11307, 11310, 11321, 11363, 11451, 11452, 11514, 11568, 11634, 11641, 11678, 11794, 11844, 11847, 11940, 11941, 11962, 11964, 12067, 12068, 12133, 12134, 12169, 12196, 12240, 12400, 12408, 12411, 12412, 12471, 12543, 12545, 12546, 12566, 12623, 12626, 12709, 12730, 12997, 13103, 13105, 13106, 13116, 13153, 13170, 13224, 13271, 13309, 13311, 13312, 13324, 13357, 13358, 13360, 13361, 13362, 13363, 13376, 13377, 13416, 13417, 13424, 13426, 13427, 20934, 21082, 21482, 21936, 22340, 22994, 44425.
P. 4414.
S. 7602.
W. 92, 286, 394, 481, 507, 755, 1091, 1121, 1140, 1174, 1354, 1447, 1452, 1542, 1606, 1705, 1874, 2132, 2162, 2493, 2589, 3301, 3392, 3606, 3819, 3840, 3926, 4190, 4247, 4288, 4408, 4475, 4485, 4741, 4878, 4813, 5131, 5339, 5585, 5614, 5620, 5865, 6079, 6581, 6623, 6884, 6892, 6936, 7018, 7245, 7580, 7587, 7619, 7638, 7883, 7905, 7933, 7991, 8083, 8338, 8472, 8597, 8781, 8929, 8974, 9117, 9220, 9374, 9518, 9556, 9712, 9902, 11174, 13261, 13441, 22012, 22796, 23596, 23668, 23992, 34902.
Z. 121, 168, 326, 370, 396, 529, 838, 898, 1205, 1278, 1325, 1440, 1711, 1901, 1914, 2219, 2387, 2943, 3292, 3356, 3551, 3673, 3741, 4104, 4201, 4460, 4727, 4778, 4937, 4946, 4977, 4991, 5037, 5066, 5157, 5163, 5417, 5445, 5509, 5598, 5642, 5670, 5932, 6027, 6187, 6326, 6371, 6408, 6409, 6450, 6686, 6687, 7139, 7178, 7308, 7367, 7894, 7962, 8049, 8091, 8139, 8193, 8221, 8304, 8307, 8366, 8423, 8503, 8504, 8524, 8567, 8647, 8666, 8702, 8746, 8922, 8923, 9035, 9284, 9368, 9418, 9453, 9704, 9708, 9861, 9881, 9934, 9992, 10084, 10147, 10321, 10450, 10458, 10772, 10955, 10985, 12384, 14090, 14378.

Distress Papers (DP)
D. 16, 73, 90 140, 162, 169, 170, 183, 226, 497, 530, 567, 577, 580, 581, 639, 660, 686, 702, 705, 747, 767, 774, 775, 800, 863, 938, 945, 1055, 1077, 1102, 1176, 1177, 1178, 1199, 1249, 1306, 1331, 1398, 1399, 1435, 1490, 1510, 1530, 1592, 1593, 1658, 1620, 1821, 1838, 1896, 1897, 2049, 2122, 2123, 2315, 2335, 2424, 2437, 2440, 2465, 2483, 2611, 2616, 2622, 2659, 2661, 2761, 2778, 2807, 2822, 2870, 2878, 2936,3003, 3018, 3022,3038, 3046, 3075, 3180, 3200, 3216, 3227, 3351, 3429, 3525, 3581, 3695, 3820,

3890, 3917, 4008, 4050, 4104, 4105, 4132, 4139, 4163, 4169, 4192, 4207, 4225, 4232,
4236, 4247, 4273, 4276, 4310, 4357, 4364, 4389, 4407, 4410, 4446, 4465, 4467, 4468,
4483, 4492, 4494, 4497, 4505, 4533, 4545, 4561, 4557, 4577, 4613, 4622, 4631, 4642,
4649, 4650, 4679, 4680, 4695, 4697, 4712, 4714, 4715, 4718, 4720, 4736, 4768, 4775,
4778, 4779, 4785, 4797, 4865, 4878, 4885, 4899, 4912, 4963, 4968, 4997, 5044, 5096,
5134, 5163, 5164, 5166, 5179, 5222, 5292, 5301, 5304, 5311, 5325, 5360, 5411, 5427,
5454, 5473, 5484, 5485, 5497, 5498, 5509, 5515, 5523, 5524, 5552, 5574, 5615, 5631,
5687, 5688, 5735, 5821, 5826, 5852, 5871, 5888, 5916, 5922, 5925, 5952, 5956, 5957,
5970, 5981, 6019, 6085, 6105, 6137, 6179, 6189, 6191, 6221, 6384, 6386, 6387, 6410,
6576, 6581, 6605, 6621, 6668, 6694, 6699, 6733, 6895, 6989, 7038, 7055, 7075, 7111,
7131, 7152, 7156, 7204, 7213, 7240, 7243, 7334, 7342, 7476, 7512, 7537, 7540, 7541,
7558, 7607, 7613, 7631, 7686, 7700, 7704, 7731, 7766, 7774, 7775, 7776, 7782, 7830,
7852, 7874, 7893, 7913, 7914, 7927, 7949, 7954, 7990, 8026, 8086, 8104, 8113, 8114,
8145, 8157, 8220, 8344, 8354, 8374, 8408, 8410, 8438, 8500, 8501, 8510, 8533, 8597,
8853, 8869, 8933, 8978, 8981, 9028, 9122, 9291, 9352, 9482, 9513. 9528, 9551, 9701,
9742, 9759, 9798, 9909, 9919, 10020, 10114, 10160, 10258, 10280,10390, 10391,
10479, 10438.

Outrage Papers (OP)
21/ 48, 53, 75, 80, 81, 83, 94, 106, 143, 149, 190, 226, 240, 242, 270, 293, 406, 444,
448, 473, 521, 23951, 26029, 30135, 30565, 35577, 37185.
26/ 16, 52, 80, 112, 117, 143, 153, 162, 198, 226, 228, 242, 268, 273, 307, 338, 22733,
26555.

Society of Friends' Famine Papers (SFFP)
2/505/2 Achonry, 22 Feb. 1847, Tubbercurry, 27 Feb. 1847.
2/505/5 Achonry, Kilmactigue, 28 Dec. 1846, Coolavin, Collooney, 2 Feb. 1847,
Ballaghaderreen, 4 Feb. 1847, Coolavin, 8 Feb. 1847, Ballisodare, Ballinacarrow, 9 Feb.
1847, Rathbarron, 12 Feb. 1847, Carracastle, 15 Feb. 1847, Swinford, 16 Feb. 1847,
Ballaghaderreen, 20 Feb. 1847, Carracastle, Loughglynn, 22 Feb. 1847, Collooney, 23 Feb.
1847, Ballina, 24 Feb. 1847, Ballymote, 25 Feb, 1847, Collooney, 26 Feb. 1847, Kilkelly,
26 Feb. 1847, Ballaghaderreen, 27 Feb. 1847, Ballaghaderreen, 4 Mar. 1847, Collooney,
Aclare, 8 Mar. 1847, Swinford, Foxford, 20 Mar. 1847.
2/505/6 Kilkelly, 22 Mar. 1947, Coolavin, Templehouse, 25 Mar. 1847, Ballaghaderreen, 30
Mar. 1847, Charlestown, 31 Mar. 1847, Kilmactigue, 7 April 1847, Aclare, Coolavin, 10
April 1847, Achonry, Ballaghaderreen, Foxford, 14 April 1847, Ballymote, 19 April 1847,
Aclare, Foxford, Swinford, 21 April 1847, Collooney, 22 April 1847, Swinford, Ballina,
Collooney, 23 April 1847, Kilkelly, 26 April 1847.
2/506/3 Loughglynn, 31 Oct. 1847.
2/506/18 Coolavin, 19 May 1848, Tubbercurry, 12 July 1848, Keash, Tubbercurry, 15 July
1848, 18 July 1848, Meelick, 25 July 1848, Achonry, 27 July 1848, Achonry, 2 Aug. 1848,
Boyle, Castlebar, 4 Aug. 1848, Kiltimagh, 7 Aug. 1848, Achonry, 17 Aug. 1848, Coolaney,
29 Aug. 1848, Keash, 4 & 28 Oct. 1848, Swinford, 8 Nov. 1848, Kiltimagh, 16 Nov. 1848.
2/506,19 Loughglynn, 1 Feb. 1847, Kilmactigue, 3 Feb. 1847, Ballaghaderreen,
Kilmactigue, 8 Feb. 1847, Coolavin, 13 Feb. 1847, Ballaghaderreen, 14 Feb. 1847,
Ballymote, 15 Feb. 1847, Achonry, 16 Feb. 1847, Corran, 17 Feb. 1847, Ballaghaderreen,
22 Feb. 1847, Kilkelly, 1 Mar. 1847, Ballina, 8 Mar, 1847, Boyle, 10 Mar. 1847,
Templehouse, Coolavin, 11 Mar. 1847, Swinford, Foxford, 18 Mar. 1847, Ardcarne, 26
Mar. 1847, Kilmactigue, Foxford, 3 April 1847, Aclare, 7 April, 1847, Achonry, Ballymote,
9 April 1847, Aclare, 15 April 1847, Swinford, 27 April 1847, Collooney, 29 April 1847,

Rathbarron, 30 April 1847, Coolavin, 4 May 1847, Ballaghaderreen, 6 & 8 May 1847, Coolavin, 11 May 1847.

2/506/20 Bohola, 16 May 1847, Belmullet, 19 May 1847, Boyle, 21 May 1847, Kilmovee, 23 May 1847, Ballymote, 24 May 1847, Ballaghaderreen, 13 June 1847, Swinford, 14 June 1847, Kilcolman, Coolavin, 16 June 1847, Ballaghaderreen, 18 June 1847, Keash, 19 June 1847, Coolavin, 29 June 1847, Loughglynn, 2 & 4 July 1847, Swinford, 5 July 1847

2/506/21 Swinford, Aclare, 12 July 1847, Achonry, 16 July 1847, Keash, 19 July 1847, Ballaghaderreen, 20 July 1847, Sligo, 23 July 1847, Boyle, 26 July 1847, Coolavin, 27 July 1847, Belmullet, 30 July 1847, Clogher, Ballaghaderreen, 31 July 1847, Kilkelly, 9 Aug. 1847, Keash, 6 Sept. 1847, Achonry, 10 Sept. 1847, Kilturra & Kilshalvey, 14 Sept. 1847, Templehouse, 17 Sept. 1847, Swinford, 18 Sept. 1847, Clogher, Ballaghaderreen, 21 Sept. 1847, Coolavin, 27 Sept. 1847, Foxford, 1 Oct. 1847, Boyle, 7 Oct. 1847, Kilmactigue, 14 Oct. 1847, Meelick, 20 Oct, 1847, Keash, 21 October 1847, Ballymote, 24 Oct. 1847, Ballina, 5 Nov. 1847, Coolaney, 6 Nov. 1847,

2/506/22 Achonry, 27 Nov. 1847, Foxford, 2 Dec. 1847, Achonry, 6 Dec. 1847, Boyle, 13 Dec. 1847, Keash, 18 Dec. 1847, Ballymote, 21 Dec. 1847, Meelick, 11 Jan. 1848, Achonry, 1 Feb. 1848, Charlestown, 8 Feb. 1848, Ballymote, 14 Feb. 1848, Clogher, Ballaghaderreen, 12 Feb. 1848, Swinford, 21 Feb. 1848, Bunninadden, Meelick, 3 Mar. 1848, Bunninadden, 23 & 25 Mar. 1848, Ballymote, 25 Mar. 1848, Ballina, 27 Mar. 1848, Achonry, 13 April 1848, Kiltimagh, 25 April 1848, 1 May 1848, Achonry, 11 May 1848, Meelick, 12 May 1848.

2/506/23 Bunninadden, 24 May 1847, Achonry, 17 May 1848, Kilkelly, 22 May 1848, Foxford, 23 May 1848, Bonninconlon, 29 May 1848, Achonry, 11 June 1848, Kiltimagh, 12 & 17 & 24 June 1848, Achonry, 29 June 1848, Kiltimagh, 7 July 1848, Clogher, Ballaghaderreen, 8 July 1848, Keash, 10 July 1848, Achonry, Sligo, 11 July 1848, Meelick, Tubbercurry, 12 July 1848, 18 July 1848, Achonry, 20 July 1848, Kiltimagh, 24 July 1848, Kiltimagh, 29 July 1848, Bunninadden, 30 July 1848, Achonry, 8 Aug. 1848, Loughglynn, 12 July 1849, Coolavin, 24 July 1849, Meelick, 29 July 1849. Achonry, 30 July 1849.

2/506/34 Charlestown, 11 Mar. 1847, Foxford, 24 Mar. 1847, Collooney, 4 Mar. 1848, Kiltimagh, 29 April 1848, Ballymote, 15 May 1848, Loughglynn, 2 June 1848, Loughglynn, 28 Aug. 1848, Coolavin, 2 Nov. 1848, Ballymote, 3 & 5 Nov. 1848, Templehouse, 18 Dec. 1848, Ballymote, 19 Dec. 1848, Swinford, n.d., Tubbercurry, n.d.

2/506/35 Templehouse, 29 Feb. 1848, Charlestown, 13 Mar. 1848, Charlestown, 22 Mar. 1848, Ballaghaderreen, 27 Mar. 1848, Ballymote, 2 April 1848, Collooney, 4 April 1848, Riverstown, 24 April 1848, Keash, 3 May 1848, Ballymote, 10 May 1848, Sligo, 12 May 1848, Clogher, Ballaghaderreen, 25 May 1848, Ballymote, 7 June 1848, Ballymote, 27 July 1848, Aclare, 4 Aug. 1848.

2/506/36 Swinford, Foxford, 18 Mar. 1847, Foxford, 25 April 1847, Coolaney, 28 April 1847, Ballaghaderreen, 8 May 1847, Tubbercurry, 19 May 1847, Coolaney, 31 May & 12 June 1847, Kilcolman, 13 June 1847, Kilmactigue, Killaraght, 19 May 1848, Kilshalvey, n.d., Kilfree & Kilcolman, n.d., Collooney, n.d.

2/506/37 Kilshalvey, 19 Dec. 1847, Loughglynn, 20 Dec. 1847, Kilcolman & Kilfree, 25 Dec. 1847, Kilmactigue, 29 Dec. 1847, Coolaney, 1 Jan. 1848, Kilmactigue, 2 Jan. 1848, Swinford, 17 Jan. 1848, Kilcolman, 19 Jan. 1848, Kilmactigue, 20 Jan. 1848, Keash, 24 Jan. 1848, Collooney, 15 Mar. 1848, Ballymote, 5 April 1848, Kilmactigue, 13 April 1848, Loughglynn, 16 May 1848.

2/507/3 Erris, 15 Jan. 1847, Foxford, 12 May 1847, Attymass, 28 Feb. 1848, Swinford, 20 June 1848.

Propaganda Fide Archives, Rome   *Italy*
Scritture riferite nei Congressi, Irlanda,(SC IRLANDA) vol. 29, ff. 166rv, 172rv, 184rv, 187r,
194r, 200, 224r, 225rv, 226r, 253r, 271r, 279, 293rv, 297r, 324, 361r, 382rv, 383r, 384rv,
670r, 783rv, 784rv, 813rv, 816rv, 817rv, 852rv, 854rv, 927rv, 988rv, 990rv, 1072r, 1076r.
vol. 30, ff. 212r.

NEWSPAPERS

Connaught Ranger
Freeman's Journal
Galway Vindicator
Mayo Constitution
Sligo Champion
Sligo Journal
Tyrawly Herald

SELECTED PRINTED MATERIAL

Achonry/Mulinabreena Developing the West Group, *From Plain to Hill. A Short History of
the Parish of Achonry* (1995)
Browne, Raymond, *The Destitution Survey. Reflections on the Famine in the Diocese of Elphin*
(1997)
*Correspondence from July 1846 to January 1847 relating to measures adopted for the relief of
distress in Ireland*
*Correspondence from January to March 1847 relating to measures adopted for the relief of dis-
tress in Ireland*
Donnelly, James S., Jr, 'Famine and Government Response, 1845-6', 'Production, Prices and
Exports, 1846-51', 'The Administration of Relief, 1846-7', 'The Soup Kitchens', 'The
Administration of Relief, 1847-51', 'Landlords and Tenants', 'Excess Mortality and
Emigration', in *A New History of Ireland,* vol. V, pp. 272-356
Farry, M, *Killoran and Coolaney: A Local History* (1985)
Glazier, Ira A., ed., *Famine Immigrants* (1986)
Goodbody, Rob, *A Suitable Channel. Quaker Relief in the Great Famine* (1995)
Kerr, Donal A., *'A Nation of Beggars'? Priests, People and Politics in Famine Ireland 1846-1852*
(1994)
— *The Catholic Church and the Famine* (1996)
Kinealy, Christine, *This Great Calamity* (1994)
Laxton, Edward, *The Famine Ships. The Irish Exodus to America 1846-51* (1996)
McTernan, John C., *Olde Sligoe. Aspects of Town and County over 750 years* (1995)
O'Connor, John, *The Workhouses of Ireland. The fate of Ireland's Poor* (1995)
O'Gallagher, Marianna & Dompierre, Rose Masson, *Eyewitness Grosse Isle, 1847* (1995)
Swinford Historical Society, *An Gorta Mór. Famine in the Swinford Union*
Tuke, J. H., *Narrative of Visits to the Distressed Districts in Ireland, Nov.-Dec. 1846*
— *A Visit to Connaught in Autumn 1847*
*Transactions of the Central Relief Committee of the Society of Friends during the Famine in
Ireland in 1846 and 1847* (reprinted in 1996)
Woodham-Smith, Cecil, *The Great Hunger: Ireland 1845-49* (1962)

Index